D0164430

Urban Economics and Real Estate

John
For Glena and Elizabeth

Daniel
For Mary, Katie, Steve, and Rob

Urban Economics and Real Estate

Theory and Policy

John F. McDonald
Daniel P. McMillen

College of Business Administration
University of Illinois at Chicago

© 2007 by John F. McDonald and Daniel P. McMillen

BLACKWELL PUBLISHING
350 Main Street, Malden, MA 02148-5020, USA
9600 Garsington Road, Oxford OX4 2DQ, UK
550 Swanston Street, Carlton, Victoria 3053, Australia

First published 2007 by Blackwell Publishing Ltd

2   2008

Library of Congress Cataloging-in-Publication Data

McDonald, John F., 1943–
Urban economics and real estate : theory and policy / John F. McDonald, Daniel P. McMillen.
p. cm.
Includes bibliographical references and index.
ISBN: 978-1-4051-3118-6 (hardcover : alk. paper)
1. Urban economics.   2. Real property.
3. Real estate development.   4. Real estate business.   5. Urban policy.
I. McMillen, Daniel P.   II. Title.

HT321.M35 2007
330.9173′2—dc22
2006021668

A catalogue record for this title is available from the British Library.

Set in 10/12pt Times
by Graphicraft Limited, Hong Kong
Printed and bound in Singapore
by C.O.S. Printers Pte Ltd

The publisher's policy is to use permanent paper from mills that operate a sustainable forestry policy, and which has been manufactured from pulp processed using acid-free and elementary chlorine-free practices. Furthermore, the publisher ensures that the text paper and cover board used have met acceptable environmental accreditation standards.

For further information on
Blackwell Publishing, visit our website:
www.blackwellpublishing.com

Contents

Preface

This textbook has been written primarily for undergraduate and master's degree students who wish to learn about the field in which economic analysis is applied to urban areas and urban real estate. The title of the book has been chosen with care. The emphasis is on economic analysis (primarily microeconomic theory), empirical studies that are based in economic theory, and the policy lessons that can be drawn from the use of economics to understand urban areas. The book includes a group of chapters on urban real estate. We believe that the economics of real estate markets and real estate investment and development are essential components of a course in urban economics. No other urban economics text includes the extensive coverage of real estate such as that included in this book.

A course in urban economics with a strong real estate component would use the chapters in the book in the order in which they are presented. An alternative is to use the book for a course in urban real estate with strong urban economics and public policy components. In this case the course would begin with Chapters 10, 11, and 12 on real estate law and institutions, real estate markets, and real estate development and investment. Students would then read Part I (Economics and Urban Areas), Part II (Location Patterns in Urban Areas), and Chapters 8 and 9 on housing. The remainder of the course should include Chapter 13 on the urban public sector and Part VI (Urban Growth). Chapter 14 on urban transportation and Part V (Urban Social Problems) would be optional.

Those who study this book should be able to conduct economic studies of an urban area and its real estate markets. We do not mean that the student can do original academic research, but that she or he can conduct a study that is informed and well organized. One implication of this purpose is that, although many policy issues are examined, a complete catalog of urban social problems is not included. Potential users of the book should note that all of the examples and data pertain to urban areas in the United States.

The book is written presuming that the student has a background that, at a minimum, includes a strong course in the principles of microeconomics and the ability to handle algebra. The student needs to feel comfortable with the use of basic mathematics because economic analysis cannot be done without it. The book does include a few mathematical derivations that are more than two or three lines in length. Students who have had a course in intermediate microeconomic theory will find that most of the mathematical and economic concepts in the book are quite familiar. The book does not require that the student has studied calculus. All of the mathematical concepts used are covered in the appendix at the end of the book. However, the student who has had a course in basic differential calculus (e.g., math for business and economics) will find that the math is easy.

The book can be used in (at least) two ways. It can serve as a text for students who are majoring in economics. These students wish to learn about the subject matter of urban economics, but they also need to gain more practice in the use of economic theory and the underlying mathematical techniques. Several more advanced sections and appendices have been included for these students, and they should review the appendix to the book while they are reading the first five chapters. The book can also serve as a text for students in related fields, such as real estate, urban planning, and urban geography, who do not intend to become experts in economic analysis, but who wish to apply their knowledge of microeconomics to the urban economy and urban real estate. These students can omit some of the more mathematical appendices to the chapters. If we were teaching students in this category, we would allocate some time in each of the first few weeks of the course to covering the material in the appendix to the book.

The book begins with four chapters that introduce urban economics as a field of study and discuss the origins and functions of cities in the United States. The rest of the book consists of sections organized around these topics:

- location patterns in urban areas;
- urban housing and real estate;
- government in urban areas;
- urban social problems;
- urban growth.

We have been teaching urban economics and real estate to undergraduate and to graduate students for many years, and this book draws upon that experience. Our experience also tells us that students need to do more than read the textbook and attend lectures. They need to learn about the main data sources in the field, they need to write, they need to read other books, and they need to go out and observe the urban area in which they live (since most of them do live in an urban area).

The main data sources in the field are available on the world wide web, and chief among the relevant web sites is that of the US Bureau of the Census (census.gov). We recommend that the instructor show the student how to surf census.gov. Another important data source County Business Patterns, which provides detailed employment data by industry for all counties in the US. Other labor market data can be obtained from the web sites of the US Department of Labor and state departments of labor or employment security. Data on urban real estate markets can be obtained from private sources which often have free web sites. Also, most of the county tax assessors now provide data on real estate parcels on the web.

We normally require that the student read other books and write a book review. Recommendations for books to use are made along the way in the text. Here we make a few suggestions of books that are readable and insightful. They are:

- William Cronon, *Nature's Metropolis*, W. W. Norton, 1992;
- Anthony Downs, *Still Stuck in Traffic*, The Brookings Institution, 2004;
- Joel Garreau, *Edge* City, Doubleday, 1991;
- Edgar Hoover and Raymond Vernon, *Anatomy of a Metropolis*, Harvard University Press, 1959;
- Jane Jacobs, *The Economy of Cities*, Random House, 1969;
- Saskia Sassen, *Cities in a World Economy*, 2nd edition, Pine Forge Press, 2000;
- Thomas Stanback, *The Transforming Metropolitan Economy*, Center for Urban Policy Research, Rutgers University, 2002;
- William Fischel, *The Homevoter Hypothesis*, Harvard University Press, 2001.

We also heartily recommend the Blackwell book of readings edited by Richard Arnott and Daniel McMillen titled *A Companion to Urban Economics*. These readings make a fine complement to our textbook treatment of the subject. The only supplement for this text is a web site hosted by Daniel P. McMillen at http://www.uic.edu/~mcmillen. There you will find any necessary exrata, updates, some new examples, and directions to useful web sites.

John F. McDonald, mcdonald@uic.edu
Daniel P. McMillen, mcmillen@uic.edu

Acknowledgements

We owe a debt of gratitude to four scholars who reviewed a draft of the book and made many valuable suggestions. We also owe much to Seth Ditchik, former editor, George Lobell, current editor, and Laura Stearns, editorial assistant, of Blackwell Publishing. They have handled the project with efficiency and good humor. We hope that we will provide a good return on their investment. And we would be remiss if we failed to note that Blackwell has a large program in urban economics, real estate, and related subjects. All students and scholars in these fields are in their debt. Figures 7.9, 7.10, 7.11, and 7.12 are reprinted from the *Journal of Urban Economics*, vol. 3, Daniel McMillen and Stefani Smith, "The Number of Subcenters in Large Urban Areas," pp. 321–38, 2003, with permission from Elsevier. Finally, we wish to thank very much the three people in the Dean's office of the College of Business Administration who helped us prepare this manuscript: Debra Bibbs, Vrinda Patel, and Yuliya Yurova.

Part I

Economics and Urban Areas

Chapter 1

Introduction to Urban Economics

A. The Nature of Urban Areas and Urban Economics

Urban economics is the study of economies that are organized as urban areas. An urban area can be defined as a place with:

- a very high population density, compared to the surrounding area; and
- a total population greater than some minimum number (to distinguish urban areas from small towns).

Most urban areas have an identifiable central point where population density is at a peak and declines with distance from that point. (A few urban areas, such as Minneapolis–St. Paul, have more than one central point.) Urban economies are based on frequent contact among people and economic activities, and high population density facilitates that contact. You will be studying economies such as the New York metropolitan area, "Chicagoland," and the Dallas–Fort Worth "metroplex."

Urban economics is also the study of cities – both the positive and the negative aspects of cities. Cities are at the heart of the modern economy and society. They are economic centers of trade and finance. They are centers of culture, innovation, and education. Cities are also the home of urban problems, including crime, traffic congestion, urban sprawl, racial segregation and discrimination. Cities are the endlessly fascinating places where nearly all of us spend our lives. Our proposition in writing this book is that your education should include a deeper understanding of the economics of cities.

The field of urban economics is closely related to other fields such as regional economics and real estate. Regional economics is the study of regions that are much larger than a single urban area but are smaller than an entire nation. Regional economists are interested in the economy of the Midwest, the Southwest, etc. But both urban and regional economists are interested in the variety of economic experience that can occur within a single nation. Both study economic units that are defined geographically, as opposed to industry units, demographic groups, occupational groups, or other possible disaggregations of the whole economy. Indeed, because both urban economics and regional economics study geographic subunits of the national economy, both make use of some of the same models and methods. Urban economics is also closely related to real estate, the field that studies real estate markets, institutions, investment, and development. An urban area consists of the people who live there and the land, buildings, and other facilities that people use. Many urban economists concentrate on the study of housing markets in urban areas, for example. Other urban economists study the urban land market, while some examine the causes and consequences of real estate developments of various types. Urban economics is also related to urban planning, urban sociology, urban politics, and urban geography. We believe that students in all of these fields can benefit from a course in urban economics that provides a solid understanding of the economics of cities and how market forces shape cities.

This book uses two different, and complementary, methods for examining the economy of an urban area. The first method is the study of location patterns within an urban area. The location decisions of households, firms, and industries within the urban area are the chief topics. For example, the study of the spatial pattern of population density in an urban area is a favorite topic in urban economics. Location decisions are influenced by many factors, including public policies regarding the provision of transportation facilities and other public goods and services, local taxation, and zoning and other forms of land use control. The second method is the examination of the urban economy in the aggregate. Spatial patterns within the urban area are largely ignored. Instead the focus is on the growth or decline of economy of the urban area. An urban economy is quite "open" in the sense that imports and exports are large fractions of its total economic activity. Most urban areas specialize in the production of a certain group of goods and services for export outside the urban area. Most urban areas thus have an identifiable economic function within the larger economy. Changes in the larger economy can have sizable impacts on an urban economy, and at times may require that the urban area undergo a significant change in its basic economic function.

These two methods for looking at an urban economy are not independent. Clearly a major change in the economic functions performed by an urban area can have implications for the location patterns within the urban area. Chicago is no longer the "hog butcher of the world," but is in fact now the center of the nation's air transportation system. Location patterns within the Chicago metropolitan area have adjusted accordingly as O'Hare Airport and its surrounding area have become a major center of employment. Further, does a significant change in the rate at which an urban area grows imply a change in location patterns? At the same time, it is possible that the location patterns within an urban area can influence its ability to grow. Is the supply of industrial sites sufficient for further industrial growth? Do those industrial sites possess good access to transportation facilities, suppliers, and needed workers? Is the urban area, (especially its downtown and other major employment centers), an attractive place that will draw to it workers who possess skills that are used in the new knowledge-based economy? In this chapter we take a brief look at New York, Los Angeles, and Chicago, the three largest urban areas in the US, to begin to see how urban growth and location patterns interact. We shall see that a metropolitan area that grows slowly will likely experience decline in its central areas along with substantial growth in the suburbs. This combination has motivated the concern about urban "sprawl." But first we offer a brief introduction to urban economics as a field of study.

B. Development of the Field of Urban Economics

Urban economics as something of a separate field of study within economics began in the late 1930s when economists started using the tools of macroeconomics to examine urban economies and their real estate markets. Basic concepts such as gross national product, exports and imports, the multiplier, and the unemployment rate were adapted to the study of urban economies. Perhaps a date for the founding of the field is 1956, the year in which the New York Metropolitan Region Study was initiated. The book that summarizes this huge study was written by two economists, Edgar M. Hoover and Raymond Vernon, and is entitled *Anatomy of a Metropolis*. This book, which was published in 1959, carries the subtitle "The changing distribution of people and jobs within the New York metropolitan region." This study of New York succeeded in gathering an enormous volume of data that were presented in a well-organized fashion. The trends observable in the data were then discussed using a variety of forces that were hypothesized to influence the location choices of firms and households within a metropolitan area. *Anatomy of a Metropolis* is a classic study, and we recommend that you read it.

Some urban economists would place the founding of the field in 1964, the date of the publication of William Alonso's book *Location and Land Use*. Alonso laid out a basic theoretical model that can be used to study the economics of location patterns within urban areas that is still used today. Alonso's method makes use of the idea that households and firms are willing to make bids for land at various locations. Location decisions and patterns of land use can be explained by comparing the bids made by different types of households and firms. The law firm outbids others for downtown locations, the electronics plant makes the highest bid for a site near the interstate highway, the family with children bids more than others for a lot in the suburbs, and so on. These ideas will be explored in detail in this book.

Since the 1960s a great deal of progress has been made in urban economics as a field of research. It is also true that urban economics is still a relatively new field of study. But what does it mean to say that progress has been made in a field of research? Research in economics can be classified as one of two fundamental types; normative and positive. Normative economics is the exploration of questions such as, "How should the economy be organized to be efficient and/or equitable?" Some ethical objective is specified, and what "ought" to be done is deduced – given the facts of life. This type of research usually makes use of formal economic theory to derive propositions such as, "The economy should have perfectly competitive markets," or "A tax should be placed on polluters." The task of positive economics is to determine the facts of economic life.

The development of positive economic knowledge in fields such as urban economics typically proceeds through five stages, which can be characterized as follows:

1   accumulation of data pertinent to the field of study;
2   systematic examination of these data in order to determine the important facts which require formal "explanation" through the development of economic models;
3   formulation of economic models which are capable of accounting for the important facts;

4   empirical estimation and testing of such economic models;
5   use of the models for forecasting, policy analysis, and normative analysis.

While research may be underway simultaneously in all five stages, often researchers at a single time focus on only one or two stages. Also, some researchers may be engaged in work that refines or makes use of the generally accepted model (stages 4 and 5), while other researchers are in the process of questioning the generally accepted model (stages 1, 2, and 3). Sometimes those who are questioning the generally accepted model will demonstrate that the older model needs to be abandoned in favor of their newer, better approach. In other cases the older and the newer models will co-exist, and the matter of which model is better will be unresolved.

Given these five stages in the accumulation of positive economic knowledge, can we determine a date for the founding of the field of urban economics? Perhaps the field begins with the accumulation of facts – the first stage listed above. If that is the case, then no date can be given because we do not (and perhaps can never) know when someone who resembled an economist began to collect data about cities. On the other hand, maybe a field of study is founded when someone begins to sort through the facts and to find patterns and trends that seem to call for an economic model. Indeed, maybe it is the *finding* of such patterns and trends that initiates a field in economic science.

Others will claim that economic science does not exist until the first economic model pertaining to those patterns and trends is actually formulated. This is why 1964, the year of the publication of Alonso's *Location and Land Use*, is often proposed as the date for the founding of the field. There is no definitive answer to this question, but a stimulating class discussion might be held to sort out the issues. How would you compare urban economics to other fields within economics, to other social sciences, and to other fields of science?

Urban economics provides several examples of competing models. For example, consider the analysis of urban economic growth. One model places emphasis on the demand for the exports of the urban area, and uses macroeconomic methods (including Keynesian multipliers) to explain trends in the urban economy. Another model puts its emphasis on the supply side. The growth of an urban economy is seen as being determined largely by its supplies of labor, capital, and infrastructure. Yet another model emphasizes the life cycle patterns of the industries that are located in the urban area. Are the industries in the urban area "mature," or are they new and vigorous? Which of these models is best at explaining the facts that need to be explained? Can these models be combined into a more comprehensive model that provides better explanations? These matters are discussed in detail in Part VI of this book. For now you have learned that a field of research can contain alternative models, and that the question of which model is "best" can be an unresolved issue.

Our purpose in writing this book is to teach you, to the best of our ability, the nature of the progress that has been made in the field of urban economics. Both normative and positive economics are covered, but it is fair to say that this book emphasizes the positive side. This reflects caution on our part; we are not sure that sufficient knowledge exists to make detailed normative statements about some urban issues. We do have some answers, but we also have many unresolved questions.

C. Tales of Three Cities: New York, Los Angeles, and Chicago

Urban areas are the subject matter of urban economics, and the New York, Los Angeles and Chicago metropolitan areas are, by far, the three largest in the US. In our opinion, all students of urban economics should have some familiarity with the basic economic facts of these three dominant urban areas. The book by Janet Abu-Lughod (1999) provides a detailed history of these three urban areas – American's global cities. This section provides a systematic presentation of some of the basic facts of metropolitan population growth and spatial patterns for the three largest urban areas in the US since 1970. The fundamental point is that there is a close relationship between the growth of an urban area and change in the spatial patterns of population and employment. Economic models to explain these facts are covered in later chapters.

The definition of the metropolitan area is the first question that must be answered in an empirical study. We wish to focus on a particular urban area viewed as an economic unit, distinct from rural areas and other urban areas. Clearly studying only the "central city" (i.e., New York City, the city of Los Angeles, the city of Chicago) will not do. The residential suburbs must be included because they are part of the economic unit. A more difficult question concerns the inclusion of nearby cities that are satellite cities, but not really residential suburbs of the main city. For example, New York has Newark, New Jersey, just across the Hudson River. Chicago has a ring of old satellite cities – Waukegan, Elgin, Aurora and Joliet (in Illinois), and Gary, Indiana. Except for Gary, these cities were founded in the nineteenth century after a railroad line was built around Chicago, intersecting the major trunk rail lines that converge on Chicago. Los Angeles has a series of cities that line the coast of the Pacific Ocean, and a line of cities that stretches to the East. The difficulty of this question is compounded by the fact that, since 1970, some satellite cities that were really economic units separate from the major city at that time have been engulfed by the spreading out of the major urban area.

The US Bureau of the Census has the task of defining the metropolitan areas. As a practical matter the Census Bureau defines metropolitan areas as groups of *counties* that contain a central city with a population of at least 50,000. A county is included in a metropolitan area if there is a significant amount of commuting to jobs in the county that contains the central city. Counties are used as the building blocks of metropolitan areas because their boundaries do not change and because a great deal of data are gathered at the county level. This procedure means that the Census Bureau changes the definition of a metropolitan area as residential and commuting patterns change. This procedure also means that there can be more than one "metropolitan division," as defined by the Census Bureau, within a metropolitan area. For example, Newark is its own metropolitan division because it is a central city of over 50,000 population and workers in surrounding counties commute to Newark. Consequently, the Census Bureau also defines what it calls a Combined Statistical Area (CSA). A CSA has a population of at least 2.5 million and at least two metropolitan divisions that are economically integrated. The Census Bureau has also defined "micropolitan areas" as consisting of a city of 10,000 to 50,000 people and the county in which the city is located (plus any adjacent counties that are economically integrated with it). Metropolitan areas and micropolitan areas together make up the list of Core Based Statistical Areas, of which there were 935 in the US and Puerto Rico in 2003.

New York, Los Angeles, and Chicago all fall into the CSA category. For purposes of this section, these three major urban areas are defined for 1970 to 2000 as given groups of counties as itemized below. This definition means that some counties are included for 1970 that cannot be considered to be part of the main urban area at that time. However, there is a benefit from studying the *same* geographic area over time. We make a small error by including some farms and an occasional satellite city in 1970, but we make sure that we encompass the entire larger urban area for the entire 1970–2000 period. We recognize what we are doing, and keep that small error in mind. The method that is followed is to define a "core" area (e.g., the central city), an inner ring of suburban counties, and an outer ring of counties.

New York

The New York Metropolitan Area consists of 22 counties in New York, New Jersey and Connecticut. New York City consists of its five boroughs [Manhattan (New York County), Brooklyn, Queens, the Bronx, and Staten Island (Richmond)]; each is a separate county.

Population data for 1970, 1980, 1990, and 2000 are shown in Table 1.1. The definitions of the core area, the inner ring and the outer ring follow Hoover and Vernon (1959), and are noted in the footnotes of Table 1.1. The population of the metropolitan area grew by 29.6% from 1950 to 1970, and reached 17.8 million in 1970. The next twenty years actually saw negative population growth; population dropped to 17.1 million in 1980, and the 1990 population was 17.6 million. But New York revived in the 1990s. Population growth from 1990 to 2000 was 1.46 million, which amounts to 8.29% growth for the decade. Table 1.1 also shows that the core of the metropolitan area [defined as New York City excluding Staten Island and adding Hudson County (Newark), NJ] had a population

Table 1.1 New York metropolitan area

	Population (thousands)			
	1970	1980	1990	2000
Core area	8,207	7,283	7,509	8,183
Manhattan	1,533	1,428	1,487	1,539
New York City	7,897	7,077	7,336	8,018
Inner ring	5,455	5,188	5,114	5,401
Outer ring	4,095	4,650	4,961	5,457
Total	17,757	17,121	17,584	19,041

Core area is defined as Manhattan, Brooklyn, Queens, the Bronx, and Hudson County, NJ. New York City includes Staten Island and excludes Hudson County. Inner ring counties include 3 counties in New York and 4 counties in New Jersey. Outer ring counties include 5 counties in New York, 4 in New Jersey, and 1 in Connecticut.
Source: Bureau of Economic Analysis, US Department of Commerce

loss of 11.3% from 1970 to 1980. All parts of the core area lost population during the 1970s. The population loss of 924,000 in the core area exceeds the population of the State of Montana (and six other states), and suggests the image of large expanses of abandoned territory in the Bronx. The next decade tells a different story for the core area; the population increased by 3.10%, and this was followed by an even larger increase in the 1990s of 8.98%. The population of the core area in 2000 had bounced back to its 1970 level of about 8.2 million.

Next consider the inner ring of eight counties that are adjacent to the core area. Population declined in this area during the 1970s and 1980s, and then regained most of this loss by 2000. The failure of population to grow at the metropolitan level meant decline for the inner ring in the 1970–90 period, but the growth in the 1990s at the metropolitan level translated into growth in the inner ring. The outer ring experienced population growth during the entire 1970–2000 period, and its rate of growth was actually greatest in the decade of the 1970s while the rest of the metropolitan area was experiencing large population losses.

The New York metropolitan area gives us a reasonably clear example of what happens to the spatial distribution of population in modern urban areas under conditions of zero growth. When there is no population growth in the metropolitan area (as in 1970–90), the core area declines rather sharply, the inner ring also declines, and the outer ring experiences growth equal to the declines in the other two areas. One might hypothesize that the data for 1970 and 1990 provide us with a pretty clear picture of the underlying trend towards the "suburbanization" of the population. Even if there is no population growth, the outer suburbs still grow for a variety of reasons such as the demand for new houses, desire to escape central city problems, local taxes, and the shift of jobs to the suburbs. The core area must cope with population decline, while the outer ring must handle rather sizable growth. The remarkable turn-around that New York experienced in the 1990s is not typical, as you will see. The rate of population growth in the core area of 8.98% actually exceeded the growth rate for the entire metropolitan area of 8.29%. New York City benefited from the economic boom of the late 1990s as sizable areas were rebuilt and employment in its financial sector boomed. New York's role as a world financial capital makes its experience in the 1990s unusual, if not unique.

Los Angeles

The Los Angeles metropolitan area consists of five counties in California. Los Angeles County contains the city of Los Angeles. The Los Angeles metropolitan area tells a story quite different from the New York story. Refer to Table 1.2. In 1950 it was a metropolitan area of 4.9 million people – only one-third the size of the New York metropolitan area and smaller than metropolitan Chicago. The post-World War II boom in California more than doubled the population of the entire metropolitan area from 1950 to 1970 (growth of 102%), and then added another 6.4 million people from 1970 to 2000. It is remarkable for a place that large to have grown so rapidly. A glance at Tables 1.1 and 1.2 suggests that Los Angeles may overtake New York as the largest metropolitan area in the US. When will Los Angeles overtake New York in metropolitan population? What is your estimate? How did you make that estimate? Is making local population forecasts fun

Table 1.2   Los Angeles metropolitan area

	Population (thousands)			
	1970	*1980*	*1990*	*2000*
City of Los Angeles	2,812	2,967	3,485	3,695
Rest of Los Angeles County	4,230	4,540	5,378	5,824
Inner ring	1,799	2,481	3,080	3,600
Outer ring	1,139	1,572	2,588	3,255
Total	9,980	11,560	14,531	16,374

Inner ring counties are Orange and Ventura. Outer ring counties are San Bernardino and Riverside.
Source: US Bureau of the Census

or what? An exercise at the end of this chapter provides several suggestions for how to make local population forecasts.

Table 1.2 shows that the growth in total population translated into growth in all areas of the metropolitan area. The city of Los Angeles increased its population by 31.4% from 1970 to 2000, and the rest of Los Angeles County grew by 37.7% over the same 30 years. But the other counties saw explosive population growth. The inner ring counties of Orange and Ventura went from 331,000 people in 1950 to 1.8 million in 1970 and 3.6 million in 2000, and the outer ring counties of San Bernardino and Riverside added over 2.1 million people from 1970 to 2000. Orange County started with 216,000 people in 1950, and had a population of 2.8 million in 2000. In short, a modern metropolitan area that experiences very rapid population growth increases the population density in its settled areas, but also spreads out in rather startling fashion. Los Angeles is a textbook case. (This is a textbook, after all.)

Chicago

Our third-largest metropolitan area is Chicago. It consists of eight counties in Illinois, two counties in Indiana, and one county in Wisconsin. The city of Chicago is located in Cook County, Illinois and the city of Gary is located in Lake County, Indiana. Metropolitan Chicago too experienced substantial population growth in the baby boom years of 1950 to 1970; the growth was from 5.6 million to 7.8 million, or 36.7%, during those twenty years. Recall that population growth in the New York metropolitan area was 29.6% during this same period. Chicago also resembles New York in that population growth in the urban area essentially came to a halt from 1970 to 1990; the growth was only 3.7% over the 1970–90 period. Chicago began the post-World War II period as the "second city" and the "second metropolitan area," but by 1970 it was no longer second in metropolitan population, and by 1990 it had lost its title of "second city" as well. The Los Angeles metropolitan population of 10.0 million in 1970 far exceeded metropolitan Chicago's 7.8 million. By 1990 the population in the city of Chicago had dropped to 2.8 million, compared to 3.5 million in the city of Los Angeles.

Table 1.3   Chicago metropolitan area

	Population (thousands)			
	1970	*1980*	*1990*	*2000*
Core	3,915	3,527	3,260	3,381
City of Chicago	3,369	3,005	2,784	2,896
Lake County, IN	546	522	476	485
Rest of Cook County	2,125	2,244	2,321	2,483
Inner ring	871	1,103	1,298	1,555
Outer ring	869	1,063	1,185	1,568
Total	7,780	7,937	8,064	8,987

Inner ring counties include DuPage and Lake in Illinois. Outer ring counties include Kane, McHenry, Will, Kendall and Grundy in Illinois, Porter in Indiana, and Kenosha in Wisconsin.
Source: US Bureau of the Census

The spatial patterns of population change in metropolitan Chicago follow what is now a familiar pattern. In the 1970–90 period, when metropolitan population was growing very slowly, the population of the core area declined, where the core area is defined as the city of Chicago plus Lake County (Gary), Indiana. Table 1.3 shows that the population of the core area dropped 16.7% from 1970 to 1990, and the city of Chicago lost 17.4% of its population. This population loss for the central city is perhaps larger than one might have expected, and can probably be attributed to the gradual adjustment to the opening of the system of radial expressways in the 1960s. The other areas in metropolitan Chicago display population growth from 1970 to 1990. The rest of Cook County (excluding the city of Chicago) was 9.2% over this period, while the inner and outer rings grew by 49.0% and 36.4%, respectively. As we shall see in later chapters, during this period the inner ring counties were the sites of substantial employment growth, partly in the form of employment subcenters. During the 1970s and 1980s metropolitan Chicago, as does New York, thus presents us with the seemingly strange combination of a core area coping with sizable decline while some suburban areas are grappling with substantial growth.

The 1990s are the turn-around decade for Chicago, but not to the same degree that we have seen for New York. Population grew by 11.4% in the metropolitan area, which exceeds the growth of the New York metropolitan area of 8.3%. However, most of this growth in metropolitan Chicago took place in the suburbs. The city of Chicago grew by 4.0% and the rest of Cook County grew by 6.8%, but the inner ring counties and the outer ring counties grew by 19.8% and 32.3%, respectively. Nevertheless, the city of Chicago gained 112,000 people. This is a dramatic reversal of four decades of population loss, and means that the city had to cope with growth in many areas and experienced decline in relatively few neighborhoods. Chicago represents a more typical case in the sense that brisk growth at the metropolitan level translated into modest growth in the central city and rapid growth in the suburbs. As Table 1.2 shows, metropolitan Los Angeles is a more extreme version of this typical pattern.

D. Employment in Metropolitan Los Angeles

The other half of the story is employment. This section is a brief look at employment location patterns and growth *by place of work* in the Los Angeles metropolitan area. Employment data can also be studied *by place of residence* of the workers. The data compiled by place of work reflect the location decisions made by businesses, rather than households. Metropolitan Los Angeles was chosen (rather than New York or Chicago) because it experienced the greatest population growth of the three. What sort of employment growth went along with the rapid population growth? Also, it was easier to compile the necessary data, which are available by county. Metropolitan Los Angeles contains only five counties, all of which are in the same state. The New York and Chicago metropolitan areas contain more counties, and both include at least one county from each of three states.

Any discussion of employment change first must acknowledge the changes that have taken place in the composition of the national economy. Employment outside of agriculture can be classified broadly into industries that produce goods, industries that produce services, and government. Goods-producing industries include manufacturing, mining and construction. Service-producing industries include wholesale and retail trade, the financial sector (including banking, insurance and real estate), services (business services, health care, et al.), and transportation, communication, and utilities. In 1970 the goods-producing sector of the American economy employed 24.8 million people and the service-producing sector had employment of 45.9 million. Non-military government at all levels provided 12.8 million jobs. Thirty years later the picture had changed dramatically. The goods-producing sector employed only slightly more workers – 29.4 million. In contrast, service-producing industries had grown to an employment level of 109.9 million, and government employment had increased to 20.7 million. Total nonagricultural, non-military employment in the United States had increased by about 93% over those thirty years, but that growth was largely in the service-producing sector – in fact, 82% of employment growth was in service production. This overwhelming fact about the nature of employment growth is an important piece of background information that you must bear in mind as you read this book.

The basic data for Los Angeles are shown in Table 1.4. Total employment in the metropolitan area increased from 4.49 million in 1970 to 9.22 million in 2000, an increase of 105.3%. Population growth over this same period was from 9.98 million to 16.37 million, which is an increase of 64%. Employment grew more rapidly than population because the baby boom generation entered the workforce, and because a larger proportion of women decided to work. Table 1.4 also shows that employment growth varied by industry; manufacturing jobs increased only by 6.4%, while jobs in the service sector grew 224.3%. The main components of the service sector are health care, business services, private educational services, and various professional services (law, accounting, etc.). See the footnotes to Table 1.4 for more details. Other sectors as a whole, including retail trade, grew by about 95%. As we know from the national data, this comparison of industry employment growth is typical – manufacturing jobs grew comparatively slowly and service sector jobs grew comparatively rapidly.

Table 1.4   Employment in the Los Angeles metropolitan area, by place of work[a]

Geographic area	Employment (1,000s)		Share (%)	
	1970	2000	1970	2000
LA metropolitan area				
Total	4,491	9,223	100	100
Manufacturing	1,018	1,083	22.7	11.7
Retail trade	714	1398	15.9	15.2
Services[b]	981	3,279	21.8	35.6
Other[c]	1,778	3,463	39.6	37.5
LA County				
Total	3,391	5,514	100	100
Manufacturing	825	663	24.3	12.0
Retail trade	522	788	15.4	14.3
Services	766	2,099	22.6	38.1
Other	1,278	1,964	37.7	35.6
Suburban counties				
Total	1,100	3,709	100	100
Manufacturing	193	420	17.5	11.3
Retail trade	192	610	17.5	16.4
Services	215	1,180	19.5	31.8
Other	500	1499	45.5	40.4

[a] Employment includes all full-time and part-time wage and salary employees and proprietors.
[b] Services include hotels, personal services, business services (advertising, data processing, etc.), repair services, health services, private educational and social services, legal services, membership organizations, and professional services (engineering, accounting, management consulting, etc.).
[c] Other employment includes construction, TCU (transportation, communication and utilities), wholesale trade, FIRE (finance, insurance and real estate), government (federal, state, and local), and all other.
Source: Regional Economic Information System, Bureau of Economic Analysis, US Dept. of Commerce

Table 1.4 also shows employment for Los Angeles County (the central county) and for the other four suburban counties. Employment in the Los Angeles metropolitan area grew very rapidly, and a good deal of that growth took place in the central county. Employment in Los Angeles County increased from 3.39 million to 5.51 million, a growth of 62.6%. This compares to population growth in the county of 35.2% (Table 1.2). But the employment growth rate in the four suburban counties was more than double the rate in the central county. Employment in the suburban counties of 1.10 million in 1970 turned into 3.71 million in 2000; a growth of 237.3%. Population growth in these suburban counties was 133.3% over the same period (Table 1.2). Recall that employment growth exceeded population growth in the metropolitan area by 41.3%, so jobs were "suburbanizing" more rapidly than were residents. Employment growth by industry shows the same pattern in both locations – manufacturing jobs grew relatively slowly and service sector employment grew relatively rapidly. Another interesting fact is that the composition of employment in the suburban counties resembled the overall composition of employment in the metropolitan area fairly closely both in 1970 and 2000.

Employment growth in Los Angeles was certainly spectacular. No wonder so many people decided to locate in Los Angeles. At the same time, one could say that population growth in Los Angeles was spectacular. No wonder they created so many jobs. Which is it? It is both, of course. People follow jobs, and jobs follow people. One important goal of this book is to explain both mechanisms.

D. Making Local Population Projections

The population figures for New York and Los Angeles suggest that there may come a time when the Los Angeles metropolitan area has the larger population. The Los Angeles metropolitan population increased by 6.39 million from 1970 to 2000, while the New York metropolitan area increased by 1.28 million. As of 2000 the New York population exceeded that of Los Angeles by 2.67 million. Given the trends we see in Tables 1.1 and 1.2, when might Los Angeles overtake New York as the nation's most populous metropolitan area?

Here are some alternative suggestions for making local population projections.

1   Assume that population continues to grow by the same absolute amount per year as it did over the prior 10 (or 20, or 30) years. For example, the Los Angeles population increased by 1.84 million during the 1990s, while New York increased by 1.46 million. But, as noted above, the longer-run picture shows that Los Angeles increased by 6.39 million in 30 years while New York increased by 1.28 million. Do we base our projections just on the data for the 1990s, or should a longer period of time be used? The decade of the 1990s appears to be unusual, but is it so peculiar going forward?

2   Assume that population continues to grow at the same percentage rate as it did over the prior 10, 20, or 30 years. In the case of Los Angeles, the increase from 1990 to 2000 was 12.7%. You can solve for the annual percentage increase by solving for r in $(1 + r)^{10} = 1.127$. The steps in the solution are:

$$(1 + r) = (1.127)^{1/10}$$
$$\log(1 + r) = 0.10 \log 1.127 = 0.00519$$
$$(1 + r) = 10^{0.00519} = 1.012$$
$$r = 0.012 \text{ (i.e., 1.2\% per year).}$$

At a growth rate of 1.2% per year, the population of Los Angeles will reach 19.1 million in 12 years. What will happen to New York?

3   Assume that the metropolitan area grows so as to be the same percentage of the nation's population as it was in 2000. The US Bureau of the Census makes projections of the US population that are updated on a regular basis. The most recent projections (made before the 2000 census) are as follows:

1990 (actual)	249,439,000	
2000	270,299,000	(281,422 actual)
2010	299,862,000	
2020	324,927,000	
2030	351,070,000	
2040	377,350,000	
2050	403,687,000	

Note that the projection for 2000 turned out to be 2.22% below the actual population count, so one might update the projections for 2010 and later years by adjusting them upwards by 2.22%. If this method is used, Los Angeles will never catch up to New York, of course.

4   However, the fraction of the population of the nation that is located in the Los Angeles metropolitan area has been *rising*. You could assume that this fraction will continue to rise as it did over the 1970–2000 period. The US population was 205,052,000 in 1970 and 281,422,000 in 2000, so the fraction of the population located in metropolitan Los Angeles was 4.87% in 1970 and 5.82% in 2000. This is an increase of 0.95% in 30 years, or an increase of 0.32% per decade. We might therefore project that the population of metropolitan Los Angeles will be 6.14% of the US population in the year 2010, which (after adjusting the US projection upwards by 2.22%) produces a projected population of 18.82 million. A fascinating fact is that the fraction of the US population located in Los Angeles did not change in the 1990s; it was 5.81% in 1990. The New York population has been declining as a fraction of the nation; it was 8.66% in 1970 and fell to 6.77% in 2000.

There is no "right answer" for how to make local population projections. It may surprise you to learn that all of the methods discussed here have been used by local demographers and others who need a local population projection.

Preview of Coming Attractions

This book is organized into six parts:

*   economics and urban areas;
*   location patterns in urban areas;
*   urban housing and real estate;
*   government in urban areas;
*   urban social problems; and
*   urban growth.

The remaining three chapters of Part I continue the introduction to the field of urban economics. Chapter 2 is a discussion of schools of thought within the field of urban economics. Urban economists come in (roughly speaking) three varieties, mainstream, conservative, and Marxist. An economist's identification with a particular school of thought can influence the research questions he or she asks, the methods used to investigate those questions, and the nature of the conclusions that are drawn from research. These matters are examined in some depth in Chapter 2. In Chapters 3 and 4 we turn from methodological matters to the economic origins and functions of cities. The focus of Chapter 3 is the location decisions of firms and how those decisions create cities, and Chapter 4 is an examination of the economic functions of cities.

Part II contains three chapters on the location patterns of economic activity within urban areas. Basic theories and facts are introduced in Chapter 5. In Chapter 5 urban areas are organized around a single central point. Chapter 6 presents some modest extensions of the basic model of the city introduced in Chapter 5, and Chapter 7 is a discussion of the multi-centered urban areas of today.

Part III contains two chapters that cover theory, problems, and policies that pertain to urban housing and three chapters that constitute an introduction to urban real estate – basic institutions, market analysis, and real estate development. Part IV contains two chapters on urban government that cover public finance and urban transportation. Part V covers additional urban social problems such as poverty (and its spatial concentration), crime, and education.

The economic growth of urban areas is treated in Part VI of the book. The focus of this part of the book is on urban area as an economic unit. As stated above, spatial patterns within the urban area are largely ignored. A wide variety of theories of urban economic growth are covered. These theories generally are of two types; one type emphasizes the demand side as a determinant of growth, and the other type concentrates on the supply side. The relationship of urban growth to forces of agglomeration in urban areas and to technical change is discussed in depth. The last chapter in the book is devoted to urban economic growth policy. The chapter discusses the process of setting general economic goals, devising strategies and supporting policies, and conducting evaluations of the results of policy.

F. Summary

This first chapter has served to introduce you to the subject matter of urban economics and to the contents of this book. Urban economics is largely an applied field of economic inquiry in which data are collected, patterns in the data are observed, economic models are formulated and tested, and then the knowledge that is gained is used for forecasting or policy-making purposes.

Urban economics is about the economics of urban areas. Urban areas are linked to the larger economy, and one critical task is to understand those linkages. The other major part of the agenda of urban economics is to understand the spatial patterns of economic activity within an urban area – and how those patterns have changed. The examples of New York, Los Angeles, and Chicago were used to illustrate some of the basic facts of modern urban areas in the US. We learned that the absence of population growth at the metropolitan level usually translates into population decline in the core of the urban area because there is an underlying trend towards suburbanization even in urban areas that are not growing. We also learned that very rapid population growth in the metropolitan area leads to an increase in population densities and to a remarkable spreading out of the urban area. And we learned some different methods for making local population projections.

One final introductory word needs to be said. Probably many students sign up for urban economics because they are interested in and concerned about a variety of economic and social problems that exist in urban areas in the US and around the world. Students are rightly concerned about poverty, homelessness, central city schools, racial discrimination, the welfare system, high taxes, and many other troubling aspects of urban life. Such students have come to the right place. It probably is true that quite a few professional economists who specialize in urban economics began their studies with similar concerns, and this book reflects the topics that urban economists have decided to study.

However, economists (and other social scientists, of course) know that concern about economic and social problems is not enough. Study and professional training are needed to turn concern into deeper understanding and useful contributions to debates over urban economic and social policy. That is why the emphasis in this book is on the fundamental methods that are used by urban economists. As you will see, there are many places where the more formal study of urban economics comes very close to being the study of an urban economic or social problem. However, there will also be many times when your study of this book seems to be pretty remote from more immediate urban problems. Be patient. Urban economists are probably more concerned about urban problems than are most people, but they also know that understanding urban problems is difficult work. A course in urban economics is, in our view, an essential part (but only a part) of the education that one needs to understand and address urban economic and social problems.

Exercise

Use the four methods discussed in Section D above to make population projections for the New York and Los Angeles metropolitan areas for 2010 and 2020. Does LA land overtake the Big Apple? If so, when does that happen?

References

Abu-Lughod, Janet, 1999, *New York, Chicago, Los Angeles: America's Global Cities*. Minneapolis: University of Minnesota Press.

Alonso, William, 1964, *Location and Land Use*. Cambridge, MA: Harvard University Press.

Hoover, Edgar and Raymond Vernon, 1959, *Anatomy of a Metropolis*. Cambridge, MA: Harvard University Press.

Chapter 2

Schools of Thought in Urban Economics

A. Introduction

Urban economics was portrayed in Chapter 1 as a field of research in which economists are busy gathering data, building and testing models, making forecasts, conducting policy analysis, and deducing new normative propositions. All of that is true, but it leaves something out. Present within the field of urban economics (and economics in general) are three rather distinct schools of thought. Students in courses in macroeconomics are introduced to different schools of thought, such as the "Keynesians" and the "monetarists." Some textbooks in macroeconomics try to give a "balanced" treatment to the different schools of thought, while other texts primarily present the views of only one school. As you will see, adherence to a particular school of thought can influence research at every phase. On the normative side, schools of thought differ in the ethical objectives that are taken as given. On the positive side, the school of thought influences the nature of the data that are gathered, the nature of the facts that are deemed important to explain, the choice of economic model to explain those facts, and the use of the models that are formed. The existence of alternative schools of thought leads to competing economic models that can co-exist. Sometimes it is not simply a matter of determining which economic model is "best," but which school of thought is "best." Often there is no answer to this question. And often it will be the case that a person's views on a particular question cannot be understood until that person's school of thought is identified.

What are the three schools of thought in urban economics? We shall refer to them as mainstream economics, conservative economics, and Marxian economics. These schools of thought in economics overlap with political views (liberal, conservative, socialist/ Marxist), so each school of thought will be discussed both as a guide to economic research and as a political philosophy. These schools of thought are mentioned in various places throughout the book. The basic ideas in this chapter can be covered by reading the next section on mainstream economics and the concluding section.

B. Mainstream Economics

Most urban economists (including your authors) belong to the school of thought that is called mainstream economics. This school of thought is presented in most intermediate textbooks in microeconomic theory, so most students are already familiar with it. The ethical objective in mainstream economics is the maximization of the utility of the members of a society, where utility depends upon the goods a person consumes and how a person spends his/her time. The society is constrained by the availability of resources, including land, capital, and (above all) the time of its members. Framing the economic question in this way as maximization subject to constraints leads to the familiar normative proposition that the marginal benefit of a particular good or activity (and hence price) should equal marginal cost. This is so because the failure to satisfy this condition makes someone needlessly worse off. For example, suppose a monopolist controls all of the taxicabs in a particular city and charges a fare that is higher than marginal cost. This means that there are some consumers out there who are willing to pay more than marginal cost (but less than the monopoly price) for a taxi ride, but they are unable to satisfy their demands. The benefit of the unsupplied taxi ride exceeds the benefit of the next-best use of resources at the margin (i.e., the marginal opportunity cost), so the consumer is made needlessly worse off. A different allocation of existing resources (more taxi rides, less of something else) could make consumers better off.

Mainstream economists believe that the allocation of resources to their various uses is, for the most part, best handled by the market. However, there are some very important exceptions to this rule that call for intervention into the economy by government. Mainstream economists argue that monopoly (and oligopoly), externalities (pollution and congestion), information problems (such as murky accounting by firms), and public goods all call for public action to improve the allocation of resources. They also acknowledge that the market economy produces a distribution of income that is unequal, and they generally favor public policies to reduce income inequality. They recognize that there may be some loss of efficiency caused by income redistribution policy, but they suggest that society might be willing to tolerate some inefficiency in order to achieve a more equitable income distribution. They believe that government intervention in these situations will improve matters. Indeed, mainstream economists also generally advocate activist macroeconomic policies as well. They believe that the government is capable of using monetary and fiscal policy to stabilize the economy in the short run and to promote growth in the long run. Government policies can be mistaken or badly timed, but on balance the policies of a democratic government can be made to improve welfare.

The research agenda of mainstream urban economists is, to a degree, influenced by membership in this school of thought. A fair amount of their research focuses of the costs and benefits of various policy actions or proposals. Consider housing for low-income households, for example. Facts are gathered concerning the operation of the urban housing market in general and the status of low-income households in the housing market in particular. Economic models of the urban housing market are formulated and estimated. Then those models are used to discover the most efficient method for improving the housing of low-income households. Mainstream urban economists think that the facts show that the construction of public housing is a very expensive method for improving the housing of low-income households. The use of housing vouchers – certificates that increase the ability of low-income households to rent decent housing in the private market – is far more efficient. The same improvement in housing quality can be achieved with a lower government expenditure on housing vouchers, and a lower expenditure of real resources as well, than on public housing.

Now the fact is that housing policy in the US, until fairly recently, included only a small program that resembles housing vouchers. What explanation did the mainstream urban economist have for this seeming anomaly? First, nearly all of the public housing was constructed before we knew that housing vouchers are better policy. We were locked into a policy that had to use the existing public housing units until they were obsolete. Recently a program was started in which some of those public housing units are being demolished and replaced with a variety of public programs, including housing vouchers. Second, the suppliers of public housing (and housing that is supplied by private suppliers under public subsidy) formed political interest groups that block attempts to turn the public money for housing over directly to the low-income households. A political battle was fought, and that battle was waged partly with the results of studies that show the efficiency of housing vouchers and the waste of public housing. Also, the final outcome involved some modification of the voucher idea to give housing suppliers some control over how the program is administered.

The appendix to this book provides a brief review of some of the major normative propositions in mainstream microeconomics, and introduces the mathematical techniques that are used in this book. You should study the first two sections of this appendix before you read Chapter 3.

C. Conservative Economics

Conservative economics will be discussed at some length here because this school of thought has been quite influential since the 1970s, and because most students may not really know how conservative economics differs from mainstream economics.

Most students know that Milton Friedman, the professor emeritus from the University of Chicago and a winner of the Nobel Prize in economics, is the most prominent conservative economist. But it was Friedrich A. Hayek (another Nobel Prize winner) who wrote what conservative economists consider to be the classic statement of their values. Hayek's book *The Road to Serfdom* was published in 1944, and it still exerts considerable influence in conservative quarters. In its Summer 1994 issue the conservative magazine *Policy Review* included a symposium entitled "Serfdom USA: Fifty Years Down Hayek's Road." The symposium coincides with the reissue of the book on its 50th anniversary.

Hayek's chief concern was with the progressive replacement of competition with planning, or the central direction of the nation's resources towards some objective. At the time he wrote he was worried about the progressive advance of socialism in western nations, especially England. His concern was with the *method* of centralized planning, even if the goals espoused by its advocates were admirable. He saw that the ultimate effect of socialism and other forms of central planning would be a return to serfdom, the condition of most ordinary people prior to their progressive liberation that began roughly with the Renaissance. For Hayek (1944, p. 14), the hallmark of Western Civilization is:

> the respect for the individual man *qua* man, that is, the recognition of his own views and tastes as supreme in his own sphere, however narrowly that may be circumscribed, and the belief that it is desirable that men should develop their own individual gifts and bents.

Conservatives think that the emergence of this respect for individual was closely associated with the development of the laissez faire market economy.

For Hayek the danger was people who advocated goals for the society other than freedom and liberty. This includes mainstream economists who advocate the maximization of utility of society's members. Hayek's central point is that the pursuit of social goals (except for those that can achieve virtually unanimous agreement), even those chosen through democratic means, must inevitably sharply restrict the freedom of individuals. The democratic decision to engage in central planning of a particular sector of the economy will lead to a delegation of substantial power to planning agencies. Hayek (1944, p. 66) stated that:

> The objectionable feature is that delegation is so often resorted to because the matter in hand cannot be regulated by general rules but only by the exercise of discretion in the decision of particular cases. In these instances delegation means that some authority is given power to make with the force of law what to all intents and purposes are arbitrary decisions (usually described as "judging the case on its merits").

The attempt to plan a substantial portion of an economy will eventually cry out for an economic dictator, someone who can get things done – make the trains run on time, etc. Free societies are governed by the rule of law, not by administrative discretion. Or, as Milton Friedman suggests, the Federal Reserve should increase the money supply by a fixed percentage per year (a rule) rather than attempt to engage in discretionary monetary policy.

Hayek wrote a new foreword for his book in the late 1950s, and there he recognized that socialism based upon the state as chief owner of the means of production was essentially a dead issue in the US and Western Europe. His updated forecast was for continued "hodge-podge" development of the welfare state that would produce restrictions on human freedom that would strongly resemble full state socialism. Increasing reliance on administrative discretion rather than the rule of law was, in his view, going to be in the cards. The desire to have a welfare state would slowly produce a psychological predilection to limiting freedom. He predicted that we would get there, just at a slower pace than if we had embraced outright socialism.

Whether you believe Hayek's prediction, Milton Friedman certainly did. His 1962 book *Capitalism and Freedom* sets down the conservative's economic creed clearly and concisely. Like Hayek, Friedman's basic proposition is that human freedom is the ultimate end, and that competitive capitalism is a system of economic freedom that is a necessary condition for political freedom. The secondary proposition is that the scope of government must be limited to functions that Friedman outlines and that governmental power must be dispersed rather than concentrated at the federal level. His basic statement (1962, p. 2) is that:

> Freedom is a rare and delicate plant. Our minds tell us, and history confirms, that the great threat to freedom is the concentration of power. Government is necessary to preserve our freedom, it is an instrument through which we can exercise our freedom; yet by concentrating power in political hands, it is also a threat to freedom.

Friedman asked (1962, p. 2), "How can we benefit from the promise of government while avoiding the threat to freedom?" His answer is that government largely should be limited to certain functions that support the competitive market economy – provision of pure public goods such as the common defense, maintenance of law and order, enforcement of contracts voluntarily made, definition and enforcement of property rights, and provision of a monetary system. He found little reason for government action to regulate or operate monopolies, or for public policy to attempt to correct for externalities (neighborhood effects) or informational problems.

Friedman's view of monopoly is instructive. Monopoly means a lack of alternatives, and therefore an inhibition of freedom. Friedman stated (in agreement with Hayek) that monopoly most often arises from government policy of some sort or through collusive agreements, so most monopoly can be avoided by eliminating the offending public support or by enforcement of the anti-trust laws. The few instances in which monopoly arises from technological factors call for one of three courses of action; private monopoly, government regulation, or government operation. Friedman suggested (1962, p. 28) that permitting the private monopoly to operate as it will "may be the least of the evils."

In matters of externalities, or neighborhood effects, Friedman follows the argument that was made by Ronald Coase, his colleague at the University of Chicago and yet another Nobel Prize winner, in a classic article (Coase 1960). Coase argued that, if property rights are fully defined and enforced, and that the costs of making "transactions" (i.e., costs of arriving at private contracts) are trivial, then externalities will not cause inefficiencies. Private negotiation can be used to arrive at an efficient allocation of resources. For example, suppose that a factory owns the right to make noise. In this case the neighbors can pay the factory owner to reduce the noise (by, perhaps, installing insulation), or they can suffer – whichever is cheaper. Or suppose that the neighbors own the right to peace and quiet. The factory owner can install insulation, or he can bribe the neighbors into accepting some noise (whichever is cheaper). Furthermore, all parties always have the option of moving away. Provided that a private agreement can be reached with minimal difficulties, there is no role for government to play in the regulation of factory noise. Besides, the attempt by government to regulate noise may make matters worse. Problems related to information are best handled by individuals because they have an incentive to make decisions based on good information.

Friedman recognized that one of society's needs is the alleviation of poverty. Here he is famous for his advocacy of the negative income tax for all poor people regardless of occupation, employment status, sex, location, etc. According to Friedman, the negative income tax has three fundamental advantages; it provides purchasing power for the poor directly, it permits markets to function in unregulated fashion, and it can be set up to provide an incentive for the poor to work. Friedman advocated the negative income tax as a more effective replacement for the myriad of programs that attempt to assist the poor. Note that Friedman's proposals follow Hayek's philosophy that we should follow simple rules of law rather than rely on the bureaucratic judgments of people such as officials of the Environmental Protection Agency and social workers. At this point you may wonder why Friedman advocates any anti-poverty policy at all. In a market economy people are paid according to their own decisions to work, obtain training for jobs, undertake risks, and so on. The income distribution is the result of choices freely made, so what's the problem? First of all, the economy is full of constraints on free choice. Equal educational opportunity is not available to all, minimum wage laws exist, and occupational licensure limits entry to various remunerative jobs. Friedman advocates doing away with all of these limitations on freedom, but in the meantime we have people in poverty. Furthermore, Friedman believes that the alleviation of poverty is a public good. As he put it (1962, p. 191):

> I am distressed by the sight of poverty; I am benefited by its alleviation; but I am benefited equally whether I or someone else pays for its alleviation; the benefits of other people's charity therefore partly accrue to me.

Given this "free-rider" problem, the alleviation of poverty must become a public program. Private charity will be insufficient to improve the welfare of *those who are not in poverty*. In this case, as in the case of other public goods, a public program enhances the personal freedom of both the poor *and* those who are not poor.

There can be no question that membership in the Conservative Economics school of thought influences one's research. These economists look for unexpected places in which the private market is working well, and they take particular delight in finding those instances in which government policy turns out to have had effects that seemingly were the opposite of those intended. In fact, George Stigler, another of Friedman's colleagues at the University of Chicago, received the Nobel Prize for founding the Chicago School of Political Economy. Members of this school concentrate some of their research efforts on the economic analysis of political decisions – equilibrium in the political marketplace for policies that help or harm certain groups. Why do public policies seem to "fail" so often? Perhaps it is because we fail to perceive the real purposes of those policies. For example, it is argued that zoning to regulate the use of urban land is needed to protect the health and welfare of the public. The legal justification for zoning in fact falls under the police power of local government. No doubt some aspects of zoning ordinances do protect the health and welfare of the public, but other aspects of zoning probably do just the opposite. Consider the requirement that some suburban zoning ordinances require that residential lots are quite large. This "large-lot" zoning has the effect of excluding households of more modest means from living in that suburb, and has little to do with health and welfare of the public. Has zoning therefore "failed"? No, because the exclusion of lower-income households was the intention of the local government in the first place.

Two of Friedman's favorite examples of urban policy are public housing and urban renewal. One argument made for public housing is that slums create negative neighborhood effects. Therefore, the argument goes, the government should tear down the slums and replace them with public housing so that the negative neighborhood effects are eliminated. Friedman replies that those negative neighborhood effects may well exist, and that Coasian negotiation cannot handle the problem. The proper policy therefore is to levy a tax on slum housing (just as we should levy a tax on polluters), and to provide the poor with more income through a negative income tax. By the way, other conservative economists doubt that there are pervasive negative neighborhood effects associated with the housing consumed by low-income households that would call for any public action at all. Friedman then suggests that the real justification for the public housing program was paternalism – policy makers thought that the poor needed better housing more than they needed other things.

Whatever the justification for the public housing program may have been, its results seem to have been disastrous. The program of the 1950s bulldozed more housing units than were constructed, and many of the units constructed under the urban renewal program were for middle-class households. The public housing units that were constructed tended to segregate the poor into public housing developments, and to concentrate and perhaps to exacerbate social problems. The actual implementation of the public housing and urban renewal programs, as opposed to the high-minded goals that were the original motivation for these programs, was the result of decisions made by local officials and real estate developers who had their own agendas.

D. Marxian Economics

Karl Marx provided the world with a sweeping interpretation of economic history that included a prophesy for capitalism. Marx taught that the ultimate outcome of capitalism is huge industrial firms owned by the capitalist class that exploit and oppress the industrial workers, the proletariat. Capitalism ultimately fails to be of benefit to the mass of workers, who rise up and defeat the capitalist class in the final battle of the war between these two dominant social classes. The overriding theme in Marxism is the class struggle between the two classes that are associated with the two primary factors of production, capital and labor.

Marxian economics survives in American universities (and a few other places), so it behooves one to understand Marxian arguments, and to be able to recognize a Marxist. Marxism has been revised and adapted to the American scene, but the theme of class struggle remains intact. According to Marxists, conventional economics, including both the mainstream and conservative varieties, omits class conflict as an important factor to consider.

What does this sort of Marxist analysis have to do with urban areas? Plenty, according to a growing group of Marxist urbanists. For them, class conflict and the role of the state in advanced capitalism play out in urban areas. In the early 1970s Marxists began to write about how, in their view, urban problems that provoke local conflicts have their roots in national, and even global, economic forces. Why has industrial investment shifted to the sunbelt and to less-developed countries? Why is the American economy shifting from an industrial to a service base? How do these forces influence class conflicts in urban areas, and what are the outcomes of those conflicts?

Marxists see class conflicts in controversies over the use of land in cities and in the funding of urban public services. Industrial workers in the US (and in other advanced capitalist countries) failed to create national revolutionary politics based on grievances at the work place, so Marxists have turned their attention to urban political economy because that is where the class conflict action is. For them capitalism will inevitably lead to class conflicts that will lead to a socialist revolution, so the questions are, "Where are the conflicts happening?" and, following Lenin, "What can Marxist intellectuals do to move the revolutionary process along?" In short, the ethical objective is socialist revolution, and the gathering of facts and the formulation of theories are guided by this goal. As the Marxist urban political scientist Michael Peter Smith (1988, pp. 64–5) puts it:

> Both structural Marxists and other critical urban theorists were forced to come to grips with the failure of the industrial working classes in advanced capitalist societies to convert concrete grievances found in the work place into a revolutionary politics. Surveying the landscape, they turned to the arena where social conflicts in the 1960s and 1970s were most evident, the arena of urban politics.

For Marxists there must be a "crisis" that reflects the inherent contradictions in the capitalist economy, but traditional Marxist analysis had not been used to examine urban areas. Marxists have disagreed over how to make Marxism fit urban political economy. This section describes three examples of Marxist analysis applied to urban areas.

Richard Child Hill (1978) provides one anatomy of that "crisis" in the context of urban America. He argues that the huge profits and the capital accumulation of large, oligopolistic firms no longer require the older, densely concentrated central cities. Capital accumulation is taking place in the suburbs. More importantly, perhaps, as profits have been squeezed since the 1980s, the major corporations have become global in scope. They seek to locate production and distribution facilities at the least expensive locations – in places such as Mexico and southeast Asia. Hill does not see all of this as a "capitalist conspiracy," but rather as inevitable outcomes of capitalism. The consequences of these trends include the loss of economic opportunity for central city residents (especially minority populations), financial decline of various central cities, and a host of social problems associated with the urban "underclass." Central cities have an enormous fiscal burden associated with maintaining some semblance of social control over their people who no longer have an economic function in the capitalist economy. The inherent contradiction is between the use of the economic surplus for further capital accumulation or measures for social control. For most people, questions of urban social policy are the ordinary stuff of local and national politics. Marxists seek to make clear the underlying "structural" reasons for social problems in our capitalist economy.

Another example of Marxist analysis of urban areas is Matthew Edel's (1972) essay on the conflict over the use of land near the downtown areas of major cities. He argued that, as new housing was built in the suburbs for upper- and middle-class households, the older housing in the central city was relinquished to the lower-income households. However, many of the jobs held by the corporate elite and their supporters continued to be located downtown. Indeed, many downtown areas experienced renewed growth in professional and white-collar jobs starting in the 1980s that has continued. The continued strength of downtown as the location of jobs held by the middle and upper classes therefore creates a conflict over the use of land near the downtown business area. Edel (1972) argued that the market is not capable of converting what many regard as slums into places where the middle and upper classes wish to live. Government action is needed, and the political struggle surrounding "urban renewal" policy and "gentrification" is an outgrowth of the market (capitalist) economy that is a conflict between social classes. Edel went on to describe examples of victories for the social elite in such land-use conflicts. Gentrification is usually defined as private residential and commercial investment in an urban neighborhood that involves an inflow of people of higher socioeconomic status (SES) than the current residents. Gentrification has its positive and negative aspects, but it is important for you to realize that Marxists view gentrification as part of the larger class struggle arising from the inherent contradictions of corporate capitalism. More discussion of gentrification is included in Chapter 8.

Andy Merrifield's book (2002) is titled "Dialectical Urbanism: Social Struggles in the Capitalist City" and takes this argument even further by asserting that conflicts over land use are conflicts over what Marx called exchange value (in which urban space becomes just another commodity with a price) and use value (urban land as concrete places where people live). Merrifield thinks that an understanding of this inherent conflict will alter how we see the world. He states (p. 170) that:

> progressives need to find ways of incorporating struggle, conflict, and contradiction into a passionate and just urban life, secretly acknowledging that the way beyond these contradictions is working through them, not around them.

Note the use of the term progressives. Evidently one does not say Marxists.

All students should learn to think critically and, in our opinion, the Marxist viewpoint must be given particularly close scrutiny. We shall illustrate with our own critique of Hill's urban crisis theory.

We must remember that some Marxists do not care whether their arguments are "right or wrong" in the ordinary sense. Following Lenin, their primary concern is whether their arguments move the society closer to the socialist revolution.

Consider Hill's (1978) attempt to link the problems of central cities primarily to the actions of major corporations. First of all, the movement of middle-class people and many jobs to the suburbs does not originate with decisions made by the elite of corporate management. Many people have a taste for living in the suburbs. The development of the automobile and the government decisions to build highways were driven by the obvious benefits that automobiles bring to people – provided that there are decent roads upon which to drive. Subsequently many employers large and small have established work places in the suburbs. As subsequent chapters show, one does not have to be a Marxist to understand why. Secondly, it is true that, since the early 1970s, many of the older American corporations have been under a great deal of pressure to cut costs and improve productivity. We have seen big increases in the foreign penetration of American markets (along with expanding American exports). As the Japanese, Chinese, German, Korean, and other economies have grown, competition in world markets has increased. Corporate "downsizing" seems to be a way of life. Changes in technology and communications have made it feasible to disperse production activity away from traditional locations in the northeastern US and create long and complex supply chains. All of these changes can be explained using the methods of mainstream economics. The social and fiscal problems of the older central cities are very troublesome, and have many causes.

Marxists such as Hill cannot have it both ways. If the problems of the central cities in the current era are the product of advanced capitalism, so too were the benefits of urban areas of just a few years ago. In the period of the 1940s to the 1960s millions of people of all races migrated to the great urban areas of the northeastern US to work in the factories, offices, and distribution centers. Members of minority groups, especially blacks, encountered racism in the cities, but still they came because life in the city was better than life in the rural areas and small towns of the South and Midwest. The machinations of the elite of corporate managers cannot be given credit for these facts, just as they cannot be given primary blame for today's urban problems. It is not clear that the notion of class conflict in "advanced capitalism" contributes to our understanding of urban economic and social problems. And racism is not a product of capitalism. Racism exists all over the world.

E. Summary

Urban economists can generally be classified as belonging to one of three schools of thought – mainstream economics, conservative economics, or Marxist economics. Mainstream urban economists take the economy as they find it. Their first task is to understand the workings of the urban economy, and then they sometimes make policy recommendations that are designed to have benefits that are greater than costs. Conservative economists normally are distrustful of the ability of government to undertake policies that enhance individual freedom. Milton and Rose Friedman, in their best-selling book *Free to Choose*, asserted that (1980, p. xix):

> In the government sphere, as in the market, there seems to be an invisible hand, but it operates in precisely the opposite direction from Adam Smith's: an individual who intends only to serve the public interest by fostering government intervention is "led by an invisible hand to promote" private interests, "which was no part of his intention."

The conservative urban economist's research agenda will often include finding out why the market outcome is the best outcome, or determining just how the Friedmans' invisible hand "theorem" operates in particular cases. In complete contrast, the Marxist economist seeks to find the locus of the crisis of advanced capitalism that will lead eventually to socialist revolution. Many contemporary Marxists think that the inevitable class struggle between capital and labor is taking place in America's central cities, and includes conflict over the use of land. Some Marxists view gentrification as a form of class struggle.

You should be able now to recognize each of these schools of thought when you meet them. And we are certain that you will meet them. Your task will always be to use your ability for critical thinking to evaluate the points of view that you encounter. It is fair to say that most of the rest of this book is devoted to mainstream urban economics. Criticisms of mainstream economic thinking are included along the way, and some references to the conservative and Marxist schools of thought are also incorporated. Our purpose in this chapter is to give you a candid introduction to the three schools of thought so that you are better prepared to engage in the debate.

Exercise

1   Select an issue of public policy that is under debate in the news media in an urban area of your choice. For example, the issue might have to do with public housing, schools, environmental protection, public transit, etc. Decide how a mainstream economist, a conservative economist, and a Marxist economist might approach the study of that issue and what the nature of their policy recommendations might be.

References

Coase, Ronald H., 1960, "The Problem of Social Cost," *Journal of Law and Economics*, vol. 3 (October), pp. 1–44.

Edel, Matthew, 1972, "Planning, Market or Warfare? Recent Land Use Conflict in American Cities," in M. Edel and J. Rothenberg (eds.), *Reading in Urban Economics*. New York: Macmillan Publishing Co.

Friedman, Milton, 1962, *Capitalism and Freedom*. Chicago: University of Chicago Press.

Friedman, Milton and Rose D. Friedman, 1980, *Free to Choose*. New York: Harcourt Brace Jovanovich.

Hayek, Friedrich A., 1944, *The Road to Serfdom*. Chicago: University of Chicago Press.

Hill, Richard Child, 1978, "Fiscal Collapse and Political Struggle in Decaying Central Cities in the United States," in W. Tabb and L. Sawyers (eds.), *Marxism and the Metropolis*. New York: Oxford.

Merrifield, Andy, 2002, *Dialectical Urbanism*. New York: Monthly Review Press.

Smith, Michael Peter, 1988, *City, State, and Market*. Cambridge: Basil Blackwell.

Chapter 3

Location Decisions, Agglomeration Economies, and the Origins of Cities

A. Introduction

Cities are formed by the location decisions of firms, households, and governmental bodies. This chapter examines the theory and some more practical aspects of how location decisions are made by firms. The chapter begins with some basic theory that explores transportation costs and other determinants of a firm's location decision. The next section takes a further step to examine the possibility that firms in a specific industry, or firms in general, may save on costs by locating together. These ideas about economies of urban agglomeration are explored theoretically in the succeeding section. The final section of the chapter uses some of the theoretical concepts to examine the origins of cities in the United States.

B. Lessons in Basic Location Theory for a Firm

The general problem faced by a firm is to choose a location at which it will assemble inputs and from which it will distribute its output to customers. Both the inputs and the customers may have dispersed location patterns, and both inputs and output are subject to transportation costs. This general problem can be very complicated, so in order to make some progress, economists emphasize two simple versions of the problem. The first version supposes that there is only one input that is used to produce the output, and that customers are located all in one place. The second version suppresses the inputs entirely, and only considers a firm that must distribute output to customers in various locations.

In the first model – the one input, one market model – the firm uses an input that is available at some location and produces an output that is sold at another location. For example, suppose that the firm's business is to take raw lumber (i.e. trees that have been cut down) available at some forest, cut the lumber into firewood, and then deliver the firewood to the market in the city. One of the things that the firm must do to maximize profits is to select the location where it cuts the trees into firewood. At any level of output that is chosen the firm can make more profits if it can cut down on transportation costs. Where does the firm perform the operation of cutting the trees into firewood? The firm could transport the raw lumber to the city first, and then produce the firewood. Or the firm could cut up the trees at the forest first, and then transport the firewood to market. Also, some point between the forest and the city could be selected.

Suppose the firm decides to produce 10 tons of firewood, and assume that it takes 12.5 tons of trees to make 10 tons of firewood. (There is 20% waste in the process of turning trees into firewood, so this is a *weight-losing* process.) The firm can use a standard stake-bed truck to carry the firewood, but hauling trees calls for a larger and more expensive truck. Either type of truck is available for rent, but the truck used to haul trees is more expensive. Now consider this problem carefully. Clearly it is cheaper to cut the trees into firewood at the forest and haul firewood to the city compared to hauling the trees to the city first. Furthermore, and here is the more subtle point, the firm will not choose a point in between the forest and the city either. Hauling 12.5 tons of trees even one mile is more expensive (in this model) than hauling 10 tons of firewood. The firm will choose to locate at the source of the raw material – the trees.

This argument can be made graphically. The firm uses an input that is located at point *I* in Figure 3.1, and produces output for the market located at point *M*. Straight line *II** shows the cost of transporting the input (12.5 tons of raw lumber) needed for 10 tons of output at various distances from *I*. The slope of this line is the cost of an additional mile of transporting the input. Straight line *MM** likewise shows the cost of transporting the output (10 tons of firewood) from various locations away from point *M*. The slope of the line is −1 times the cost of transporting the output one more mile. The negative slope means that this component of transportation cost declines as distance to the market *declines*. The entire transportation cost for 10 tons of output is the sum of these two costs, which is line *M*I**. Where would you locate your firewood firm? Given the transportation costs displayed in Figure 3.1, you would choose to locate at point *I* because the point minimizes transportation costs.

The appendix to this chapter contains a mathematical model for this location problem that connects the model to the standard theory of the firm. This appendix is recommended for those students who are familiar with microeconomic theory.

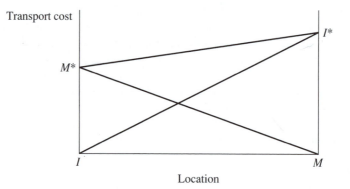

Figure 3.1   Transportation cost and location

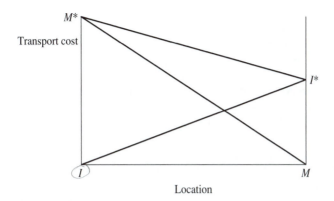

Figure 3.2   Transportation cost and location

The example shown in Figure 3.1 leads to the firm's location choice at *I*, the input location. It is easy to construct cases in which the firm decides to locate at the market. Consider the case of Coca Cola. The "secret" formula syrup is produced at point *I* and is the main input. The other input is water. The market for bottles of Coca Cola is at point *M*. It is much cheaper to transport the input (syrup) than it is to transport the bottles of output. Figure 3.2 illustrates the matter. This is a case of a *weight-gaining* production process, and the transportation costs throw the firm to the market location.

What does this have to do with cities? Note that the firm chooses to locate either at the input location or at the market, and not at intermediate points. Firms are drawn to their inputs or to their markets. Either location might become a city. Obviously a *market-oriented firm* (as in Figure 3.2) will locate in a city, where the consumers are located. Also, an *input-oriented firm* (as in Figure 3.1) would locate in a city if the input happens to be located there. For example, the main input might be some sort of specialized labor rather than a raw material. The cumulative effect of these location decisions would create cities.

The next basic location theory model considers a firm that must distribute output to customers in various locations. It is assumed that input and production costs do not vary from place to place. The simplest version of the model presumes that customers are located along a straight line – space is only one dimensional. Figure 3.3 shows seven customers (*A* through *G*) arrayed along a road. Each customer purchases one unit of the good. Ignore customer *G'* for now. The rules of the game are that the firm must select *one* location at which production takes place, and then deliver the product to each customer. Furthermore, there is one delivery round trip per customer. We can assume that either the firm's delivery person or the customer makes the trip. The classic example is that of an ice cream vendor on a (linear) beach.

Where should the firm locate to minimize transportation costs? The firm should follow the *principle of median location*, which states that transportation costs are minimized

Figure 3.3   Customers on a road

if the firm is located at the median customer. In this case the median customer is customer D. Three customers are located to the left of D and three are located to the right of D. Why does the median customer determine the minimum for transportation costs? Consider any other point – point C, for example. Assume that the distance from D to C is 1/2 mile. Point C has a higher transportation cost than point D because, in moving to C, the firm is nearer to three customers (A, B, and C) and saves 3 miles in round trips, but is farther away from four customers (D, E, F, and G) and adds 4 miles to total delivery cost. A similar argument holds for any other point along the line. By a similar argument, the best location cannot be off the line either. Why?

One interesting and perhaps unexpected implication of the model is that the location of the most distant customer makes no difference to the choice of location. Suppose that customer G moves to location G' in Figure 3.3. Point D is still the best location. Total delivery costs have increased, of course, but there is nothing the firm can do about that.

The principle of median location works best if there is an *odd* number of customers. If there is an *even* number of customers, the firm's location is not determined precisely. For example, suppose that customer G (and G') is eliminated. Now with six customers the firm is indifferent to all locations from C to D. As the firm hypothetically moves from C to D, it gets closer to three customers and farther away from three customers. But moving outside this range will increase transportation cost – a move away from D towards E puts the firm closer to only two customers and farther away from four.

The two basic location models for the firm in this section seem to offer contradictory advice. The one-input, one-market model leads to the conclusion that the firm should locate at the input source or at the market. However, the principle of median location tells us that the firm should locate in some sense in the "middle" of its customers. Upon closer examination the two models are not offering contradictory advice. Consider a firm with only two customers (with inputs suppressed). Such a firm is indifferent to all locations along the route from one customer to the other – provided that the cost of delivery per mile is the same for the two customers. Now suppose that the per-mile delivery cost is higher for one customer than for the other. This delivery cost difference makes the firm prefer to locate at the site of the customer with the higher delivery cost. This result is essentially the same as the result obtained in the one-input, one-market model. In short, the model that generates the principle of median location can easily be transformed into one that closely resembles the one-input, one-market model.

The principle of median location provides a reason why cities grow. Suppose that a new product is invented, and a firm decides to provide the product to the market shown in Figure 3.4. The market has five customers (A through E) located together in a city and three customers located in the "hinterlands" (F, G, and H). The median location is between customers D and E – in the city. The city attracts the new firm based on access to the customers.

Figure 3.4   Customers on a road

A slightly more complex model than the two discussed so far can be used to explain the existence of port cities. A port city is a city at which goods are transferred from one mode of transportation to another. There is a cost of transferring cargo from one mode to another. For example, wheat is transported from the farms to the port by train, and then exported by ship. Or foodstuffs are transported to the port by ship, and then distributed by truck. In each case the cargo must undergo the costly operation of being unloaded and then loaded. These natural breaks in the transportation system, called transshipment points, become likely locations for cities. A transshipment point, by definition, requires a labor force for the loading and unloading operations. In addition, a transshipment point can become the location of production activity.

Consider the case of wheat production for export shown in Figure 3.5. Wheat is produced along rail lines R_1, R_2, and R_3. The market for wheat and wheat products is located at point M, and the port is point P. The distance from P to M must be traversed by ship. Now imagine that you are going to locate a flour mill somewhere in Figure 3.5. There are two locations that are likely candidates, M and P. It might be cheaper to ship raw wheat all the way to M and produce flour at the market. Because flour-milling is a weight-losing process, it is more likely that it will be cheaper to mill flour at point P and ship flour to M. Note that you would not assemble your raw material at some other point along the routes to R_1, R_2 or R_3. Such a location would require greater shipping distances for both the wheat *and* the flour than does point P. The port thus becomes a center for production activity as well as transportation. Indeed, most of the major cities in the US began as ports or transshipment points and grew into major centers of production. This group includes Boston, New York, Philadelphia, Baltimore, Chicago, Cleveland, Pittsburgh, New Orleans, St. Louis, Los Angeles, San Francisco, and Seattle.

The possible importance of a transshipment point can also be demonstrated in the simple one input, one-market model. In this model it is assumed that a transshipment point exists somewhere between the location of the raw material and the location of the market. The cargo must be transferred from one transport mode to another at that point, so the costs of unloading and loading must be paid in any case. It is also assumed that there are loading and unloading costs incurred at the location of the raw material and the market, respectively. In this case clearly the firm would never wish to locate at any point other than the location of the raw material, the market, or the transshipment point because such a location would mean adding an unloading-loading operation that is unnecessary.

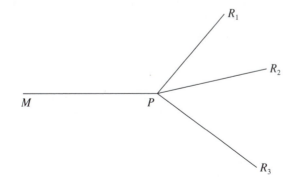

Figure 3.5   Production of wheat for export

For simplicity assume that loading and unloading are the only transportation costs for the firm – the cost of moving the cargo is trivial compared to loading and unloading costs. The problem now boils down to a comparison of three alternatives:

- loading raw material at its source, unloading and loading raw material at the transshipment point, and unloading raw material at the production point (market);
- loading final output at the raw material source, unloading and loading final output at the transshipment point, and then unloading at the market; and
- loading raw material at its source, unloading raw material and loading final output at the transshipment point, and unloading final output at the market.

Any of these three alternatives could turn out to be cheapest, depending upon the various loading and unloading costs at the three locations. The point is that the transshipment point has become one of the options for the location of the production facility.

C. Other Factors in the Location Decision

The models discussed so far only consider transportation costs, but there are many other factors that enter into a firm's location decision. Indeed, improvements in transportation and communication have made these other factors more important than they were in the past. This is the day of interstate highways, air travel, rapid airfreight, fax machines, and the internet. A manufacturer of a product for a wide market has a large range of possible locations from the standpoint of transportation and communication costs. What can narrow that choice?

Labor costs

One critical factor is labor. The wage rate (before taxes) that must be paid is important, but the quality of the workforce can be even more important to the firm. Firms seek locations where the workers with the needed skills are available. They also seek locations where the business climate is such that work rules can be designed to enhance the efficiency of the operation. If all of the needed skills are not available at a particular location, then workers must be recruited and moved. How difficult will it be to attract these workers from other urban areas? Wage rates (after taxes) matter again, of course, but another set of factors lumped into a category called "quality of life" is also quite important. Quality of life depends upon positive things such as fine weather, sports and cultural amenities, good schools, recreation opportunities, universities, quality of medical care, attractive natural terrain and architecture, historical sites, and good shopping. These things are called locational amenities. Negative factors such as crime and pollution also play a role. Clearly the San Francisco metropolitan area wins. What do you particularly value on this list? What would you add to the list? A good set of locational amenities will help the firm to recruit the needed workers. All of this can get quite complicated because different types of workers may prefer different groups of locational amenities.

Other inputs: energy, capital, and land

The cost and availability of other inputs may also be important. Energy costs are particularly important for the industries that require substantial amounts of this commodity. The most energy-intensive manufacturing industries are paper mills, chemicals, petroleum refining, primary metals (e.g., steel and aluminum), and stone, clay, and glass products. These industries can be expected to pay attention to energy costs. The availability of capital can be an important consideration for smaller firms. Large firms raise capital in the national capital market, but smaller firms may have to rely on local sources of loans. Do local financial institutions understand the firm's line of business? Is venture capital available? These questions can be important in particular cases. Labor, energy and capital have been discussed. What about land and real estate? Are good sites available at reasonable prices? Do those sites have environmental problems lurking under the ground? Are needed buildings (offices, warehouses, industrial facilities) available?

Intermediate inputs

In addition to the primary inputs, firms are also concerned with the cost and availability of goods and services that are intermediate inputs to the business in question. This can be a long list of raw materials, parts, and business services such as specialized legal, accounting, and computer services. These intermediate inputs are normally purchased from other firms, and many of them may be available in the local economy.

The knowledge input

Another category of inputs can be called knowledge of the industry. Is a proposed location one where the firm can more easily keep up with the latest trends in the industry? A firm may need to have rapid access to information about changes in products and/or production technologies in order to survive and thrive. Television and movie producers locate in Los Angeles. Fashion designers prefer New York (and Paris and Milan). Information about these industries is "in the air" in such places.

Taxes and public services

The activities of the state and local governments can also be important to firms. Governments impose taxes and provide the standard public goods and services. The level of taxation imposed on the firm and the quality of the public goods and services provided to the firm must be considered. There has been disagreement about the importance of taxes and routine public services in the location decisions of firms, but a recent survey of research by Newman and Sullivan (1988) shows that, when other factors are equal, taxes do matter. This result is found consistently in studies of location choice within an urban area. Taxes show up as a significant location factor less often in studies of location choice from among a group of urban areas. There are additional factors beyond the normal functions of state and local governments. Nearly all states and localities offer incentive programs for business. Businesses may be offered tax breaks, low-interest loans, job training programs targeted to their needs, construction of needed infrastructure (e.g., a highway interchange), and other inducements. Incentives for business are a part of location decisions in the modern economy. These kinds of programs are discussed at length in later chapters. Local governments also engage in a variety of regulatory activities such as building codes, zoning ordinances, and environmental regulations. Are local governments prepared to be cooperative with business?

This section has discussed a lengthy list of factors other than transportation costs that influence the location decisions of firms. Implicit in the discussion of many of these factors is the idea that a firm may be attracted to a location because the location possesses an agglomeration of economic activity that creates a favorable economic environment for that firm. A more systematic discussion of agglomeration factors is needed.

D. Agglomeration Economies

The notion of an economy of agglomeration is one of the central concepts in urban economics, and it means that cost reductions occur *because* economic activities are *located* in one place. The original idea is attributed to Alfred Marshall (1920, Book 4, Chapter 10). Marshall never used the term agglomeration economies; instead he referred to "localized industries." He devoted an entire chapter to this concept, but the following passage (Marshall 1920, p. 225) may give you the flavor of his discussion:

> When an industry has thus chosen a locality for itself, it is likely to stay there long: so great are the advantages which people following the same skilled trade get from near neighborhood to one another. The mysteries of the trade become no mysteries; but are as it were in the air, and children learn many of them unconsciously. Good work is rightly appreciated, inventions and improvements in machinery, in processes and the general organization of the business, have their merits promptly discussed: if one man starts a new idea, it is taken up by others and combined with suggestions of their own; and thus it becomes the sources of further new ideas. And presently subsidiary trades grow up in the neighborhood, supplying it with implements and materials, organizing its traffic, and in many ways conducing to the economy of its material.

This statement, and the rest of Marshall's chapter on the subject, includes factors that are external to the individual firm but internal to the local industry (e.g., if one man starts an new idea), as well as factors that are external to the local industry but internal to the local economy (e.g., subsidiary trades grow up). Also, Marshall mixed factors that mean lower costs in a static sense with factors that create continuing decreases in costs. A more systematic approach was needed.

Bertil Ohlin (1933), in his classic volume *Interregional and International Trade*, provided most of what is now the standard system for classifying agglomeration economies. Ohlin (1933, p. 203) suggested that it is meaningful to set of the following categories of agglomeration economies:

- economies of scale within the firm;
- localization economies, which are external to the individual firm and arise from the size of the local industry; and
- urbanization economies, which are external to the local industry and arise from the size of the local economy.

Hoover (1937) used the terms localization economies and urbanization economies to refer to the last two of Ohlin's categories. Ohlin's categories refer to *static*, rather than dynamic, agglomeration economies. Dynamic agglomeration economies are important for the growth of an urban area, and this topic is discussed in detail in Part VI of this book. Ohlin added one more category to the list because an agglomeration of firms in an urban area may be the result of:

- Interindustry linkages, which arise from transportation cost savings in purchases of intermediate inputs (i.e., inputs other than the primary inputs – labor, capital, land, and entrepreneurship). Input-output analysis, a method for taking account of all interindustry linkages, is discussed in Chapter 19.

More recently Rosenthal and Strange (2003) have proposed a system for classifying the dimensions of agglomeration economies as:

- *industry*, which can vary from localization economies within a single industry up to urbanization economies (size of the urban area), where all points in between are possible sources of agglomeration effects;
- *geographic*, where the effect is attenuated by distance between two establishments;
- *temporal*, where the effect takes place over time; and
- *organization of industry*, in which the level of competitiveness has a positive effect on productivity.

Rosenthal and Strange (2003) surveyed the rapidly growing empirical literature and found evidence for all of these types of agglomeration economies. Their survey is discussed in greater depth in Chapter 20.

Economies of scale within the firm refer, in this context, to economies that are created by expanding production at a single location. Average cost declines as output at that location increases. Other economies of scale may arise when the firm increases in size by adding establishments at new locations. This latter notion of economies of scale is not an agglomeration economy as here defined. The agglomeration economy called economies of scale can arise for a variety of reasons, including the spreading of a fixed cost over a larger output, greater specialization and division of labor, and cost reductions through bulk purchases. This form of agglomeration economy is discussed rather extensively in general courses in microeconomics, but there is a need to pursue the topic a bit more here.

In a classic article, Edwin Mills (1967) asked us to imagine an economy with *no* economies of scale. It turns out that this is difficult to do because it is an economy without cities. All goods and services can be produced in very small quantities at minimum cost, so everything is produced everywhere. What sort of economy is this? One idea is that the feudal economy of medieval times may have approximated such an economy.

Each feudal manor was nearly a self-sufficient entity that produced its own food, clothing, housing, furniture, tools, weapons, livestock, medical care, religious services, and so on. Roads basically did not exist, and there was very little trade.

Now suppose that someone invents a process that creates economies of scale in some line of production. Suppose that the product involved is cloth. People on the feudal manor raise sheep, sheer them, and make wool cloth for clothing. They use simple technologies for these tasks, and the making of cloth consumes a great deal of time. This particular example has been chosen because it should sound familiar. Have you ever been to a reconstructed pioneer village, or a museum with articles from America of the first half of the nineteenth century? You undoubtedly have seen a spinning wheel. What on earth were people doing with a spinning wheel in the middle of the nineteenth century? They were making their own thread so that they could make their own cloth, of course. In fact, most of the soldiers in the Confederate army in the Civil War wore clothing that was "homespun." By the way, clothing made out of homespun cotton cloth had a distinctive "butternut" color. Most of the Confederate soldiers did not wear the stylish grey uniforms that we see in the movies.

Suppose that cloth can now be made by using a manufacturing production process that embodies significant economies of scale. What happens? Someone builds a factory of some size and hires workers. The cost of producing cloth in the factory is far less than the cost of making it at home. The cost of making cloth at home is the opportunity cost of spending time spinning and weaving. People on the farms can do better by growing more crops and trading the foodstuffs for cloth. The people who work in the cloth factory get paid wages, with which they buy food from the farmers. What is more, the factory is located at some particular site. To save time getting to work, the workers reside near the factory. A market place is set up so that people can make the exchanges that are needed. Voila, a town has been created.

How large will this town be, and how much cloth will be produced there? The answer depends upon the extent of the economies of scale, the cost of transporting the cloth to the consumers, and the population density out in the agricultural area. Suppose that the economies of scale are not very great; the cost of producing in the factory even at its most efficient size is not very much less than the cost of homespun. Further suppose that transportation costs are high (e.g., no roads exist and people walk). These assumptions mean that the output of the factory will be small, the town will be small, and the area to which the factory sells its output will be small as well. The farmers cannot save much by buying cloth from the factory, and transportation costs (in terms of time spent) are high. Beyond some rather short distance the farmers will simply decide to make their own cloth because this option is cheaper. These are the reasons why the pioneers in the first half of the nineteenth century made their own cloth even though there were sizable textile industries in New England and England at the time. On the other hand, if the economies of scale are large and transportation costs are cheap, then the factory can sell its output over a wide area.

Localization economies are external to the firm, and arise because of the size of the local industry. The static notion of localization economies presumes that there is a limit to the cost saving that arises from the size of the local industry, or otherwise there would be cumulative declines in costs for that industry. The larger the local industry gets, the lower are costs, and the larger the industry gets. The first point that one might make is that firms in some (indeed, many) industries have no interest at all in locating near other firms in the same industry. Firms in the same industry are in competition. If you wish to start a grocery store, you are probably not going to locate your store next to a big supermarket. You look for a possible gap in the network of grocery stores. The same thing can be said for drug stores, video rental stores, dentists, and many others. These examples are what are called *convenience goods* in the Census of Retail Trade. But the Census of Retail Trade also has another category called *shopping goods*. Shopping goods are goods for which the consumer invests some time comparing prices and qualities before the purchase is made. Think about purchasing an automobile. The consumer probably engages in fairly extensive comparison shopping before such a major purchase is made. Now think again about where the auto dealers are located. Many of them are located near other auto dealers! There are major streets or highways that are lined with one auto dealer after another. This spatial arrangement facilitates the comparison shopping that consumers are going to do. Many auto dealers want to be a stop on that comparison shopping trip, so they are willing to locate near their competitors. Note that auto dealers are willing to locate near dealers who sell *other* makes of autos. A Buick dealer does not wish to locate near another Buick dealer. Indeed, the Buick Division of General Motors does a careful analysis of the local market and the spatial arrangement of Buick dealers before they grant a license for another Buick dealer. In any event, this sort of shopping behavior creates an incentive for businesses in an industry to cluster together because they can save on advertising and promotion costs, the costs of attracting customers. These shopping effects can apply to an entire industry in an urban area. If you are a wholesale buyer of clothing for a department store, you can go to New York, Paris, and Milan to see the products that are available.

Other forms of localization economies are created if there are economies of scale in the provision of inputs specific to the industry. Suppose that the industry requires workers who need some specific form of training. The workers can be trained by the firm itself, but that might be expensive. If there are enough firms in the local industry, then it will be worthwhile for someone to set up an educational or training program that does the job. These programs can be set up by labor unions, private training firms, public institutions of higher education (e.g., junior colleges or universities), or local governments through the use of job training funds provided partly by the federal government. A training program that is not run as part of one of the firms is created precisely because it is the cheaper option. Or, as Marshall put it, if the local industry is large enough, the skills that are required for that industry are just "in the air." People in Los Angeles really do talk the movie business. At least some people in Chicago really do discuss the futures and options markets in their spare time. A larger local industry also creates a larger pool of labor with the requisite skills, so it may be easier for an individual firm to fill open positions. That pool of labor is created partly by people who migrate to the urban area in the hope of finding a job in that particular industry.

Economies of scale can also exist in the other inputs. These items were discussed in the previous section, but not in the context of economies of scale. The provision of capital for the industry may require specialized knowledge of the industry by lending officers and others who make lending decisions. If there are enough firms in the local industry, then it will be worthwhile for some financial institutions to develop that specialized knowledge. The same thing goes for various types of business services such as legal advice, accounting, advertising, management consulting, and computer services. The needs of an industry may be special, and an agglomeration economy is created when it pays someone to become the specialized lawyer, accountant, media buyer, management consultant, or computer consultant. The lawyer or accountant can work more efficiently if she works only for movie producers (or fashion designers or commodity traders) than if she has a general practice that requires jumping from type of work to another. Other intermediate inputs can be subject to economies of scale as well. The industry may require specialized machinery and parts. The specialized machinery may require highly skilled and specialized maintenance and repair services, which in turn may require specialized training courses as well.

The last three paragraphs are written in a rather informal style, but they contain some powerful specific reasons for the existence of localization economies. Similar arguments can be made for urbanization economies, cost reductions for an industry that arise from the size of the entire local economy. We have places called shopping centers within an urban area. These are places that offer a wide range of goods, so shoppers hope to be able to buy everything of their lists in a single place. Similarly, shoppers such as wholesale buyers are attracted to an urban area that offers a wide range of products. Economies of scale exist in the provision of inputs that are not specific to a particular industry. An important example is the general urban infrastructure. Much of this infrastructure is provided by the public sector, and other parts are provided privately. Transportation facilities such as airports, ports, and railway service are subject to economies of scale. Air and water transportation services are provided jointly by the public and private sectors. The public sector provides the terminal facility (the airport and the port), and private firms provide the transportation services. A larger urban area provides more frequent service and a longer list of destinations that is served directly. Freight railway service is provided by private firms, but the same idea applies. The larger urban area has more convenient service.

The larger urban area also offers a deeper and more diverse set of goods and services for businesses – the interindustry linkages. Does your firm need a patent attorney, an architect who can design an office building, or an economic consultant? If your firm is located in a smaller urban area, you can hire a local attorney who does not specialize in patent work, or you can bring in someone from a larger urban area who does. The quality of the work may be suspect in the former case, and the latter option may be inconvenient and expensive. The firm that is located in the larger urban area does not face these problems. The theory of the hierarchy of urban areas is discussed in the next chapter. The basic point is that large urban areas are not just larger versions of small urban areas. The large urban areas offer goods and services that do not exist in small urban areas.

Other important features of large urban areas are cultural and recreational amenities. Large urban areas have more museums, more live theatre and musical performances, and more sporting events to attend. These amenities can make it easier to attract the workers that are needed by an industry.

These are some examples of urbanization economies, but there is a "downside" to urbanization. Large urban areas also suffer from higher levels of congestion, pollution, and social problems. Competition for central locations drives up office rents and housing prices. Given that there are both benefits and costs to the size of the urban area, some researchers have tried to determine whether there is an optimal size for urban areas in general. At what point do the costs to everyone in the urban area of additional urban size outweigh the added benefits? In other words, at what level of urban size are the marginal costs equal to the marginal benefits? The research has not reached any clear conclusions. It is fair to say that we do not know the optimal size for urban areas, and it is also not likely that a general answer exists. A more meaningful way to ask the question is whether there is an optimal size for an individual urban area that performs a particular set of economic functions. Given the economic functions that each urban area performs, should New York, Los Angeles, and Chicago be larger or smaller than they are? Maybe the television and movie capital of the world should be larger than the financial capital of the western hemisphere (or maybe not). This question has not been investigated.

There is a good deal of empirical evidence concerning the existence of localization and urbanization economies. The idea is to measure the effects of both the size of the local industry and the size of the local economy as a whole on the costs in that local industry. One careful study by Henderson (1986) examined labor productivity for 1972 in manufacturing industries in US urban areas. Labor productivity is measured as output in the local manufacturing industry divided by the total labor input. Clearly the wage rate is the first variable that determines labor productivity. The standard result in microeconomic theory is that workers are hired by an industry up to the point at which the wage rate is equal to the value of the marginal product of the last worker. The value of the marginal product is the price of output times the marginal product. Henderson (1986) assumed that the price of output in a manufacturing industry is the same for all urban areas in the US, so the marginal product for an urban area is higher if the wage rate is higher. Note that labor productivity is defined as *average* product, but the average product and the marginal product should change together. Henderson further hypothesized that, given the wage rate, labor productivity will depend upon localization and urbanization economies. The localization effect is measured as full-time employment in the local industry, and urbanization is measured by total local population. Henderson studied 16 manufacturing industries, and found statistically significant localization economies in eight out of 16. These industries are:

- primary metals;
- electrical machinery;
- non-electrical machinery;
- petroleum refining;
- apparel;
- wood products;
- pulp and paper products; and
- food products.

Henderson also found that the localization economies die out once the local industry has reached some critical size. Localization economies in these manufacturing industries do not go up without limit. The other manufacturing industries did not exhibit localization economies in US urban areas, and they are;

- textiles;
- leather products;

- printing and publishing;
- furniture;
- fabricated metals;
- rubber and plastics;
- chemicals; and
- stone, clay and glass products.

One industry in the group of 16 exhibited urbanization economies. That industry is stone, clay, and glass products.

What are we to make of Henderson's (1986) results? One implication is that those industries that are subject to localization economies should be found to cluster in a relatively small number of urban areas rather than being spread out over a large number of urban areas. Henderson (1986) found evidence of a tendency for the eight industries with localization economies to cluster, and the other eight industries did not cluster. In addition, the fact that localization economies do not go up without limit means that there will be several urban areas in which an industry clusters, and not just a few. The general absence of urbanization economies in manufacturing industries means that firms in these industries have no particular incentive to locate in the largest urban areas. Of course, Henderson's findings do not mean that urbanization economies do not exist in other industries, such as those that produce business services or financial services. Unfortunately, the output data required for Henderson's empirical tests are available only for manufacturing industries.

Research by Rosenthal and Strange (2001) explored the factors that cause agglomeration of manufacturing industry in the US. Their findings indicate that labor-market pooling has a positive impact on agglomeration at the state, county, and zip-code levels. Measures of knowledge spill-overs have an effect, but only at the zip-code level. Measures pertaining to the shipping of goods (interindustry linkages pertaining to manufactured inputs, access to required resources, and perishability) influence agglomeration only at the state level. One can infer from these results that there are indeed several sources of localization economies in manufacturing as hypothesized above, but that the geographic level at which the localization effect operates can vary.

Another study by Henderson (2003) examined output at the plant level in two industries and found that the count of other plants in the same industry has a strong positive effect in high tech, but not in machinery. High-tech single-plant firms benefit from the scale of previous activity in the same industry (i.e., dynamic agglomeration economies). He found little evidence that plants benefited from either diversity or the scale of economic activity in the urban area outside the own industry. In short, he found evidence for both static and dynamic localization economies.

E. Static Theory of External Economies and Diseconomies

The previous section has examined the possibility that external economies are an important feature of urban areas. External diseconomies of urban areas were also mentioned briefly. The basic idea in each case is that the person who is making an economic decision, such

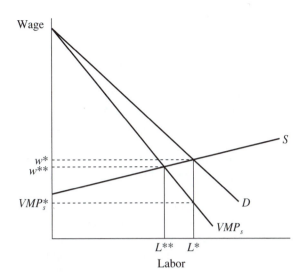

Figure 3.6   External diseconomies of urbanization

as whether to produce more output, makes that decision on the basis of his own marginal costs and marginal benefits, and ignores costs or benefits that affect others. The familiar case is the external diseconomy of air pollution. The individual firm makes an output decision based on its own marginal cost, which does not include a cost of air pollution. But the marginal cost to the entire urban area must also include the cost of additional air pollution that is caused by that firm. A diagram can depict the situation. Figure 3.6 shows the case of the case of external diseconomies of urbanization. The diagram depicts a perfectly competitive market for labor in an urban area. Employment in the urban area will represent the size of the urban area for this purpose. Labor is demanded by the firms in the urban area for use in producing goods and services for export or for local use, and the demand curve for labor is denoted D. The supply curve of labor that is faced by the firms in the urban area is S, which is drawn with a positive slope. If employment in the urban area is to expand, a higher wage rate must be paid. A market equilibrium wage is established at w^*, and the employment level is L^*. Wage w^* is the wage rate that firms use to decide how many workers to hire.

External diseconomies can be introduced into the urban labor market model on the demand side. Recall that the demand curve for labor is the same thing as the value of labor's marginal product, which equals the price of output times the physical marginal product of labor. Now suppose that when a firm hires one more worker, that worker produces a marginal product for the firm *and* causes output at other firms to decline. How can this happen? The water pollution example works well. The firm decides to produce more output, so another worker is hired. That decision adds more pollution to the river. Firms that are located downstream and use the water must now use more resources to clean up the water before it can be used. A given amount of resources employed by those downstream firms will now produce a smaller quantity of output. In effect, the decision by the upstream firm to hire another worker has reduced the output of the downstream firms. Another example is traffic congestion. The decision to hire another worker means that there will be more traffic in the urban area. Truck drivers who work for the various firms will now have to spend more time in traffic, so they will produce less in a day's work. If phenomena of this type apply to all firms in the urban area, the value of the marginal product of labor to the urban area as a whole should be drawn as curve VMP_s in Figure 3.6. Curve VMP_s is below demand curve D by the amount of the external diseconomy at the margin. At employment level L^* the wage rate is equal to the value of the marginal product of labor that accrues to the firm that hired the last worker, but the actual value of the marginal product of that last worker for the urban area as a whole is only VMP_s^*.

Left to their own devices, the firms hire "too many" workers and the urban area is too large. This is a normative proposition of the kind discussed in Chapter 1. Exactly what is wrong with employment level L^*? Employment level L^* is *inefficient* because the last worker hired generated a marginal benefit to the firms in the urban area that is less than marginal cost. A firm paid wage w^* to hire the last worker, but the firms as a group only reaped a benefit of VMP_s^*. This creates a situation in which it is possible to make some firms better off and no one else worse off. For example, suppose it is possible for the firms in the urban area, excluding the one that hired the last worker, to take up a collection and bribe that firm and the worker not to work. The firm does not need much inducement because the profits earned from hiring the last worker are small. Furthermore, the marginal worker *is* the marginal worker because the opportunity cost of his or her time is just slightly less than the wage rate. Small bribes will do for both. The firms in the urban area have amount w^*-VMP_s^* available for bribery, and that is more than enough to do the trick. If this bribery scheme could be organized, everyone can be made better off.

As you already might have concluded, the efficient level of employment for the urban area is L^{**}, where the supply curve of labor crosses the value of labor's marginal product to the entire group of firms. At this point workers earn wage rate w^{**}, and the firms as a group gain output worth that same amount by hiring the last worker.

Now consider the less familiar case of an external economy. Henderson (1986) found evidence of localization economies, so the analysis will focus on an individual industry in an urban area. Supply and demand for this industry are shown in Figure 3. The industry faces the usual sort of demand curve, labeled D. The industry is made up of a large number of small, competitive firms. Each of these firms is assumed to have a long-run average cost curve that has a minimum point at some level of output. In the long run the output of the industry expands by adding more firms of this optimum size. If there is no external economy, then the long-run supply curve of the industry is just horizontal line S in Figure 3.7. The market price is set equal to long-run average and marginal cost. This is the model that students learn in the introductory microeconomics course. Now suppose that there is an economy that is external to the firm, but internal to the industry. The expansion of industry output, through the addition of another firm, will lower the average costs for the other firms. The price at which the firms in the industry will offer the good for sale now drops to the lower average cost.

The critical relationship is between the average and marginal costs of output for the industry. Define TC as the total cost in the industry, which equals the number of firms (n) times the total cost in each of those firms (tc), or

$$TC = n(tc).$$

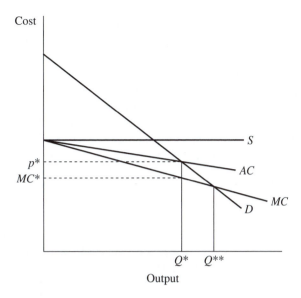

Figure 3.7   Localization economies

Total cost in each firm is the firm's average cost (ac) times output (q), or

$$tc = q(ac).$$

Note that the average cost for the industry (AC) is the same as the average cost for each of the firms because

$$AC = TC/nq = tc(n)/nq = tc/q = ac.$$

If one firm is added to the industry, the change in total cost is

$$\Delta TC = \Delta nq(ac) + \Delta ac(nq) + \Delta qn(ac).$$

Here the Δ symbol stands for "change in." Assume that the optimal output for each firm does not change, so $\Delta q = 0$. The marginal cost (MC) for the industry is the change in total cost for the industry as the number of firms increases, divided by the output of the additional firm; therefore

$$MC = (\Delta TC/\Delta n)/q = q(ac)/q + (\Delta ac/\Delta n)(nq)/q$$
$$= ac + n(\Delta ac/\Delta n)$$
$$= AC + n(\Delta ac/\Delta n).$$

The existence an external economy means that $\Delta ac/\Delta n$ is less than zero; average cost declines as the industry expands. This result is very clear. It says that the marginal cost of output *for the industry* is the initial average cost minus the change in average cost in each firm times the number of firms. In other words, the marginal cost for the industry is less than average cost by the amount $n(\Delta ac/\Delta n)$. Curves for AC and MC are shown in Figure 3.7.

Which of the two curves (AC or MC) is the supply curve of the industry? The supply curve is AC because firms in a competitive industry must make a price equal to average cost to make a normal profit. At price p^* the firms will offer quantity Q^*, and this is the equilibrium solution for the market. The supply curve AC is called "forward falling" because the offer price declines as industry output expands. But you probably already have realized that the equilibrium price for the output exceeds its *marginal* cost, which is the cost to the entire industry of producing one more unit of output. Clearly output level Q^* is an inefficiently low output. At Q^* the benefit of producing another unit of output is p^*, but the cost to the industry of doing so is only MC^*. This industry expands by adding firms, but at price p^* no new firm will enter *unless it is bribed to do so.* At price p^* the firms in the industry are just making a normal profit. Equilibrium output will remain at Q^* even though the optimal level of output is at Q^{**}. Output level Q^{**} is the point at which the marginal benefits of the good (the price) are equal to the marginal costs. It is in the interest of the consumers of the product (i.e., the rest of society) to bribe firms to enter the industry to produce more output. At output level Q^{**} the price is below average cost, so the firms in the industry will lose money unless they are subsidized.

Figure 3.7 has produced an important theoretical result. Society will benefit by subsidizing the expansion of an industry that possesses localization economies. The matter of subsidization will be discussed further in Part VI of the book.

F. Economic Origins of Urban Areas in the United States

The history of urban areas is a fascinating subject. If you enjoy reading history, then you probably will also enjoy reading about the history of urban areas in general and the histories of specific urban areas. Cities around the world have their origins in a wide variety of political, military, religious, social, and economic reasons. A classic book that was published in 1961 and that still appears on many college reading lists is Lewis Mumford's *The City in History*. Mumford's book is 576 pages in length, and he does not get around to discussing the market economy until page 410. Unlike Mumford's book, the purpose of this section is not to summarize the stories of the world's major cities. Rather, the idea is to take a brief look at major urban areas in the United States. This decision narrows the focus to the more recent past, and it also means that the economic reasons for cities can be emphasized. Except for Washington, DC, and some of the former and current state capitals, urban areas in the United States have origins that are almost purely economic in nature.

In 1790, the year of the first Census of Population, only 5.1% of the population of 3.9 million lived in urban places, which are defined as having a population of 2,500 or more. The United States was an agricultural nation. The largest urban areas were really nothing more than towns: New York had a population of 49,000, Philadelphia had 29,000, 18,000 people resided in Boston, and Baltimore weighed in with 14,000.

These and most of the other towns began life in colonial days as ports that were used to ship agricultural products out and various goods in. Ports were built where a major river empties into the ocean. A port represents a transshipment point, as discussed above in section B, and ports are subject to economies of scale, as mentioned in section C. Transshipment points are not spread out all up and down the coast, but are concentrated at a few points. The New York harbor was and is, by far, the best port on the east coast. The harbor is sheltered from the ocean by Long Island and, flanked by the East River and the Hudson River, the Island of Manhattan provides a great deal of space for docking facilities. What is more, the navigable Hudson River reaches far into the agricultural hinterland. It is difficult to imagine a better setup, given the transportation methods of the time.

The transportation methods of the time are critical. In 1790 cities were small partly because of limitations imposed by a transportation system that consisted of boats without steam power, horses, and feet. The next 70 years produced what economic historians call the transportation revolution. First came improvements in transportation by water. Robert Fulton's steamboat completed its first upstream voyage from New York City to Albany in 1807, and regular service was initiated. The earliest canal projects were also completed in the first decade of the nineteenth century. The value of steamboats for use on the Ohio and Mississippi Rivers was immediately apparent, and the steamboat made its first appearance on these western waters in 1811. Regular service on the western rivers was initiated in 1817, and by 1825, 80 steamboats were operating there. At the same time the era of canal building got underway. Most of the canals were financed by state governments. The Erie Canal, which was completed in 1825, was the most important one. It connects the Hudson River with the Great Lakes (at Buffalo, on Lake Erie), and thereby provided a cheap freight connection between the upper Midwest and the East Coast. Many other canals were built in the first six decades of the nineteenth century. Most of the canal mileage was in the states of New York, Pennsylvania and Ohio. The economic historian Douglas North (1973) shows that canal and upstream river freight rates declined by over 90% between 1800 and 1840.

The canal era overlaps with the era of the railroad. The first railroad was opened in England in 1825, and the Baltimore and Ohio began operation in 1830 with 23 miles of track. Total mileage of main track reached 4,600 in 1845, and then the industry exploded to 30,600 miles in 1860. North (1973) shows that freight rates on the railroad dropped by over 50% from 1845 to 1860. Railroad rates were far greater than canal or river boat rates, but the railroad was much faster, could run in all seasons and in all weather conditions, and reached places that were inaccessible by water. The speed and reliability of rail service meant that timetables could be kept, and meant that people, probably for the first time, had to pay close attention to the time of day. The system of standard time zones was created by the railroads in 1881.

We are fond of using anecdotes from the life of Abraham Lincoln to illustrate the economic history of this period. His first job after he left his father's household in 1830 was to transport a farmer's crop from central Illinois down river for sale in New Orleans. He used an unpowered flatboat, and the first leg of the journey was on the Sangamon River. The Sangamon River is little more than a wide creek. He had not gone very far when the boat became stalled on a small dam next to a new pioneer village named New Salem. He cleverly freed his flatboat from its predicament, and a man who was watching told him that he had a job waiting for him in New Salem when he returned from New Orleans. Lincoln eventually made his way back to New Salem and took the job as store-keeper and postmaster. The job left him plenty of time to study law and to get elected to the Illinois General Assembly. Thirty years later President-elect Lincoln left nearby Springfield by train. He rode to Chicago, and then to Baltimore and Washington, DC.

The transportation revolution had transformed the nation by making enormous areas of fertile agricultural land accessible and by reducing dramatically the cost of moving agricultural commodities, manufactured goods, and people. People knew very well that the eastern half of the nation was going to be settled very quickly, and that an entire system of towns and cities would spring up. They knew that agricultural settlement and the growth of towns and cities would go hand-in-hand. Furthermore, they knew that the cities would be very large by the standards of the early years of the nineteenth century. Any clue as to where the large cities would be located was valuable information. For example, the *announcement* in 1829 that a canal would be built at Chicago to connect the Great Lakes to the Mississippi River system set off a tremendous land boom in what was a minor trading post.

How did people know all of this? In short, they knew that the new transportation system would lead to urban agglomeration economies. The water and rail transportation systems themselves provided services under conditions of substantial economies of scale. The emerging manufacturing industries based on steam power and standardized parts possessed some internal economies of scale. Many of the business services required by an agricultural economy, such as banking, insurance, and marketing of agricultural products, also possessed economies of scale. The economies of scale in water and rail operations tended to centralize economic activity, and the cheap freight rates permitted urban manufacturing and business services to cover a wide area. The economies of scale in manufacturing production activity became an even larger factor in urbanization after the Civil War, but the level of urbanization in 1860 is still impressive.

The percentage of the population residing in urban places increased slightly from 5.1% in 1790 to 8.8% in 1830, the year in which Lincoln struggled down the Sangamon River. When the President-elect traveled to Washington, DC, 19.8% of the American people lived in urban places. This increase in urbanization was coupled with a huge increase in the total population of the nation. The total population in 1830 was 12.9 million, and the waves of immigrants from Germany and Ireland, coupled with a very rapid natural rate of increase, produced a population of 31.4 million in 1860. These figures mean that the population in urban places was 1.1 million in 1830 and 6.2 million in 1860, an increase of *464%*. Of these 6.2 million, 1.37 million lived in New York and Philadelphia. Recall that the total population of these two cities was 78,000 in 1790. At the end of the Civil War decade in 1870 the two cities had a total population of 2.13 million. The other major cities – Baltimore, Boston, Buffalo, Chicago, Cincinnati, New Orleans, and St. Louis – were also growing rapidly. In 1860, 42.4% of the urban population lived in the 9 largest cities, each of which had populations in excess of 100,000.

Cities of such size also generated substantial diseconomies. The sanitation problems were staggering. The threats of fire and communicable diseases were ever present. The movement of both people and freight within an urban area was still rudimentary. Some of the early photographs of urban areas show traffic jams that defy description. (Note that early photographic technology required that the subjects must stand still for a lengthy period. Photographs of urban traffic jams were possible nonetheless.)

Between 1790 and 1860 Americans settled almost half of the nation. Because of the transportation revolution, and innovations in the production urban goods and services, that settlement was coupled with very rapid urbanization after 1830. The first real cities in the United States were created in this period, and the economic models of this chapter provide good explanations for this first phase of urbanization.

G. Summary

This chapter is an introduction to the economic theory of location choice by firms. The role of transportation costs for inputs and outputs was examined first, and then several other factors were considered. The costs of labor, land, capital, and intermediate inputs can vary over space. For some firms in some industries these costs can vary because of the level of:

- economies of scale internal to the firm's operation at a single location;
- economies of scale external to the firm, but internal to the local industry;
- economies that are external to the local industry that arise from the size of the urban area; and
- economies arising from inter-industry linkages.

These are called agglomeration economies; the second and third are called localization economies and urbanization economies, respectively. In addition, the size of the urban area may cause diseconomies such as pollution and congestion.

Empirical evidence indicates that localization economies occur in several manufacturing industries, but that urbanization economies in manufacturing industry are rare. These findings imply that those manufacturing industries with localization economies should be observed to cluster in a relatively small number of urban areas, and that those urban areas are not necessarily very large. Henderson's (1986) findings are consistent with these hypotheses.

The existence of diseconomies of urban size and localization economies was investigated theoretically. Diseconomies of urban size generate an urban area that is inefficiently "too large," given its economic functions. Localization economies lead to an industry in an urban area that is inefficiently "too small." It would be worthwhile for the public to bribe firms to enter the local industry to create additional economies.

The chapter concluded with a brief discussion of the creation of urban areas in the United States in the first sixty years of the nineteenth century. Urbanization was particularly rapid during the 1830–60 period as firms took advantage of the transportation revolution and agglomeration economies arising from economies of scale in manufacturing production and business services. On the eve of the Civil War, 19.8% of the population of the United States lived in urban places, and 42.4% of the urban population lived in nine large cities.

Appendix to Chapter 3: Mathematics of the One Input, One Market Model

In the one input, one market model the firm uses an input that is located at point I in Figure 3.1. The input is available at a given price at point I. The firm produces output for the market located at point M, and the firms faces a downward-sloping demand curve for output at the market. The firms must decide how much to produce and where to produce it. For example, suppose that the firm's business is to take raw lumber (i.e., trees that have been cut down) available at the forest at point I, cut the lumber into firewood, and deliver the firewood to the market at point M. Where does the firm perform the operation of cutting the trees into firewood? As discussed in the text, the firm could transport the raw lumber to point M first, and then produce the firewood. Or the firm could cut up the trees first at point I, and transport the firewood to market. Also, some point between I and M could be selected. The decision depends upon transportation costs.

Suppose that the firm takes 1.2 tons of raw lumber to produce 1 ton of firewood. The production process involves a little waste, so the product is known as *weight losing*. The cost of transporting 1.2 tons on raw lumber is a per mile, and the cost of transporting 1 ton of firewood is b per mile. Cutting the raw lumber into firewood requires L units of labor at a wage of w per unit. The price of output at the market is p per ton, and the price of raw lumber at point I is R per ton. Denote the distance from point I to the firm's location as x. This is the distance the raw lumber is transported. Let y stand for the distance from the firm's location to the market; y is the distance the output is transported. Obviously $z = x + y$ equals the distance from I to M. Either x or y is permitted to be zero. Let us restate the definitions of the variables:

p = price of output at the market, point M,
a = cost per mile of transporting 1.2 tons of raw lumber,
b = cost per mile of transporting 1 one of firewood,
w = wage rate per unit of labor,
L = amount of labor needed for one ton of firewood,
R = price of raw lumber at the forest, point I,
x = distance raw lumber of transported,
y = distance firewood is transported, and
$z = x + y$ = distance from I to M.

Given these definitions, and letting Q stand for output, the firm's profit can be written

profit = total revenue minus total costs
$$= pQ - 1.2RQ - wLQ - Q(1.2ax + by).$$

Total revenue is pQ, and the three components of total cost are:

$$1.2RQ = \text{cost of raw lumber},$$
$$wLQ = \text{cost of labor, and}$$
$$Q(1.2ax + by) = \text{transportation cost}.$$

The firm maximizes profits by selecting the output level at which the marginal change in profit is zero. In other words, Q is selected so that

change in profit = marginal revenue − marginal cost
$$= p\Delta Q + Q\Delta p - 1.2R\Delta Q - wL\Delta Q - 1.2ax\Delta Q - by\Delta Q = 0.$$

Here ΔQ stands for a marginal change in Q, and Δp is the marginal change in p. Marginal revenue for a change in output of out unit is $p + Q\Delta p/\Delta Q$. The condition above reduces to the usual statement that marginal revenue equals marginal cost, or

$$MR = p + Q\Delta p/\Delta Q = 1.2R + wL + 1.2ax + by = MC.$$

Marginal cost consists of the cost of raw lumber per ton of output ($1.2R$) plus labor cost (wL) plus transportation costs per ton of output ($1.2ax + by).

The firm must also choose its *location* so as to maximize profits. Consider Figure A3.1. Straight line II^* shows the cost of transporting the input (raw lumber) needed for one ton of output at various distances from I. The slope of this line is $1.2a$. Straight line M^*M likewise shows the cost of transporting the output (firewood) from various locations away from point M. The slope of line M^*M is $-$b$, meaning that this component of costs declines by b per mile for each ton of output. The entire transportation cost for a ton of output is the sum of these two costs, which is line M^*I^*. In algebraic form, transportation cost per ton is $1.2ax + by$. Where would you locate your firewood firm? Given the transportation costs displayed in Figure A3.1, you would choose to locate *at* point I because this point minimizes transportation costs per ton of output.

You can further convince yourself that point I is the correct choice by returning to the equation for profits. Rewrite the profit equation;

$$\text{profits} = pQ - 1.2RQ - wLQ - Q(1.2ax + by).$$

Clearly for profits to be at a maximum at whatever output level is chosen, the firm must minimize transportation costs per unit of output, which equals $1.2ax + by$. Point I, with $x = 0$ and y equal to the total distance from I to M, is the cost-minimizing point.

The analysis is complicated slightly by the fact that output depends upon price, which depends upon marginal cost. And marginal cost (MC) depends upon location. Recall that

$$MC = 1.2R + wL + 1.2ax + by.$$

The point is that, in order to maximize profits, the firm must minimize marginal costs. Given that R, the price of raw lumber, and w, the price of labor, are constant, marginal costs are at a minimum if $x = 0$ (location I is chosen).

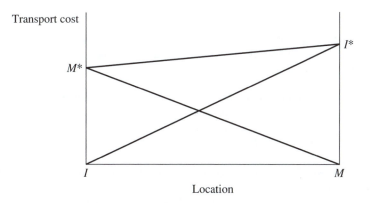

Figure A3.1   Transportation cost and location

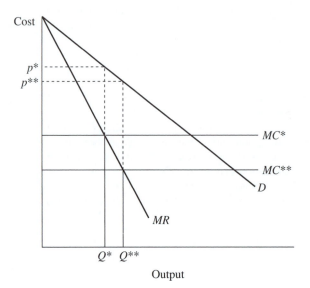

Figure A3.2   The Firewood Firm

Consider the alternative. Suppose that some other location and output level have been chosen. The firm can increase profits (at that output level) by reducing transportation costs. Furthermore, the lowering of marginal cost by selecting the best location will also stimulate the firm to produce more output and earn even greater profits. This point is illustrated in Figure A3.2. The firm begins with the "wrong" location and marginal cost level MC^*. Profit-maximizing price is p^* and output is Q^* given demand D and marginal revenue MR. Selection of the correct location lowers marginal cost to MC^{**}. If output is held at Q^*, profits increase by the amount $Q^*(MC^* - MC^{**})$. However, the firm will decide to increase output to Q^{**} because, at the lower output Q^*, marginal revenue exceeds the new marginal cost. Therefore, selection of the correct location increases profits on two counts.

Exercises

1   You own a firewood business that involves chopping down trees, cutting the trees up into firewood, and transporting to the market. You can cut the trees up into firewood where they are cut down, or you can transport the trees to the market and then cut them into firewood. The costs of the various operations are as follows:

Cutting down trees	$25 per ton
Cutting trees into firewood	$100 per ton
Transporting trees to market	$50 per ton
Transporting firewood to market	$35 per ton

(a)   Where should the trees be cut into firewood to minimize costs? Why? What data did you need to make this decision?

(b)   Suppose that the price of firewood at the market is $150 per ton. Where should the trees be cut into firewood now? What if the price increased to $175 per ton?

2   A business has customers located in Lubbock, Amarillo, and points in between as follows:

Lubbock	10 customers
10 miles from Lubbock	1 customer
25 miles from Lubbock	3 customers
50 miles from Lubbock	1 customer
70 miles from Lubbock	2 customers
Amarillo	6 customers

(a)   Suppose that a separate trip must be made to each customer and that transportation costs per mile are the same for all trips to any customer. Where does the business locate to minimize transportation costs?

(b)   How does the solution change if our more customers are added in Amarillo? Why?

(c)   How does the solution change if four more customers are added in Lubbock? (Assume six customers in Amarillo.) Why?

3   Imagine that there are two ice cream vendors on a linear beach 100 yards long. We assume that

- Consumers are evenly distributed along the beach, located at the endpoints and spaced 10 yards apart.
- Production costs are zero.
- Both vendors sell ice cream for p cents.
- The cost to consumers of travel is $1/2$ cent per yard (money equivalent of consumer's time).

(a)   What are the profit-maximizing equilibrium locations for the two vendors? What do aggregate travel costs equal?

(b)   What are the socially optimal locations (to minimize travel costs)? How much are aggregate travel costs reduced compared to the answer in part a?

4   Consider an industry in an urban area that is subject to localization economies. The industry faces the demand curve

$$P = 59 - 0.05Q,$$

Where P is price and Q is the output of the industry. Each firm in the industry has an average cost function of

$$ac = 10 - 0.001Q.$$

The firms in the industry behave as competitive firms.

(a)   What is the average cost function of the industry?

(b)   What is the marginal cost function of the industry? (Hint: First find the total cost function.)

(c)   What is the output level that this competitive industry would produce in the absence of any bribes or subsidies? What is the difference between average cost and marginal cost at this output level?

(d)   What output level would be produced if there were no localization economy for the industry? (Hint: The coefficient of Q in the average cost function is zero.)

References

Henderson, Vernon, 1986, "Efficiency of Resource Usage and City Size," *Journal of Urban Economics*, vol. 19, pp. 47–70.

Henderson, Vernon, 2003, "Marshall's Scale Economies," *Journal of Urban Economics*, vol. 53, pp. 1–28.

Hoover, Edgar, 1937, *Location Theory and the Shoe and Leather Industries*. Cambridge, MA: Harvard University Press.

Marshall, Alfred, 1920, *Principles of Economics*, 8th edn. London: Macmillan and Co.

Mills, Edwin, 1967, "An Aggregative Model of Resource Allocation in a Metropolitan Area," *American Economic Review, Papers and Proceedings*, vol. 57, pp. 197–210.

Mumford, Lewis, 1961, *The City in History*. New York: Harcourt, Brace, and World.

Newman, R. and D. Sullivan, 1988, "Econometric Analysis of Business Tax Impacts on Industrial Location: What Do We Know and How Do We Know It?" *Journal of Urban Economics*, vol. 23, pp. 215–34.

North, Douglas, 1973, *Growth and Welfare in the American Past*. Englewood Cliffs, NJ: Prentice-Hall.

Ohlin, Bertil, 1933, *Interregional and International Trade*. Cambridge, MA: Harvard University Press.

Rosenthal, Stuart, and William Strange, 2001, "The Determinants of Agglomeration," *Journal of Urban Economics*, vol. 50, pp. 191–229.

Rosenthal, Stuart and William Strange, 2003, "Evidence on the Nature and Sources of Agglomeration Economies," in J. Henderson and J. Thisse (eds.), *Handbook of Regional and Urban Economics*, vol. 4. Amsterdam: North Holland.

Chapter 4

The Economic Functions of Cities

A. Introduction

It is obvious that urban areas are arranged in fairly regular patterns. There are many small towns, fewer large towns, even fewer cities, and a small number of major metropolitan areas. Clearly there is a hierarchy of urban areas that is shaped roughly like a pyramid. Also, there are geographic regularities. As you know from Chapter 1, the three largest metropolitan areas in the United States are New York, Los Angeles, and Chicago (with Los Angeles gaining rapidly on New York). They are, of course, located on the east coast, the west coast, and in the middle of the nation, respectively. The urban areas that have populations in excess of 2.0 million by rank are shown in Table 4.1.

Notice how many of the largest urban areas are now located in the sunbelt. If Seattle/ Tacoma/Bremerton and Portland/Salem are included in the "sunbelt," – a dubious assumption because of all of the rain in the Northwest, then 11 of the top 23 urban areas are located in the sunbelt. Large urban areas are now seemingly scattered around the nation in a pattern that surely has some regularity. Urban areas vary widely in size and in economic function; the task of this chapter is to gain an understanding of the patterns in urban size and function. The approach to this task is to examine the system of urban areas in the contemporary US economy. These population data show that the list of the largest metropolitan areas is far from static; changes in rank from 1980 to 2000 are:

Higher rank	*Lower rank*
San Francisco/Oakland/San Jose	Philadelphia/Wilmington/Trenton
Dallas/Fort Worth	Detroit/Ann Arbor
Atlanta	Washington, DC
Seattle/Tacoma/Bremerton	Houston/Galveston/Brazoria
Phoenix	Cleveland/Akron
Minneapolis/St. Paul	St. Louis
San Diego	Baltimore
Denver/Boulder/Greeley	Pittsburgh
Tampa/St. Petersburg/Clearwater	
Portland/Salem OR	

Table 4.1   The top 23 urban areas in the US

Urban area	1980 population (millions)	2000 population (millions)
New York/Newark	16.95	19.05
Los Angeles/Long Beach	11.50	16.37
Chicago/Gary	7.89	8.90
San Francisco/Oakland/San Jose	5.37	7.04
Philadelphia/Wilmington/Trenton	5.65	6.19
Boston/Worcester/Lawrence	5.12	5.82
Dallas/Fort Worth	3.05	5.22
Detroit/Ann Arbor	4.82	5.02
Washington, DC	3.48	4.92
Houston/Galveston/Brazoria	3.12	4.87
Atlanta	2.23	4.11
Miami/Ft. Lauderdale	2.64	3.88
Seattle/Tacoma/Bremerton	2.41	3.55
Phoenix/Mesa	1.60	3.25
Minneapolis/St. Paul	2.20	2.97
Cleveland/Akron	2.94	2.95
San Diego	1.86	2.81
St. Louis	2.41	2.60
Denver/Boulder/Greeley	1.74	2.58
Baltimore	2.20	2.55
Tampa/St. Petersburg/Clearwater	1.61	2.40
Pittsburgh	2.57	2.36
Portland/Salem OR	1.58	2.26

Except for Minneapolis/St. Paul and Denver/Boulder/Greeley, all of the metropolitan areas that achieved a higher population rank are located in the sunbelt (or West Coast, to include the cases of Seattle/Tacoma/Bremerton and Portland/Salem). And, except for Houston/Galveston/Brazoria, all of the metropolitan areas with a lower rank are located in the northeast quadrant of the nation. Houston lost only one place in rank – from ninth to tenth as its population increased by 56% in twenty years. The shift of the population to the sunbelt is evident. We see that San Francisco/Oakland/San Jose moved into fourth place – ahead of Philadelphia/Wilmington/Trenton – and appears to be gaining on Chicago/Gary for third place. Dallas/Fort Worth moved from tenth place to seventh place, and by nearly doubling its population in twenty years, Atlanta moved from 16th place to 11th place. Phoenix/Mesa actually did double in population to move into 14th place. It is quite possible that, at some time in the twenty-first century, California will be home to the largest and the third-largest metropolitan areas in the nation.

The first section of the chapter takes a look at a simple geographic theory of an urban hierarchy that is based on market-oriented goods and services. This theory has severe limitations, but it points out the important relationship between economies of scale and the economic functions performed by urban areas of various sizes. The next section is an empirical investigation of the economic functions performed by urban areas. What are their basic functions and how can they be measured? These questions are answered, and then the next section of the chapter makes use of a system for measuring fundamental economic functions to classify urban areas into three general categories and more specific groups. The general categories are:

- diversified service centers;
- production centers; and
- specialized service centers.

The field of urban economics lacks a comprehensive theory of the urban hierarchy that can explain most of the real-world pattern, but the categorization exercise is useful and may lead to a new theory. The chapter concludes with a close look at the economy of Des Moines that makes use of the classification schemes that are introduced.

B. Theory of the Urban Hierarchy

Basic model

There is a reasonably simple theory, based on the location decisions of market-oriented firms, that leads to a hierarchy of urban areas. The theory has several weaknesses that are discussed later, but for now it is useful to examine the theory in detail. The theory that is discussed in the next few paragraphs is known as central place theory. The book by Lösch (1954) is the most important discussion of the theory.

The first assumption of the theory is that an agricultural population lives on a plain at a population density that does not vary by location. Transportation costs are equal in all directions. Suppose that the agricultural population purchases and consumes two goods; one good can be supplied by small firms and, because of significant economies of scale, the other must be supplied by large firms. Furthermore, because of agglomeration economies such as shared roads and other public infrastructure, firms in the two industries have an incentive to locate together whenever possible. The firms in both industries are assumed to be market oriented; their inputs are assumed to be available everywhere at constant prices.

As an example, suppose that gas stations serve an area containing 1,000 households, and that department stores serve an area of 7,000 households. These market sizes enable the firms to make a normal profit, and firms with market sizes much in excess of these numbers will induce more firms to enter. What will happen? First, gas stations will locate at regular intervals sufficiently small to create markets of 1,000 households. The markets tend to be circular in shape, and the households located in a given market will, in order to minimize travel, purchase gasoline at the gas station that is located in that market. Likewise, department stores will locate so as to establish market areas of 7,000 households each. Recall that department stores also have a strong incentive to locate next to a gas station in order to share infrastructure. Therefore, one in seven gas stations will be accompanied by a department store. Each firm requires a workforce, of course. The workers and their families create towns. This model has created a simple hierarchy of retail "towns" with small towns that contain only a gas station and larger towns that include both a gas station and a department store. There is one larger town for every six small towns.

Suppose that the gas station in the larger town supplies the gasoline needed by the department store workers, and that the department store supplies its good to the workers in the seven gas stations that fall within its market area. Also, farmers pay for their gasoline and department store goods with agricultural produce, which the workers in the towns consume. Finally, farmers produce and consume their own food, gas station workers buy gasoline at their own stations, and department store workers purchase goods at their own stores. Incomes and expenditures are in balance for these groups of workers.

More goods and services can be added to the model. For example, suppose that a hospital can provide comprehensive care to 49,000 households and all of the other people who live in 42 small towns and seven larger towns. One of those seven larger towns will then also contain a hospital (so that infrastructure can be shared), and will therefore be larger than the other six. The hierarchy is now one "city" for every six larger towns and for every 42 small towns. Further, assume that one hospital in seven contains a university that educates doctors and nurses for its own employ and for the other six hospitals in its area. One could keep on going with the exercise, but the point is now clear.

Rank-size rule for urban areas

The basic theory of the urban hierarchy as presented above is roughly consistent with what is known as the "rank-size rule" of urban areas. Suppose that urban areas are ranked by population from the largest to the smallest (New York is number one, etc.). The rank-size rule says that, for any urban area, its rank times its population size is a constant number. For New York,

$$\text{rank} \times \text{size} = 1 \times 19.0 \text{ million} = 19.$$

However, for Los Angeles,

$$\text{rank} \times \text{size} = 2 \times 16.4 \text{ million} = 32.8,$$

and for Chicago,

$$\text{rank} \times \text{size} = 3 \times 9.0 \text{ million} = 27.$$

Clearly rank times size is not equal for 19 for the next two urban areas. Try out a few of the other large urban areas listed above in section A. You will note that rank times size generally is a number larger than 28 million. (For example, Baltimore is 18×2.38 million = 42.84.) The rank-size rule does not work particularly well because New York is, oddly enough, "too small." The rule would work better if we regard New York and Los Angeles as "tied" for first, with Chicago ranked number two.

Why is the urban hierarchy theory roughly consistent with the rank-size rule? Return to the simple model with six small towns and one larger town. The six small towns just contain one gas station, which serves 1,000 rural households and the people who live in the town. The basic equation for the size of the small town is

$$p_1 = k(r + p_1),$$

where p_1 is the size of the small town, r is the size of the rural population that it serves, and k is the number of gas station workers needed to serve one household. The input coefficient k is most likely a small number such as 0.015; 15 gas station workers can serve 1,000 households. The solution for the size of the small town is

$$p_1 = rk/(1 - k).$$

If $r = 1,000$ and $k = 0.015$, then $p_1 = 15.2$. Note that the kp_1 term is quite small (the number of gas station workers needed to serve the small town itself), and it will be ignored for simplicity. In this case we have

$$p_1 = rk.$$

Now consider the larger town. It contains a department store that serves seven rural areas, six small towns, and its own population. The larger town also contains a gas station that serves one rural area and its own population. Let us assume that a department store, as does a gas station, requires 15 workers per 1,000 households served ($k = 0.015$). How large is the larger town? First of all, determine the number of workers in the department store. This works out to be

$$7kr + 6kp_1 + kp_2 = 7kr + 6k^2r/(1 - k) + kp_2,$$

where p_2 is the population of the larger town. However, the last two terms of this expression are quite small and can be ignored for the sake of simplicity. The number of workers in the gas station is

$$k(r + p_2),$$

but, once again, the kp_2 term is quite small and can be ignored.

The size of the larger town is approximately

$$p_2 = 7kr + kr = 8kr,$$

or one department store plus one gas station. Given that $k = 0.015$ and $r = 1,000$, $p_2 = 120$. The ratio of the population of a small town to the population of the larger town is

$$p_1/p_2 = kr/8kr = 1/8.$$

The larger town has a rank of one among the seven towns and a population that is sufficient to staff one department store and one gas station. The small towns have a population that is sufficient to staff one gas station and ranks of 2 through 7 (average rank of 4). Rank times size for the larger town is 120, and rank times size for the average small town is $15 \times 4 = 60$. What went wrong? Clearly the outcome of the model depended, among other things, on the number of department store workers needed to serve 1,000 households. This number was assumed to be 15, but instead suppose it is 7. In this case the number of workers in the department store is $0.007(7r)$, and the size the larger town is

$$0.007(7r) + 0.015r = 64.$$

This change in input coefficients makes the rank-size rule work almost exactly. Clearly the rank-size rule is only a very rough approximation of the relationship between the size of an urban areas and its rank.

Shortcomings of the urban hierarchy model

The basic urban hierarchy theory (or central place theory) does a good job of providing an explanation for a spatial hierarchy of towns and cities for retailing and consumer services. The theory can also include manufacturing and producer services provided that they are market oriented rather than input oriented. For example, suppose that a textile mill and an accompanying apparel factory use the cotton produced everywhere by farmers to produce clothing for people who live in the market area of 42 small towns, six larger towns, and one city discussed above. Where will these manufacturing firms locate? They most likely choose to locate in the one city because of urbanization economies arising from shared urban infrastructure. However, if infrastructure is not important for them, then it is conceivable that they will locate in one of the towns.

Clearly the critical feature of the model is economies of scale. As discussed in Chapter 3, if there were no economies of scale in the production of anything, then each farm household would be a self-sufficient producer of all of its consumer goods and services. Households would produce their own food, clothing, shelter, tools, medical care, etc. There would be no reason for towns and cities. In this world no one specializes in the production of anything. But as soon as we introduce the notion of specialization, we start to get reasons for towns and cities.

Consider the making of tools. Suppose initially that each farmer spends one hour out of a workday of eight hours making tools. Next, consider a tool making "specialist" who makes tools for himself and seven other farmers. The seven farmers can now devote eight hours per day to farming, and the eighth man is the toolmaker. However, this arrangement is better only if output increases as a result of specialization. Output will increase if the toolmaker can make more and better tools (in eight hours) than the eight farmers can (each spending one hour on tool making). Furthermore, the increased output of tools (and the resulting increase in farm products) must be sufficient to compensate for the travel time expended by the farmers to get their tools from the toolmaker. But it is clear that specialization does generate economies of scale, and that economies of scale are indeed very powerful forces. In the previous example of a hierarchy of urban places, imagine what would happen if each "larger town" (with a gas station and a department store) tried to have a "comprehensive" hospital staffed by one doctor who does everything. Or imagine what would happen if every hospital tried to have medical and nursing schools with a very small faculty.

The urban hierarchy theory is useful, but it leaves out some very important features of the real-world economy. Firms that are resource oriented (or input oriented in general) make location decisions, as discussed in Chapter 3, which are not based on the locations of customers. Steel once was produced exclusively where one could assemble the necessary resources – iron ore, coal, and limestone. (Now steel scrap, an input that is virtually ubiquitous, is used to produce some steel. This fact makes the steel industry tend to be more oriented to the market.) Second, the urban hierarchy theory leaves out the geographic features of real transportation systems. In particular, the theory ignores the importance of transshipment points and the port cities that are created along the lines discussed in Chapter 3. Recall that most of the major urban areas in the United States began as ports. Third, the urban hierarchy theory leaves out localization economies. Firms in the same industry avoid each other in the urban hierarchy theory. They set up separate market areas, a result that makes sense for gas stations and (probably) for department stores. However, we know that firms that sell "shopping goods" have an incentive to locate together to facilitate the activity of shopping. All of the other arguments made in Chapter 3 regarding localization economies apply. Finally, the theory leaves out special cases such as government capitals, military centers, resort cities, and retirement communities.

Chicago is a good example of a complex case. Metropolitan Chicago began as the place where the Great Lakes water transportation system could be linked to the Mississippi River (via the Chicago River, a canal, and the Illinois River). Because of its location, by the 1850s Chicago had also become a center of the rail transport system in the Midwest region. All of this meant that Chicago could become a production center for goods that are market oriented and subject to very large economies of scale. It could also become a center for the production of goods that required the assembly of inputs at a transshipment point. Chicago became a center for exporting various agricultural products from the Midwest and for importing goods to the Midwest from the factories of the East. Last, but not least, Chicago became a gateway for people coming to the Midwest from Europe and from the other regions of the United States. Real-life urban areas that are larger than small towns usually represent complicated combinations of various location forces, of which the urban hierarchy theory presented in the section is only one. Enough information has already been presented in this book about Los Angeles to enable you to make a preliminary attempt at telling its story in the same terms we just used to discuss Chicago. This would make an excellent question for your first examination in this course, would it not?

C. Industry Clusters in Urban Areas

The theory of the urban hierarchy reaches the conclusion that the economic functions performed by an urban area are determined by its place in the hierarchy. The previous section also noted that the basic urban hierarchy model leaves out urban areas that are centers of resource-based production, mining-based cities, transshipment points, governmental centers, military centers, centers of production for goods with localization economies, resorts, or retirement communities. The task of this section and the next is to provide a comprehensive and realistic method for classifying urban areas according to their economic functions. The first step is to enumerate the basic economic functions performed by urban areas. Methods for performing this task are discussed here. The next section presents a functional classification of the urban areas in the United States for 1990. Recall the discussion in Chapter 1 of the creation of economic knowledge in an applied field such as urban economics. The tasks that are being undertaken in the remainder of this chapter involve the collection of data about urban areas and the systematic examination of the data to find important patterns and trends. The next step would be to develop a more comprehensive theory of the urban hierarchy but, alas, that is a step that cannot be included in this text. It is a step that has not been taken.

Noyelle and Stanback (1983) have proposed a scheme for the enumeration and measurement of the fundamental economic functions performed in an urban area. Table 4.2

Table 4.2   Basic economic functions performed by urban areas

		SIC code
1	Agriculture, extractive, construction	01–09
2	Manufacturing	20–39
3	Distributive services	
	Transportation, communication, and utilities	40–9
	Wholesale trade	50–1
4	Complex of corporate activities	
	Central administrative offices and auxiliary establishments	A&A[a]
	Finance, insurance, and real estate	60–7
	Corporate services	
	Business services	73
	Legal services	81
	Membership organizations	86
	Misc. professional services	89
	Social services	83
5	Nonprofit services	
	Health	80
	Education	82
6	Retailing	52–9
7	Consumer services	
	Hotels, etc.	70
	Personal services	72
	Auto repair, garages	75
	Misc. repair services	76
	Motion pictures	78
	Amusement and recreation services	79, 84
	Private household services	88
8	Government and government enterprises	91–7

[a] A&A stands for administrative and auxiliary employment, and can pertain to any industry group.
Source: Adapted from Noyelle and Stanback (1983, pp. 9, 60–1)

summarizes their method of classification by type of output. The system that they used to classify output and hence define industries is called the Standard Industrial Classification (SIC) that was developed by the US Department of Commerce. Noyelle and Stanback group industries into eight basic functional areas, and the SIC code for each industry is shown in Table 4.2. The first category of agriculture, extractive, and construction includes industries that are not necessarily urban in character, although a few urban areas specialize in one of these industries. The other seven functional areas typically are urban functions. They include the manufacturing of goods and the distribution of goods and services. Next comes the area that Noyelle and Stanback call the complex of corporate activities. The large and important urban sector includes central administrative offices; finance, insurance and real estate (FIRE); and corporate services that include business, legal, social and other professional services as well as membership organizations. In short, the complex of corporate activities includes the "command and control" portions of large and medium-sized companies along with the services those companies need for planning, financing, managing risk, operating within the law, expanding, and interacting with each other.

The other basic economic functions of urban areas are performed by the nonprofit services (health and education), retailing, consumer services, and government sectors. The sectors are all quite substantial in size. The health care sector alone constitutes 14% of GNP (and should probably not be called "nonprofit"). Retailing and consumer services both deal directly with consumers, but retailing involves the sale of goods (including restaurant meals and beverages). In contrast, consumer services include services such as hotel rooms, hair styling, auto repairs, amusements, et al. Finally, government includes the federal, state, and local levels. Everything from local public schools to the US military is lumped into this category, which constitutes 35% of the economy.

Stanback (2002) updated the Noyelle–Stanback system to 1990, and added high-tech manufacturing and services as another category. Stanback's definition of high-tech actually includes industries that are part of the broader categories listed in Table 4.2, and it includes:

High-tech manufacturing
- drugs;
- computer and office equipment;
- communications equipment;
- electronic components and accessories;
- aircraft and parts;
- guided missiles, space vehicles, and parts;
- instruments for such purposes such as detection, guidance, control, surgery, and so on.

High-tech services
- telephone communications services;
- computer programming, data processing, and so on;
- motion picture production;
- engineering and related services;
- research, development, and testing services.

The Noyelle and Stanback system permits the analyst to break down the economy of an urban area into a relatively small number of economically meaningful sectors. However, the Noyelle and Stanback system displayed in Table 4.2 is not based on an empirical examination of urban areas. Rather, it is a system based on an *a priori* classification of output into types. It would be helpful to know if the industries included in each of the eight categories in Table 4.2 tend to cluster together in urban areas. A finding that the industries tend to cluster as shown in Table 4.2 would lend credibility to the Noyelle and Stanback system.

Research on this issue was conducted by McDonald (1992) and O'hUallachain (1992) and reported in Mills and McDonald (1992). They computed "location quotients" for the 150 largest urban areas in the United States in 1980 using employment data at the two-digit SIC code level – the same type of data used by Noyelle and Stanback to devise their classification system. A location quotient is a measure of the extent to which an urban area specializes in a particular industry. It is defined as the percentage of total employment in an urban area engaged in a particular industry divided by the corresponding percentage for the nation as a whole. In algebraic form,

$$LQ = (e_i/e)/(E_i/E),$$

with the notation that

e_i = employment in industry i in the subject urban area,
e = total employment in the subject urban area,
E_i = employment in industry i in the US, and
E = total employment in the US.

A location quotient that is appreciably greater than one indicates the urban area probably is producing the good or service for export outside its own area. A location quotient smaller than one suggests that the urban area imports the good or service.

For example, manufacturing employment in the Des Moines metropolitan area in 1980 was 26,303 out of a total of 154,178 jobs in the private sectors; jobs in manufacturing were 17.1% of the private-sector total. The corresponding figure for the US is 1980 was 28.3%, so the location quotient for manufacturing in Des Moines was 0.60. This figure indicates that Des Moines did not specialize in manufacturing. In contrast, employment in wholesale trade for Des Moines was 9.2% of total private employment. The corresponding figure for the US was 7.0%, so the location quotient for this sector was 1.31. Such a location quotient that is substantially greater than 1.0 indicates that the Des Moines metropolitan area specializes in this industry and therefore is providing this service for a wider area.

The location-quotient data were then used to find statistical associations among the two-digit SIC code industries. The statistical method determined whether urban areas with large location quotients for one particular industry had large location quotients for other industries – whether there were of industries that tended to cluster together. The results of this exercise are shown in Table 4.3. Thirteen industry clusters emerge, although only the first seven are of importance to most urban areas. The first cluster is manufacturing as a whole. However, the fact is that not all 20 manufacturing industries cluster together. A separate examination of manufacturing was completed and is reported in the appendix

Table 4.3   Clustering of industries in urban areas[a]

1   Manufacturing
2   Financial and legal services
        Finance, insurance and real estate
        Transportation by air
        Communication
        Legal services
3   Business and professional services
4   Distribution
        Trucking and warehousing
        Wholesale trade
        Administrative offices, wholesale and retail trade
5   Health, social services, and education
        Health services
        Education
        Social services
        Government, state and local
        Local passenger transit
6   Retail trade
        Retail trade
        Personal services
        Auto repair
        Special trade contractors
7   Recreation services
        Hotels, etc.
        Amusement and recreation services
        Museums, etc.

---

[a] There are six more clusters that appear in selected urban areas; wood products, manufacturing headquarters and cultural activities, construction, the port cluster, the mining and oil cluster, and apparel manufacturing and distribution.
Source: Adapted from McDonald (1992)

to this chapter. The second and third clusters are financial and legal services and business and professional services. The groupings presented in Table 4.3 differ somewhat from the Noyelle and Stanback system in Table 4.2, but the basic ideas are similar. The complex of corporate activities includes two groups of supporting industries – one is largely financial in nature and the other provides business and professional services.

The distribution sector in Table 4.3 is more narrowly defined than is the corresponding Noyelle–Stanback sector, but the systems are quite similar. The health, social service, and education sector in Table 4.3 corresponds to the nonprofit services sector defined by Noyelle and Stanback, with the main exception that state and local government is included in the cluster defined in Table 4.3. The retail trade and recreation services clusters in Table 4.3 correspond pretty closely to the combination of the retailing and consumer services groups defined by Noyelle and Stanback. In summary, the Noyelle and Stanback system does not correspond exactly to groupings based on statistical associations, but the results in Tables 4.2 and 4.3 are quite similar.

The Standard Industrial Classification (SIC) system used by County Business Patterns and in this section had existed for many years, but it was replaced in 1998 by the North American Industrial Classification System (NAICS). These two systems are similar, but not identical. There is a very large manual that compares the two systems, but we have concluded that 1998 represents a break in County Business Patterns data. To be on the safe side, we recommend that, unfortunately, studies based on County Business Patterns data should now use 1998 as the base year. Comparisons with previous years are tricky. However, the good news is that the data for 1998 and subsequent years are available on the County Business Patterns web site for free. The web site is very user-friendly, and provides amazing industry detail under the NAICS system. One of the exercises at the end of this chapter involves making use of County Business Patterns data. All students of urban economics should become familiar with this valuable and accessible source of data.

D. The Noyelle–Stanback Classification System

The book by Noyelle and Stanback entitled *The Economic Transformation of American Cities* (1983) uses the system for the classification of industry sectors, as shown in Table 4.2, to classify urban areas according to their economic functions. This study was updated to 1990 by Stanback's *The Transforming Metropolitan Economy* (2002), and this section draws from his book. Now let us examine their use of that industry classification system to develop a functional topology of urban areas in the US.

The theories discussed in Chapter 3 and in this chapter lead to the conclusion that the mix of economic activity will vary from urban area to urban area. Stanback (2002) measured that mix as of 1990, and assigned all 317 urban areas to different functional categories. The basic data consisted of employment location quotients for urban areas for the industry groups defined above in Table 4.2. He searched statistically for groupings of *urban areas*.

Stanback found that, using the location quotient data, urban areas tended to cluster into seven reasonably distinct groups. These groups are given titles in Table 4.4. The first group is called diversified service centers, which can pertain to the national, regional, or sub-regional level. These urban areas all tend to have location quotients in excess of 1.10 for the corporate complex (administrative offices, FIRE, and corporate services), and the distribution sector (transportation, communication and utilities, and wholesale trade). The larger diversified service centers also have concentrations in high-tech manufacturing and services.

The next three groups of urban areas are production centers. Functional-nodal centers specialize in manufacturing and corporate administration and business and professional services within the complex of corporate activities, but they do not specialize in FIRE or distribution. They also have high concentrations of high-tech manufacturing and services. Manufacturing/service metropolitan areas have high location quotients in manufacturing and non-profit services (such as higher education or health care). The manufacturing group has high concentrations of manufacturing employment only. As we know from Chapter 3, this group of urban areas is consistent with Henderson's (1986) finding of localization economies in several manufacturing industries.

Table 4.4 Functional typology of metropolitan areas

Number of metropolitan areas		Important industry sectors (LQ > 1.1)
Diversified service centers		
Very large (> 2 million)	16	Distribution, corporate complex, high tech
Large (1–2 million)	18	Distribution, corporate complex, high tech
Medium (250,000–1 million)	22	Distribution, corporate complex
Small (under 250,000)	32	Distribution, retailing, insurance, health services
Production centers		
Functional nodal	22	Manufacturing, business/professional services, headquarters
Manufacturing/service	56	Manufacturing, nonprofit services
Manufacturing	27	Manufacturing
Specialized service centers		
Government/service	62	State, local government
Government/military	37	Federal government, consumer services
Resort/retirement	25	Retail, FIRE agents and brokers, consumer services, construction

Source: Adapted from Stanback (2002)

The government/service group consists of centers of government (e.g., state capitals) combined in most cases with employment in universities. Government/military centers specialize in government (federal civilian or military), retailing, and consumer services. The last group, resort/retirement centers, have employment concentrated in retailing, FIRE agents and brokers, consumer services, health services, and construction – the last reflecting rapid recent growth. Which urban areas fall into these groups? The three largest urban areas (New York, Los Angeles, and Chicago) are diversified service centers. Indeed, most of the top urban areas are diversified service centers. Smaller diversified service centers include Memphis, Syracuse, Omaha, Des Moines, Lubbock, La Crosse (Wisconsin), and Casper (Wyoming). Readers who are familiar with some of these smaller urban areas will recognize this as a group of commercial centers with more limited spheres of influence.

The production centers include the functional-nodal group. This group combines manufacturing with corporate administrative employment, and the only major urban area in this group is Detroit. The group also includes smaller urban areas such as Hartford, Rochester (New York), Akron, and Peoria. The manufacturing/service group includes Providence (the largest member of the group) and smaller urban areas such as Toledo, Ann Arbor, Waco, and Wausau (Wisconsin). The members of manufacturing group are urban areas such as Grand Rapids (Michigan), Gary, Flint, Rockford (Illinois), and Kokomo (Indiana).

The government/service group includes Washington, DC, of course, and several state capitals such as Sacramento, Albany, Austin, Baton Rouge, and Madison. Government/military areas are headed by San Diego, Norfolk, and San Antonio. Resort/retirement areas include Tampa, Ft. Lauderdale, Orlando, and Las Vegas.

Table 4.5   Employment shares and location quotients: 1974 and 1997

	Shares of total US employment (%)		Location quotients			
			Diversified Service Centers, very large		Prod. Centers Functional nodal	
	1974	*1997*	*1974*	*1997*	*1974*	*1997*
Construction	4.95	4.38	1.06	0.91	1.05	0.95
Manufacturing	25.47	14.81	0.95	0.85	1.42	1.45
TCU[a]	5.07	4.96	1.20	1.17	0.83	0.87
Wholesale trade	5.56	5.41	1.20	1.23	0.92	1.06
Retail trade	15.51	17.49	0.97	0.89	0.95	0.96
FIRE[b]	5.43	5.85	1.39	1.34	0.97	1.01
Bus./prof services	3.69	9.75	1.51	1.35	0.93	1.10
Nonprofit services	7.80	14.37	1.11	1.04	0.99	0.98
Consumer services	3.88	5.20	1.00	1.05	0.82	0.78
Government	21.79	17.31	0.81	0.78	0.72	0.74
Total	100.00	100.00				

[a] Transportation, communication, and utilities.
[b] Finance, insurance, and real estate.
Source: Adapted from Stanback (2002)

The data supplied by Stanback (2002) also permit us to take a closer look at how the nature of employment has changed in the nation and in particular types of urban areas. Table 4.5 shows the shares of total employment by industry for 1974 and 1997 for the nation. The large increases in the shares of employment in Business and Professional Services (3.69% to 9.75%) and in Nonprofit Services – largely health care (7.80% to 14.37%) are clear. These increases in shares came at the expense of Manufacturing (25.47% to 14.81%) and Government (21.79% to 17.31%). Table 4.5 also shows the location quotients for the 16 very large diversified service centers. We can see that these urban areas in both 1974 and 1997 specialized in (by size of location quotient) Business and Professional Services, Finance, Insurance, and Real Estate, Wholesale Trade, and Transportation, Communication, and Utilities. The composition of employment in the 22 functional nodal production centers is quite different. These urban areas specialized only in Manufacturing in both years. Given that the national share of employment in Manufacturing dropped by 10.66 percentage points, these urban areas such as Detroit, Rochester, Akron, and Peoria were fighting an uphill battle.

In summary, the Noyelle–Stanback system produces a functional hierarchy for modern urban areas, and classifies urban areas according to their dominant economic functions. There is no simple theory that explains fully the patterns that Noyelle and Stanback (1983) and Stanback (2002) uncovered. The simple urban hierarchy model of market-oriented activities based on specialization and economies of scale tells part of the story. Localization economies appear to be important for some industries, including both manufacturing and non-manufacturing industries. Urbanization economies appear to be important too, but they may have been more critical in the early history of large urban areas than they are today. As shown in the appendix to this chapter, input–output linkages are also important, and emerge as factors in the clustering of manufacturing industries. The complex of corporate activities also clearly involves input-output relationships between corporate offices and business and financial services.

Information and labor market factors surely create further urban agglomeration. But at this point we do not know the relative importance of these agglomerative forces. Finally, large urban areas are large because they grew rapidly during some previous time periods. What role does each of the forces of agglomeration play in urban *growth*? A discussion of this question is deferred to Part VI of the book.

E. A New Category: The Global City

The most recent development in studies of the urban hierarchy is the idea that some major cities are joining a new category, called global cities. The rapid expansion of international trade and financial operations since the 1980s has meant that these cities must perform new functions. Saskia Sassen is prominent among the scholars of global cities, which she (2000, p. 21) defines as "strategic sites for the management of the global economy and the production of the most advanced services and financial operations." Global cities are the places from which the global economy is managed. They attract the headquarters of companies that operate globally, and they house the financial institutions and other sectors that support global trade and investment. Financial and legal services play particularly important roles in the global economy, and London, Tokyo, and New York are the world's leading financial and legal centers and the leading global cities. However, Sassen (2000) observes that a world-wide network of global cities has emerged that now includes perhaps three or four dozen cities. This network of cities is needed to facilitate global trade and investment, including investment in the global cities themselves. It has become quite fashionable for local officials in these cities to be concerned about the position their city occupies in the global economy, and to initiate measures to enhance that position. In short, mayors of major cities have become players in the global economy who interact directly with each other. The mayor of Chicago goes to meet with the mayor of Shanghai to discuss mutual interests. The business of being a global city is changing rapidly.

F. An Examination of the Des Moines Economy

A good theory is a useful theory. Good classification systems are also useful. This chapter has presented two systems for classifying industries in urban areas and one functional classification of urban areas themselves. These systems can be of use to anyone who wishes to gain some insight into the economy of a particular urban area. Since most people do not live in global cities, this section makes use of these systems to take a look at a more typical local economy, the economy of Des Moines, Iowa. The choice of Des Moines is

Table 4.6   Employment in Des Moines (Polk County), Iowa

Sector	1980			1987		
	Employment	% share	LQ[a]	Employment	Share (%)	LQ
Total private employment	154,178			171,945		
Manufacturing	26,303	17.1	0.60	22,850	13.3	0.60
Retail cluster	37,595	24.4	1.00	40,477	23.5	0.89
Financial & legal services[b]	23,147	15.0	1.74	30,796	17.9	1.83
Business & prof. services	7,604	4.9	0.94	11,770	6.8	0.91
Distribution	21,647	14.0	1.46	22,727	13.2	1.40
Health, educ. & social services	17,744	11.5	1.11	23,026	13.4	1.11
Other	20,138	13.1	0.97	20,299	11.8	0.93
Government	28,800	15.8	0.88	30,600	15.3	0.89

[a] *LQ* stands for location quotient, which equals the local share for the industry group divided by the corresponding figure for the nation. For the private sectors, percent share and *LQ* pertain to private employment only.
[b] Industry group includes FIRE (SIC 61–7) plus legal services (SIC 81), air transportation (SIC 45) and transportation services (SIC 47).
Sources: County Business Patterns (US Dept. of Commerce) and Employment and Earnings (US Dept. of Labor)

purely arbitrary, although Des Moines has the advantage of being almost entirely contained in one county, Polk County, Iowa. What follows is an examination of this county.

From the previous discussion we already know that Des Moines was classified by Stanback (2002) as a diversified service center of the smaller variety. Des Moines is grouped with urban areas such as Mobile, Spokane, and Knoxville (Tennessee). Diversified service centers in this group tend to specialize in the distribution sector and the complex of corporate activities. The population of Des Moines was 389,000 in 1980.

Total employment in Polk County has been broken down into the industry clusters in Table 4.6 using the McDonald (1992) scheme. Employment data for 1980 and 1987 for the top six clusters are shown in Table 4.6. Des Moines is the state capital of Iowa, so government employment is a separate category in Table 4.6. Table 4.6 also displays the fraction of total private employment for each private industry cluster and location quotients for each private industry cluster. These figures are restricted to private industries because of the presence of the state government in Des Moines.

Table 4.6 shows that Stanback (2002) had it just about right. Des Moines specializes in financial and legal services and in the distribution cluster. The employment level of 23,147 in financial and legal services for 1980 translates into a share of 15.0% and a location quotient of 1.74. These are high numbers indeed. By 1987 employment in this sector had grown to 30,796 for a share of 17.9% and a location quotient of 1.83. This sector is a winner! The distribution cluster employed 21,647 in 1980. Its share was 14.0% and the location quotient was a relatively high 1.46. However, this cluster did not keep pace with financial and legal services. Employment grew to 22,727 in 1987, but its share dropped to 13.2%, and the location quotient also fell to 1.40. These two sectors are examined in more detail below.

Table 4.7 Employment growth in Des Moines (Polk County), Iowa and in the US: 1980–1987

Sector	Des Moines (%)	US (%)
Total private employment	11.5	14.2
Manufacturing	−13.1	−10.2
Retail cluster	7.7	23.4
Financial & legal services[1]	33.0	30.7
Business & prof. services	54.8	64.2
Distribution	5.0	12.5
Health, education & social services	29.8	32.8
Other	0.8	7.5
Government	6.2	7.2

Industry group includes FIRE (SIC 61–7), legal services (SIC 81), air transportation (SIC 45), and transportation services (SIC 47).

The health, education and social services cluster had a location quotient of 1.11 in both 1980 and 1987, which is only slightly in excess of 1.0. Note that, in order to maintain its location quotient of 1.11 over these years, the sector had to grow from 17,744 to 23,026 workers and increase its share from 11.5% to 13.4%. This sector includes health care, and the sector will be examined in more detail below.

Table 4.6 also shows the lack of prominence of manufacturing in the Des Moines economy. The location quotient for manufacturing was 0.60 in both 1980 and 1987, and both its level and share of employment dropped. With one exception, the other sectors listed in Table 4.6 are rather unremarkable; they show up with location quotients that are equal to or slightly less than 1.0. The exception is business and professional services. This sector has a location quotient that is less than 1.0, but it grew very rapidly in Des Moines (and in the rest of the nation, as well). Table 4.6 did not take very long to construct, and it provides a nice overview of the main sectors of the Des Moines economy and how well they have been doing.

A comparison for Des Moines of employment growth by industry cluster with the US is shown in Table 4.7. Private employment in the US grew by 14.2% from 1980 to 1987, and Des Moines almost matched that growth with a figure of 11.5%. However, the patterns of that growth for the Des Moines and the national economies were very different. The retail cluster grew much more rapidly at the national level, and national employment growth in business and professional services and in distribution also exceeded their growth in Des Moines by a fair margin. Remember, this last cluster is one in which Des Moines specializes. Perhaps we need to take a more detailed look at these sectors so that we can pinpoint the both the sources of robust employment growth and the sources of lackluster performance.

The more detailed look at the sectors is shown in Table 4.8. The data source is *County Business Patterns*, which provides employment figures by county down to the four-digit SIC code level. Most of the data shown in Table 4.8 is taken from the two-digit SIC industry level, but a few three- and four-digit SIC figures are used to examine some

Table 4.8   Important industries in Des Moines (Polk County), Iowa

Industry	Employment		Growth (%)
	1980	*1987*	
Financial & legal services	23,147	30,796	33.0
SIC 60 Banking	2,696	2,958	9.7
SIC 61 S&Ls	1,879	3,390	80.4
SIC 62 Security brokers	499	733	46.9
SIC 63 Insurance carriers	12,434	15,237	22.5
SIC 64 Insurance agents	1,220	2,293	88.0
SIC 65 Real estate	2,242	2,584	15.3
SIC 66–7 Other real est. & investment	432	702	62.5
A&A Administrative	298	643	115.8
SIC 45, 47 Transportation	347	701	102.0
SIC 81 Legal services	1,100	1,555	41.4
Distribution	18,630	21,647	16.2
SIC 42 Trucking & warehousing	5,418	5,390	−0.5
SIC 50–1 Wholesale trade	12,462	14,122	13.3
A&A in retailing	750	2,135	184.7
Business and professional services	7,604	11,770	54.8
SIC 73 Business services	6,140	10,075	64.1
734 Services to buildings	1,064	1,670	57.0
736 Personnel supply	1,217	1,898	56.0
737 Computer, data processing	880	2,262	157.0
7374 Data processing	841	1,821	116.5
SIC 89 Prof. services	1,464	1,695	15.8
Health, education & social services	17,744	23,026	29.8
SIC 80 Health services	13,041	13,854	6.2
SIC 82 Education services	2,366	4,064	71.8
SIC 83 Social services	1,910	3,843	101.2
SIC 41 Local transit	427	1,265	195.6

Source: County Business Patterns (US Dept. of Commerce)

additional details. Four sectors will be examined in turn – financial and legal services, distribution, business and professional services, and the health, education and social services group.

Table 4.8 tells us immediately that the financial and legal services cluster is dominated by the insurance industry – the insurance carriers, as opposed to local insurance agents. Insurance carriers (SIC 63) made up 53.7% of the cluster in 1980, and that percentage fell slightly to 49.5% in 1987. It would certainly not come as news to anyone in Des Moines that insurance is big business there, but the importance of this industry is highlighted in Table 4.8. Clearly insurance services are being exported to a wide area. What are the localization economies at work? This is a question that should be investigated by those who are vitally concerned with the Des Moines economy. However, it is also true that the other components of the financial and legal services cluster grew substantially during the

1980–7 period. As a group their growth was far greater than the growth in the insurance industry. Employment in insurance (SIC 63) grew by 22.5% over these seven years, but employment in the rest of the financial and legal services cluster grew by 45.2%. This finding perhaps tells us that the Des Moines economy is branching out into other areas of financial and legal services, a trend that is probably a good thing. A local economy perhaps relies so heavily on a single industry at its peril.

The other major specialty for Des Moines is the distribution cluster, which consists of trucking and warehousing, wholesale trade, and administrative offices in retail trade. Table 4.8 shows that wholesale trade alone contributed 14,808 jobs to the Des Moines economy in 1987. Des Moines clearly is a center of distribution of goods to its sub-region, and it also serves as a collection point for exports from Iowa. The growth in this cluster was a rather modest 5.0% during 1980–7. Trucking and warehousing added 455 jobs, and wholesale trade added 686. Why did this sector experience this lackluster performance, when the sector as a whole grew by 12.5% at the national level? What impact did the deregulation of the trucking industry in the early 1980s have on Des Moines? These questions need some answers.

The business and professional services cluster is not a specialty for Des Moines, but it experienced an impressive growth of 54.8%. This cluster has only two industries at the two-digit SIC level, business services (SIC 73) and professional services (SIC 89). Table 4.8 shows that the cluster in Des Moines is dominated by business services. Nearly all of the growth in the cluster from 1980 to 1987 was in business services. Table 4.8 shows the major components of business services (SIC 73) in Des Moines. These are services to buildings (SIC 734), personnel supply (SIC 736), and computer and data processing services (SIC 737). This last industry is dominated by data processing (SIC 7374). Services to buildings (SIC 734) means janitorial, maintenance and repair services. This industry has been growing as building owners have decided to have their buildings serviced by a more professional company. This kind of service is particularly prevalent in office buildings, and clearly office employment and the office building industry has been growing in Des Moines. Personnel supply (SIC 736) consists of firms that supply temporary workers to a variety of clients. The temporary workers are usually considered to be employees of the supplying firm (e.g., Manpower, Inc.). Growth in this industry in Des Moines is part of the national trend towards hiring temporary rather than permanent workers. Firms seem to require more of the flexibility that temporary workers can provide. Finally, Des Moines experienced huge growth in data processing (SIC 7374) of 116.5% in just seven years. Almost 1,000 jobs were created in this industry alone. Why did this happen? Could this growth have continued?

The fourth and final cluster that is examined in Table 4.8 is health, education, and social services. Recall that this cluster grew rapidly enough to maintain its location quotient of 1.11. That growth was 5,282 jobs over seven years. Table 4.8 shows that, perhaps surprisingly, the lion's share of the growth was *not* in health services. Health services made up 73.5% of the cluster in 1980, but that proportion had fallen to 60.2% in 1987. Most of the growth took place in the education services and social services industries. Once again, the people of Des Moines needed to find out why this growth took place and whether more of the same could have been expected. This section in effect has presented a report on the status of the Des Moines economy that might be of use to local officials and industry leaders. It shows a great deal of what makes the Des Moines economy tick, but it also raises some questions that need to be answered. This is certainly one valid purpose for a short report of this kind – to raise questions that are critical to a deeper understanding of the local economy.

G. Summary

This chapter is a discussion of the economic functions of urban areas. An urban area fits into the system of urban areas in particular ways. The urban hierarchy model for market-oriented industries explains some of the patterns that are observed, but that model has severe limitations. Those limitations include not taking account of resource-based industries, industries that are subject to localization economies, and various types of special-purpose urban areas. The real features of the transportation system are also ignored. Unfortunately, there is no comprehensive theory that can replace the urban hierarchy theory.

In the absence of a comprehensive theory, researchers and practitioners have turned to classification systems that are based on statistical associations. Noyelle and Stanback (1983) provided an innovative classification scheme for the top 140 urban areas in the United States based on economic functions broadly defined, and this study was updated by Stanback (2002). McDonald (1992) and O'hUallachain (1992) have introduced a classification system for industries that is based on statistical association. These classification systems can be used to gain some insights into the functions performed by a local economy, and the Des Moines economy was used as an example. At the top of these classification systems rests a new category called global cities (Sassen, 2000) that are the strategic points from which the global economy is managed and financed. Indeed, Sassen (2000) posits that a hierarchy of global cities has emerged, wherein each global city performs its functions as part of the global network. The notion of a system of global cities will surely attract much discussion and research in the coming years.

Appendix to Chapter 4: Clustering of Manufacturing Industries

It was noted in the text that not all manufacturing industries tend to cluster together. Manufacturing industries cluster in urban areas if they have strong input–output relationships or other forms of agglomeration economies, as discussed in Chapter 3. McDonald (1992) found that the two-digit SIC code manufacturing industries tended to group together statistically in 1986 as shown in Table A4.1. The procedure followed was to compute the 20×20 matrix of simple correlations of employment shares in total manufacturing. Of the 190 simple correlations, eighteen are positive and statistically significant (at the 99% level of statistical significance). None of these simple correlations is negative and statistically significant. The 18 simple correlations led to 15 industry clusters of 2 industries each and 1 cluster of 3 industries.

The clusters clearly are largely based on input–output relationships or on particular combinations of available basic resources. For example, the first cluster is food and kindred products (SIC 20) and stone, clay, and glass products (SIC 32). This cluster is consistent with the idea that food products and food containers, dishes, etc. tend to be produced in the same urban areas. Part of the correlation probably stems from the use of glass containers as packaging for food items. In contrast, the second cluster is tobacco (SIC 21) and furniture (SIC 25). Urban areas that produce both of

Table A4.1   Major manufacturing clusters

	SIC Code
1 Food and containers	
Food and kindred products	20
Stone, clay, and glass products	32
2 Tobacco and furniture	
Tobacco	21
Furniture	25
3 Textiles and apparel	
Textile mill products	22
Apparel	23
4 Textiles and furniture	
Textile mill products	22
Furniture	25
5 Furniture and fixtures	
Furniture	25
Fabricated metal products	34
6 Petrochemicals	
Chemicals and allied products	28
Petroleum and coal products	
7 Chemical products and containers	
Chemicals and allied products	28
Stone, clay, and glass products	32
8 Machinery I	
Rubber and plastic products	30
Fabricated metal products	34
Machinery, except electrical	35
9 Metals	
Primary metal products	33
Fabricated metal products	34
10 Transportation equipment	
Fabricated metal products	34
Transportation equipment	37
11 Machinery II	
Machinery, except electrical	35
Electric and electronic equipment	36

[a] Clusters based on correlations of employment shares.
Source: Adapted from McDonald (1992), from *County Business Patterns* (US Dept. of Commerce) data

these products are located in the southeastern region of the nation, which has an abundance of the raw materials used in both industries. The presence of tobacco farms and forests in the same general area is simply a coincidence of nature. The third cluster of textiles and apparel is obviously based on a strong input–output relationship. The fourth cluster consists of textiles and furniture, which combine and input–output relationship (use of textile mill products in furniture) and coincidental resource availability (cotton and wood from forests).

One can proceed through the list of cluster in Table A4.1 in this fashion and note that all of the remaining clusters are based in substantial measure on input–output relationships. For example, cluster 9 has chemicals, which need petroleum and coal products as inputs. Cluster 15 includes transportation equipment (autos, trucks) and the fabricated metals products needed for such equipment. However, one cluster stands out as unusual. Cluster 13 includes leather and leather products (SIC 31) and electric and electronic equipment (SIC 36). There is no obvious input–output relationship between these two industries, nor is there nay other clear agglomerative force that brings these two industries together. However, it is also true that leather and leather products are one of the smallest manufacturing industries in terms of employment (only tobacco and petroleum and coal products are smaller). Therefore, this cluster is probably not very important, and is simply a statistical coincidence that was generated by the data from a handful of urban areas.

This appendix has shown that manufacturing industries have clear tendencies to cluster together based largely on input–output relationships. Table A4.1 provides a summary of these clusters.

Exercises

1   Collect data on employment for an urban area of your choice and for the entire US using *County Business Patterns* for private employment and *Employment and Earnings* for public employment. Create a table that shows employment by major NAICS industries for 1998 and 2002. The major NAICS industries are:

   11   Forestry, and so on
   21   Mining
   22   Utilities
   23   Construction
   31   Manufacturing
   42   Wholesale trade
   44   Retail trade
   48   Transportation and warehousing
   51   Information
   53   Real estate & rental & leasing
   54   Professional, scientific & technical services
   55   Management of companies and enterprises
   56   Admin. support, waste managment, remediation services
   61   Educational services
   62   Health care and social assistance
   71   Arts, entertainment & recreation
   72   Accommodation and food services
   81   Other services (except public administration)
   95   Auxiliaries
   99   Unclassified establishments.

   Compute the location quotients for your urban area (relative to the US). Which industries in your urban area grew rapidly? Which industries had an increase in the location quotient? Is the same list of industries the answer to both questions? Why or why not?

2   Update the study of Des Moines by looking at County Business Patterns data for 1998 to 2002. What changes have occurred in that economy? Why do you think those changes happened?

3   Select two global cities as suggested by Sassen (2000). Global cities in the US include New York, Los Angeles, Chicago, San Francisco, Miami, and Houston. Use County Business Patterns data to compare the composition of employment in two of these metropolitan areas. How are they the same? How do they differ?

References

Henderson, J. Vernon, 1986, "Efficiency of Resource Usage and City Size," *Journal of Urban Economics*, vol. 19, pp. 47–70.

Lösch, August, 1954, *The Economics of Location*. New Haven: Yale University Press.

McDonald, John, 1992, "Assessing the Development Status of Metropolitan Areas," in E. Mills and J. McDonald (eds.), *Sources of Metropolitan Growth*. New Brunswick, NJ: Center for Urban Policy Research, Rutgers University.

Mills, Edwin and John McDonald (eds.), 1992, *Sources of Metropolitan Growth*. New Brunswick, NJ: Center for Urban Policy Research, Rutgers University.

Noyelle, Thierry and Thomas Stanback, Jr., 1983, *The Economic Transformation of American Cities*. Totowa, NJ: Rowan & Allanheld.

O'hUallachain, Breandon, 1992, "Economic Structure and Growth of Metropolitan Areas," in E. Mills and J. McDonald (eds.), *Sources of Metropolitan Growth*. New Brunswick, NJ: Center for Urban Policy Research, Rutgers University.

Sassen, Saskia, 2000, *Cities in a World Economy*, 2nd edn. Thousand Oaks, CA: Pine Forge Press.

Stanback, Thomas M., 2002, *The Transforming Metropolitan Economy*, New Brunswick, NJ: Center for Urban Policy Research, Rutgers University.

Part II

Location Patterns in Urban Areas

Chapter 5

Introduction to Urban Location Patterns: Static Analysis

A. Introduction

In this chapter we introduce the static theory of the location of economic activity within urban areas. Conventional textbooks in microeconomics present theories designed to answer the following conventions. *What* is produced? *How* is it produced? *For whom* is it produced? *How much* is produced and at what price? Urban economics is a branch of microeconomics that also asks: *Where* are the various economic goods produced within urban areas? *Where* do people choose to live? *How* do prices and the quantity produced vary *spatially* within an urban area?

The market for urban land is of central importance to the theory of urban location patterns. The urban land market is a highly regulated market, but it is still very useful to employ the tools of competitive market analysis to understand how land is allocated to its various potential uses. Furthermore, land is an important input into the production of all goods and services. It is obvious that housing uses a great deal of land as an input. Manufacturing and commercial activities also use land. The public sector uses a great deal of land for transportation facilities (roads, highways, and airports) as well as for parks, schools, and other public buildings. The amount of land that is used to produce outputs can vary enormously – from tall downtown office buildings to vast suburban shopping malls. The land market not only determines what is produced at a particular site but also influences how much is produced (per unit of land).

The standard urban spatial model is known at the *monocentric city model*. As the name implies, the standard model is based on an assumption that the city revolves around a single center. The center is referred to as the *central business district* (or "CBD"). The CBD is the center of the stylized city's economic life. All jobs are located there, and people commute from the surrounding residential areas to their jobs in the center. Later, we will consider extensions of the model in which jobs are also located outside the CBD. But the simple monocentric city model is still the most important theoretical model in urban economics. Despite its simple assumptions, it provides a great deal of insight into the spatial arrangement of urban economic activity. And the tools developed for the model can be used to analyze many interesting and realistic extensions.

B. Agglomerations of Economic Activity in Urban Areas

The theory of the urban land market begins with the observation that economic activity tends to be concentrated in certain locations within an urban area. The modern urban area contains several types of economic agglomerations: the downtown central business district, major airports and other transportation and distribution centers, industrial areas, large shopping centers, hospitals and related medical facilities, educational institutions, and government offices and facilities. An urban area contains a collection of such centers of economic activity that depends upon its economic history and its functions in the modern economy. The types and sizes of urban areas were discussed in Chapter 4.

All of the major urban areas in the United States were founded prior to the 1920s, the beginning of the age of the automobile. Indeed, except for a few that began as railroad junctions, most urban areas began as ports. For example, Chicago and its central business district are located at the mouth of the Chicago River because this small, lifeless river was once the best of a bad set of choices for the location of a port on Lake Michigan. Similarly, New Orleans is first site upriver from the mouth of the Mississippi that has a small area of land above sea level. St. Louis is located at a site just downriver from a set of rapids that once forced ships carrying goods downriver to stop, with the goods making their way past the rapids on land. Other major urban areas, such as New York, Boston, Philadelphia, Miami, Houston, Los Angeles, San Francisco, and Seattle, began economic life as ports and continue to be ports in the world economy.

The layout of the port facility tended to dictate the nearby location of other commercial activities, such as wholesale trade, banking, and insurance companies as well as important parts of manufacturing production. The coming of the railroad in the latter half of the nineteenth century usually meant that rail lines were focused on an existing port and its related concentration of economic activity. For these reasons, many urban areas in the late nineteenth and early twentieth centuries can be considered to be monocentric. In most urban areas, the traditional CBD continues to be the single largest concentration of economic activity today, even though it may have formed over a century ago.

There are important early exceptions to monocentric cities. The largest urban areas, such as New York, Philadelphia, and Chicago, had outgrown their original downtown districts well before 1900. Important parts of the urban economy had taken up residence in other locations. The early examples of suburbanization of employment usually involved one of the large-scale manufacturing facilities that date from the late nineteenth century. Chicago's Union Stockyards provide a good case in point. Chicago had a large number of small stockyards and meatpacking plants that grew rapidly in the early 1860s. These companies were located at various spots near the downtown area and very quickly ran out of space. The Union Stockyards was formed in 1865 by a consortium of meat packers and railroad companies. A single site was chosen at what was then the periphery of the urban area, about 5 miles to the southwest of downtown. This site was provided with both rail and water transportation and it almost instantly developed into a huge agglomeration of industrial activity. Did the Chicagoans of the day decry the loss of jobs from the inner city? No. Rather, there was a great feeling of relief because cattle and hogs do not make very good urban neighborhoods. Besides, the Chicago economy was growing rapidly.

The basic message here is that the analysis of an urban land market for some point in time begins with the enumeration of the important focal points for economic activity. In many cases, these centers of activity are still located at the initial site of a port or a railroad center. In some cases, it is still sufficient to assume a monocentric urban area. In other cases, two or three centers of employment are important enough to merit separate attention. The number and types of employment centers are matters for more detailed examination in Chapter 7. Only rarely is employment so dispersed within an urban area that the insights of the monocentric model are simply not applicable.

C. Sectors in the Urban Economy

One of the first things that a student in elementary economics learns is that the economy can be divided into the household and business sectors. Households supply labor to businesses, and businesses produce products that are channeled ultimately into investments made by businesses. This simple characterization of an economy that is without a government is completely closed to the rest of the world. A basic model of the urban economy and its land market could be based on this elementary picture. However, this model would miss some very important features of real urban areas.

It is critical to recognize that urban areas engage in a great deal of importing and exporting. This trading activity is not necessarily foreign trade – trade with foreign countries – but is simply trade with people who are located outside the urban area. Philadelphians "import" much of their food from outside their metropolitan area. There are many firms in Philadelphia that manufacture food items for Philadelphians, but these firms must purchase their basic inputs of grains, vegetables, meats, and so on, from outside the area. Also, most of Philadelphia's food-processing firms export some of their output to people who live outside the metropolitan area. Therefore, it is necessary to specify at least three business sectors: businesses that produce for export, businesses that import, and businesses that exist to produce for the local population. Some businesses may in fact engage in all three types of activities, but this complication will be ignored for now.

Another type of categorization of business sectors was introduced in Chapter 1 and used extensively in Chapter 4. The US Department of Commerce classifies businesses by type of industry into the following categories:

- agriculture, forestry, and fisheries;
- mining;
- construction;
- manufacturing;
- transportation, communication, and public utilities;
- wholesale trade;
- retail trade;
- finance, insurance, and real estate;
- services.

Obviously, the first two categories are not important in most urban areas, but the other seven are. Furthermore, each of these seven major sectors has numerous, very different components. There are 20 basic types of manufacturing industries, eight categories of retail trade establishments, and services consist of everything from hotels and personal services to health care, legal services, engineers and architects, accountants, and educational services. How many business sectors should be enumerated to gain a good understanding of urban location patterns and the urban labor market? The answer is that no one is entirely sure because it depends on the nature of the questions that one is trying to investigate.

Suppose that you are mainly interested in the market for industrial land and the location patterns of manufacturing activity and employment. In this case, you might divide manufacturing activity into two categories, such as heavy industry and light industry, keep a separate category for transportation, communication, and public utilities, and lump all other industries into a "commercial" category consisting largely of warehouses, stores, and offices. On the other hand, if you are interested primarily in studying whether downtown activities such as banking and finance, business and professional services, and retail trade have moved into other parts of an urban area, you would set up business sectors differently.

The household also consists of many components. Households differ by type (married couple with or without children, single individual, single parent with children), race, age of household head, and income level. Different schemes for the categorization of households can be used depending on the purpose at hand. One might wish to examine household location patterns and the residential land market for various racial or income incomes. We examine this matter in detail in Chapter 8.

So far the role of government in an urban area has been ignored except to note at the beginning that government is a major user of land for streets, public buildings, parks, and other things. Furthermore, the government regulates the use of land. Any model of the urban land market that claims to be reasonably comprehensive cannot afford to ignore the various roles of government. The role of government as a major employer cannot be ignored either.

Large urban areas have professional planners who, among other things, collect information on the use of land. A standard set of categories for urban activities includes the following:

- residential;
- manufacturing;
- transportation, communication, and public utilities;
- commercial;
- public buildings;
- public open space;
- parking;
- streets;
- vacant;
- unusable (including bodies of water).

As a practical matter, analysis of an urban land market may be constrained by such data collection efforts.

D. The Role of Transportation Infrastructure

One way to write a history of urban areas is to focus on the methods used to transport people and goods inside cities. Major changes in transportation are associated with great changes in the layout of an urban area. Historians usually emphasize the importance of the technical changes in long-distance transportation that began in the early nineteenth century when steam power was adapted for use in ships and railroad locomotives. Prior to that time people traveled over land on horseback or by wagon (stagecoach) – or on foot. Goods moved by wagon over land and by sailing vessel over water. Roads were usually bad or nonexistent. Long-distance travel was very costly and risky as well. The steam engine began to change all that.

Travel within urban areas until the 1850s was rudimentary. People "commuted" on foot, and goods moved by wagon. In fact, livestock also moved on foot. Telephones did not exist, so messages had to travel on foot. Streets were often narrow and became muddy quagmires when it rained. Something had to change or the urban transportation bottleneck would prevent cities from taking advantage of emerging economies of scale in production.

The first thing that was done in some of the world's major cities was to improve the street system. Streets needed to be widened, straightened, and paved. Paris underwent a massive facelift that became the inspiration for urban officials in many other places. The streets in Chicago were raised above the muck and mire. (This required raising the buildings too.) Eventually the people, horses, cattle, and hogs could walk around Chicago without sinking into mud.

The next step was to devise a system for moving people around an urban area at faster than walking speed. The first systems were horse-drawn trolley cars – they ran on rails embedded in the streets. This was an improvement over walking, but not much. The latter half of the nineteenth century saw the steady improvement of rail systems for the movement of people. The railroads mainly concentrated on the movement of freight over long distances, but they also began to offer commuter service in large urban areas such as London, Paris, New York, Philadelphia, and Chicago. In those days the railroads had major terminals near the downtown areas anyway, so it was natural to provide passenger service in the morning and evening that would permit downtown workers to reside several miles from the workplace. Also, steam power was used for a few years on rail systems that moved people shorter distances within urban areas.

A major change in technology occurred in the 1890s when urban transit systems were converted to electric power. Electricity made for a more efficient and less noxious transit system, and permitted urban areas to build subway systems. Anyone who has eaten a sandwich at a certain chain of sandwich shops knows that a certain John McDonald was the builder of New York's first subway system in the 1890s. As far as is known, the author of this book is not related to this important figure in urban history.

At the same time rail systems were being built that facilitated the movement of goods within urban areas. The idea was to build a system of "beltway" rail lines and rail yards for the assembly and disassembly of trains to supplement the existing radial rail lines. Such a system meant that a factory could be located anywhere near a beltway rail line. The factory would have its own rail spur line and, when it had produced a carload of output to be shipped somewhere, a small work train could pick up the car and take it to a nearby rail yard. A train would then be assembled for a destination outside the urban area. The factory's output would not necessarily have to be moved to the downtown area first. Rail yards could be located at the periphery of the urban area. The construction of this type of system greatly expanded the area that could be used for manufacturing enterprises.

Rail systems dominated urban transportation until the 1920s. The development of the internal combustion engine, and its widespread use after World War I, changed the face of urban areas. The automobile provided remarkable freedom of choice in both trip origin and destination. People were no longer tied to the fixed routes of the urban rail system. Likewise, the truck provided an efficient vehicle for the movement of freight within urban areas that was not tied to existing rail lines. As more and more cars and trucks were put into use, the bottleneck once again became the urban street system. The field of traffic engineering was founded, and urban freeways, traffic control devices, and one-way streets were invented.

Street and bridge improvements were made on a wide scale in the 1920s. Many of the facilities constructed at that time are still in use, but urban highway construction reached its zenith in the late 1950s and early 1960s. A large portion of today's urban freeway systems in the US were built at this time with the help of funds from the federal government under the Interstate Highway program. It became possible, in the absence of traffic congestion, to drive through an urban area at a speed of 65 miles per hour. The new radial and circumferential freeways opened up vast amounts of land to urban use. In some ways the nation is still in the process of adjusting to this boom in freeway construction that ended in the 1960s.

A model of urban location patterns must begin with a careful examination of the urban transportation system. People only have so much time in a day, and generally they do not particularly enjoy spending time commuting to work or making trips for other purposes. Some people can conduct business on the car phone, and others can really accomplish something while riding on the commuter train. But time spent in travel is simply not as enjoyable as time spent at home or as productive as time spent at work. The transportation system shapes the urban area as nothing else.

E. Theory of Rent, Land Rent, and Bid Rent

Basic and intermediate textbooks in microeconomics barely mention land, and if they do, the reference is usually to agricultural land. Furthermore, in the standard texts rent is defined as the price paid per year (or per month) for the services of a factor of production that is fixed in supply. *Rent* is thus a term that can be applied to the earnings of land, the price for the services of uniquely talented people, or the earnings of some other inelastically supplied input. Rent in this sense is sometimes called *pure economic rent* to emphasize that it is payments per year to an input beyond the payment needed to call forth the existing supply. Babe Ruth earned $125,000 per year to play baseball (in the 1920s!), and his alternative occupation (let us suppose) was to be a bartender at a salary of $3,000 per year. His pure economic rent was $122,000. Figure 5.1 illustrates the determination of

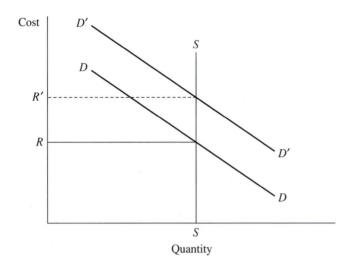

Figure 5.1   Determination of pure economic rent

rent in this kind of situation in a competitive market. The fixed supply is vertical line *SS*, and the demand is *DD*. Market equilibrium rent *R* is determined by the height of the demand curve. An increase in demand to *D'D* gets translated directly into an increase in rent to *R'*.

The rent as illustrated in Figure 5.1 can be translated into the market value of the asset that is being rented. The market value is simply the present value of the stream of rents that the asset will earn. In a competitive market for the asset, the value would be set so that the buyer would not earn a higher return on his purchase than could be earned in another investment of equal risk. In equation form:

$$V = \frac{R_1}{1+r} + \frac{R_2}{(1+r)^2} + \frac{R_3}{(1+r)^3} + \dots, \tag{1}$$

where R_1 is the rent for the first year, R_2 the rent for the second year, R_3 the rent for the third year, and r is the going interest rate (in decimal terms such as 0.5 for 5%). The stream of rents last for the life of the asset.

If the rent is expected to be the same amount R each year, then

$$V = \sum_{i=1}^{n} \frac{R}{(1+r)^i} \tag{2}$$

where Σ refers to the sum, which runs from year 1 to year n. Furthermore, if the asset has a life of infinite length, then

$$V = \frac{R}{r}. \tag{3}$$

This equation implies that an asset's value is proportional to its rent when the rent is constant over time. By definition, a market is in equilibrium when there is no tendency toward change in prices or quantities. Therefore, rents will not be changing over time in a market that is equilibrium, and values will be proportional to rent. In a static model, we do not need to distinguish between rent and value as the two concepts are related directly by equation (3).

Early theories of land rent

The first economist to develop a theory of land rent was David Ricardo (1821, pp. 33–45), who turned his attention to agricultural land. His theory is a steppingstone on the way to the modern theory of urban land rent, so it is interesting to examine his theory as he presented it. Ricardo (1821, p. 34) defined land rent as "that compensation which is paid to the owner of land for the use of its original and indestructible powers." This statement refers to the fertility of agricultural land, which of course is not truly indestructible. For now, assume that the fertility of land is a given.

Ricardo's fundamental insight was to realize that agricultural land is not all of the same utility. He supposed that there is a fixed supply of land of the best fertility, which he called No. 1 land. Land with a somewhat lower level of fertility was called No. 2 land, and it was fixed in supply as well. Land with even lower levels of fertility (No. 3, No. 4, etc.) was also fixed in supply. Ricardo assumed that with equal employment of capital and labor, No. 1, No. 2, and No. 3 land would yield a net produce of 100, 90, and 80 units of corn per acre.

Now consider what happens when the county under consideration is young and has a small population. A sufficient amount of No. 1 land exists to feed the entire population, with some No. 1 land left over. In this case, the land rent is zero. (The most fertile land is a free good because its supply exceeds its demand, even at a price of zero.) But as Ricardo (1821, p. 35) put it, "when, in the progress of society, land of the second degree of fertility is taken into cultivation, rent immediately commences on that of the first quality, and the amount of that rent will depend on the difference in the quality of these two portions of land." No. 2 land produces 90 units of corn per acre for an equal application of capital land labor. For capital (and labor) to earn the same amount on both types of land, 10 units of corn must be paid to the owner of the No. 1 land. Therefore, land rent exists because land varies in fertility and because land of a given fertility level is fixed in supply.

Further "progress of society" will bring No. 3 land into cultivation, which will mean that No. 1 land will now receive land rent of 20 units of corn per acre and No. 2 land will earn land rent of 10 units per acre. The modern economist would add that competition among farmers generates the result. A farmer who is cultivating No. 3 land would pay up to 20 units of corn to occupy No. 1 land, so farmers who actually occupy No. 1 land must pay 20 units or lose their lease.

Ricardo (1821) introduced several crucial concepts in the theory of land rent:

1 Land varies in its natural endowment or advantage for the user.
2 Land of a given level of natural endowment or advantage is fixed in supply.

3   The land market is governed by perfect competition.
4   Land rent is determined by the natural endowment or advantage of land.

However, Ricardo's agricultural theory must be modified to explain the spatial variation of land rents in urban areas. Land in Midtown Manhattan would probably be quite fertile if it could be farmed. But it is not valuable because of its fertility; it is valuable because it is at the center of the New York metropolitan area.

Even in an agricultural area, land rent reflects more than just the fertility of the soil. Ricardo ignored location, but assumed that land varied in fertility. Writing a few years later, Von Thünen (1826) reversed the assumption – land varies in location but fertility is the same everywhere – to show how land rent varies by distance to a central marketplace. Von Thünen assumed that farmers shipped their output to town to sell it at the marketplace. If the quality of every farmer's product is the same, then all farmers will receive the same price for their product, no matter how far they have to ship it. Therefore, the farmers bear the entire cost of shipping their product to the marketplace.

Now consider the decision-making process of farmers who need to decide where to farm. Farmers who locate near the marketplace will not have to pay as much in shipping cost as those who locate in more distance spots. The land is equally fertile in all locations, so farmers will clearly be willing to pay more for land near the marketplace. Unfortunately, not all the farmers can located right next to the marketplace. The farm closest to the market will get the highest price, the next closet farm will get the next highest price, and so on. At some point, transportation costs have eaten up all of the a the farmer's profits, and land simply remains fallow.

Von Thünen's fundamental insight is that competition among the farmers for sites with low shipping costs means that land rent will be higher closer to the marketplace, even when the fertility of the soil does not vary. In equilibrium, all farmers must be equally well off in all locations. In modern economic jargon, "equally well off" means that farmers receive zero profits at all locations. Competition implies that land rent falls as the cost of shipping to market increases.

The urban land market

It should not take much imagination to see how Von Thünen's model applies to urban areas. If you must pay to commute to your workplace, you have an incentive to find a home that is close to your job. If everyone works in the CBD, then all workers have an incentive to locate as close to the city center as possible. Competition for sites close to the workplace assures that land values will be higher near the CBD. A simple re-labeling of Von Thünen's model produces a viable model of urban land rents.

Although Ricardo's theory of land rent appears less relevant than the Von Thünen model for urban areas, it also provides some important insights. Ricardo's model is driven by the notion of *scarcity*: No. 1 land is valuable because there are not enough sites with high-fertile soil to produce corn for everyone. As with other forms of economic rent, land rents exist because land is in fixed supply. To a certain extent, the assumption of fixed supply is literally true: the total land area of the earth is fixed except for minor additions in Holland, land-fill areas, and erosion of coastlines. But it also is true that the market value of much of the earth's land is zero. You may have heard of Will Rogers' fatuous remark, "Land is a good investment: they ain't making any more of it." Buy land in the Sahara, Gobi, or Mojave Desert and see what a good investment you have made. Unless there happens to be oil under your sand, you will lose your money. Besides, if there were oil under the ground, you would want to buy the mineral rights, not the land itself. A better fatuous remark is that there are three principles in the determination of land values: location, location, and location. The locations may vary in terms of fertility – an important element of any theory attempting to explain the value of farmland – or they vary in terms of access to the city center or other characteristics that are valued by urban residents. What is fixed in supply is the amount of land within 5 miles of 42nd Street and Fifth Avenue in New York. There is only so much land in San Francisco's peninsula.

The land that is fixed in supply is the land with particular locational attributes. This corresponds to Ricardo's assumption that there is a fixed supply of land of a given level of fertility (natural endowment or advantage). However, the supply of land for a particular *use* is *not* fixed in supply. The supply of land for urban use has expanded rapidly. Also, land within an urban area can be converted from one use to another. Sometimes land-use conversion is expensive, but it can be done. For example, in the 1950s and 1960s a great deal of urban land in a variety of uses was converted to urban highways to facilitate the movement of auto and truck traffic. At this moment, urban land developers are converting to commercial and residential uses land in older industrial cities that once housed factories.

The fundamental concept that is used in the theory of the urban land market is *bid rent*. Land rent as defined above is a market price, but bid rent is only a hypothetical price. Bid rent for a household for a particular urban site is the maximum rent per unit of land that the household can pay to reside at location x and maintain some given level of utility. Similarly, bid rent for a business is the maximum rent per unit of land that it can pay for a particular urban site and maintain a given profit level. This idea corresponds to the bid that Ricardo's farmer on No. 3 land would make for the use of No. 1 land. A bid-rent function for a household depicts the relationship between location and bid rent at a given utility level. There is a bid-rent function for each hypothetical utility level of the household, and there is a bid-rent function for the firm at each hypothetical profit level. The bid rent for a household changes as location changes so as to keep utility constant, and the bid rent for a firm changes as location changes so as to keep profits constant. In other words, bid rent can be thought of as a residual amount that is paid for land once the attributes of a location have been taken into account.

Bid-rent theory for firms

The theory of bid rent for a firm is easier to explain than the bid rent for households. Suppose that a firm in an urban area is in business to produce a particular product that is sold for export at the port in the center of the urban area. For simplicity we shall assume that the firm occupies exactly 1 acre of land and produces Q^* units of output no matter where the firm decides to locate. The firm uses labor and capital (along with land) to produce the output, and the average cost of labor and capital for each unit of output is c dollars. The output is sold at the port at a price of p dollars per unit, but before the output can be sold, it must be transported from the plant site to the port. Assume that transportation cost is t dollars per mile for each unit of output. Finally, the firm must pay land rent R for its 1 acre of land. Notice that these assumptions closely match the Von Thünen model: instead of farmers paying to ship their corn to a marketplace, we have firms shipping their product to the port.

Given these assumptions, the firm's profits can be written as

$$\text{Profit} = pQ^* - cQ^* - txQ^* - R,$$

where x is the distance (in miles) from the plant site to the port. The basic idea of a bid-rent function is to set profit at some level and then trace out how land rent varies. *The bid-rent function shows the maximum amount of land rent that a firm can pay and still have profit a given level.* In this case, land rent can vary with distance to port (x). Set profits at some arbitrary level K, and solve for land rent as follows:

$$K = pQ^* - cQ^* - txQ^* - R,$$
$$R = (p - c)Q^* - K - (tQ^*)x.$$

Recall that R is the bid rent for 1 acre of land, so R is the bid rent per acre. This bid-rent function is depicted in Figure 5.2. The intercept of the function is $(p - c)Q^* - K$, and the slope of the (linear) function is $-(tQ^*)$. The intercept of the function indicates the bid rent at the port site – a distance of $x = 0$. The slope of the function says that bid rent declines by tQ^* dollars as distance from the port increases by 1 mile.

There is economic intuition behind the bid-rent function. At all locations, the firm receives pQ^* in revenue, and it incurs cQ^* in variable costs. The firm does not incur any shipping cost if it locates right at the port. With no land rent, the firm's profit would simply be revenue minus variable costs, or $(p - c)Q^*$. Land rent is set to the level that assures that profit equals K after the firm pays for its land use, so $K = (p - c)Q^* - R$. The bid-rent function simply turns this equation around to solve for the level of land rent that

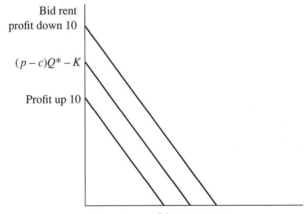

Figure 5.2 Bid-rent functions for firms

implies this level of profit. When a firm moves one mile away from the port, it must pay tQ^* dollars to ship its product. The shipping cost leads to lower profits unless something else changes. To keep profit a K, rent must fall by exactly the amount of the shipping cost, so at a distance of $x = 1$, we have $R = (p - c)Q^* - K - tQ^*$. Rent continues to fall by tQ^* with each additional mile from the port in order to exactly offset the additional shipping costs. It is important to note that if rents follow the bid-rent function, a firm is indifferent between all locations: rents vary by exactly the amount that gives the firm the same level of profit everywhere.

A family of bid-rent functions can be derived by varying the level of profits that is assumed. An increase in the level of profits from K to $K + 10$, for example, will shift the bid-rent function *down* by 10 dollars – higher profits are associated with *lower* rent payments. Similarly, a decrease in the level of profits from K to $K - 10$ will shift the bid-rent function up by 10 dollars. A particularly important bid-rent function is the one that corresponds to a profit level of zero. If the firm that is depicted in the model is a member of a competitive industry, that firm will make zero economic profits in the long run. Each of the inputs into production (labor and capital) will earn its opportunity cost (competitive) return and no more.

Suppose that the firm does indeed earn zero economic profits. In this case, the bid-rent function is just

$$R = (p - c)Q^* - (tQ^*)x.$$

This bid-rent function is shown in Figure 5.3. Why is this case so important? This bid-rent function is the one that is forced upon the firm by the competition for land among all of the firms in the industry. Suppose that the rent at a site is lower than the amount given by the zero-profit bid-rent function. To be precise, suppose that the current rent at a site allows firms to make a profit of $100. Then some firm will certainly think to offer $10 more in land rent – the firm would still be making $90 profit. But then another firm would still find it worthwhile to offer still $10 more. This process would continue until firms make zero profits everywhere. Competition for land – firms seeking out

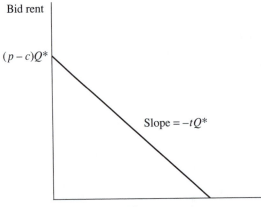

Figure 5.3   Bid-rent function with zero profit

locations that allow them to make economic profits – ensures that, in the end, firms make zero profit everywhere. However, it is important to remember that zero economic profit still allows firms to make normal rates of return. Although the firm makes accounting profits, it does not earn any economic profit.

Substitution in production

So far we have assumed that the firm produces a given amount of output Q^* on an acre of land, and this quantity does not vary with distance from the port. This assumption is unrealistic because it means that land cannot be substituted for other inputs. There is always a fixed ratio of output to land. A more realistic model would assume that land and other inputs can vary. In particular, firms can change the amount of capital and labor per unit of land by building a taller building. Firms that face a higher land rent would then substitute away from land and use more of other inputs to produce a given level of output, so the ratio of output to land is higher if land rent is higher (and as a result, building are taller). What does this modification imply for the bid-rent function?

Consider point A along the linear, no-substitution, bid-rent function in Figure 5.4. This point shows the rent that leaves the firm with zero profit when it locates at a site x miles from the port. Now suppose the firm considers moving to a site 1 mile closer to the port. Shipping costs fall by tQ_0 since the change in x is 1, and in a competitive market rent rises by exactly this amount to keep profit at zero. But suppose the firm can vary the mix of capital and land that it uses to produce its product. With higher land rent at site $x-1$, the obvious thing to do is to use a bit less land, compensating for the loss in this input by increasing its use of capital. As a result of this substitution of capital for land, output per acre of land rises to Q_1. Under the linear bid-rent function, land rent had increased by exactly the amount that led to zero profits under both locations. But the amount of the increase was based on an assumption that output per acre stayed at Q_0 at both locations. If the firm substitutes away from land and toward capital when it moves to location $x-1$, it can now make economic profit. All firms that can substitute capital for labor would

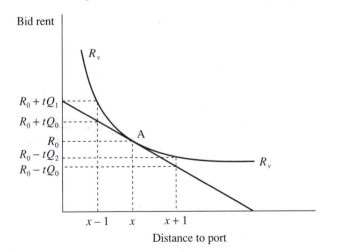

Figure 5.4   Bid-rent function with substitution

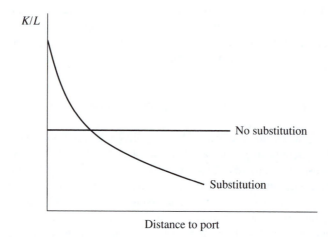

Figure 5.5   The capital to land ratio

want to move closer to the port. Therefore, rent has to rise above $R_0 + tQ_0$ to keep profit at zero. In fact, land rent will rise to $R_0 + tQ_1$. The slope of the bid-rent function has increased from tQ_0 to tQ_1 as output per acre increases at the site closer to the port, where land is more valuable.

The same argument works in reverse. Suppose the firm considers a move from x to a site one mile farther from the CBD. If the firm cannot substitute between capital and land, output per acre remains at Q_0. The firm incurs an additional tQ_0 in shipping cost at the more distant location, so land rent falls to $R_0 - tQ_0$ to keep profit at zero. But lower land rent gives the firm an incentive to substitute away from capital and toward land. Output per acre falls to Q_2. If land rent remains at $R_0 - tQ_0$, the firm is now able to make some profit. All firms would want to make the move to site $x + 1$. Therefore, rent has to rise above $R_0 - tQ_0$ to profit at zero. Rent is now $R_0 - tQ_1$ – lower than at x but higher than the amount paid for a firm that cannot substitute between capital and land in production. In general, the more firms can substitute between capital and land in production, the "more curved" is the bid-rent function. $R_v R_v$ is the bid-rent function for a firm that is able to substitute between capital and land in production.

Substitution between capital and land implies another important result. As land rent rises closer to the port, firms substitute away from land and toward capital. And as land rent falls farther from the port, firms substitute toward land and away from capital. Therefore, the ratio K/L is higher near the port. Figure 5.5 shows this relationship. In the case where firms cannot substitute between capital and land, the ratio K/L does not vary by distance from the port. Substitution implies a smooth, downward-sloping function that looks very similar to the bid-rent function.

Shifts in the bid-rent function

So far, we have only described the shape of the bid-rent function. Urban theory also provides interesting implication for how rents change when the values of several important

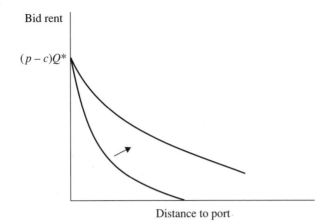

Figure 5.6   Effect of a reduction in transportation costs on bid rent

variable change. Recall that the bid-rent function is $R = (p - c)Q^* - (tQ^*)x$. The position of this function depends on the price of output (p), the average production cost (c), the transportation cost per mile per unit of output (t), and the level of the firm's output (Q^*). You should verify that the following statements are correct:

1   An increase in the price of output (p) shifts the bid-rent function up in a parallel fashion.
2   An increase in the average of production cost (c) shifts the bid-rent function down in a parallel fashion.
3   A reduction in transportation cost (t) makes the bid-rent function flatter but does not change the intercept.
4   An increase in output per acre shifts the intercept of the bid-rent function up and makes the function steeper.

In all of these cases, profits remain at zero. You might think that an increase in output price, a reduction in average production cost, a reduction in transportation costs, and an increase in output per acre would all tend to increase a firm's profits. But an increase an in profit means that a firm will have to pay more for land. In the end, firms are just as well off (or badly off!) as before the changes – profits equal zero before and after.

These results mean that *landowners* benefit when the price of output rises and lose when average production costs increase. Landowners reap the benefits of reductions in transportation costs per mile, where that benefit is greater at greater distances from the port in the center of the city. This case is depicted is shown in Figure 5.6. Finally, an increase in output per acre could occur because of an increase in the productivity of the inputs. The increase in output per acre could occur because of an increase in the productivity of the inputs. The increase in output increases the bid rent next to the port because the firm has more revenue (per acre). However, the increase in output per acre also means that the firm's transportation costs are greater because more output must be transported. As shown in Figure 5.7, there is some distance x^* at which the old bid rent and the new bid rent are equal and beyond which the old bid rent is higher.

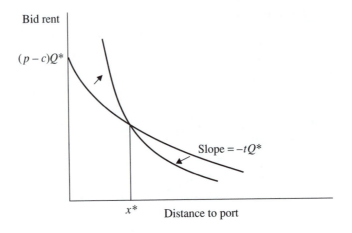

Figure 5.7   Effect of an output increase in bid rent

Bid-rent theory for households

Now let us turn to the theory of bid rent for households. The concepts are similar to those used for firms. Suppose that the only attribute of land that matters to a household is distance to the downtown workplace. Greater distance to the workplace means that the household must spend more money and time to get to and from work. The household therefore bids less for land at greater distances to maintain its utility level. In particular, suppose that the time and money costs can be expressed as a single dollar value t. For utility to remain constant as the household moves 1 mile, bid rent must adjust to make the marginal benefit of distance to the workplace equal to marginal cost. The marginal benefit of moving 1 mile more distant is the *change* in bid rent times the amount of land occupied by the household. This amount of money is what the household would save if its bid were accepted.

This basic condition can be expressed in equation form as

$$t = -\frac{dR}{dx}L$$

Where dR/dx is the change in the bid rent as distance to the workplace x changes by 1 mile, and L is the amount of land occupied by the household. The negative sign appears on the right-hand side of the equation because dR/dx is a negative number. The basic condition can be rewritten as

$$\frac{dR}{dx} = -\frac{-t}{L}$$

The *slope* of the bid-rent function is −1 times the marginal cost of distance (t) divided by the amount of land occupied. For example, suppose that the annual cost of commuting 1 extra mile is $150. This amount is plausible given that the commuter must travel to work

250 days per year. A total of 500 miles is added to annual commuting. If the household occupies 1,500 square feet of land, the slope of the bid-rent function is $150/1,500, or 10 cents per square foot per mile. This many not sound like much, but convert it to dollars per acre. An acre contains 43,560 feet, so bid rent changes by $4,356 per acre per mile. And if the going interest rate is 10%, the value per acre that the household bids changes by $43,560 per mile.

Bid rent can also be a function of other variables, such as distance to other employment centers, location of shipping districts, the quality of the public schools, distance from environmental disamenities, and a variety of other factors. But the basic point holds: there is a relationship between bid rent and location defined for a given utility level for a household (or profit level, in the case of the firm). For example, suppose that there is an environmental disamenity (e.g., air pollution) that is generated in the CBD. In this case, households can avoid the disamenity by locating at greater distances from downtown. However, commuting costs still matter. The slope of the bid-rent function is now a combination of two effects: the increase in commuting cost and the decrease in the disamenity as distance to downtown increase. In equation form:

$$\frac{dR}{dx} = -\frac{t}{L} + \frac{dR}{dE}\frac{dE}{dx}$$

where dE/dx is the change in the amount of the environmental disamenity as distance increases and dR/dE is the effect of an additional amount of this disamenity on bid rent (per square foot). Both of these additional terms are negative numbers, so their effect is to make the slope of the bid-rent function flatter than just $-t/L$. Moving farther from the CBD is bad because it increases commuting cost, but it is good because it moves the household farther from the disamenity. Indeed, if the effect of proximity to downtown on exposure to the disamenity is very large near the CBD, the net effect of distance from downtown on bid rent could even be positive over some range of distance. Over this range of distance, households value the avoidance of the environmental disamenity more than they value the increase in commuting cost.

Figure 5.8 shows a family of bid-rent functions for a particular household. In this case, we assume that bid rent at any given utility level declines with distance to downtown because the household's sole worker is employed in a downtown business, and no other variable other than commuting costs (such as an environmental disamenity) matters. Bid-rent function R_1R_1 corresponds to some utility level U_1. Bid-rent function R_2R_2 is higher than R_1R_1 and therefore corresponds to a lower level of utility U_2 – higher rents are associated with lower utility.

The bid-rent functions shown in Figure 5.8 are drawn so that they become flatter as distance to downtown increases. This shape is an immediate consequence of the result from above that $dR/dx = -t/L$. The slope (dR/dx) gets flatter as distance x increases because L (land occupied by the household) increases as distance increases. L increases as distance increases because the price of land (bid rent) declines with distance; as with any consumer good, the lower price causes the quantity to increase. Note that this result is similar to the bid-rent function for the firm that permits output acre to vary with land rent. The more households are willing to substitute land for other goods, the "more curved" is this bid-rent function.

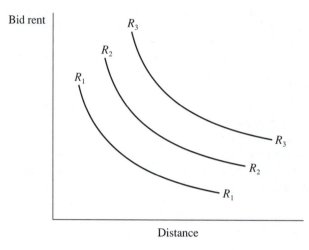

Figure 5.8   Bid-rent function for a household

What happens to the bid-rent function when commuting cost per mile (t) decreases? Rent is unaffected at a distance of zero: if you do not have to commute at all, commuting cost is zero no matter the cost per mile. Thus, the bid rent of a household at a $x = 0$ will be unaffected by the change in commuting cost. But for households located farther away, the reduction in commuting cost leaves them with more money to spend on land and other goods. If rents do not change, they will have enjoyed an increase in utility. But bid-rent is defined for a *given* level of utility. To keep utility at the given level, rents will have to increase at all sites with $x > 0$. Figure 5.9 shows the change in the bid-rent function as commuting cost per mile falls. The bid-rent function rotate from R_1 to R_2.

An urban area includes many different types of households. Do different types of households have bid-rent functions with different shapes? An answer to this question can be obtained by examining carefully the equilibrium condition

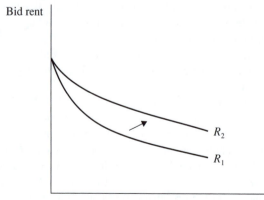

Figure 5.9   Change in the bid-rent function when commuting cost declines

$$\frac{dR}{dx} = -\frac{-t}{L}$$

This condition says that the slope of the bid-rent function equals the ratio of commuting cost per mile (t) to land occupied by the household (L). How do households differ depending on these two determinants of the bid-rent functions? First, consider a larger household with children versus a smaller household without children. Imagine that they have the same level of utility; they differ only in the presence of children. The household with children is likely to want land. Suppose that commuting cost is the same for both households. (Both households have one worker who commutes, and both workers have the same value of time.) If all of these presumptions are true, then the increased demand for land will lead the larger household to have the flatter bid-rent function because t/L is smaller when L is larger. The bid-rent function for the household with children is labeled R_2 in Figure 5.9, while the bid-rent function for the childless household is labeled R_1.

Alternatively, consider two types of households that differ only by income level. If land is a normal good, the households with the large income will demand more land at any given land rent. However, households with larger incomes probably also have *higher commuting costs*. Why might this be? Recall that commuting involves the expenditure of both money and time. We can presume that monetary expenditures per mile do not vary much, if at all, with income. However, higher-income households place a higher value on time than do lower-income households. A person's time is the ultimate scarce resource, and people with more money regard the time spent commuting as having a higher monetary value. Therefore, both the numerator and the denominator in t/L increase with income. The bid-rent function for the higher-income households may be flatter, steeper, or have the same slope as the one for households with lower income. The answer depends upon whether the value of commuting time or land consumption increases more with increases in income. In particular, the result is provided in the appendix to this chapter that t/L decreases (gets flatter) as income rises if the income elasticity of demand for land is greater than the income elasticity of the cost of commuting, or if

$$\frac{dL}{dy}\frac{y}{L} > \frac{dt}{dy}\frac{t}{t}$$

where y is income. The bid-rent function gets steeper if the opposite condition holds. At this time there is no evidence to suggest that one of these elasticities is clearly larger, so there is no evidence to suggest that higher-income households have flatter (or steeper) bid-rent functions.

Finally, what about households with two consumers (as opposed to one)? Suppose that we are comparing households with equal income levels; each worker in the household with two commuters earns half the amount of the worker in the one-commuter household. The household with two commuters has a higher time cost of commuting and, let us suppose, the same demand for land as the household with one commuter. Therefore, the two-commuter household has the steeper bid-rent function; t/L is larger. In Figure 5.9, R_1 represents the bid-rent function for the two-commuter household and R_2 is the bid-rent function for the one-commuter household. It is important to remember that the reason the two functions have the same intercept is because we have assumed that both households achieve the same level of utility. Also, note that the curves will be different if the one-commuter household views the opportunity cost of the commuter's (i.e., worker's) time as being double the opportunity cost of time for each worker in the two-commuter household.

F. The Bid Rent and Land Use Nexus

The model of the urban land market presented in this section uses a simple characterization of how land uses and market land values are determined. Each urban site is allocated to the sector with the highest bid rent, and land value is just the discounted value of the stream of highest bid rents. As discussed above, the real world contains many types of business and household sectors. This section discusses how these sectors have different bid-rent functions. Then a simple three-sector model of the land market is presented; equilibrium land rent and land use patterns are described.

Different types of businesses may have very different bid-rent functions. Some businesses, such as financial institutions, law firms, and advertising agencies, have very high bid rents for downtown locations and relatively low bid rents for locations in the rest of the urban area. These businesses need the opportunities for immediate face-to-face communication with customers, suppliers, government agencies, and others that is offered by the downtown location. Some manufacturers also have this sort of bid-rent function. High-fashion clothing manufacturers and publishers need the immediacy of the downtown location. Other manufacturers such as printers bid for downtown locations, but find that their bids are not high enough. Instead, they may locate on the fringe of the downtown area or nearby. They can serve the huge downtown demand for printed material without being located right in the downtown district. Or consider other types of manufacturers such as food products, furniture, fabricated metals, instruments, machinery, and electrical equipment. There may be no particular need to locate factories and workshops for these industries in the downtown area. They bid for the land in industrial districts in various locations around an urban area. Locations near highways, rail lines, an industrial labor force or a major airport may be advantageous for these kinds of firms. Indeed, suburban locations are increasingly popular choices for "light" industry. Lastly, heavy industry such as primary metals, oil refining, transportation equipment (e.g., auto assembly), and chemicals usually require locations near water, rail and highway transportation. The inputs and/or outputs are bulky, and therefore require heavy-duty transportation facilities. Bid rent is determined accordingly. Different types of firms and the various clusters of employment they create in urban areas are discussed in Chapter 7.

The bid-rent function for the residential sector includes access to downtown employment, shopping, and various services. Residential bid rent may also depend upon access to other workplace locations, shopping, health services, and other attractions. Government services such as school, police and fire protection, and parks and recreation are also important. Negative factors include crime, environmental pollution, congestion, noise, and taxes (given a level of public services). Different types of households also exhibit different bid-rent functions. Single adults or couples without children may make relatively high bids for land located near the downtown area with its attractions, but make low bids for suburban locations where they would feel isolated. On the other hand, families with children will bid relatively more for the spaciousness and safety of suburban locations. Given that most employment is in fact not located downtown, bid rent for the same site varies across households because workplaces vary across households. And bid rent for a site by a household of a particular racial or ethnic group may depend upon who lives near the site. It is a fact of life in the US that many white households will make low bids for sites located in all-black neighborhoods.

Clearly there are many different bid-rent functions for households and businesses. How does the land market operate to allocate sites to the many types of possible users? Prior to the 1920s the allocation of land was largely left to the private market. The general laws pertaining to nuisances were used on a case-by-case basis to handle particular conflicts in land use, but there was no general policy to regulate the use of land. For simplicity suppose that there are three sectors in the urban economy; commercial and financial business, manufacturing, and households. Further assume that the bid rent for each sector is *only* a function of access to downtown.

In this case bid rent in each sector depends only on access to downtown, but the shapes of these functions are different. The commercial/financial sector places a very high value on the downtown location and, given a normal profit rate, its bid rent drops off sharply as distance to downtown increases. Compared to the commercial/financial sector, manufacturing enterprises place a lower value on the downtown location, and bid rent at a normal profit rate declines less as distance to downtown increases. Of the three, the residential bid-rent function for a given utility level includes the lowest bid for downtown land and the flattest slope with respect to distance to downtown. These three bid-rent functions are shown in Figure 5.10. A bid rent for the agricultural (non-urban) sector is also shown in Figure 5.10 at a constant level R_a.

The competitive market allocates land to the use with the highest bid rent, so land up to distance x_c in Figure 5.10 is allocated to the commercial/financial sector. Land between distances x_c and x_m is in manufacturing use, and the residential sector occupies land from distance x_m to distance x_a. Beyond distance x_a the land is devoted to agricultural use. Land use thus forms a set of concentric rings, and the equilibrium land rent function is a combination of the three bid-rent functions. Equilibrium land rent follows the commercial/financial bid rent up to distance x_c, moves along the manufacturing bid rent from x_c up to distance x_m, and is the residential bid rent from x_m to the fringe of the urban area at distance x_a.

Now recall our earlier discussion of bid-rent functions for different types of households. It was concluded, for instance, that larger households with children will have flatter functions than those of smaller households without children. Bid-rent functions for these two types of households are shown in Figure 5.11, and we can see (as in Figure 5.10) the sector with the flatter bid-rent function will be located at the greater distances to the central point. Recall also that households with two commuters probably have steeper bid-rent functions than households with only one commuter, so "DINKS" (double income, no kids) will reside nearer downtown than will single-commuter households with kids. Finally, recall that higher income can make the slope of the bid-rent function flatter or steeper (or have no effect at all). Therefore, using this model based on commuting costs

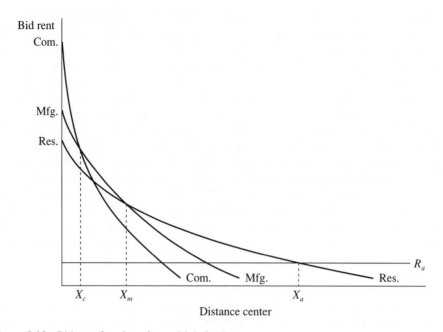

Figure 5.10   Bid-rent functions for multiple land uses

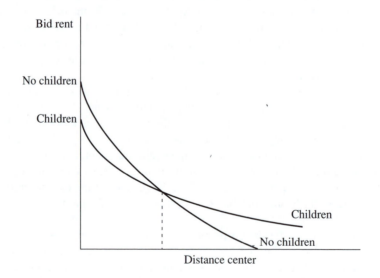

Figure 5.11   Bid-rent functions for different household types

alone, we cannot conclude that households with higher incomes will live farther from (or closer to) downtown. However, we can predict with reasonable certainty that households with different incomes will want to locate in *different* places. But we cannot say for certain whether these location are closer or farther from downtown. In addition, schools are generally better in the suburbs; crime is usually lower in the suburbs; suburbs have new houses and the central city has old houses; and so on. These and other factors are discussed at length in the succeeding chapters. Even with all of these extensions, the simple bid-rent function remains a useful tool for understanding location patterns.

G. Summary

A great deal of ground has been covered in this chapter (pun intended). You have learned that the economic sectors of the urban area have different bid-rent functions that express a willingness to pay for land at various locations. In a monocentric city – a city with a single focal point – the bid rent declines with distance to that central point. The decline in bid rent depends on the costs of travel in the urban area, and great changes have taken place in the methods used to get around town. People used their feet in the small cities of 1800 that were discussed in Chapter 3. Urban residents graduated to horse-drawn vehicles, then steam-powered commuter trains, and then electric trains and streetcars. Modern subways were built in some urban areas, and commuter trains switched to diesel power. But most of all, we switched to the auto. Urban transportation is the topic of Chapter 14.

This chapter has developed the basic tools that are used to analyze the spatial arrangement of urban areas. We have seen that a very simple extension of standard microeconomics models of household behavior produces a rich set of predictions. Land values are predicted to decline with distance from the city center. If firms substitute between land and capital in production and households substitute between land and other goods in consumption, then rents will fall a decreasing rate with distance – we will have curves rather than straight lines. We also have predicted that the ratio of capital to land – or buildings heights – will decline with distance from the city center. Finally, we have shown how the model can be used to predict where different types of households will locate.

We have not yet show how to *use* the model to generate useful predications. Nor have we analyzed any of the empirical tests of the model. We turn to these issues in Chapter 6. Finally, we extend the model to the case of multiple employment centers in Chapter 7. All of our extensions will make extensive use of the tools developed in this chapter.

Appendix to Chapter 5: Income and the Slope of the Bid-Rent Function

Section E of the chapter includes an analysis of the effect of an increase in household income on the slope of the residential bid-rent function. This appendix provides a proof of the statement that a higher income elasticity of commuting cost compared to the income elasticity of demand for land leads to a steeper bid-rent function as income rises.

Recall that the slope of the bid-rent function $R(x)$ is

$$\frac{dR}{dx} = -\frac{t}{L}$$

where x is distance to the central business district, t is the commuting cost per mile, and L is the land rented by the household. By the assumptions that time and land are normal goods, both t and L are positive functions of income (y), so

$$\frac{dR}{dx} = -\frac{-t(y)}{L(y)} \tag{A1}$$

The problem is to determine the change in dR/dx as y increases.

Rewrite equation (A1) as

$$\frac{dR}{dx} = R' = -t(y)[L(y)]^{-1}.$$

Now use the product rule and the chain rule (from the appendix to the book) to determine the change in dR/dx with respect to a change in y, or

$$\frac{dR'}{dy} = -t'(y)[L(y)]^{-1} + t(y)[L(y)]^{-2}L'(y) \tag{A2}$$

where $t'(y)$ and $L'(y)$ are dt/dy and dL/dy. Factor $1/L(y)$ out of both terms of equation (A2) to obtain

$$\frac{dR'}{dy} = -\left(\frac{1}{L}\right)\left[t'(y) - \frac{L'(y)t}{L}\right]. \tag{A3}$$

The quantity t/y can be factored out of the terms inside the brackets to yield

$$\frac{dR'}{du} = \frac{-t}{yL}\left[t'(y)\left(\frac{y}{t}\right) - L'(y)\left(\frac{t}{L}\right)\left(\frac{y}{t}\right)\right]$$

$$= \frac{-t}{yL}\left[\frac{dt}{dy}\left(\frac{y}{t}\right) - \frac{dL}{dy}\left(\frac{y}{L}\right)\right] \tag{A4}$$

The sign of equation (A4) is determined by the two terms inside the brackets because (t/yL) is a positive number. And one can see immediately that $(dt/dy)(y/t)$ is the elasticity of commuting cost with respect to income, or

$$E_{ty} = \frac{dt/t}{dy/y}$$

Also, $(dL/dy)(y/L)$ is just the elasticity of land demand with respect to income, or

$$E_{Ly} = \frac{dL/L}{dy/y}.$$

If E_{ty} is greater than E_{Ly}, then dR'/dy is negative, and the bid-rent function gets steeper (i.e., more negative). In other words, if the income elasticity of commuting cost is greater than the income elasticity of demand for land, the bid-rent function gets steeper as income rises. If E_{Ly} is greater than E_{ty}, then dR'/dy is positive, and the bid-rent function gets flatter (its slope moves toward zero). An income elasticity of demand for land that is greater than the income elasticity of commuting cost means that the bid-rent function gets flatter as income rise.

Exercises

1   Return to the model of pure economic rent depicted in Figure 5.1. Recall that the market value V of an asset such as land that lasts forever is $V = R/r$, where R is the annual rent and r is the going interest rate. Let $R = \$10,000$ and $r = 0.05$. Now introduce an annual property tax that is a proportion t of the market value of the asset. In other words, the owner of the assert must now pay tax in the amount of tV each year, where the tax rate t is 0.03 (i.e., a 3% tax on market value). What is the market value of the asset now?

2   Consider an industry in a circular city. The industry produces a good for export, and the export point is the center of the city. The price of the good at the point of export is \$10 per unit. Transportation costs within the city are 25 cents per mile per unit of the good, and other costs (labor and capital) are \$5 per unit. Firms in the industry produce 100 units of the good per acre of land. The land market is perfectly competitive, which implies that the users of land bid enough to reduce their economic (excess) profits to zero.

   (a)   Find the bid-rent function for the industry that corresponds to zero economic profits.
   (b)   Assume that agricultural bid rent is \$100 per acre at all locations. At what distance does agricultural bid rent equal the industry's bid rent?

3   Suppose that a household resides in an urban area at a distance to downtown of 8 miles. The household occupies 3,000 square feet of land, and at this distance land rent is \$1.50 per year per square foot. Land rent declines by \$0.05 per square foot as distance to downtown increases by 1 mile. A member of the household must travel downtown to work five days per week (50 weeks per year). The cost of this trip is \$4.00 per day, which includes both money cost and the time cost converted to money.

   (a)   Assume that the marginal and average costs of distance from downtown are equal. What is the marginal cost of distance?
   (b)   Is the household in locational equilibrium? How do you determine the answer to this question? If the household is not in locational equilibrium, which direction should it move to improve its welfare? (Hint: Compare the costs and benefits of moving 1 mile closer to downtown and of moving 1 mile away from downtown.)
   (c)   What would the slope of the land-rent function have to be for the household to be in locational equilibrium?

References

Ricardo, David, 1821, *Principles of Political Economy and Taxation*. Reprinted in 1963. London: Everyman Library.
Von Thunen, Johann, 1826, *The Isolated State*. Reprinted in 1966. New York: Pergamon Press.

Chapter 6

Using the Monocentric City Model

A. Introduction

A model is by definition a simplification of reality. The monocentric city model relies on simple assumptions to produce important insights into the workings of urban land markets. So far, we have developed in some detail the basic tool behind the monocentric city model – the bid-rent function. Two simple assumptions – that firms must pay to ship their product to a port and that each household's workers must pay the cost of commuting from their home to job – generate a rich set of predictions. We have seen that bid rents for both firms and households are predicted to decline with distance from the city center. We have also seen that the rate of decline is highest near the city center, and that it tails off in locations farther from the city center. The simple bid-rent model predicts that building heights will be higher near the city center. It produces realistic predictions about where different types of households will live within an urban area.

All of these predictions are generated by a very simple model whose assumptions appear unrealistic at first glance. This simplicity is a virtue. It shows that the simple tradeoff between the desire to have more space and the desire to avoid commuting is all that is needed to produce reasonable predictions for the spatial arrangement of urban areas. The simplicity is also useful because it allows the model to serve as a base for generating interesting extensions. The tools developed in Chapter 5 apply in many more situations than in a simple monocentric city. For example, suppose there is a nice park in a neighborhood, or that a city is set on a beautiful coastline. If people primarily work in the city center, then we would still expect land values to decline with distance from the CBD. But we also would expect prices to rise near the park and near the coastline. The fundamental insight of bid rents – that people will pay a premium to be near any amenity you care to define – continues to hold. The park or coastline may generate a *local peak* in the bid-rent function. Within the area defined by this peak, land prices and capital/land ratios are relatively high. It is not the monocentric structure of the city that produces this result; rather, it is the combined assumptions of a competitive land market along with spatial variation in desirable characteristics.

We begin this chapter by pushing the monocentric city model to its extreme. In the extreme version of the model, *all* employment is at the city center. Firms ship their product to the port at the center of the city. As we have seen in Chapter 5, this assumption implies that the firms' bid rents will decline with distance from the port. Each household has a worker who commutes each day to the center of the city. Households, too, will have bid-rent functions that decline with distance from the CBD. We shall assume that the household bid-rent function is flatter than the firms' function. This assumption implies that firms outbid households for land in the CBD. The city ends where farmers outbid households for land.

This extreme version of the monocentric city model allows us to make interesting predictions regarding the spatial layout of an urban area when several important variables change. The changes we consider are the following:

- a reduction in the cost of commuting within the urban area;
- a decline in the agricultural land rent at the fringe of the urban area;
- an increase in population (and labor supply) in the urban area;
- an increase in the income of every household in the urban area.

Each of these changes leads to predictions of changes in land values, house prices, building heights, and population density. And all of these "comparative statics" predictions can be generated using the simple model of bid rents that was developed in Chapter 5.

Following this set of four exercises, we show how the model can be extended to analyze other interesting extensions. What effect does zoning have on urban areas? Do pollution and crime affect the spatial layout of a city? What effect does racial prejudice have on the housing market? We also summarize the empirical evidence on the monocentric city model.

B. The Traditional Monocentric City Model

The bid-rent model of Chapter 5 forms the basis for the traditional monocentric city model. The earliest version of the model was developed by Alonso (1964), who also developed the bid-rent function technique. In Alonso' original formulation of the model, households received utility directly from land, along with other goods. Extensions of the model were later produced by Muth (1969) and Mills (1972). These extensions added housing to the model. Households do not get utility directly from land; rather, they get utility from housing, and housing is produced by combining land and capital. This extension of the model allows us to analyze house prices and building heights, as well as lot sizes. Although Muth and Mills worked independently, this version of the monocentric city model is often referred to as the "Muth–Mills" model.

It is assumed that the urban area produces a good for export and that the good is sold at a given price on the open market. The nature of transportation costs within the urban area is such that this good is only produced in the central business district. The all-purpose consumption good is imported at the going price and is sold at retail stores that are also located in the CBD. The urban area's workers work in either the export industry or the retail stores. The number of households residing in the urban area is assumed to be fixed, and all of the households are identical.

Each worker contains one worker, who travels to the CBD to work and to purchase the all-purpose consumption good. Therefore, each household makes the same number of trips to the CBD each year. The cost of an additional mile from the CBD is a constant t, measured in units of money. Each worker in both industries makes the same wage W, and this is the entire income of the household. Hours of work are fixed. The monocentric urban area is assumed to be circular. Transportation costs are equal in all directions. A fixed proportion of the space at each distance outside the CBD has been allocated to transportation facilities, so a fixed proportion of space is available for residential use at each distance.

Households

Households in the urban area maximize utility subject to the budget constraint in which wage income (W) equals the amounts spent on housing, the all-purpose consumption good, and commuting. The households' utility level depends on its amount of housing and the all-purpose consumption good. The amount spent on commuting does not add or subtract directly from utility. However, higher commuting costs indirectly lower utility by leaving less to spend on housing and the consumption good.

The choice problem for the household can be depicted in Figure 6.1. The household has a set of indifference curves for the two goods, housing and the all-purpose consumption good. We assume that both goods are normal goods; an increase in income will increase the consumption of both goods. The budget constraint is defined by the equation

$$W - tx = G + P_H H,$$

where x is the distance from the edge of downtown, G is the amount of the all-purpose good, H is the consumption of housing, and P_H is the price of one unit of housing. You

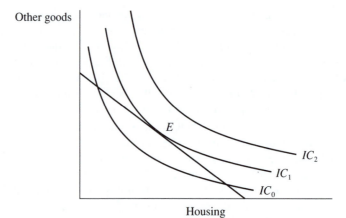

Figure 6.1   Household equilibrium

may find it helpful to think of H as square footage, while P_H is the price per square foot. For example, a house with 2,000 square feet that sells for $200,000 has $H = 2,000$, $P_H = \$100$. Home *value* is the product $P_H H$. However, H includes any relevant housing characteristics, including square footage – lot size, the number of rooms, the presence of air conditioning, a 2-car garage, and so on.

The household's choice problem can be reduced to a simple indifference curve diagram, with H on the horizontal axis and G on the vertical axis. The slope of the budget constraint can be found to be $-P_H$ by writing

$$G = (W - tx) - P_H H.$$

At a given distance x_1, the household has $W - tx_1$ to spend on the two consumer goods. The relevant budget constraint is shown in Figure 6.1. Given this income and the prices of the two goods (1 and P_H), the household maximizes utility on indifference curve IC_1 by choosing point E.

What if the household were located at some other distance x_2, where x_2 is greater than x_1? The theory of bid rent and equilibrium for the household both require that the household achieve the identical level of utility at both distances. At distance x_2, the household has $W - tx_2$ to spend on the two consumer goods, an amount that is less that $W - tx_1$. Therefore, for the household to reach the same indifference curve as before (IC_1), the price of a unit of housing at distance x_2 must be less than at distance x_1 – prices decline with distance from the CBD. Figure 6.2 shows both of these budget constraints. The fact that $P_H(x_2)$ must be less than $P_H(x_1)$ means that the budget constraint at distance x_2 is flatter than the one at x_1. The household now chooses point E'' rather than E'. The household purchases more housing and less of the all-purpose consumption good at the greater distance to downtown. In more specific terms, you might think of this substitution as people who live close to downtown consume less housing, but they compensate for it by going out to dinner and seeing shows more often.

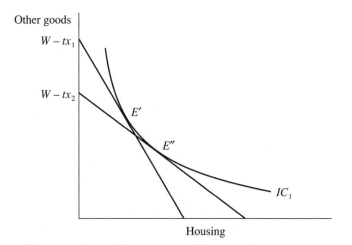

Figure 6.2   Household equilibrium at alternative locations

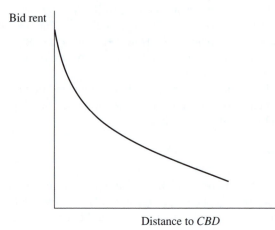

Figure 6.3   Bid-rent function for housing

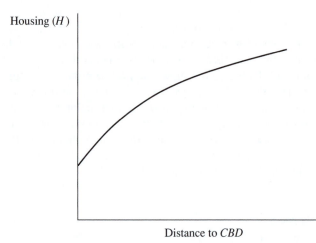

Figure 6.4   Housing consumption

The information in Figure 6.2 can be translated into a bid-rent function for housing. Figure 6.3 shows the bid-rent function. The price for a unit of housing is high near the city center and is low farther away. The curvature of the function is a direct result of the shape of the indifference curves: the more the household is willing to trade off between housing and other goods, the more curved is the bid-rent function. As we have also seen, the consumption of housing is high where the price of housing is low, and housing consumption is low where the price is high. Figure 6.4 shows the implied shape of the function for housing consumption. Figure 6.5 shows the implied shape of the function for the consumption of the all-purpose good (G). When the price of a unit of housing is high near the CBD, consumers substitute away from housing and toward other goods. When the price of a unit of housing is low, consumers substitute toward housing and away from

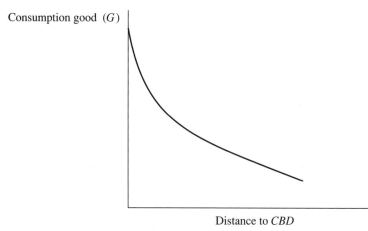

Figure 6.5   All-purpose consumption good

the all-purpose consumption. Therefore, the consumption of G varies across the urban area; it peaks at the CBD boundary and falls smoothly with distance.

At this point, students are occasionally disturbed by the implication that the price of housing is higher near the city center. In some urban areas, housing is more expensive in the suburbs, so how can we argue that the price of housing is higher near the CBD? The answer is that the student is confusing the price of a unit of housing (P_H) with the value of a house ($P_H H$). Mathematically, P_H falls while H rises with distance, so we cannot say for certain what happens to the product. Consider the following experiment. Take a million-dollar home in a suburb of New York. It may be on an acre lot and have 4,000 square feet of living. Now take the same home and place it in the middle of Manhattan. The home would instantly be demolished, and a skyscraper worth millions of dollars would be built on the site. The overall value of the lot and building are far, far more expensive in Midtown Manhattan than in any suburb.

More fundamentally, the student has now introduced an additional variable into the model. Recall that we have so far assumed that all households are identical. We will relax this assumption later. But so far, the model has predicted only that for a given income level, the bid-rent function for housing declines with distance from the CBD. The question of where the expensive homes are is really a question of where high-income and low-income households choose to locate. The model will not have anything to say about income sorting until we expand it to include different income groups.

Housing production

Housing is produced by combining capital (K) and land (L). The production function for housing is $H(K, L)$. In the Muth–Mills version of the model, consumers do not value either capital or land directly. The same amount of housing can be produced by using a small amount of capital on a large lot, or by using a lot of capital to compensate for having a small amount of land. The producers rent the housing to households at the price given by household bid rent, P_H. Therefore, revenue is given by $P_H H(K, L)$. The housing producers make rent payments for both land and capital. The rental price of capital is P_K and land rent is R. Total costs are the sum of the rent payments to land and capital: $P_K K + RL$. The producer's profit is

$$\text{Profit} = P_H H(K, L) - P_K K - RL.$$

The demand for land is derived from the household's willingness to pay for housing. Households are willing to bid more for sites close to the city center because these sites lead to low commuting costs. The amount that households pay for housing is the revenue received by the housing producers. Unless land prices are higher near the CBD, the producers will all want to build houses at sites close to the city center so that they can rent it to households at high prices.

In equilibrium, producers are indifferent between all locations for building the houses. Profits will be equal to zero everywhere. As in Chapter 5, the bid rent function is found by setting profit to zero and solving for land rent per acre:

$$R = \frac{P_H H - P_K K}{L}$$

The shape of the bid-rent function is similar to the shape of the household's bid-rent function. Land rent is high where house prices are high, that is, close to the CBD. Therefore, even if producers cannot substitute between land and capital in the production of housing, the bid-rent function for land will look much like the bid-rent function for housing as shown in Figure 6.3: it will be a smooth curve, with a higher rate of decline in the city center than at sites farther away from the CBD.

Substitution between land and capital makes the bid-rent function for land "more curved." Producers will pay more for land near the city center because households will pay more for land in those locations. As land prices increase near the CBD, producers will substitute away from land and toward capital. This substitution leads to further increases in the prices of land to ensure that profits equal zero everywhere. In the end, we have a bid-rent function for land that is more curved than the bid-rent function for housing. As you approach the CBD, the rate of increase in land prices is even greater than the rate of increase in house prices.

The bid-rent function for land is shown in Figure 6.6. As we saw in Chapter 5, higher bid-rent functions are associated with lower levels of profit. Since land rents are high near the CBD, producers substitute away from land and toward capital in these locations. Therefore, the capital/land ratio is higher near the city center. Although we could present a graph of the function for the capital/land ratio, there is no need to do so because it is identical qualitatively to the bid-rent function shown in Figure 6.6. Indeed, there are no qualitative differences between the graphs for four of the variables we have discussed – the price of a unit of housing (P_H), the quantity of the consumption good (G), land rent per acre (R), and the ratio of capital to land (K/L).

The housing production sector is not a well developed part of the Muth–Mills model. Producers combine land and capital to make housing – labor does not appear to be involved. The housing production sector uses land to produce housing, but it does not

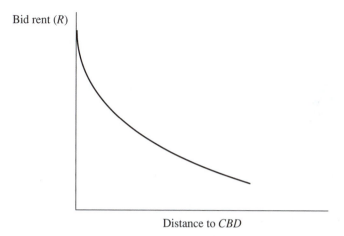

Figure 6.6   The bid-rent function for land

directly use any land of its own. They rent land that is used in housing, but they do not pay any of the residents of the city for it. Similarly, while households pay rent on the homes they occupy, the rent does not go to other residents of the urban area. We know that residents of the urban area do not receive any of these payments because then this form of income would have to be in the model. Instead, it must have been assumed that all land and housing rents are paid to owners who live somewhere else, not in the urban area. You can think of housing producers as the out-of-town landowners, who swoop in, build the housing, and collect their rent payments while continuing to make land rent payments to others who also live out of town. Although the assumption of out-of-town ownership is not particularly appealing, it makes the model easier to understand. Various ways of relaxing this assumption are discussed in detail in Fujita (1989). Although they make the model appear more realistic, the effect on the results is trivial yet the additional mathematical complexity is tremendous. The unrealistic assumption of out-of-town owner-ship makes the model much easier to analyze without affecting the important results – the very definition of a useful simplifying assumption.

The residential sector

We can now put together the household and production sides of the residential sector. Nearly everything can be summarized by a single, downward sloping function. We have already seen the general form of this function three times, in Figures 6.3, 6.5, and 6.6. What other variables can this function represent? The units obviously differ, but the qualitative results are the same for each of the following variables:

- the price of a unit of housing (P_H);
- land rent per acre (R);
- the ratio of capital to land (K/L);
- the quantity of the consumption good (G);

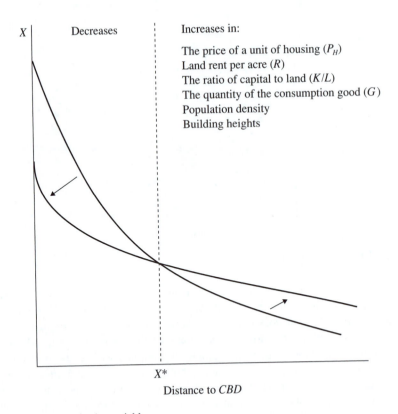

Figure 6.7 Changes in the variables

- population density;
- building heights.

Except for population density and building heights, we have discussed each of these variables at length. Population density follows automatically from the other results. At the household level, population density can be defined as the number of people in the household divided by the land area occupied by the household. If all households have the same number of people and lot size increases with distance from the city center, then population density must be higher farther from the CBD. The prediction for building height also follows directly from our other results. One way to substitute capital for land in production is to build a taller building.

Although the model includes many variables, the results are easy to sort through because all of these variables change in the same direction. Suppose that there is a change in the urban area that causes the house price function to rotate counter-clockwise, as shown in Figure 6.7. For some reason, house prices fall near the city center and increase at sites far from the CBD. In Figure 6.7, x^* is the boundary between locations where house prices increase and where they decrease. The increase in the bid-rent for housing to the right of x^* leads housing producers to bid more for these locations. Higher house

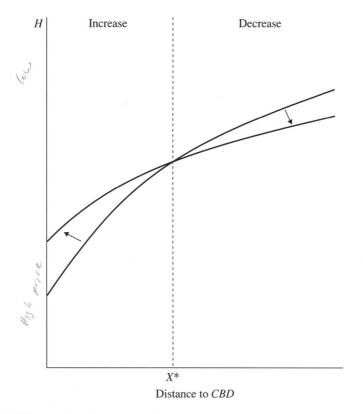

Figure 6.8   Change in housing consumption

prices lead households to substitute away from housing and toward other goods in consumption. Higher land rents lead producers to substitute away from land and toward capital in production, which leads to a higher capital/land ratio. Higher capital/land ratios mean taller buildings and higher population density. All of these changes simply work in reverse to the left of x^*. Once we have developed the model, all of these changes can be inferred simply by looking at the change in one of the bid-rent functions.

The once exception to this rule is the function for housing consumption, which was shown in Figure 6.4. Fortunately, this function is simply the mirror image of the other functions. When house prices are high, housing consumption is low, and housing consumption is high where house prices are low. Therefore, when the bid-rent function for housing rotates counter-clockwise, the function showing the consumption for housing rotates clockwise. This change is shown in Figure 6.8. The observant reader might also assume that Figure 6.8 also represents the change in lot size. We certainly would expect higher land rents to lead to lower lot sizes. But remember that lot size is determined by combining land and capital to produce housing. In the theory of the firm, it turns out that we do not get clear predictions regarding the levels of the inputs – capital and land – we only get a clear prediction that their ratio, K/L, will be high where land rents are high.

The central business district

The final piece of the model is the central business district. The employment sectors require land for their activities in the CBD. It would be simpler to assume that the employment sectors do not need land and therefore that the CBD is a dimensionless point. Would such an assumption be helpful or grossly inaccurate? We know that major urban areas have central business districts of nontrivial size in which few people reside, so a simple non-residential land market will be included. Assume that each employee in both the retail and export industries requires a fixed amount of land l_e. This assumption means that the total area of the CBD is $l_e H$, where H is the total number of workers and households. The radius of the CBD is therefore written

$$x_c = (leH/\pi)^{1/2}$$

The requirement for land for the central business district establishes the distance at which residential land begins. Given that x_c has been determined, we can select the bid-rent curve that is consistent with the number of households H that live in the urban area and have a member who works in the CBD.

   We can now put all of the sectors together on a single diagram. Figure 6.9 shows three functions. We label as "commercial" the bid-rent function (R_cR_c) for the export and retail trade industries. This function shows the maximum amount that these industries will pay for an acre of land. We are assuming that the commercial sector is willing to pay more for land than the residential sector at the city center, and that the commercial sector declines rapidly with distance from the center. The bid-rent function for land in the residential sector (RR) is lower than the commercial function up to distance x_1. After x_1, housing

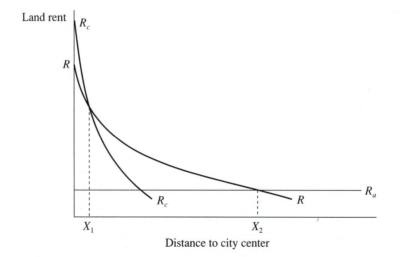

Figure 6.9   The monocentric urban area

producers will bid more for land than the commercial firms will. Therefore, the boundary between the commercial and residential areas is at distance x_1. The urban area ends at the point where farmers will pay more for the land than will housing produces. We assume that the agricultural land rent, R_a, is a constant that does not vary with distance from the city center. The urban area therefore extends to distance x_2.

Why did we choose to use the bid-rent functions for land in Figure 6.9, rather than the bid-rent for housing? The reason is simple: whoever pays the most for a parcel of land gets it. The commercial firms are not bidding for housing; they are bidding for land.

C. Changes in Commuting Cost, Income, Agricultural Land Rent, and Population

We are now ready to use the model to analyze changes in important variables. Figure 6.9 will serve as our starting point. We then will change one of the exogenous variables and sort through how it affects the other variables of interest. You should refer back to Figure 6.7 for this list of endogenous variables. (Recall that an "exogenous" variable is one that is given to us outside the model, while an "endogenous" variable is one that is implied by the results from the model.)

First, we have not yet discussed an important detail. We are assuming a "closed" city, the alternative being an "open" city. Technically, these assumptions are two different ways of closing the model. In a closed city, the number of firms and the total residential population are taken as given. A variable that tends to make people better off, such as a reduction in commuting cost, will not attract migration into the urban area. People will, in fact, enjoy an increase in utility after a reduction in commuting cost. In contrast, in an open city, utility does not change but population does. After commuting cost declines, people will move into the city. This immigration continues until utility is restored to its original level. However, population has increased. In general, the results do not differ much for closed and open cities (although we obviously cannot analyze the effects of an increase in population in an open city because this variable is an endogenous variable when the city is open). The results are easier to derive using the closed city model, however.

Which assumption – closed or open cities – is more appropriate? The answer depends on the question one wishes to analyze. Suppose a city adds a highway that makes commuting less costly. Will this investment attract residents from other cities? If it does, then an open city model may be the right assumption. Most of the changes we consider, such as increases in income or declines in commuting costs, have been enjoyed by all urban areas over time. When all cities are experiencing the same changes, the closed city assumption may be more appropriate. Alternatively, if migration does not take place quickly, we might think of the open city model as more appropriate for the long run while the closed city version of the model shows the changes in a shorter amount of time. Usually the distinction is a technical one that makes little substantive difference. We shall briefly review the results of an open city model when we analyze changes in commuting cost, after which we suspect that most readers will prefer not to see the distinction come up again.

Decrease in commuting cost (a decline in t)

What happens to our stylized urban area when commuting costs decline? Let us assume that the decline in commuting cost only affects the residential sector. It costs less to commute from your home to your job, but in the export sector there is no difference in the cost of shipping their product to the port. Historically, we might think of the progression from walking to streetcars to train lines to highways. Although commuting is still quite costly, the cost is much lower than it was in the past.

In Chapter 5, we saw that a decline in commuting costs gives the bid-rent function a flatter slope, although in Figure 5.9 the intercept is the same as before the change in commuting cost. Figure 5.9 is drawn so that the households get the same utility before and after the decline in commuting cost. In a closed city, utility will *rise* after a commuting cost declines. Therefore, the new bid-rent function will have a lower intercept than before. The intuition behind this result is simple. The urban area has the same population before and after the change in commuting cost. If commuting cost falls yet house prices do not change, everyone in the city will find it worthwhile to move farther from the city center. The demand for housing falls near the city center and it rises farther from the CBD. Everyone enjoys some increase in utility after the commuting costs change, but utility does not increase as much as it would if rents did not change.

We have established that, in a closed city, the house-price function rotates such that prices fall near the CBD and rise farther out. How does this result affect the bid-rent function for land? If households are willing to pay more for housing farther away from the city center, then housing producers will be willing to pay more for land at these locations. And housing producers will offer less for land near the CBD because households are no longer willing to pay as large a premium as before for houses in those locations. In Figure 6.10, the residential bid-rent function rotates from R_1R_1 to R_2R_2. Land rents increase at distances greater than x_b, and they decline at distances less than x_b. The residential sector has bid some land away from the farmers, but it gives up some land to the commercial sector. If there were no further changes, the boundary between the commercial and residential sectors would have moved farther from the CBD (from distance x_1 to x_1^*) and the boundary between the residential and agricultural sectors would also have moved farther from the city center (from x_2 to x_2^*). Some farmers have lost their farms.

There are no further changes in the agricultural sector because, by assumption, there is a single prevailing price for agricultural land. Although some farmers have been displaced, they can find more land elsewhere outside the city at the same price. Things are not so simple in the commercial sector, however. As households retreat from the area near the CBD, more land becomes available for commercial use. The reduced competition for the land allows the commercial firms to make winning bids for land near the old commercial/residential boundary. With no change in shipping cost for the commercial sector, the new commercial bid-rent function has the same slope as before, but commercial bid rents fall everywhere. This secondary effect of the decline in commuting cost causes the commercial bid-rent function for land to shift from R_cR_c to the dotted line parallel to it in Figure 6.11. Instead of expanding to x_1^*, the commercial district only expands out as far as distance x_1^{**}. We could extend this analysis a bit further and

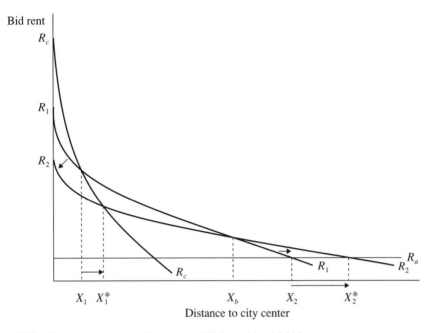

Figure 6.10   Decrease in commuting cost – shift in residential bid rent

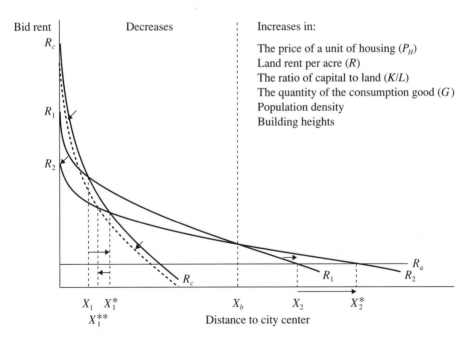

Figure 6.11   Decrease in commuting cost – secondary shift in commercial bid rent

consider another minor effect on the residential bid-rent function, but it would simply complicate the analysis. The equilibrium looks like the one shown in Figure 6.11.

There is trick in drawing these curves properly. If you shift the commercial bid-rent function back too far, you will end up predicting that the area covered by the commercial district gets smaller even as households are moving away from the city center. Such an outcome clearly does not make sense, and it is, in fact, not an equilibrium result. The trick is to only shift the commercial function a small distance. This small shift also makes economic sense: it does not take a large shift in bid rents to absorb the new commercial land near the old boundary when land is being used intensively and rents are already quite high.

Our results imply that land rents increase at distances greater than x_b, and they decrease at sites closer to the city center, including at sites within the commercial district. The urban/rural boundary has shifted out, and the commercial district is also bigger than before. The shift in the urban/rural boundary is greater than the shift in the commercial/residential boundary, so the amount of land occupied by the residential sector has increased. *Average* population density has gone down. But what about the other variables? For these predictions, we return to Figure 6.7. To the right of x_b, we have the following changes:

- the price of a unit of housing (P_H) increases;
- land rent per acre (R) increases;
- the ratio of capital to land (K/L) increases;
- the quantity of the consumption good (G) increases;
- population density increases;
- building heights increase.

At points closer to the city center ($x < x_b$), all the changes are reversed:

- the price of a unit of housing (P_H) decreases;
- land rent per acre (R) decreases;
- the ratio of capital to land (K/L) decreases;
- the quantity of the consumption good (G) decreases;
- population density decreases;
- building heights increases.

One way to look at this outcome is to say that the urban area has become more *decentralized*. Density used to be very high near the city center. It then tailed off rapidly with distance. Now, the urban area extends out farther, density is lower near the city center, but it tails off less rapidly and is actually higher than before sites beyond distance x_b. Across the entire urban area, average density has gone down because the same number of people are occupying more land area, but density has actually increased at distant sites.

The open city version

The closed city results are easy to figure out because they are a straightforward application of supply and demand. When commuting cost declines, the demand for housing increases at distant sites as housing demand falls near the city center. Therefore, the bid-rent function for housing rotates around a point at some distance x_b. The same results take an additional step to obtain using the open city model. Lower commuting costs lead to a flatter slope for the bid-rent function for housing. They also lead to higher levels of utility if population remains the same. But the open city model is based on an assumption that population changes to keep utility constant. The increase in utility causes people to move into the urban area from other places. With a given number of firms offering employment, the increased supply of labor leads to a lower wage. Lower wages cause the bid-rent function to shift down a bit. We end up with the same outcome as shown in Figure 6.11.

The open city model requires an additional step beyond the straightforward supply and demand analysis of the closed city model. In some situations, the open city model is somewhat more realistic. However, any additional realism comes at the cost of introducing modeling one more sector, the labor market. For the rest of this chapter, we will confine our attention to the closed city version of the model.

Increase in income (W up)

The effect of an increase in income is identical to a decline in commuting cost if the income elasticity of demand for housing is greater than the income elasticity of commuting cost. In the extreme case, suppose that commuting requires only money, rather than time. Your income doubles but monetary commuting costs are the same as before. You now have a clear incentive to move farther from the CBD, where you can indulge your taste for more housing. After all, commuting only involves money, and you now have a lot of it. If everyone is the same, then the increase in income increases the demand for housing at distant locations, and it reduces the demand in sites close to the city center. The change in the bid-rent function for housing means that the housing producers will bid more for land at distant sites, and less for land near the CBD. In Figure 6.10, the residential bid-rent function again rotates from R_1R_1 to R_2R_2.

The situation is completely reversed if the income elasticity of demand for housing is less than the income elasticity of commuting cost. In this case, households really dislike spending time commuting. When their income increases, they all try to reduce their commuting time by moving closer to the city center. Housing is more expensive, but they do not have to endure the same lengthy commute. The move toward the CBD increases the demand for housing near the city center and reduces housing demand at more distant sites. Housing producers bid less for distant sites and more for land near the city center. The bid-rent function rotates in the opposite direction as before – from R_2R_2 to R_1R_1. This change causes the city to contract from distance x_2^* to x_2. The increased competition from the residential sector for sites closer to the city center takes land away from the commercial sector. Commercial firms are forced to offer higher rents for land near the city center, and the commercial bid-rent function shifts from the dotted line *up* to R_cR_c. The commercial districts contracts from distance x_1^{**} to x_1.

Empirically, the results for a change in income hinge on the relationship between the income elasticity of demand for housing and the income elasticity of commuting cost. Unfortunately, the handful of empirical studies is out of date. We will address this issue in more detail later in the chapter.

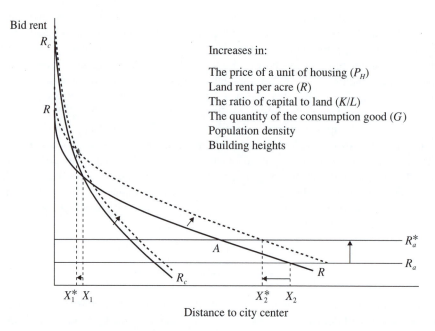

Figure 6.12   Increase in agricultural land rent

Increase in agricultural land rent (R_a *up)*

It is very easy to model the effects of an increase in agricultural land rent. In Figure 6.12, the bid-rent function for agriculture shifts up from R_a to R_a^*. Many households at the edge of the urban area have suddenly had their homes bought out, torn down, and plowed under. In our closed city, they are forced to make higher bids for housing than before. Their utility level falls, and the bid-rent function for housing shifts up. Housing producers are getting more revenue from their houses, so their bid-rent function for land also shifts up and parallel to the old one. In Figure 6.12, the new bid-rent function for land is the dotted line parallel to *RR*. The shift in the bid-rent function restores some of the land that was taken away by farmers, but the new boundary between the urban area and the agricultural periphery has moved closer to the city center – from x_2 to x_2^*.

The upward shift in the residential bid-rent function means that some housing producers find it worthwhile to convert land at the commercial/residential boundary from commercial use to housing. As the stores and offices are converted to houses, the commercial sector must make higher bids for land near the city center. The commercial bid-rent function shifts up from R_cR_c to the dotted line parallel to it. Again the trick is to draw make only a small shift in the commercial bid-rent function. In the end, the new boundary between the commercial and residential sectors is at distance x_1^*, which is closer to the city center than the old boundary at x_1.

The new equilibrium has high land rents in all locations. The urban area is more compact than before. The commercial district also covers less land area. House prices are higher than before everywhere. Household utility falls and commercial profits decline because everyone has to pay more for land. The increase in land rents leads producers to substitute away from land and toward other inputs in production. Therefore, building heights and the capital/land ratio increase everywhere. Population density increases at all distances from the city center because households are living in taller buildings on smaller lots. The increased price of housing leads households to substitute away from housing, so the consumption of other goods increases. These changes are summarized in Figure 6.12.

Increase in population

Our last exercise in comparative statics is to analyze the effect of an increase in population. An increase in the number of households raises the demand for housing in all locations. We assume (somewhat unrealistically) that the population increase has no effect on commuting costs or on the going wage rate. If these assumptions are correct, then the bid-rent function for housing shifts up and parallel to the original function. The increases in house prices lead the producers of housing to bid more for land at all locations. In Figure 6.13, the bid-rent function for land shifts from R_1R_1 to R_2R_2. The urban area expands by buying up farms at the urban fringe. In Figure 6.13, the urban/rural boundary shifts from distance x_2 to x_2^*.

As housing producers bid for building sites, they are able to outbid the commercial sector for sites near the old commercial/residential boundary at x_1. The boundary would shift to x_1^* if there were no change in the commercial sector. But the commercial sector reacts to this increase in competition by bidding more for land in the central business

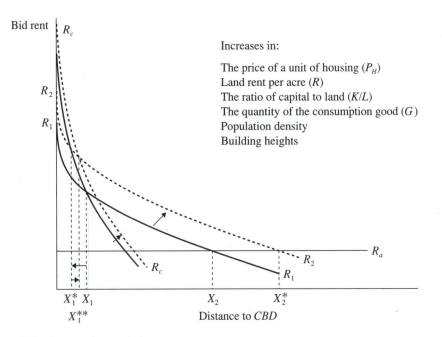

Figure 6.13 Increase in population

district. The bid-rent function shifts from R_cR_c to the dotted line that is parallel to it. (Again, draw only a small shift in the commercial bid-rent function.) This shift in the commercial bid-rent function restores some, but not all, of the land back to commercial use. In equilibrium, the commercial zone contracts to a distance of x_1^{**}, which is closer to the city center than the old boundary at x_1.

With prices rising everywhere, we have the same qualitative results as we obtained before when we analyzed the effects of an increase in agricultural land rents. The major results are

- the price of a unit of housing (P_H) increases;
- land rent per acre (R) increases;
- the ratio of capital to land (K/L) increases;
- the quantity of the consumption good (G) increases;
- population density increases;
- building heights increase.

What if commuting costs rise as population increases? We have already analyzed the effects of a decline in commuting costs. An increase in t works the same way but in reverse: the bid-rent function for residential land becomes steeper. We can analyze the effect of a simultaneous increase in commuting cost and increase in population by simply combining the two effects. First, the population increase causes the bid-rent function to shift up, parallel to the old one. Second, the increase in commuting cost causes the new function to pivot; the steeper slope implies that prices are higher near the CBD and lower farther away that would be the case if only population increased. It should be clear that the boundary between the commercial and residential areas has gotten closer to the city center. What is unclear is what happens to the boundary between the residential and agricultural areas. Whereas higher commuting costs lead people closer to the center, greater population tends to cause the urban area to expand into the agricultural periphery. The net effect is unclear. The important point is that you can analyze two changes by considering each one separately and combining the two effects. The order does not matter – you would end up at the same result if you first considered the effect of the increase in commuting cost and then consider the increase in population. We leave this analysis as an exercise to the reader.

Pollution and bid rents

Commuting costs, income, agricultural land rents, and population are all exogenous variables in the closed city version of the monocentric city model. Our comparative statics exercises involve changing the values of these variables and tracing out the effects on the endogenous variables – the price of unit of housing, land rent, the capital/land ratio, the quantity of the consumption good, population density, and building heights. Now we will consider a fundamental change in the assumptions behind the model. So far, we have assumed that both firms and households want to live close to the city center in order to reduce their shipping and commuting costs. But what if the firms in the CBD generate some sort of negative externality that makes living near the city center less attractive?

Sites near the CBD may have higher levels of air pollution, noise, and crime. What happens to the spatial layout of our monocentric city?

A reasonable assumption is that the effects of these externalities dissipate with distance. Air pollution is most severe at its source. Noise is easy to avoid by moving away from it. Your probability of being the victim of a crime is likely to be lower if you live farther from a high-crime area. When the externalities dissipate with distance from the city center, moving farther away from the CBD has two advantages. In the spirit of the monocentric model, the first advantage is that more distant sites have lower prices for a unit of housing. The second advantage is sites farther from the city center have lower levels of pollution, noise, and crime. Let us suppose that the monetary cost to the household of these externalities declines by $c per mile with distance from the city center. Before we considered the effects of these externalities, the benefit of living one mile farther from the CBD was negative. The marginal benefit was $-t/L$, which is the slope of the bid rent function. Now the marginal benefit is at least closer to being positive; it is now $c - t/L$. As long as c is small, the bid-rent function continues to have a negative slope. With mild pollution, noise, or crime, it is still preferable to live closer to the city center; the disadvantages of a distant location just are not as great as they were before.

Mild externalities can be modeled in precisely the same way as a decrease in commuting cost. Compared to the same city with no externalities, households will be willing to pay more for housing farther from the city center and less for sites near the CBD. Therefore, housing producers will bid more for sites farther from the city center, and less for sites near the CBD. In Figure 6.14, the residential bid-rent function for land rotates from $R_1 R_1$ to $R_2 R_2$. The urban/agricultural boundary expands from distance x_2 to x_2^* as households move away from the source of the externalities. Their movement reduces the competition for land near the old commercial/residential boundary at x_1. This reduced

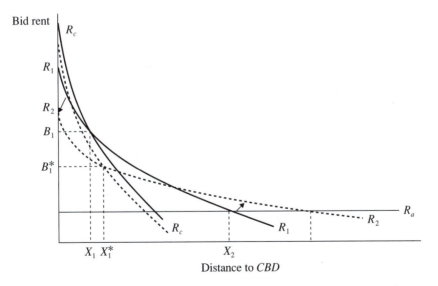

Figure 6.14   Mild pollution at the city center

competition allows commercial firms to bid less for land at all locations. Commercial firms get higher profits. The commercial bid-rent function shifts from R_cR_c to the dotted line parallel to it. Although the downward shift in the commercial bid-rent function restores some land back to the residential area, the boundary between the commercial and residential areas is still farther away from the center than before: x_1^* instead of x_1. In equilibrium, we have a larger, more decentralized urban area than before.

Somewhat ironically, the attempt by all households to get farther away from the source of the externalities has left some households right next to the CBD again. However, they are compensated for the externality with lower house prices than before. The bid-rent for land has fallen from R_1 the old commercial/residential boundary to R_1^* at the new boundary. Another ironic result is that the firms are made better off by the movement of households away from the city center, in spite of the fact that it is presumably the firms who are generating the negative externalities. Profits are now higher for firms on the new bid-rent rent function because they do not have to pay as much as before for land (and they are assumed to not care directly about the level of the externalities). The equilibrium is not optimal in this situation. The firms who are generating the externalities are neither being taxed nor are the households being subsidized for the harm they incur. A potential solution would be to compensate a household who locates at site x the cx dollars of damage that they incur. By charging firms an amount equal to the externality incurred by each household, this form of tax restores optimality to the land market.

The situation changes when the externalities are severe. In Figure 6.15, we assume that households will pay a premium to get away from the externalities being generated at the city center. The gain from avoiding the externalities is so large that it offsets the commuting

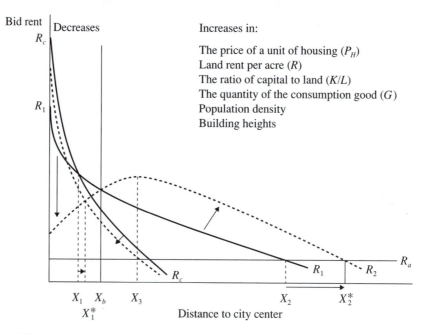

Figure 6.15   Severe pollution at the city center

costs that households must incur by moving farther from the center. Severe pollution thus produces an initial positive slope to the bid-rent function. However, pollution eventually dissipates. At some point, the level of the externality falls to a point that commuting costs again become the most important factor in location decisions. In Figure 6.15, distance x_3 is the point where the externalities are no longer so severe as to more than offset commuting costs. Up to x_3, the bid-rent function has a positive slope as households will pay a premium to get away from the source of the pollution. Beyond x_3, the bid-rent function has the usual negative slope because pollution is no longer severe and households prefer to be closer to their workplace in order to save on commuting costs.

The bid-rent function with severe pollution intersects the no-pollution bid-function at a distance of x_b. Severe pollution causes house prices to fall closer to the city center because the demand for housing falls in areas that expose households to severe levels of pollution. The households that continue to live in these locations are compensated for their exposure to pollution with low home prices. (Note that if R_a is high and pollution is severe, there may actually be a strip of agricultural land that serves as a buffer between commercial and residential land uses.) The pollution also leads to higher house prices at distances beyond x_b as households move into these locations to avoid some of the exposure to pollutants. Land rents rise as house prices fall near the city center, and they fall at distances beyond x_b. Near the city center, building heights, population density, and the capital/land ratio fall as firms substitute away from capital and toward land as a result of the reduction in land rents. Beyond x_b, opposite changes take place: building heights, population density, and the capital/land ratio rise because increased housing demand leads to higher land rents, which cause firms to substitute away from land and toward capital in the production of housing. As in the case of mild negative externalities, severe pollution leads to a city that is larger than the optimum. The boundary between urban and agricultural land uses shifts out from x_2 to x_2^*.

D. Zoning and Land Use

The first general zoning ordinance was adopted in New York City in 1916, and most urban areas had zoning laws by the end of the 1920s. The major exception is Houston, which does not have a zoning ordinance. (Voters in Houston defeated a proposed zoning ordinance in 1993.) How do zoning laws influence the allocation of land to the various possible uses?

Zoning laws do several things. They regulate the height and bulk of the buildings permitted on each site. They contain certain set-back requirements so that buildings are not located "too close" to the property boundaries. They often require that residential lots be of a certain minimum size. But first and foremost zoning laws specify the basic use for each lot in a jurisdiction. Use can be specified in greater or lesser detail. Some zoning ordinances simply break private land use down into three categories; residential, commercial and industrial. Other zoning ordinances specify two or more categories within each of these three basic sectors. Residential use might be: (1) single-family detached houses and duplexes, (2) residential structures with up to six housing units, and (3) apartment buildings with more than six units. Commercial use might be broken down into (1) retail trade, (2) offices, and (3) wholesale trade. Industrial use is often split into two or more categories depending upon the extent of the possible nuisances created. The zoning ordinance then proceeds to allocate all privately owned land to one of these eight or more separate categories. Does this flurry of administrative activity have any sizable effect on the allocation of land?

The answer is, "Yes, it probably does." It is clear that, at least in many suburban jurisdictions, single-family housing is the preferred use of land. Preferred by whom? Preferred by the current residents of the jurisdiction, and therefore preferred by the zoning officials. Suburban zoning officials often provide limited amounts of space for apartment housing even in the face of strong demand for apartments. Less obviously, they also often restrict commercial and industrial uses to areas adjacent to major high-ways and/or freight rail lines. This kind of decision for non-residential uses would seem to follow the market, but there is evidence provided by McMillen and McDonald (1989) that zoning officials do not follow the market closely. Sometimes the unregulated market would have allocated more land (than did the zoning officials) for commercial and indus-trial use at locations away from the highways and rail lines. The role of the zoning official is to try to anticipate conflicts in land use and to plan accordingly in the interests of the existing residents. Indeed, some of these officials earn university degrees (in urban planning) which train them in such matters. Urban planners learn that commercial and industrial uses conflict with residential use, especially when the residential use involves middle (and higher) class residents. They also learn that the "character" of residential neighborhoods should be maintained.

On the other side of the ledger, suburban officials worry about taxes and public spend-ing on schools and other functions of local government. These matters are discussed at length in Chapter 14, but for now it is important to note that commercial and industrial land uses generally generate more tax revenue than they cost the local jurisdiction in expenses for public services. The main fact is that commercial and industrial land uses do not demand public schools, but that residential land use does. Zoning officials thus face a trade-off between the quality of the local environment and tax revenues. Shopping centers bring traffic, noise, and a lot of people who do not live in the community. They also may not be physically very attractive. Office buildings also bring in traffic, especially during the morning and afternoon rush hours. Industrial land use adds to traffic and, depending upon the nature of the industry, can contribute to other environmental problems. Empirical studies, such as Erickson and Wollover (1987) have investigated how communities respond to this trade-off. One finding is that communities with higher incomes tend to zone less land for commercial and industrial use – environmental quality is a normal good (demand increases as income rises).

What about land use in the older central cities? Has the adoption of zoning laws altered the allocation of land there? It is not clear that zoning has had any major impact in areas that were already built up prior to the adoption of the zoning ordinance. The use of the downtown area and most of the major industrial and commercial areas of central cities predate the zoning law. However, one minor impact often occurred. Prior to the zoning laws there was some tendency to mix light manufacturing and commercial uses in with residential use on the same block. Provided these uses did not generate appreciable nuisances, this mixing of land uses might well have been of benefit to the residential population by providing ready access to retailing, services, and employment. Zoning ordinances usually ended this mixing of land uses over a period of years. Blocks were zoned exclusively for residential use, and conditions were set up for the elimination of "non-conforming" uses. Separate areas along the busier streets were zoned for commercial and industrial uses. Most of these areas were already being used by businesses, but the zoning laws excluded new residential use.

McMillen and McDonald (1993) studied land use and land values in Chicago prior to the adoption of its first zoning ordinance in 1923. Their empirical results for 1921 showed that the mixing of small commercial and industrial uses with housing did not have a negative effect on land values. Indeed, the results suggest that close access to shopping and employment opportunities was of benefit to residents. One must remember that this result was obtained for 1921, a time when very few people owned automobiles. However, in a later study, McMillen and McDonald (2001) find that zoning may still have increased land values in residentially zoned areas even though mixed land use did not appear to have caused any negative effects prior to the zoning ordinance. Between 1921 and 1924, land values grew faster in areas that were zoned residential, regardless of the initial use of the land. Even when mixed land use usually does not harm land values, the possibility still exists in a free land market that a severe problem may move in next door. Zoning offers some insurance against nuisance neighboring land uses.

The allocation of urban land is thus influenced both by the bid rents of the various sectors and by zoning. Zoning officials sometimes alter market allocations of land for apartment, commercial, and industrial uses. This is not to say that zoning officials are completely unresponsive to market forces. Changes in zoning occur all of the time in response to requests from land owners. Requests for zoning changes are granted unless the requested change would lead to a conflict among land uses. It is fair to say that market forces operate through the zoning process, and that zoning will occasionally alter market allocations.

Zoning and bid-rent functions

Many zoning policies can be analyzed using the tools provided by the monocentric city model. Figure 6.16 is an example. Suppose that we have a monocentric urban area with two income groups. In the absence zoning, the land bid-rent function for the low-income group is LL and the high-income bid-rent function is HH. The high-income group outbids low-income households for sites at more distant locations. The boundary between the two groups is at distance x_1. Low-income households are located at sites where $x < x_1$.

Now suppose that the city adopts a form of "exclusionary" zoning. Exclusionary zoning policies include such practices as minimum one-acre lot sizes or zoning for very low densities. Exclusionary policies make it difficult to build housing at a cost that is affordable to low-income households. In drawing Figure 6.16, we assume that the restrictions are ironclad: no low-income housing can be built at any distance greater than x_b. It is illegal, of course, for a city to use income as an explicit criterion for zoning. A suburb cannot write an ordinance that forbids households from living there unless their annual total income is at least $100,000. However, the objective of excluding low-income residents may nonetheless be achieved with a minimum one-acre lot size if land is very expensive.

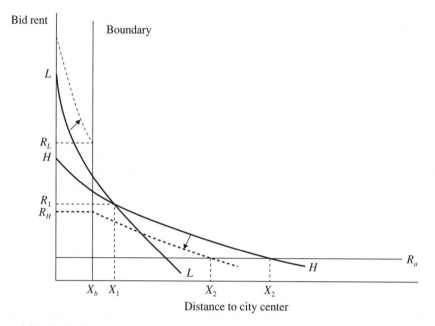

Figure 6.16   Exclusionary zoning

The exclusionary zoning ordinance confines the low-income group to a smaller area than would have been the case if the zoning policy had not been adopted. In a closed city, this restriction forces the low-income group to bid more than before for housing in the area in which they are allowed to live. The higher bid rent for housing leads to higher bid rents for land within this area. The new land bid-rent function for low-income households is the dotted line parallel to *LL* within the area where $x < x_b$. High-income households now have less competition for land because the area between x_1 and x_b has become available to them. The high-income bid-rent function for land shifts down to the dotted line parallel to *HH*. Bid-rents are now higher everywhere within the low-income area $(x < x_b)$. Bid-rents fall everywhere within the high-income area $(x > x_b)$. House prices, land rents, population densities, capital/land ratios, and building heights are higher in the low-income area after the zoning policy is adopted. In contrast, the high-income area experiences a drop in all of these variables.

Is the result shown in Figure 6.16 an equilibrium outcome? At the boundary between the high- and low-income districts (x_b), land rents are much higher for low-income households. At the boundary, the land rent is R_L for low-income homes and it is R_H for high-income homes. Therefore, landowners just to the right of x_b have a huge incentive to get the zoning on their land changed. The outcome shown in Figure 6.16 could not be equilibrium in a private market. Housing producers would bid to take land away from the high-income households and convert it over to the type of housing preferred by low-income households. This process would continue until land rents are equal at the boundary between the two groups. In other words, a private market would work to restore the original equilibrium with bid-rent functions *HH* and *LL* intersecting at distance x_1.

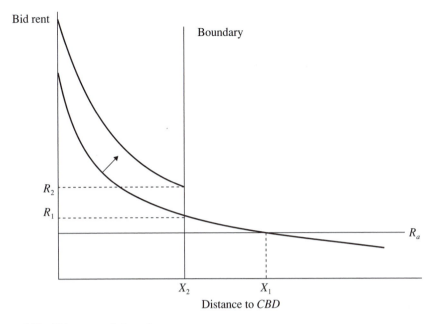

Figure 6.17   Urban growth boundary

Only the power of the state is able to enforce the exclusionary zoning policies that impose the boundary at x_b. Over time, landowners will lobby the local government to ease up on the zoning restrictions. The greater the difference between the rents at the boundary (R_H v. R_L), the more incentive the landowners have to get the zoning changed. The large difference in rents is hard to maintain over time.

Figure 6.17 presents a similar analysis for the case of an Urban Growth Boundary. An urban growth boundary is a restrictive zoning practice that confines urban development to areas closer to the city center than would be the case if development were left to the private market. In places such as Oregon and Colorado, these policies are explicit, and developers are simply not allowed to build homes in areas beyond distance x_2. In other places, the restrictive zoning is accomplished by refusing to extend services such as roads, water, electricity, and sewage disposal to areas where $x > x_2$. In Figure 6.17, the boundary between the urban area and the agricultural periphery would be at distance x_1 in the absence of a boundary. The boundary at distance x_2 leads to an upward shift in the bid-rent function as the same number of households is forced to compete for a smaller land area. House prices, land rents, population densities, capital/land ratios, and building heights are all higher within the urban area after the urban growth boundary is imposed.

Some households may enjoy the increase in house prices and land rents caused by the urban growth boundary. Landowners and homeowners have experienced capital gains. Others are less likely to be happy – first-time homebuyers, or people who were considering moving to this urban area. The people who own land just beyond the urban growth boundary are particularly likely to be upset. Land rent is R_2 on the urban side of the boundary, compared with R_1 on the non-urban side. Landowners just to the right of x_2 are

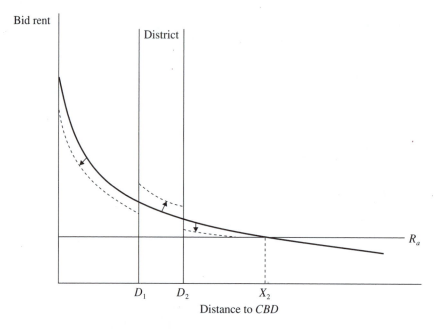

Figure 6.18 High-quality school district

likely to lobby to move the boundary farther out so that they can build houses on their land. Somewhat ironically, it is often the farmers near the urban area who are most upset by the growth boundary. Although the policy may be promoted as a means of protecting farmers by preventing urban "sprawl", the policy has reduced the value of some farmers' land by removing the possibility that it can be sold to housing developers. Again, we find that zoning leads to a discontinuity between rents at the boundary between land uses. Developers bid this discontinuity away in a private market. It breeds dissatisfaction and lobbying when zoning is highly restrictive.

Figure 6.18 shows a somewhat more complicated case where a district is in the middle of the urban area rather than at one of the two ends. In this case, suppose that a district with unusually high-quality schools is created between distances D_1 and D_2. Bid-rents rise within this district as people move to take advantage of the high-quality schools. Bid-rents drop in other areas as people are drawn to the new district. Again, the policy has created discontinuities at the boundaries between districts. Landowners just to the left of D_1 and just to the right of D_2 will want their parcels added to the high-quality district. People within the district pay for their high-quality schools with higher home prices and land rents.

It is important to understand the difference between our results for pollution and the results for zoning practices. When we analyzed the effects of pollution, we assumed that the land market was competitive. In a competitive market, every parcel of land goes to the highest bidder. Pollution reduces residential bids near in areas close to the source. This shift in the residential bid-rent function leaves more land available to the industrial firm. Land rents are equal at the boundary between residential and industrial uses. Residential households near the industrial area are compensated for their exposure to pollution by getting low land rents and house prices. The allocation of land uses is stable – there is no tendency toward change – because the industrial sector expands up to the distance where land rents are just the same in industrial use as they are in residential use.

Zoning uses the power of the state to create boundaries between land uses. The boundaries increase land rents for the restricted sector and lower rents for the sector that is left with more land than before. Zoning creates a discontinuity between land rents at district boundaries. A large difference in land rents creates an incentive to change the zoning policy. Landowners will attempt to get their parcels added to the district if restrictive zoning raised land rents. In the long run, zoning officials may well have an incentive to follow the market as landowners lobby to have their parcels zoned for the use that produces the highest land rents.

E. Summary

This chapter has shown how the monocentric city model can be used to predict how changes in key variables affect the spatial arrangement of economic activity in an urban area. A decline in commuting costs leads to a more decentralized city with higher housing prices and land rents in more distant locations and lower housing prices and rents near the city center. Population densities, capital/land ratios, and building heights also increase at distant locations while falling near the city center. In contrast, a population increase or an increase in agricultural land rents simply leads to a more densely populated urban area, with higher housing prices, land rents, population densities, capital/land ratios, and building heights at *all* locations.

The effect of income on the spatial layout of the monocentric is more complex. An increase in income has two opposing effects. Since the demand for housing increases with income, higher incomes push households toward distant locations where the price of a unit of housing is low. However, higher-income households will want to reduce their commuting time if time is a normal good. If the income elasticity of demand for housing is greater than the income elasticity of commuting time, an increase in income has the same effect as a decrease in commuting costs. The city becomes more *decentralized*, with higher housing prices, land rents, population densities, capital/land ratios, and building heights at distant sites and lower values of these variables at locations close to the city center. The effects are exactly the opposite if the income elasticity condition is reversed. If the income elasticity of demand for housing is less than the income elasticity of commuting time, an increase in income causes the city to becomes more *centralized*, with lower housing prices, land rents, population densities, capital/land ratios, and building heights at distant sites and higher values of these variables at locations close to the city center.

We have seen in this chapter that bid-rent functions may be upward sloping in some areas of the city. If negative externalities such as pollution, noise, and crime are concentrated near the city center, then bid rents may increase with distance from the center until the point the problems are no longer severe. Negative externalities are likely to lead to decentralized cities that cover more ground than is optimal.

Finally, we have seen that the effect of many zoning policies can be analyzed using the monocentric city model. Zoning often leads to discontinuities between land rents at the border between districts. For example, if zoning restricts the area that is available for low-income housing, low-income housing prices and land rents are higher than they would have been without this form of exclusionary zoning. At the same time, house prices and land rents fall in high-income areas. Landowners at the boundary between the zones have an incentive to try to get their parcels included in the low-income district, where land rents are high. This discontinuity in the land-rent function does not occur in a market where land use is determined by simply allowing the people who bid the most for land to use it as they please. Sharp differences in land rents at district boundaries tend to make zoning unstable as landowners lobby the local zoning board for changes in zoning designations.

Exercises

1 Add a second industry to exercise 2 from Chapter 5. This industry produces a good for export at a price of $20 per unit at the point of export, and transportation costs are $1 per mile per unit of output. Other costs (labor and capital) are $10 per unit. Output is 75 units per acre.

   (a) Find the bid-rent function for this industry that corresponds to zero economic profits.
   (b) Where do the first (from Exercise 2 in Chapter 5) and the second industries locate in the city?

2 Assume the following

   • The population and lot size are fixed
   • All households occupy the same amount of land K.
   • All households must travel to and from downtown once per day.
   • The marginal cost of travel is $\$t$ per mile; thus the marginal cost of distance to downtown is $\$2t$.
   • Households are identical.
   • The number of households is P.
   • The CBD is a dimensionless point in the middle of a circular city.
   • All land is used for residential use.
   • The area of the city is PK.
   • Land rent at the edge of the city is zero.

   (a) Derive the bid-rent function. This is the pattern of land rents that makes all households indifferent to all locations in the city. In particular, people who live at the edge of the city are just as well off as those who live right downtown.
   (b) Compare aggregate land rent and travel costs in the city. (Hint: The volume of a cone is $(1/3)bh$, where b is the area of the base and h is the height of the cone.)
   (c) What is the effect on land rent of a decline in the marginal transportation cost?
   (d) If you answered c correctly, you found that land rents generally declined in response to a fall in transportation costs. How can this be? Are not improvements in transportation supposed to bring about increases in land rents and values?

3 The market for residential land in an urban area can be described by the following set of equations:

(1) $L_D(x) = BR(x)^\theta$ Individual household's demand curve for land at distance x
(2) $L_D(x) = N(x)L_D(x)$ Market demand for land at distance x
(3) $R'(x)L_D(x) + t = 0$ Condition for locational equilibrium of the household
(4) $R(x)^* = R^*$ Land rent at edge of city
(5) $L_S(x) = 2\Pi x$ Supply of land at distance x, circumference of a circle
(6) $L_S(x) = L_D(x)$ Market equilibrium at each distance x

It is further assumed that the total number of households in the urban area is fixed at N. The variables in the model are:

$L_D(x)$ = quantity of land demanded by a household
$R(x)$ = land rent at distance x
θ = price elasticity of demand for land
B = a constant
$N(x)$ = number of households located at distance x
$R'(x) = dR/dx$ = slope of the rent function
t = commuting cost incurred by residing one mile farther from the CBD

The model incorporates the following assumptions:

- Households consume land, and consume less land per household where rent is higher [equation (1)].
- All households must commute to the CBD, a dimensionless point at which all employment is located.
- All land is consumed by households. No land is needed for transportation facilities [equation (5)].
- The market for land is perfectly competitive. In equilibrium the rent at each distance [$R(x)$] equates supply and demand in that annulus.

Have you got all of that? Now here are the questions.

(a) What is the meaning of equation (3)? Where does this equation come from?
(b) Assuming that $\theta = -1$ (unitary price elasticity of demand for land), derive the land-rent gradient $R(x)$. This is actually a very simple question if you understand how to do it. If you find yourself performing an elaborate mathematical derivation, you are on the wrong track.
(c) Derive the population density gradient $N(x)/L(x)$.
(d) What happens to the distribution of population over space if t (marginal transportation cost) rises?
(e) How does this little mathematical model relate to the graphical model in Figure 6.7?

References

Alonso, William, 1964, *Location and Land Use*. Cambridge, MA: Harvard University Press.
Erickson, Rodney and E. Wollover, 1987, "Local Tax Burdens and the Supply of Business Sites in Suburban Communities," *Journal of Regional Science*, vol. 27, pp. 25–38.
Fujita, Masahisa, 1989, *Urban Economic Theory*. Cambridge, UK: Cambridge University Press.
McMillen, Daniel and John McDonald, 1989, "Selectivity Bias in Urban Land Value Functions," *Land Economics*, vol. 65, pp. 341–51.

McMillen, Daniel and John McDonald, 1993, "Could Zoning Have Increase Land Values in Chicago?" *Journal of Urban Economics*, vol. 33, pp. 167–88.

McMillen, Daniel and John McDonald, 2002, "Land Values in a Newly Zoned City," *Review of Economic and Statistics*, vol. 84, pp. 62–72.

Mills, Edwin, 1972, *Studies in the Structure of the Urban Economy*. Baltimore: Johns Hopkins University Press.

Muth, Richard, 1969, *Cities and Housing*. Chicago: University of Chicago Press.

Chapter 7

Empirical Testing of the Monocentric City Model

A. Introduction

The monocentric city model produces many empirically testable propositions. Is the distance from the city the most important factor explaining the spatial variation in land rents, house prices, capital/land ratios, population density, and building heights? The model predicts that each of these variables declines smoothly with distance from the city center. Moreover, the model predicts that the functions should be curves rather than straight lines. These predictions are easy to check using simple regression procedures. Another way to test the model is to check whether the functions shift in the expected way when commuting costs, income, population, and agricultural land rents change. There are two ways of going about testing these comparative statistics predictions. First, we can use data from a single city over many years to test whether the estimated functions shift up and get flatter over time as commuting costs decline and population increases. Second, we can use data for multiple cities to see whether the functions are higher and flatter in city with lower commuting costs, greater population, and higher agricultural land rents.

We shall see that the empirical evidence is consistent with these predictions in many cities. Most researchers focus on population density, although there also is some evidence on land rents and capital/land ratios. Unfortunately, many researchers have attempted to test the model using data on house prices. In Chapter 5, we saw that the model predicts that the price of a unit of housing declines with distance from the city center, while the quantity of housing rises with distance. In practice, we can only directly observe the product – the cost of a home rather than its unit price. The model does not produce testable predictions regarding the spatial variation in the cost of homes.

Real cities are, of course, more complicated than assumed for the monocentric city model. Many real-world complexities can be handled by adding some variables into the estimated functions. For example, we might add a variable for distance to a coast line or a variable indicating that a site has a scenic view. Although such variables are not explicitly included in the monocentric city model, they are minor extensions that can be incorporated easily into the model. Much recent research has focused on a more significant extension of the model. *Polycentric* cities have multiple employment centers, rather than only one. At the end of the chapter, we show how to identify secondary employment centers and how to incorporate their effects into estimated functions.

B. The Intensity of Land Use: Population Density

The intensity of land use is the amount of economic activity that takes place on a unit of land. An investigation of the location of economic activity must examine land-use intensity as well as the allocation of land to the various uses. There are many ways to measure land-use intensity. For example, employment per acre, building heights, and floor-area ratios are all readily available measures. The most important measure of land-use intensity is population density. At the household level, population density can be defined as the number of people in the household divided by the land area occupied by the household. The general definition of population density is simply

population ÷ land area

This definition can be used for land areas of any size, from individual lots and residential blocks to entire states and regions. One needs to measure the land area in question and the population that resides on that land. The US Census of Population and Housing provides the necessary population data every 10 years. Population is enumerated at the block level, and these blocks are also aggregated into what are known as Census Tracts, which are census enumeration areas that contain approximately 4,000 people. The Census of Population and Housing also provides a great deal of social and economic data at the level of the Census Tract. Breakdowns of population by sex, household type, race, and age are provided. The economic data include the distribution of household income and the distributions of estimated house values and contract rents. The population data from the Census, coupled with the measure of total land area of the Census Tract, generates the measure of land-use intensity known as *gross population density*, so called because the total land area of the Census Tract is used as the denominator. The density measure is population per unit of land, where *all* land uses are included in the measure of land area.

Numerous empirical studies of gross population density have established that the typical pattern is as shown in Figure 7.1. The boundary between the commercial and residential areas is at distance x_c. Although we have assumed so far that all land is commercial in the central business area and all land is residential at distances beyond x_c, the contrast is not so stark in real cities. Some land is residential even in the middle of a large commercial district, and stores and small offices are located in primarily residential areas. Residential buildings are typically built at a very high density – tall buildings with many units built atop small land parcels. Population divided by *residential* land area – *net density* – is very high in the area where $x < x_c$. However, population divided by *total* land area – *gross density* – tends to be low because most of the land is commercial. Since the amount of land devoted to residential use tends to rise farther from the city center, the population density tends to rise with distance in the area between $x = 0$ and $x = x_c$. This initial upward-sloping segment is *not* evidence against the monocentric city model. If we

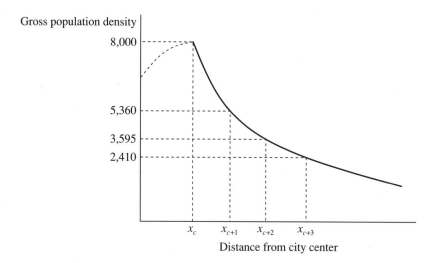

Figure 7.1   Gross population density functions

could observe net density rather than gross density, we might very well observe a smooth, downward sloping function everywhere, which is the pattern implied by the model. The initial upward-sloping segment is the dotted line in Figure 7.1. Although the upward-sloping segment does not exist in all cities, it is nonetheless a common finding.

Outside the central business district, gross population density declines with distance to downtown in the nonlinear fashion shown in Figure 7.1. Density declines rapidly near x_c and drops more gradually at greater distances from the center. This shape for the gross population density function can be expressed in mathematical form as the exponential function

$$D(x) = D(x_c)e^{-g(x-x_c)}.$$

In this equation, $D(x)$ is gross population density as a function of x, distance to the edge of the central business district. $D(x_c)$ is gross population density at the edge of the CBD (this is the greatest value for density). The symbol e stands for the base of the natural logarithms, which is approximately 2.718. The letter g stands for the value of the population density gradient, which is the percentage decline in density per unit of distance (i.e., per mile) from the central business district. In practice, most researchers assume that $x_c = 0$. Looking at Figure 7.1, it should be clear that the result of this assumption – which clearly is incorrect – is to flatten the slope of the estimated function. The initial low values of population density pull down the intercept and produce a flatter function. However, this problem is not severe when the central business area is small.

An understanding of the population density equation can be gained through numerical example. First, suppose that x_c is 1 mile. The central business area has a radius of 1 mile, which is fairly typical for an urban area of medium size, 250,000 to 500,000 population. Next, suppose that $D(x_c)$ is 8,000 per square mile, or that gross density per square mile 8,000 per square mile at a distance of 1 mile from the center. Finally, assume that the gradient is 0.4, or that population density declines by 40% per mile. These values mean that the gross population density at distance x from the city center is

$$D(x) = 8,000 \times 2.718^{-0.4(x-1)}$$

For example, population at the edge of the central business district ($x = 1$) equals 8,000 because 2.718 raised to the zero power is 1. At distance $x = 2$, $D(2)$ equals 5,360 because 2.718 raised to the -0.4 power equals 0.67. Other numerical values of $D(x)$ are displayed in Figure 7.1. The basic mathematics of this density function is discussed in the appendix to this book.

Why does gross population density decline with distance to the central business district? The monocentric city model provides the answer. As we saw in Chapter 5, residential bid rent declines with distance to the central business district to compensate for commuting costs. Lower rents at greater distances mean that households use more land as distance increases. The basic law of demand says that when the price of a good declines, people purchase more of it. Land is not different in this regard. Holding other relevant factors constant (income and tastes), households that live where land rents are lower occupy more land. Lower land rent means that population density is lower.

This standard explanation for the decline in gross population density with distance to the center leaves one loose end. The argument really pertains to net rather than gross density. Remember that net population density is defined as population per unit of land that is allocated to residential use. For example, consider a square mile that houses 1,000 people. Suppose that 40% of that square mile is in residential use; the rest is allocated to streets, commercial and industrial use, parks and public buildings, and so on. Gross population density is 1,000 people per square mile, but net population is 2,500 per square mile because the 1,000 people actually live on 0.4 square miles of land.

There have been many empirical studies of urban population density based on the exponential function discussed above. Taking the natural logarithm of both sides of the equation produces the linear equation

$$\ln D(x) = \ln D(x_c) - g(x - x_c)$$
$$\text{or } \ln D(x) = [\ln D(x_c) + gx_c] - gx$$

where ln stands for logarithm to base e. The intercept of this equation, $\ln D(x_c) + gx_c$, is treated as a simple parameter in estimation. What is actually estimated is the equation

$$\ln D(x) = \alpha - gx$$

In many studies, data are gathered for a sample of census tracts in an urban area and then the data are used to estimate this linear equation. The Census provides data on population; what is left is to measure distances and the area of each census tract. Geographic information system software programs make these calculations easy.

Table 7.1 shows estimated values of g for 25 large US cities. The gradients are estimated using data on Census Tracts from 2000. We include all Census Tracts whose center points are within 30 miles of the primary CBD in the metropolitan area. Although a single point must be specified for the site of the city center, the approximate location is not difficult to

Table 7.1 Population density gradients: 2000

Metropolitan area	Population (millions)	Gradient	T-Value	R^2
New York	17.6	0.124	44.518	0.345
Los Angeles	13.8	0.051	19.124	0.134
Chicago	8.6	0.087	31.009	0.365
Washington, DC	6.8	0.073	17.498	0.228
San Francisco–San Jose–Oakland	6.1	0.069	15.008	0.203
Philadelphia	6.7	0.080	18.460	0.200
Boston	4.5	0.100	23.424	0.406
Detroit	4.6	0.072	21.446	0.287
Dallas	5.0	0.046	9.154	0.089
Houston	4.5	0.082	13.030	0.183
Atlanta	4.2	0.069	14.789	0.278
Miami	3.6	0.028	5.892	0.059
Seattle–Tacoma	3.4	0.059	11.170	0.165
Phoenix	3.1	0.064	7.694	0.083
Minneapolis–St. Paul	2.9	0.111	18.978	0.342
Cleveland	3.1	0.063	13.611	0.196
San Diego	2.8	0.057	9.472	0.145
St. Louis	2.5	0.088	12.288	0.241
Denver	2.6	0.085	10.341	0.158
Tampa–St. Petersburg	3.1	0.021	3.295	0.019
Pittsburgh	2.7	0.088	16.680	0.298
Portland, OR	2.2	0.091	9.007	0.165
Cincinnati	2.5	0.080	11.424	0.222
Sacramento	2.5	0.079	8.304	0.153
Kansas City	1.9	0.074	7.345	0.102

determine in most places. The results of the equations are not sensitive to small changes in the exact location of the city center. In urban areas with several large cities, we measure distance from the traditional center. For example, we take the city center of San Francisco–San Jose–Oakland to be the center of San Francisco, even though San Jose actually has more residents than San Francisco. The gradients range from 0.021 in Tampa–St. Petersburg to 0.124 in New York. These estimates imply that gross population density declines by 12.4% with each additional mile from the center of New York (taken to be Midtown Manhattan) and 2.1% with each additional mile from the center of Tampa.

How well do these results support the predictions of the monocentric city model? The *t*-values and R^2s help answer this question. Remember that we are estimating the value of *g*; we do not know its true value. How confident are we that the actual value of *g* is equal to the value that we have estimated? Even more important, how confident are we that the true value of *g* is not negative? A negative value of *g* is completely inconsistent with the monocentric city model. The *t*-value provides a measure of the precision of the estimates. Roughly speaking, *t*-values in excess of 2 are evidence that we can be very confident that the true value of *g* is not equal to zero (or negative). Every *t*-value in Table 7.1 is much larger than 2. This result supports the model; population density declines with distance

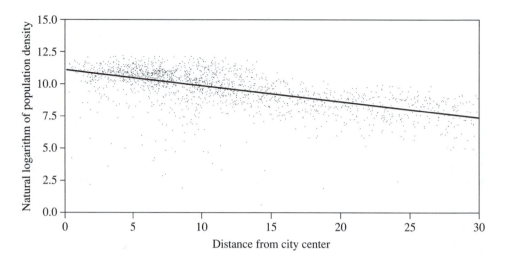

Figure 7.2   Population density in New York

from the traditional city center even in urban areas such as California's Bay Area. However, the fact that the gradient is positive does not necessarily mean that distance from the city center does a good job of explaining the variation in population density. The R^2 of a regression is a measure of the overall fit of the equation: how much of the variation in the natural logarithm of population density is explained by distance from the city center? The R^2s range from 0.019 in Tampa–St. Petersburg to 0.406 in Boston. These values imply that 40.6% of the variation in the natural logarithm of population density is explained by distance from the city center in Boston, compared with only 1.9% in Tampa–St. Petersburg. Whether an R^2 is "good" or "bad" depends on the context. Suffice it to say that 40.6% is not bad, while 1.9% is very low indeed. The monocentric city model does a reasonably good job of explaining the spatial variation in traditional cities such as Boston and New York. It does a very poor job of explaining densities in cities such as Tampa–St. Petersburg and Miami.

Many observers have suggested that the relatively low R^2s found for many of the urban areas in Table 7.1 are evidence that the model no longer offers much explanatory power. It is clear that cities such as Tampa–St. Petersburg require a different model to explain the variation in population densities across the full urban area. However, the model's apparent failure is often exaggerated. New York provides a useful illustration. Figure 7.2 shows the raw data and the estimated regression for New York using data on Census Tracts from the 2000 Census. It does not take much imagination to fit a downward-sloping line to the raw data. The overall trend in the natural logarithm of population clearly fits the model's predictions. The problem is the large number of points that are well below the estimated regression line. These points are in places where population density is well below the level predicted by the regression. Is this under-predication because the model has failed or is it because we are observing gross densities instead of net? These "outliers" may be places with parks or large commercial districts that lower the amount of land available for residential use. Alternatively, they may be locations that simply are at odds with the model's predications. We cannot really say whether the

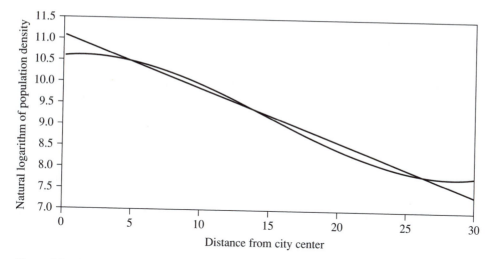

Figure 7.3   Cubic versus linear

model does or does not explain these points. The model is not designed to explain densities at every block; it is designed to explain the overall trend. In explaining overall trends, an R^2 of 0.345 is not bad: we have explained more than a third of the variation in population density with a single variable, even when the density has actually been measured incorrectly.

The equation $\ln D(x) = \alpha - gx$ is referred to as a "negative exponential function". It is a very simple function, it is easy to estimate, and it often fits the data well. However, the theory does not necessarily imply such a simple function. The theory implies only that densities are a smoothly declining function of distance, and much more complex functional forms may be more appropriate. Figure 7.3 shows the difference in the estimates implied by the simple negative exponential function and the function $\ln D(x) = \alpha + g_1 x + g_2 x^2 + g_3 x^3$. The negative exponential function is a linear equation in the dependent variable, $\ln D(x)$, whereas the new equation is a cubic function of distance. Figure 7.3 shows that the cubic equation allows population density to decline more slowly near the city center than implied by the negative exponential function. Densities then flatten out at a distance of about 25 miles from the city center. In the case of New York, this change does not help improve the explanatory power much – the R^2 only rises form 0.345 to 0.354. In other urban areas, adding some nonlinearity makes a big difference.

Another important point to recognize is that the quality of urban data sets has improved over time. The New York metropolitan area has 3,761 census tracts within 30 miles of the city center that have some residents. (Although Census Tracts are supposed to have a population of about 4,000, a surprising number have no residents.) Studies from the 1960s often employed data sets covering much larger land areas: the same area might be divided into 50 zones rather than 3,761. Regressions tend to fit the data much better when the zones are big. As an example, consider what happens when we mimic the approach taken by Colin Clark (1951) in his classic study of population densities in 1951. Clark divided cities into one-mile rings around the city center. He measured the total population living in each ring and divided it by the total land area in the ring. Restricting his

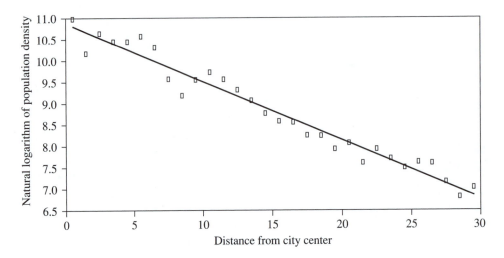

Figure 7.4   One-mile bands

attention to only the first 10 miles around the city center, Clark showed that the simple
negative exponential function does a remarkably good job of explaining the spatial variation in population densities in many cities throughout the world going back as far as the
first half of the nineteenth century. Figure 7.4 shows what happens to the New York data
when we aggregate the Census Tract data into one-mile rings round the city center. With
some variation, we come very close to a perfect fit. The R^2 for this regression with 30
observations is 0.960, which means that 96% of the variation in the natural logarithm of
population density is explained by distance from the city center alone. Any theory that
can explain 96% of the spatial variation in densities by a single variable is doing very
well. The estimated gradient is 13.6%, which is close to our original estimate of 12.4%.

The moral of this exercise is that the answer to the question of how well does the
monocentric data explain the spatial variation in population density is, "it depends."
The model does not explain densities well at all in cities such as Tampa–St. Petersburg or
San Francisco–San Jose–Oakland. These urban areas grew by merging together formerly
distinct cities. They need to be modeled explicitly as "polycentric" urban area. A polycentric
urban area is an urban area with multiple centers, rather than the single center of
monocentric city. The model does not do a good job of explaining micro-level details
in densities for any urban area. However, it was never designed for this purpose. It was
designed to explain the overall spatial variation in such important variables as population
densities. If we divide our data set into one-mile rings, it explains New York well despite
the fact a 30-mile radius around the center of New York includes parts of three states
and contains several important employment centers in New Jersey and Long Island. The
model explains broad spatial trends well in many modern urban areas.

So far we have only attempted to determine how well the model fits the data for
individual urban areas at one point in time. We can ask whether the model helps to
explain the variation in population densities (1) across different cities at one point in time
and (2) over time for individual urban areas. The first question has been investigated by
several researchers. The results have been summarized by McDonald (1989). It can be

concluded that urban areas with larger population have flatter gradients, older urban areas often have steeper gradients, and other variables are not consistent in their impact on the gradient. The fact that a larger urban population is associated with a flatter gradient needs some explanation. Some researchers argue that a larger urban population generates a greater decentralization of employment and hence of population. Others suggest that the supply of housing is more elastic at the urban fringe. Consequently, an increase in urban population means that population growth will be greater at the fringe. The observation that older urban areas have steeper gradients appears to require a model in which housing that was constructed in the past to accommodate high population densities lives on in the present. Some empirical evidence appears to support some other statements, but these statements are weak statistically. These statements include:

- employment concentration is associated with a steeper gradient;
- substandard housing and black population in the central city are associated with a flatter gradient.

The central density also has been found to have systematic variations across urban areas. Central densities tend to be greater in larger urban areas and in older urban areas. One study by Edmonston and Guterbock (1984) found that central densities are high in smaller urban areas; central density declines with the size of an urban area up to a point, and then increases. These are the results that one would have expected.

The second question – how does the population gradient vary over time for an individual urban area? – has been investigated extensively. Two of the most important findings are that both central density and the gradient have become smaller over time. These results apply to virtually every urban area in the United States since the end of World War II (and probably before that). Population density functions for the Chicago urban area were estimated by McDonald (1979) and updated to 2000. The trend in the gradients is shown in Figure 7.5. The graph shows that the gradient has declined steadily over time since 1880. The decline in the gradient was particularly rapid between 1880 and 1900 and

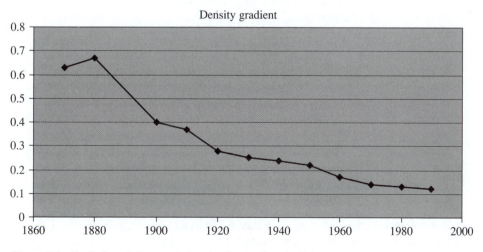

Figure 7.5 Evolution of the population density gradient in Chicago

for 1950–70. These are periods of rapid change in the nature of the urban transportation system. The last two decades of the nineteenth century saw the introduction of reasonably modern public transportation facilities that covered a wide area, and the period after World War II is, of course, the age of the automobile (and the expressway). Central density has also declined since 1950 as the introduction of the automobile on a large scale, the expressway system, and the end of population growth in the urban area formed a three-pronged assault on the central density.

The overwhelming trend of the last century and a half is the decline in transportation cost. First rapid transit and later the automobile reduced commuting costs dramatically. Population density declines very sharply with distance when people have to walk to work. It declines much less rapidly in a city with an extensive expressway system. The marked decline in the population density gradient is precisely what the monocentric city model predicts. It also is the reason that the model no longer explains the spatial variation in urban economic activity as well as it did in the past. The broad trend in variables such as population density is much flatter than in the past. Explaining the variation in densities with a high degree of accuracy now requires a consideration of more local factors such as access to the transportation network, the quality of schools, and the location of parks and scenic areas that increase land rents locally.

C. Other Measures of the Intensity of Land Use

Although population density patterns are important, urban planners and economists also use several other measures of the intensity of land use. Additional measures of the residential sector are considered first, and then the commercial and industrial sectors are discussed.

Urban planners use physical measures of density such as housing units and residential floor space per unit of land area. The term *floor-area ratio* refers to the ratio of floor space to land area. Some zoning ordinances regulate land per unit and the floor-area ratio directly. For example, the zoning ordinance in the City of Chicago contains the following residential zoning categories and regulations.

Category	Permitted use	Floor-area ratio	Lot area per unit (ft^2)
R-1	One-family detached	0.5	6,250
R-2	Same as R-1	0.5	5,000
R-3	One- and two-family	0.7	2,500
R-4	R-3 plus apartments	1.2	900
R-5	Same as R-4	2.2	400
R-6	Same as R-4	4.4	200
R-7	Same as R-4	7.0	145
R-8	Same as R-4	10.0	115

The R-1 category requires a lot size of a least 6,250 square feet (e.g., 50 feet by 125 feet) and limits the square footage of a house to 0.5 of the lot size (3,125 for a lot of 6,250 square feet). A one-story house can have 3,125 square feet, or a two-story house can have

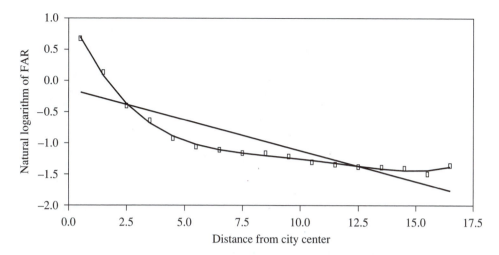

Figure 7.6   Floor-area ratios in Chicago

1,562.5 square feet on each floor. If you want a larger house than that, you need to buy a larger lot. The categories run up to R-8, which permits an apartment building with floor space 10 times the size of the lot. In other words, a 20-story building can cover 50% of the lot, and a 40-story building can cover 25% of the lot.

Figure 7.6 shows the spatial pattern of floor-area ratios in the City of Chicago. We followed Colin Clark's method in constructing this graph. Using more than 230,000 sales of single-family homes that sold in Chicago between 1983 and 1999, we calculate the total square footage in each one-mile ring around the city center and the total land area. We then calculate the (gross) floor area ratio by dividing the total square footage by the land area. The scatter of points shown in Figure 7.6 is a smooth curve when the natural logarithm of the floor-area ratio is shown on the vertical axis. The estimated equations are shown in Table 7.2. The simple negative exponential function implies that floor/area ratios fall by 9.9% with each additional mile from the city center. It is clear from Figure 7.6, however, that this estimated gradient understates the decline near the city center and overstates the decline farther out. It turns out that the data shown in Figure 7.6 closely follow the predictions of a fourth-order polynomial. The explanatory variables for a fourth-order polynomial are x, x^2, x^3, and x^4, where x represents distance from the city center in this case. The fourth-order polynomial provides a nearly perfect fit for the natural logarithm of the floor/area ratio. The R^2 of 0.997 implies that 99.7% of the variation in the log of the floor/area ratio is explained by this polynomial in distance. The predictions of the monocentric model hold nearly perfectly for this data set, even though floor-area ratios pertain only to single-family houses and are also influenced by Chicago's zoning ordinance.

Employment density and the floor-area ratio are conventional measures of land-use intensity in the commercial and industrial sectors. These variables can be measured in net or gross terms. Data on these measures can be used to estimate exponential functions that describe their spatial patterns. Some examples of net density functions for Chicago in 1956 and 1970 are shown in Table 7.3. In 1956 the manufacturing sector in the city of

Table 7.2   Floor-area ratios in Chicago

Variable	Negative exponential	Fourth-order polynomial
Constant	−0.128	1.093
	(0.783)	(21.931)
Distance	−0.099	−0.840
	(−5.976)	(−20.552)
Distance squared		0.120
		(12.308)
Distance cubed		−0.008
		(−9.093)
Distance^4		0.0002
		(7.449)
R^2	0.704	0.997

T-values are in parentheses below the estimated coefficients.

Chicago had a central net density for floor area of 153,000 square feet per acre, and this density measure declined by 22.3% per mile. The net employment density function in manufacturing had a central density of 403 workers per acre, and the gradient was 28.2% per mile. Because the net employment density function was steeper than the floor space density function, these findings mean that the floor space per worker increased with distance to the central business district. From 1956 to 1970 the floor area density function in manufacturing changed to a lower central density and a flatter gradient. Older facilities near the downtown that were built at high densities were abandoned or torn down during this period in which the expressway system was opened. However, the net employment

Table 7.3   Examples of net density functions for Chicago

Year and category	Central density	Gradient
1956		
Manufacturing		
Net floor area	153,000 sq. ft./acre	0.223
Net employment	403 per acre	0.282
Transp., comm. & utilities		
Net floor area	44,000 sq. ft./acre	0.292
Net employment	52 per acre	0.253
1970		
Manufacturing		
Net floor area	116,000 sq. ft./acre	0.157
Net employment	437 per acre	0.295
Transp., comm. & utilities		
Net floor area	8,000 sq. ft./acre	0.204
Net employment	12 per acre	0.131

Source: McDonald (1986)

density function did not change between 1956 and 1970. This was a period in which manufacturing employment in the city of Chicago held fairly steady, and the net employment density function reflects that fact. Dramatic declines in manufacturing employment in the city of Chicago began immediately after 1970.

The results for the other employment sector shown in Table 7.3 are different from the manufacturing story. The other sector is the transportation, communication and utility (TCU) sector. This sector is much smaller than the manufacturing sector; manufacturing employment in Cook County (the county that contains the city of Chicago) was 748,000 in 1963, and the TCU sector was only 137,000 at that same time. The decentralization of this sector from 1956 to 1970 is striking. The net floor area density gradient dropped from −29.2% per mile to −20.4% per mile, and the net employment density gradient changed from −25.3% to −13.1% per mile. Both measures of central density fell drastically.

Researchers who study net density must take care that the measures of economic activity (e.g., manufacturing employment) match the measure of land area. For example, some employment in manufacturing firms is located in offices, which might be classified as commercial land use.

D. Land Values, House Prices, and Land Area

Directly estimating the bid-rent function for land would appear to be the most direct way of testing the monocentric city model. Unfortunately, good data on land values are hard to find. Vacant land is rare in a built-up urban area, and even when it exists, it may not be a good approximation to the value of land in other locations. The price of a home includes the value of a building as well as the land that it sits on. There have been only a few attempts to estimate urban land-value functions. Coincidentally, these studies have focused on Chicago because two remarkable data sources exist for this city. The first data source is Homer Hoyt's classic book, *One Hundred Years of Land Values in Chicago* (1933). Hoyt's book is both a history of Chicago and a thorough analysis of the real estate market as the city evolved during its first century. He combed through government records of land transactions in the city to estimate the value of land in every square mile of the city in 1833, 1857, 1873, 1892, 1910, and 1928. The second data source is *Olcott's Land Values Blue Book of Chicago*, which was published annually for most of the twentieth century. Although it is unclear exactly how *Olcott's* obtained its data, the books are unrivaled in the breadth of their coverage. *Olcott's* reported land values for *every block* in the city and many of the suburbs, and began to report zoning categories in the 1930s.

Figure 7.7 shows the raw data and estimated land-value functions for Hoyt's 1873 data. Table 7.4 presents the estimated regression equations. The year 1873 is particularly interesting because it is shortly after the Great Chicago Fire of 1871, when the city was nearly entirely destroyed. The simple negative-exponential function, which is the straight line in Figure 7.7, explains 64.8% of the variation in the natural logarithm of land value per square mile. The gradient is very high at 0.311: each additional mile from the city center reduces land values by 31.1%. A cubic equation implies an even greater rate of decline near the city center, and the R^2 rises to 0.751. Notice that several points in

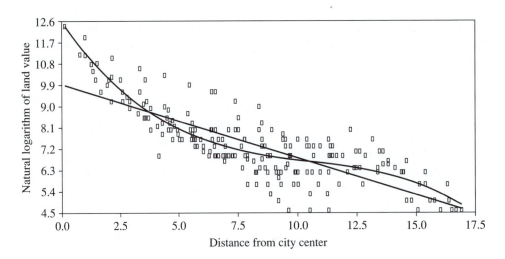

Figure 7.7   Chicago land values in 1873

Figure 7.7 are well above the estimated functions. It turns out that these areas tend to be locations near Lake Michigan, which is a local amenity in Chicago. Distance to Lake Michigan adds still more explanatory power to the equation. In the last column of Table 7.4, we find that the combination of a distance to Lake Michigan and a cubic function of distance to the city center explains 82.2% of the spatial variation in land values in Chicago in 1873. It also is worth pointing out that the city did not extend 17 miles from the CBD in 1873. In fact, it probably did not extend much more than five miles from the center at this time. Thus, the apparent upturn in land values at a distance of about 10 miles form the city center has no implications for the monocentric city model, which is not, after all, a model of farmland.

Table 7.4   Land value functions: Chicago in 1873

Variable	Negative exponential	Cubic	Cubic with distance to Lake Michigan
Constant	9.930	12.557	12.552
	(69.690)	(39.424)	(46.494)
Distance	−0.311	−1.421	−1.258
	(−19.801)	(−10.050)	(−10.382)
Distance squared		0.123	0.115
		(6.684)	(7.397)
Distance cubed		−0.004	−0.004
		(−5.536)	(−6.417)
Distance to Lake Michigan			−0.192
			(−9.150)
R^2	0.648	0.751	0.822

T-values are in parentheses below the estimated coefficients.

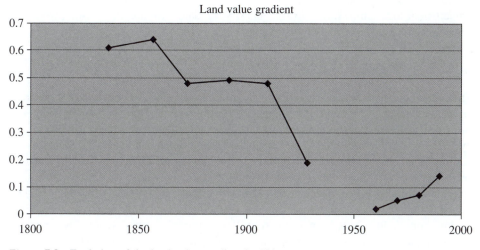

Figure 7.8   Evolution of the land value gradient in Chicago

Although the 1873 data are consistent with the predictions of the monocentric model, updated estimates are not as supportive of the model. Figure 7.8 shows the evolution of the land-value gradient from the 1830s to 1990. Up to 1928, the data come from Hoyt's book. After this time, the data are drawn from *Olcott's*. The long-term decline in the land-value gradient is consistent with the predications of the model: declines in commuting costs lead to flatter land-value functions. However, in 1960 the gradient had fallen to zero. In fact, McDonald (1979) shows that land values increased with distance in the area just outside the central business district. A significant gradient has been reestablished recently, though. By 1990, the gradient was back to 13.4%. McMillen (1996) shows that adding some nonlinearity and a few other variables – distance from Lake Michigan and distances from O'Hare and Midway airports – is sufficient to produce an R^2 of 0.873. The central business district still dominates Chicago's land market.

Many researchers have attempted to test the monocentric city model using data on house prices, which are far easier to obtain than data on land values. Unfortunately, much of this research is based on a faulty interpretation of the model's implications. Recall from Chapter 5 that the model predicts the price per unit of housing, P_H, declines with distance from the city center. The model also predicts that the quantity of housing, H, increases with distance. What about the product, $P_H H$? The product is the cost of a home. All that the model predicts for this variable is that house prices are high where high-income households live. As we have seen, the model's predictions are ambiguous for the location of high-income households.

We might be able to use house prices to test the model if we could measure all relevant housing characteristics. Suppose that the price of a unit of housing follows the negative exponential function,

$$\ln P_H(x) = \alpha - gx$$

where x represents distance from the center. The cost of a home is $V = P_H H$. By the properties of logarithms, $\ln V = \ln P_H + \ln H$. Since data on V are easy to find, we might consider estimating the following equation:

$$\ln V(x) = \alpha - gx + \ln H$$

The problem is that H is not observed. It might be thought of as a function of a group of variables Z, so that $H = H(Z)$. But we cannot control for all of the plethora of characteristics that make up a house. For example, suppose that we are missing a variable "quality." High-quality homes tend to be demanded by high-income households. Suppose that high-income households tend to live far from the city center. Then high values of quality are correlated with high values of x. If quality is not measured accurately, then each additional mile from the city center will have two effects: (1) it directly lowers $\ln V(x)$ by g, and it indirectly raises it by the value of the additional "quality" demanded by high-income households. A regression of $\ln V(x)$ on x combines the two effects, and it is distinctly possible that the estimated gradient will have the wrong sign. The wrong sign for the estimated distance gradient simply indicates that some variables are missing and that high-priced houses are located at greater distances. In general, home sales cannot be used to test the predictions of the monocentric city model.

A final approach to testing the prediction of the monocentric city model is offered by Brueckner and Fansler (1983). These authors analyze the total land area covered by a group of 40 urbanized areas with 1970 populations ranging from 52,000 to 275,000. The land area covered by urbanized areas is determined by the intersection of the bid-rent functions for land and the agricultural land rent. In the simple version of the model in which there are no time costs of commuting, the income elasticity of demand for housing is (trivially) greater than the income elasticity of commuting cost. In this case, the model predicts that urbanized land areas will be higher when commuting costs are lower, incomes are higher, the urban population is higher, and agricultural land rent is lower. Brueckner and Fansler's results are shown in Table 7.5. As expected, land areas increase with population and income, and they fall with agricultural land values. Commuting cost is a difficult variable to measure. Brueckner and Fansler try two measures – the percentage of commuters using public transit and the percentage of households with one or more cars. The idea is more people use public transit when commuting is costly, and commuting tends to be cheaper when more households have cars available. Though the coefficients for these variables have the right sign, they are not statistically different from zero. Perhaps the results for commuting cost would improve if the variable were measured more accurately.

The R^2s of the estimated equations in Brueckner and Fansler (1983) imply that nearly 80% of the variation in urbanized land areas is explained by just these four variables. To quote them directly:

> The results of this paper justify a dispassionate view of urban sprawl. By showing that urban spatial area is related to population, income, and agricultural land rent in the manner predicted by the model, the empirical results suggest that sprawl is the result of an orderly process rather than a symptom of an economic system out of control. In this context, it is interesting to note that by demonstrating the negative impact of agricultural land rent on urban size, the

Table 7.5   Brueckner and Fansler's estimates for total urban land area

Variable	Coefficient	
Constant	−41.0723	−63.4691
	(−2.277)	(−1.244)
Population	0.0004	0.0004
	(10.030)	(9.876)
Median agricultural land value in county	−0.0303	−0.0289
	(−3.090)	(−2.888)
Household income	0.0062	0.0062
	(3.033)	(3.050)
% of commuters using public transit	−0.2444	
	(−0.4056)	
% of households with one or more cars		0.2475
		(0.4604)
R^2	0.7982	0.7985

T-Values are in parentheses below the estimated coefficients.

empirical results undermine the sprawl critic's claim that the transfer of a farmland to urban uses represents the "waste" of a valuable resource. By showing that high-quality, high-priced farmland is more resistant to urban expansion than poor-quality land, the empirical results establish that the land market balances the gains and losses from urban sprawl, restricting spatial growth when the process consumes a valuable resource. As well as providing a measured view of urban sprawl, the results of this paper constitute further evidence of the empirical robustness of the Muth–Mills model. Although the model's excellent performance in predicting the internal structure of cities is widely recognized, the present results show its ability to successfully explain intercity differences in urban spatial structure. (Brueckner and Fansler, 1983, pp. 481–2)

E. Urban Employment Centers and Spatial Patterns for Urban Industries

The basic economic functions performed in urban areas were outlined in Chapter 4. Noyelle and Stanback (1983) defined the types of goods and services produced in urban areas according to the following classification system:

1 agriculture, extractive, construction;
2 manufacturing;
3 distributive services;
4 complex of corporate activities:
   (a)   central administrative offices and auxiliary establishments,
   (b)   finance, insurance, and real estate,
   (c)   corporate services;

5   nonprofit services;
6   retailing;
7   consumer services;
8   government

In this section, we discuss for each of these sectors the nature of its spatial pattern within an urban area, which includes distinctive features such as the central business district, the airport and its surrounding area, industrial zones, major shopping malls, and suburban office agglomerations. Changes in the geography of urban employment are discussed along the way. In addition to this section, you will enjoy reading the part of Hoover and Vernon's *Anatomy of a Metropolis* (1959), in which these topics are discussed for New York in the 1950s.

The agriculture, extractive and construction sector is not given a detailed treatment because it does not really follow an overall coherent pattern. Agricultural activity in urban areas tends to be located at the urban fringe, of course. Extractive activity (mines, oil wells, quarries) has a location pattern determined by natural resources. For example, there are oil wells in downtown Oklahoma City. Also, construction activity takes place in areas of physical growth, which usually are located in outer suburbs. (One exception is the downtown office building boom of the 1980s in many of the larger urban areas.)

Manufacturing

Most large urban areas in the United States began as trading centers, but by the late nineteenth century, many had become centers of manufacturing. Manufacturing of that day was tied to water and rail transportation systems. Indeed, manufacturing was tied to water transport routes before the development of the rail network in the 1850–90 era. Railroads freed manufacturing location decisions to a remarkable degree and in a manner not unlike the interstate highways in the 1960s and 1970s. For example, Inland Steel is a maker of basic steel that was founded around the turn of the century at a location in the Chicago urban area that is several miles removed from Lake Michigan and major waterways.

For our present purposes, manufacturing can be divided into two basic categories: heavy and light. *Heavy manufacturing* involves the assembly of bulky raw materials or semi-finished products for the manufacture of a bulky product. Included in this category are:

1   primary metals (SIC 33);
2   chemicals (SIC 28);
3   petroleum and coal products (SIC 29);
4   transportation equipment (SIC 37);
5   paper and allied products (SIC 26);
6   textile mill products (SIC 22).

Recall from Chapter 6 that Henderson (1986) found evidence of localization economies in primary metals, petroleum and coal products, paper and allied products, and textiles. He did not conduct a test for transportation equipment, so four out of five heavy manufacturing industries tested display localization economies. Heavy manufacturing to a considerable degree still occupies locations that are adjacent to water transportation and are also served by rail. The sharing of transportation facilities may be the source of the localization economies. These shared transportation facilities provide access to the raw materials that are important to these industries. But increasingly, some of these industries have reduced their intakes of raw materials and their reliance on water transportation. Railways and highways are sufficient to support auto assembly plants and auto parts manufacture (transportation equipment), mini-mills (steel), and chemical plants of various types, for example. Some of the old industrial districts in urban areas such as Pittsburgh, Detroit, Chicago, Cleveland, Buffalo, and New York City have been more than decimated – they have been virtually abandoned.

The rest of manufacturing can be called *light manufacturing*. It consists primarily of food products, apparel, printing and publishing, plastics, fabricated metal products, machinery (electrical and non-electrical), and instruments. For these industries, many of the location factors discussed in Chapter 3 come into play. Location choice within the urban area depends on access to the market for the product, which can be partly local in nature. Access to labor is important, as is access to intermediate inputs. Access to knowledge is especially important for many of these industries. After all, electrical machinery includes computers and their components. Silicon Valley, the area around San Jose that is the home of the nation's computer industry, is perhaps the leading example of the importance of access to knowledge in a manufacturing industry. Access to knowledge is important in the high-fashion apparel business too. The actions of local governments can also influence the location choices of these industries in an urban area. The general quality of the neighborhood in which the facility is located can play a role. In addition, there is a factor that has not been discussed yet – room for expansion. Studies of industrial relocation show that relocation is most often prompted by running out of space. It is logical to conclude that the choice of location will depend in part on the availability of room for expansion.

Henderson's (1986) list of manufacturing industries that exhibit localization economies includes four in the above list of light manufacturing industries – food products, apparel, electrical machinery, and non-electrical machinery. With examples such as the Silicon Valley phenomenon in the computer industry and the high-fashion apparel industry, it is clear that localization economies sometimes lead to a clear cluster of an industry within an urban area. In other cases it seems that presence in the urban area is sufficient to reap the benefits of localization economies. However, this is only a conjecture that needs to be tested.

Some other clusters of light manufacturing have existed in the past, and some of these clusters continue to exist. Smaller firms in a variety of light manufacturing sectors have tended to cluster in the denser areas near the central business district, where there is ready access to space, labor, and a variety of business services. These are more properly considered to be economies of urbanization that exist in particular locations within the urban area.

Another type of cluster was formed by the printing and publishing industry in some urban areas. This industry is really two industries – printing and publishing. Printing tends to cluster near central business districts because much of the demand for printing was in the central business district. Many special printing jobs require rapid completion, so printers must be in close contact with their customers. The attraction of the central business district for printers has diminished in recent years, but many urban areas contain what was once a printers' district near downtown. For example, an area adjacent to the Chicago central business district called "Printers' Row" contains old-fashioned industrial loft buildings that have since been converted to a variety of other uses, including residential use. Publishing is the industry in which writers write, editors edit, and marketing departments sell. There is a sense in which this industry does not seem to be manufacturing, but that is how it is classified. For many years, this industry responded to localization economies by being concentrated in the central business districts of a few major urban areas. Publishing is still big business in New York, of course. Some of the publishing houses have relocated to New Jersey and even to places such as San Diego. The publishing industry relies on sources of information, and much of that information is not easily interpreted without face-to-face contact. Publishing also relies on the talents of highly skilled people, so labor-market economies of localization are at work too. Perhaps Henderson (1986) failed to find evidence of localization economies in printing and publishing because these two very different industries were lumped together.

The other sectors in the light manufacturing group correspond to one's image of the modern factory located in the suburbs. Larger firms in industries such as food products, machinery, plastics, fabricated metals, and instruments build factories that may be only one story (or two or three stories) in height. These facilities are surrounded by parking lots and, in many cases, by grass and trees. They are happy with convenient access to a highway, a good workforce nearby, a pleasant environment, and room to expand. Firms in some of these industries led the charge to the suburbs beginning in the 1950s. The completion of the expressway systems in urban areas accelerated the movement of these types of firms to the suburbs. Some of the smaller firms in these industries still require the external economies of locations near the central business district, but it is also true that those external economies of available space, labor supply, and business services can now be found elsewhere in the urban area.

The impact of zoning can also be seen in the location patterns of light manufacturing, especially in suburban jurisdictions. Suburbs sometimes trade off the fiscal benefits of industrial land use and environmental quality. The amount of space made available to manufacturers depends on how local officials view this tradeoff. Given that a local jurisdiction has decided to make some land available for manufacturing use, there are clear patterns in the allocation of land. A detailed study of land allocations in zoning ordinances by McMillen and McDonald (1990) shows that land in suburban Chicago is more likely to have been allocated to manufacturing if it is:

- near a limited-access highway;
- near a freight rail line;
- near a commuter rail line;
- closer to the major airport (O'Hare);
- at a greater distance from the village hall;
- at a greater distance from downtown Chicago.

The list includes very local effects and more regional patterns. Immediate access to highway and rail is important, and local officials evidently dislike zoning land for industry near the village hall, which is usually near the center of the village. Villages that are closer to O'Hare Airport provide more land for industry, as one would expect. This list also includes the tendency, holding all of these other factors constant, for land zoned for manufacturing to increase with distance to downtown Chicago. This result perhaps is evidence of a desire to put new manufacturing facilities on the outer fringe of the suburb. Finally, the study by McMillen and McDonald (1990) found that more land was zoned for manufacturing by older suburbs than by newer suburbs. As is explained below, newer suburbs are trying to attract commercial activity because of the lack of growth in manufacturing employment in recent years. Older suburbs were, at least at some time, trying to attract manufacturing activity.

The distribution sector

The Noyelle–Stanback (1983) distribution sector includes wholesale trade and transportation, communication, and utilities. McDonald (1992) prefers a narrower definition of the distribution sector: wholesale trade and trucking and warehousing. Clearly, this more narrowly defined distribution sector will usually locate near highways, rail lines, and airports. Some agglomerations of wholesale trade activity, such as fresh fruits and vegetables and meats, select a central location as a convenience to their customers. In some major urban areas, there are agglomerations of wholesalers in apparel, furniture, and other durable goods so as to cater to the buyers from retail stores, many of whom come from outside the urban area. These agglomerations might be located downtown or near the airport. The airport is, of course, the center of the air transportation industry. Transportation services, such as travel agents, air freight companies, and other services, tend to cluster in the downtown area or at the airport.

The communication industry includes TV and radio broadcasters and the telephone company. TV and radio broadcasters often locate in the downtown district to maximize their access to the entire urban area. The telephone company has a central office and local offices to serve customers. The electric company has power-generating facilities that resemble heavy manufacturing. Most power plants burn coal or oil and therefore must be located near transportation facilities that are used to deliver the basic fuel. The transportation facilities include water routes, rail lines, and oil pipelines. Power plants often are located in the same districts as heavy manufacturing. The natural gas utility has a major facility located near the natural gas pipeline. Both utilities also have a network of facilities to serve the local population.

The story of the changes in location patterns in this sector is instructive. Transportation and wholesale trade were once concentrated in or near the downtowns of most urban areas. Many urban areas, and their downtowns, began life as ports. And remember those old railroad stations? Those railroad stations also came equipped with railroad yards, where trains were assembled and disassembled. Early trucking terminals were also located near the downtown areas. Wholesale trade was not usually located right in the downtown area, but used sites near the transportation facilities in the vicinity of downtown. Wholesale trade was much more centralized within an urban area than was retail trade. Finally, the earliest airports were located as close to downtown as possible. Airports require a lot of space, but LaGuardia in New York, Ronald Reagan National Airport in Washington,

DC, Love Field in Dallas, and Midway Airport in Chicago are all good examples of early airports that are located only a few miles from downtown.

As the urban areas grew along with the entire nation, the demand for the services of the distribution sector grew as well. The sites near the downtown area were not large enough to handle the demand, so new facilities had to be built on the periphery of the urban area. Rail yards became too small and congested. New rail yards were built at the periphery of the urban area. Later, even more rail yards were built at the new periphery of the urban area. The older, larger urban areas have a collection of rail yards that date from various times in their histories. Trucking terminals also became outdated, and new ones have been established partly by the deregulation of the trucking industry in the 1980s. Under the old regulations, trucking terminals had to be located inside the commercial trucking zone that had been set up by the Interstate Commerce Commission.

In like manner, the air transportation industry outgrew the first set of airports. A second set of airports has been built, and these are located at what was the periphery of the urban area at the time of their construction. We now have Kennedy Airport and Newark Airport for New York, Dulles Airport in the vicinity of Washington, DC, Dallas–Fort Worth Airport, and O'Hare Airport in Chicago. The wholesale trade sector is attracted to these newer transportation facilities. Indeed, in some instances, a great deal of economic activity is attracted to the newer airports. Some urban areas have recently or are now facing the issue of where to build the *next* airport. New airports require an enormous amount of space, and that kind of space can only be found at rather great distances from the downtown area.

Complex of corporate activities

This sector consists of corporate offices, financial services, and business and professional services. All of this is office-based employment, and office buildings can vary from one to 100 stories in height. This is the sector that has been, and still is to a large degree, located downtown. Some parts of this sector, such as banks, insurance agents, and real estate brokers, have always located in residential areas because they are really providing services at the retail level. Beyond these functions, the necessity for face-to-face contact led this sector to locate downtown. Indeed, the strength of the attraction of downtown was underestimated by some analysts. During the 1980s, many of the downtown areas experienced unprecedented booms in the construction of office space. Employment in these sectors was growing rapidly and, contrary to the predictions of many people, the downtowns of major urban areas were the recipients of some of that growth. For example, employment in FIRE (finance, insurance, and real estate) almost doubled, from 3.6 million in 1970 to 6.7 million in 1990. Downtowns in places such as Baltimore and Cleveland have come back from the dead. Other places, such as Los Angeles and Phoenix, were thought by some people not to have downtowns. That thought turns out to have been wrong. Downtown provides economies of agglomeration of all the types discussed in Chapter 3.

The growth of the complex of corporate activities has yielded growth for many downtowns, but even more spectacular is the creation of what journalist/author Joel

Garreau has called *Edge Cities*. Garreau's 1991 book *Edge City* is both insightful and entertaining. He points out that we built monocentric city models roughly between the years 1840 and 1920. Since then we have mainly been building suburbs, and the growth of suburbs has passed through three stages. First came the bedroom communities that permitted the downtown workers to live in a more pleasant setting. The next stage began in the late 1940s and brought shopping malls and industrial parks to the suburbs. The shopping malls grew to serve the rapidly growing suburban population, and the industrial parks attracted manufacturing plants that needed large amounts of relatively cheap land and ready access to highways. These developments changed the nature of suburbs, but there was still a heavy reliance on the economy of the central city. In the third stage, corporate offices and many other activities have moved to suburban centers that Garreau calls edge cities. This stage began in the early 1970s, and it represents something entirely new. Just what is an edge city, and why is it so important?

Garreau does not use the terminology of Chapter 3, but clearly he means that an edge city is a large cluster of economic activity that includes a substantial amount of office-based employment and possesses economies of agglomeration. He calls them edge *cities* because of the existence of agglomeration economies. As you know, suburban shopping malls and industrial parks have agglomeration economies, too, but Garreau would contend that the agglomeration economies of the new edge city are far greater and more pervasive. Garreau contends that the agglomeration economies in edge cities rival those in the central business district. Economic growth is being created in edge cities. The primary physical manifestation of economic growth of the American economy since the 1970s is the construction of edge cities near the edge of every major urban area in the nation. How are edge cities formed, and how do they work?

Garreau's book is a work of journalism rather than science. He interviewed hundreds of people who have been involved in creating edge cities, and he reported on their motivations and the guidelines that they used. First, it is clear that edge cities form at the intersections of major highways. Not every intersection has an edge city, but nearly every edge city has an intersection of major, limited-access highways. It is also clear that the highway intersection usually has reasonable access to an airport. A highway intersection may already have a shopping mall or an industrial park nearby, but often the precipitating event in the creation of an edge city is the decision of a major corporation to move some or all of its headquarters operation to that location. The headquarters operation might include the research and development facility, which employs people with high levels of education and training. The major corporation did not need agglomeration economies that are external to the firm. Firms such as IBM, AT&T, and Motorola brought much of their own supporting services with them. Their choice of location was driven by the convenience of their managers, scientists, and other critical personnel. Other large companies might then choose the same location largely for convenience in commuting. The crucial next phase in the creation of an edge city is the decision of smaller companies to locate in the vicinity. These firms might have some connection to the large corporation as supplier or consultant, but the critical difference is that they require extensive supporting services. Their agglomeration economies are external to the firm. Those supporting services include restaurants, hotels and conference facilities, office supply stores, lawyers, accountants, computer experts, financial services, engineering consultants, and a host of other activities. Once all of these kinds of enterprises are there, more new businesses are created because the supporting services are there.

Garreau has found that people really like edge cities. What are their reasons? Convenience in commuting for the important employees has already been mentioned. People regard commuting by public transportation as an unpleasant experience, so edge cities are based on the automobile. Edge cities have been created partly in response to the increase in the number of women who have entered the labor force since the early 1980s. What is more, people like the pleasant environment of the edge city. They like green grass and trees, and they like to live in suburban communities that have greenery as well. Garreau points out that edge cities cannot form unless some suburban housing already exists in the vicinity. An edge city is a nice compromise between the desires to live and work in a pleasant location and to have a productive career. The edge city corporate "campus" includes ball fields, picnic grounds, tennis courts, and jogging tracks. The nearby suburban communities provide good housing at decent prices and good public schools. An edge city and its surrounding residential areas provide safety, especially for women and children.

The big central city comes with dirt, crime, subways, stress, congestion, high taxes, and poor public schools. Edge cities are not immune to all of these problems (especially congestion), but for now they largely avoid most of them. Edge cities are subject to a certain amount of traffic congestion, but their developers have methods of ameliorating some of the problems. For one thing, they build parking garages. The construction of the first parking garage is an important event in the life of an edge city because a parking garage is a signal of the fact that the edge city has reached a certain size and status. Also, an edge city that has become large enough to create its own traffic jams will soon develop at an intensity of land use that permits a person to walk, rather than drive, to lunch and shopping.

Edge cities are new and important features of modern urban areas, and we are just beginning to study them. Some of the empirical research on edge cities is discussed in the next section.

Retailing and consumer services

You already know that retailing and consumer services are of two types: convenience goods and shopping goods. Convenience goods and services follow residential location patterns closely, so little needs to be said about them because they are not major forces in the shaping of an urban area. Shopping goods are a different story. Once upon a time nearly everyone in an urban area went downtown to shop for clothing, jewelry, shoes, furniture, house wares, appliances, and most other things of a durable nature. Downtown shopping still exists in most urban area (although not in Detroit, for example), but most shopping has shifted to the suburban shopping malls.

The rapid growth of residential suburbs in the 1950s brought convenience goods almost immediately, and branch stores of the downtown department stores soon followed. As suburban growth continued and as more highways were constructed, it became economically feasible to build huge suburban shopping malls. Huge shopping malls are designed to capture the externalities that were discussed in Chapter 3. The shopping malls contain "anchor" department stores and a large variety of smaller stores that specialize in particular lines of business. These big shopping malls are in competition with downtown *and* with the smaller shopping centers that were built in the 1950s and 1960s. In the process, many downtown stores have folded, and many of the early suburban shopping centers have also been converted to other uses. All of this has been made possible by the automobile. A study by McDonald (1975) of retailing in Detroit in the early 1960s showed that for people who owned a car, the probability of shopping downtown declined sharply with distance from home to downtown. In contrast, most people who did not own a car shopped downtown, and that tendency did not decline with distance to downtown. Public transportation is centered on downtown, so those who do not own cars travel downtown to shop. The increase in auto ownership caused downtown shopping to decline.

The story for downtown is not entirely one of gloom and doom. The growth of downtown office-based employment of the 1980s has helped to create some opportunities for downtown retailers. Successful downtown retailers have changed to cater to the downtown worker. And some downtowns have been and still are tourist attractions. Included on a list of such downtowns are New York, Chicago, Boston, San Francisco, Washington DC, Seattle, and perhaps a few others. Some other downtowns have been promoted as tourist attractions without much success. After General Motors decided to close its plants in Flint, Michigan, the community attempted to turn its downtown area into a tourist attraction by building a fancy downtown hotel, a "festival market" facility, and an indoor amusement park named Auto World. The hotel and the festival market facility were not successful and closed recently, and Auto World closed within a few months of its opening.

Nonprofit services and government

Nonprofit services include health care, which is in fact very big business in the modern economy. The location patterns of hospitals and other health-care facilities are important parts of the urban economy, and some big changes have occurred in recent years. Health-care facilities are now organized according to a reasonably clear hierarchy. The offices of doctors and dentists in private practice and small health clinics are located in or near the residential areas that they serve. The next level of the hierarchy includes the smaller hospitals and larger clinics that serve an area but do not offer the full range of medical services that is available only in the large hospitals. Often, those large hospitals are attached to or affiliated with a medical school.

Major changes are taking place in the systems used to deliver health care. The use of health maintenance organizations and other forms of "managed care" is growing rapidly, even without any direction from the federal government. The old model of health-care delivery was one in which doctors in independent private practice were affiliated with an independent, nonprofit hospital. Cases that could not be handled at that level were referred up the hierarchy to the large hospital with the staff of surgeons, cancer specialists, and medical researchers. The doctors and hospitals were reimbursed by private insurance companies based on fees for services rendered. This system resulted in a rate of inflation in medical costs that spelled trouble. The average rate of inflation from 1970 to 1990 for all consumer goods and services was 6.1%, but the price of medical services increased by 7.9% per year. From 1980 to 1990, the rate of inflation as a whole averaged 4.6%, but the inflation of medical services was 7.8%.

The concern with the rising cost of medical care has prompted large employers to seek more efficient and cost-conscious providers, and the market has responded. A health maintenance organization (HMO) is a private company that operates or a profit. It hires salaried doctors and other medical professionals to provide care for a large group of people, such as the employees of a large firm. The contract drawn up between the HMO and the firm stipulates that the HMO is paid a certain amount to provide health care for the clients. The HMO is not paid on the basis of fees for services rendered. Cases that cannot be handled by the HMO staff are contracted out to the large hospitals. Clearly, this type of system gives the HMO a strong incentive to keep costs down.

The shift to managed care has meant that many of the old nonprofit hospitals in urban neighborhoods have been under a great deal of pressure. Many of the smaller hospitals have closed. In other cases, they have been taken over by HMOs or other for-profit health-care providers. Some of the doctors who were in private practice have gone to work for HMOs at a salary. These changes in the organization of health care have probably stimulated growth in large medical centers. The large hospitals, with their huge staffs and comprehensive set of services and medical education, have set up their own HMOs or managed-care organizations. They have also set up contracts with HMOs to provided the specialized care that the cost-conscious HMO will not supply directly. The hypothesis is that the shift to managed care has been beneficial to the organizations at the top of the hierarchy. In addition, the public is demanding improvements in health care through public and private funding of medical research and development. The large hospital/medical complexes are the recipients of most of this funding for research. These medical complexes are important parts of the urban economy.

Where are these major medical centers located in an urban area? Often they are located near the center of the urban area because that is where the hospital or medical school was founded. Major medical complexes are located adjacent to downtown in Chicago, Cleveland, and New Orleans, for example. Others, such as the Mayo Clinic in the Minneapolis–St. Paul urban area, have sought a location in a nearby smaller city (Rochester). Major medical complexes can be located in a variety of places within the urban area, and they will continue to exert major impacts on location patterns.

Government employment was 16.6% of all nonagricultural employment in 2003, so the location patterns of government are important to an urban area. Much of local government serves the population directly, so location patterns are driven by the location of the population. Other parts of local government, as well as state and federal government, often locate in downtown office buildings. Courthouses have traditionally been part of downtown, and that tradition remains in force to a considerable degree. However, the growth of suburban counties has meant that there are now large centers of county government in the suburbs. In a few other cases, major government employment centers exist for historic reasons. Some urban areas are centers of military employment, and the location of the naval base or other military post will influence location patterns. The analyst who seeks to understand location patterns in an urban area must take government into account.

F. Empirical Studies of Employment Centers

Empirical researchers only recently have begun to recognize the importance of urban employment centers other than the central business district. Somewhat surprisingly, the central business district itself has been the subject of only a modest amount of research. Urban economics has tended to concentrate on distance to the central business district as a crucial variable in theoretical and empirical models of the spatial patterns of an urban area (as in Chapter 5), but the content of the CBD has been the subject of fewer studies. The reason for this relative lack of studies is a lack of data on employment *by place of work* enumerated for small geographic zones. This section begins with a brief look at the central business districts of Los Angeles and Chicago, and then the other employment centers in those urban areas are examined.

The Los Angeles urban area can be studied in detail because the data gathered by the 1980 census of population include information on the journey to work for 17% of households. These data were gathered by place of residence and then transformed to employment data by place of work. Giuliano and Small (1991) used the data to identify employment subcenters in the Los Angeles urban area, and their findings are discussed below. The first thing that they discovered is that the central business district was, by far, the most important center of employment. Downtown Los Angeles in 1980 had an employment level of 469,000 out of a total employment 4.65 million in the entire urban area, so downtown contained 10.1% of total employment. The area that is traditionally used as the definition of the CBD is rather small and contained only 152,000 workers, but Giuliano and Small (1991) believe that an area of about 2.5 miles in radius is the better definition of the CBD. Clearly, a downtown that is 19.6 square miles in area is not a downtown made for walking. Here is clear evidence that some downtowns are spreading out, so travel within the downtown area is an emerging problem. Giuliano and Small (1991) examined downtown employment by industry and found a strong concentration in public employment and FIRE (finance, insurance, and real estate). Downtown contained about 20% of the urban area's employment in these two sectors, and downtown manufacturing employment was relatively low.

Data for the Chicago CBD permit an examination of the changes in downtown employment over time. These data are based on reports filed by employers to the state unemployment insurance system. This kind of data exists for all states, but Illinois makes a special effort to provide summary data for the public. The Northeastern Illinois Planning Commission provides summaries of the employment data by quarter section. A quarter section is a $\frac{1}{2} \times \frac{1}{2}$ mile square, or an area of $\frac{1}{4}$ square miles. The Chicago CBD has been spreading out over time. The definition that is used here is an area that is about 4 miles long (in the north–south direction) and 2 miles wide. The Chicago CBD is smaller than the Los Angeles CBD because Chicago is served by an extensive system of public transit and commuter rail lines that brings most of the workers downtown. Developers of downtown office buildings must provide reasonable proximity to the transit and commuter rail systems.

Data on employment by industry for the Chicago CBD are shown in Table 7.6. Total employment in downtown Chicago was 783,440 in 1970, a figure that was 24.7% of total employment in the urban area. Note that as one would expect, downtown Chicago

Table 7.6   Employment in downtown Chicago

Industry	1970		1980		1990		2000	
	Workers (thous.)	% of urban area	Workers (thous.)	% of urban area	Workers (thous.)	% of urban area	Workers (thous.)	% of urban area
Total	783.4	24.7	582.0	18.2	611.4	16.8	630.7	15.4
Manufacturing			66.6	8.0	46.4	7.0	26.4	4.3
TCU			80.2	18.0	58.1	11.6	55.3	10.4
Retail			79.1	15.4	60.2	10.1	51.0	8.0
FIRE			111.0	50.4	134.7	45.8	121.8	39.4
Services			155.5	23.9	237.0	24.0	291.3	21.4
Government			78.6	30.6	62.9	22.7	56.9	19.9
Other	–	–	11.0	–	12.1	–	28.0	–

The columns labeled "% of urban area" show employment in the *CBD* divided by employment in the industry in the urban area.
Source: Northeastern Illinois Planning Commission

contains a larger proportion of total employment in the urban area than does downtown Los Angeles. In contrast to the Los Angeles CBD's 19.6 square miles, Chicago's downtown covers only 8.9 square miles. Yet employment in downtown Chicago was 24% higher than in Los Angeles in 1980. It is an impressive feat for the transportation network to bring more than 700,000 workers into such a small area each day. Downtown employment fell by 25.7% during the 1970s, and its percentage of total employment in the urban area fell to 18.2%. This downward trend partially reversed after 1980 as the downtown added jobs. The number of downtown jobs rose by 8.4% between 1980 and 2000. However, the Chicago area added more jobs to the area outside the CBD. Despite the increase in then number of downtown jobs between 1980 and 2000, the percentage of jobs in the urban area that are downtown fell from 18.2% in 1980 to 15.4% in 2000.

Table 7.6 shows that downtown employment in Chicago is heavily concentrated in FIRE (finance, insurance, and real estate) and services. These two sectors made up 45.8% of downtown employment in 1980, and they grew to 65.5% of downtown employment in 2000. Services grew particularly rapidly, nearly doubling in the number of jobs between 1980 and 2000. All of the other industries declined between 1980 and 2000. During the 1980s, office space in the downtown area increased from 68 million square feet with an occupancy rate of 95% to 109 million square feet with an occupancy rate of 90% (McDonald and McMillen 1990). Downtown contained 50.4% of all FIRE employment in 1980, and that fraction had dropped to 39.4% in 2000. Employment in the service sector is more dispersed; 23.9% of service sector employment was located downtown in 1980, and this figure dropped slightly to 21.4% in 2000. The only other sector that is heavily concentrated downtown is the government. More than 30% of the urban area's government workers were located downtown in 1980. However, both the number of workers and the percentage of government workers who are downtown fell sharply between 1980 and 2000.

Downtown employment in major urban areas is heavily concentrated in the FIRE, service, and public sectors, but what about other centers of employment in the urban area? An examination of other urban employment centers requires first that they be identified using some criteria. There is no standard set of criteria that everyone uses to identify employment centers. For example, Garreau (1991) defined an edge city as a place with at least 5 million square feet of office space, 600,000 square feet of retail space, and more workers than residents. Furthermore, Garreau required that the place was nothing like a city in 1960. Clearly, Garreau was focusing on newer concentration of office-based employment. His definition misses other kinds of employment centers that concentrate in manufacturing, distribution, or transportation. Garreau's definition seems to run into trouble because he tried to establish boundaries for his edge cities. Sometimes his edge city is so dispersed that there are no clear boundaries, and in other cases the edge cities are so close together that it is not clear where one ends and the other begins. Using this definition, he listed edge cities for 36 urban areas. The New York area contains 17 edge cities and four traditional downtowns. Four additional edge cities appeared to be emerging. The Los Angeles urban area was found to have 16 edge cities, two traditional downtowns, and nine more edge cities that seemed to be emerging. In contrast, the Chicago urban area is very simple. Garreau found only one traditional downtown and four edge cities. No more edge cities appeared to be emerging in the Chicago area.

Other researchers have recognized that most employment in an urban area is rather dispersed, and this fact will frustrate the attempt to delineate precise boundaries for employment centers. For example, Giuliano and Small (1991) showed that 68.0% of all employment in the Los Angeles urban area in 1970 was not located in identifiable employment centers. McDonald (1987) proposed that employment centers be identified as peaks in gross employment density. The idea is that an employment center has a peak gross employment density that is greater than the employment density in the surrounding area. Gross employment density is used rather than net density because it is possible that a high level of net employment density reflects the fact that a small amount of land has been devoted to employment. Giuliano and Small (1991) agreed with this criterion and added the proviso that total employment must exceed some critical value; they define an employment center as a set of contiguous tracts that each have a minimum of density of at least 10 employees per acre and together have at least 10,000 employees. There seems to be agreement that a local peak in gross employment density serves as a reasonable criterion for establishing the location of an employment center. Researchers such as Craig and Ng (2001) and McMillen (2001) have used this idea to propose more complicated procedures that take into account the overall trend in employment density in an urban area. The idea behind these procedures is that the size of the local peak that qualifies an area for status as an employment center is higher in areas with generally high levels of density.

Giuliano and Small (1991) used these criteria and identified 29 employment centers in the Los Angeles urban area outside the CBD in 1980. The largest of these centers is located about 10 miles west of downtown Los Angeles and had employment of 176,000. The next-largest centers are Santa Monica and Hollywood, and each had employment of about 65,000 in 1980. Another important center, with employment of 59,000, is the Los Angeles Airport area. Guiliano and Small (1991) had data on employment by industry, so they classified the employment centers according to function as follows:

Economic function	Number of centers	Important industries (%)	
Specialized manufacturing	7	Manufacturing	73
Mixed industrial	9	Manufacturing	45
		Service	14
		TCU	11
Mixed service	8	Service	30
		Retail	16
		FIRE	15
Specialized entertainment	2	Service	33
		Entertainment	21
Specialized service	3	Service	57

McMillen (2003) used a similar procedure to identify employment in the Chicago urban area, and used a formal cluster analysis to characterize their employment mix. He finds 32 employment centers outside the CBD in 2000, up from 15 in 1990. The employment centers cluster into categories that are dominated by employment in a single sector. In 2000, there were six employment centers that specialized in manufacturing; four in retail; 10 in services; five in transportation, communication, and utilities; one in FIRE; and six in government employment. These studies show that employment centers differ widely in economic function. The number of centers that specialize in a small collection of industries suggests that localization economies operate at this level. However, it should be borne in mind that the majority of employment in both Los Angeles and Chicago is not located downtown or in any of these centers.

Research on office rents in employment subcenters had just begun. An excellent study by Sivitanidou (1995) shows that office rent in the employment subcenters in the Los Angeles urban area varies systematically with the characteristics of the subcenter. Office rent declines with distance to the central business district, the nearest airport, and distance to the Pacific Ocean (i.e., distance to the beach). Office rent is higher if the subcenter has better access to freeways, lower crime, and more retail space. Holding other factors constant, office rents are also influenced by the degree of land-use regulation. A more severe limitation on the height of buildings (or on the permissible ratio of floor area to land area) leads to a higher office rent. The limitation on building height restricts the supply of office space in the subcenter so office rents are higher.

Subcenters are not entirely a new phenomenon. McDonald and McMillen (1990) identified four employment centers in the Chicago urban area in 1956. All four were centers of manufacturing and related distribution activities, and all four were inside or close to the boundaries of Chicago. Figures 7.9–7.12 show McMillen and Lester's (2003) maps depicting the evolution of Chicago's subcenters over time. In 1970, Chicago had nine subcenters. These included an area around O'Hare Airport, education centers in Evanston and Hyde Park, and several large manufacturing districts. Over time, more and more of Chicago's employment has been concentrated in suburban employment centers. By 2000, it is sometimes unclear where one subcenter starts and another stops. The area around O'Hare Airport has very large concentrations of jobs, and even quite distant suburbs have high-density areas that qualify as subcenters.

What determines the number of subcenters in an urban area? Theoretical studies by authors such as Anas and Kim (1996) and Fujita and Ogawa (1982) suggest that subcenters

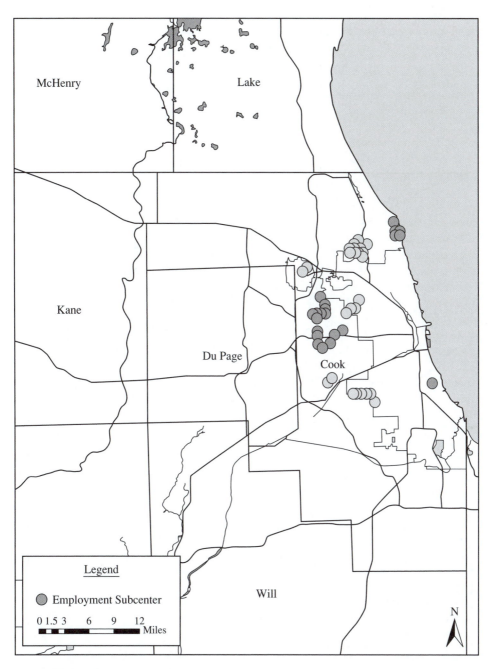

McHenry

Lake

Kane

Du Page

Cook

Will

Legend

● Employment Subcenter

0 1.5 3   6   9   12
▬▬▬▬▬▬▬▬ Miles

N

Figure 7.9   Employment centers in 1970
Source: Reprinted from *Journal of Urban Economics*, vol. 3, Daniel McMillen and Stefani Smith,
"The Number of Subcenters in Large Urban Areas," pp. 321–38, 2003, with permission from Elsevier

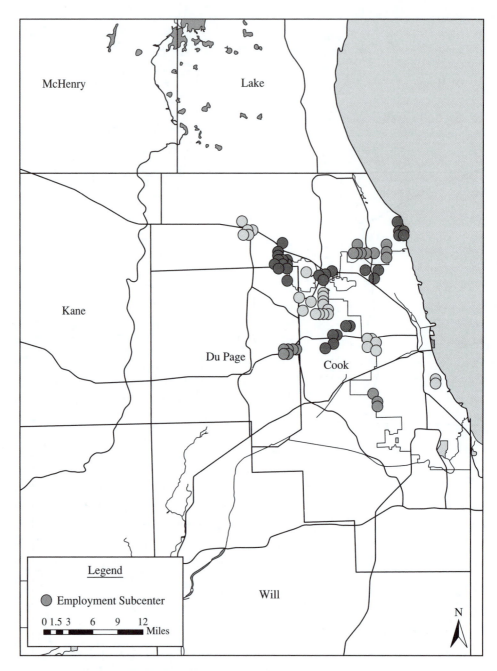

Figure 7.10 Employment centers in 1980
Source: Reprinted from *Journal of Urban Economics*, vol. 3, Daniel McMillen and Stefani Smith,
"The Number of Subcenters in Large Urban Areas," pp. 321–38, 2003, with permission from Elsevier

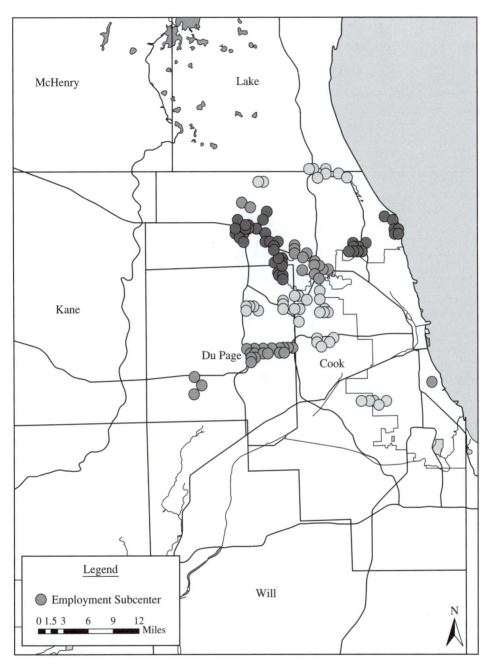

Figure 7.11 Employment centers in 1990
Source: Reprinted from *Journal of Urban Economics*, vol. 3, Daniel McMillen and Stefani Smith,
"The Number of Subcenters in Large Urban Areas," pp. 321–38, 2003, with permission from Elsevier

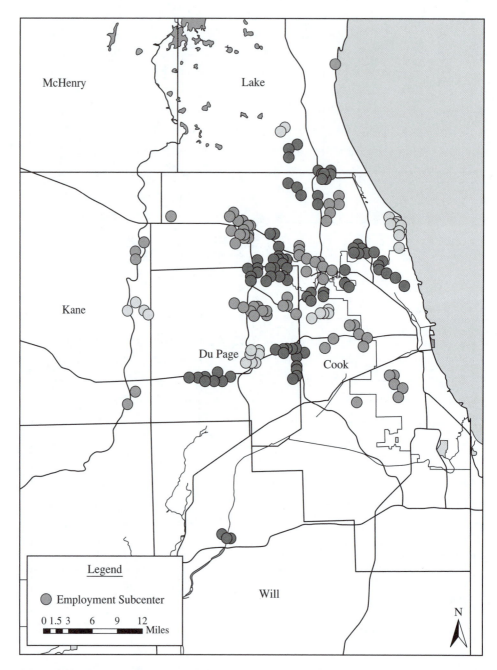

Figure 7.12 Employment centers in 2000
Source: Reprinted from *Journal of Urban Economics*, vol. 3, Daniel McMillen and Stefani Smith, "The Number of Subcenters in Large Urban Areas," pp. 321–38, 2003, with permission from Elsevier

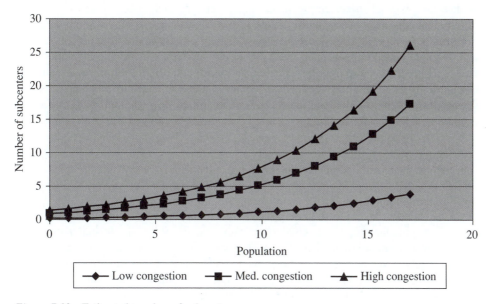

Figure 7.13   Estimated number of subcenters
Source: McMillen and Smith (2003)

will tend to form when an urban area gets large enough and levels of congestion are bad enough that firms find it worthwhile to leave the central business district and form employment concentrations in the suburbs. Subcenters offer several advantages to firms. They allow the firm to pay lower wages to workers who live close by because commuting costs are lower for these workers. They offer significantly lower land prices than the central business district. However, the advantage of the CBD is that it offers significant agglomeration economies. Subcenters are a middle ground – lower land prices, commuting costs, and wages than the CBD, but at least some degree of agglomeration economies when compared with non-subcenter suburban sites. McMillen and Smith (2003) identified subcenters in 62 urban areas and used the results to try to predict when a city would begin to form subcenters. Figure 7.13 summarizes their results. According to McMillen and Smith (2003), an urban area with low congestion levels develops its first subcenter when its population reaches 2.68 million and its second subcenter at a population of 6.74 million. Large metropolitan areas with high congestion levels are virtually certain to have a least one subcenter. As predicted by theory, larger urban areas with higher levels of congestion are more likely to have subcenters.

This section has shown that the central business districts of major urban areas are dominated by employment in the FIRE (finance, insurance, and real estate), service, and public sectors. Employment in the CBD has grown as these sectors have grown, and that growth has caused the CBD to spread over a wider area. The CBD in Los Angeles now has a diameter of 5 miles. Large urban areas probably have always had centers of employment outside the CBD. Prior to the 1970s, these other centers were most likely to be manufacturing centers that were partly based on access to the freight railroad system (and/or to the water transportations system). Garreau (1991) pointed out in a popular book a new type of urban employment center has emerged since the 1970s. Garreau called them edge cities because they seem to possess agglomeration economies that are external to the firm that are located there. They are based on immediate access to the highway system and on reasonable access to air transportation. Edge cities contain office-based employment in corporate headquarters, services, and FIRE. Edge cities do not have boundaries that can be clearly defined. It is better to think of edge cities as peaks in gross density. Suburban employment centers are an important new phenomenon, and urban economics are currently working to gain a better understanding of them.

G. Summary

The monocentric city model is a simplification of reality. It uses a simple idea – people will pay a premium to avoid lengthy commutes – to predict the spatial patterns of population and employment density, house prices, land values, building heights, and floor-area ratios. We have seen in these chapters that most of these predictions stand up to empirical testing. Population density, land values, employment density, building heights, and floor-area ratios do tend to decline with distance from the city center. Over time, the functions have flattened and urban areas have become increasingly decentralized as commuting costs have declined. But the central business district still is the largest single employment site in most cities, and it exerts a powerful influence on the spatial layout of urban areas.

We have also presented a discussion of the urban location patterns of various industries. With its concentration of corporate offices, FIRE services, and public employment, downtown remains an important feature of urban areas. Shopping malls and industrial areas are also important parts of the economic geography. However, a relatively new phenomenon is the suburban employment center, based on corporate offices, FIRE, and services. Garreau (1991) has called these new types of centers edge cities, and there is evidence that they possess significant agglomeration economies.

A good criterion for identifying employment centers is a local peak in gross employment density. If employment centers are characterized by economies of agglomeration, bid rents in employment sectors should be high in those locations. High bid rents in employment sectors result in land being allocated to those sectors *and* in high land values and net employment densities. Employment centers with economies of agglomeration should therefore be characterized by high levels of gross employment density.

Appendix 1 to Chapter 7: A Mathematical Model of Bid Rent

Proximity to an employment center that possesses agglomeration economics will lead to higher land values and levels of employment density. The next step in the analysis is the proposition that proximity to such an employment center increases the bid rent offered by firms in the relevant industries. The purpose of this appendix is to develop a mathematical model of bid rent that has this implication. Your first reaction to this purpose might be something like: "Aren't you doing it backwards? You are purposely setting up a model that has the implication you are seeking. Isn't it better to set up a model using the best assumption that you can muster and see where it leads?" If you were to say all of this, you would be correct. However, economists do what is done in this appendix all the time. The idea is to find one set of assumptions that leads to a particular conclusion. The next step is to determine whether these assumptions are correct.

Consider firms in a competitive industry in an urban area that produces a good or service that is sold for a price of p^*. This price does not vary by location within the urban area. If the good or service is exported outside the urban area, the assumption of a constant output price is based on ubiquitous interurban transportation (e.g., trucking) at a constant price. If the good is consumed locally, a constant output price is justified by assuming that the consumers are highly mobile and eliminate any price differences.

The critical assumption in the model is on the production (supply) side. Assume that output (value added) is a function of two inputs, labor and land, *and* distance to a central point, or

$$Q = f(E, L, x)$$

where Q is the output, E the labor, L the land, and x the distance to the central point. The central point may be the central business district or one of the of Garreau's (1991) edge cities. It is assumed that greater distance to the central point reduces output, holding other inputs constant. In other words, inputs are more productive if the firm is located closer to the central point. The central point is a center of information about markets and technology and provides legal, financial, and other services. Proximity to these intermediate inputs (purchased and unpurchased) makes the primary inputs more productive.

The production function can assume many forms. One convenient form with which you are familiar is the Cobb–Douglas function, which for this model shall be written

$$Q(x) = A(x)E^\alpha L^{1-\alpha}.$$

Here output is a function of x, distance to the central point, through a shift term $A(x)$. It is assumed that $dA(x)/dx < 0$, so that, holding other inputs constant,

$$\frac{dQ(x)}{dx} < 0$$

Now the bid-rent function can be derived. The firms are in a competitive industry, so it is assumed that each firm will make only a normal profit in the long run. Economic profits are zero, so a bid-rent function shall be derived for this level of profit. Recall from Chapter 4 that there is a bid-rent function for each level of profit, but in this case only one bid-rent function is relevant in the long run. If economic profits for a particular period of time are zero, total revenue minus total cost is zero:

$$p^*Q(x) = wE + v(x)L,$$

where w is the wage rate and v is the cost of using land for one time period. Note that v is assumed to be a function of x but w is not. The bid-rent function is derived by increasing distance to the central point, holding total revenue equal to total cost. This derivation is accomplished mathematically by considering a marginal change in x as follows:

$$p^*\left(\frac{dQ}{dx}\right) = L\left(\frac{dv}{dx}\right).$$

The firms change their offer price for the use of land as distance to the central point increases according to

$$\frac{dv}{ds} = p* \frac{(dQ/dx)}{L} < 0$$

Bid rent declines with distance to the central point because the productivity of the inputs declines with that distance (i.e., because dQ/dx is less that zero from the discussion above).

The model in this appendix has demonstrated the following conclusion. If agglomeration economies at a central point enhance the productivity of the primary inputs, and if the effect of those agglomeration economies declines with distance to the central point, bid rent offered by the relevant industries also declines with distance to the central point. The industries that are relevant are, of course, the ones that benefit from the agglomeration economies. Is this a reasonable model? The model seems to be sensible in light of the discussion of agglomeration economies in Chapter 3, but it needs to be tested empirical.

Appendix 2 to Chapter 7:
Economic Analysis of Employment Density

Employment density has been used as an important indicator of the spatial patterns in an urban area in both Chapter 5 and in this chapter. This section presents an economic model of production on urban land that leads to some propositions concerning employment density. Land is at the heart of urban economics. The study of location patterns within an urban area requires that the production function introduced in the appendix at the end of the book be amended to include land.

The usual production function used in economics considers output to be a function of labor and capital inputs. Output is measured as value added, so intermediate inputs are ignored. However, land is one of the basic inputs (along with labor and capital) that produces value added. The simplest approach might be to add land as an input in the usual production function, and write

$$Q = f(N,K,L)$$

where labor is N, capital is K, and land is L. However, this specification ignores the special relationship that land has with some of the capital. In particular, some capital is in the form of structures (buildings) that are constructed on the land. The rest of the capital consists of equipment (machines, computers, telephones, trucks, etc.) and inventories that can be moved around fairly easily. In fact, buildings and land are normally called real estate. There are separate markets for buildings and the land upon which the buildings are situated called real estate markets. Here we are interested in the markets for commercial and industrial real estate.

This line of argument suggests that the basic inputs used by a firm are labor, equipment capital, structure capital, and land. Furthermore, structure capital and land can be grouped together and called real estate. Therefore, the production function can be written as

$$Q = f(R,N,E),$$

where R is real estate, E is the equipment capital, and N is the labor, as above. The input real estate is itself a function of structure capital and land, or

$$R = g(S,L).$$

Structure capital is S and L is land, as above. This production function for real estate requires that you stretch your imagination a bit and suppose that there is some commodity called real estate that is bought and sold in the real estate market. You must imagine that along an isoquant, there are various combinations of structure capital and land that produce the same amount of this thing called real estate. A couple of examples may help.

A simple case is real estate to be used for parking cars. You wish to provide parking for 250 cars. This can be done with a parking lot that is covered by asphalt – a lot of land and vary little capital. Alternatively, a two-story parking garage can be built that uses a lot more capital and about 50% as much land. Or, a three-story parking garage can be built with even more capital and even less land. All three options provide parking for 250 cars. The story can be retold using office buildings that house office workers. There are alternative combinations of land and capital that house the same number of workers. Taller buildings can also be built to conserve on the use of land in the retailing or in the manufacturing sectors as well. However, one suspects that it is easier to substitute capital for land in office buildings than in manufacturing facilities or shopping centers. The worlds' tallest buildings are office buildings.

Now you are convinced that real estate is an input. Indeed, real estate is an input into everything! The production of all goods and services requires that workers and their equipment (if any) be located somewhere. That somewhere could be on bare land, or it could be in a 100-story office building. A particularly convenient form for the production function is

$$Q = AR^{\alpha}E^{\beta}N^{1-\alpha-\beta}.$$

This function is known as the Cobb–Douglas production function, and the A term and the exponents in the equation are constant parameters of the function. This production function exhibits constant returns to scale because the exponents of the inputs sum to 1.0. To see this, suppose that all of the inputs are doubled and write

$$A(2R)^{\alpha}(2E)^{\beta}(2N)^{1-\alpha-\beta} = 2AR^{\alpha}E^{\beta}N^{1-\alpha-\beta} = 2Q.$$

The production function for real estate shall also be assumed to be a Cobb–Douglas function of the form

$$R = BS^{\mu}L^{1-\mu}.$$

We are now ready to explore the economics of land-use intensity. Recall from the appendix to the book that to be efficient in its use of inputs, the firm uses inputs so that the ratio of their prices equals the ratio of their marginal products. The prices of the inputs are denoted as follows: w is the price of labor (N), q the price of equipment capital (E), r the price of structure capital (S), and v the price of land.

Consider first equipment capital and labor. The marginal product of equipment capital is

$$MP_E = \frac{\partial Q}{\partial E} = \beta AR^{\alpha}E^{\beta-1}N^{1-\alpha-\beta} = \frac{\beta Q}{E}.$$

Similarly, the marginal product of labor is

$$MP_N = \frac{\partial Q}{\partial N} = (1-\alpha-\beta)AR^{\alpha}E^{\beta}M^{-\alpha-\beta} = \frac{(1-\alpha-\beta)Q}{E}.$$

This ratio of the two marginal products can be found and set equal to the input prices as follows:

$$\frac{MP_E}{MP_N} = \left(\frac{\beta}{1 - \alpha - \beta}\right)\frac{N}{E} = \frac{q}{w}.$$

This equation can be rearranged to read

$$\frac{N}{E} = \left(\frac{1 - \alpha - \beta}{\beta}\right)\frac{q}{w}.$$

In short, the ratio of labor to equipment capital is a constant times the ratio of the price of equipment capital to the wage rate. This result has three important implications. The ratio of labor to equipment rises when the price of equipment rises, and it falls when the wage rises. In addition, the ratio of labor to equipment does *not* depend on the price of real estate, which depends on the prices of structure capital and land. We can say that the decision regarding the ratio of labor to equipment is *separable* from the real estate input.

The production function for real estate can be used to derive the equation for the ratio of structure capital to land. The marginal product of structure capital in the production of real estate is the derivative of R with respect to S:

$$\frac{\partial R}{\partial S} = \mu B S^{\mu-1}L^{1-\mu} = \frac{\mu R}{S}.$$

Similarly, the marginal product of land in the production of real estate is

$$\frac{\partial R}{\partial L} = (1 - \mu)\frac{R}{L}.$$

You should derive this result on your own. Setting the ratio of marginal products equal to the ratio of prices yields

$$\frac{(1 - \mu)R/L}{\mu R/S} = \left(\frac{1 - \mu}{\mu}\right)\frac{S}{L} = \frac{v}{r}.$$

The ratio of structure capital to land is essentially the height of the buildings and is a constant times the ratio of the price of land to the price of structure capital, or

$$\frac{S}{L} = \left(\frac{\mu}{1 - \mu}\right)\frac{v}{r}.$$

One can presume that the price of structure capital does not vary within an urban area, so the height of buildings depends directly on the price of land.

The next step is to derive an equation for employment density. To do this, first substitute the production function for real estate into the production function for output, or

$$Q = A(BS^{\mu}L^{1-\mu})^{\alpha}E^{\beta}N^{1-\alpha-\beta}$$
$$= AB^{\alpha}S^{\alpha\mu}L^{\alpha(1-\mu)}E^{\beta}N^{1-\alpha-\beta}.$$

The marginal product of land is

$$MP_L = \frac{\partial Q}{\partial L} = \alpha(1 - \mu)AB^{\alpha}S^{\alpha\mu}L^{\alpha(1-\mu)-1}E^{\beta}N^{1-\alpha-\beta}$$
$$= \frac{\alpha(1 - \mu)Q}{L}.$$

The ratio of the marginal product of land to the marginal product of labor is set equal to their price ratio, written

$$\frac{MP_L}{MP_N} = \frac{\alpha(1 - \mu)Q/L}{(1 - \alpha - \beta)Q/N} = \frac{v}{w}$$

or

$$\left[\frac{\alpha(1 - \mu)}{1 - \alpha - \beta}\right]\frac{N}{L} = \frac{v}{w}.$$

Net employment density can now be written as

$$\frac{N}{L} = \left[\frac{1 - \alpha - \beta}{\alpha(1 - \mu)}\right]\frac{v}{w} = Z\left(\frac{v}{w}\right),$$

where Z is the collect of constant parameters from the production function collected in the brackets. Note that this is an equation for net employment density because only land used in the production process in question is included in the analysis. The equation says that employment density is a constant times the ratio of the price of land to the wage rate. In natural logarithmic form, the equation is

$$\ln \frac{N}{L} = \ln Z + \ln v - \ln w$$

The equation for net employment density is important because it says that employment density is high where land values are high. Recall from above that the ratio of structure capital to land (i.e., the height of the buildings) is also a direct function of the price of land. As you know from Chapters 5 and 6, land values are high where bid rents are high, and bid rents are high in the central business district because office-based firms find the agglomeration economics of this location advantageous. If Garreau (1991) is correct, edge cities also produce relatively high land values because of agglomeration economies. Appendix 1 of this chapter presented a mathematical model of bid rent with this implication. These high land values produce high levels of net employment density compared to the surrounding areas. In addition, the theory in Chapter 5 says that the use of land will be determined by the market forces expressed through bid rent. The market will allocate land to the highest bidder, so much of the land in the central business district and in the edge cities will be allocated to commercial use (i.e., office buildings). In other words, gross employment density will also be high in the CBD and the edge cities.

Gross employment density can be defined as net employment density times the fraction of land devoted to employment use, or

$$\frac{N}{L}\left(\frac{L}{L_T}\right),$$

where N/L is the net employment density from above, L_T is the total amount of land in the urban zone in question, and L/L_T is the fraction of that land devoted to employment. Both parts of gross employment density are at high levels in the CBD and at the center of an edge city. This theory of employment density is the reason that authors such as Giuliano and Small (1991) and McDonald and McMillen (1990) used data on gross employment density to identify employment centers.

Exercises

1 Suppose the gross population density function for an urban area is estimated to be

$$D(x) = 7,500e^{-0.2x},$$

Where x is distance to downtown.

(a) In this case downtown has an area of zero, so population density has what value at distance zero?

(b) Fill in the following table

Distance	Gross density
0	
1	
2	
4	
10	
	4,000
	1,514

(Hint: the easiest way to do this problem is to use a calculator with a natural log key (LN) and to convert the density function to natural log form.)

2 Select an urban area of your choice and think about its downtown. What has happened to downtown retailing over the long run? Has downtown experienced much growth in office space since the 1970s? Does downtown have a business association that tries to promote the use of downtown? If so, this group can be a useful source of information. Also, you can probably call up the local Chamber of Commerce to obtain some information on these questions. Further, think about the fringe, or outer ring, of downtown. What tends to locate just outside the downtown area proper? Does one find wholesale trade (e.g., fresh meat and produce) and light manufacturing along with old houses. Or does one find new condos? What has been happening to these areas over time?

3 Select an urban area of your choice. Based on your knowledge of where things are, does it have employment subcenters? Where are they in relationship to downtown and to each other? Does the local airport create an agglomeration of employment that is large enough to be called an employment subcenter? Do the employment subcenters you have identified tend to specialize in any particular line of business? For example, is there an older manufacturing center, a newer center of corporate headquarters and research and development, a distribution center (trucking and warehousing), a health care center, and so on? Check Garreau (1991) to see if he included your urban area in his appendix where he lists the edge cities. How might you determine the locations of employment subcenters more systematically?

References

Anas, A. and I. Kim, 1996, "General Equilibrium Models of Polycentric Urban Land Use With Endogenous Congestion And Job Agglomeration," *Journal of Urban Economics*, vol. 40, pp. 232–56.

Brueckner, J. K. and D. A. Fansler, 1983, "The Economics of Urban Sprawl: Theory and Evidence on the Spatial Sizes of Cities," *Review of Economics and Statistics*, vol. 65, pp. 479–82.

Clark, C., 1951, "Urban Population Densities," *Journal of the Royal Statistical Association Series A*, vol. 114, pp. 490–6.

Craig, S. G. and P. Ng, 2001, "Using Quantile Smoothing Splines to Identify Employment Subcenters in a Multicentric Urban Area," *Journal of Urban Economics*, vol. 49, pp. 100–20.

Edmonston, B. and T. Guterbock, 1984, "Is Suburbanization Slowing Down? Recent Trends in Population Deconcentration in US Metropolitan Areas," *Social Forces*, vol. 62, pp. 905–25.

Fujita, M. and H. Ogawa, 1982, "Multiple Equilibria and Structural Transition of Non-Monocentric Urban Configurations," *Regional Science and Urban Economics*, vol. 12, pp. 161–96.

Garreau, J. 1991, *Edge City: Life on the New Frontier.* New York: Doubleday.

Giuliano, G. and K. A. Small, 1991, "Subcenters in the Los Angeles Region," *Regional Science and Urban Economics*, vol. 21, pp. 163–82.

Henderson, J. V., 1986, "Efficiency of Resource Usage and City Size," *Journal of Urban Economics*, vol. 19, pp. 47–70.

Hoover, E. and R. Vernon, 1959, *Anatomy of a Metropolis.* Cambridge, MA: Harvard University Press.

Hoyt, H., 1933, *One Hundred Years of Land Values in Chicago.* Chicago: University of Chicago.

McDonald, J. F., 1975, "Some Causes of the Decline of Central Business District Retail Sales in Detroit," *Urban Studies*, vol. 12, pp. 229–33.

McDonald, J. F., 1979, *Economic Analysis of an Urban Housing Market.* New York: Academic Press.

McDonald, J. F., 1987, "The Identification of Urban Employment Subcenters," *Journal of Urban Economics*, vol. 21, pp. 242–58.

McDonald, J. F., 1986, "The Intensity of Land Use in Urban Employment Sectors: Chicago 1956–1970," *Journal of Urban Economics*, vol. 18, pp. 261–77.

McDonald, J. F., 1989, "Econometric Studies of Urban Population Density: A Survey," *Journal of Urban Economics*, vol. 26, pp. 361–85.

McDonald, J. F., 1992, "Assessing the Development Status of Urban Areas," in E. S. Mills and J. F. McDonald (eds.), *Sources of Metropolitan Growth.* New Brunswick, NJ: Center for Urban Policy Research, Rutgers University.

McDonald, J. F. and D. P. McMillen, 1990, "Employment Subcenters and Land Values in a Polycentric Urban Area: The Case of Chicago," *Environment and Planning A*, vol. 22, pp. 1561–74.

McMillen, D. P., 1996, "One Hundred Fifty Years of Land Values in Chicago: A Nonparametric Approach," *Journal of Urban Economics*, vol. 40, pp. 100–24.

McMillen, D. P., 2001, "Nonparametric Employment Subcenter Identification," *Journal of Urban Economics*, vol. 50, pp. 448–73.

McMillen, D. P. and T. W. Lester, 2003, "Evolving Subcenters: Employment and Population Densities in Chicago, 1970–2020," *Journal of Housing Economics*, vol. 12, pp. 60–81.

McMillen, D. P. and J. F. McDonald, 1990, "A Two-Limit Tobit Model of Suburban Land Use Zoning," *Land Economics*, vol. 66, pp. 272–82,

McMillen, D. P. and S. C. Smith, 2003, "The Number of Subcenters in Large Urban Areas," *Journal of Urban Economics*, vol. 53, pp. 321–38.

Noyelle, T. and T. Stanback, Jr., 1983, *The Economic Transformation of American Cities.* Totowa, NJ: Rowan & Allanheld.

Sivitanidou, R., 1995, "Urban Spatial Variations in Office-Commercial Rents: The Role of Spatial Amenities and Commercial Zoning," *Journal of Urban Economics*, vol. 38, pp. 23–49.

Part III

Urban Housing and Real Estate

Chapter 8

Housing in Urban Areas

A. Introduction

Housing bulks large in the household budget, and it occupies more space in urban areas than anything else. According to the *Economic Report of the President*, in 2002 housing expenditures, including the imputed rent of owner-occupied houses, were $1,145 billion, 15.5% of all personal consumption expenditures. The costs of household operation (electricity, gas, insurance, etc.) were $408 billion, another 5.5% of total consumption. Furniture and other household equipment added another $324 billion (4.4% of total consumption). All together, the expenses related to the home amounted to 25.4% of all consumption expenditures. Neidercorn and Hearle (1963) examined studies of land use in 48 urban areas and found that, on average, 29.6% of all land and 39.0% of developed land in an urban area is the spatial pattern of its housing stock.

Table 8.1 offers a snapshot of housing in the 322 metropolitan areas in 2003. There were 93 million housing units at that time. Of those 93 million units: 8.7% were vacant, 60.1% were owner-occupied, 30.7% were occupied by renters, 37.6% were located in central cities and 62.4% in suburbs, and 66.4% of occupied units were owner-occupied and 68.7% of owner-occupied units had mortgage loans.

Table 8.1 provides data for owner-occupied and rental units located in both central cities and suburbs. The median size of units in central cities was 1,669 square feet, and the median size in the suburbs was 1,847 square feet. Owner-occupied units were larger than rental units in both locations. The median cost for units in the central cities was $678 per month, and the figure for the suburbs was $798. Rental units cost less, on average, than owner-occupied units in both locations. Very few housing units were crowded, where crowded is defined as more than 1.0 person per room. More units lacked plumbing for exclusive use than were crowded, but the numbers are still pretty small. In central cities 2.2% of the units lacked plumbing for exclusive use, while 1.4% of suburban units had this deficiency. Vacant units were the most likely to have this plumbing deficiency in both locations. More troubling is the fact that 15% of households in central cities reported that crime was a problem in their neighborhoods (compared to 6% of households in the

Table 8.1   Housing in metropolitan areas: 2003 (units in millions, other data are medians)

	Central cities			Suburbs		
	Total[a]	Occupied own	Occupied rent	Total[a]	Occupied own	Occupied rent
Units	35.0	16.7	14.6	58.1	39.7	14.0
Sq. ft.	1,669	1,766	1,306	1,847	1,906	1,462
Cost/mo.	$678	$748	$642	$798	$961	$726
Mortgage		68%			69%	
Crowded[b]	3.1%	1.8%	5.0%	2.0%	1.2%	5.0%
No plumbing[c]	2.2%	1.3%	2.3%	1.4%	0.8%	1.9%
Crime bothersome	15%	12%	18%	6%	5%	10%
Cost/income	24%	18%	31%	22%	18%	30%
Cost > 30% income	41%	27%	56%	34%	26%	55%
Year built	1961	1962	1961	1975	1976	1973

[a] Vacant units in central cities; 3.7 million units with median square feet of 1,413, 6.1% with no plumbing for exclusive use, median year built of 1958. Vacant units in the suburbs; 4.4 million units with median square feet of 1,462, 4.9% with no plumbing for exclusive use, median year built of 1975.
[b] Crowded is defined as persons per room exceeds 1.0.
[c] Unit does not have plumbing for exclusive use.
Source: American Housing Survey 2003

suburbs). These results show that housing units in urban areas in the United States are large on average, and that few have the basic problems of crowding or lack of plumbing. However, the average cost of housing is rather high, $8,136 per year in central cities and $9,576 per year in the suburbs.

The problem of cost is shown further in Table 8.1. One measure that is used is the ratio of monthly housing cost to monthly income for the household. In the data reported in Table 8.1 all forms of cash income before taxes are included in the definition of income. Welfare payments are counted as well as wages, business income, retirement income, and so on. The survey shows that the median for the ratio of housing cost to income was 24% for households in central cities and 22% for households in the suburbs. However, the median ratio was only 18% for households that owned their homes and 31% (central city) or 30% (suburbs) for renters. Renters clearly are paying a higher percentage of their incomes for housing than are homeowners, and this fact is underscored by the last line in Table 8.1. This line shows the percentage of households who spent more than 30% of their incomes on housing. Over half of renters fall into this category; 56% of central city renters and 55% of suburban renters spent at least 30% of their incomes on housing. The 30% figure is generally used to define a problem with *affordability* of housing. The message in Table 8.1 is now pretty clear. Urban Americans generally have a housing stock of fairly high quality, but housing has a high cost both in absolute terms and relative to income. The apparent high cost of housing relative to income is particularly evident among renters in urban areas.

Be that as it may, the idea of affordability as determined by some ratio of housing cost to current income is a slippery concept that should be used with caution. For one thing, the demand for housing is more properly considered to be a function of income averaged over a period of years rather than just current income. A household's current income can fluctuate around a longer-run average. It is likely that one would always observe some percentage of households with a ratio of housing costs to current income in excess of some figure (such as 30%) even though there is no problem with affordability because no household exceeds the 30% figure in the longer run. For another thing, some households may simply freely choose to spend a high percentage of income (in the longer run) on housing. So long as the children are receiving adequate care and no laws are being broken, why should anyone else care? Indeed, spending a lot of money on housing may have positive external effects on the neighborhood!

The real social problem behind the idea of affordability needs to be defined more precisely. The social problem arises when households with lower incomes over the longer run *must* spend a high fraction of that income on housing to obtain a decent, minimal domicile. The cost of a decent house or apartment is high relative to their ability to pay in the long run. The nature and extent of the problem depends, of course, on the standard for decent housing that is used. Also, local governments play a role in determining the ratio of housing costs to income for low-income households. Nearly all municipal governments in urban areas have ordinances called building codes and housing codes that impose minimal requirements on the housing that can be offered for sale or rent in that jurisdiction. Zoning ordinances often impose minimum lot sizes and other requirements that affect housing. All of these laws can mean that the minimal housing unit set by law costs more than some households with low incomes would choose to spend if left to their own devices. In short, some households would choose to live in housing of relatively low quality, but the municipal government will not permit them to make this choice because of concern for the health and safety of the public and/or an interest in the overall quality of the neighborhood. These matters are examined more fully below.

Housing is a big part of people's lives and a big part of an urban area, but it is also unique among consumer goods in other respects. Housing is potentially *very* durable. A useful life for a house routinely is 70 years, and many last far longer than that. With careful maintenance and periodic modernization, a well-built house can last indefinitely. But misuse and lack of maintenance can also shorten the life of a house. The high degree of durability means that the market for housing is dominated by existing housing units. New construction adds, at most, about 2% to the nation's existing stock of housing in a year, although the housing stock grows more rapidly in urban areas with high growth rates. Housing is also immovable. (Even mobile homes are not moved very much.) When one selects a particular housing unit, a choice of residential location has been made as well. The neighborhood surrounding the house contains neighbors, schools, and many other things that people care about. The analysis of the market for housing in an urban area cannot be divorced from neighborhood factors. Finally, houses and apartments are very complicated commodities that contain numerous features that have value for the consumer. The housing market is a market that is characterized by complicated, highly durable units each of which is located in a neighborhood with many attributes. This statement makes it sound as if each housing unit is unique, and there is considerable truth in that thought. However, it is also true that the housing market functions. Every day houses and apartment buildings are bought and sold, and housing units are rented. How do the actors in the housing market simplify things so that transactions can be made on a routine basis?

B. Appraisal and the Determination of Housing Values

One good way to understand the housing market is to examine the process through which a house is sold. This section provides a brief overview of the functioning of the housing market. Chapters 10–11 provide lengthier discussions of the details on the operation of the market for housing. A course in real estate is recommended for those who are interested in learning more about real estate markets. The appraisal of house value is part of the sale process.

The owner who decides to sell a house typically will contact a real estate broker, a person who operates a business that specializes in selling houses. A listing contract is drawn up between the seller and the broker. This contract stipulates the price that the seller is willing to accept, the fee that the broker will receive when the house is sold, and the time limit on the contract. The broker's commission is usually 6% of the sale price and is paid by the seller. It is important to remember that the real estate broker is working on behalf of the *seller*. The broker employs real estate agents who engage in marketing activities designed to sell the house.

Potential buyers contact the broker or his or her agents. If a potential buyer wishes to make an offer to the seller, a contract for sale is drawn up. This contract stipulates the price to be paid, the date at which ownership will be transferred and payments made, and several other terms and conditions for the sale. The potential buyer signs the proposed contract, thereby accepting the offer, or draw up another proposed contract that is a counterproposal. Because contracts for the sale of real estate are rather complex documents with many provisions, there are many opportunities for the parties to bargain. Eventually, the buyer and the seller agree on a set of terms, and the contract for sale is signed by both parties.

The most important term in the contract for sale, the price, is determined by the bargaining process. The original listing contract included a price that the seller was willing to accept, and this figure was probably based on the broker's comparative market analysis of the property (plus a little more added on, perhaps). The broker is familiar with the current market prices for houses in the area, so the seller will normally defer to the broker's expertise. The buyer may base an offer on information provided by the broker, or he may hire someone else to perform a comparative market analysis that can serve as the basis for an offer. Recall that the broker is working for the seller and is paid a commission that is larger the higher is the selling price.

In most cases the next step is the arrangement of financing by the buyer. The typical buyer must arrange for a home loan from a financial situation such as a savings and loan association or a bank. Conventional home loans usually require a down payment of 20% of the purchase price, so a loan of 80% of the price is a standard financing package. However, some government home loan programs permit the buyer to make a down payment that is far less than 20% of the price. These programs are discussed in the next chapter.

The basic contract for a home loan, a mortgage contract, stipulates that if the buyer fails to make the required payments on the loan, the financial institution can *foreclose*. Foreclosure means that the financial institution has assumed ownership of the property for the purpose of selling it to recover the amount loaned. Before the financial institution offers a loan to a buyer, a formal appraisal of the value of the property is conducted. An appraisal is an estimate of the market value of the property if it were to be sold under normal conditions. The appraisal will tell the financial institution whether the price as set by the buyer and seller is reasonable and therefore whether the financial institution will be able to recovery its money if a foreclosure becomes necessary. The appraisal is performed by an appraiser, a professional who specializes in this kind of work. The basic idea is to gather data on three houses that have been sold recently that are also comparable to the subject house. The selling price of each "comparable" is adjusted up or down for any differences between it and the subject house. For example, if the comparable property is larger that the subject house by 100 square feet, the price of the comparable is adjusted *downward* by the market value of 100 square feet to make it more identical to the subject property. The techniques used in appraisal are discussed in Chapter 10.

The last step in the process of selling the house is the closing. At the closing the deed, the document that is evidence of legal title is transferred from the seller to the buyer. The buyer's lender pays the seller, and the buyer writes a check for his or her part of the price (and any other expenses). The buyer also signs the mortgage contract. The seller pays off the balance on any loans that were outstanding on the property and walks away with the selling price minus the final loan payment and any expenses (including the broker's commission).

C. Owning versus Renting and Discrimination in Mortgage Lending

We saw in Table 8.1 that 66.4% of occupied housing units in urban areas are owner-occupied – and that 33.6% are rented. The percentage rented in central cities is 46.6%. Households must make the basic decision whether to own or rent the housing unit. This section presents the economics of the decision to own or rent, and then turns to the matter of discrimination in access to the credit needed to become a homeowner. While there are good economic reasons to be a renter rather than an owner, housing researchers have found consistently that minority households face some discrimination in access to mortgage financing. This section concludes with a brief review of these findings, based on the comprehensive study by Ross and Yinger (2002).

In order to consider the own versus rent decision, assume that a household can either own or rent identical houses. One is for sale, and the other is for rent. The real economic costs of both units are the same. The difference in the cost of the two units has two sources; there is a substantial "transaction" cost associated with purchasing a home, and the federal income tax law treats homeowners and renters differently. Home purchase typically costs about 10% of the price of the house (including 6% to the real estate brokers – half of that to the listing broker and half to the selling broker), but federal taxes favor homeowners. Owning is cheaper than renting if the household lives in the house long enough so that the transactions cost is spread out over time.

The federal income tax permits homeowners to deduct from income the amounts paid in local property taxes and mortgage interest. Suppose that V is the value of the house and t is the annual real estate tax rate as a percentage of house value. For simplicity assume that the homeowner borrows 100% of the value of the house at interest rate r. The real economic cost of the house per year is

$$C = tV + rV + dV,$$

where d is the annual cost of maintenance and depreciation. A landlord would have to set annual rent at this level to cover costs. Assume that the homeowner faces federal income tax rate T. Because both property taxes and mortgage interest are deductible, the annual cost of the house to a homeowner is

$$C_O = (1 - T)tV + (1 - T)rV + dV.$$

The property taxes paid are still tV, of course, but the homeowner gets to reduce the federal tax payment by TtV. The point is identical for mortgage interest payments. Consequently, the favorable income tax treatment reduces the cost of homeownership by

$$C - C_O = (t + r)TV.$$

A typical property tax rate is 2.5% of house value, and current mortgage interest rates are about 6%. Many homeowners face a federal tax rate of 35%, so the saving from being a homeowner is about 3% of house value per year for such a household. If maintenance and depreciation are about 2.5% per year, the real economic cost per year is 11% of house value per year. This would mean that homeowners save 27% of the annual cost because of the favorable tax treatment. Given that the transaction cost of becoming a homeowner is 10% of house value, it will be cheaper to own rather than rent if the household lives in the house for more than 10% divided by 3% equals 3.33 years.

Homeownership has advantages besides the favorable tax treatment. It is the most widely used method for accumulating wealth, and it also gives the household access to the best communities with good public services such as schools. The ability of a household to become a homeowner is closely linked with its access to mortgage credit. Lack of access to mortgage credit can therefore have serious negative consequences for the household. Ross and Yinger (2002, p. 2) note that there are large ethnic differences in homeownership rates. In 2001 74.3% of white households owned their homes, but only 47.7% of African American and 47.3% of Hispanic households were owners. This gap is caused by many factors other than discrimination, such as income differences, differences in credit risk, and so on. However, careful research has documented the existence of discrimination in access to mortgage credit.

Concern about discrimination and possible "red-lining" led to the adoption of the Home Mortgage Disclosure Act (HMDA) in 1975. Red-lining is the practice of drawing red lines on the map of a city to define areas in which a bank would not provide mortgage loans. The original HMDA required lenders to report the location of mortgage applications and the disposition of those applications. HMDA was amended in 1989 to require that lenders provide information on the race and ethnicity of each applicant. This requirement means that lenders now disclose the loan approval rates by racial and ethnic group and by location as well. These data enable researchers to study possible discrimination in lending in much greater depth. The most extensive study was conducted by researchers at the Boston Federal Reserve Bank, and published as Munnell, et al. (1996). This study of mortgage lending in the Boston metropolitan area combined HMDA data with detailed records from loan applications that were provided by the lenders. The study pertains to the year 1990, and includes a sample of about 3,000 loan applications, including 1,200 applications from African American and Hispanic households. The study found that, controlling for a large number of variables that are thought to influence the decision to approve an application, the loan denial rate was 8.2% higher for African American and Hispanic applicants than for white applicants. The denial rate was 10% for white applicants, so the denial rate for these minority applicants was 82% greater than for whites. In response to numerous critics of the Boston Fed study, Ross and Yinger (2002) conducted an extensive review of the data and the empirical methods, and concluded that the denial rate for minority applicants was 5.6% to 7.7% greater than for whites. In short, Ross and Yinger (2002) confirmed the Boston Fed results reported by Munnell et al. (1996) that discrimination exists that cannot be justified by rational underwriting standards. The results obtained by Ross and Yinger (2002), and other researchers too, suggest that the enforcement of anti-discrimination laws is insufficient at this time. This issue remains unresolved.

D. What Is Housing?

Any study of housing begins with the definition of what housing is. The literature is organized around two definitions. At one end of the spectrum, Richard Muth (1969) defined housing as a bundle of services that is produced by stocks of housing capital and land, and defined the price of housing as the expenditure needed to purchase a standardized quantity of those services. In effect, Muth collapsed housing to a unidimensional service. At the other end of this spectrum is the idea from Lancaster (1966) and Rosen (1974) that housing is fundamentally a multi-dimensional product. Households value goods according to their characteristics, and market demands and supplies of characteristics determine the particular bundles bought and sold at any given place and time. These two somewhat opposing models might be called the House of Lancaster/Rosen and the House of Muth. The House of Muth has many uses, and (as we shall see in Chapter 9) is the basis for conventional studies of the income and price elasticities of demand for housing as well as studies of supply elasticity, population density patterns, and patterns of land-use intensity. The House of Muth was the basic model used in Chapters 5–7. The House of Lancaster/Rosen has led to literally hundreds of statistical studies of house values and a revolution in the methods used by real estate appraisers and tax assessors. Let us further consider the House of Lancaster/Rosen. The appendix to this chapter provides a theoretical discussion of this model.

Suppose that you work as an appraiser of residential property and the files in your office contain data on hundreds of sales. Suppose also that you had a statistics course in college. Your job is to estimate the market value of a subject house given its location and the attributes of the house and lot. Most likely it would occur to you that the data base in your office could be used to estimate a statistical model of house prices that would make your job easier. You know the attributes, locations, and selling prices of many properties. You might also have data on the important features of the neighborhood in which each house is located. All of this information can then be used to estimate an equation that can be used to predict the price of a subject house. The statistical model of house prices estimated using such a database is called a *hedonic model*, a term derived from the word *hedonism*, which is the idea that one should pursue pleasure. The idea is that a house consists of numerous components that add to one's pleasure, and that each of these components has a price. The market price of the house is the sum of the market prices of its component. Consider a very simple model of house value in which the components are the size of the house (interior square feet), the size of the lot (exterior square feet), and the proximity to employment. The market value of houses (V) can be specified as a linear equation

$$V = a_0 + a_1 F + a_2 L + a_3 x + e,$$

where F is the number of square feet of interior space, L the number of square feet of exterior space, x the distance to employment, and e is a random error term. The coefficient a_1 is the market value of an additional square foot of interior space, a_2 the market value of a square foot of exterior space, and a_3 the reduction in value that is associated with greater distance from employment. The random error term reflects the fact that the three variables do not completely account for variations in the value of houses. Each house in the database has its own individual error term, which is a collection of other influences on value that are not included in the equation.

Suppose you use the multiple regression program that came with the computer in your office to estimate the foregoing linear model of house prices. You have just finished this task when a client walks in the door and asks you to appraise a house with 1,500 square feet of interior space on a lot that is 50 by 100 feet and located 5 miles from the CBD. It takes you about 2 minutes to compute an estimate of market value $V*$ as

$$V* = a_0 + a_1(1,500) + a_2(5,000) + a_3(5).$$

Appraisers are not permitted to perform appraisals in this manner. They must follow the procedure discussed in Chapter 10. However, hedonic models are useful tools for appraisers because they indicate the market value of particular attributes. For example, suppose that the subject property and the comparable properties used for appraisal purposes differ in the amount of interior space they provide. The estimated coefficient a_1 tells you the magnitude of the adjustment to the price of the comparable property that is needed in the standard appraisal. Another use of hedonic models is for property tax assessment. The task of the county tax assessor is to determine an assessed value for every house in the county. Many assessors estimate a hedonic model based on a sample of houses and then use it to "predict" the market value of all the houses in the county. Assessed value is then based on this predicated market value.

Scores of hedonic studies of house prices have been published in academic and professional journals. A study is deemed worthy of publication if it adds something to our knowledge of the determinants of housing values, but they all include a fairly standard list of variables. Most hedonic studies of house prices use an exponential function rather than a linear function of the form

$$V = \exp(a_0 + a_1 F + \ldots + a_n X + e),$$

where $\exp(\cdot)$ means that the base of the natural logarithms is taken to the power shown in parentheses. The natural log of the price is then the dependent variable in a linear hedonic model of the form

$$\ln V = a_0 + a_1 F + \ldots + a_n X + e.$$

This log-linear equation usually fits the data better than does the conventional linear equation in which V is the dependent variable. Recalling the discussion from Chapter 5, the coefficients in the log-linear model (a_1 to a_n) indicate the *percentage* change in V associated with a change in the independent variable.

A typical example of such a study is one by McMillen and McDonald (2004) of houses on the southwest side of Chicago sold in the late 1990s. Data were provided by the county tax assessor and the US Bureau of the Census. Other studies are based on data provided by the local realtors' multiple listing service (MLS). The results obtained by McMillen and McDonald (2004) are shown in Table 8.2. The mean selling price for

Table 8.2 Hedonic model of house values: southwest side of Chicago in 1997–1999 (dependent variable is natural log of selling price)

Variable	Mean	Price effect
Selling price	$116,000	
Building area	1,060 sq. ft.	0.25% for 1% increase
Lot area	3,670 sq. ft.	0.22% for 1% increase
Age	59 years	−0.5% per year
Bedrooms	2.61	2.1% per room
Over one story	0.18	−7.8% compared to 1 story
Masonry construction	0.60	2.1% compared to frame
Basement	0.68	−1.0% (not stat. significant)
Finished basement	0.18	2.8%
Attic	0.46	0.1% (not stat. significant)
Finished attic	0.11	4.2%
Central air conditioning	0.12	−0.9% (not stat. significant)
Garage, one car	0.31	5.7%
Garage, two cars	0.45	7.4%
Proportion Hispanic	24%	−0.5% per 1% increase
Proportion black	6%	−0.5% per 1% increase
Near transit line	0.04	−3.3% within 1/8 mile
Distance to downtown	7.2 miles	4.7% per mile
Distance to transit station	0.8 miles	−9.8% per mile

Source: Table compiled from data obtained from McMillen and McDonald (2004)

houses in the sample was $116,000. The average house has 1,060 square feet of interior space and a lot area of 3,670 square feet (e.g., 30 feet wide and 125 feet deep), and was 59 years old. This is an inner city area with older, smaller houses on relatively small lots. Most of the houses are one story.

The results show that an increase in interior space of 10% (106 square feet, on average) increased the selling price by 2.5% (i.e., $2,900). A 10% increase in lot size (367 square feet) increased the price by 2.2%. The selling price was reduced by 0.5% for each additional year of age. An additional bedroom added only 2.1% to the price, but remember that this holds constant the total interior space of the house. The market attached 7.8% higher value to one-story houses compared to two-story (or taller) houses, Masonry construction added 2.1% to value, compared to frame construction. The presence of an unfinished basement or attic added nothing to the value, but a finished basement and a finished attic added 2.8 and 4.1% to value, respectively. A garage added to value – 5.7% for a one-care garage and 7.4% for a two-car garage.

The results for the southwest side of Chicago also show that prices were somewhat lower in minority neighborhoods: 0.5% lower as either the percentage of Hispanic or black population increased by 1%. Reasons for this finding are discussed in the next section. The study shows that proximity to the stations of a new rapid-transit line increased selling price, but that houses adjacent to the line itself were lower in price. Access to stations is a good thing, but a location next to the line is not good – because of its noise and relatively unattractive appearance. Finally, McMillen and McDonald (2004) found that selling prices increase with distance to downtown by 4.7% per mile. Here the results are probably reflecting positive housing and/or neighborhood features that increase with distance to downtown, but are not measured in the study. This idea was introduced in Chapter 6

E. Housing Prices, Neighborhood Characteristics, and Racial Segregation

In the preceding section we established that the price of a house reflects the attributes of the house and lot and the characteristics of the neighborhood in which the house is located. The price is established through the process of negotiation between buyer and seller, but there is no sale unless the buyer makes a bid. Buyers base their bids on many factors, and the purpose of this section is to discuss the neighborhood characteristics that influence bids. This section also introduces the idea that different types of households may make different bids for the same property. Not everyone places the same value on a given bundle of attributes and neighborhood characteristics. As in Chapter 5, the household with the highest bid occupies the property. If there are systematic differences in the bids made by different types of households, there will be clustering of households of particular types.

What neighborhood factors have been found to influence the selling price of a house? No doubt the following list is not complete, but its length gives you some idea of how many variables seem to matter to people. These variables have been found to have a statistically significant impact on the selling price of houses in at least one study:

1   quality of local school (positive effect);
2   crime rate in area (negative effect);
3   property tax rate (negative effect);
4   neighborhood income, size of houses in neighborhood, etc. (positive effect);
5   air pollution (negative effect);
6   airport noise (negative effect);
7   proximity to contaminated areas (negative effect);
8   proximity of nuclear power plant (negative effect);
9   proximity to a park (positive effect);
10   industrial noise (negative effect);
11   heavy traffic on street (negative effect);
12   location in a floodplain (negative effect);
13   distance to employment (negative effect);
14   distance to shopping (negative effect);
15   distance to airport (negative effect);
16   rating of the quality of houses next door and on the block (positive effect);
17   within walking distance of public transit or commuter rail station (positive effect);
18   adjacent to rail line, highway, or transit line (negative effect);
19   proximity to highway interchange (positive effect);
20   proximity to a church (negative effect);
21   existence of zoning or restrictive covenants versus their absence (positive effect);
22   previous price increase in neighborhood, to capture expectation of future price increases (positive effect).

This is a pretty bewildering list of variables. Each variable makes sense individually, but how can a person possibly take all of these factors into account in formulating a bid for a house, or for that matter, in doing an empirical study of house values? It is fair to say that researchers in the field are busy making the list longer rather than shorter. The typical study will gather data on selling prices, include several attributes of the house and lot, and measure a few neighborhood characteristics. The focus of the study will usually be on some neighborhood characteristic that has not previously been studied, and the results of the study will be published because a statistically significant result has been obtained for that new variable. This procedure for research settles few issues because no one ever includes *all* of the neighborhood characteristics that have been found to be statistically significant in previous studies. If all of these variables were included, would the addition of another variable add to the explanatory power of the model? This question is difficult to answer, but perhaps it would not.

The individual household obviously cannot take all of these factors into account at once. A sensible procedure is to restrict the search to areas with reasonable access to work where it is known that many potential neighborhood problems do not exist. The household probably specifies a desired set of characteristics in the housing unit itself and a price range, and the real estate agent identifies units that meet these criteria. If a subject house meets the basic criteria, the household will take a look at the neighborhood characteristics that are regarded as most important (e.g., school quality, access to shopping, and the like).

It is worthwhile to understand how the appraiser deals with this problem of the large number of potentially relevant neighborhood characteristics. The appraiser first seeks comparable properties that are in the same neighborhood as the subject property. If comparables must be used from another neighborhood, the appraiser estimates the difference in value attributable to location by use of paired observations from the two neighborhoods. In either case, the appraiser does not need to know anything about the various neighborhood characteristics to do the job. The appraiser relies on the market to do the job for him and whatever the market says will be used.

The foregoing list of neighborhood characteristics is very long, but leaves out the one characteristic that has captured more attention among researchers, and probably among the general public also, than any other. That characteristic is the racial composition of the neighborhood. There is a large and growing body of evidence to support the notion that the demand for housing expressed by white households is influenced by the racial composition of the area in which the house is located. In particular, the importance of the black residential population on white demand has emerged in several studies. It appears that white demand is reduced both by the percentage black population in the area immediately surrounding a house and by proximity to the closest predominantly black neighborhood. Both of these effects arise from racial prejudice, an aversion to an individual member of a racial group regardless of the attributes of that person. Furthermore, there is evidence of discriminatory behavior against blacks that takes the form of exclusion and price discrimination on the part of housing sellers. The purpose of this section is to review some studies of these phenomena.

King and Mieszkowski (1973) first pointed out that it is important to separate the effects of demand and supply factors on racial price differences. If prejudice on the part of white households is the only racial factor operating, the aversion of whites for blacks will lead to supply adjustment, which brings about lower housing prices for blacks than for whites who avoid blacks. However, if housing suppliers discriminate against blacks by limiting access as black demand increases, for example, we may find that blacks pay more than whites for equivalent housing while white demand for housing some areas is reduced by racial prejudice. To untangle these various effects, King and Mieszkowski (1973), in their study of rents in New Haven during 1968–9, examined the rents paid by white and black households in two types of areas, the black interior and the racial boundary, compared to rents paid by whites in the white interior. The results of estimating the hedonic equation show that white rents in the boundary areas were 7% lower than rents in the white interior. Rents paid by blacks in the boundary areas were equal to white interior rents, so there was a 7% difference between white and black rents in the boundary area. This is their estimate of the effect of racial prejudice, the aversion of whites for blacks. Both white and black rents in the black interior were about 9% higher than white interior rents, suggesting limitations on the expansion of the black residential areas during a period of demand growth.

The study by King and Mieszkowski has been followed by a few more studies that separate the depressing effect of black neighbors on white housing demand from the effect of supply restrictions imposed by blacks. One influential study of housing prices in Chicago for 1968–72 by Berry (1976) found that prices were lower in white areas near black and Latino areas than in white areas that were removed from the racial borders. However, Berry (1976) also found that prices were lowest of all in the traditional black and Latino neighborhoods. Prices in the zones of recent black and Latino expansion were about equal to prices in the white border areas. In contrast to the King–Mieszkowski study, the race of the individual household is unknown. What can account for the pattern in Berry's (1976) results?

Berry argued that in the 1950s and early 1960s, the black and Latino population were expanding rapidly, but that the stock of housing available to these groups was expanding slowly because of racial discrimination on the part of white sellers, which was no doubt partly created by the racial prejudice of their neighbors. At this point it is appropriate to recall the image of Martin Luther King leading housing integration marches in Chicago in the summer of 1966. Those marches yielded angry reactions from whites in Chicago.

According to Berry (1976), the situation had changed considerably by the end of the 1960s. Berry (1976) pointed out that 482,000 new housing units were built in the Chicago urban area during the 1960s, but the number of households increased by only 285,000. As a result, 128,000 units were transferred from white to black occupancy and 63,000 units were demolished. The number of black households in the city of Chicago increased by 80,000, while the number of white households declined by 119,000. The Latino population increased by 35,000 households. Berry argued that these massive changes in the racial geography of the city, as the whites relinquished neighborhood after neighborhood to blacks and Latinos, resulted in substantially lower prices for blacks and Latinos than whites in their traditional neighborhoods. This combination of results suggested to Berry that, in effect, the model of white prejudice was operating and that there were no barriers to a rapid increase in the aggregate supply of housing available to blacks and Latinos. The timing of Berry's study is important, because he examined the housing market just after completion of the expressway system in Chicago. Whites were moving to the suburbs in large numbers as new suburban housing was being built. The general effects of new construction are discussed in more detail below.

Smith (1981) strongly questioned Berry's conclusion that blacks and Latinos paid less for housing than did whites. Smith's (1981) study of Chicago housing prices in 1972 found that prices were lower in traditional black areas and zones of recent black expansion than in white interior areas. Also, prices were lowest in the black–white border areas. However, Smith attributes these seeming racial price effects to differences in crucial neighborhood characteristics that Berry failed to take into account properly. In particular, black areas had significantly higher crime rates and levels of air pollution. Smith's general conclusion is that blacks paid less for housing because they purchased housing in inferior neighborhoods. The discussion of racial segregation below suggests that black households do not necessarily prefer the option of lower prices and inferior neighborhoods. Smith even questioned the conclusion that after controlling properly for other neighborhood characteristics, prices are really lower in the black–white border areas. The results in Table 8.2 show the price differential as of the late 1990s on the southwest side of Chicago, but do not explain it.

If the empirical evidence on racial differences in housing prices and rents is somewhat ambiguous, the segregation of the races is not. A book by sociologists Douglas Massey and Nancy Denton (1993) with the title *American Apartheid* documents the degree of segregation in urban areas in America. One measure of segregation is the percentage of blacks who would have to move to achieve an equal percentage of blacks in all census tracts. (Blacks who hypothetically move are hypothetically replaced by whites who move.)

This index of segregation as reported by the US Bureau of the Census on its web site for the top 10 urban areas (as of 2000) for 1980 and 2000 is as follows:

	Segregation index for:	
	1980	*2000*
New York	81.2	81.0
Los Angeles	80.8	66.4
Chicago	87.8	79.7
San Francisco	67.5	60.0
Philadelphia	78.1	73.0
Washington, DC	68.7	62.5
Boston	76.3	65.8
Detroit	87.4	84.6
Dallas–Ft. Worth	77.1	58.7
Houston	75.4	66.3

The average segregation index for 1980 for these 10 urban areas was 78.9, and the average fell to 70.0 in 2000. The segregation index in 1980 was generally smaller in the sunbelt urban areas of Los Angeles, San Francisco, Dallas–Fort Worth, and Houston. The greatest declines in the segregation index occurred in the sunbelt urban areas of Los Angeles and Dallas–Fort Worth. Three of the five largest urban areas of the northeast (New York, Philadelphia, and Detroit) had little change in segregation over these decades.

What are the causes of racial segregation? The study of racial segregation is more within the province of urban sociology than urban economics, and Schwab (1992, ch. 12) provides a good introduction to the topic. A list of the factors that cause racial segregation would include:

1 segregation by social and economic status, caused by tastes for social linkages;
2 segregation related to ethnic group, which may in part stem from the timing of arrival of immigrants to the urban area;
3 segregation caused by active discrimination against certain racial groups;
4 segregation caused by prejudice against certain racial groups.

The first two causes on this list bring about voluntary segregation of groups, but the last two involuntarily segregate the victims of discrimination and prejudice. The studies reviewed by Massey and Denton (1993) indicate that voluntary segregation can explain very little of the high degree of segregation of the black population in urban areas. A study by Miller and Quigley (1990) of the San Francisco urban area found that almost none of the racial segregation in both 1970 and 1980 could be attributed to segregation by type of household (household composition and income).

Segregation through prejudice often involves a process called neighborhood *tipping*. Consider an all-white neighborhood that is adjacent to a black neighborhood. Houses are put up for sale on a regular basis because people change jobs, retire, and so on. The process begins when a black household buys a house in the adjacent all-white neighborhood. The purchase may have been made because of demand growth in the black portion of the housing market. This household may be subjected to racial discrimination and antisocial behavior, or maybe nothing happens. White households continue to buy houses in the neighborhood because they are not influenced by the presence of one black household. However, soon more black households buy homes in the formerly all-white neighborhood. Now some potential white buyers "avoid" this area, and more and more of the houses that are put on the market are sold to black households. What we really mean is that potential white buyers make lower bids than do potential black buyers *because of the presence of blacks in the area*. The *tipping point* is defined as the percentage of houses in the neighborhood occupied by black households at which potential white buyers begin to avoid the area for racial reasons (i.e., make lower bids than potential black buyers). If a neighborhood has crossed the tipping point, transition to a neighborhood that is largely occupied by black households will occur. Some white households may remain, and some white households may purchase homes in the area, but their number will not be great enough to prevent the racial transition.

F. The Filtering Model of the Housing Market

The discussion of racial prejudice, discrimination, and segregation included the idea that new houses were built in the suburbs for white households, and this led to an expansion of the residential areas occupied by minority households, especially black households. Housing researchers have observed that this kind of mechanism is at work in any housing market that includes a variety of both household and housing types. The filtering model of the housing market has been devised to take both types – households and housing units – into account.

The presentation of the model will begin by ignoring location and neighborhood characteristics. This assumption is relaxed later. As a beginning, suppose that all housing units can be arrayed in a hierarchy from best to worst. The array goes from the fanciest mansion to the run-down, single-room apartment. Further, suppose that households are arrayed in order of the amount of housing that they demand. Households with higher incomes demand more housing, so the order of the household in the array will be strongly correlated with income. The housing market assigns each household to a housing unit and determines prices for the various units. Now let us simplify the picture by grouping the households and their assigned housing units according to the quality level of the housing unit. For concreteness, suppose that the housing units are grouped into the top, middle, and bottom thirds. We now have set up a model with markets for three general types of housing units: high-quality units, medium-quality units, and low-quality units. These three markets are interrelated because they are markets for goods that are, to some degree, substitutes.

The basic three-market model is depicted in Figure 8.1. The initial demand functions for high-, medium-, and low-quality units are denoted D_H, D_M, and D_L. The supply of high-quality units initially is H, and M units of medium-quality units are supplied. These supplies are fixed (for the moment), and it is assumed that there are no vacant units in these two markets. The number of low-quality units in the market is L, but the short-run supply curve is S_L, to reflect the fact that the number of units actually offered in the market depends on the housing rent. Given the market demands, the initial equilibrium housing rents are R_H, R_M, and R_L. In addition, the number of vacant units of low-quality housing is $L - Q_L$.

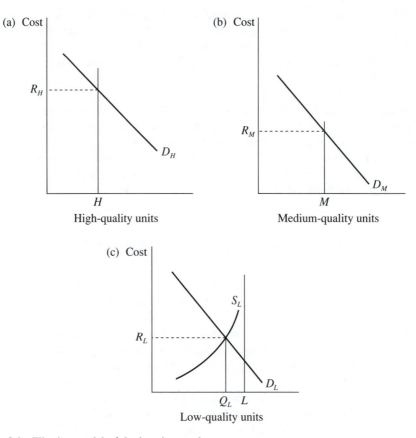

Figure 8.1   Filtering model of the housing market

The model in Figure 8.1 has many uses. Perhaps the standard exercise is to introduce an increase in the supply of high-quality units. Why might this supply increase occur? One possible reason is a reduction in the cost of building these units. The increase in the supply of high-quality units is shown in Figure 8.2 as a shift from H to H^*. Given the demand for high-quality units has not changed, the housing rent must decline from R to R^* so that the additional units will be occupied. Who occupies those units? The obvious candidates are households who occupy medium-quality units. Since high- and medium-quality units are substitutes, the demand curve for medium-quality units shifts to the left (decreases) as the rent in high-quality units falls. In Figure 8.2 the demand for medium-quality units shifts to the left by the increase in high-quality units. The decline in rent in high-quality units must be enough to shift D_M to D_M^*. Some households who occupy units of medium quality move up to high-quality units. What happens next? Housing rents in units of medium quality fall and cause the demand for low-quality units to decrease. Some households who occupy low-quality units move into the vacated medium-quality units. Housing rents in medium-quality units fall to R_M^*. Finally, housing rents in low-quality units fall to R_L^*, and there is an increase in the number of vacant low-quality units equal to the increase in high-quality units.

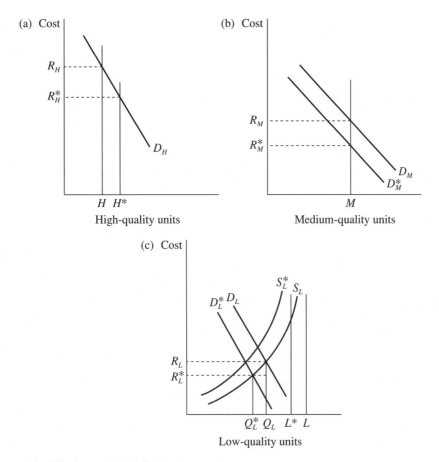

Figure 8.2 Filtering model of the housing market

Note carefully what happened. The increase in high-quality units has set off a series of changes in which all housing rents declined and some households "filtered" up in the quality hierarchy. In fact, the number of households who moved up in quality is, in this case, equal to two times the original increase in high-quality units. This appears to be a good thing for everyone, but what can go wrong? For one thing, the process is initiated by an increase in supply of high-quality units *relative to demand*. The filtering process will not occur if new construction at the top end only matches the growth in high-income households. Furthermore, the results are altered if the number of households can expand in response to lower housing rents. Suppose that some of the households who live in medium-quality units can split into two households. One of these households moves into a vacant high-quality unit and the other household stays put. This can mean that the demand for medium-quality units does not decline at all, and the housing rent for these units does not decline. No occupants of low-quality units move up in quality. This is an extreme example, but the creation of new households from the same population tends to choke off the filtering process.

Next consider the market for low-quality units. The housing rent has declined and the vacancy rate has increased. Do the suppliers of low-quality housing react to these changes? Eventually they will, because a high vacancy rate will mean that some units will be vacant for lengths of time that are too great to make them economically feasible. A unit is no longer economically feasible if the housing rents cannot cover the variable costs of operating the unit as housing. This is the usual decision to shut down a business. Clearly, units will be withdrawn from the housing stock, but just exactly how does that happen? If there is a good alternative use for the land under the unit, the owner will demolish the housing and convert to another use, such as commercial, parking lot, and so on. The withdrawal of units from the low-quality stock will shift supply to the left (to L^* and S_L^*) and cause housing rents to rise at this end of the market. This reduction in supply and increase in housing rents can be a good thing because they ensure that the remaining low-quality units are now economically feasible. The occupants of low-quality housing must pay the higher housing rents, of course.

One more feature of housing needs to be added to the model. Housing is durable, but it is not infinitely durable. Some households move up in housing quality, but the units that they occupy may not remain at the original quality level. Medium-quality units eventually may become low-quality units, and high-quality units can become units of medium quality. The improvement in housing quality generated by the filtering mechanism may well not be permanent. Indeed, note that the rents paid for both high- and medium-quality units have declined. These declines in rents will probably lead landlords to cut back on maintenance expenditures, which will eventually lead to a decline in the quality of some units. Some high-quality units will be turned into medium-quality units, and some medium-quality units will be turned into low-quality units. The entire housing market may eventually return to the original price and quantity for each level of quality.

So far the model has generated reductions in the stock of low-quality housing by demolition, but a drive around older central cities will demonstrate that many units are removed from the stock simply by being abandoned. The owner walks away from the building and leaves no forwarding address for the property tax collector and the building inspector. Abandonment can be a good choice for the owner. The abandonment of a property means that the housing rents cannot cover variable costs *and* that the value of the land, less any demolition costs, is zero (or less). Given that the value of land in some inner-city areas has collapsed virtually to zero, abandonments can be expected to result from increases in the supply of high- or medium-quality housing.

Abandonment may be a good decision for the owner, but it is often a disastrous decision for the society. Abandoned units cost something to demolish, and usually the municipal government must pay the cost. Before the demolition can be accomplished, the abandoned unit can be a source of negative external effects in its neighborhood. Abandoned units hurt the appearance of a neighborhood, are fire hazards, and can be places of criminal activity. Abandoned units are red flags which indicate that the neighborhood is in trouble. It appears that abandonment can beget more abandonment as many factors interact to reduce the quality of the neighborhood further unless the city government can keep on top of the problem with timely demolition. Central cities sometimes have lost the race against abandonment, but in some cases the city is its own worst enemy. A study by White (1986) showed that the most important factor in housing abandonment in New York City during the late 1970s was a high property tax bill compared to the rents the building can earn. The property tax bills loomed large as a percentage of rent because the city had failed to adjust assessed values downward as rents declined. Landlords were pushed over the edge by high property tax bills. The economics of the property tax are discussed in Chapter 13.

Now let us put location into the filtering model. The fact is that most of the newer and high-quality housing is in the suburbs, and most of the low-quality housing is the old housing located in the inner city. Mieszkowski and Mills (1993) argue that the filtering model provides a primary reason for the movement of population to the suburbs and for the concentration of low-income households in central cities. They call the model the natural evolution theory. The construction of the expressways in the 1950s and 1960s, coupled with federal policies that encouraged new construction and homeownership (discussed below), opened the floodgates for movement of (mostly white) middle-class people to the suburbs. As we have already seen, the movement of employment to the suburbs in great numbers came later. Rising real incomes, at least up to the 1970s, stimulated new construction as well. In this kind of housing market in the suburbs, the filtering mechanism worked and neighborhood after neighborhood was relinquished to the growing minority populations. The old minority neighborhoods increasingly became areas of abandonment. A good research project would be to examine the data on census tracts in an urban area with which you are familiar for the years 1960, 1980, and 2000. Do you see evidence of the filtering process at work? How has the racial geography of the urban area changed over these 40 years? As a supplement to the data work, ask someone over the age of 60 who has always lived in the urban area where the "old neighborhood" is. Find out where that person lives now.

It is true that the old housing in the central cities eventually wears out and must be demolished and replaced even in the absence of the construction of high-quality units. However, the construction of high-quality units in the suburbs in excess of the growth of the number of households ultimately leads to demolition (or abandonment) of some units in the inner city *without replacement*. Vast areas of some of the older central cities, such

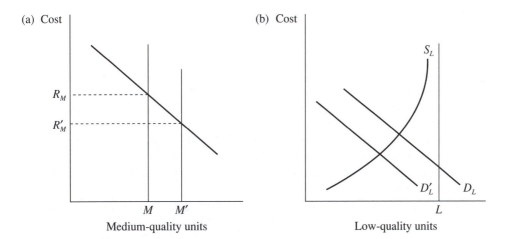

Figure 8.3 Filtering model of the housing market

as New York, Detroit, Chicago, Milwaukee, St. Louis, and others, are vacant and awaiting redevelopment (although some of redevelopment took place in the 1990s). Furthermore, the central city has lost middle-class households and their tax base in the process. The lost of tax base, in both the residential and nonresidential categories, puts pressure on the budget of governments in the central city. The model of filtering as in Figure 8.1 has other uses. For example, one aspect of housing policy in the United States is the subsidization of the construction of housing units that fall within the medium-quality category. In an increase in the quantity of medium-quality units from M to M' causes housing rents to fall to R'_M, and the demand for low-quality units to drop as people move up in quality to these new units. Here it is being assumed that the market for high-quality units is not affected by this increase in medium-quality units. The impacts on the market for low-quality units include reduced housing rents and increased vacancies and, ultimately, removals of units from the stock and restoration of the rent level. The construction of medium-quality units on a large scale might very well lead to the abandonment of areas that contain the old low-quality units unless that construction is managed to preserve those neighborhoods.

G. Residential Construction

This section presents a reasonably simple model of new residential construction in urban counties that is based on the study by McDonald and McMillen (2000). We noted above that new construction adds at most about 2% to the stock of housing units per year. In fact, the data on residential building permits from the US Bureau of the Census for 696 urban counties over the 1990–7 period show a mean "permit rate" of 1.53% per year, and some of these units simply replaced units that wore out.

Consider the housing market in an urban county in the initial period in question (e.g., 1990). Quantity demanded (Q_d) equals quantity supplied (Q_s) at the current price of housing. Quantity supplied is less than the total housing stock (K) by the number of vacant housing units; the actual vacancy rate (V_a) is defined as

$$V_a = (K - Q_s)/K.$$

If the current price of housing is greater than the long-run supply price, builders will apply for building permits and new additional units will be constructed until the current price is driven down to the long-run supply price. If the current price of housing is equal to the long-run supply price, then the vacancy rate equals the "natural" rate (V_n) at which there is no incentive to build more units (other than to replace units that wear out). Finally, if the current price of housing is less than the long-run supply price there is no incentive to build more units and, in the long run, units will be abandoned, demolished, or converted to other uses.

We hypothesize the percentage change in the housing stock is a constant times the difference between the actual vacancy rate and the natural vacancy rate,

$$\Delta K/K = b(V_a - V_n),$$

where $b < 0$. Because the natural vacancy rate is not known, this equation is rewritten

$$\Delta K/K = -bV_n + bV_a$$

so that the natural vacancy rate and its coefficient become the constant term. Building permits (B) are issued to replace worn-out units as well as to add to the housing stock, so a model of the building permit rate is

$$B/K = (r - bV_n) + bV_a$$

where r is the percentage of units that are replaced. The change in the housing stock is, of course, also driven by changes in demand. We use the population growth rate to measure the change in demand for housing units. Other demand variables could be used, but our objective is to develop models that make use of data that are routinely available to local planners and analysts. Our basic model is

$$B/K = (r - bV_n) + bV_a + cG,$$

This model was estimated for 696 urban counties over the 1990–7 period, with the average annual permit rate over this period as the dependent variable. The estimated equation is:

Permit rate $= 0.917 - 0.044V_a + 0.675G.$

All variables are highly statistically significant, and the R^2 for the estimated equation is 0.737. The equation says that an annual population growth rate that was one percentage point higher increased the average annual permit rate by 0.675%. A vacancy rate that was one percentage point higher in 1990 reduced the average annual permit rate over seven years by 0.044%. In short, housing construction is driven by population growth, moderated slightly by the initial vacancy rate.

Recall that the intercept term in the estimated equation equals $(r - bV_n)$, the permit rate for replacement units minus bV_n (where $b < 0$). If we assume that the mean vacancy rate of 8.3% is equal to the natural vacancy rate, then the estimated equation implies that

$r = 0.917 - (8.3)(0.044) = 0.552.$

The estimated equation implies that the building permit rate for replacement units is 0.55% per year on average in urban counties. This finding is consistent with the result in the hedonic study in section C that showed a depreciation in value of 0.5% per year for houses.

H. Affordable Housing and Gentrification

The issues of affordable housing and gentrification are much on the minds of the public, public officials, and economists. In this section we review current research and try to home in on the most important problems. We find that the problem of the affordability of housing is confined mainly to low-income renters in urban areas and that, in some places, gentrification has contributed to the increase in housing costs experienced by this group.

Quigley and Raphael (2004) provide a clear overview of the issue of housing affordability. Their first finding is that, for the two-thirds of households that own the home, there is no evidence that the annual cost of housing increased in the 1990s. The basic point is that mortgage interest rates have been low and stable over this period. However, rates of home ownership are low for non-elderly, low-income households. For example, Quigley and Raphael (2004, p. 193) show that only 32% of low-income (in the bottom 20%) households with a household head aged 35 to 44 own the home. This can be compared to a 66% homeownership rate (as it happens, the overall national average) for all households in this age group. Given that low-income households have low rates of homeownership, the next task is to examine the rental housing market.

The Quigley–Raphael (2004) study of rental housing shows the following:

- In 2000 the poor renter household spent, on average, 64% of income on housing and 77% of the renter poor devoted more than 30% of their income on housing. The poor represent about 12% of all households.
- Renter households in the lowest 20% of the income distribution experienced a large increase in the ratio of rent to income – from 0.47 in 1960 to 0.53 in 1980 to 0.55 in 2000. The proportion of this group that spent more than 30% of income on rent increased from 62% in 1960 to 69% in 1980 to 79% in 2000.

What are the causes of these trends? Quigley and Raphael (2004) show that this decrease in affordability in the 1980s and 1990s can be attributed almost entirely to increases in rents rather than decreases in income of the low-income population. Some of the increase in rents can be attributed to increases in the quality of rental housing. Rental units are larger and very few lack plumbing facilities or adequate electricity or heating. The increase in quality can partly be attributed to government restrictions – building codes and housing codes that mandate standards. It is possible that low-income households would have chosen housing units of lower quality than required by the building and housing codes imposed by local governments. In the extreme case, some households choose to be homeless. Homelessness is discussed in Chapter 16 in the section of the book on urban social problems.

While some of the increase in rents stems from increases in quality, it is also true that rents increased after adjusting for quality. The trend in rents depends upon factors that influence the overall supply of rental housing. The filtering model discussed above implies that rents for housing at the bottom of the housing supply continuum depend upon supplies of all types of housing. Malpezzi and Green (1996) showed that the growth in the quantity of low-quality housing units depends upon the quantity of new, higher-quality units supplied. Any factor that reduces the rate of housing construction is implicated; growth controls, land-use and zoning regulations, generous provisions for open space, and stringent building codes. We find it ironic that some of the same people who are concerned about housing affordability are also in favor of growth controls and strong land-use regulation. Making rental housing more affordable will depend upon increasing housing supply and increasing the income of poor households. Housing policy is discussed in detail in the next chapter.

Does gentrification contribute to the problem of housing affordability? Vigdor (2002) has considered this question at length. As we noted in Chapter 2, gentrification is defined as private residential and commercial development (usually in the central city) that includes the movement into the neighborhood of households with larger incomes than the current residents. Vigdor's detailed study of Boston shows that gentrification as defined does not necessarily mean that poor households suffer a decline in living standards. In Vigdor's view gentrification is a result of broader trends that affect the poor rather than a direct cause of any change in the well-being of the poor. As we have seen, housing in urban areas has become less affordable for the poor over time, and this trend has numerous underlying economic causes. Gentrification is a symptom of the broader trends in the urban economy. Furthermore, gentrification tends to increase the tax base of the central city and might therefore lead to improvements in public services. Gentrification might increase employment opportunities in the central city and reduce the concentration of poverty as well. Vigdor (2002) finds no evidence that low-income households move out of their housing units. He finds that poor households are more likely to leave poverty than to be displaced from the housing units by higher-income households. But low-income households in Boston generally have experienced reductions in housing affordability without compensating changes in public services or neighborhood quality. In essence, Vigdor (2002) has found that there is a general problem of housing affordability among the low-income renters in Boston. This finding matches the conclusion of the Quigley–Raphael (2004) study of the entire nation.

I. Summary

This chapter has examined the operation of housing markets in urban areas. The next chapter discusses urban housing policy objectives and programs. A summary of the two chapters appears at the end of Chapter 9.

Appendix to Chapter 8: The Hedonic Housing Model

The house price models discussed in Sections D and E are examples of a *hedonic* model. This model, which came into widespread use after the publication of a theoretical paper by Rosen (1974), is used to recover the implicit price of a multi-faceted good. How much does an additional bedroom add to the sales price of a house? Do higher average student test scores increase the value of homes within the school district? Do higher crime rates reduce house prices? This appendix is an introduction to this more advanced topic.

In the hedonic model of housing, households are assumed to receive utility from each of the many characteristics that comprise a house. Housing producers attempt to build homes that reflect the tastes of consumers. It is costly to add square footage, another room, or more elaborate design components to a house. The basic insight of the hedonic model is that the marginal price of a characteristic – the additional charge for one more unit – can be estimated by regressing the sales

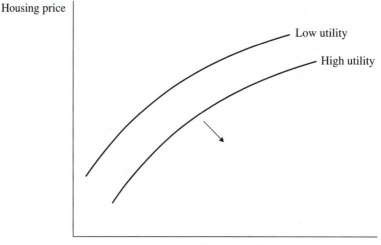

Figure A8.1   Household bid curves

price of a home on its characteristics. In equilibrium, the marginal price is equal to the household's marginal willingness to pay for an additional unit. The marginal price is also equal to the marginal cost of the good on the part of producers.

Although the theoretical model appears quite complicated, it can be simplified by focusing on the choice of a single housing characteristic. A home includes basic characteristics of the structure, e.g., square footage, the number of stories, room size, and so on. It also includes characteristics of the location, such as school quality and crime rates. Holding all these factors constant, let us focus on the choice of the quality of the design, which we assume can be simplified down to a single measure. Homes can be built with expensive hardwood floors, marble countertops, and outdoor landscaping, all of which add to the amount of the composite good "housing" as well as the price. For simplicity, we will treat all of these components together as though they are a single good called "design quality."

Figure A8.1 shows the household's bid function for this good. Like the overall bid-rent function for housing, it shows the maximum amount that a household will pay for the level of design quality indicated on the horizontal axis, holding other factors constant. This maximum bid increases at a decreasing rate with the quality of the design. Initial amounts – a better kitchen design, some grass in the yard – add a lot to the amount households will pay for the house. But eventually this levels off as we move into the "luxury" range. As was the case with the bid-rent function for housing, the position of the bid curve for an individual housing characteristic depends on the level of utility received by the households. Higher levels of utility are associated with higher design quality and lower house prices. Two bid curves are shown in Figure A8.1, representing "high" and "low" levels of utility. As indicated by the arrow, utility rises as we move toward lower bid curves.

A high-quality design comes at a cost. Producers will be willing to install luxurious design components, but only if they are compensated for the installation cost. Figure A8.2 shows the offer curves for a representative producer. The offer curve shows combinations of house price and design quality that lead to the same level of profit for the producer. The offer curves are assumed to increase at an increasing rate with the level of design quality because additional increments to quality become more and more expensive to add to a home. Producers find it less costly to

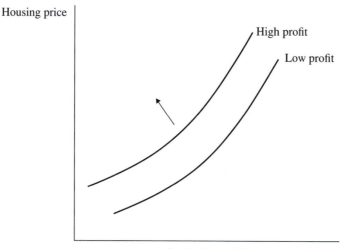

Figure A8.2   Product offer curves

build homes with lower quality, and they earn higher profit when house prices are high. Thus, as indicated by the arrow in Figure A8.2, higher profits levels are associated with higher offer curves.

Figure A8.3 shows an equilibrium combination of bid and offer curves. Given the level of the bid curves, producers have reached the highest offer curve – the highest level of profit – that they can attain. Similarly, households have reached the highest level of utility they can attain given the location of the offer curve. Of course, there are many other combinations of bid and offer curves

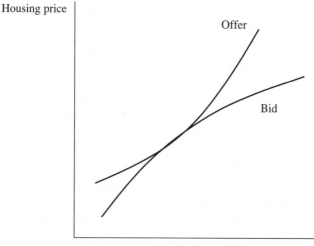

Figure A8.3   Hedonic equilibrium

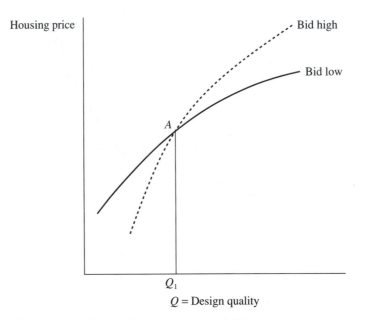

Figure A8.4   Bid curves for high- and low-demand households

that also are consistent with equilibrium in the housing market. But all equilibrium combinations will end up with the bid curve for households being tangent to the offer curve for firms.

If Figure A8.3 were the full story, the hedonic housing model would not be particularly useful or interesting. The hedonic model becomes interesting once we recognize that households differ in their tastes for housing characteristics and that producers may differ in their cost structure. Figure A8.4 represents two different types of households. To understand this diagram, start from point A, the intersection of the two bid curves. The households represented by the dotted line will pay more for an additional unit of design quality than households represented by the solid line. Similarly, the bids drop off more sharply for dotted-line households when design quality is reduced below Q_1. The households represented by the dotted bid curve clearly value design quality more than the solid-line households. In general, steeper bid curves imply that households value the housing characteristic more highly in the sense that they will pay more for an additional increment of the good.

Figure A8.5 shows the offer curves for two firms that differ in their cost structures. Again start from the point labeled A. The firm represented by the dotted line requires more compensation for increasing the design quality beyond Q_1, where the additional compensation comes in the form of a higher house price. Similarly, if the firm represented by the dotted line were to reduce design quality below Q_1, it would have reduced its costs by enough that it could significantly reduce the housing price and still come out with the same level of profit. Thus, the firm represented by the dotted line is the high-cost producer: it requires a greater addition to the price of housing to compensate it for having to add more design quality.

The analysis becomes interesting when we match our high- and low-cost producers to the high- and low-demand households. Intuitively, we would expect households who place a high value on design quality to seek out housing producers who are able to provide that level of design relatively inexpensively. And firms that find it costly to produce high levels of design quality will offer discounts for lower quality levels that attract low-demand households. This outcome is exactly as

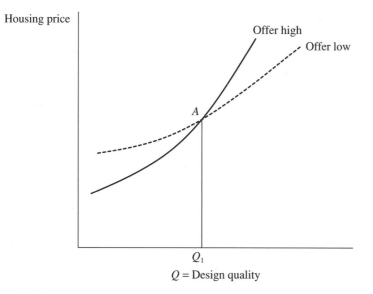

Figure A8.5   Offer curves for high- and low-cost producers

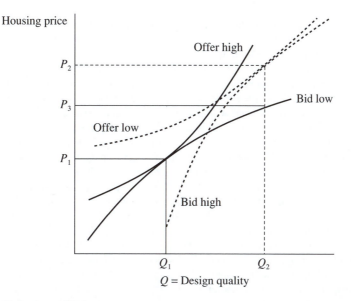

Figure A8.6   Hedonic equilibrium

predicted by the model. Figure A8.6 represents an equilibrium outcome. The two dotted lines – high-demand households and low-cost firms – are matched in equilibrium with a high level of design quality. The two solid lines – low-demand households and high-cost firms – are in a match with low design quality. High design quality comes at a price: high-demand prices pay P_2 for Q_2 units of design quality, whereas low-demand households pay the lower amount P_1 for Q_1 units. But

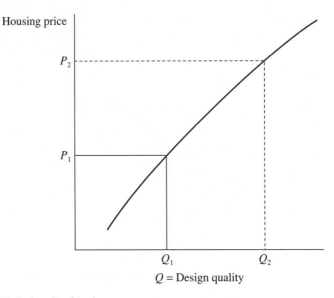

Figure A8.7   Hedonic price function

notice that the price paid by each household is significantly lower than what they would have to pay to get the same level of design quality from the other type of producer. This matching process is an important prediction of the hedonic model.

It does not take much imagination to extend Figure A8.6 to include a wide variety of household and producer types. The set of tangencies between bid and offer curves forms a set of equilibrium price–quantity combinations. The curve that connects these tangencies is called the "hedonic price function." Figure A8.7 shows a hedonic price function that is consistent with the matching equilibrium of Figure A8.6. The hedonic function shows that the price of housing rises with design quality. The slope of the hedonic price function is a direct result of our assumptions that (1) consumers are willing to pay more for high levels of design quality, and (2) producers find it costly to produce higher-quality houses. An important feature of the hedonic price function shown in Figure A8.7 is that it is *not* linear. In this case, the hedonic price function increases at a decreasing rate with the level of design quality. This implies that it costs less per unit of design quality to have a high-quality home than a home with a lower level of design quality. A nonlinear pricing structure is one of the predictions of hedonic theory.

The matching process is important to keep in mind when interpreting the results of hedonic models. At Q_1, the slope of the hedonic price function is equal to the slope of the low-demand households' bid function and the high-cost firms' offer function. Thus, this marginal price represents the marginal willingness to pay for another unit of design quality on the part of low-demand households. It also represents the marginal cost of production for high-cost firms. It does *not* represent the marginal willingness to pay on the part of high-demand households or the marginal cost to low-cost firms. To see this, look at the slopes at Q_1 for the high-demand bid curve and the low-cost offer curves (the dotted lines). At Q_1, the marginal willingness to pay for another unit is higher for high-demand households than it is for low-income households, and the marginal cost for low-cost firms is lower than for high-cost firms. Thus, the marginal price implied by the hedonic price function is the right measure of marginal willingness to pay and marginal cost only for those households and firms who have chosen that quality level.

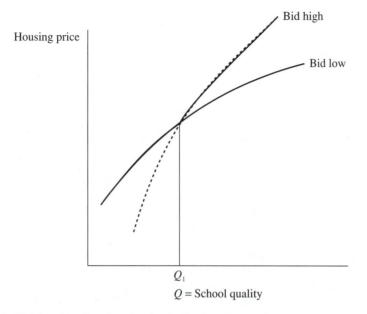

Figure A8.8   Bid functions for given levels of school quality

The matching process has important implications for cost–benefit analyses of housing policies. Suppose the local government decides to adopt stringent building codes that effectively require a minimum level of design quality. Coincidentally, suppose this minimum design quality is given by Q_2 in Figures A8.6 and A8.7. Armed with estimates of the hedonic price function, you might think that the value of this high level of design quality is the difference between P_2 and P_1 for households who are living in low-quality homes. After all, the hedonic price function implies that households are willing to pay $P_2 - P_1$ to increase design quality from Q_1 to Q_2. However, low-demand households are willing only to pay P_3 for this increase in design quality. If they are forced to consume Q_2 units, they will have to pay P_2, and this higher price will leave them at a lower level of utility than they had before. In a competitive hedonic market, this type of quality regulation will actually make low-demand households worse off even though they end up living in higher-quality homes.

The housing characteristic we have analyzed to this point, design quality, is representative of any characteristic that is added to a house by producers. Other variables – school quality, crime, access to employment opportunities – are part of the location and cannot be varied readily by the producer. The hedonic model is simplified somewhat when the supply of the characteristic is fixed because we need only consider the households' bid functions. Consider the case of school quality. Housing producers do not directly choose the quality of the schools in a neighborhood. But many studies show that school quality is capitalized into house price because people will bid more for homes in neighborhoods with good schools.

To simplify the diagrams, assume that we have two types of households. The first household type places a higher value on school quality than the second type. The bid functions for the two households are shown in Figure A8.8. The trick to analyzing the shape of the equilibrium price function is the same as we used before to analyze bid-rent function: the household type that bids more for a home is the one who buys it. Thus, homes in neighborhoods with low school quality, $Q < Q_1$, are occupied by low-demand household – households with a relatively low demand for school quality. Homes in neighborhoods with $Q > Q_1$ are occupied by high-demand households.

The hedonic price function is the upper envelope of the two bid functions, i.e., the bold line segments in Figure A8.8. At each point along this function, the marginal price of housing is equal to the household's marginal willingness to pay.

Estimates of hedonic price functions are pervasive in the urban economics literature. Interesting examples include Coulson and Leichenko (2001), Downes and Zabel (2002), and Hite et al. (2001). Sheppard (1999) presents a good review of hedonic theory.

The hedonic model just described is useful when analyzing a single metropolitan area. Within a single metropolitan area, it is reasonable to assume that any differences in such goods as school quality, parks, and environmental quality are reflected directly in house prices. Using only house prices may not be enough when comparing the situation across metropolitan areas. Suppose that city A has better schools, better parks, and higher environmental quality than city B (think of "A" and "B" as grades). Then people are willing to pay more to live in A than to live in B: as predicted by the hedonic model, house prices will reflect the "quality of life" as indicated by school quality, parks, and environmental quality. However, looking at house prices alone may not be enough to calculate the full benefits of living in A because people may be willing to accept lower *wages* to live in city A. If residents of city A have accepted both higher house prices and lower wages to live there rather than in city B, then analyzing only house prices will understate the benefits of living in city A. Ignoring wages is most likely not a problem when analyzing a single metropolitan area because most metropolitan areas share a common labor market: wages do not adjust to reflect differences across suburbs because workers can easily commute between them. Ignoring the labor market is a problem when analyzing difference across metropolitan areas because workers seldom commute from one urban area to another.

Roback (1982) extended Rosen's hedonic model to include both housing and labor markets. The Roback model is mainly employed in two ways. First, it is used as an analytical tool to predict how wages and house prices adjust to differences in amenities across urban areas. Second, it is used to develop indexes for both the quality of life and the quality of the business environment. The model is based on an assumption that firms and households move across cities to attain the highest possible profit (firms) and utility (households). In equilibrium, neither profits nor utility levels will vary across urban areas. Thus, if a city has amenities that make it an appealing place to live, it will attract households until some combination of higher house prices and lower wages eliminates the inducement to move there. Similarly, a good business environment will lead to a combination of higher land rents and increased wages for firms. In the end – in equilibrium – both firms and households are equally well off in all locations, and there is no incentive to move. As we discuss in Chapter 18, some researchers have questioned the validity of the assumption that urban labor markets routinely attain this equilibrium because migration flows may operate with a long lag.

The Roback model can be illustrated using simple diagrams showing the tradeoffs between wages and land rents that provide firms with identical levels of profit and households with identical levels of utility. Constant-utility curves for households are shown in Figure A8.9. The curve labels A_1 shows the combination of wages and land rents that lead to equal levels of utility when a city's amenities are fixed at the level A_1. The upward slope means that households are willing to pay higher land rents when they receive higher wages. If the city's level of amenities increases to A_2, then the curve shifts up: for any given wage level, a household is willing to pay higher land rents to live in a city that offers a higher level of amenities. Both curves are associated with the *same* level of utility.

On the firm side, we must distinguish between "productive" and "unproductive" amenities. Roback labels an amenity "productive" if it lowers costs for the firm. For example, a good climate may directly lower the cost of production for a firm because it reduces air conditioning or heating bills. An "unproductive" amenity is the opposite – something that raises firms' costs even though valued by households. For example, a remote mountainous area that is desirable to households may lead to high shipping costs for firms. The case of a productive amenity is illustrated in Figure A8.10.

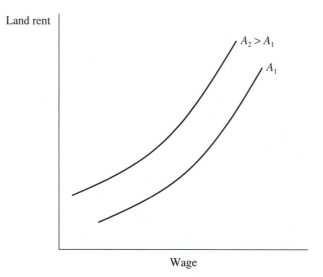

Figure A8.9   Roback model – households

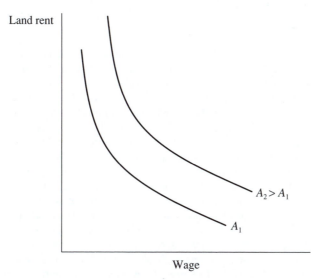

Figure A8.10   Roback model – firms, productive amenity

The isoprofit curves show combinations of wages and land rents that lead to identical levels of profits for firms. The curves are downward sloping because both land rents and wages are bad to a firm: to endure higher land rents, a firm must be compensated with lower wages in order to keep the same level of profit. For a productivity amenity, the isoprofit curve shifts up when the amenity level increases from A_1 to A_2: for each wage, the firm is now willing to pay a higher land rent because the higher amenity level has lowered costs otherwise. Both curves are associated with the *same* level of profit.

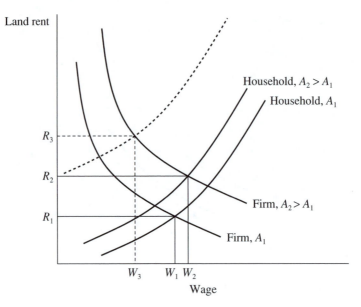

Figure A8.11 Equilibrium with productive amenities

Figure A8.11 combines the firm and household sides of the market. The figure is drawn for the case of two urban areas. The first urban area has the amenity level at A_1, while the second urban area has the higher amenity level of A_2. The equal-utility curve intersects the isoprofit curve at a wage of W_1 and land rent of R_1 in the urban area that has the amenity level at A_1. The equal-utility and isoprofit curves are both higher in the second urban area that has a higher level of the amenity $(A_2 > A_1)$. Equilibrium land rents and wages are R_2 and W_2 in the second urban area. Thus, Figure A8.11 predicts that both wages and land rents will be higher in the city with a higher amenity level. It is important to bear in mind that residents of both urban areas have the same level of utility and firms have the same levels of profit. Wages and rents are higher in the second urban area by exactly the amount that leaves firms and workers equally well off in locations.

Although our results so far appear quite reasonable – higher amenities mean higher wage and land rents – matters are actually more complex than we have shown. The solid lines in Figure A8.11 represent a situation where the higher amenity level matters more to the firm than to the household in the sense that the firms' isoprofit curves have shifted more than the households' equal utility curves. Suppose that instead the household curve shifts all the way to the dotted line. Land rents still have risen even more – up to R_3. But wages have *fallen* to W_3. It turns out that our prediction for what happens to wages is ambiguous – they can go either way – while we can say confidently that land rents will be higher in urban areas with higher levels of a productive amenity.

The intuition behind this result is actually quite easy to understand. If the amenity is productive, then both firms and households prefer to locate in the urban area with the higher level of the amenity. As they move to the high-amenity location, they bid up land rents. The increase in the number of households in the high-amenity urban area raises the supply of labor there. An increased supply of labor puts downward pressure on wages. But if the amenity is productive, then firms too prefer the high-amenity urban area. More firms moving to an area increases the demand for labor, which places upward pressure on wages. Which effect dominates – increased labor supply or increased labor demand – depends on the relative strengths of the two effects. Intuitively, if the

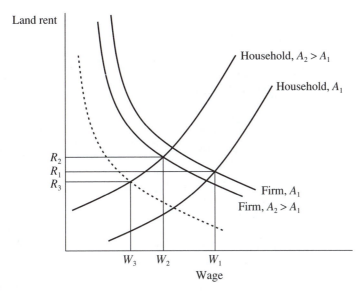

Figure A8.12   Equilibrium with unproductive amenities

amenity is valued much more highly by households than by firms, then households are more attracted to the area than firms, and wages tend to fall because labor supply has risen more than labor demand. But if the amenity is valued more highly by firms, then wages may rise. Either way, the migration of firms and households into the high-amenity urban area increases land rents.

The case of an unproductive amenity is shown in Figure A8.12. Again, the amenity is valued by households, so the equal-utility curve shifts up when the amenity level is A_2 rather than A_1. Other things being equal, this upward shift will tend to raise land rents and lower wages. But other things are not equal if the isoprofit curve shifts. When the amenity is unproductive, firms prefer to be in the low-amenity location as production costs are lower there. Thus, the isoprofit curve shifts down: for any given level of wages, firms are willing to pay less for land when the amenity level is at A_2. Other things being equal, this tendency for firms to avoid the low-amenity location tends to lower land rents and reduce wages. If households are more sensitive to differences in the amenity levels than are firms – the solid lines in Figure A8.12 – then the wages fall from W_1 to W_2 while rents rise form R_1 to R_2. In this case, so many households are entering the urban area that land rents rise even though firms prefer to be elsewhere. But if the firms' isoprofit line falls all the way to the dotted line, then rents will fall to R_3 while we again have the unambiguous prediction that wages fall (this time to W_3). At the end of the process, equilibrium is reached when there is no further incentive to relocate and both households and workers are indifferent between the two locations.

Figures A8.11 and A8.12 provide some interesting insights into patterns across urban areas. If you live in an urban area with low wages and low house prices, it is clear that it does not score highly on the list of urban amenities: both firms and households find it undesirable (or "unproductive"). If you live in an urban area that has both high levels of wages and high house prices, it is clear that it scores low on the list of urban amenities. Wages may be high while house prices are low if firms value the characteristics offered by an urban area while households prefer to avoid them. And wages may be low while house prices are high if households value the amenities offered by an urban area yet firms find them unproductive. Beeson and Eberts (1989) have used this approach to classify urban areas. Table A8.1 summarizes their results:

Table A8.1   Classification of US urban areas

	Low wages	High wages
Low rents	Kansas City MO	Atlanta GA
	New Orleans LA	Baltimore, MD
	Phoenix AZ	Cincinnati OH
	Sacramento CA	Cleveland OH
	Salt Lake City UT	Indianapolis IN
	San Antonio TX	Philadelphia PA
	Tampa FL	Pittsburgh PA
High rents	Denver CO	Anaheim CA
	Fort Lauderdale FL	Chicago IL
	Miami FL	Detroit MI
	Portland OR	Houston TX
	Riverside–San Bernardino CA	Los Angeles CA
	San Diego CA	Minneapolis MN
		Nassau–Suffolk NY
		New York NY
		Newark NJ
		St. Louis MO
		San Francisco CA
		San Jose CA
		Seattle WA
		Washington DC

Source: Beeson and Eberts (1989)

Although their study is somewhat old (it uses data form 1980), it provides some interesting insights into the quality of life and the quality of the business environment in different cities. At the risk of overgeneralization, cities like Anaheim and Chicago are good places to work and live; cities like Atlanta and Cincinnati are better places to work than to live; and cities like Denver and Fort Lauderdale are better to places to live than to work. Both households and firms appear to be avoiding places like Kansas City and New Orleans, at least as of 1980.

The Beeson and Eberts study is an example of the use of the Roback model to develop indexes of the quality of life or the quality of the business environment offered by different urban areas. Other good examples are Blomquist, Berger, and Hoehn (1988); Gabriel and Rosenthal (2004); and Kahn (1995). The basic approach used to develop such an index is easy to explain. We begin by collecting data on wages and house prices for different urban areas. It would be better to have data on land rents, but they are not readily available. We also need data on various amenities; examples include heating degree days, average annual snowfall and rainfall, and indicators for whether the city is on a coast or in a mountainous area. Let A represent this group of amenity indicators. To simplify matters, assume that we just have two amenities, A_1 and A_2. We estimate the following house price and wage regressions:

$$P = c_p + a_{p1}A_1 + a_{p2}A_2 + bZ$$
$$W = c_w + a_{w1}A_1 + a_{w2}A_2 + dX$$

where W is the annual wage rate, P is annual housing expenditures, and X and Z are controls for worker and house characteristics. (For example, X might include age and education, while Z includes square footage and land area.) using combined data from many urban areas. For households, the marginal willingness to pay for an additional unit of A_1 is just $a_{p1} - a_{w1}$: households value A_1 more highly if they are willing to pay higher house prices and accept lower wages to get more of it, i.e., $a_{p1} > 0$ and $a_{w1} < 0$. Similarly, the marginal willingness to pay for an additional unit of A_2 is $a_{p2} - a_{w2}$.

These estimates of the marginal willingness to pay provide weights that are then used to form an estimate of the quality of life in different urban areas. On the margin, households are willing to pay $a_{p1} - a_{w1}$ for another unit of A_1 and $a_{p2} - a_{w2}$ for another unit of A_2. If they actually receive A_1 of the first amenity, then the value they place on this amenity is $(a_{p1} - a_{w1})A_1$. Similarly, the value they place on the second amenity is $(a_{p2} - a_{w2})A_2$. Finally, the total value they place on all the amenities offered in their urban area is QOL $= (a_{p1} - a_{w1})A_1 + (a_{p2} - a_{w2})A_2$. We make this calculation separately for each urban area, setting A_1 and A_2 to the values offered by each location. Finally, we rank the urban areas from highest to lowest according to QOL; the result is a simple ranking of the "quality of life." Of course, this approach only works if we have successfully identified the most important amenities offered by urban areas, and if we have successfully controlled for differences in worker and housing characteristics. Varying the list of amenities can lead to significant differences in the implied quality of life ranking.

The same approach can be used to estimate an index for the quality of the business environment. We again estimate wage and land rent equations. The wage regression is not changed because the same wages were being received by households as are being paid by firms. However, the house prices are not really the right measure of land rents for firms. In the absence of actual measures of land prices, we might like to substitute real estate values for commercial or manufacturing establishments. Such data are hard to obtain. In practice, researchers have used house prices to measure the land prices for firms. Thus, our two estimating equations do not change at all. We simply change the weights. The marginal benefit to the firm of an additional unit of A_1 is simply $a_{p1} + a_{w1}$. For households, it was $a_{p1} - a_{w1}$. The difference is that higher wages are a bad thing to the firm. The marginal benefit to the firm of an additional unit of A_2 is simply $a_{p2} + a_{w2}$. The total benefit to the firm of the package of amenities offered in the urban area being studied is QOBE $= (a_{p1} + a_{w1})A_1 + (a_{p2} + a_{w2})A_2$. Finally, we rank these from highest to lowest to rank the quality of the business environment.

Table A8.2 presents Gabriel and Rosenthal's rankings of quality life and quality of the business environment offered by various American cities. The data are averages over 1977–95. Note that urban areas can differ significantly in the quality of life and the business environment rankings. For example, Miami appears to be a good place to live but not a good place to do business. In contrast, Detroit appears to be a much better place to do business than to live.

Table A8.2   Gabriel and Rosenthal's rankings of quality of life and quality of the business environment

Metropolitan area	Quality of life	Quality of business environment
Miami	1	34
San Diego	2	10
Los Angeles–Long Beach	3	5
San Francisco	4	2
Tampa–St. Petersburg–Clearwater	5	37
New York	6	7
Albany–Schenectady–Troy	7	28
Greensboro–Winston-Salem–High Point	8	35
Sacramento	9	18
Norfolk–Virginia Beach–Newport News	10	30
Seattle–Bellevue–Everett	11	6
Denver	12	15
Newark	13	3
San Jose	14	1
Minneapolis–St. Paul	15	12
Fort Worth–Arlington	16	31
Birmingham	17	36
New Orleans	18	25
Chicago	19	8
Indianapolis	20	33
Rochester	21	16
Pittsburgh	22	29
Dallas	23	20
Columbus	24	26
Washington DC	25	4
Milwaukee–Waukesha	26	14
Philadelphia	27	13
Baltimore	28	11
Cincinnati	29	23
Atlanta	30	19
Cleveland–Lorain–Elyria	31	21
Akron	32	27
Kansas City	33	32
Houston	34	22
St. Louis	35	24
Gary	36	17
Detroit	37	9

Source: Gabriel and Rosenthal (2004)

Exercises

1 Compute the market value of a rental house given the following assumptions:

*The annual rent is $6,000.
- The annual expenses (taxes, maintenance, and so on) are $4,000.
- The annual maintenance expenses permit the house to last forever.
- The discount rate is 5%.

(a) Compute the market value of the house.
(b) Now compute the market value of the same house assuming that the buyer will sell it after 3 years for $40,000. Assume that the house is purchased at the beginning of year 1, rents are received at the end of years 1, 2, and 3, and house is sold at the end of year 3.
(c) What is the current value of the house if its price at the end of year 3 is expected to be $50,000 instead of $40.000?

2 For an urban area of your choice, use the Census Bureau web site (census.gov) to find the extent of racial segregation in 2000 (and 1990, if possible). Do you know the borders of the submarket that is occupied by the black population? Are housing prices and rents generally higher or lower in the black submarket than in areas occupied by the white population? Are there areas that can be identified as Hispanic submarkets?

3 Use the model of filtering in the housing market depicted in Figure 8.1 to determine the effects of

(a) Demolition of some high-quality housing.
(b) Demolition of some low-quality housing.

References

Beeson, Patricia and Randall Eberts, 1989, "Identifying Productivity and Amenity Effects in Interurban Wage Differentials," *Review of Economics and Statistics*, vol. 71, pp. 443–52.

Berry, Brian, 1976, "Ghetto Expansion and Single-Family Housing Prices: Chicago, 1968–1972," *Journal of Urban Economics*, vol. 3, pp. 297–323.

Blomquist, Glenn, M. Berger, and J. Hoehn, 1988, "New Estimates of the Quality of Life in Urban Areas," *American Economic Review*, vol. 78, pp. 89–107.

Coulson, N. Edward and R. Leichenko, 2001, "The Internal and External Impact of Historical Designation on Property Values," *Journal of Real Estate Finance and Economics*, vol. 23, pp. 113–24.

Downes, Thomas and J. Zabel, 2002, "The Impact of School Prices on Housing Prices: Chicago 1987–1991," *Journal of Urban Economics*, vol. 52, pp. 1–25.

Gabriel, Stuart and S. Rosenthal, 2004, "Quality of the Business Environment Versus Quality of Life," *Review of Economics and Statistics*, vol. 86, pp. 438–44.

Hite, Diane, W. Chern, F. Hitzhusen, and A. Randall, 2001, "Property Value Impacts of an Environmental Disamenity: The Case of Landfills," *Journal of Real Estate Finance and Economics*, vol. 22, pp. 185–202.

Kahn, Matthew, 1995, "A Revealed Preference Approach to Ranking City Quality of Life," *Journal of Urban Economics*, vol. 38, pp. 221–35.

King, A. Thomas and P. Mieszkowski, 1973, "Racial Discrimination, Segregation, and the Price of Housing," *Journal of Political Economy*, vol. 81, pp. 590–606.

Lancaster, Kelvin, 1966, "A New Approach to Consumer Theory," *Journal of Political Economy*, vol. 74, pp. 132–57.

McDonald, John F. and Daniel P. McMillen, 2000, "Residential Building Permits in Urban Counties: 1990–1997," *Journal of Housing Economics*, vol. 9, pp. 175–86.

McMillen, Daniel P. and John F. McDonald, 2004, "Reaction of House Prices to New Rapid Transit Line: Chicago's Midway Line, 1983–1999," *Real Estate Economics*, vol. 32, pp. 463–86.

Malpezzi, Stephen and Richard Green, 1996, "What Has Happened to the Bottom of the US Housing Market?" *Urban Studies*, vol. 33, pp. 1807–20.

Massey, Douglas and Nancy Denton, 1993, *American Apartheid*. Cambridge, MA: Harvard University Press.

Mieszkowski, Peter and Edwin Mills, 1993, "The Causes of Metropolitan Suburbanization," *Journal of Economic Perspectives* vol. 7, no. 3, pp. 135–47.

Miller, V. P. and J. Quigley, 1990, "Segregation by Racial and Demographic Group: Evidence from the San Francisco Bay Area," *Urban Studies*, vol. 27, pp. 3–21.

Munnell, Alicia, Lynn Browne, James McEneaney, and Geoffrey Tootell, 1996, "Mortgage Lending in Boston: Interpreting the HMDA Data," *American Economic Review*, vol. 86, pp. 25–53.

Muth, Richard, 1969, *Cities and Housing*, Chicago: University of Chicago Press.

Niedercorn, John and E. Hearle, 1963, "Recent Land-Use Trends in Forty-Eight Large American Cities," RM-3663-1-FF. Santa Monica, CA: The Rand Corporation.

Quigley, John and Steven Raphael, 2004, "Is Housing Affordable? Why Isn't It More Affordable?" *Journal of Economic Perspectives*, vol. 18, pp. 191–214.

Roback, Jennifer, 1982, "Wages, Rents, and the Quality of Life," *Journal of Political Economy*, vol. 90, pp. 1257–78.

Rosen, Sherwin, 1974, "Hedonic Prices and Implicit Markets: Product Differentiation in Pure Competition," *Journal of Political Economy*, vol. 82, pp. 34–55.

Ross, Stephen L. and John Yinger, 2002, *The Color of Credit*. Cambridge, MA: MIT Press.

Schwab, William, 1992, *The Sociology of Cities*. Englewood Cliffs, NJ: Prentice-Hall.

Sheppard, Stephen, 1999, "Hedonic Analysis of Housing Markets," in P. Cheshire and E. Mills (eds.), *Handbook of Regional and Urban Economics*, vol. 3, Amsterdam: North Holland.

Smith, Barton, 1981, "A Study of Racial Discrimination in Housing," in J. V. Henderson (ed.), *Research in Urban Economics*, vol. 1. Greenwich, CT: JAI Press.

Vigdor, Jacob, 2002, "Does Gentrification Harm the Poor?" *Brookings-Wharton Papers on Urban Affairs*, vol. 3, pp. 133–60.

White, Michele, 1986, "Property Taxes and Urban Housing Abandonment," *Journal of Urban Economics*, vol. 20, pp. 312–30.

Chapter 9

Housing Policy in the United States

A. Introduction

The housing market is the one market for a consumer good that is subjected to more policy initiatives than any other. The main actor is the federal government, but local governments are deeply involved in administering federal programs and in creating their own programs, such as rent controls. We include in this section a brief history of federal housing policy since the first program was begun in 1934. Federal policy is of two basic types: policies designed to enable middle-class households to own their own homes, and policies aimed at upgrading the housing of lower-income households. Before the details of various programs are discussed, it is worthwhile to consider the reasons why society has singled out housing as a good that people are encouraged to consume.

As you might have guessed, economists of the conservative school of thought have serious doubts about the wisdom of policies designed to increase the consumption of housing. As discussed in Chapter 2, conservatives will acknowledge that there is a poverty problem and that there is a good case for cash transfer payments to the poor, couched in a system with strong incentives to work. If low-income households have a decent amount of cash, they can decide how to spend it. There is no particular reason to encourage housing consumption. To the conservative economist the housing market appears to be a competitive market that does not need intervention by the government. Furthermore, as Milton Friedman would say, attempts by the government to "do good" in the housing market will probably end up with the opposite result. How do the advocates of housing policy respond?

Several theoretical arguments are made. The housing market contains both positive and negative externalities in neighborhoods. The quality of one housing unit can have either positive or negative effects on the value of neighboring units and the living conditions of the neighbors. As discussed above, abandoned housing units are unsightly, create fire hazards, and attract crime. At the other extreme, a neighborhood filled with nice, well-maintained houses (and filled with decent people) creates a strong positive effect. Some economists and housing advocates go further and argue that there are additional serious imperfections in the housing market that arise from racial discrimination. Racial discrimination circumscribes the choices that minority households have in the housing market, and this reduction in choices limits the ability to minorities to consume good housing and to reside in locations that are easily accessible to suburban workplaces. In addition, many argue that there is overt discrimination in the markets for mortgage loans and housing insurance that limits the ability of minority households to maintain and upgrade the housing stock in their racially segregated neighborhoods. Recent detailed empirical research by economists at the Federal Reserve Bank of Boston and discussed above in Chapter 8 (Munnell et al. 1996) has documented what appears to be discrimination in the mortgage market. They have found that minority households are rejected for mortgages at a higher rate than are white households, even after the effects of a large number of variables (income, employment stability, credit rating, etc.) are included.

Other advocates of housing policy go even further and argue that housing is a *merit good*, a good that society views as more important than allowed for by individual choices. A merit good is a good that creates benefits for the community as a whole, and housing, health, recreation, and education are often mentioned as being in this category. It is fair to say that conservative economists take a very dim view of the idea of merit goods. They see the idea of merit goods as a vague justification for all sorts of ill-considered interventions into the private economy. Because of this criticism, the use of the term *merit good* has fallen into disuse. Nevertheless, the idea of a merit good is based on externalities. The question is whether the externalities in the housing market are strong enough to justify intervention and, if they are, what sort of interventions is indicated. The answers to these questions are much in dispute among economists and the public at large.

One point that is more persuasive pertains to the support of housing for lower-income households. In accordance with a general negative externality argument, cities have housing codes and building codes that establish minimum standards for housing units. These codes come under the police power of local government to protect the health, safety, and welfare of the public, but they mean that some households have great difficulty affording housing at the minimum standards. The minimum rent implied by the housing and building codes exceeds the amount that some households would choose to pay of their own accord. For example, some poor single men would choose to live in shabby single-room occupancy hotels or rooming houses, but local governments regard such buildings as unsafe and have forced them to close down. Housing subsidies can then be viewed as a method of compensating the low-income households for being forced to make an allocation of their incomes not of their own choosing (or to be homeless). With these points in mind, let us turn to the actual policies.

B. Housing Policies for the Middle Class

Middle-class Americans are encouraged to own their homes through two long-standing policies: federal mortgage insurance and federal income tax deductions for mortgage payments and local property taxes. The Federal Housing Administration (FHA) was established in 1934 to provide mortgage lenders with a guarantee that the default of a borrower will not cost them money. Prior to the creation of FHA, most home loans had high down payments and were of rather short duration by today's standards – 5 to 15 years. Those loans required repayment in full at the end of the term of the loan, which meant that the household usually had to obtain another loan to repay the first loan. This kind of loan is called *nonamortizing* because the monthly payments do not include an amount that reduces the principal of the loan to zero by the end of the term. During the early years of the Great Depression, which began in 1929, many households lost their homes because they could not qualify for the new loan that was needed to pay off the old loan. High unemployment and declining wages meant that monthly incomes were insufficient to make the loan payments. Other households simply defaulted on their existing home loans because of the drop in income, and the decline in the market value of the house caused by the depression left the lender unable to recover the principal amount.

Policy makers at the FHA decided that a good solution to these problems was to create a mortgage loan instrument that had a long term of 25 to 30 years that would also be fully amortizing. A loan that is fully amortizing eliminates the need to find new financing. If the loan is to be fully amortizing, the longer term for the loan will reduce the size of the monthly payment needed to pay back the loan. Furthermore, policy makers wanted to encourage ownership of homes by having lower down payments. FHA officials reasoned that lenders would not agree to low down payments and long terms for the home loan unless there was a guarantee. FHA loans were thus formulated as loans with maximum 30-year terms, low down payments, full amortization, and mortgage insurance that is purchased by the borrower. The insurance premium can be paid in a lump sum at the beginning, or it can be included in the loan amount and thus paid over the term of the loan. FHA loans are limited in their amount, so expensive houses cannot be bought under the FHA program. However, the FHA loan guarantee program demonstrated that loans of this type were feasible, and private lenders soon began to offer the same type of loan (but with higher down-payment requirements) to any borrower. The conventional home loan is for 25 to 30 years, is fully amortizing, and requires a down payment of 20%. It is fair to say that once the Great Depression and World War II era had ended, the creation of this new type of home loan enabled many households to become owners of homes in the suburbs. Many may wonder today about the wisdom of encouraging suburban home-ownership, but clearly the FHA program has been highly successful in addressing the problems as they existed in the 1930s.

The other major housing program aimed at the middle (and upper) class is the favorable treatment of owner-occupied housing in the federal income tax. The owners of homes are permitted to deduct from income their expenses for mortgage interest and state and local taxes. They are not permitted to deduct loan payments that reduce principal – only the interest payments are deductible. The effect of these deductions on the cost of owning compared to the cost or renting was examined in Chapter 8. American taxpayers also get to avoid paying the capital gains tax on the increase in the value of their homes. No capital gains tax is paid if the homeowner used the house as main residence for two years and the gain is less than $250,000 ($500,000 for married couples filing joint returns). This favorable treatment of capital gains is an incentive to "invest" in one's home rather than other assets.

The economic impact of these tax provisions can be examined through the use of a framework developed by King and Fullerton (1984) to study the taxation of income from capital. In this case the income is the implicit (or imputed) housing rents that are created by an investment in an owner-occupied house. Obviously, the house generates a flow of housing services that has market value. Note that the homeowner does not report imputed rent on the owner-occupied house on the federal tax form but may deduct interest and property taxes, which are two of the main expenses incurred in producing housing services. (Imputed rent is reported in Italy, and it used to be reported in Sweden and the United Kingdom.) The King–Fullerton framework uses two basic concepts: (1) the marginal effective tax rate, and (2) the cost of capital.

The marginal effective tax rate is defined as

$$t = (p - s)/p,$$

where p is the homeowner's before-tax real rate of return on the marginal investment (net of depreciation), and s is the after-tax real rate of return to the saver who supplied the financing for the investment. The simple difference $p - s$ is known as the *tax wedge*. The real rate of return p is in the form of imputed net rents. This equation for marginal effective tax rate can be written $t = 1 - s/p$. The assumption used in the King–Fullerton model is that p is equal to some constant such 10%, so

$$t = 1 - 10s.$$

The before-tax real rate of return is held constant so that differences in tax provisions can be compared at a given real rate of return for housing investment. The finding that a change in tax regimes lowers the effective tax rate will, of course, provide an incentive for greater investment in housing capital.

The saver who supplied the financing for the house earns a real rate of return after taxes of

$$s = i(1 - m_L) - \pi - w,$$

where i is the nominal discount rate, m_L the saver's marginal tax rate, π the expected rate of inflation, and w the marginal personal tax rate on wealth. All of these variables that determine s, with the exception of i, are known. The trick is to estimate i.

King and Fullerton (1984) assume that investors in housing invest up to the point at which p is equal to the cost of capital net of depreciation. Assuming that one knows the nominal discount rate, the cost of capital varies with the details of the tax code. The cost of capital net of depreciation can be written

$$c = (1 - A)(i - \pi + \varphi) + (1 - B)w + z(\pi - \Omega),$$

with the additional terms in the equation defined as follows: A is the present value of tax allowances for owner-occupied housing (e.g. mortgage interest deduction), φ the tax rate on imputed rental income, B the present value of tax allowances that offset the wealth tax (i.e., income tax deduction for property taxes), Ω the real rate of depreciation, and z the tax rate on capital gains.

Consider this equation for the cost of capital net of depreciation very carefully. It says that the cost of capital net of depreciation includes the real discount rate $(i - \pi)$ and the tax rate on imputed net income φ, all multiplied by the factor $(1 - A)$ to reflect tax benefits provided to owner-occupied housing. The cost of capital also includes the wealth rate w (with offset factor B) and the tax rate on nominal capital gains after depreciation has been allowed $[z(\pi - \Omega)]$. This last term assumes that the house appreciates in value at the same rate as the expected inflation rate π. Clearly the tax benefits A and B lower the cost of capital.

The King–Fullerton procedure assumes that $c = p = 10\%$, and solves for i, the nominal discount rate. The value for i is then inserted into the equation for s, the real after-tax rate of return to the saver who supplied the housing finance. Actually, all of this can be performed in one operation. Consider the simple tax regime in which A, φ, B, and z are all equal to zero and where savers are not subject to the wealth tax rate w (homeowners are subject to the wealth tax). This is, in fact, the system that exists in Canada, and the cost of capital net of depreciation is just

$$c = 0.1 = i - \pi + w,$$

which means that $i = 0.1 + \pi - w$. The result for the effective tax rate is

$$t = 1 - 10[(0.1 + \pi - w)(1 - m_L) - \pi].$$

For example, suppose that π (expected inflation) is 0.05, w (property tax rate) is 0.02, and m_L (marginal tax rate for savers) is 0.30. For this example, suppose that the house is financed entirely by debt (i.e., by borrowing from people who face a marginal tax rate on their savings of 0.30). The marginal effective tax rate is 0.59 if the house is financed by debt. The interpretation is that 59% of the imputed return to a marginal investment in owner-occupied housing is taxed away.

The system in the United States permits tax deductions for interest and property taxes (i.e., $A = B$), so with 100% debt finance,

$$c = 0.1 = (1 - A)(i + w) - \pi.$$

In this case

$$t = 1 - 10\{[(0.1 + \pi)/(1 - A)](1 - m_L) - w(1 - m_L) - \pi\}$$

The only difference is that $0.1 + \pi$ is divided by $(1 - A)$, but the effective tax rate is changed dramatically. If $A = m_L = 0.30$ and the other numerical values remain unchanged, t falls to 0.14! Now the imputed rent of owner-occupied housing is taxed very lightly, which provides a strong incentive to invest compared to the Canadian system without the favorable tax deductions. In addition, the research reported in the book edited by Jorgenson and Landau (1993) shows that owner-occupied housing in the United States has a very low effective tax rate compared to other forms of private investment. Analogous computations for regular corporate investment show that the effective tax rate in 1990 was in the range of 30 to 45%, compared to an estimated effective tax rate on owner-occupied housing of 11%. How can one invest in more owner-occupied housing? The usual procedure is to build more of it in the suburbs.

Table 9.1   Subsidized housing units in urban areas: 2003 (thousands)

	Central cities		Suburbs		Total
	Occupied rental	*Vacant rental*	*Occupied rental*	*Vacant rental*	
Total	14,599	1,593	14,041	1,333	31,566
No subsidy	11,418	1,311	11,635	1,135	25,499
Rent controlled	650	22	184	9	865
Public housing	946	92	498	26	1,562
Govt. rent subsidy	2,052	78	1,762	15	3,907
Not reported	182	102	146	79	509

Some units are included in more than one total.
Source: American Housing Survey, US Department of Housing and Urban Development, 2004

C. Housing Policies for Lower-Income Households

The goal of housing policy in the United States is, as stated in the Housing Act of 1949, to "provide a decent, safe, and sanitary living environment . . . for every American." The pursuit of this goal has spawned an array of federal programs, and the purpose of this section is to review briefly the history of federal low-income housing programs. Housing programs, or programs targeted at any other consumer good, can be classified as programs that function on the supply side or on the demand side of the market. For example, in the case of food, the government could produce the food and then give it away to poor households (supply-side program), or it could give the poor households food stamps that are spent on food (demand-side program). The general theme of this brief discussion is that federal policy began by supplying housing for low-income households directly and has, over the decades, gradually shifted to subsidies that operate on the demand side. Table 9.1 has been constructed to show the numbers of housing units in urban areas that are covered by the various housing programs in 2003.

The first federal program was begun under the Housing Act of 1937, which created federally funded public housing. Under this program local governments were authorized to set up public housing authorities that would receive federal funds to build public housing. The federal government set up the eligibility criteria for residents of public housing, who then paid a low rent to the local public housing authority. The program was expanded under the Housing Act of 1949, the law that also created the urban renewal program. The 1949 act authorized the construction of 800,000 units of public housing. The urban renewal program set up local urban renewal authorities that received federal funds for the purchase of slum properties. Under the urban renewal program the local urban renewal authority demolished the slum buildings, assembled land into usable parcels, and then sold the land at below-market prices to housing developers. Sometimes that land was turned over to the local public housing authority for the construction of public housing, but most of the land parcels were sold to private developers that built a variety of types of housing. Table 9.1 shows that as of 2003, there were 1.56 million public housing units in urban areas in the United States and that 66% of those units were in central cities. Public housing makes up 1.7% of the 93 million housing units in urban areas. The number of public housing units is declining – from 1.78 million in 1991 to 1.56 million in 2003. Demolition of old public housing has been underway in Chicago and other cities.

Housing policy branched out in the 1960s to encourage the construction of housing for low-income households by private developers. Also, a small program of rent supplement for low-income households was created in 1965. Another new program in 1965 permitted public housing authorities to lease existing private housing units and subsidize low-income households to live in them. The 1960 Census of Population and Housing showed that 17% of housing units were either dilapidated or deteriorating, that 12% were over-crowded, and that affordability was a problem. Furthermore, the baby-boom generation would soon form their own families and overwhelm the limited housing stock unless the nation acted to meet its housing needs. Analysts at the US Department of Housing and Urban Development (HUD) estimated that 26 million units would be needed between 1969 and 1978, and set a goal of 6 million subsidized units. The Housing Act of 1968 adopted this goal and created programs whereby below-market interest rates were offered to apartment developers to enable them to offer below-market rents to low and moderate-income tenants. Another part of the 1968 Act offered below-market interest rates to eligible home buyers under the FHA mortgage insurance program. During the 1970–3 period 1.7 million subsidized units were added to the stock of housing. There were problems with the implementation and costs of these new programs, and after he had won a landslide election victory in 1972, President Nixon called for a thorough review of housing policy.

The result of this review was the 1974 Housing and Community Development Act, which included the section 8 low-income rental assistance program, a revision of the programs that were created in 1965 and mentioned above. This program had separate elements for new construction, substantial rehabilitation, and existing housing. Under the new construction and substantial rehabilitation parts of the program, private and nonprofit developers obtained their own FHA-insured financing, and HUD entered into a long-term contract of 20 to 30 years to subsidize the difference between fair-market rent and 25% (30% after 1981) of the tenant's income. In recent years some of these long-term contracts expired, and controversy surrounds the issue of whether those contracts should be extended. The Section 8 program for new housing was eliminated in 1983 because the program was too expensive. According to the US Department of Housing and Urban Development (1982), the annual subsidy per unit was over $6,000.

In contrast to all of the programs described so far, the Section 8 program for existing housing is a demand-side program. An eligible tenant obtains a rent certificate from the local housing authority and then shops for suitable housing that meets the quality stand-ards and a rent limit set by HUD. The local housing authority retained some control over location and assisted with the lease negotiation. The actual payments go directly from the local housing authority to the landlord. The tenant pays rent that is no more than 30% of income.

Table 9.1 shows that as of 2003, there were 3.9 million subsidized housing units of various types in urban areas in the United States (up from 2.2 million in 1991). Most are federally subsidized rental units (i.e., Section 8 units) and some are subsidized by state or local governments. About 55% of these units are located in central cities, but 1.77 million subsidized units are located in the suburbs. Subsidized rental units, together with public housing, made up 5.9% of the total housing stock and 17.3% of the rental housing in urban areas in 2003. Some 19.6% of the rental housing in central cities is either public housing or subsidized rental units. Therefore, while publicly subsidized housing makes up a small fraction of the total urban housing market, it plays a significant role in the rental housing market in central cities.

The other program shown on Table 9.1 is rental units that operate under rent controls put in place by local governments. As of 2003, 865,000 units were under rent control, the vast majority (78%) in central cities. The largest number of rent-controlled apartments is in New York City, which has had rent control since World War II, but more recently, Boston, Washington, DC, Los Angeles, San Francisco, and many other places that experienced rapid increases in rents have instituted rent controls. Economists generally take a dim view of rent controls that remain in place for any extended length of time. Rent controls that are truly effective discourage maintenance and can ultimately lead to the withdrawal of units from the housing stock. Rent control is discussed in detail in section E.

Despite all of these programs aimed at providing housing for lower-income households or controlling rents, there is serious problem of housing affordability among households in poverty. In 2003 there were 13.960 million units (13.2% of all occupied housing units in the nation) occupied by households with incomes below poverty level. The official poverty level of income for a family of four in 2003 was $18,810. Of those in poverty, 36% reported housing costs that were 30% to 99% of their incomes. (Many households in poverty report no income or do not pay rent. These are excluded from this computation.) The median ratio of housing costs to income for these households was 42%. In other words, if a family of four with an income of $18,810 (in 2003) spent 42% of that income on housing rent, $10,910 was left for all other purposes. The failure of wages to grow since 1973 for less-skilled workers, coupled with increases in housing rents, has created a housing problem among the low-income population.

D. The Demand for Housing and Demand-Side Housing Policies

Rent certificates became a significant part of federal housing policy in the 1974 Housing and Community Development Act, but the idea of demand-side subsidies was not new. Such a program was discussed and rejected in the formulation of the Housing Act of 1937, and they were reconsidered and rejected during the congressional discussions that led up to the Housing Act of 1949. In 1968 the President's Committee on Urban Housing argued in favor of demand-side programs and recommended that the government undertake an experiment to determine the feasibility of such programs. Advocates of demand-side programs argued that:

1   Housing provided directly or indirectly by the public sector is more expensive than private-sector housing.

2   Demand-side subsidies are more equitable because the same amount of money can be used to serve more households.
3   Demand-side subsidies give households freedom to choose their own housing and location.

Opponents of demand-side subsidies include housing suppliers who argue in their own self-interest, but there are other opponents who make theoretical arguments in favor of supply-side programs. Some argue that the best way to make sure that the low-income households actually improve their housing is for the public sector to have housing built for them. For example, Friedman and Weinberg (1982) noted that low-income minority households largely failed to participate in the experiments that tested the effects of housing vouchers similar to the section 8 existing housing program. Others point out that once built, public housing and other units that are directly subsidized cannot be removed or canceled. A program of demand-side subsidies is just money, and Congress can take away the money at any time. Advocates of supply-side policies also point out that increasing demand for housing through the use of demand-side subsidies might cause an increase in housing rents for all low- and moderate-income households.

Theory of housing demand and demand subsidies

Before we examine research on the effects of demand-side subsidies, it is helpful to think through various policy options using the basic economics of housing demand. Consider a household with a relatively low income. The household allocates its income to housing or to other consumption goods. To keep the theory simple we assume that expenditures on all other goods can be lumped together. The household has preferences for housing and other goods that can be depicted on the standard indifference curve diagram shown in Figure 9.1. Indifference curves are labeled IC_1, IC_2, and so on. Housing is assumed to be a commodity that can be measured in standard units of housing services. The combinations of housing and other goods that are on the same indifference curve yield equal levels of utility for the household. As explained in the appendix to this book, the slope of the indifference curve is the rate at which the household is willing to trade one commodity (housing) for the other (expenditures on other goods) and stay at the same level of utility. The household has a family of indifference curves; indifference curves farther to the northeast on the diagram pertain to higher levels of utility.

Now let us add the household's budget constraint to the model. The household has a particular level of income Y and faces a price per standardized unit of housing services of R. The "price" of expenditures on all other goods is $1, of course. These pieces of information determine the position of the budget constraint. Write the budget constraint as

$$Y = RH + G,$$

where H is the number of units of housing services purchased and G is expenditures on other goods. This equation can be manipulated to yield

$$G = Y - RH,$$

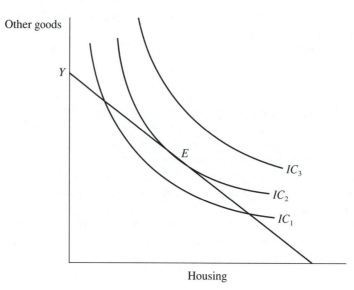

Figure 9.1   Household choices of housing and other goods

so the budget constraint in Figure 9.1 has an intercept of Y and a slope of $-R$.

Given its preferences as represented by the indifference curves and its budget constraint, the household selects the combination of housing services and other goods represented by point E in Figure 9.1. At this point the slope of the budget constraint $(-R)$ is equal to the slope of indifference curve IC_2, the highest indifference curve that is attainable.

The household depicted in Figure 9.1 may well be spending a rather high proportion of its income on housing, or it may not. The household is simply doing the best it can with what it has. Now let us suppose that the municipal officials enact building and housing codes that, in effect, require a low-income household to consume some minimum quantity of housing services (or move elsewhere). If that minimum is less than the amount of housing services shown in Figure 9.1, nothing has happened.

Figure 9.2 shows the result. The household moves from point E to point E', consumes more housing and less other goods, and suffers a loss of utility as shown from a move from indifference curve IC_2 to IC_1. Now here we have something that might be called a housing affordability problem. On its own, the household chooses to purchase less than the minimum amount of housing deemed suitable by the local government. The policy of forcing the household to consume the minimum amount of housing reduces its utility. One solution to this problem would be to give additional income until its consumption of housing freely chosen equals the minimum required by the local government. This option is shown in Figure 9.2 as the move of the budget constraint from Y to Y'. To its delight, the household now achieves the utility level on indifference curve IC_3 at point E''. Comparing points E and E'', the household has increased its consumption of housing and other goods as well. However, a general income subsidy may be an expensive method for the government to induce the household to increase its housing consumption.

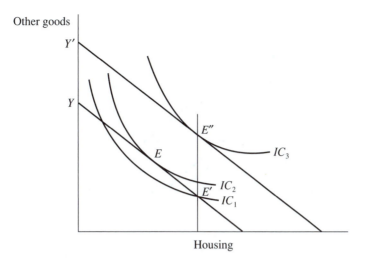

Figure 9.2   Effects of a minimum standard

The same apparatus can be used to examine the effects of the section 8 existing housing program – the rent certificate program. The rules of the program specify that the participating household pays 30% of its income on housing, and the government pays the difference between the actual rent and the household's contribution. Actual rent cannot exceed some estimated fair market rent for a dwelling of the required level of quality. This program tells the household that it will not be spending more than 30% of its income on housing. The new budget constraint for the household is shown in Figure 9.3 as line *YAB*; the *AB* portion of the constraint is horizontal up to housing consumption level *H** because the household never has to spend more than 0.3*Y* on housing. Obviously, the household maximizes utility by choosing point *B*. The government has paid a subsidy to the landlord equal to distance *CB* because the cost of *H** units of housing services is, in Figure 9.3, equal to 0.3*Y* + *CB* (and the household paid 0.3*Y*).

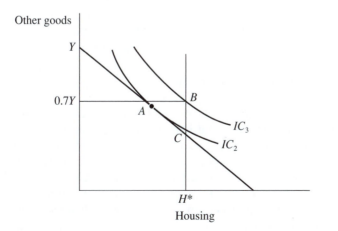

Figure 9.3   Rent certificate program

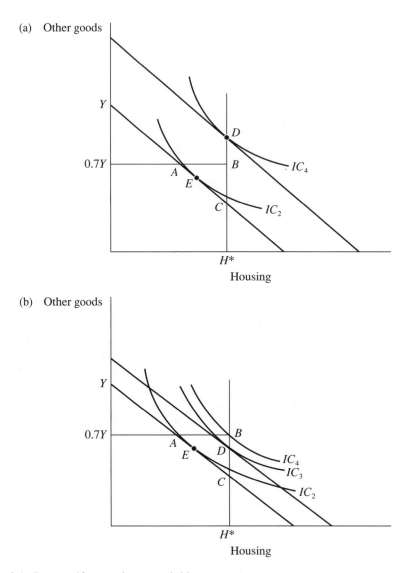

Figure 9.4   Rent certificate or income subsidy

Is this a cheaper method than an income subsidy for inducing the household to increase its consumption of housing to H^*? It is if the situation is as depicted in Figure 9.4a. In this figure an income subsidy of DC is needed to induce the household to increase housing consumption of H^* (compared to the smaller rent certificate BC).

However, in Figure 9.4b the household has a different set of preferences, and the required income subsidy of DC is smaller than the rent certificate BC. What is the difference between Figure 9.4a and b? In the first case the household has a relatively low income elasticity of demand for housing, and in the second case the income elasticity is higher. Which figure depicts the more likely outcome? Note that Figure 9.4b depicts the case in which the household responds to an income subsidy by increasing its expenditures on other goods by only a small amount. In other words, the income elasticity of demand for all other goods as a group (food, clothing, appliances, entertainment, etc.) must be rather low. This is not likely, especially for low-income households. Indeed, numerous empirical studies indicate otherwise. Figure 9.4a therefore depicts the real case, and the rent certificate program is the cheaper method for inducing the household to increase housing consumption to H^*.

In response to the recommendation of the President's Committee on Urban Housing, the 1970 Housing and Urban Development Act directed HUD to carry out a major experimental study of demand-side housing allowances. Two issues were of immediate concern. First, if low-income households were given housing allowances (also called *housing vouchers*) that reduced the housing rent that they pay, how much improvement in their housing standards would result? Second, if all low-income households received housing allowances, will housing rents rise (and by how much)?

The empirical literature on the demand for housing at the time did not provide clear answers to the question of price and income elasticities of demand for housing. The estimation of price elasticity is particularly problematic because there is no market "price" for a unit of housing services. The prices that are observed in the market are actually household expenditures on housing (either the market price of a house or the housing rent; i.e., price times quantity). The estimation of income elasticity was not so problematic, although clearly the relevant income concept is permanent (or longer-run) income rather than just current income. Short-run fluctuations in current income cannot be expected to have a major impact on housing expenditures because it is costly to move and adjust one's housing consumption bundle.

The Housing Allowance Demand Experiment was designed to address these methodological problems. As discussed by Friedman and Weinberg (1982), the experiment enrolled about 1,200 families in housing allowance programs in each of two sites (Pittsburgh and Phoenix) during a three-year period beginning in 1974. The experiment also included 500 families in each site as control groups. The experiment tested two types of programs. One program reduced the rent paid by the household by a fixed percentage, such as 30%. The other type of program was similar to the section 8 existing housing rent certificate program that is discussed above. The crucial experimental variable is the size of the subsidy received by the households. The experiment was designed so that the experimenters could manipulate the price of a unit of housing services or the amount of the rent certificate and observe the results of price changes. For example, suppose that the members of the experimental group received a rent subsidy of 30%, so the price of a unit of housing services is 70% of its market price.

The effects of this rent subsidy can be depicted graphically. Figure 9.5 shows the same initial household equilibrium at point E as does Figure 9.1. The rent subsidy reduces the price of a unit of housing services by 30%, so the budget constraint rotates to line YE'. The consumption of housing services has increased for two reasons. First, the price of housing relative to other goods has been reduced. The budget constraint has become flatter, and this change in slope pushes the household to consume more housing and less of other goods. The effect of the change in *relative prices* is called the *substitution effect*. Second, the rent subsidy has caused the household to have a higher income in real terms. The household's money income (Y) has not increased, but the amount it must pay for its

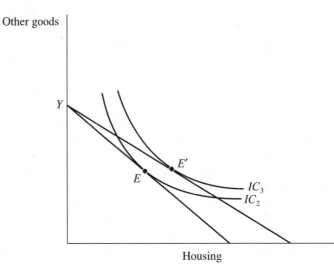

Figure 9.5   Rent subsidy program

bundle of consumer goods has been reduced. This increase in real income generally causes an increase in the consumption of all goods, including housing, and this effect is known as the *income effect*.

Following the analysis in Figure 9.5, suppose that the demand for housing H can be specified for a household as

$$H = AY^b p_h^c$$

or

$$\ln H = \ln A + b \ln Y + c \ln p_h,$$

where H units of housing services, Y the household's permanent income, and p_h the price of a unit of housing services. The coefficients b and c are the income and price elasticities of demand. To see this, write the change in H as

$$\Delta H = (bAY^{b-1} p_h^c)\Delta Y + (cAY^b p_h^{c-1})\Delta p_h = (bH/Y)\Delta Y + (cH/p_h)\Delta p_h.$$

Therefore, income elasticity can be derived as

$$\Delta H/\Delta Y = bH/Y$$

so

$$e_y = (\Delta H/H)/(\Delta Y/Y) = b.$$

Similarly, price elasticity of demand can be found from

$$(\Delta H/\Delta p_h) = cH/p_h$$

so that

$$e_d = (\Delta H/H)/(\Delta p_h/p_h) = c.$$

The variables H and p_h are not directly observable. Housing expenditures E are p_hH, so

$$\ln E = \ln p_h + \ln H = \ln(p_hH), \text{ and}$$
$$\ln E = \ln A + b \ln Y + (1 + c) \ln p_h$$

The experimental housing allowance reduces p_h to $(1 - a)p_h$, where a is the subsidy amount (ranging from 0.2 to 0.6 for the various experimental groups and zero for the control group). Substitution of $(1 - a)p_h$ for p_h yields

$$\ln[(1 - a)p_hH] = \ln A + b \ln Y + (1 + c) \ln[(1 - a)p_h],$$

or

$$\ln(1 - a) + \ln E = \ln A + (1 + c) \ln p_h + b \ln Y + (1 + c) \ln(1 - a).$$

Subtraction of $\ln(1 - a)$ yields the equation

$$\ln E = [\ln A + (1 + c) \ln p_h] + b \ln Y + c \ln(1 - a).$$

The variable p_h is still not observable, but it can plausibly be assumed to be constant within the same housing market (e.g., within the same neighborhood). The equation can therefore be estimated with $\ln Y$, $\ln(1 - a)$, and neighborhood control variables included. The coefficient of $\ln(1 - a)$ is the price elasticity of demand for housing services.

Friedman and Weinberg (1982, p. 32) reported that the price elasticities estimated for low-income households in Pittsburgh and Phoenix are -0.18 and -0.23, respectively. These estimates mean that a 30% reduction in the price of housing leads to an increase in housing consumption of about 6%. In other words, a program that reduces housing rents by 30% will increase the quantity of housing by only 6%, and expenditures on housing out of the household's own income decrease. The elasticity of the change in expenditures on housing that result from a price can be written

$$(\Delta E/\Delta p_h)(p_h/E) = (p_h/E)(\Delta p_hH/\Delta p_h) = (p_h/p_hH)[H + p_h(\Delta H/\Delta p_h)]$$
$$= 1 + (\Delta H/\Delta p_h)(p_h/H) = 1 + e_d,$$

where e_d is the price elasticity of demand. If demand is inelastic $(0 > e_d > -1)$, expenditures increase when the price increases. If the price of housing is *cut*, housing expenditures *fall* by $(1 + e_d)$. If the price of housing is cut by 30% and e_d is -0.2, expenditures on housing fall by $0.3 \times 0.8 = 0.24$, or 24%. The estimated income elasticities (based on income averaged over three years) are 0.33 for Pittsburgh and 0.44 for Phoenix. These responses are less than overwhelming, but they are based only on a three-year experiment. Perhaps, the responses would have been larger if the program had been permanent. However, it is plausible to argue that most households in the experiment were already living in housing that is more or less acceptable and that the real housing problem is one of affordability. A reduction in housing rent mainly enabled households to save money on their housing so that other goods and services could be purchased, although a small improvement in housing quality was also observed.

While the housing allowance experiments were under way, other housing economists were making progress on estimating housing demand functions using nonexperimental data. One particularly good study by Polinsky and Ellwood (1979) specified the demand for housing as

$$\ln H = \beta_0 + \beta_1 \ln Y + \beta_2 \ln p_h + \beta_3 \ln p_o,$$

where p_o is the price of all other goods besides housing. We know from basic demand theory that $\beta_1 + \beta_2 + \beta_3 = 0$ because doubling income and all prices leaves the quantity demanded unchanged. Doubling each variable means, for example $\ln 2Y = \ln 2 + \ln Y$, or adding $\ln 2$ to $\ln Y$, $\ln p_h$, and $\ln p_o$, so the result follows. The demand function can now be written as

$$\ln H = \beta_0 + \beta_1 \ln Y + \beta_2 \ln p_h - (\beta_1 + \beta_2) \ln p_o.$$

Housing expenditures divided by the price of other goods can be found as

$$\ln(p_h H/p_o) = \beta_0 + \beta_1 \ln Y + (\beta_2 + 1) \ln p_h - (\beta_1 + \beta_2 + 1) \ln p_o,$$

or

$$\ln(E/p_o) = (\beta_0 - \beta_1 - \beta_2) + \beta_1 \ln(Y/p_o) + (\beta_2 + 1) \ln(p_h/p_o)$$

Housing expenditures and income are observable. The price of other goods is the index of consumer prices (excluding the price of housing) for the metropolitan area in which the household is located, and the price of housing is predicted using a model in which the price of land and the price of construction determine the price of a unit of housing. Note, that the coefficient of $\ln(p_h/p_o)$ is the price elasticity of demand plus 1.

Polinsky and Ellwood (1979) estimated the model using a sample of 10,054 households in 31 urban areas that purchased housing through the FHA mortgage guarantee program. Their estimate of β_1 (income elasticity) is 0.57; and their estimate of $\beta_2 + 1$ is 0.28, so the estimated price elasticity of demand is -0.72. Polinsky and Ellwood (1979) think that their estimate of income elasticity is a bit low because the FHA program has an upper limit on the size of the loan that can be insured. Some people with high incomes who wish to be part of FHA program must therefore reduce the amount that they otherwise might spend on housing. Their final estimate of income elasticity is therefore adjusted upward to 0.80. These estimates pertain to the general population, and the price and income elasticities can be different for different groups. However, there is general agreement that the demand is inelastic with respect to price and that income elasticity is less than 1.

The federally sponsored housing research of the 1970s also included two tests of housing allowances that were designed to determine whether housing rents would be driven up by a general housing allowance program. Two sites were chosen – Green Bay, Wisconsin and South Bend, Indiana – and housing allowances were made available to any household that qualified on the basis of income and family size. The result of these field tests were as follows:

1 Participation of eligible households was rather low, with only about 40 to 45% of those eligible enrolled.
2 Participating households increased their housing consumption by small amounts (as in the Pittsburgh and Phoenix experiments).
3 Housing rents in the two markets did not rise.

Because the participation in the Green Bay and South Bend projects was rather low, these results probably cannot be generalized to all housing allowance programs. Surely there are situations in which inundating a local housing market with housing allowances would lead to increases in housing rents.

E. Rent Control

Table 9.1 shows that as of 1991, there were 865,000 housing units in the United States under some form of rent control, or about 2.7% of the total stock of rental housing. Rent control has existed in New York City since World War II, and many other large and small cities have instituted rent-control programs since the 1970s. The list of cities includes Los Angeles, Washington, DC, Boston, San Francisco, Cambridge (Massachusetts), and New York. The number of units under rent control has declined – from 1.2 million in 1991 to 865,000 in 2003. Rent control programs come in many forms. Some programs froze rents, while other programs permitted rent increases according to some formula based on general inflation or increases in landlord expenses. Some early rent control programs controlled rents on all rental units, but more recent programs exempt new construction and/or units of very high quality. In addition, some programs permit rent to adjust to the market when the unit is vacated. The purpose of this section is use basic microeconomic theory to examine some of these programs. Most economists agree that the old-fashioned rent controls discouraged new construction, caused abandonment, reduced maintenance and mobility, created mismatches between tenants and housing units, caused rental units to be converted to owner-occupied housing, stimulated black markets and other methods for getting around controls, and potentially led to greater racial discrimination. However, one prominent urban economist [Arnott (1995)] has a mildly dissenting view. Arnott believes that a well-designed version of the newer form of rent control (with exemptions for new construction, rent adjustments for inflation and verifiable increases in expenses, and regulations regarding maintenance) can be beneficial.

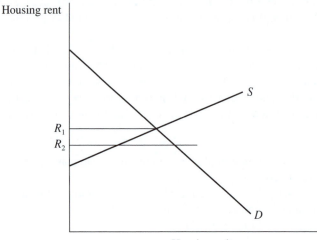

Figure 9.6   Old-fashioned rent control

The conventional analysis of old-fashioned rent control uses a simple supply and demand model, as shown in Figure 9.6. In this model all housing units are identical. The current supply of units is S and the current demand for units is D. As always, supply and demand are functions of the real price of the good, the opportunity cost in terms of other goods. Rent is frozen on all units in *nominal* terms at the current level R_1. Consider first what happens when the costs of supplying housing rise in nominal terms but the rent is still frozen in nominal terms. The result is a reduction in the real rent that is permitted to R_2. (The supply and demand curves do not shift. Why?) This reduction in real rent creates shortage of housing units in this market by both increasing quantity demanded and reducing quantity supplied. In the short run the quantity of units supplied will not change much because housing is very durable, but in the longer run some rental units will be removed from the rental stock. Some units will be converted to owner-occupied units and others eventually will be demolished because the full cost of owning and operating the units cannot be covered. If the elasticity of supply is large enough and the reduction in real rent is great enough, the stock of rental housing in this city could disappear entirely!

Rent control has an impact on the distribution of income. The winners in the game are those tenants who continue to live in the remaining rental housing stock – their rents in real terms have declined. Landlords of those remaining units suffer a loss of real income, and the real market value of rental units also drops. Some tenants are displaced be the withdrawals of units from the rental housing stock, and they must pay the cost of searching for and moving into a new unit in some other city. Rent control as depicted in Figure 9.6 has some other interesting effects. Rent control will cut down on the mobility of tenants because the existing tenants know that the shortage of rent-controlled units means that many households are out there waiting for the chance to get a low rent. Tenants know that if they move out, there is a slim chance that they will be able to rent another unit that is under control. Rent control therefore leads to anomalous situations such as retired couples (or widows) living in large apartments while families with children are unable to find a rent-controlled unit. In addition, when a rent-controlled unit does become vacant, the lucky new tenant may find that it was necessary to pay additional fees to secure the unit. Such a fee is sometimes called *key money* or a *finder's fee*. Under some rent control laws such fees are illegal, but they exist nonetheless. In other cases the long list of households desiring to move into a rent-controlled unit may enable the landlord to screen tenants heavily on the basis of income level, race, and so on.

This basic model is consistent with evidence from some cities that have introduced rent controls. For example, Santa Monica and four cities in California introduced rent controls in 1979 that prohibited rent increases when the apartment turns over. Newspaper accounts describe how a new tenant must pay a big finder's fee – or that vacated apartment goes to a relative of the landlord. Many units have been boarded up and withdrawn from the market. Tenants in some buildings are paying maintenance expenses. In response to such stories the state of California in 1995 enacted a law that prevents cities from prohibiting rent increases when a unit turns over.

Now let us change the game and impose what Arnott (1995) calls "second-generation" rent control. This program permits landlords to raise rents because of general inflation and verifiable increases in costs, and newly constructed units are exempt from controls. In this case the problem arising in Figure 9.6 from a decline in real rent cannot occur. Let us, instead, examine the effects of an increase in the demand for rental units. In Figure 9.7 demand has increased from D_1 to D_2. An uncontrolled market will respond with an increase in quantity from H_1 to H_2 and an increase in rent on all units from R_1 to R_2. With old-fashioned rent control the market will not respond to this increase in demand, and a shortage of units exists. With second-generation rent control the rent on the old units will remain at R_1 but the quantity supplied will increase to H_3 and rent on

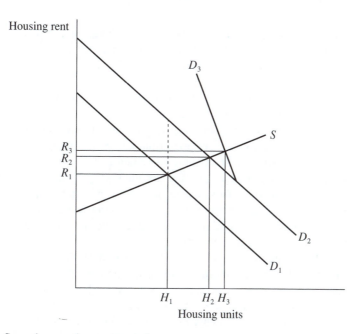

Figure 9.7   Second-generation rent control

new units will be R_3 because with this program demand has actually increased to D_3. New units have been built without the redistribution of income from the old tenants to the old landlords that would accompany the uncontrolled market response. Furthermore, more new units have been built and rents in new units have increased more compared to the uncontrolled market. Why does this happen? Without rent control the quantity of housing units demanded by the *old* tenants falls, but with rent control these old tenants continue to demand quantity H_1.

Fallis and Smith (1984) provided empirical evidence for the Los Angeles housing market that rents in the uncontrolled portion of the market increased more with rent control that they would have without rent control.

Second-generation rent control has some of the problems of old-fashioned rent control. Tenant mobility can still be reduced, and mismatches between tenants and units therefore can be created with the passage of time. In addition, the nature of any adjustment of rent with unit turnover presents a dilemma. Do we permit real rents to adjust upward at that time, thereby giving the landlord an incentive to get rid of the current tenant? Or do we prohibit the adjustment and create the black market, the waiting lists, and the key money payments?

The harmful effects of old-fashioned rent control, as depicted in Figure 9.6, are not in dispute, but the jury is still out on second-generation rent control programs. Some of these programs have prevented income redistribution from tenants to landlords while encouraging new construction.

F. Summary

In Chapters 8 and 9 we have examined both the workings of the private market for housing in urban areas and the history of housing policy in the United States. The main points made in the two chapters can be outlined as follows.

1   Housing is the biggest part of the household's budget for many people, and it is the largest use of land in urban areas as well.
2   Housing is a complicated commodity that is very durable and immovable.
3   The housing market has its own set of institutions for recording ownership, buying and selling, and borrowing money to purchase a house. The urban economist needs to understand these institutions and the role that they play in determining the market value of residential property. This chapter includes a brief introduction to residential real estate transactions, and more details are provided in Chapters 10 and 11. Students interested in pursuing these topics in greater depth and/or interested in a career in real estate should take a course in real estate.
4   A useful model of the urban housing market is based on the idea of filtering. The housing stock can be arrayed in order of quality, with households arrayed in order of their demand for housing. The housing market assigns households to housing units and determines housing prices and rents. An increase in the supply of housing at or near the top of the quality hierarchy, for example, provides opportunities for households to improve the quality of their housing by filtering up.

5   There is clear evidence of racial prejudice and discrimination in urban housing markets. The level of segregation of the black population from other groups is far higher than can be attributed reasonably to voluntary segregation. During the period of the 1950s to the 1970s when the black population in urban areas was growing very rapidly, housing rents were often observed to higher for black households than for white households. However, at this time housing rents in black neighborhoods may actually be lower than rents in white neighborhoods largely because black neighborhoods have fewer amenities and higher crime rates. The same may be true in Hispanic neighborhoods as well.

6   Housing policy in the United States has encouraged the ownership of homes by the middle class and has attempted to improve the housing occupied by low-income households. The policies of home mortgage guarantees and income tax incentives for homeowners have been successful in promoting the ownership of homes. Furthermore, the quality of the housing units occupied by the vast majority of urban Americans is quite good. However, urban households with low incomes have a serious problem with affordability of urban housing. Federal housing policy has failed to make much progress on the affordability issue, but the idea of demand-side subsidies (i.e., housing allowances) holds some promise. Demand-side housing subsidies are a growing program that must compete with many other programs for federal funds. The total number of subsidized rental units increased form 2.2 million in 1991 to 3.9 million in 2003, an increase of 77%. The empirical studies suggest that when a low-income household is given a housing allowance, it reduces expenditures of its own income on housing in order to have more money to spend on other things. Given the high cost of housing relative to income among low-income households, this is an altogether reasonable choice.

7   Rent control exists in several local housing markets around the country, especially in New York and California. The old form of rent control, which froze rents in nominal terms, clearly was harmful on many counts. New construction and maintenance were discouraged, and units were abandoned. However, newer forms of rent control, which Arnott (1995) calls second-generation programs, have been designed to permit landlords of existing units reasonable increases in rents and to encourage construction by exempting new units. These provisions tend to mitigate some, but not all, of the adverse effects of rent control.

Exercises

1   Consider the King–Fullerton analysis of the taxation of income from capital as applied to owner-occupied housing. Use the same model and numerical magnitudes as in the text. What would happen to the effective tax rate on implicit rent if the income tax rate in the US were increased from 0.3 to 0.4?

2   Suppose that the demand for housing by low-income households is

$$H = AY^b p^c$$

Here b is the income elasticity of demand and c is the price elasticity of demand. Let $A = 0.0333$, $b = 1$, and $c = -0.5$.

(a)   If Y is \$15,000 and the price of housing is \$100, how much housing is purchased, and what is the level of housing expenditures?

(b)   Now let income increase to \$20,000, with all other data constant. How much housing is purchased, and what is the level of housing expenditures?

(c)   Assume that income returns to \$15,000. What happens to housing purchased and housing expenditures if the price of housing is reduced by 30% (to \$70)?

References

Arnott, Richard, 1995, "Time for Revision on Rent Control?" *Journal of Economic Perspectives*, vol. 9, pp. 99–120.

Fallis, George and L. Smith, 1984, "Uncontrolled Prices in a Controlled Market: The Case of Rent Controls," *American Economic Review*, vol. 74, pp. 193–200.

Friedman, Joseph and D. Weinberg, 1982, *The Economics of Housing Vouchers*. New York: Academic Press.

Jorgenson, Dale and R. Landau (eds.), 1993, *Tax Reform and the Cost of Capital*. Washington, DC: The Brookings Institution.

King, Mervyn and D. Fullerton (eds.), 1984, *The Taxation of Income from Capital*. Chicago: University of Chicago Press.

Munnell, Alicia, L. Browne, J. McEneaney, and G. Tootell, 1996, "Mortgage Lending in Boston: Interpreting the HMDA Data," *American Economic Review*, vol. 86, pp. 25–53.

Polinsky, A. Mitchell and D. Ellwood, 1979, "An Empirical Reconciliation of Micro and Grouped Estimates of the Demand for Housing," *Review of Economics and Statistics*, vol. 61, pp. 199–205.

US Department of Housing and Urban Development, 1982, "HUD Subsidized Housing Overview," in *Major Themes and Additional Budget Details: 1983 Budget of the United States*. Washington, DC: US Government Printing Office.

Chapter 10

Real Estate Law and Institutions

A. How a House is Sold

This chapter is an introduction to the law of real estate and the institutions that are used to engage in the sale of residential real estate. A basic course in real estate will provide you with much more depth on the topics that are covered here, but this chapter will give you familiarity with some of the peculiar terminology and procedures that are used in the real estate business. This first section is a discussion of the process used to sell a house. The following sections cover the appraisal of residential real estate, the basic mechanics of home mortgage loans and some background on the mortgage loan industry, and the appraisal of income-producing property such as commercial or industrial buildings.

The process of selling a house begins when the owner decides to sell. The owner is selling the physical property (the house and the lot) *and* the legal rights of ownership. There are many forms of real property ownership, or estates, which are recognized in law. A fundamental distinction is between ownership by one party (estates in severalty) and more than one party (concurrent estates). The term "estates in severalty" designates a single owner because that owner's estate is *severed* from those of others. Estates in severalty can be of indefinite duration (freehold estates) or of definite duration set by private contract (leasehold estate). The most common leasehold estate is the rental of an apartment. Freehold estates can be "of inheritance" or "not of inheritance." Freehold estates of inheritance means that the owner has the legal right to transfer ownership as he or she sees fit (e.g. by sale or will), and a freehold estate that is not of inheritance does not include this right. An example of the latter is the life estate, wherein the owner possesses the rights to the property during his or her lifetime, but upon the death of the owner the estate passes to some other owner as stipulated in the private contract that set up the life estate.

Ownership of real estate that involves more than one owner is called concurrent estates. The two basic forms of concurrent estates are direct co-ownership and indirect co-ownership. Direct co-ownership can be one of the following:

- Joint tenancy, where the owners have right of survivorship in which, upon the death of one owner, the co-owners divide the property of the deceased among themselves. All owners must agree if one wishes to sell his/her portion.
- Tenancy by the entirety, the term used when a husband and a wife are the joint tenants. Husbands and wives often use this form of ownership of the home in states that are not "community property" states. This form of ownership is used in Illinois.
- Tenancy in common, which does not include right of survivorship. Owners may will their ownership to heirs or sell his/her share.
- Community property, in which the husband and the wife are equal partners. California is a community property state.
- Condominium and cooperative, which involve co-ownership of the common property (stairways, common grounds, and so on).

Indirect co-ownership may be of the following forms:

- Tenancy in partnership, with one partner designated as the general partner (with liability that is greater than his/her investment) and the others are limited partners (with limited liability).
- Corporations, which can be standard C corporations or S corporations (with 35 or fewer shareholders). S corporations are not subject to the corporate income tax.
- Real estate investment trust, a special corporation set up for the purpose of owning and operating commercial real estate. These companies must distribute 95 percent of net earnings to the shareholders, and are exempt from the federal corporate income tax.

The most common form of freehold estate of inheritance is called fee simple absolute estate, the form of ownership that provides the maximum legal rights of ownership that are consistent with the laws of the land. Those legal rights include the aforementioned right to transfer ownership as one sees fit (the right of disposition), the right of exclusive possession and control, and the right of quiet enjoyment. These legal rights apply regardless of the physical nature of the property involved. The right of exclusive possession and control means that the owner can control entry to the property, collect damages in case of trespass, and use the property as collateral for loans. The right of quiet enjoyment has nothing to do with an absence of noise; it means that the owner is legally protected from unfounded claims about the validity of the title to the property. The owner with a fee simple absolute estate is still subject to restrictions imposed by government – zoning laws, building codes, taxes, and eminent domain. Under the power of eminent domain, the government (usually a local government) has the right to force the sale of property for just compensation if the property is needed for a public purpose. The term "fee simple" is a legal term that combines fee, which is an inheritance in legal terminology, and simple, which means unconditional.

The owner decides to sell the residential property and the accompanying fee simple absolute estate. Legal title to the physical property and the legal rights are evidenced by a *deed* that is in the possession of the owner. A copy of the deed is on file with the county's recorder of deeds. The deed is one of the following:

- general warranty deed, which warrants good title, no encumbrances, quiet enjoyment, and the existence of no superior title;

- special warranty deed, which provides a warrant only for the term of ownership of the immediately previous owner;
- bargain and sale deed, which provides no guarantees.

Another type of deed is a quit-claim deed, which states that a party "quits" an ownership claim that may have existed. This device is used to clarify and consolidate ownership.

The next step ordinarily is for the owner to draw up a listing contract with a real estate broker, a person who operates a business that specializes in selling real estate. The listing contract will stipulate the price that the owner is willing to accept, the commission that the broker will receive if the property is sold, and a time period for the listing contract. Indeed, if the broker produces a qualified buyer who is willing to pay the listing price, the owner must pay the commission (or face the penalty stated in the listing contract). There are different types of listing contracts, but the one used most often in residential real estate is the exclusive right of sale listing. With this type of listing the broker is due the commission if the property is sold during the time period of the contract *regardless of who sells the property*. This type of listing is used by brokers who are members of multiple listing services (MLS) because, under MLS agreements, the brokers share listings. If another broker sells the house, the entire commission is paid to the listing broker, who, by prior agreement, splits the commission with the selling broker. The normal commission is a stated percentage of the selling price of the property. A commission of 6% is pretty common, but the commission rate is always subject to negotiation prior to the signing of the listing contract. Under the listing contract the broker promises to market the property through the appropriate media and to employ real estate agents who show the property to potential buyers and help negotiate a contract for sale. Other types of listing contracts include:

- Open listing, which permits anyone to sell the property. The listing broker is paid no commission if he/she does not sell the property.
- Exclusive agency listing, in which the owner reserves the right to sell the property and not pay a commission.

The contract for sale is often called the most important document in real estate. Contracts in real estate are governed by the state's general law of contracts. Legally binding contracts all have the following features:

- The parties to the contract are legally competent to act, e.g., the seller actually owns the property.
- The parties have legal objectives.
- There is an offer and an acceptance.
- There is value given or a promise made by each party. This is called statement of consideration, and legally binding contracts impose obligations on both parties. In this case the seller promises to deliver the property upon payment of a sum of money, and the buyer promises to deliver the money.
- There must be no defects to mutual agreement, e.g., no one is under duress.

In addition, contracts in real estate must be in writing and must include a legal description of the property, i.e., its location in precise terms.

Contracts for the sale of real estate are fairly complicated documents, and normally include the following additional provisions:

- date of the closing;
- financing terms for the buyer;
- condition of building and its equipment;
- brokerage commission;
- earnest-money deposit; and
- remedies for breach of contract.

The contract states a date upon which the actual transfer of ownership will take place (date of closing). By that date the buyer must have acquired the financing as stated in the contract. For example, the contract states that the buyer will obtain a loan for 80% of the purchase price of the property at an interest rate of 7% or less. If the buyer, after reasonable effort, is unable to obtain the financing as stated, the contract for sale says that the sale is void. The buyer puts up earnest money when the contract for sale is signed. The earnest money is usually a small percentage of the purchase price (e.g., 1%), and this money is held by the broker in a separate bank account until the date of closing.

How do the buyer and seller arrive at the purchase price that is then written in the sale contract? This is the crucial question. The determination of the price begins with the listing contract, where the seller states the price that is acceptable. The "listing price" is set in discussions with the real estate broker. The broker's real estate agent will conduct a comparative market analysis to determine the price at which the house is likely to sell. The real estate agent is familiar with the market in the immediate neighborhood, and knows the prices at which houses are selling. However, the houses that have been sold recently may differ from the subject house in some respects; e.g., size of the house, size of the lot, and appearance of the neighborhood. The real estate agent will make adjustments to those prices to make them pertain more accurately to the subject house. This process is described below. The broker will take the real estate agent's estimate of selling price and boost it a little as a bargaining tactic. Remember that the broker is the *seller's* agent. The seller can take the broker's recommendation for listing price, or the seller can insist on some other price. It is fair to say that sellers sometimes insist on an unrealistically high listing price – at first. Hope springs eternal.

The buyer enters the picture by making contact with the real estate agent. The real estate agent will assist the buyer in finding the house that meets his or her needs and also fits within the buyer's budget. Once the buyer has found a house, an offer is made in writing using a proposed contract for sale. But how does the buyer determine the price that is offered? Naturally the buyer discusses the offer with the real estate agent (who, you will recall, is working for the seller). The broker and real estate agent do not get paid unless there is a sale, so they have a strong incentive to get the two parties together. However, since the commission is usually a percentage of the selling price, they also get paid more the higher is the price. Under these circumstances, it is advisable for the buyer to seek additional advice from another professional in the business. The buyer's attorney often plays this role. If the buyer is making a particularly large purchase, a buyer's real estate agent may be hired to carry out the search and handle the negotiations. These advisors may conduct their own comparative market analysis to help determine the offer price.

The price that is agreed upon is, of course, the present discounted value of the stream of housing services that the housing unit will provide. In equation form, the selling price is determined in the usual present-value formula, written

$$V = R_1/(1 + r) + R_2/(1 + r)^2 + R_3/(1 + r)^3 + \ldots + R_n/(1 + r)^n,$$

where R_1 to R_n is the stream of implicit housing rents, r is the discount rate, and n is the number of years remaining in the economic life of the house. It is not assumed that the rent stream is a constant. Indeed, because a house deteriorates over time, the rent in real terms (corrected for general inflation) should fall. By the way, if the projected rent stream is stated in real terms, then the discount rate also should be corrected for inflation. Current nominal interest rates include the rate of inflation that is expected. The real discount rate is the nominal rate minus that expected inflation rate – whatever that may be.

Once the sale contract has been signed, the buyer arranges for financing with some lender. The lender is usually a financial institution, such as a savings and loan company or a bank, that specializes in home loans. The lending institution will make its own independent assessment of the market value of the property because the buyer may default on the loan. If default occurs, the lender recovers the value of the loan by forcing the sale of the property (foreclosure), so the lender needs to know the price at which the property can be sold. The lender normally will require a professional appraisal of the market value of the property. The government regulations that apply to lending institutions also require that appraisals be performed in most instances. In addition, the seller, the buyer, or both might have engaged the services of a professional appraiser in the process of determining the listing or offer price.

B. Appraisal of Residential Real Estate

How are appraisals performed? The task is to estimate the market value of the property, assuming that the property is being sold by a "normal" seller to a "normal" buyer under "normal" market conditions. The professional appraiser has extensive training and, if the appraisal is done properly, makes use of procedures that are actually quite scientific. The appraisal process for a residential property is very standardized; in fact the appraiser fills out a standard form that meets the requirements of government agencies. The standard appraisal of a house is based primarily on a sales comparison approach that is supplemented by two other methods, called the income capitalization and the cost-less-depreciation methods. The income capitalization method is similar to the method used for commercial properties, except that a market rent for the house must be estimated from rental market data. The cost-less-depreciation method begins with the cost of reproducing the structure today. Standard sources on construction costs, such as Marshall and Swift's *Residential Cost Handbook*, are used to determine this cost, and then allowances are made for the depreciation of the structure's value. An estimate of the value of the land is added on. Let us focus on the sales comparison approach because this is the method that all parties to the transaction primarily rely upon.

Table 10.1   The sales comparison approach to appraisal

	Comparable sales			Subject property
	#1	#2	#3	
Sale price	$125,000	$130,000	$140,000	
Data source	MLS	MLS	MLS	
Square ft.	1,500	1,600	1,600	1,500
Price per sq. ft.	$83.33	$81.25	$87.50	
Adjustments for conditions of sale	none	none	none	
Financing concessions	none	none	−1,000 (reduced payment, year 1)	
Date of sale	+3,750 (1 year ago)	+1,950 (6 months ago)	none	
Location	none	none	none	
Site/view	none	none	none	
Design	none	none	none	
Quality of construction	none	+5,000 (frame)	none (brick)	brick
Age	+3,125 (8 years)	+1,300 (5 years)	none (3 years)	(3 years)
Condition	none	none	none	excellent
Rooms	none	none	none	3BR
Bathrooms	+1,500 (a bath)	none	none	$1\frac{1}{2}$
Heating/cooling	none	none	none	gas/AC
Garage/carport	none	none	none	garage
Porch, patio, pool	none	none	none	porch
Fireplaces	+1,500 (none)	none	none	one
Other	none	none	none	
Total adjustment	9,875	125	−9,750	
Indicated value of subject	134,875	130,125	130,250	

The formal, professional appraisal process requires that three actual sales of comparable properties be used. Detailed data on the subject property and the three "comparables" are gathered, and the use of the data is described below and in Table 10.1. The basic idea in appraisal is to adjust the actual selling price of the comparable property so that the adjustments make the comparable property as close as identical to the subject property as is possible. After the price of the comparable property has been adjusted, the adjusted selling price is an estimate of the market value of the subject property. The critical step is the *selection* of comparable properties so that the adjustments to their selling prices do not have to be very large and, therefore, less subject to error. In the example in

Table 10.1 three comparables have been selected that are located close to the house in question and are very nearly the same size (1,500 or 1,600 square feet of living area, with a garage, and so on).

The sequence of adjustments to the selling prices that appraisers follow is shown in Table 10.1. The first adjustment that must be considered is called "conditions of sale." The sale of a comparable property may not be a conventional arm's length transaction. For example, transactions involving members of the same family may not really be a fair market price. The appraiser should select only comparables that are straightforward arm's length sales. The next adjustment is made to account for the effect of any special financing arrangements. For example, suppose that the seller loans some of the purchase price to the buyer at an interest rate that is below the rate that prevails in the market. This sort of concession will tend to boost the selling price of the house, so the effect on the price of a financing concession must be *subtracted* from the actual selling price, as is done for comparable #3. Remember that the idea is to estimate the market value of the subject property under normal selling conditions. The third possible adjustment is for the date of sale of the comparable property. If the comparable was sold six months ago and it is known that prices are increasing over time, then the price must be adjusted upward by a percentage to reflect the price increase. This price adjustment should be based, if possible, on data for the immediate neighborhood of the comparable property. Price trends can be quite different in different parts of the same urban area. At this point we have an estimate of the price of the comparable property if it were to be sold today under normal selling conditions. Here we know that prices are rising by 3% per year, so comparables #1 and #2 are adjusted upwards by 3% and 1.5%, respectively.

The next task is to adjust the price of the comparable property to match the subject property. The first adjustment that must be made is for location. If the comparable and the subject properties are located in the same immediate neighborhood, no location adjustment is needed. However, if the comparable property is located in a different local school district, or is located in what is clearly another neighborhood, then a location adjustment should be made. The location adjustment is made by finding two actual sales – one near the subject property and one near the comparable property. If the appraiser is lucky, these two sales are identical properties *except for the location factor*. The difference in their sales prices is computed in percentage terms, and that percentage is used to adjust the price of the comparable property. If it is required, the location adjustment is obviously a critical step. The appraiser hopes that comparable properties can be found that are all in the same neighborhood as the subject property.

Now come the adjustments for the actual physical characteristics of the comparable and subject properties. Table 10.1 lists the factors that are taken into account. Again, the appraiser hopes to find comparables that are *very* similar to the subject property on these features. An adjustment must be made if the comparable and the subject properties are not identical on a feature. For example, suppose that the comparable is ten years older than the subject property. It is known that houses in the market in question decline in value as they age by 0.5% per year, so the price of the comparable must be *increased* by 5% because it is the older property. The appraiser has this knowledge because of previous comparisons of value that have been made. As another example, suppose that the subject property does not have central air conditioning, but that the comparable property does have this feature. From previous comparisons, the appraiser knows that central air conditioning adds about 12% to the value of houses of this type. This means that the sales price of the comparable must be *reduced* by 12% to make it match the subject property. The adjustments in Table 10.1 include an adjustment for a half bath (comparable #1 does not have one), gross living area (comparables #2 and #3 have 100 square feet more than the subject property), and a fireplace (comparable #1 does not have one). The sum of all of the adjustments is computed, and the indicated value of the subject property is shown at the bottom of the table.

The final step in the sales comparison approach is to use the sample of three "indicated values" to estimate the market value of the subject property. The usual approach is to compute the mean of the three indicated values, which in Table 10.1 results in an estimated value of $131,750. However, there are times when more weight might be put on one of the comparable properties. For example, if the comparable property is the house directly across the street from the subject property, then substantially more weight should be placed on this indicated value. However, the appraiser must not put 100% of the weight on the comparable from across the street because that would mean relying on a sample of one. The vagaries of negotiating a sale price may have made this sale somewhat unusual in a way that has not been measured. The other two comparables provide additional information that should be used. Indeed, you may be asking, "Why three comparables? Why not five, or ten, or twenty?" Three is the number required for professional appraisals by convention, but why not a bigger sample indeed?

The work of the appraiser is sent along to the lending institution and, assuming that the subject property is really worth about as much as the price agreed to by the seller and the buyer, the application for the loan is approved. The last step in the process of selling the house is the closing. The lender's agent makes sure that all of the details are in order. The deed has been prepared, and the seller has obtained a title insurance policy to guard against any possible legal defects in title. The mortgage contract has been prepared for the buyer's signature, and a check has been prepared by the lender for the seller. The lender's agent prepares the closing statement, which is a comprehensive list of debits and credits for both the seller and the buyer. The lender has made payment to satisfy any remaining balance that the seller has on a home loan, and a statement of satisfaction of the old mortgage has been obtained. When the transaction has been completed, the buyer and seller will probably find that the costs of making the transaction (broker's commission, lawyers' fees, loan fees, document preparation, title search and title insurance, etc.) are about 10% of the value of the property. The real estate market has high transactions costs.

C. Financial Analysis of Mortgage Amortization

The home loan obtained by the typical buyer includes the feature that it is fully amortizing, which means that the loan payments that are made each month both pay the interest on the loan and retire the debt itself. Loans used in commercial real estate often are not fully amortizing; the payment schedule does not pay off the loan, so a "balloon" payment is due at the end. Another application of the same idea of full amortization is the computation of the annual cost of capital that includes opportunity cost of the funds tied up in the capital *and* the depreciation of the capital itself.

Two preliminary steps are needed before the relevant formula can be derived. The first idea is the present value of a one-time payment that is made at the *end* of year *n*. A one-time payment made at some point (end of year *n*) in the future is called a reversion. Suppose that the payment is $1; its present value is

$$PV = 1/(1 + r)^n,$$

where *r* is the discount rate. A series of reversions is called an annuity, and the present value of an annuity of $1 per year for *n* years in duration can be written

$$PV_a(n) = 1/(1 + r) + 1/(1 + r)^2 + \ldots + 1/(1 + r)^n,$$

where it is assumed that each reversion is paid at the end of the year.

There is a standard financial formula for the present value of an annuity, and it is found as follows. First multiply both sides of the equation for present value by $(1 + r)$, or

$$(1 + r)PV_a(n) = 1 + 1/(1 + r) + \ldots + 1/(1 + r)^{n-1}.$$

Subtraction of the present value equation from this equation yields

$$(1 + r)PV_a(n) - PV_a(n) = 1 - 1/(1 + r)^n, \text{ so that}$$
$$PV_a(n) = \{1 - [1/(1 + r)^n]\}/r.$$

This is the present value of an annuity of $1 per year for *n* years. Note that, if *n* is infinitely large, then $PV_a(n)$ simply is $1/r$. However, if *n* is some number of finite size, then the term $[-1/(1 + r)^n]$ adjusts the present value down from $1/r$.

Now we are ready to consider the mortgage loan that is fully amortizing. We seek the constant annual payment that will pay the interest and retire the debt. Suppose that the original loan amount is $1. In this case the constant annual payment is called the mortgage constant because it is the payment that is needed for each dollar of the loan. The mortgage constant is also called the capitalization rate because the annual payments include the return on the investment and the recapture of capital by the end of *n* years, assuming that the useful life of the capital is *n* years. In this case the present value of the annuity in question is $1 because the stream of payments must have a present value equal to the original loan amount of $1; therefore

$$PV_a(n) = 1 = R/(1 + r) + R/(1 + r)^2 + \ldots + R/(1 + r)^n,$$

where *R* is the constant annual payment that is made at the end of each year. The borrower is borrowing $1 in the first year, and pays the interest on a loan of $1 for one year at the end of the year. However, that payment of *R* also includes an amount that goes to retire the debt.

The trick is to solve for *R*, the annual payment. Once again, multiply by $(1 + r)$ to obtain

$$(1 + r)PV_a(n) = 1 + r = R + R/(1 + r) + \ldots + R/(1 + r)^{n-1}.$$

Subtraction yields

$$1 + r - 1 = r = R - R/(1 + r)^n = R\{1 - [1/(1 + r)^n]\}.$$

The solution for R is

$$R = r/\{1 - [1/(1 + r)^n]\}.$$

The formula for the mortgage constant is the inverse of the formula for the present value of an annuity of \$1 per year for n years at interest rate r. If the loan is of infinite duration (or the capital is of infinite life), the $R = r$. The annual payment per dollar of loan is just equal to the discount rate, which is the opportunity cost of the capital. However, if the loan is of some finite duration n, then the annual payment must be increased above r to amortize the loan.

Consider a simple example in which you borrow \$1 for three years at an interest rate of 5%, and make annual payments at the end of each year. In this case the term $1/(1 + r)^n$ is

$$1/(1.05)^3 = 0.8638.$$

The annual payment is

$$R = 0.05/(1 - 0.8638) = 0.05/0.1362 = 0.3671.$$

The annual payment is 36.71 cents on the \$1 loan. (If you borrow \$1,000, then the annual payment is \$367.10.) At the end of the first year you make that payment, which consists of an interest payment of 5 cents and a payment that goes to retiring the debt of 31.71 cents. In the second year you are borrowing only $1 - 0.3171 = 0.6829$ dollars. At the end of the second year you make the same payment of 36.71 cents, of which $0.05 \times 68.29 = 3.41$ cents is interest and 33.30 cents goes to retire the debt. In the third year you are borrowing 34.99 cents because the loan has been reduced from 68.29 cents to this amount. The payment of 36.71 cents at the end of the third year consists of $0.05 \times 34.99 = 1.75$ cents in interest and 34.96 cents to retire the remaining debt of 34.99 cents. The computation is off by 0.03 cents because of rounding errors.

Financial calculators or financial tables exist to enable you to compute the mortgage constant for a loan of any length and any interest rate. Also, mortgage payments are normally made on a monthly basis rather than on an annual basis. In this case you are borrowing the money for one month at a time and paying an interest rate of $r/12$ at the end of each month. The formula for the monthly mortgage constant is

$$R = (r/12)/\{1 - [1/(1 + r/12)^{12n}]\}.$$

The formula for the present value of an annuity of \$1 can be used to determine the balance that remains on the loan at any time during the term of the loan. The trick is to realize that the remaining loan balance B is the present value of the remaining payments, or

$$B = R/(1 + r) + R/(1 + r)^2 + \ldots + R/(1 + r)^m,$$

where m is the number of years that remain on the term of the loan. The annual payment R is known, so

$$B/R = PV_a(m),$$

where $PV_a(m)$ is the present value of a $1 annuity that extends for m years at interest rate r. The remaining loan balance is simply the annual payment R times this factor. Recall that the mortgage constant is the inverse of the present value factor, so

$$B = R/R_m,$$

where R_m is the mortgage constant for a loan of $1 for m years at interest rate r.

Return to the numerical example of the $1 loan at 5% interest for three years. The mortgage constant is 36.71 cents. Now consider the remaining loan balance after one year. We already know that the remaining loan balance is 68.29 cents after the first payment has been made. In this case the computation of R_m is

$$R_m = r/\{1 - [1/(1 + r)^2]\} = 0.05/(1 - 1/1.1025) = 0.5376.$$

The remaining loan balance is therefore

$$B = R/R_m = 36.71/53.76 = 0.6828 \text{ dollars.}$$

As an exercise, compute the remaining loan balance after two years. Did you get 34.99 cents (or close it)?

One additional financial formula that is very useful and related to the mortgage constant is the sinking fund factor. The sinking fund factor is the amount that must be set aside at the end of each year to yield a certain amount at the end of year n, given an interest rate r. For example, you know that you must replace your roof at the end of 10 years, and you want to know how much should be set aside each year to pay for the new roof at that time. The amount that is set aside each year will earn interest at rate r per year. The sinking fund factor is derived assuming that the goal at the end of n years is $1. The future value ($FV$) of the accumulated money is to be $1, so

$$FV = 1 = A + A(1 + r) + \ldots + A(1 + r)^{n-1},$$

where A is the amount set aside at the *end* of each year. Because of the timing, the last amount set aside earns no interest, and that the first amount set aside earns interest for $n - 1$ years. The solution for A proceeds as before; multiply both sides of the equation by $(1 + r)$ to get

$$(1 + r)FV = 1 + r = A(1 + r) + A(1 + r)^2 + \ldots + A(1 + r)^n.$$

Subtraction yields

$$(1 + r)FV - FV = r = A(1 + r)^n - A = A[(1 + r)^n - 1].$$

Therefore, the sinking fund factor is

$$A = r/[(1 + r)^n - 1].$$

Suppose that you need \$1 at the end of three years, and that the interest rate is 5%. How much do you need to set aside at the end of each year? You know that 33.33 cents at the end of each year will more than do the job because you will earn interest on the first two payments. In this case

$$A = 0.05/[(1.05)^3 - 1] = 0.05/0.1576 = 0.3173,$$

or 31.73 cents per year.

D. The Business of Residential Mortgage Lending

Loans for the purchase of residential real estate are provided by a very large and sophisticated industry. Some of the features of this industry were discussed in Chapter 9 as part of the examination of federal housing policy for the middle class. The financial institutions that provide housing loans include commercial banks, savings and loan institutions (called "thrifts"), and mortgage companies. Mortgage companies create mortgage loans that are immediately sold on the secondary mortgage market; they earn a fee for creating the loan. Commercial banks and savings and loan institutions are depository institutions that accept deposits from the public, pay interest on those deposits, and lend the money to borrowers. Commercial banks were prohibited from paying interest on demand deposits (i.e. checking accounts) under the Banking Act of 1933, and this prohibition remained in force until 1980. The Banking Act of 1933 created the Federal Deposit Insurance Corporation (FDIC) to insure deposits in commercial banks. Deposits in savings and loan institutions were insured by the Federal Savings and Loan Insurance Corporation (FSLIC) under the National Housing Act of 1934.

The fundamental flaw in the business of residential lending is that lenders take in short-term deposits – demand deposits and certificates of deposit – and use the deposits to make long-term loans with typical durations of 30 years. The lending institution holds mortgage loans as assets, and these loans normally pay a fixed rate of interest. The liabilities of the lender are the deposits. As long as the interest rate paid on the mortgage loans exceeds the interest paid to depositors, the lending institution is solvent – has a positive net worth and is making a profit. However, if a lender is sitting there with assets consisting largely of long-term fixed-rate mortgages, then the institution is subject to what is known as interest rate risk. If short-term interest rates rise, then the payments from the borrowers are insufficient to pay the interest to the depositors and the lender is insolvent. (A lender can also become insolvent if the borrowers are unable to make their interest payments, as happened in the Depression of the early 1930s. In this case the institutions go out of business and the depositors lose their money. Deposit insurance arose from the Depression banking disaster.)

This basic flaw in the mortgage lending business was recognized and several steps were taken to reduce interest rate risk. The Federal Housing Administration (FHA) was created in 1934 to set up a mortgage insurance program to guarantee mortgage payments to the lender from borrowers who did not have funds for a down payment in an amount regarded as sufficient to protect the lender (e.g., 20% of the sales price). The Federal National Mortgage Association (Fannie Mae) was created in 1938 for the purpose of borrowing funds to purchase mortgages from lenders, thereby increasing the supply of funds for housing finance. The Federal Home Loan Mortgage Corporation (Freddie Mac) was formed in 1970 with the same function. The Government National Mortgage Association (Ginnie Mae) was established in 1968 to provide a secondary market for FHA and Veteran's Administration mortgages. These three institutions create "pass-through" securities that enable investors to invest in bundles of home mortgages that are purchased from the original lenders. Courses in real estate finance examine in detail the secondary market for home mortgages.

The business of home mortgage lending became more sophisticated in the 1960s and 1970s with the growth of the secondary mortgage market, but this development did not prevent what is known as the savings and loan debacle of the early 1980s. The book by Lawrence White (1991) provides a blow-by-blow account. As long as interest rates remained low and stable, banks and savings and loans could operate on the 3-5-3 principle; take in deposits paying 3% interest, make home mortgage loans at 5%, and be on the golf course by 3 P.M. The first signs of trouble occurred in the mid-1960s when federal deficits drove nominal interest rates up. The first response of Congress was to pass the Interest Rate Control Act of 1966, which gave authority to federal regulators to set ceilings on interest rates paid by thrifts. The Federal Reserve Bank had been regulating the interest rates paid by banks since 1933, including the prohibition of interest on demand deposits. This policy worked to protect thrifts and banks from interest rate risk through the 1970s, but the sharp increase in nominal interest rates in the late 1970s made attempts to regulate rates paid by banks and thrifts self-defeating.

Here is a short version of the debacle, as provided by White (1991). The interest rate on three-month treasury bills stood at 6.49% in January 1978, reached 9.35% in January 1979, broke the 10% barrier in September, and remained in double digits for almost three years. The highest three-month bill rate was 15.61% in August 1981. Money market mutual funds were created so that ordinary investors could invest in treasury securities, and this drained deposits from the banks and thrifts. Federal regulators decided to permit banks and thrifts to pay market interest rates on six-month certificates of deposit in June 1978, but this left the banks and thrifts with a cruel choice; pay high interest rates on deposits and suffer operating losses, or refuse to pay high rates on deposits and watch the deposits migrate to the money market mutual funds and other investment vehicles. The departure of deposits forces the banks and thrifts to sell off their mortgage loans at drastically reduced market values. Huge losses could not be avoided.

The policy responses included two major acts of Congress, the Depository Institutions Deregulation and Monetary Control Act of 1980 (DIDMCA) and the Garn–St. Germain Act of 1982. These laws included the following provisions:

- Thrifts were permitted to offer adjustable-rate mortgages (ARMs), with interest rates that adjust upwards (and downwards) with the general level of interest rates.
- The types of loans permitted to federally chartered thrifts were greatly expanded to include credit cards and consumer loans (up to 30% of assets), commercial real estate loans (up to 40% of assets), and other commercial loans (up to 11% of assets).

These thrifts were also permitted to take equity positions in ventures through a subsidiary.

• Regulation of interest rates payable to depositors was phased out.
• Interest on checking accounts (NOW accounts) was authorized for banks and thrifts.
• The DIDMCA increased to $100,000 the maximum insured deposit amount for banks and thrifts.

Regulations pertaining loans of to state-chartered thrifts were relaxed, especially in Texas, Florida, and California.

Some of these new rules were quite sensible (introduction of ARMs, elimination of interest rate regulation on deposits, increased maximum on insured deposits), but the net effect of the new system was to induce many thrifts to take on excessive risk, with disastrous consequences for themselves and for the FSLIC, the deposit insurance agent for thrifts. The thrift industry expanded rapidly in the mid-1980s into new areas of lending. In many instances, as White (1991, p. 260) put it, "thrifts' executives were overly optimistic, excessively aggressive, careless, ignorant, and/or outright criminal or fraudulent." The agency that regulated the thrifts tightened its regulations regarding safety and soundness during 1985–7, but by then it was too late. About one-third of the thrift industry had become insolvent, and the FSLIC became insolvent in January 1987. The FSLIC had insufficient funds to pay all of the depositors in the failed thrifts, and disposed of 205 thrift institutions in 1988 alone.

This debacle led to passage of the Financial Institutions Reform, Recovery, and Enforcement Act of 1989 (FIRREA). FIRREA provided funds for dealing with the costs of disposing of the remaining insolvent thrifts, put deposit insurance for thrifts under FDIC (with new insurance premium rules), created the Resolution Trust Corporation (RTC) to handle the disposal of insolvent thrifts, and created the Office of Thrift Supervisions (OTS) to tighten the safety and soundness regulation of thrifts in several ways. The total cost of the clean up of the thrift industry has turned out to be approximately $300 billion. And it was all because of interest rate risk faced by mortgage lenders. In the early twenty-first century the industry seems to be on an even keel as interest rates have been low and stable and homeownership has reached record levels. The only cloud on the horizon has to do with the safety and soundness practices of Fannie Mae and Freddie Mac, the big intermediaries in the secondary mortgage market, but that is a story for another day in another course.

E. Markets for Commercial and Industrial Real Estate

Most students have had some experience with the market for rental housing (including dorm rooms), and some have had experience with buying or selling residential property. Most of you probably are not familiar with the markets for commercial and industrial property. There are markets for offices, retail space, industrial property, warehouses, restaurants, parking lots and garages, hotels and motels, auto service stations and repair shops, and other types of properties for business use. Each of these types of property can be rented or purchased, and each type of property has its own set of market procedures and institutions. Commercial and industrial real estate can be a fascinating subject, and we recommend that you take a course in real estate if you are considering this field. People with knowledge of urban economics can find interesting and rewarding careers in commercial and industrial real estate.

The purpose of this section is to provide a brief introduction to the markets for commercial and industrial real estate in urban areas. Commercial and industrial properties produce a stream of income, and the market value of such property is based on that stream of income. The first step in the analysis of the market for income-producing property is to look carefully at the income stream.

Leases for commercial and industrial property are usually very complicated documents, and the provisions in leases can vary a great deal. A fundamental distinction is the gross lease versus the net lease. The gross lease is a lease in which the contract rent includes the tenant's share of all operating expenses of the building. The tenant pays only the contract rent, called gross rent, and the landlord is responsible for paying the property taxes, insurance, utilities, maintenance, replacement and repairs, and management fees. Alternatively, a net lease is a lease in which the contract rent does not include the operating expenses. Instead, operating expenses are passed through to the tenant as a direct expense. The tenant pays net rent to the landlord. In addition, landlords have begun to use the term effective rent to refer to the rental income received after accounting for operating expenses and various concessions granted to tenants. An oversupply of real estate of a particular type, such as office space in the early to mid-1990s, will lead to a proliferation of concessions to tenants to get them to sign a lease. The most popular concessions are months of free rent, extra allowances for finishing and decorating the space, moving allowances for tenants who are moving into the building, and payments to the new tenant's old landlord to cover part of the old lease. This last concession is called lease assumption cost. The value of a building is based on the actual stream of income that it generates, so concessions in leases must be taken into account.

The job of the real estate appraiser is to estimate the market value, or most probable selling price, of a subject property. Appraisers usually estimate the value of income-producing property using the income capitalization approach. Capitalization means the conversion of expected future income into a current lump-sum amount. The general expression for the income capitalization approach is

$$V = I/r,$$

where V is the estimated market value, I the expected future income, and r the capitalization rate. The appraiser must estimate both the expected future income and the capitalization rate. Each of these is discussed in turn.

The expected future income that is relevant to the determination of the market value of a property is called net operating income (NOI). Net operating income is closely related to the idea of effective rent, the net rent corrected for concessions to tenants. Refer to Table 10.2 to see how appraisers determine net operating income. Numerical examples of net operating income are provided in Chapter 12. The first step is to estimate the potential gross income (PGI) of the property. PGI is the total of gross rents that would be produced if the building were fully occupied and tenants paid the gross rent prevailing in the market for this type of real estate. The second step is to correct PGI for the vacancy rate

Table 10.2   Estimation of net operating income

Potential gross income (*PGI*)
   Market rent per square foot times the total amount of space available for rental plus any other
   income generated by the building (parking fees, vending, and so on)

Effective gross income (*EGI*)
   PGI less vacancy allowance. Vacancy allowance is the expected amount of vacant (in square
   feet) times the market rent per square foot.

Net operating income (*NOI*)
   EGI less
      Operating expenses
      Fixed expenses
      Reserves for replacement
      Tenant concessions (annualized basis)

that can be expected, yielding an amount called effective gross income. The third step is to deduct expected annual operating expenses and concessions to tenants from effective gross income. Operating expenses include fixed expenses, variable expenses, and reserves for replacement of parts of the building that wear out. Fixed expenses include real estate taxes and insurance. Variable expenses consist of utilities, repairs, maintenance, and management fees. Tenant concessions that can be expected must be converted to an average annual figure. For example, a landlord might grant a tenant three months of free rent in the first year of a five-year lease, but the estimation of net operating income requires a figure for the average annual expense for tenant concessions. Net operating income is the bottom line of Table 10.2. Note that net operating income does not involve subtracting interest paid by the landlord on any loans taken to acquire the property. Also, income taxes paid by the landlord are not deducted. These two items count as part of the income generated by the property.

The estimated future net operating income in the formula $V = I/r$ is presumed to be a long-run average for the property. However, there may be reason to think that net operating income will vary over time. Accurate appraisal will then require estimation of the varying stream of net operating income out into the future, as show in section A above. This can be a difficult task. However, if the market for real estate is functioning as a competitive market so that market values accurately reflect expected future income, a simpler solution is at hand. In this case one uses current net operating income (or perhaps *NOI* expected for next year) plus the expected change in the market value of the property. The valuation formula is now

$$V = (NOI + \Delta V)/r,$$

where ΔV is the change in value predicted for the coming year. This result can be demonstrated easily for a two-period example. Suppose that the property earns NOI_1 in the first year, NOI_2 in the second year, and nothing thereafter. The discounted present value of the property at the beginning of period one is

$$V = NOI_1/(1 + r) + NOI_2/(1 + r)^2.$$

The change in the value of the property from the beginning of period one to the beginning of period two is

$$\Delta V = NOI_2/(1 + r) - V.$$

Dividing this equation by $(1 + r)$ and rearranging terms produces

$$NOI_2/(1 + r)^2 = (V + \Delta V)/(1 + r).$$

Substitution of this result into the discounted present value formula yields

$$V = NOI_1/(1 + r) + (V + \Delta V)/(1 + r).$$

Solving for V produces

$$V = (NOI_1 + \Delta V)/r.$$

The other half of the process is the estimation of the capitalization rate for the type of property that is being studied. Professional appraisers generally use data on similar properties that have actually been sold recently to estimate the rate at which net operating income is being converted into market value. Suppose that the appraiser has a sample of properties for which the market value (V) is known and sufficient information exists to be able to construct a good estimate of expected net operating income (NOI). These data can be used to estimate the capitalization rate that is prevailing in the market via the equation

$$r^* = NOI/V.$$

Estimates of current market capitalization rates for various types of property are available from commercial real estate research services. The basic idea is that the capitalization rate equals the risk-free rate of return plus an adjustment for the risk associated with this type of property. That adjustment for risk equals the "beta" for the property type times the market risk premium, so

$$r = r_f + \beta(r_m - r_f),$$

where r_f is the risk-free rate of return (e.g., the rate of return on short-term government bonds), r_m is the return to a portfolio consisting of all risky assets in the economy (proxied by the S&P 1,000 stocks, for example), and β is the covariance of the rate of return of property type in question with the return to the market portfolio divided by the variance of the rate of return to the market portfolio. This is the standard result presented in courses in corporate finance.

The final step in the appraisal is to divide the estimated *NOI* for the subject property by the capitalization rate that is prevailing in the market for this type of property; $V = NOI/r^*$. The estimate of market value that is produced is the selling price of the property that can be expected under a normal sale to a typical buyer. The actual selling price can vary from this estimate because of simple randomness in the market. Special circumstances can arise when the seller must sell very quickly and cannot take the time needed to generate an offer that reflects full market value. Also, the contract for sale might include other considerations, such as financing to be provided by the seller at below-market interest rates. This sort of special financing usually will cause the selling price of the property to be above its appraised value. Finally, the appraised value is just an estimate of value. Not every conceivable factor that can influence selling price has been taken into account, to the actual selling price can vary from appraised value in a random fashion.

F. Summary

This chapter has presented an introduction to residential property markets, the mechanics of mortgage loans, and the appraisal of income-producing property. The next chapter is a more technical discussion of how markets for real estate function in the short run and in the long run. The final chapter in this part of the book examines the financing of real estate in greater depth and takes the reader through the real estate development process.

Exercises

1   This project is to perform what the real estate agents call a comparative market analysis. Select a subject property (e.g., your family's single house) for which you obtain an estimate of market value. The idea is to find three houses that have been sold recently that are very similar to the subject house. You can visit a local real estate agent and ask for the "closing book," the book that records the recent sales in the vicinity. Real estate offices now obtain this information from a centralized computer. You may also be able to find selling prices of "comparables" on the web by going to the real estate site supported by a major newspaper, for example. Find your three comparables and make the adjustments to their market prices so as to make them as close to the subject property as possible. See Table 10.1 for the details. This project may take you some time and legwork, but it literally can be a very valuable exercise.

2   You have been given the task of estimating the market value of an office building, and you have been given the following information.

- The building contains 150,000 square feet of rentable space, and the current market rent is $15 per square foot per year. The current vacancy rate is 10%.
- Annual fixed expenses include property taxes of $350,000 and insurance of $250,000.
- Annual operating expenses include repairs and maintenance of $100,000, utilities of $200,000, and a management fee of 5% of effective gross income. There are no tenant concessions.
- The current capitalization rate for this type of building is 10%.

(a)   Estimate the potential gross income and the effective gross income. What a assumptions are you making?

(b) Compute the net operating income.

(c) Estimate the market value of the building. What happens to value if the capitalization rate increases to 11%?

Reference

White, Lawrence, 1991, *The S&L Debacle*. Oxford: Oxford University Press.

Chapter 11

Real Estate Markets

A. Introduction

The purpose of this chapter is to present a simple equilibrium model of a real estate market that includes a vacancy rate. The model is then used to examine recent trends in residential and commercial markets. A further purpose of the chapter is to show that this simple model is consistent with some recent models of search in real estate markets that generate a natural vacancy rate. The model in this chapter is in some contrast to the Fisher–DiPasquale–Wheaton property market model (Fisher, 1992; DiPasquale and Wheaton, 1992; Achour-Fischer, 1999), which does not incorporate a vacancy rate. Indeed, market models used in some standard textbooks (e.g., Ball et al., 1998, Corgel et al., 1998, DiPasquale and Wheaton, 1996, and Geltner and Miller, 2001) typically do not include a vacancy rate. However, these texts also introduce the concept of the natural vacancy rate, the vacancy rate that prevails in long run equilibrium when supply and demand are in balance. The model developed in this chapter determines a long-run natural vacancy rate along with rent, occupied space, and total space supplied in the long run. The presentation is based on McDonald (2000).

   A basic diagrammatic model of a real estate market is set forth in the next section. The two critical features of this model are the demand for vacant space (in addition to the demand for occupied space), and the long-run equilibrium condition that annual net rent times the occupancy rate equals the annual cost of capital. A mathematical version of this model, with a numerical example, is presented next. The following section shows that models of search in real estate markets, such as those presented by Arnott and Igarashi (2000) and Geltner and Miller (2001), are consistent with the basic diagrammatic model. Relevant empirical literature and data are then examined from the theoretical perspective in the chapter. Sections B and F present the basic model and some empirical tests. Sections C, D, and E contain more advanced material and can be skipped without loss of continuity.

B. Rent, Vacancy, and Equilibrium: A Simple Model

Consider a market for a particular type of real estate, such as office space, commercial space, or industrial space. The quantity demanded and supplied in the market is measured as square feet of usable space (a continuous variable). The market price per square foot is *net* rent; i.e., rent that excludes current operating expenses. Net rent is the price paid for use of the capital – one square foot of space – for the period in question (e.g., one year).

The cost of an additional square foot of space is κ, the cost of construction. It is assumed that, once constructed, a square foot of space lasts for $1/\delta$ years, where δ is the rate at which the stock of space wears out. (The value of δ is, for example, 0.025 and the life of a square foot is 40 years.) This assumption permits the stock of space to adjust in the downward direction in response to changes in demand.

The demand for occupied space in the current period is a function of net rent per square foot, and this demand shifts in response to changes in the demand for the goods and services produced by the economic sectors that make use of the type of real estate in question. The demand for occupied space is actually a function of gross rent – net rent plus operating expenses. However, it shall be assumed that operating expenses per square foot are a constant amount. The demand schedule for occupied space can therefore be drawn as shown in Figure 11.1 either as D_g (the quantity of occupied space demanded as a function of gross rent) or as D_n (quantity demanded as a function of net rent).

A crucial feature of this model is the assumption that there is a demand for vacant space, a demand that is expressed by the owners of the real estate (the landlords). Clapp (1993, pp. 31–2) has stated well the informal rationale for assuming the existence of a demand for vacant space; some excerpts are as follows:

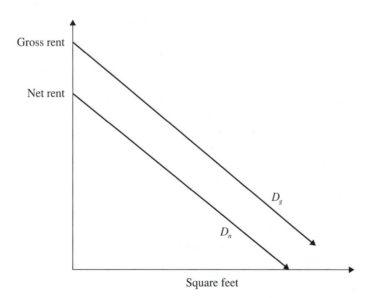

Figure 11.1   Demand for occupied space

Landlords want or need to hold some vacant space (i.e., they are willing to rent this space only under certain conditions that are not currently met).

Vacant space is like an inventory of goods held by a merchant. Landlords hold vacant space so that they can quickly satisfy the needs of those seeking to rent space.

Landlords need to hold some vacant space to prepare it for rental to tenants. Part of this "frictional" vacancy is the need to search for tenants who can be relied upon to pay rent.

Of course, it is expensive for landlords to keep space vacant. They must continue to pay property taxes, insurance, interest on their mortgage, and other expenses even though no rental income is received on the space. Thus, landlords must balance the cost of holding vacant space against the benefits just discussed.

The demand for vacant space is closely related to the notion from the management science field that there is a demand for slack capacity. Standard texts in operations analysis such as Nahmias (1993) present various models that lead to the conclusion that there is an optimal amount of slack capacity. For example, the expansion of capacity to meet growing demand will exhibit slack capacity if there are economies of scale in capacity construction. Demand uncertainty leads to a demand for slack capacity that will permit the firm to respond to demand surges. In the standard "newsboy" problem (Nahmias, 1993) the newsboy carries a stock of newspapers Q^* such that the probability that demand Q does not exceed some $F(Q^*)$ is equal to

price/(price plus cost of an unsold newspaper).

If the price that can be charged and the cost of an unsold newspaper are equal, then the optimal stock is set so that $F(Q^*) = 0.5$. The newsboy has extra papers only 50% of the time. However, if the price exceeds the cost of an unsold paper, then $F(Q^*)$ exceeds 0.5 and the newsboy will have excess capacity more than 50% of the time. Also, demand uncertainty leads to a demand for vacant space based on the theory of real options. The landlord may be able to rent all available space now, but the decision to do so may eliminate the option to wait for better conditions. The greater is the volatility in rents, the greater is the value of the option to wait. Consideration of this option value is particularly important if the normal practice is to sign long-term leases. A more formal model along these lines presented by Geltner and Miller (2001) is discussed below.

In this chapter it is assumed that the demand for such vacant space is a function of net rent; the higher is net rent, the lower is the demand for vacant space. Net rent is the opportunity cost of holding space vacant for the current period.

The variables in the model are:

K = the total inventory of space in the market, measured in square feet;
Q = the amount of space occupied by tenants;
V = the amount of vacant space;
r = the discount rate;
δ = the depreciation rate;
R = net rent per square foot of occupied space;

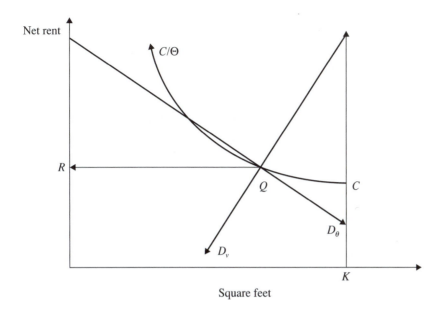

Figure 11.2   A real-estate market in long-run equilibrium

κ = construction cost per square foot;

$v = V/K$, the vacancy rate;

$\Theta = Q/K$, the occupancy rate; and

C = the annual cost of capital, which is a function of κ, r, and δ. (If there is no depreciation, then C is just equal to $r\kappa$. With $\delta > 0$, C is slightly larger than $r\kappa$.)

Given these definitions,

$$K = Q + V, \text{ and} \tag{1}$$
$$1 = v + \Theta. \tag{2}$$

Figure 11.2 depicts the market in long-run equilibrium. The current demand for occupied space is known and denoted D_Θ, and is the usual downward-sloping demand curve. The current inventory of space is K, and a vertical line is drawn at this amount. The demand for vacant space is D_v, and is drawn using the vertical line at K as the vertical axis. As noted above, the demand for vacant space can be based on uncertainty about future demand. Given the current inventory of space K, the demand for vacant space D_v is also the current supply of occupied space. Equilibrium Q, V, and R are determined by the intersection of D_Θ and D_v. Given K, equilibrium Q and V establish the equilibrium occupancy rate and vacancy rate (Θ and v).

Figure 11.2 depicts long-run equilibrium because, at the intersection of D_Θ and D_v, net rent R equals C/Θ. The long-run equilibrium price must ensure that there is neither an incentive to build additional space nor an incentive not to replace the space that wears out each year. This condition is that

$$\Theta R = C, \tag{3}$$

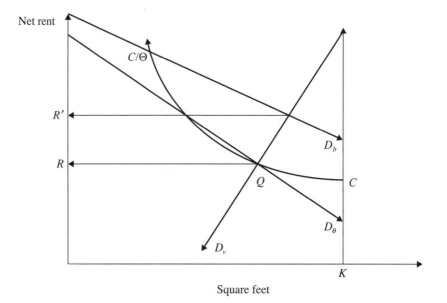

Net rent

Figure 11.3   A real-estate market in long-run disequilibrium

which states that the annual cost of capital equals net rent corrected for the occupancy rate. The curve labeled (C/Θ) shows the combinations of net rent R and occupied space Q that meet this condition. For example, if occupancy is 100%, then $R = C$ satisfies the condition. If occupancy is 75%, then $0.75R$ must equal C for long-run equilibrium. As drawn in Figure 11.2, curve (C/Θ) passes through the point of intersection of D_Θ and D_v.

The equilibrium vacancy rate depicted in Figure 11.2 is the natural vacancy rate, the vacancy rate that is consistent with a net rent that provides no incentive to change the size of the stock of space. This is so because (we assume that) potential suppliers of additional space look at this market and presume that the expected annual income from a marginal unit of space is ΘR, which equals the annual cost of capital. Furthermore, those landlords who would consider not replacing a marginal unit of space that wears out also see that the expected annual income is ΘR.

Figure 11.3 depicts a market that is not in long-run equilibrium. In Figure 11.3 the intersection of D_b and D_v is a short-run equilibrium, but equilibrium net rent R' so determined exceeds C/Θ. (Ignore demand curve D_θ for now.) An incentive to build more space exists, so the total inventory of space K will increase until a new long-run equilibrium is established.

Figure 11.3 provides some illumination on the process of market adjustment. Suppose that the market is out of long-run equilibrium because demand for occupied space had increased to D_b from D_Θ. This increase in demand increased both net rent and the occupancy rate (Q/K) in the short run. Empirical evidence, which will be discussed below, indicates that the occupancy rate usually adjusts more rapidly than rent because of the long-term nature of many existing leases. This suggests that net rent in the short run responds to an increase in the occupancy rate; the *change* in rent is a function of the *change* in the occupancy rate (i.e., a negative function of a *change* in the vacancy rate).

Net rent continues to adjust until it reaches R', the new short-run equilibrium. In the long run the stock of space adjusts upward because net rent R' exceeds C/Θ. In this situation the vacancy rate has dropped below the natural vacancy rate. If the stock can adjust fully in one time period, the size of the addition to the stock depends upon the size of the drop in the vacancy rate below its natural rate in the previous period. However, adjustments to the stock take more than one time period for some types of real estate. The construction of large office buildings takes several years, for example. In this case, the more general statement is that the amount of construction that takes place in the current year is a more complicated function of previous changes in the vacancy rate.

C. A Mathematical Version of the Model

The model in the previous section consists of three equations; a demand function for occupied space, and demand function for vacant space, and the long-run equilibrium condition that net rent equals the cost of capital divided by the occupancy rate ($R = C/\Theta$). The model has three unknowns; net rent R, the amount of occupied space Q, and the amount of vacant space V. The total amount of space is then just determined as $K = Q + V$, and the occupancy and vacancy rates follow as well. The short-run version of the model is examined first (K fixed), and then the long-run model is presented.

The short run

In the short run the inventory of space is fixed, so the model reduces to two equations and one identity; in linear form the demand for occupied space is

$$Q = Q_o - bR, \tag{4}$$

the demand for vacant space is

$$V = V_o - \beta R, \tag{5}$$

and the identity is

$$K - Q = V. \tag{6}$$

Both b and β are positive numbers. Substituting $K - Q$ for V in Eq. (5) and solving equations (4) and (5) for R yields

$$R = (Q_o + V_o - K)/(\beta + b). \tag{7}$$

This equation shows the usual result that increases in demand for either occupied or vacant space (increases in Q_o or V_o) will increase rent. In addition, the effect of an increase in the inventory of space is (using subscripts for partial derivatives)

$$R_k = -1/(\beta + b) < 0. \tag{8}$$

Substitution for R into the demand functions yields the short-run solutions

$$Q = (\beta Q_o - bV_o + bK)/(\beta + b) \tag{9}$$

and

$$V = (bV_o - \beta Q_o + \beta K)/(\beta + b). \tag{10}$$

Note that, with an increase in the inventory of space,

$$Q_k + V_k = [\beta/(\beta + b)] + [b/(\beta + b)] = 1. \tag{11}$$

An interesting question is whether the model implies that the occupancy *rate* (Q/K) falls if there is an increase in K. The change in the occupancy rate with respect to a change in K can be written

$$d(Q/K)/dK = [Q_k/K - Q/K^2]$$
$$= (1/K)[Q_k - \Theta], \tag{12}$$

which states that the occupancy rate falls if the marginal change in occupied space Q_k is less than the original occupancy rate Θ. Substitution for Q_k yields the condition that, for the occupancy rate to fall as K increases,

$$b/(\beta + b) < \Theta, \text{ or}$$
$$b < \beta\Theta/v, \tag{13}$$

where v is the vacancy rate $(1 - \Theta)$. The condition does not hold if b (the slope of the demand for occupied space) is very large relative to β (the slope of the demand for vacant space). However, one would suppose that this condition will often hold if occupancy rates are at normal, reasonably high levels. For example, if $\Theta = 0.84$ and $v = 0.16$, then b can be up to 5.25 times β and the condition still holds. Empirical tests can investigate the slopes of the two demand functions, or they can test for the effect of K on Θ directly. Empirical studies are reviewed below, but no study was found that examined this question. Let us now turn to the long run.

The long run

In the long run the condition must hold that $\Theta R = C$. This condition can be rewritten as

$$\Theta = C/R, \tag{14}$$

which states that the long-run equilibrium occupancy rate equals the cost of capital divided by the long-run equilibrium net rent. This occupancy rate can be called the "natural" occupancy rate (and the corresponding vacancy rate is the natural vacancy rate). The problem is to solve for long-run equilibrium R.

The solution can be found by writing the long-equilibrium condition as $K = QR/C$, and writing equation (5) as

$$V = K - Q = Q[(R/C) - 1] = V_o - \beta R. \tag{15}$$

Substitution for Q from equation (4) produces

$$(Q_o - bR)[(R/C) - 1] = V_o - \beta R. \tag{16}$$

The equation for R is therefore a quadratic equation;

$$-(b/C)R^2 + [b + \beta + (Q_o/C)]R - (V_o + Q_o) = 0. \tag{17}$$

The quadratic formula states that, for quadratic equation

$$a_o R^2 + b_o R + c_o = 0,$$
$$R = [-b_o + \text{or} - (b_o^2 - 4a_o c_o)^{1/2}]/2a_o.$$

The solutions for R are found by inserting

$a_o = -(b/C),$
$b_o = b + \beta + (Q_o/C),$ and
$c_o = -(V_o + Q_o).$

There can be two positive, real solutions for R for realistic values of the parameters, and it is possible that both of these solutions produce positive values for Q, V, and K. (Sometimes one solution for R implies negative values for Q, V, and K – but a positive value for Θ so that $R = C/\Theta$ holds.) The economic relevance of the solutions must be judged for each case.

Consider a numerical example that is intended to approximate the office market in the Chicago central business district. Assume that

$Q = 160 - 4R,$
$V = 25 - R,$ and
$C = 15$ (dollars per year).

The constants in the demand functions are the amounts of space demanded if the net rent is zero, measured in millions of square feet. (Actual occupied space in 1998 was 98 msf and vacant space was 12 msf.) These parameter values imply that

$R = 16.37$ or $42.38.$

The larger value for R produces negative values for Q and V. The smaller value for R produces a natural occupancy rate of

$\Theta = C/R = 15/16.37 = 0.916$

and solutions for Q, V, and K of

$Q = 94.52$,
$V = 8.63$, and
$K = 103.15$.

This market therefore has a long-run equilibrium with net rent of $16.37 per square foot per year, an inventory of space of 103.15 million square feet, and a natural occupancy rate of 91.6% (natural vacancy rate of 8.4%).

D. Search in Real Estate Markets

The purpose of this section is to present briefly two models of search in real estate markets developed by Geltner and Miller (2001) and Arnott and Igarashi (2000), and to show that the latter model can be depicted as in Figure 11.2. In short, there are more formal theoretical justifications for the model presented in this chapter. It will also be shown that the Arnott–Igarashi model contains the long-run equilibrium condition for net rent that $R = C/\Theta$.

A simple model of optimal search by landlords for tenants has been provided by Geltner and Miller (2001, pp. 829–33). This model is based on the theory of real options. In this model potential tenants arrive at an average rate of one per month, and each has an ex ante normal probability distribution of maximum rent that he or she is willing to pay. All leases are for five years. The landlord's problem is to set the asking rent to maximize the value of a given building. If the tenant refuses the landlord's asking rent, the landlord has to wait until the next potential tenant arrives and the space remains vacant. Clearly a higher asking rent implies a longer wait and a higher vacancy rate. Variations in the asking rent trace out the demand for occupied space. The optimal asking rent implies an optimal vacancy rate for the building. Geltner and Miller (2001) found that, in this model, the optimal asking rent and the optimal vacancy rate are higher the greater is the variance of the distribution of rents that the potential tenants are willing to pay.

A set of search models in housing markets has been developed by authors such as Anas (1997), Arnott (1989), Wheaton (1990), Read (1988), Igarashi (1992), and Arnott and Igarashi (2000). Because housing units are heterogeneous and households have idiosyncratic tastes, households search for a housing unit until a "good match" is found. Search is more efficient if there are more vacant units, so vacancies are of benefit to society. These models generate a natural vacancy rate in the long run at which landlords make no economic profit. Landlords set price above cost to cover the cost of providing vacant units.

Tenant arrivals at the market are generated by a random Poisson process with exogenous rate Γ. Each tenant who arrives demands one unit of space, but a tenant's tastes for specific features are idiosyncratic and private information. Each tenant has an ideal combination of characteristics. The model assumes that tenants and actual space have the same uniform distribution of characteristics.

The pool of searchers is denoted S, and there is a matching search technology in which landlords of vacant space and searchers create what Arnott and Igarashi (2000, p. 252) call "opportunities to match." These opportunities to match are generated by another Poisson process with the aggregate rate of

$$\Omega = \Omega(S,V) = (SV)^{1/2}. \tag{18}$$

Clearly vacant space makes search more effective. For the individual searcher the opportunities to match arrive at rate

$$\Omega_s = (V/S)^{1/2}, \tag{19}$$

the "marginal product" of searchers. Opportunities to match for vacant units of space arrive at rate

$$\Omega_v = (S/V)^{1/2}, \tag{20}$$

the "marginal product" of vacant space. The "tightness" of the market is measured by S/V, the ratio of searchers to vacancies (both measured in square feet). The tenant match rate is ΩX, where X is the probability that the tenant accepts an opportunity to match. The higher is the probability that a tenant will accept an opportunity to match, the higher are mismatch costs – the costs associated with occupying space that is not "ideal." Tenants establish a reservation level of mismatch costs, which are measured as probability X. The "full rent" paid by a tenant is $X + R$. Search costs are s_o per period, which includes the cost of temporary accommodations.

Tenants exit the market at aggregate rate μQ, where μ is the exogenous rate of exit for tenants that is also governed by a Poisson process. Internal mobility, in which tenants move to space that better matches their tastes, is ruled out by assumption.

The analysis is restricted to the stationary state, where equilibrium net rent is R^*, probability of match is X^*, and equilibrium reservation full rent is $R^* + X^*$. In the stationary state the rate at which tenants enter the market is equal to the rate at which matches are made, which also equals the rate at which tenants exit the market, so

$$\Gamma = (SV)^{1/2}X^*, \text{ and} \tag{21}$$
$$= \mu Q. \tag{21'}$$

The amount of occupied space is therefore Γ/μ. Consider, for example, an office market with 100 million square feet (msf) of occupied space. If the arrival rate is 10 msf per period, then the exit rate must be 0.10.

For our purposes the model can also be depicted on the same sort of diagram as was used above. Equations (21) and (21') combine to determine the quantity of occupied space $Q = \Gamma/\mu$. This is shown as a fixed amount on Figure 11.4. Tenants set reservation mismatch costs, and then landlords set net rent R^* and supply vacant space. Equilibrium net rent R^* is shown on Figure 11.4, and then the quantity of vacant space supplied in equilibrium is determined according to

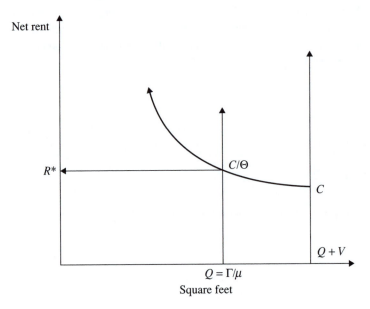

Figure 11.4   The Arnott–Igarashi model

$$V = Q(R^* - C)/C. \tag{22}$$

For example, if (from the example above), $Q = 94.52$ msf, $C = 15$, and $R^* = 16.37$, then $V = 8.63$ msf. This amount of vacant space is shown in Figure 11.4, and the curve that connects R^* at quantity Q to C at quantity $Q + V$ is labeled C/Θ as in Figure 11.2.

E. A Brief Review of Empirical Studies of Office Markets

As Clapp (1993) and Ball, Lizieri, and MacGregor (1998) have noted, much of the early empirical research on office markets attempted to estimate the natural vacancy rate by estimating an equation for rent dynamics written (ignoring other independent variables)

$$R_t - R_{t-1} = \alpha_o(v_{t-1} - v_n), \tag{23}$$

where v_n is the natural vacancy rate and $\alpha_o < 0$. Since v_n is unknown, the equation is estimated as

$$R_t - R_{t-1} = \beta_o + \alpha_o v_{t-1}, \tag{24}$$

and the natural vacancy rate is computed as

$$v_n = -\beta_o/\alpha_o. \tag{25}$$

Equation (23) is based on the plausible notion that, if the actual vacancy rate is at the natural rate, rent will not change. And if the vacancy rate falls below (rises above) the natural rate, rent will rise (fall). Equation (23) is based on the hypothesis that, in the short run, rents adjust with a lag to a deviation in the vacancy rate away from its natural rate. For example, if the market begins in long-run equilibrium, a shift upward in the demand for occupied space will increase both the rent and the occupancy rate in the short run. Equation (23) presumes that the occupancy rate adjusts first, and the adjustment in rent follows with a lag.

As Wheaton and Torto (1994), Hendershott (1996), and others have pointed out, equation (23) lacks theoretical justification. As shown above, an increase in the demand for occupied space will increase both the rent and the occupancy rate until a new short-run equilibrium is reached. The vacancy rate has dropped below its natural rate, but there is no further incentive for rents to rise. Equation (23) states that rents will keep on rising whenever the vacancy rate is below its natural rate, but the market model presented in this chapter shows that a new (short-run) equilibrium rent will be reached. Indeed, once a new short-run equilibrium has been reached in response to an increase in the demand for occupied space, the market adjustment in the long run will increase the supply of space, increase the vacancy rate, and *reduce* rent from its short-run equilibrium level. As the supply of space is increased, the vacancy rate will begin to rise and rent will begin to fall. However, until a new long-run equilibrium is reached, the vacancy rate is still below its natural rate. Equation (23) states that rent will continue to rise until the natural vacancy rate is reached, but rent must fall to reach its new long-run equilibrium.

Recent studies have recognized the deficiencies of this model and developed and estimated more complete models of a commercial real estate market. However, these studies are not consistent with the model in this chapter because they do not include a demand function for vacant space.

Wheaton and Torto (1994) proposed a model in which equilibrium rent $R*$ is a function of what they call the tenant flow rate (the arrival rate in the search model) and the *actual* vacancy rate. Rent then adjusts to its deviations from this equilibrium rent. In equation form,

$$R* = R(\Gamma, v), \text{ and}$$
$$R_t - R_{t-1} = z_o(R* - R_{t-1}),$$

so

$$R_t - R_{t-1} = z_o[R(\Gamma, v)] - z_o R_{t-1}.$$

In the empirical model Γ and v are entered in linear form. The model pertains to the short run, so clearly the short-run equilibrium rent is (inversely) related to the vacancy rate. However, as the equilibrium model in this paper implies, both the rent and the vacancy rate in the short run are jointly dependent variables. Wheaton and Torto (1994) treat the vacancy rate as an exogenous variable. Also, the rent adjustment equation used by Wheaton and Torto (1994) specifies the change in rent as a function of the vacancy rate, which is equation (23) in a slightly different guise.

The econometric studies of office and industrial markets presented in the book by DiPasquale and Wheaton (1996, ch. 12) and in Wheaton, Torto, and Evans (1997) use the same rent adjustment model as in Wheaton and Torto (1994). Equations for absorption and new construction are added to the model. Absorption is hypothesized to be a function of employment growth, the lagged vacancy rate, and the amount of occupied space. New construction is a function of lagged absorption, vacancy, the lagged stock of space, and lagged construction.

Hendershott (1996) develops a model of rent adjustment by first specifying an equation for long-run equilibrium gross rent g^* which states

$$g^*(1 - v_n) = C + \exp,$$

where exp are operating expenses. This equation is, of course, the gross-rent equivalent of the long-run equilibrium condition used throughout this chapter. Data from the Sydney office market were obtained that provide an independent estimate of g^*. Gross rent is then hypothesized to adjust to the deviation of gross rent from g^* *and* to the natural vacancy rate minus the actual vacancy rate according to:

$$(g_t - g_{t-1})/g_{t-1} = \alpha_o(v_n - v_{t-1}) + \alpha_1(g^* - g_{t-1}).$$

The signs of α_o and α_1 were found to be negative and positive, respectively. This equation is essentially equation (23) supplemented by the deviation of rent from its long-run equilibrium level. A rent below (above) long-run equilibrium results in a rent increase (decrease), so this variable is capturing long-run adjustment. Hendershott's equation would be a valid specification for rent adjustment in the long run if the vacancy rate variable were dropped from the model. Hendershott et al. (1999) use the same rent-adjustment equation to study the London office market. The model for London also includes a space–demand equation and an equation for office space completions. Space demand is a function of employment and rent. Office space completions are modeled as a function of the lagged gap between long-run equilibrium rent and actual rent.

F. Rent and Vacancy in Commercial Real Estate Markets

Hotel rooms

The model presented in this chapter is most readily applied to the market for hotel rooms. Analysts of the market actually refer to "revenue per available room" (RevPAR), which is simply the occupancy rate times the room rate per day; i.e., θR in the model. Occupancy, average daily rate, and RevPAR for the national hotel market for the first five months of recent years are as follows:

	Occupancy (%)	Daily rate ($)	RevPAR ($)
1998	62.0	78.59	48.73
1999	61.5	81.63	50.20
2000	61.9	85.03	52.63
2001	60.3	88.27	53.23
2002	58.0	84.51	49.02

These data show that, from 1998 to 2000, the daily rate was increasing while the occupancy rate remained roughly constant over the first five months of the year. The data for these three years are consistent with the idea that the demand for hotel rooms was increasing, and the short-run supply curve was vertical. Hotel owners were taking the increase in demand in the form of increases in the daily rate rather than increases in occupancy. Revenue per available room increased steadily. Then in the first five months of 2001 the occupancy rate actually fell while the daily rate increased by $3.24, suggesting that the short-run supply curve might be "backward-bending." Perhaps it is best to realize that one year does not make a trend. Then we come to 2002. The 9/11 attack produced an immediate decline in the demand for hotel rooms because travel declined. We see the effect in the data. Occupancy dropped 2.3% and the daily rate declined by $3.76. Here we see that a sudden drop in demand resulted in declines in both occupancy and the daily rate, just as the model predicts. Revenue per available room fell by $4.21, essentially wiping out the gains from the previous four years. It will come as no surprise to you that the market price of hotels declined at the same time.

Office space

The same model can be used to study the market for office space, with two modifications. First, the quantity of office space is measured in square feet, rather than rooms. Second, the rent charged for office space can be quite complex. The rent in the model is "net" rent, the rent that does not include operating expenses (heating, lighting, janitorial service, and so on). The difficulty is that true net rent is usually not reported to those who study office markets. Commercial leases can include a variety of concessions to tenants that will create an appreciable discrepancy between "stated" net rent and effective rent. These concessions include months of free rent, extra allowances for finishing and decorating the space, moving allowances, and payments to the tenant's old landlord. A reliable measure of effective net rent is thus a critical ingredient in a study of the rent/occupancy relationship. Office rent is stated in terms of dollars per square foot per year.

We have conducted studies of net effective rent for the office market in downtown Chicago, and the data for 1993–1999 are as follows:

	Effective net rent ($)	Occupancy rate (%)
1993	0.55	78.4
1994	1.29	80.4
1995	2.41	82.5
1996	1.98	82.8
1997	4.23	86.2
1998	6.10	88.1
1999	8.06	88.9

The 1990s were a time during which the stock of office space in downtown Chicago remained constant, which should come as no surprise given that effective net rents were very low as the economy came out of the recession of the early 1990s. Consequently, these data trace out the short-run supply curve of office space quite nicely. Simply using the end-points in the data, an increase in effective net rent of $7.51 per square foot per year was associated with an increase in occupancy of 10.5%. New construction of office space in downtown Chicago commenced in 1999 (but was then blind-sided by the 9/11 attack in 2001). Unfortunately, our studies of net effective rent ended in 1999.

McDonald (2002) used the data from the study by Hendershott, Lizieri, and Matysiak (1999) that was discussed above to estimate the model presented in this chapter for the London office market. Supppose that the demand for occupied space in linear form is:

$$Q_t = Q_0 - b_1 R_t + b_2 E_t,$$

where R is rent per square foot, E is office employment, and t refers to the time period (a year from 1977 to 1996). At a given level of mobility in the market, the demand for vacant space is:

$$V_t = V_o - \beta R_t.$$

An increase in mobility would shift the demand for vacant space upward. Given that the total amount of space is the sum of occupied and vacant space, these two equations can be solved for short-run equilibrium Q, V, and R. In particular, equilibrium rent is a function of employment, the stock of space, and the parameters from the two demand functions:

$$R_t = (Q_o + V_o)/(\beta + b_1) + [b_2/(\beta + b_1)]E_t - [1/(\beta + b_1)]S_t.$$

This equation for rent was estimated with the result that

$$R_t = 7.030 + 0.096E_t - 0.00257S_t.$$

Rent is measured in pounds per square foot per year, employment is in thousands, and the stock of space is in thousands of square meters. The coefficients of both E and S are statistically significant. The demand function for space is estimated as:

$$Q_t = 3,832.480 - 160.625R_t + 23.892E_t.$$

The coefficients of R and E are both statistically significant in this equation. The coefficient of rent of -161 implies that the elasticity of demand for occupied space is -0.23. Finally, an equation for new construction was estimated for London. New construction is a function of the change in office employment in London lagged five years and the gap between actual rent and long-run average rent lagged two years, but only when the gap is positive. Otherwise the rent gap variable is zero.

G. Summary

The purpose of this chapter was to develop a simple equilibrium model of rent and vacancy for commercial real estate markets. The model is presented in diagrammatic and algebraic forms. In short-run equilibrium, net rent and the amounts of occupied and vacant space are functions of the total inventory of space (taken as given) and the underlying parameters in the demand functions for occupied space and vacant space. In the long run, net rent is a function of the cost of capital and the underlying parameters in these two demand functions. Net rent then determines the quantities of occupied and vacant space and, hence, the natural vacancy rate. Therefore, the natural vacancy rate is shown to be a function of the cost of capital and the parameters in the demand functions for occupied and vacant space.

The chapter then considers two models of search and equilibrium in real estate markets developed recently by Geltner and Miller (2001) and Arnott and Igarashi (2000). Both models imply that there exists an optimal vacancy rate for landlords. The latter model can be presented on a diagram that is identical to the diagram used for the model developed in this chapter. The chapter then considers some of the recent econometric studies of commercial real estate rent and vacancy. It is concluded that none of these studies is fully consistent with the basic model of equilibrium presented here because none includes an estimate of the demand for vacant space. Further econometric studies are needed. The chapter concludes with some practical examples of real estate market analysis from the commercial sector.

Exercises

1 Suppose that the demand for office space (measured in millions of square feet) is

$$Q = 150 - 3R.$$

The demand for vacant space is

$$V = 25 - R$$

The total amount of space is 110 msf. The cost of capital is 12.5 dollars per square foot per year.

(a) Solve for rent, quantity of occupied space, quantity of vacant space, and the vacancy rate in the short run.
(b) Given these answers, is there an incentive to build more space?
(c) What are the long-run equilibrium rent, total stock of space, and vacancy rate in this market?

2 Go to a web site for a commercial real estate firm that provides (free) office market data. C. B. Richard Ellis, Cushman and Wakefield, and Grubb and Ellis are good choices. If one does not work, try another. Select a metropolitan area and prepare a short report on the recent past and current state of the downtown and suburban markets. Be careful to note the concepts of rent and vacancy that are being used in their reports.

References

Achour-Fischer, D., 1999, "An Integrated Property Market Model: A Pedagogical Tool," *Journal of Real Estate Practice and Education*, vol. 2, pp. 33–43.

Anas, A., 1997, "Rent Control with Matching Economies: A Model of European Housing Market Regulation," *Journal of Real Estate Finance and Economics*, vol. 15, pp. 111–37.

Arnott, R., 1989, "Housing Vacancies, Thin Markets, and Idiosyncratic Tastes," *Journal of Real Estate Finance and Economics*, vol. 2, pp. 5–30.

Arnott, R. and M. Igarashi, 2000, "Rent Control, Mismatch Costs and Search Efficiency," *Regional Science and Urban Economics*, vol. 30, pp. 249–88.

Ball, M., C. Lizieri, and B. MacGregor, 1998, *The Economics of Commercial Property Markets*. London: Routledge.

Clapp, J., 1993, *Dynamics of Office Markets*, Washington, DC: Urban Institute Press.

Corgel, J., H. Smith, and D. Ling, 1998, *Real Estate Perspectives*, 3rd edn. Boston: Irwin McGraw-Hill.

DiPasquale, D. and W. Wheaton, 1992, "The Markets for Real Estate Assets and Space: A Conceptual Framework," *AREUEA Journal*, vol. 20, pp. 181–97.

DiPasquale, D. and W. Wheaton, 1996, *Urban Economics and Real Estate Markets*, Englewood Cliffs, NJ: Prentice-Hall.

Fisher, J., 1992, "Presidential Address," *AREUEA Journal*, vol. 20, pp. 165–80.

Geltner, D. and N. Miller, 2001, *Commercial Real Estate Analysis and Investments*, Upper Saddle River, NJ: Prentice-Hall.

Hendershott, P., 1996, "Rental Adjustment and Valuation in Overbuilt Markets: Evidence from the Sydney Office Market," *Journal of Urban Economics*, vol. 39, pp. 51–67.

Hendershott, P., C. Lizieri, and G. Matysiak, 1999, "The Workings of the London Office Market," *Real Estate Economics*, vol. 27, pp. 365–87.

Igarashi, M., 1992, "The Rent–Vacancy Relationship in the Rental Housing Market," *Journal of Housing Economics*, vol. 1, pp. 251–70.

McDonald, John, F., 2000, "Rent, Vacancy, and Equilibrium in Real Estate Markets," *Journal of Real Estate Practice and Education*, vol. 3, pp. 55–69.

Nahmias, S., 1993, *Production and Operations Analysis*, 2nd edn. Homewood, IL: Irwin.

Read, C., Price Strategies for Idiosyncratic Goods: The Case of Housing, *AREUEA Journal*, vol. 16, pp. 379–95.

Wheaton, W., Vacancy, 1990, "Search, and Prices in a Housing Market Matching Model," *Journal of Political Economy*, vol. 98, pp. 1270–92.

Wheaton, W., and R. Torto, 1994, "Office Rent Indices and Their Behavior Over Time," *Journal of Urban Economics*, vol. 35, pp. 121–39.

Wheaton, W., R. Torto, and P. Evans, 1997, "The Cyclic Behavior of the Greater London Office Market," *Journal of Real Estate Finance and Economics*, vol. 15, pp. 77–92.

Chapter 12

Real Estate Development and Investment

A. Introduction

This chapter provides an introductory overview of the real estate development process, techniques to determine the financial feasibility of proposed developments or other types of real estate investments, and examination of some development case studies. You will learn the details of the real estate development process and the steps in financing a proposed development. You will also learn the basic methods developers use to determine financial feasibility of a proposed development, and then see how to apply those methods to actual developments. Many colleges offer separate courses in real estate development and investment, and textbooks on the subject are available. Our goal in this chapter is to provide you with enough information to decide whether you wish to pursue the subject further.

The chapter begins with an examination of the property development process, including stages in the real estate development process, the role of the lender, the numerous contracts that must be executed, and the business of land development. This is followed by a discussion of market analysis used to investigate proposed development projects. The largest portion of the chapter is devoted to financial analysis for real estate development and investment. The methods included progress from simpler to more complex procedures that are followed as the proposed development progresses from initial to later stages. The chapter concludes with case studies.

B. The Real Estate Development Process

Real estate development is a broad concept, usually taken to mean taking a parcel of land and adding improvements to produce a completed, operational property.

Land development is acquisition of "raw" land, addition of some infrastructure, subdividing, and selling off the lots to real estate developers. In other cases land development involves the assembling of smaller parcels of land into a larger parcel, and selling the larger parcel to a developer. *Plottage value* arises if the value of several parcels, when combined, exceeds the sum of the values of the individual parcels under separate ownership.

A goal of real estate development is to develop the land for its "highest and best" use, the use that will produce the highest net return to the land (given legal and physical constraints). The completion of a real estate development may take several years. During this time there will be "carrying costs" associated with the land (e.g., property taxes). Sometimes a parcel of land will be devoted to some temporary use, such as a parking lot, while the site is awaiting development.

The legal constraints on real estate development usually are determined by the zoning ordinance, which determines the permissible use of the land. A zoning variance or other type of change possibly can be obtained to change the permissible use, but otherwise zoning is set and determines use. The timing of that use is up to the developer.

The stages in the development process include the formulation of plans – from a preliminary to the final version – and project management. Throughout the process the lender is a critical partner. And, at each stage, there are various contracts that must be executed and approvals that are needed.

Role of the lender

Lenders take a risk because decisions of potential tenants are unknown. The developer is a speculator who produces a product in advance of orders – unless the lender requires that tenants shall be identified before the project begins. The lender takes the risk that the project can be built on schedule and on budget, and then sold, rented, or financed to pay back the borrowed money. Developers need external financing. In most cases external financing will be needed, in the form of:

- equity partnership;
- debt financing; or
- combination of the two.

Equity partners can provide seed money, and help spread the risk. Real estate investment trusts issue stock in order to undertake development projects (and to purchase existing properties as well). Debt financing can be obtained from banking institutions (commercial banks and thrift institutions), insurance companies, financial services companies, foreign banks, and (to some extent) Wall Street.

Loans for real estate development are of two basic types: construction loans and permanent take-out commitments.

Construction loans run to completion of improvements and, possibly, to the sale of the property. Lenders require that the construction loan be the first lien on the property, which means that land development lenders sometimes become equity partners. Interest rates are 2% to 5% above the prime rate. Interest accumulates and is paid off with the loan balance with the proceeds of the permanent loan.

The total amount of a construction loan is not paid out at the outset. Funds are paid out in installments at agreed stages of construction. Lender's representative will inspect and certify that satisfactory progress is being made prior to each payout.

Obtaining a construction loan requires a permanent "take-out" commitment from a long-term lender. The *permanent take-out commitment* is an option-like agreement that permits the developer to borrow at a specified interest rate within a set time period. Permanent take-out commitments include contingencies such as:

- maximum period for developer to obtain construction loan;
- completion date for construction;
- minimum leasing requirements (e.g., 60% to 70% leased) before loan proceeds are fully disbursed;
- interest rate set at the time funds are disbursed equal to a rate on a prespecified benchmark security;
- provisions for gap financing;
- expiration date of permanent loan commitment, with provisions for extensions;
- approval by permanent lender of design changes or substitution of building materials.

Gap financing is needed if the permanent lender decides to advance only partial funding because of cost overruns or failure to meet minimum leasing requirements. A typical *floor-to-ceiling* commitment specifies the full amount of the loan (the ceiling) and the amount disbursed (the floor) should the leasing requirement not be met. A commitment for gap financing is usually required by the *construction lender*.

Construction lenders face the risk that the borrower will be unable to repay because of unforeseen problems such as strikes, weather, design problems, material supply problems, or loss of contractor or subcontractor. When project costs exceed the value of the project, the developer may abandon the project rather than invest additional equity. The construction lender may have to foreclose on the property.

An *open-ended construction loan* is a loan granted without a permanent takeout commitment. These loans are very risky, carry high interest rates, and often involve foreclosure.

Mini-perm loans are loans that cover the construction period, the lease-up period, and a few years beyond the lease-up period. Developers expect to sell the project before the end of the mini-perm loan. These loans have been widely used.

Alternative real estate development loan packages are illustrated in the following table. Three separate time periods are relevant for lenders: the construction period, the lease-up period, and the period of stable operations. Loan package A includes a construction loan followed immediately by a permanent loan. That permanent loan is relatively risky because it starts at the beginning of the lease-up period. Loan package *B* has a construction loan followed by a gap loan for the lease-up period. In this case the permanent loan is less risky because it begins at the end of the lease-up period. Loan package *C* has a very risky open-ended construction loan followed by a safe permanent loan, and package *D* uses a mini-perm loan that goes a few years beyond the lease-up period.

Summary of alternative loan packages for development projects

	A	B	C	D
Construction period	Construction loan	Construction loan with take-out	Open-end construction loan	Mini-perm loan
Lease-up period	Risky permanent loan	Floor amount or gap loan		
Stable operations		Safe permanent loan	Safe permanent loan	Safe permanent loan

Land development

Land development involves the acquisition of land with the intention of constructing utilities and surface improvements, and then reselling some or all of the developed sites to project developers or homebuilders. Structuring loan agreements and repayment schedules and estimating interest carrying cost for land development projects are complex processes.

The land developer must have a general development concept that has evidence of feasibility even if the land development company is not going to construct improvements on the developed sites. In residential land development companies specialize in the acquisition and development of raw land on the fringe of the urban area. The land development plan contemplates the nature of the housing to be constructed (e.g., single family, multi-family, cluster housing) and constructs streets, sewers, and utilities accordingly.

Stages of the land development process are as follows:

Stage 1: initial contact by land broker
• site inspection;
• preliminary market study;
• preliminary cost estimates;
• option contract with land owner, where price of option can be applied to purchase price.

Stage 2: option period
• soil studies, engineering;
• feasibility, appraisal, and design strategy;
• negotiating with contractors, subject to closing;
• submit plan for public approval;
• submit package for financing.

Stage 3: development period
• purchase land;
• close on land development loan;
• implement financial controls;
• coordinate with contractors, consultants, public sector.

The land purchase may be by:

• cash (with loan for site improvements);
• down payment and loan from seller (with loan for site improvements);
• loan from lender to cover all costs, where loan amount is based on a percentage of appraised value of land plus improvements (e.g., 75%).

A land development loan from a lender requires information about:

• capacities of third parties to perform (contractors, etc.);
• verification by public sector that use and density proposed conform with zoning ordinances and capacities of utilities on site;
• verification that third parties bear unforeseen risk (e.g., performance of contractors).

A crucial part of land development loan pertains to estimating the interest carrying cost. The land developer "draws" from development loan on a schedule, and pays a variable interest rate (2–3% over prime lending rate). This interest accumulates, and the loan is paid off on a schedule that had been negotiated.

Stage 4: sales period
- implement marketing program;
- implement design controls with builders;
- implement facility management and/or begin homeowner association.

In summary, land acquisition and development loans are made with the purpose of acquiring, subdividing, and making improvements to raw, undeveloped land. Land is sold to individual developers. Land developers, in conjunction with local planning officials, make decisions on lot sizes, land use, traffic circulation, and amenities. Land development loans are repaid as lots are sold, and are the riskiest loans of all real estate loans. As each lot is sold the developer is given a release statement in which the lender waives all liens on the parcel sold, permitting clear title to pass from developer to buyer of the parcel. Acquisition, development, and construction loans (ADC loans) are available sometimes, but most lending institutions are unwilling to make them.

The call option model of land value and real estate development

The land developer starts by obtaining an option to purchase the land. This indicates that options, and the pricing of options, have an important role to play in land and real estate development. An option is the right, without obligation, to obtain something of value upon payment. The owner of land (or a developer who holds an option to purchase the land) has a "real" option to develop now or to develop later. In other words, the timing of development is a matter of exercising an option.

Somewhat paradoxically, it is uncertainty about the future that can create option value. Consider the following example in which a property can be developed today with a value of $1 million, or can be developed next year with a value of $600,000 with probability 60% or value of $1.6 million with probability 40%. If the developer decides to wait until next year, the project is undertaken only if its value turns out to be $1.6 million. In other words, the uncertainly is eliminated by waiting. Under these assumptions it is worthwhile to wait until next year because the present value of the land today is higher with the "wait" decision compared to the "build now" decision.

	Today	Next year	
Probability	100%	60%	40%
Value of developed property (1,000s)	1,000	600	1,600
Development cost (excluding land)	800	900	900
NPV of exercising option	200	−300	700
Future values		0	700
		(don't build)	(build)
Expected values	200	280	
	(1 × 200)	(0.6 × 0 + 0.4 × 700)	
PV @ 20% discount rate	200	233	

Land value today = Max (200, 233) = 233.

Contracts and approvals

Many contracts are executed and a number of approvals are obtained from government in the process of developing real estate. Here is an attempt to list them.

- Acquisition of development rights (alternatives):
  - option;
  - contract for sale with contingencies;
  - binder;
  - letter of intent.
- Partnership agreements with equity partners.
- Financing:
  - permanent take-out commitment;
  - construction;
  - gap financing.
- Tax increment financing agreement with local government.
- General contractor and construction manager contracts.
- Leases with major tenants.
- Zoning approval.
- Building permits.
- Environmental approvals.
- Payment of development impact fees.
- Utility approvals.
- Sale of developed property:
  - listing agreement;
  - contracts for sale.

Given this imposing list of contracts, it is best to have a real estate attorney as part of the real estate development team.

C. Market Analysis

Market studies attempt to analyze and predict future demand for real estate and relate that demand to existing supply conditions. The data developed in a market study form the basis for the economic feasibility and physical design stages of the planning process.

Housing

A residential market analysis answers six basic questions:

1 What are the indirect economic constraints (zoning, building codes, local concerns, permits, approvals) and the physical constraints of the proposed site?

2   What is the size of the future market, and what percentage of the overall market can be *captured* by the proposed development?
3   What is the market-determined price range?
4   What type of unit is justified by market demand?
5   How large should the units be?
6   What amenities should be provided?

A housing market analysis case study: luxury high-rise development

The case comes from the downtown area of a major northern city, and involves a high-rise rental and/or condo development.

The market study consisted of four steps:

1   Generate projections and analyze demographic trends:
    – projection of population for metro area, city, and groups that would be likely to be attracted to relatively expensive downtown units;
    – estimation of location preferences, marketable unit sizes, amenities, and building services;
    – projection of residential demands by socioeconomic group;
    – estimation of annual absorption rates by type of unit (disregarding price and competitive environment).
    Demographic projections for 10 years out were made for 9 socioeconomic groups (3 income categories times 3 family types – families with children, households under age 65 without children, and households over age 65 without children). Young and old, upper and middle-income childless households are the relevant market for the proposed project. Researchers used previous data to estimate the percentage of this market that can be captured by downtown. This produced an estimate of the demand for downtown luxury units for the next 10 years.
2   Site analysis of proposed subject property:
    – physical characteristics of site and environs;
    – analysis of attractiveness as a residential site;
    – design suggestions to ameliorate unfavorable location characteristics.
    Site analysis noted access to employment as a big plus, and identified problems such as:
    – area lacks social activity;
    – security is a concern;
    – traffic;
    – lack of greenery.
    This analysis produced recommendations for amenities in the building and requests to the city for some planning in the surrounding area.
3   Study competitive environment and document potential effective demand:
    – study inventory of existing units to determine rents, prices, unit sizes, vacancy rates, building amenities, services, fees;
    – personal interviews with owners, managers, residents;

– develop socioeconomic profile of potential condo owners who could be attracted to site.

4   Recommendations of market analysis:
   – suitability of site for condo development;
   – number and mix of units;
   – price range;
   – actions to enhance attractiveness of site;
   – development timetable;
   – marketing strategies.

Recommendations were to include both condo and rental units to broaden market, design to appeal to childless couples, and set prices and rents to be compatible with the area. Activity generators such as a restaurant and theater should be incorporated. Plaza with green space should be included. Superior security system included. Units should be designed for ultimate conversion to condo. Project should be developed in two phases to avoid glutting the market.

Commercial development market analysis

A commercial market analysis answers these questions:

1   What are the indirect economic constraints?
2   How many square feet can be leased annually? This depends upon demand projections for the sector (e.g., retail, office) and supply projections, scaled down to the specific area in question.
3   What should be the lease rate per square foot?
4   What specific types of activities are likely to be attracted? Design of project depends upon the nature of the likely tenants.
5   For retail development, what is the sales volume per square foot likely to be?
6   What amenities must be provided?

D. Financial Analysis for Real Estate Development

Financial analysis for real estate development serves both the developer and the lender, and determines the conditions under which a proposed project becomes economically viable. This section of the chapter lays out a sequence of analytical tools that corresponds not only to the real estate development process, but also to the quality of information available at each stage. During the development process the quality of the information improves.

Projects should be attractive to sources of debt and equity financing. Requirements for debt sources for both interim and permanent financing are easy to determine. Equity yield requirements depend upon circumstances – especially risk.

The first step in financial analysis involves a simple "back of the envelope" comparison of cost to value.

The second step involves applying debt and equity return requirements to gauge the *adequacy* of the project's cash flows in the first year of normal operations. We will consider this step at length.

The third step is a more complete analysis of cash flows over time and use of the present discounted value criterion. In this third step the issue can become one of profit maximization, rather than adequacy of cash flows.

Step 1: Comparison of cost to value

This comparison is normally done of a per-square-foot basis for commercial real estate or a per-unit basis for housing. An estimate of the total development cost per square foot is compared to the current market value per square foot of comparable, new developments. A more sophisticated version would use a forecast of value per square foot for the time the project is to be completed. For example, at this time an estimate of the cost of developing office space in and around downtown Chicago is $250 per square foot. What is the market value of such space?

An equivalent approach is to compare

Net rent per square foot times *occupancy rate*
versus
Annualized cost per square foot

Step 2: Financial feasibility

There are two basic approaches to financial feasibility.

The first is the "front door" (cost approach) in which the cost of the project is used to generate the revenue stream required to justify the development. This required revenue stream is then compared with the best estimate of the actual revenue stream that can be expected.

The second approach is the "back door" (market approach) in which the expected revenue stream of the project is used to compute the project's land and development cost that can be justified. This justified cost is then compared to the actual cost of the project.

These methods can test whether the proposed project comes close to being financially feasible, i.e., whether the annual revenues cover annualized costs once the project is up and running.

The front door method

The front door method is implemented by first estimating the total capital budget for the project. This total capital amount is then converted into an annual revenue stream that is needed to justify the capital budget. The steps are:

Site cost + Capital improvements + Indirect and soft costs

= Total capital budget

Total capital budget

Times loan to cost ratio	Times one minus loan to cost ratio
= Allowable mortgage amount	= Cash equity requirement
Times mortgage constant	Times before tax rate of return
= Annual debt service	= Required cash throw off

Annual debt service + Required cash throw off = Net operating income

Net operating income (NOI) + Operating expenses + Property taxes

= Effective gross income (EGI)

Effective gross income + Vacancy allowance + Credit loss

= Gross potential revenue required

Gross potential revenue required is then compared to estimated actual
gross potential revenue (i.e., total leasable space times gross rent)

Figure 12.1   The front door method

1   Split the capital budget into two parts, the mortgage loan and the cash equity shares.
2   Compute the annual amounts needed to service the mortgage loan and the equity. The annual loan payment is found by using the mortgage constant for the interest rate and term of the loan. The annual return to equity is the before-tax rate of return required for investments of this type.
3   The annual debt service plus the required return to equity together equal the net operating income (NOI) of the project.
4   NOI plus operating expenses and property taxes equal effective gross income. Effective gross income plus the vacancy allowance (and any credit loss) equal gross potential revenue required.
5   Gross potential revenue required is then compared to estimated actual gross potential revenue.

The method is illustrated in Figure 12.1.

The back door method
The back door method is the reverse of the front-door method. We begin with estimated annual gross potential revenue and convert that into a justified capital budget amount, which is then compared to the actual cost of the project. The first steps are to estimate net operating income (NOI) by subtracting the vacancy allowance, operating expenses, and property taxes from gross potential revenue. The crucial step is to convert NOI into cash available for debt service by using the applicable required debt coverage ratio. This is the ratio of NOI to annual debt service, and lenders normally require this to be at least 1.2 to 1.4:

Gross potential revenue – Vacancy allowance and credit loss

= Effective gross income

– Operating expenses and property taxes

= Net operating income (estimated actual NOI)

Net operating income

Divided by required debt coverage ratio

| NOI minus annual debt service | = Cash available for debt service |

= Available before tax cash throw off

| Divided by required before tax | Divided by mortgage constant rate of return |

| = Justified equity investment | = Justified mortgage amount |

Justified equity investment + Justified mortgage amount

= Justified project investment

– Anticipated improvement budget

= Justified land purchase

Justified land purchase is then compared with the actual purchase price of the land

Figure 12.2   The back door method

Debt coverage ratio = NOI/annual debt service = 1.2 to 1.4; i.e.,
Cash available for debt service = NOI/DCR.

Cash available for debt service is converted to the justified mortgage loan amount by dividing by the mortgage constant.

Net operating income minus the annual debt service equals the cash available as return to equity before income taxes. Dividing this annual return to equity by its required rate of return yields the justified equity investment.

The justified mortgage loan plus the justified equity investment equal the justified project investment. Subtraction of the cost of improvements from the justified project investment yields the justified land purchase amount. This last figure is then compared to the actual cost of the land to determine financial feasibility. See Figure 12.2 for a summary of these steps.

Step 3: Discounted cash-flow analysis

The front door and back door approaches are widely used by developers. They are simple and sound enough for preliminary analysis. However, the real estate development decision is a capital investment one that must be compared with other possible uses of the funds invested in the project. Should the developer select the project in question in order to maximize his/her wealth?

The more correct approach is to lay out all of the costs and revenues over a period of several years, up to the point at which the development is sold. Then the Discounted Net Present Value of the Project is computed so that it can be compared with NPV of other possible projects the developer might undertake.

Real estate development has special features:

- *Time to build*: Investment cash outflow is spread over time
- *Construction loans* are used.
- *Phased risk regimes*: Risk is greatest in the construction phase, followed by the lease-up phase, and least in the long-term phase.

We recommend the following general procedure.

1 Define two points in time:
   (a) time zero, when the development decision must be made;
   (b) time T when construction is complete and construction loan is due.
2 Compute the investment cost at time zero (land cost plus other upfront costs and fees); call this C.
3 Estimate NPV of the project as of the time construction of the project is complete, excluding C. This *NPV* is the value of the physically complete project at time T *minus* the balance due on the construction loan.
4 Discount the *NPV* of the project at time T back to time zero using the opportunity cost of capital for the development phase. Compare this *NPV* at time zero with C, the investment cost at time zero.
5 The opportunity cost of capital for the development phase is relatively high because of risk. Various methods are available for estimating this opportunity cost. For example, one might use the long-term return earned by publicly traded firms that specialize in real estate development activity. One source states that the rate to use during the construction phase might be 15% to 20%, and 10% to 12% during the lease-up phase (if there is one).

Consider the following reasonably simple example.

- The time zero cost of land is $2,000,000, and there are $200,000 in upfront design fees and developer costs.
- The construction phase takes three years, the construction contractor is paid in three annual payments of $1,500,000 at end of each year.
- The construction loan is obtained at a rate of 7.5% with $20,000 upfront origination fee. The loan covers the entire $4,500,000 and is due at end of year 3.
- Opportunity cost of capital in the development phase is 20%.
- Lease-up phase is 2 years, with expected net cash flow of negative $100,000 in year 4 and positive $400,000 in year 5.
- Opportunity cost of capital during the lease-up phase is 3% higher than for fully operational property.

- The property is fully operational in year 6 and after, with net cash flow of $800,000 in year 6, and growing at 1% per year.
- Discount rate of 9% is used for fully operational property.

These assumptions produce these data.

End of year	Net revenue	Discount rate (%)
0	−2,200,000	NA
1	−1,500,000	20
2	−1,500,000	20
3	−1,500,000	20
4	−100,000	12
5	400,000	12
6	800,000	9
7	808,000	9

and so on.

The solution to the problem involves the following computations.

Value of property at end of year 5 = $10,000,000, found as
800,000 ÷ (0.09 − 0.01) = 800,000/0.08 = 10,000,000

Value of property at end of year 3 = $8,201,531, found as
(−100,000/1.12) + (400,000/1.12*1.12) + (10,000,000/1.2544)

Construction loan due at end of year 3 = $4,845,938, found as (compounding forward)
1,500,000(1.075*1.075) + 1,500,000(1.075) + 1,500,000

Net present value of the project at time of completion is
8,201,531 − 4,845,938 = 3,355,593

Net present value of project at time zero is $1,941,894, found as
3,355,593 ÷ 1.2*1.2*1.2 = 3,355,593/1.728.

Time zero cost is $2,200,000, which exceeds NPV of project at time zero. Therefore, this project is not recommended.

Risk analysis and financial leverage

The analysis should consider the various risks in each phase of the project. What if construction takes longer than planned or costs more? What if the lease-up phase takes longer? And so on. A "pessimistic scenario" should be run to find out how bad it can get.

Financial leverage can be used to increase the rate of return to equity – at the price of increased risk. In the previous example, suppose that the $10,000,000 property is purchased with 50% debt and 50% equity, and that the interest rate on the loan is 6%. The debt service is (about) 6% of $5,000,000, or $300,000 per year, leaving an expected return to equity in the first year of

500,000/5,000,000 = 10%.

Instead, suppose that the loan is for 80% of the purchase price. Now the equity is 2,000,000, debt service is $480,000, and the expected return to equity in the first year is

3,200,000/2,000,000 = 16%.

If the loan is 50%, debt service is $300,000 out of the expected net operating income of $800,000 – a debt coverage ratio of 2.67. However, if the loan is 80%, debt service is $480,000 out of the expected $800,000, for a debt coverage ratio of 1.67.

Needless to say, the net operating income of $800,000 is not guaranteed. If the actual net operating income falls short of the debt service, the project itself is bankrupt. (However, if a firm owns this project and several others, the firm is not necessarily bankrupt.)

The greater loan means greater risk that the net operating income of the property will fail to cover the debt service. Indeed, if the financial markets are perfect, the additional expected return is the "correct" compensation for the increased risk.

E. The Real Estate Investment Decision

This section examines in detail the mechanics of making profitable commercial real estate investment decisions. Real estate is purchased (perhaps using debt financing) in order to acquire the rights to the future income from the subject property. The steps are:

- forecasting cash flows from operations;
- forecasting cash proceeds from sales;
- taking taxes into account;
- deciding on the appropriate discount rate;
- considering the use of financial leverage;
- computing net present value;
- making the investment decision.

Cash flows from operations

Primary objective in cash flow forecasting is estimating *net operating income* (NOI), which is income produced by the property after all operating expenses are deducted, but before debt service and income taxes. Debt service and income taxes are not related to the property's basic income-producing ability. Relevant data come from comparable properties and the historical experience of the subject property.

Basic procedure is to reconstruct an operating statement as follows.

Reconstructed operating statement

	Potential gross income (PGI)	Total space × gross rent
Minus	Vacancy and collection (VC)	Vacancy rate × gross rent
Plus	Miscellaneous income (MI)	Vending, parking, etc.
Equals	Effective gross income (EGI)	
Minus	Fixed operating expenses	Property tax
		Insurance
Minus	Variable operating expenses	Utilities, supplies maintenance,
		Repairs, management
Equals	Net operating income (NOI)	
Minus	Below-line costs	
	Leasing expenses	Tenant improvements,
		Rental agent commission
	Replacement of capital	Replace roof, etc.
Equals	Cash flow before debt service	
	and income tax	

Note: The below-line costs are to some degree discretionary, they can be quite significant, and should not be ignored.

This statement then serves as the basis for forecasting NOI for the holding period of some period of years, after which the property will be sold.

Proceeds from sale

The second major source of cash flow is from the sale of the property at the end of some holding period. Sale is often called a reversion.

Expected selling price is estimated by:

- assuming a growth rate of property value over time; or by
- assuming a constant ratio of NOI to property value (the reversion capitalization rate or the "going out" cap rate, in industry parlance).

Selling expenses are subtracted from expected selling price to get

Net sale proceeds (NSP)

Here's what we have so far
We have a estimated NOI for several years (n) into the future, and estimated NSP for the date of sale. In other words, we have:

NOI(1), NOI(2), NOI(3), . . . , NOI(n), NSP(n)

Income taxation and real estate

Alas, income taxes must be paid. The measure of most relevance to the investor is the present value of after-tax cash flow. Now is not the time to have a complete course in federal income taxation. We'll keep it simple.

We need to adjust the NOI series and the NSP for income taxes.

(1) First, we need to compute tax liability for each year of operation, as follows:

	Tax liability from operations
	Net operating income (NOI)
Minus	Depreciation (DEP)
Minus	Interest expense (INT)
Minus	Amortized financing costs (AFC)
Equals	Taxable income (TI)
Times	Tax rate (TR)
Equals	Tax liability (TAX)

Notes: *Depreciation* is based on a formula as follows:

  Depreciable basis times recovery rate

Currently commercial real estate uses "straight-line" depreciation with a Recovery Rate equal to one divided by the recovery period. The recovery period is 27.5 years for apartment buildings and 39 years for other commercial real estate.

Interest Expense depends upon the amount borrowed and the interest rate. Other financing costs paid at the beginning of the holding period can be amortized over time.

Tax Rate depends upon the investor's tax bracket.

(2) Second, we need to compute after-tax cash flow (ATCF) for the years of operation, as follows:

	After-tax cash flow
	Net operating income (NOI)
Minus	Interest expense (INT)
Minus	Principal amortization (PA)
Equals	Before-tax cash flow (BTCF)
Minus	Tax liability (TAX)
Equals	After-tax cash flow (ATCF)

(3) Third, we need to compute taxes due on sale:

	Taxes due on sale
	Net sale proceeds (NSP)
Minus	Adjusted basis (AB)
	AB is original purchase price
	Minus total depreciation taken
Equals	Taxable gain
Times	Tax rate on capital gains
Equals	Tax due of sale

Note: Subtraction of adjusted basis means that you pay capital gains tax on the depreciation that you took over your holding period.

(4) Fourth, we need cash flow from sale, which is:

	Cash flow from sale
	Net sale proceeds
Minus	Remaining mortgage balance (RMB)
Equals	Before-tax equity reversion (BTER)
Minus	Tax due on sale
Equals	After-tax equity reversion (ATER)

Here's what we have after income taxes

ATCF(1), ATCF(2), . . . , ATCF(n), ATER(n).

The discount rate

The use of the discounted cash flow method requires a discount rate. If the cash flow were riskless, then we could simply use the risk-free rate of return for the time period in question, such as the rate on Treasury bonds of the same maturity as the holding period n.

But real estate cash flows are risky. The theory capital asset pricing establishes that the rate of return expected by an investor is positively related to the riskiness of an investment. Therefore, we use the *risk-adjusted discount rate* to accomplish two objectives:

- discount future cash; and
- account for risk.

Algebraically, the risk-adjusted discount rate is

$$E(R) = R_f + \text{RP},$$

where $E(R)$ is the expected or required rate of return, R_f is the risk-free rate (i.e., rate on Treasury securities), and RP is the risk premium.

The question is then, how do we figure the risk premium? Elaborate financial theories have been formulated to answer this question. Here's a summary.

The risk premium

Can the risk premium be determined just by considering the riskiness of the investment itself – by measuring the standard deviation of its return? If investors have the ability to diversify away any *unsystematic risk* by having a portfolio of investments, the answer is no. Investments have some degree of risk that is unique to that investment, and this kind of risk can be eliminated by having a portfolio of many investments. It's like an insurance company offering life insurance. If the insurance company has thousands of policy holders, you can forecast the amount of benefits paid in any year very accurately.

In fact, in a competitive market, investors should not expect to be rewarded for bearing unsystematic risk because properties will be priced to yield a rate of return that is just sufficient to provide for the typical (that is, well-diversified) investor with an adequate rate of return.

The question then is, to what extent does the investment add to the risk of the typical well-diversified portfolio? Note that the investment might actually reduce the risk of a well-diversified portfolio, in which case the "risk premium" would be a negative number.

Here's the basic answer. The entire market of risky assets such as the S&P 1,000 stocks have a *market risk premium*, an expected rate of return that exceeds the riskless rate. Call this MRP. The risk premium on the investment in question moves up and down with the market risk premium. For example, if the market risk premium rises by 2%, the risk premium on your proposed investment may rise by 1.5%. The ratio of these two is called the *BETA* of the invesment. In other words,

$$RP = \beta\, MRP. \qquad \cdot$$

In this example BETA is 0.75. BETA equals 1.0 if the risk premium of the asset matches the market risk premium, and BETA is greater than 1.0 if the risk premium on the investment fluctuates more than the market risk premium.

An investment with a BETA of zero adds nothing to the risk of the diversified portfolio, so the proper discount rate is just the risk-free rate. What should we actually use? Real Estate Research Corp. (RERC) does a survey of *before-tax* returns (BTR) expected of a sample of large real estate investors, and this required return tends to be 4% to 6% above the return on 10-year Treasury securities. RERC issues this report quarterly, so one can obtain the latest number from them. For example, if the rate on 10-year Treasuries is 5%, then the before-tax return expected on real estate investment would be 9% to 11%.

The *after-tax* return (ATR) expected would be

$$ATR = BTR(1 - t),$$

where t is your (marginal) tax rate.

So, if the before-tax return expected is 10%, then the after-tax return would be 6.5% if you are in the 35% tax bracket.

Financial leverage

So far the analysis has assumed that the investor obtains a loan of some given percentage of the value of the investment (such as 80%). It was presumed that this is the "optimal" loan in some sense.

An investor (and the lender) might consider alternative loan amounts. The basic idea is that a larger loan means a greater commitment to debt service and therefore both a greater expected return and a greater risk attached to the rate of return to equity. This is the idea of financial leverage. Also, interest expenses are deductible.

Here's an example. Suppose a property worth $100,000 is purchased with 50% debt @ 6% and 50% equity. Expected net operating income is $8,000 per year. Debt service is $3,000 per year. The expected after-tax return to equity (with 35% tax rate) is:

$$0.65(5,000)/50,000 = 6.5\%.$$

Now suppose that the loan is increased to 80% @6.5%. Debt service is $5,200, and the expected return to equity is

$$0.65(2,800)/20,000 = 9.1\%.$$

Needless to say, the increase in the debt service from $3,000 to $5,200 means that there is a greater risk that the equity will earn nothing in any given year. Indeed, if the NOI is less than debt service, the project is bankrupt.

A greater loan amount also represents a greater risk for the lender too – where the risk is that the borrower will be unable to pay the debt service. Lenders normally charge a greater rate of interest for a larger loan (as a percentage of the value of the investment), or they require greater security. For example, commercial real estate loans in excess of 90% of value often must be *recourse loans*, loans whereby the borrower pledges the property itself *and* all other assets as security for the loan.

The optimal amount of financial leverage is the loan amount that just balances the benefits of borrowing (including the tax deduction for interest) against the higher interest rate that will be charged by the lender and the greater risk faced by the owners.

F. Case Studies

Office building example with five year holding period

This case study uses the methods presented in the previous section to examine a possible real estate investment.

The price of building is $885,000.

Net operating income in year 1

Potential gross income	180,000
Vacancy and collection	18,000
Effective gross income	162,000
Operating expenses	
Fixed (property tax, insurance)	28,000
Variable	45,000
NOI	89,000

NOI and value of property are projected to increase 3% per year. Selling expenses will be 6% of the selling price.

Before-tax cash flow is

Year 0	−885,000
Year 1	89,000
Year 2	91,670
Year 3	94,420
Year 4	97,253
Year 5	100,170
Plus net sale proceeds of $1,025,957 − 6%	964,400

Now we have to compute after-tax cash flow.

The building is purchased with a 75% loan at 7% interest.

Equity is $221,250. Annual debt service is

$0.75(885,000)(0.080586) = 53,489$; interest in year 1 is $46,463 and principle is reduced by $7026. The borrower borrows $656,724 in year 2 and pays interest of $45,971, and so on.

After-tax cash flow
Tax liability in years 1 through 5

	1	2	3	4	5
NOI	89,000	91,670	94,420	97,253	100,170
INT	46,463	45,971	45,444	44,881	44,279
DEP	18,154	18,154	18,154	18,154	18,154
TI	24,383	27,545	30,822	34,218	37,737

Rate = 0.35

TAX	8,534	9,641	10,788	11,976	13,208

Depreciation is based on 80% of the property (land is 20% and not depreciable), and is $1/39 = 2.5641\%$ per year.

After-tax cash flow in years 1 through 5

	1	2	3	4	5
NOI	89,000	91,670	94,420	97,253	100,170
INT + AMORT	53,489	53,489	53,489	53,489	53,489
TAX	8,534	9,641	10,788	11,976	13,208
ATCF	26,977	28,540	30,143	31,788	33,473

Taxes due on sale

Net sale proceeds	964,400
Adjusted basis	794,230
Original price	885,000
Total depreciation	90,770
Taxable gain	170,170
Tax rate = 20%	
Tax due on sale	34,034

Cash flow from sale

Net sale proceeds	964,400
Remaining mortgage balance	623,338
(PV of remaining 25 years of payments)	
Before-tax equity reversion	341,062
Tax due on sale	34,034
After-tax equity reversion	307,028

After tax cash flow

		Discounted value*
Year 0	−221,250	−221,250
Year 1	26,977	25,331
Year 2	28,540	25,163
Year 3	30,143	24,954
Year 4	31,788	24,710
Year 5	33,473	24,431
ATER	307,028	

Net present value = −221,250 + 348,683 = 127,433.
  *After-tax discount rate is 0.65(10) = 6.5%.
  This looks like a very good investment indeed!

Problem (to be done in class)
Commercial real estate investment, to be held *one* year (to keep it simple).

Price	100,000
NOI	10,000

Selling price in one year is expected to be 105,263. Selling costs are 5% of the selling price. Investor borrows 50% of the price at an interest rate of 6%, and the entire loan is repaid after one year (interest and principle). Equity investment is 50% of the price.
  The before-tax discount rate is 10%. The income tax rate is 35%, and the capital gains tax rate is 20%. Depreciation can be taken on 80% of the purchase price (the value of the structure) at a rate of 1/39 per year. (Hint, this amounts to $2,051.)

Question: Is this a good investment after taxes? Compute the after-tax cash flow and compute the net present value of the equity investment.

Shopping center project

This is a case study of a shopping center project that was constructed in the northwestern suburbs of the Chicago metropolitan area. The project is 76,366 gross square feet, 75,536 net leasable square feet. Enough data are available to use the front door and the back door methods.

Costs

Land	4,270,622
Structure	13,677,184
Soft costs	3,190,000

Total development cost: 21,137,806

(Added cost from a restaurant tenant is 3,892,000, paid by tenant.) Development cost is $280 per square foot on leasable square feet.

Front door method (75% loan)

Total capital budget		21,137,806	
Equity	5,284,452	Loan (75%)	15,853,354
10% return	528,445	7%, 25 yr. factor	0.085811
		Debt service	1,360,392

Required net operating income: 1,888,837
   Net rent required per sq. ft. (10% vacancy): 27.78
   Year one profit estimate: 1,836,763 (But will it grow?)

Note: Gross asking rent for retail space in the western suburbs is $17.00 to $21.00 per square foot as of 4th Quarter 2001 (CB Richard Ellis).
   Even assuming a very optimistic net rent figure, this project does not appear to be profitable with a 75% loan.

Front door method (80% loan)

Total capital budget		21,137,806	
Equity	4,227,561	Loan (80%)	16,910,244
10% return	422,756	7%, 25 yr. factor	0.085811
		Debt service	1,451,085

Required net operating income	1,873,841
Year one profit estimate	1,836,763

The project appears not to be profitable with the 80% loan.

Back door method

Net operating income		1,836,763 (est.)	
Debt service	1,469,410	Debt coverage ratio	1.25
Before tax cash	367,353	Debt service	1,469,410
Before tax return	10%	Mortgage constant	0.085811
Equity	3,673,530	Mortgage	17,123,795
Justified project investment		20,797,325	
Improvement budget		16,867,184	
Justified land purchase		3,930,141	
Actual land cost		4,270,622	

Note: Debt service = 1,836,763 divided by 1.25. Because 1.25 = NOI divided by debt service is the debt coverage ratio.

Housing adjacent to downtown Chicago

We now turn to a case that illustrates the realities of real estate development in a major city. The case is the story of how a new residential neighborhood, Dearborn Park, was created just south of downtown Chicago. The sources for this story are the books *At Home in the Loop* by Lois Wille (1997) and *American Pharaoh* by Adam Cohen and Elizabeth Taylor (2000). The case illustrates the instrumental role of favorable financing terms; both the construction loan and the permanent mortgage loans carried interest rates that were significantly below market rates.

Dearborn Park occupies an area that had been rail yards since the nineteenth century. Mayor Richard J. Daley's original 1958 plan for the rail yards was for the University of Illinois at Chicago campus, but this plan fell apart because the railroads would sell only at a price that was too high for the city.

In 1973 a group called the Chicago Central Area Committee drafted their Chicago 21 Plan (for twenty-first century) with the purpose of making the downtown area more attractive as a place for the middle class to live. This group was a private organization that had been founded in 1956 with Mayor Daley's active cooperation. Planning, both public and private, for the use of the site had been going on since the late 1960s.

By the early 1970s the railroad land was available. A group of downtown business executives, led by Thomas Ayers of Commonwealth Edison and John Perkins of Continental Bank, formed a corporation to build a "new town" in the rail yard area. Daley and his planning commissioner worked closely with the business community on the project. Private funds were used to purchase the land and construct the buildings, but the city agreed to pay to build new streets, schools, and sewers. The Chicago 21 Corporation was incorporated on January 14, 1974. A total of $14 million had been raised from downtown businesses, including a million each from Commonwealth Edison, Continental Bank, First Federal Savings and Loan, Illinois Bell Telephone, Peoples Gas, Sears, and Standard Oil. Investors were limited to an annual return to

6.5%. Initial plans were for 100 housing units per acre, a density that turned out to be much too large.

In the meantime George Halas had been working on purchasing 51 acres of the land for a stadium for the Chicago Bears. The city dithered throughout 1974 and 1975 on plans for the stadium, leading Halas to announce he was pulling out of the idea in April 1975. Halas had an option with the railroads on 51 acres at a price of $3.25 per square foot, which was a bargain price.

The Chicago 21 Corporation purchased the Halas option on the 51 acres, and the city finally pledged to provide infrastructure. The cost of the initial 51 acres was only $7.3 million. The corporation changed its name to Dearborn Park Corporation in December 1976, and four days later Mayor Daley died of a heart attack. Purchase of the land took place in early 1977, after the US Interstate Commerce Commission approved discontinuation of the land for railroad purposes. (Yes, railroads were regulated in detail by the federal government in those days.) The Chicago Plan Commission gave approval to the Planned Unit Development application on June 23, 1977. This was the necessary zoning change.

The design of the project was difficult, and went through several phases. The final plan, drawn up in March 1978, was for 939 townhouse and apartment units at a total cost of $36.9 million ($39,300 per unit). Sales were to begin in early 1979. The actual cost of construction actually turned out to be $40.8 million – not too bad considering that inflation was very high in those days, and given that some units were upgraded from rental to condo during construction.

First Federal S&L and Continental Bank went together on a construction loan of $45 million at the prime rate plus 1.5%, with the provision that the rate shall at no time exceed 10%. During 1978 the prime rate rose to 11.75%, and when the construction loan matured in 1981 the prime rate had reached 18.9%. Construction began in early 1978. Clearly the construction loan contract was instrumental in creating Dearborn Park.

Tentative prices were set in late 1978:

- rents of $310 per month for studio apartments to $750 for a three-bedroom unit;
- prices of $49,000 for a 780 square foot condo to $110,900 for a four-bedroom townhouse with 1,706 square feet and $145,900 for a four-bedroom unit with 1,900 square feet in a mid-rise building;
- prices were set to be 4% to 10% lower than comparable prices in the general area.

Sales began on July 21, 1979. Two-thirds of the first 341 units offered for sale were reserved by $1,000 deposits in the first weekend. By September only a few of the rental units were available. Virtually the entire first phase of 939 units had been reserved or rented within two months.

Ferd Kramer of Draper and Kramer Realty arranged for a pool of permanent mortgage financing. By August 1979 the pool had grown to $23 million for 30-year fixed rate mortgages at 10%, with a 1.5% service charge (points). At that time conventional mortgage rates were 12 to 12.5%, and when the pool ran out of money in 1981 the rates were at 16.5%. Once again the favorable financing terms were instrumental in creating Dearborn Park.

The first residents moved in on November 1, 1979. At that time the Dearborn Park Corporation was busy with plans for the next phase of 517 units.

G. Summary

This chapter concludes the introduction to urban real estate. You have studied the basics of real estate law and institutions, examined how real estate markets function both in the short run and in the long run, and learned about real estate development and its financing. For some of you, this is enough for now. We hope that the appetites of others of you have been whetted so that you will continue your study of real estate.

Exercises

1 Complete the problem in the text that was noted "to be done in class."
2 Redo the front door and back door analysis of the shopping center case using a loan amount of 50% of the total capital budget.
3 Read the business section of your major local newspaper and find an article on a prominent real estate development. Determine whether that development is profitable from the information provided in the newspaper. For example, you might be able simply compare the cost per square foot of the project with the current market value of such space. Prepare a report on this development that discusses it in the context of the evolving real estate market in the urban area (i.e., do a basic market analysis).

References

Cohen, Adam and Elizabeth Taylor, 2000, *American Pharaoh*. Boston: Little, Brown, and Company.
Wille, Lois, 1997, *At Home in the Loop: How Clout and Community Built Chicago's Dearborn Park*. Carbondale, IL: Southern Illinois University Press.

Part IV

Government in Urban Areas

Chapter 13

The Public Sector in Urban Areas

A. Introduction

The public sector performs many functions in urban areas. These many roles are carried out by a variety of governmental institutions. One goal of this chapter is to provide you with the ability to understand the complex system that is local government in the United States. Another goal of the chapter is to explore the effects that the local public sector has on the spatial patterns of the urban area. The field of local public finance is itself a large and diverse subject that could be (and is, in some colleges) a separate course. This chapter cannot cover all aspects of local public finance, but it concentrates on those general aspects of the local public sector that influence spatial patterns. Transportation facilities are discussed in Chapter 14. We shall begin with a general discussion of the functions of local government, and then turn to some official data to get an idea of the magnitudes of local taxation and spending. The next step is to examine the economic theories that have been advanced to try to explain the outcomes that we observe.

Two prominent theories stand side-by-side in the field of local public finance. One theory is based on the idea that people in an urban area can change their residential locations easily, and therefore express their demands for local public services by "voting with their feet." They set up local governmental jurisdictions to satisfy these demands, and people join the "club" that most closely matches their preferences. The other theory is based on the notion that residents are not particularly mobile and/or cannot change local jurisdictions very easily. In this theory jurisdictions contain a variety of people, and decisions regarding the local public sector are made through the political process of setting up interest groups, running candidates, voting, and so forth. An important book by Fischel (2001) argues that the dominant voters at the local level are home owners, who vote to preserve the value of their homes. Clearly both of these theories contain a great deal of truth and have implications for urban spatial patterns. One important task of this chapter is to determine which theory is applicable in different situations.

A critical feature of local government is its system for raising revenues. Local governments rely largely on the local property tax, but they also charge fees for various services and receive revenues from the state and federal governments. The first order of business on the revenue side is to examine the role of the property tax in the two theories mentioned in the previous paragraph. Then the other sources of funds will be discussed.

Local governments do much more than tax and spend. They also regulate our lives to a considerable degree. They pass building codes, zoning ordinances, and many other laws. They enforce laws, and they plan for the future. Chapter 6 included an examination of some of these functions.

B. The Roles of the Urban Public Sector

You have probably already learned that mainstream economists put the economic functions of government into three categories. The public sector has programs to:

*   allocate resources to public goods and services;
*   redistribute income in accordance with the decisions made by the society; and
*   promote economic stability and growth.

This three-way categorization was invented by the eminent public finance economist Richard Musgrave (1959), and he called them the allocation branch, the distribution branch, and the stabilization branch. Musgrave's system comes straight from the standard microeconomic and macroeconomic theory courses. In microeconomic theory you learn the principles of efficient allocation of resources, including the principles that apply to goods and services that include external costs or benefits or are public. Goods and services that are public have two features: they are consumed jointly by a large number of people, and it is costly to exclude people from enjoying them. In microeconomics you also learned that the society may decide that there should be a policy regarding the distribution of income. In theory the efficient use of resources and the distribution of income can be separate considerations, but nearly all policies in the real world have impacts on both resource allocation and income distribution. In macroeconomics you learned about the business of macroeconomic policies aimed at reducing unemployment, promoting price stability, and providing for future growth.

You may also have already learned that the different levels of government in a federal system, such as we have in the US, will logically assume different roles within Musgrave's three-part system. The federal system of government in the US is the result of over two hundred years of experience; it goes back to the founding of the country. The original thirteen colonies were separate entities that originally looked first to England. Once they had decided that there was mutual interest in setting up a separate nation, it was necessary to devise a central government that carefully preserved the powers of the individual states. The first attempt to create a central government, under the Articles of Confederation, did not work well. The federal government under this system did not have enough power to carry out its basic functions, including the power to tax and to provide for the common defense. The United States as we know it was created by the adoption of the Constitution, which (as amended) defines the powers of the federal government and leaves to the states the power over matters that are not mentioned. It may be difficult to believe, but all of the expansions of the role of the federal government had to have been consistent with the Constitution. Under the Constitution a great deal of power resides with the state governments. A major responsibility of state governments is to set up the system of local government in the state. Local governments, even the cities of New York, Los Angeles, and Chicago, are creatures of their state governments.

From adoption of the Constitution the duties of the federal government have included the sole power to regulate the money supply, international trade and interstate commerce. These powers have grown into the responsibility for promoting the economic stability of the nation, which was formally stated in the Employment Act of 1946. In the 1950s and 1960s the macroeconomic policy agenda was expanded to include economic growth as well, and the Employment Act was amended in 1978 by the Full Employment and Balanced Growth Act. However, most states and many local governments have undertaken the job of trying to promote growth and stability in their economies. There is nothing in the Constitution that prevents them from promoting their own economies, and this topic will be discussed extensively in Chapter 21. For now we shall set aside the topic of the role of local government in fostering economic stability and growth.

We also think of policies regarding income distribution as the province of the federal government. As a practical matter, this is largely true. The largest income redistribution programs are Social Security (income for the elderly) and Medicare (medical care for the elderly). However, the basic welfare programs for non-elderly people are Temporary Assistance for Needy Families (TANF) and Medicaid (medical care for the poor). These programs are run by the states, and the benefit levels are set by the states. The federal government set up the programs and covers roughly half of their cost, but the fact that the programs are run by the states has resulted in widely different benefit levels from state to state. It might appeal to one's sense of logic to have income distribution programs be entirely a federal responsibility, but the fact is that these programs are a joint responsibility of the states and the federal government.

Is income distribution policy a local responsibility? Prior to the great depression of the 1930s, public welfare was one of the roles of local government (and private charities). At this point, however, very few people would argue that local governments should set up and finance their own income redistribution programs beyond temporary emergency relief. People can move and easily overwhelm a program set up at the local level. Nevertheless, local governments do set up limited public welfare programs (e.g., homeless shelters and general assistance), and they operate income distribution programs such as TANF, food stamps, public housing, and medicaid.

This discussion leaves the allocation of resources to public goods and services as the primary function of local government. These public goods and services include:

- education;
- hospitals and health care;
- transportation (streets, highways, public transportation);
- public safety (police, fire protection, public health);
- parks and recreation;
- community development and planning;
- water, sewerage, and solid waste management (garbage); and
- other parts of local infrastructure.

By far the largest of these functions is the provision of public education. All states have created a system of school districts to provide free high school education, and most have also set up a system of local junior college districts to provide two years of college at low cost to qualified students. Many local junior colleges also provide a wide variety of adult education courses at low cost. The provision of four-year colleges and universities with graduate programs is a responsibility that the states assume themselves, with the notable exception of the City University of New York. The quantity and quality of the goods and services delivered by local governments vary enormously. Some local governments do not provide all of the items on the above list. For example, local governments in some rural areas do not provide fire protection except by voluntary subscription. In these cases the property owner is not compelled to pay taxes for a fire department, but can join a fire protection club if he or she wishes. The reason for this seemingly odd system is that an isolated building that is on fire will not cause a problem for neighboring property. Fire protection becomes a public service when the possibility of external costs arises. My burning house setting your house on fire is perhaps the ultimate negative externality. After saving lives, the first job of the fire department is to prevent the spread of a fire to other properties. We are concerned with local governments in urban areas, so the case of the rural fire department is not relevant.

With one exception, it is pretty clear that each of the items on the above list is best considered a public good or service in urban areas. That one item is education, the largest item. Is it not true that the individual student benefits from education? How much "spillover" benefit to other members of the community could there be? It is clear that education is regarded as a public good in the United States, and it is worthwhile to review the arguments briefly. First of all, the consumer of education up to grade 12 is a child, a person who largely is not held responsible for making major decisions. The decision-maker is not the consumer of the education services (the child), but the parents. The *states* have decided that school attendance is compulsory up to age 16 to protect children from irresponsible parents (and from their own immature judgments). In addition, there are spillover benefits to other members of the society. The current and future families of the student benefit from the student's education in many ways – from enhanced earning power to increased ability to handle family matters. The larger local community also benefits from a more educated citizenry. People with more education tend to have a better understanding of public issues and create fewer social problems such as delinquency and crime. People with more education are less apt to be unemployed or need public assist-ance. A more educated citizenry creates a greater demand for more and better information (newspapers, books, etc.), and information has some public goods features. These are powerful arguments for considering education, perhaps up to 12th grade, to be a good with a substantial public component.

A more difficult issue to decide is whether education for children should be *provided directly* by government agencies, i.e., public schools. Conservative economists, and many others, argue that we should separate the notion of education as a good with substantial public benefits from the idea that the education should be in a public school. They think that education for children should be subsidized by the public sector, but that the parents should have wider choice to send children to a variety of schools (provided those schools meet certain standards). The conservatives advocate the public provision of education "vouchers," or certificates worth a certain amount of money when spent at the school of the parents' choice. As the discussion in Chapter 2 would tell you, conservatives argue their case on the basis of personal freedom. They think of the local public school system as sort of a monopolist, and point out that a voucher system would create competition among providers of education, which would promote the more efficient provision of educational services as well. As we shall see in the next section, the theory of the local public sector in which people "vote with the feet" tends to undermine this argument in suburban areas (but not as much in the case of large school systems in the central cities). Nevertheless, the idea of education voucher programs has become more popular in recent years, and this topic has become one of the biggest issues in local public economics. Additional discussion of this matter is in Chapter 18.

A brief overview of local government expenditures and revenues is provided in Table 13.1. Data are presented for three fiscal years – 1966–7, 1986–7 and 2001–2. Expenditures per capita increased in real terms over those 30 years from $895 to $1,479 to $1,942 (in 1982–84 dollars), an increase of 117%. During this same period personal income per capita increased from $9,522 to $15,475 (in 1982–4 dollars), for an increase of 62.5%. Therefore, expenditures per capita by local governments grew by an average of 3.15% per year compared to the growth of personal income per capita of 1.63% per year. Table 13.1 shows that the particular categories of spending that grew most rapidly were public safety (police, fire, and correctional facilities), environment and housing, administration (including the courts and general administration), and interest and miscellaneous expenditures. The proportions of local expenditures for these functions increased, and the fraction devoted to public schools dropped from 48.0% to 43.8%. However, this decline in the proportion spent on schools still involved an increase in real expenditures per capita from $430 to $851 (1982–4 dollars), an increase of 98% (average increase of 2.77% per year). Clearly local governments have increased their expenditures on public safety and the courts, and had to pay higher interest rates on their borrowed funds. They also spent more on community development and general administrative functions.

Sources of general revenue are also shown in Table 13.1. In 1966–7 local governments obtained 65.3% of general revenue from local sources. The largest local source was the property tax, which accounted for 43.2% of all general revenue. Funds received from state government contributed 31.7% of general revenue. In 2001–2 local governments were still raising 60.1% of general revenue from local sources, but now the property tax was only 27.1% of general revenue. Other taxes had increased from 6.7% to 10.1% of general revenue, and charges and fees jumped from 15.4% to 22.9% of the total. The proportion of revenue received from intergovernmental sources increased by 5.3%, with both state and federal sources exhibiting increases. Clearly the biggest change on the revenue side is the reduction in the reliance on the property tax, and the increased use of charges and fees. The real estate tax was still the largest single source of revenue raised from local sources in 2001–2, but intergovernmental grants from the state had become the largest source of funds for local governments around the nation.

Table 13.1 pertains to all local governments in the nation, including governments in rural areas as well as urban areas. The patterns of expenditures and revenues vary depending upon whether the local government serves the central city or the suburbs. Local governments that serve the central city (or central county) of a metropolitan area tend to spend more per capita in total but less on public schools than do their suburban counterparts. Local governments in the central county tend to spend greater proportions of their

Table 13.1   Local government expenditures and revenues: all local governments

	1966–7	1986–7	2001–2
Direct general expenditures			
Education	48.0%	42.3%	43.8%
Health and welfare	12.4	12.9	12.1
Transportation	8.7	7.2	6.4
Public safety	8.0	9.8	10.5
Environment and housing[a]	9.8	11.0	10.6
Administration	3.6	5.4	5.4
Interest and misc.	9.5	11.4	10.4
Per capita direct general expenditures	$299	$1,680	$3,494
1982–4 dollars	$895	$1,479	$1,942
General revenue			
Local sources	65.3%	62.0%	60.1%
Property tax	43.2	28.3	27.1
Other taxes	6.7	10.1	10.1
Charges and misc.	15.4	23.6	22.9
Intergovernmental	34.7	38.0	40.0
State	31.7	33.3	35.7
Federal	3.0	4.7	4.3

[a] Includes parks and recreation, housing and community development, sewerage, and other sanitation.
Source: Census of Governments (1967, 1987, 2002)

budgets on health and welfare programs, transportation (including the public transportation system), public safety, and environment and housing programs. It would appear that the greater demand for such services in central counties, compared to suburban counties, has a detrimental effect on spending for schools. This conclusion was reached by Luce and Summers (1987) in a study of local government in the Philadelphia urban area; spending on schools in the city of Philadelphia had to compete with heavy demands for other public services. On the revenue side, central counties rely less heavily on general revenue from local sources and more intergovernmental revenues, compared to suburban counties. Local governments in central counties therefore rely less heavily on the local property tax than do suburban counties. Intergovernmental revenue programs are discussed in more detail later in this chapter.

We turn now to economic theories that are designed to shed some light on local government expenditure decisions.

C. The Tiebout Model of Urban Public Finance

The Tiebout, or "vote with the feet," theory of urban public finance was invented by Charles Tiebout (1956) in a celebrated paper that is entitled "A Pure Theory of Local Expenditures." Tiebout did not intend to set out a complete theory of how resource allocation decisions are made by local governments, but his theory has become a very influential tool for studying those decisions. Tiebout's article was written in response to the classic articles by Paul Samuelson (1954 and 1955) on the pure theory of public expenditures. In those articles Samuelson defined a public good as a collective consumption good; one individual's consumption of the good does not subtract from any other individual's consumption of the good. If X is the total amount of a public good supplied, X_i is the amount consumed by individual i, and X_j is the amount consumed by individual j, etc., then

$$X = X_i = X_j = \ldots = X_n,$$

where there are n individuals in the society in question. This definition is in sharp contrast to the normal private good Y, where the total amount consumed is the sum of the amounts consumed by the individuals;

$$Y = Y_i + Y_j + \ldots + Y_n.$$

If Y is hamburgers, every one I eat cannot be eaten by anyone else.

Samuelson's definition of a public good really includes two criteria: the good is jointly consumed *and* there is no easy method available for excluding people from consuming the good. Consider a football game played in a stadium with 60,000 seats. This good is consumed jointly by those in attendance, but it is easy to exclude people – just build a fence around the stadium and sell tickets. Now suppose that the game is being televised. Anyone with a television set can tune into the game for free. But wait! Suppose that the game is being carried on television with a scrambled signal, and only those who pay for a signal unscrambler can watch. Technology can change a public good into a jointly consumed private good. Indeed, there is a strong incentive for the invention of technologies to do just that.

Samuelson's point is that, for a public good, the optimal amount is found where the marginal cost of the good equals the *sum* of the marginal benefits of the good's consumers. Should the United States purchase another aircraft carrier for the Navy? That decision depends upon the cost of the carrier versus the sum of the amounts that each of us is willing to pay for it.

Consider Figure 13.1, which depicts the demand curves for a public good by three individuals, person A, person B, and person C. Samuelson says that, to find the total demand for the public good, we should add the individual demand curves *vertically* to find out how much the three people as a group would be willing to pay for the public good at each possible quantity. This total demand curve is shown in part (d) of Figure 13.1. An economically efficient quantity of the public good is set by equating the marginal cost of the good to its marginal benefit, which is the height of the total demand curve. At quantity X^* the marginal cost of the public good is equal to the marginal benefit of the good to the group – the amount that the *group* is willing to pay for another unit of the good, which is MB^* in Figure 13.1. Note that all members of the group then consume the same amount of the public good, X^*, and that the marginal benefit of the public good to each person is shown by the height of the individual demand curves at X^*. For example, person A consumes quantity X^* and has a marginal benefit for the public good of MB_a^* at that quantity.

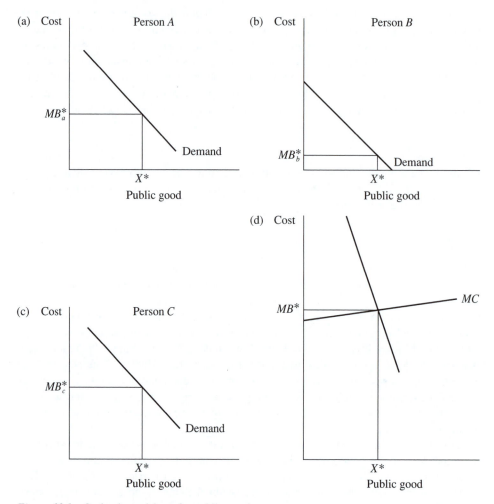

Figure 13.1 Optimal provision of a public good

   For Samuelson there is one fundamental implication that follows from this theorem. Individuals have no incentive to reveal how much they are really willing to pay for more of a public good. They have an incentive to try to be "free riders," people who do not pay but benefit from the public good anyway. (The demand curves depicted in Figure 13.1 are the true demand curves, but individuals have no incentive to reveal what these demand curves are.) This lack of incentive to reveal demand means that the private market is not capable of supplying an efficient level of a public good. People may be willing to pay a private firm some amount of money to supply a public good (i.e., voluntary contributions), but contributions will not be enough to generate an efficient level of output (where marginal cost equals sum of marginal benefits). This lack of incentive to reveal preferences also means that the public provision of a public good is problematic. The public sector has the power to tax, so it does not have to rely on voluntary contributions. Resource allocation decisions in the public sector regarding public goods are made through the political process, but there is still no method available to induce consumers to reveal their true preferences. An efficient outcome is far from assured. Mainstream and conservative economists agree on this point.

Tiebout took this unsettling result as his starting point, and wondered if there is a mechanism that could force consumers to reveal their true preferences for public goods, could supply those public goods in the same sense that the private market supplies goods, and could levy a tax on consumers equal to the value of benefits received. His answer created a revolution in the way mainstream and conservative economists think about local public finance.

Tiebout (1956) instructed us to consider the class of public goods that are local in nature. His local public goods benefit only those people who live in the particular local jurisdiction that supplies the public goods in question. There are no spillovers to other people in other jurisdictions. His model further assumes that consumer-voters are freely mobile and will move to the local jurisdiction with the supplies of local public goods that best match their preferences. The consumer-voters are not constrained in their movements by other factors such as employment location. The consumer-voters have complete knowledge of the spending and taxation policies of the local jurisdictions, and a large number of these jurisdictions offer a range of choices. Let each of those jurisdictions be operating at the minimum of average cost for the combination of public goods chosen, and assume that the households in a jurisdiction each pay an amount in local taxes equal to total expenditures divided by the number of households. Given all of these assumptions, which Tiebout admits are unrealistic, consumer-voters will reside in the jurisdiction that best matches their preferences for local public goods. They will each pay a local tax for a marginal unit of the public good equal to its marginal benefit.

To see this last result, return to the public good X defined above. Suppose that there are 3 consumer-voters in the local jurisdiction, and that each unit of X costs p. Suppose that the quantity of X is set at X^*. These facts are shown in Figure 13.2, a set of diagrams that is similar to Figure 13.1. The total amount of taxes collected is pX^*, and each household pays $pX^*/3$. In effect, each household pays a "tax price" of $p/3$ for each unit of X. Each household that chooses to locate in this jurisdiction has a marginal benefit for the public good (at quantity X^*) equal to its "tax price," or

$$MB_i = p/3$$

for each household i among the 3 households. Other households for whom this condition is not true at the quantity X^* choose to locate elsewhere. This is true because quantity X^* is not the amount that these other households would choose at the tax price of $p/3$. These other households would set up their own local jurisdictions so that tax price for the public good *will* equal marginal benefit.

The condition for the efficient provision of the public good is marginal cost equal to the sum of the marginal benefits,

$$\sum MB_i = MC.$$

In Figure 13.2 the summation runs over the households from 1 to 3. Because all households in the jurisdiction face the same "tax price" for a marginal unit of the public good

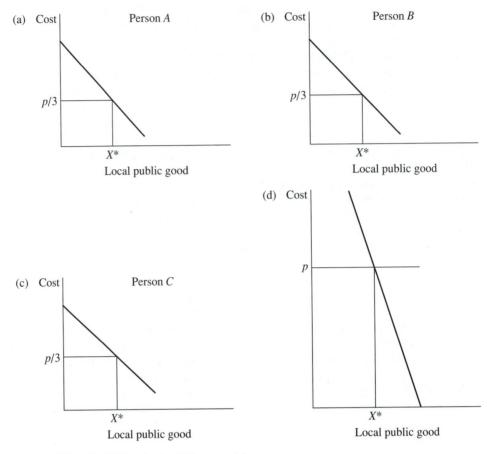

Figure 13.2 Equilibrium in the Tiebout model

of $p/3$, the sum of the marginal benefits is just $3(MB)$, where MB is the marginal benefit for each household. Therefore

$$\sum MB_i = MB^* = 3(MB) = 3(p/3) = p = MC.$$

This idealized interpretation of how local governments operate produces an efficient level of the local public good. Under this kind of local government, decisions regarding local public goods are made unanimously. Everyone who has chosen to live in a particular jurisdiction has the same marginal benefit for the local public good, so there are no disagreements (at least on resource allocation matters).

Tiebout has thus responded to Samuelson's (1954, p. 388) contention that "no decentralized pricing system can serve to determine optimally these levels of collective consumption." For Tiebout local public goods are being provided by a system that is, in effect, a decentralized pricing system. His system works if households can sort themselves according to the amount of the local public good demanded. Remember the football game that is being played in a stadium in front of 60,000 spectators? This good is jointly consumed, but the consumers pay for the good by buying tickets. There are no free riders. Those who are unwilling to pay the price of a ticket do not go to the game. This example resembles the Tiebout model in that he has, in effect, turned a local public good into a private good that is consumed jointly. The local head tax is the price of admission.

Tiebout recognized that the system he described is not a perfect allocator of resources because the real world does not match all of his assumptions. One obvious problem with the Tiebout model as presented thus far is that local taxes are equal for each household in a jurisdiction. The tax system implicitly in use is a type of "head tax." Each household has one head of the household, and that person has one head. Taxes are not assessed in that manner in the real world, of course. In fact, the real estate tax is the largest local tax, and it is assessed on the value of real estate property. This method of taxation creates an obvious problem for the operation of the Tiebout model. People can try to be free riders. Suppose that a group of people wishes to set up a local jurisdiction with a high level of a local public good, but also suppose that their only means of collecting taxes is through a real estate tax. These people know that, once the jurisdiction is set up, other people will want to build cheap houses and move into the jurisdiction so as to benefit from the public good and pay little in taxes. This line of thinking will lead the members of the original group to think, "Why should I reveal my true preferences for this public good? My better course of action would be to become a free rider in some other jurisdiction." We are back to Samuelson's problem – people will not reveal their true preferences for public goods, and they will be undersupplied by local governments.

The solution to this problem was devised by Bruce Hamilton (1975). He proposed that, when the group sets up its local jurisdiction, it can prevent free riders by imposing a requirement that each household own a certain minimum amount of real estate. Local jurisdictions cannot impose a precise minimum requirement for real estate (land plus buildings), but it *can* impose a minimum lot size in a zoning ordinance and require that houses meet quality requirements set out in a building code. If the real estate tax were only a tax on the quantity of land, setting a minimum lot size would create a perfect Tiebout mechanism. The minimum lot size would also become the maximum lot size because those people who want larger lots and the same level of the public good would set up their own jurisdiction (with a larger minimum lot size). The Hamilton (1975) mechanism requires that households must sort themselves along two dimensions – amount of the local public good demanded, and lot size – rather than just one. Furthermore, the Hamilton mechanism is not perfect because a minimum lot size requirement does not impose complete uniformity in real estate value, which is the base of the real estate tax. Zoning ordinances are adopted for a variety of reasons, including protection of health and safety of the public, maintenance of community character, and planning for growth. Nevertheless, it surely is true that local officials in the suburbs of large urban areas recognize the use of zoning as a method for ensuring some minimum real estate tax payment. Zoning ordinances were discussed at some length in Chapter 6.

Hamilton (1975) provided the Tiebout mechanism with a more realistic method for collecting taxes, but there are other problems that cause the real world to depart from the Tiebout theory. It may be true that households are neither as mobile nor as informed as Tiebout assumed. In my view these criticisms are not compelling. Households in the United States are highly mobile, and they pay close attention to the quality of local public services, especially schools. It would appear that racial discrimination is the most serious limitation on household mobility in large urban areas in the US. The problem is particularly serious because minority households are primarily confined to the central city in the major urban areas. The problem of the central city in the Tiebout model is discussed below. The Tiebout model also requires that there be a large number of local jurisdictions to provide for the efficient sorting of households. There may not be enough local jurisdictions to match everyone's preferences precisely, but there certainly is a large number of jurisdictions in any major urban area. Tiebout's assumption is not obviously wrong on this count.

Formal efficiency in the Tiebout model also required that there be no spillovers of benefits from one jurisdiction to others. If there are significant spillovers, then the solution is to set up jurisdictions that are large enough to contain the spillovers. We should set up public transportation districts, environmental protection districts, mosquito abatement districts, etc. In fact, we do just that. In many cases county governments provide some of these services that cover a wider area. In other instances special governmental units are created for these purposes. However, the creation of such larger districts reduces the number of choices available to households. Suppose I do not care for the options available in the two mosquito abatement districts in my urban area. My choices are to move to another urban area (not a sensible option), or to engage in political activity to get my mosquito abatement district to conform more closely to my preferences. The latter option is the subject of the next section.

The criticisms of the Tiebout model discussed in the previous paragraph have some substance, but we think that the two most important limitations of the Tiebout model are:

- the existence of the large central city; and
- the fact that the property tax is collected on commercial and industrial real estate.

Major urban areas are not simply collections of small jurisdictions; they all contain a major central city. Given the trend towards suburbanization, the major central city has a diminished importance in the local economy, but it still provides local public services to a large number of people with diverse preferences, real estate holdings, and income levels. Residents of the central city are provided with roughly the same level of public services. Indeed, the mayor can count on hearing complaints when people perceive that they are *not* receiving that level of services. The connection between local taxes paid and the quality of public services received may not be very close in the central city. The property tax is a tax, rather than the charge for benefits received as envisioned by Tiebout and Hamilton. For this reason, resource allocation decisions by central city governments are based primarily on the political process that is discussed in the next section.

The other major problem with the Tiebout–Hamilton model is the existence of non-residential real estate. This is a major omission indeed. Commercial or industrial real estate normally generates a fiscal surplus for the jurisdiction in which it is located – the taxes and fees paid exceed the cost of providing the services needed by these types of real estate. For example, one study by Bernhard and Strott (1977) of revenues and costs by type of land use for Milwaukee in 1975 showed that commercial and industrial properties contributed 32% of local revenues, but represented only 14% of local expenditures. Households paid 68% of local revenues, but created 86% of the costs. What is more, households with children in the public schools paid 31% of the revenues, but were the source of 61% of the costs. Households without children in public school provided 37% of the revenue and imposed only 25% of the costs. One might argue that households without children in public school potentially are users of these schools, but clearly commercial and industrial properties are not. (The owners of non-residential properties may use public schools, of course. But they also pay residential real estate taxes.)

How do commercial and industrial real estate change the Tiebout–Hamilton story? As Hamilton suggests, the crafting of the zoning ordinance for the local jurisdiction is a critical part of the model. Now the local zoning officials must decide upon the amount of land to be allocated to commercial and industrial activities. Given that these activities provide a fiscal surplus, the basic idea is that there is a trade-off between environmental quality and tax base. Communities that value environmental quality highly will zone little land for commercial or industrial use. Following state law, most local jurisdictions must impose the same property tax rate on all classes of property. In some cases local jurisdictions are permitted to impose different real estate tax rates on different classes of property. Permission to charge different property tax rates usually means that local officials decide that commercial and industrial property will face higher tax rates than residential property, which will create an even larger fiscal surplus from these uses of land. Even if the property tax rate must be uniform over classes of property, the addition of commercial and industrial property to the model means that the local officials in a Tiebout–Hamilton jurisdiction now face a more complex set of decisions. We can imagine that they must simultaneously determine the level of local public goods, set the allocation of land to the various uses, set minimum lot size, and set the property tax rate – all to match the preferences of the households whom they intend to attract to their "club." They must do all of this while recognizing that the location decisions of commercial and industrial activities are probably sensitive to the property tax rate. Furthermore, the requirement that commercial and industrial real estate must pay a property "tax price" for public goods that exceeds the value of the marginal benefit of those goods means that the outcome is no longer an efficient allocation of resources. The exception to this conclusion occurs if the tax price faced by commercial and industrial real estate exceeds the marginal benefit of public goods by the amount of the external cost imposed by these activities on the rest of the jurisdiction. The tax price could be an efficient price after all, but this is not likely to be the case because the local jurisdiction also wants to use the fiscal surplus generated to fund local public goods for its households. Efficient pricing of external costs is not the only motive, and may not even be a very important motive, for taxing commercial and industrial real estate at rates that exceed the marginal benefits of public goods.

Is the addition of commercial and industrial property an important consideration? The answer clearly is "yes." Local jurisdictions vary widely in the amount of commercial and industrial real estate they contain, and it is clear that they respond to the size of the fiscal surplus that is generated. As an example we shall examine a study of 30 elementary school districts is DuPage County, Illinois in 1990 (McDonald et al. 1991). DuPage County is a suburban county located in the Chicago urban area, and it generally contains middle-class households who value good schools. These 30 school districts vary enormously in the proportion of the tax base that is residential and in the assessed value of real estate per pupil. The district with the most commercial and industrial property had only 30.2%

Table 13.2   Mean expenditure per pupil by DuPage County grade school districts: 1990

Total assessed value per pupil	% residential tax base				
	Low[a] (49.0%)	*Medium* (73.4%)	*High* (90.0%)	*All*	
Low[a]	$3,859[b]	3,720	3,701	3,724	($106,900)
	(1)	(4)	(5)	(10)	
Medium	4,772	4,447	4,096	4,404	($153,400)
	(3)	(3)	(4)	(10)	
High	5,346	4,243	6,146	5,095	($273,500)
	(6)	(3)	(1)	(10)	
All	5,025	4,095	4,104	4,408	
	(10)	(10)	(10)	(30)	

[a] Figure in parentheses is the median for the group.
[b] Figure in parentheses is the number of school districts in the group.
Source: McDonald et al. (1991)

of its tax base as residential property. At the other extreme, 91.2% of tax base of another district was residential. The median for the group of 30 districts was 73.4% residential tax base. Table 13.2 shows the relationships between expenditure per elementary school pupil and two variables; the percentage of the tax base that is residential and the total assessed value per pupil. Spending per pupil clearly rises with assessed value per pupil, as one would expect. However, spending per pupil falls with the percentage of the tax base that is residential. The ten districts with the lowest percentage residential in the tax base spent an average of $5,025 per pupil, while the other 20 districts spent an average of $4,100 per pupil. The former group of districts clearly perceive a lower tax price for schools because of the presence of commercial and industrial property.

The point can be made more precisely by using the data shown in Table 13.2 to estimate a multiple regression model. A simple linear equation fitted to the data is

$$E = 4,600 - 12.79R + 3.68AV.$$

The variables are defined as:

E = expenditures per pupil,
R = percentage of the tax base that is residential, and
AV = total assessed value per pupil ($1,000s).

This equation explains statistically 57% of the variance of expenditures per pupil. The equation says that expenditures per pupil fall by $12.79 if the percentage of the tax base that is residential increases by 1 percent, and rise by $3.68 if the assessed value per pupil is $1,000 greater.

Econometric studies of the demand for local public services have confirmed the existence of the wealth and tax price effects and, as suggested by the data in Table 13.2, the wealth effect is usually the stronger of the two. One reason for this result is that residents do not view the business tax base as immobile. One particularly interesting study by Ladd (1975) confirmed this idea. Ladd studied school expenditures in the Boston metropolitan area in 1970. Her results show that these spending decisions are based on the assumption that commercial and industrial property will exhibit some mobility in response to increases in property tax rates. Her adjusted measure of the *perceived* residential share of the tax base is $1 - aC - bI$, where C is the actual percentage commercial, I is the actual percentage industrial, and a and b are parameters representing the shares of the commercial and industrial tax bases that are perceived not to burden local residents. If a and b are both 1, then none of the business tax burden falls on residents. Ladd estimated a to be 0.79 and b to be 0.45, which means that voters did not act as if commercial and industrial property taxes had no cost to residents. Given these estimates of a and b, residents apparently believed that the industrial tax base was more sensitive to tax rates than was the commercial tax base because increases in the commercial tax base reduce the perceived residential share by more than increases in the industrial tax base. Nevertheless, Ladd's results show that the existence of commercial and industrial property does reduce the resident's perceived tax price and contributes to higher expenditures.

Where do the chief criticisms of the Tiebout–Hamilton model leave us? Clearly a Tiebout mechanism for the efficient provision of local public goods is not at work in the large central cities. But what about the suburbs? Clearly the Tiebout–Hamilton mechanism is at work here. However, the addition of commercial and industrial property to the real estate base makes the problem that must be solved by officials in a local jurisdiction much more complex, and probably destroys the efficiency of the outcome. Local officials can try to attract commercial and industrial activity in order to "oversupply" their jurisdictions with local public goods. Does this actually happen? Research needs to be done on this question because nearly all of the studies of the Tiebout model have ignored commercial and industrial property.

D. The Median Voter Model

If the Tiebout mechanism is working perfectly, the residents of a jurisdiction all want the same level of local public goods and the same real estate tax rate. If the Tiebout mechanism is not working very well, then the residents have diverse views about these matters. Local spending and taxation policies must be decided by a political process in which diverse points of view are included. The actual method in a representative democracy is to elect a mayor and members of the city council (or officials of other local governmental jurisdictions), and to delegate to them the responsibility for setting local policy. If a majority of voters does not like their decisions, then the voters can elect someone else in the next election. People vote for a candidate for many reasons, and a candidate can embody a complex bundle of opinions, intentions, and abilities. What is more, many people do not vote at all. Does this mean that they are satisfied with the way things are, or does it mean that they perceive that their votes are meaningless? All of these complexities are more properly the subject matter of political science, but economists and political scientists have ventured into this briar patch and proposed a simple model of voting and local

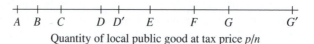

Quantity of local public good at tax price p/n

Figure 13.3   The median voter model

public finance. The model is called the median voter model, and it does provide considerable explanatory power at the local level.

The basic conclusion of the median voter model is that decisions regarding local
spending and taxation will mimic the preferences of the median voter, the person who is
right in the middle of the range of opinions on these matters. The median voter model
bears a strong resemblance to the principle of median location that was presented in
Chapter 3. The pizza parlor selects a location in physical space next to the median
customer. The winning local candidate selects a location in political space next to the
median voter. A leading book on this theory by Enelow and Hinich (1984) is entitled
The Spatial Theory of Voting. Let us see how the model works in a simple case.

Suppose that the decision at hand is the provision of a single local public good. As we
assumed in section C above, suppose that this local public good can be purchased by the
local jurisdiction at a constant cost of p, and that each household pays an equal share of
that cost. As before, each household faces the tax price of p/n, where n is the total number
of households in the local jurisdiction. In the Tiebout model, given this tax price, everyone in the jurisdiction prefers the same quantity of the local public good; they all equate
marginal benefit to the tax price at the same quantity. In the median voter model, the
quantity of the local public good demanded by households at tax price p/n varies. Suppose that those quantities demanded at some given price p/n are as shown in Figure 13.3
for voters A through G. Ignore points D' and G' for now.

Figure 13.3 depicts the preferences of the voters. Now let us suppose that an election is
held between two candidates, and that those candidates are running on a platform that
includes only a single plank – how much of the local public good to provide. Candidate
M is a crafty politician, and proposes the quantity of the local public good that matches
the preferences of voter D, the median voter. Candidate L proposes a quantity that
matches the preferences of voter C. The election is held, and candidate M wins by a vote
of 4 to 3. Voters D, E, F, and G vote for candidate M because he is closer to their
preferences than is candidate L. Alternatively, suppose that the M's opponent is candidate
H, who proposes a quantity that matches the preferences of voter E. Now candidate M
wins by a vote of 4 to 3 because he now gets the votes of voters A, B and C (in addition
to the vote of voter D). What if both candidates propose the quantity that coincides with
the preferences of voter D? In this case the preferences of the median voter prevail again,
and it does not matter who wins. The quantity of the public provided in Figure 13.3 is D.
The outcome of the median voter model is not sensitive to extreme points of view.
Suppose that voter G "moves" to point G'. Voter D is still the median voter, and candidate
M still wins. However, this result reveals an important aspect of the median voter model.
There is nothing to guarantee that the level of the local public good (X^*) provided will be
the efficient level in the usual sense, i.e., where

$$\Sigma MB_i = p,$$

where index i runs from voter A to voter G. The move of voter G to G' means that he or she has an increased marginal benefit (demand) for the local public good at its current level D ($\sum MB_i$ increases), but the political process does not respond by increasing the quantity provided. This result is similar to the outcome in the principle of median location model in Chapter 3. (However, remember that the decision of the pizza parlor not to change location is also efficient.) The quantity will increase only if the demand of the median voter increases. If voter D moves to point D', then that crafty politician M will follow. No one else has any influence, unless he or she becomes the median voter. For example, if voter C (instead of voter D) were to shift his or her demand to point D', then candidate M would follow.

You can now see that the median voter model offers the very specific prediction that resource allocation decisions regarding local public goods will follow the median voter, and no one else. The only problem is to identify the median voter! Just who is that person? One approach that is often used is to assume that preferences for the local public good follow household income, so that the median voter has the median household income. This assumption will introduce inaccuracy if preferences for the local public good also depend upon other variables such as age and number of children. Numerous empirical studies of various types of local public goods have been done, and Inman (1979) summarized the results. Inman's summary is that the elasticity of demand for total local public expenditures with respect to median income varies from 0.34 to 0.89. The income elasticities of demand for specific public goods, such as education, police and fire and public works, generally fall in this range. However, the income elasticity of demand for parks and recreation is larger, falling in the range of 0.99 to 1.32. Another prediction of the median voter model is that the preferences of other voters, who are clearly located far from the median, do not influence the outcome. For example, the preferences of the very poor or the very rich should not matter. Inman (1978) tested this implication, and found two things. First, the median voter is more accurately portrayed as a homeowner with the median income *and* a child in the local public schools. Second, the budget that was chosen depended not only on the preferences of this median voter, but also on the number of renters, elderly, and families with children in private schools. In short, voters who are not the median voter also exert some influence. The median voter model is too simple to capture the whole story.

An important recent book by William Fischel (2001) titled *The Homevoter Hypothesis* asserts that the median voter is a homeowner, and that this voter is very concerned about preserving the value of the home because the typical household has little opportunity to diversify its asset holdings. Most of the wealth of a homeowner is in the house. This concern with property values leads them to make sacrifices for public schools and good local amenities. And it leads them to very jealous of their power to make decisions about taxes and expenditures at the local level. Fischel's book is important and well written, and we recommend that you add it to your reading list.

The median voter model obviously is a gross simplification of political reality, but it does have considerable explanatory power in matters of local public finance. It may be that local issues are primarily decisions over taxes and spending largely unclouded by political ideology or other complicating factors. The median voter model also has value at the national level. Prior to the 2004 election, there was much talk about how a candidate from the Democratic party can challenge President Bush by "moving to the center."

E. The Property Tax

Recall from Table 13.1 that 27.1% of the revenue raised by local governments in 2001–02 was through the property tax. Property tax collections were 45.1% of all revenues raised from local sources. All other taxes (sales, income, and licenses) accounted for only 16.8% of locally raised revenue in 2001–2. The property tax is, by far, the most important tax that is levied by local government. Who actually pays this tax? What are its effects on location patterns? These are critical questions and the topics of this section.

Mechanics of the property tax

The first step in answering these questions is to understand the mechanics of the property tax. There are two independent parts of the system. The first half of the process is the determination of the size of the tax base for each property owner and for a jurisdiction as a whole. This task is usually undertaken by an official called the county tax assessor. This office of county government has the job of determining the *assessed value* of each parcel of real estate in the county. The assessed value by state law is set as some percentage of fair market value. This percentage is known as the assessment ratio, and figures of 0.33 or 0.50 are fairly common. The county assessor uses standard techniques of real estate appraisal to obtain an estimated market value, and then applies the assessment ratio to this figure. Many counties revise assessments every year, but others do it less frequently. When the assessor has completed the job, the property owners are notified of their assessed values. This notification is *not* a tax bill, but the time to protest is when one's assessment notice arrives. County assessors provide for a time period in which the property owner can challenge the assessor's judgment. It is possible to have one's assessed value reduced, but it usually requires proof that the assessor was inconsistent in assessing the property in question. This proof normally consists of evidence that other, identical, properties were assessed for lower amounts.

Once the time for appeals has passed, the assessor then sends notice to each local jurisdiction of the size of its tax base for the next fiscal year. A county contains several municipalities, school districts, park districts, and other types of local governments. The boundaries of these jurisdictions normally do not coincide, so the assessor must figure out the size of the tax base for each local governmental jurisdiction by keeping track of which jurisdictions contain each parcel of real estate. An example may astound you. Local government in Illinois is more complicated than in most places. Professor McDonald resides in the following local jurisdictions:

- School district 90 (elementary)
- Village of River Forest
- Village of River Forest Library District
- River Forest Park District
- Triton Community College District
- Consolidated High School District 200
- Des Plaines Valley Mosquito Abatement District

- Metropolitan Water Reclamation District of Greater Chicago
- General Assistance, River Forest
- Township of River Forest
- Consolidated Election Commission
- Suburban T B Sanitarium
- Forest Preserve District of Cook County
- County of Cook
- Cook County Health Facilities District.

The county assessor keeps track of all of this for each real estate parcel in the county.

The second half of the process starts with the determination of the amount of revenue to be raised by each unit of local government. Each jurisdiction starts by determining its expenditure level and the amount of revenue that will be received from other sources in the coming fiscal year. The other revenue sources vary by type of jurisdiction. For example, school districts will receive funds from the state through the state's school aid formula and (perhaps) from the federal government through grants for various programs. Municipalities receive funds from the state and federal governments for a variety of purposes, and they also levy several charges and fees. The difference between proposed spending and anticipated revenues from other sources is the amount of the real estate tax levy. Each local jurisdiction then determines its official real estate tax rate by dividing its tax levy by the total assessed value in the jurisdiction, or

Official tax rate = Tax levy / total assessed value.

The official tax rate is usually expressed in mills (tenths of a cent) per $100 of assessed value. One therefore often hears the term "mill rate" in reference to the property tax. The county assessor then takes the official tax rates for all the local jurisdictions and computes the tax bill for each parcel of real estate in the county. Recall that the county assessor knows *all* of the local jurisdictions in which a particular parcel of real estate is located. The county assessor uses all of the official tax rates that apply to each property, and sends out the tax bills to the property owners. These bills list each unit of government to which the property owner pays taxes, but payment is simply made to the county assessor. The assessor's office then sends the money to the local jurisdictions. The property tax bill also shows the total of the official tax rates for the parcel of real estate. For example, the official real estate tax rate that Professor McDonald paid to the total of 15 different local jurisdictions listed above was 10,645 mills in 1993. In other words, I paid $10.645 per $100 of assessed value.

We have told you Professor McDonald's official tax rate. At 10.645% this tax rate sounds very high, but this number really is meaningless. The meaningful figure is the real estate tax as a percentage of the market value of the property. In this case we estimate that this "real" tax rate is approximately 2.15%, which is a fairly standard rate. The real tax rate is figured as

Real tax rate = (Tax bill/assessed value) × (Actual assessment ratio).

The actual assessment ratio is the assessed value divided by the appraised value of the property. The actual assessment ratio may differ from the assessor's official assessment ratio if the assessor's office uses an inaccurate appraisal of the property in question. In this case you can determine that we have estimated the actual assessment ratio to be 20.2% (i.e., 2.15/10.645).

Economic effects of the property tax

Now we can consider the economic effects of the local property tax. The tax is levied on residential, commercial, and industrial property. The previous discussion showed that the economically meaningful way to specify the tax is as a percentage of market value. We shall first consider the tax on residential property. Residential property includes rental units as well as owner-occupied housing. The tax is levied on the owners of the property, but is the tax shifted forward to tenants? What is the real incidence of the tax? The answer to the question requires an economic model of the housing market. One sort of model of the urban housing (or residential land) market has been introduced in this book in Chapters 5 and 6. This model emphasizes the location patterns of housing and population in an urban area, but a simpler model can be used that does the job. We shall use a model that can be formulated as supply and demand curves.

Consider the market for housing in a local jurisdiction. The demand for housing is a demand for the services of housing in a given time period. The price that is paid for these services is housing rent, an amount that a tenant pays to the landlord or that the homeowner implicitly pays to himself. Assume that the number of households in the local jurisdiction is fixed (an assumption that will be changed later). These households have a demand for housing services, and this demand curve is shown in the upper half of Figure 13.4. On the other hand, the supply of housing is best considered to be a function of the market value of houses. The supply of housing cannot be altered a great deal in the short run, but in the long run housing units can be added to or subtracted from the stock of housing. The addition or subtraction of units depends upon the market value of those units. In this model we shall use the notion that the stock of housing consists of a large number of units of standardized quality. Both an increase in the quantity and in the quality of houses increases the supply of "housing" as defined here. It shall also be assumed that the quantity of housing services supplied by a given stock of housing is proportional to the size of the stock. The supply of housing as a function of the value of a standardized unit of housing is shown in the bottom half of Figure 13.4. The demand and supply curves are on different diagrams, so how do we get them together?

The crux of the model is the relationship between housing rent and market value. The market value of a unit of housing is the present discounted value of the stream of rents that the unit will generate. If those rents are expected to be constant at R per year, and if the real estate tax as a percentage of market value is t, then market value V is

$$V = \Sigma_i (R - tV)/(1 + r)^i,$$

where r is the rate of discount and i is the number of years into the future. In this discussion the rate of discount will be assumed to be fixed by the preferences of the public for future income versus current income. This is known as the rate of time preference.

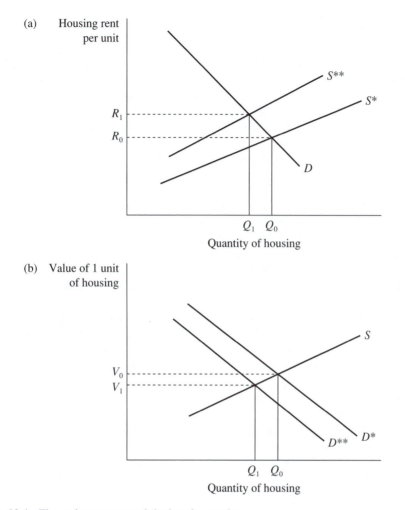

Figure 13.4   The real estate tax and the housing market

If the housing unit lasts forever (i.e., goes to infinity), the equation for market value simplifies to

$$V = (R - tV)/r,$$

which becomes

$$V = R/(r + t).$$

The term $r + t$ is known as the capitalization rate (or "cap" rate) – the rate that converts gross (before tax) annual housing rent into market value.

   Now return to the model in Figure 13.4. Given that the quantity housing services consumed (in the top half of the diagram) is proportional to the quantity of standardized housing units supplied, we can define a unit of housing services so that the two are numerically identical. The two diagrams can therefore be read vertically. We are now ready to perform two conversions. First convert the supply of housing units in the lower half of the diagram into a long-run supply of housing services in the upper half. This conversion is accomplished, at a given quantity, by multiplying V on supply curve S by $r + t$ to obtain the corresponding value of R. This supply curve is denoted S^*. The other conversion needed to translate demand in the upper half of the diagram into long-run demand in the lower half. This conversion is done, at a given quantity, by dividing R by $r + t$ to obtain the appropriate V. This long-run demand curve is labeled D^* in the lower half of Figure 13.4. Equilibrium quantity, housing rent, and value are denoted Q_0, R_0, and V_0. Recall that $V_0 = R_0/(r + t)$.

Now we are ready to play the game of increasing the real estate tax rate in the local jurisdiction. An increase in the real estate tax rate does not change the position of the demand curve for housing services in the upper half of Figure 13.4, nor does it shift the supply curve of standardized units of housing in the lower half of the diagram. Demand is still the same function of gross housing rent, and supply is still a function of market value. A change in the real estate tax rate *changes the capitalization rate $r + t$*. A higher value for t means that we must redo the conversions that were performed in the previous paragraph. First consider the supply curve. At a given quantity we now multiply V on supply curve S by a larger capitalization rate $r + t'$, and obtain the supply curve in the upper half of the diagram denoted S^{**}. Similarly, the new demand curve for the lower half of the diagram is found by dividing R on demand curve D by the larger number $r + t'$. This shifts the demand curve down to D^{**}. Note that the new equilibrium values for quantity, housing rent, and value are Q_1, R_1, and V_1.

The effects of an increase in the property tax can now be seen clearly. The quantity of housing (measured as standardized housing units) has declined, housing rent has increased, and the value of a unit of housing has decreased. In other words, the rents paid by tenants (per unit of housing services) have gone up *and* property values for owners have gone down. Another important conclusion is that the size of the tax base is sensitive to the tax rate. An increase in the tax rate reduced both the quantity of the housing stock and the value of each unit. The tax base is VQ, and both terms in this product have declined along supply curve S. The general conclusion regarding tax incidence is that the real estate tax is paid by both tenants and owners. This is a general result, but some special cases are of interest.

First, consider the possibility that the supply of housing is highly elastic. This would be the case if property owners can move their capital (in the long run, of course) in order to avoid suffering a capital loss and that would mean making a rate of return on capital that is below the rate that is available in other locations. Examine Figure 13.5, which depicts the housing market as in Figure 13.4. The supply curve in the lower half of the diagram is horizontal because, if a unit of housing is not worth V_0 in this urban area, it will be moved to some other location where it is worth V_0. This movement can occur over time as the quality of units declines in the urban area depicted in the diagram and new units are built elsewhere. Supply curve S is translated to the upper half of the diagram by multiplying V_0 by $r + t$, so this supply curve is also horizontal. The demand curves in Figure 13.5 are the same as in Figure 13.4.

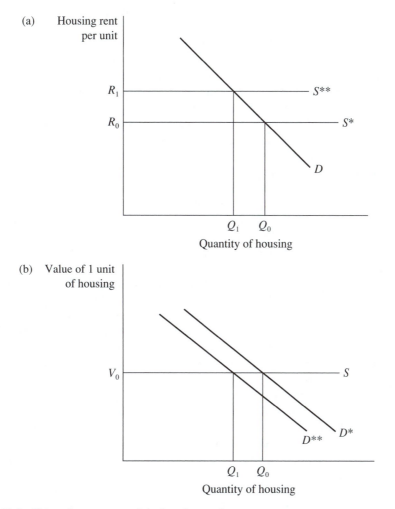

Figure 13.5   The real estate tax and the housing market

Now increase the real estate tax rate from t to t'. The supply curve in the upper half of Figure 13.5 shifts upward, and the demand curve in the lower half shifts downward as before. The market value of housing units remains at V_0, but the housing rent rises from $R_0 = (r + t)V_0$ to $R_1 = (r + t')V_0$. The quantity of housing units (and services) declines from Q_0 to Q_1. In this case only the consumers of housing services pay the real estate tax. The property owners escape the increase in the tax by being able to move capital around freely. Many people think that tenants pay the entire real estate tax. Figure 13.5 shows the conditions under which this claim is true. The tenants pay the tax if they are immobile and the capital is mobile.

Another alternative case is created if we assume that households are mobile to some extent, but that capital is not mobile. In the extreme case households are perfectly mobile, and housing rent cannot rise in response to an increase in the real estate tax. Housing rent is pegged at R_0, but the value of a unit of housing will fall from $V_0 = R_0/(r + t)$ to $V_1 = R_0/(r + t')$. The immobile capital pays the tax and loses value as a result, but the mobile housing consumers escape the tax. As an exercise, draw a set of diagrams to depict this case. In drawing your diagrams, assume that the demand curve for housing services in the urban area is horizontal, but that the supply curve has a positive slope as in Figure 13.4.

So far we have considered an isolated increase in the property tax. The tax was increased in one local jurisdiction, while all other locations held their tax rates constant. Furthermore, the tax rate was increased without any increase in spending on local public goods. The conclusions of the model are valid if these assumptions are correct. Suppose instead that the property tax is a tax on all capital (and land) in the economy, and that the tax is increased everywhere. Mieszkowski (1972) posed this version of the model and reached the conclusion that, if the total supply of capital is fixed, the owners of capital will bear the entire burden of the increase in the tax in the form of a reduction in its market value. The reason is that there is no place for capital to hide to escape the increase in the tax. The imposition of this increase in the tax on all capital will have no impact on the allocation of resources.

The expenditure side of the local public sector should also be considered. In a Tiebout world with only residential property, an increase in the property tax in a local jurisdiction presumably is matched by an increase in local public goods of equal value, so the simultaneous and equal increases in the tax and public goods will have no effect on housing rents, values, or quantity of housing units. However, consider the more realistic case in which the property tax is increased on residential, commercial and industrial property in order to provide residents with more of the local public good. These changes mean that residential property gains benefits of the local public good that exceed the increase in taxes, but that commercial and industrial property simply are taxed more heavily. The effects on the commercial and industrial sectors can be depicted in Figure 13.4. If Figure 13.4 applies, the increase in the tax rate is at least partly capitalized into lower market values for commercial and industrial property. The tenants who occupy those properties also bear a portion of the increase in the tax.

The story is different on the residential side. Residential property receives a benefit that exceeds the increase in the tax, so residential property values increase. To see this implication, suppose that the market value of a unit of housing is now

$$V = (R - tV + bV)/r$$

where bV represents the value of the local public goods provided to the housing unit in question. These benefits are expressed as a constant times the value of the housing unit, so

$$V = R/(r + t - b).$$

The assumption is that both t and b increase, but that the increase in b is greater than the increase in t. This means that $r + t - b$ declines. A decline in $r + t - b$ is the same thing as cutting the tax rate in Figure 13.4, so the implications can be found by running the model in reverse; use the shift in supply in the upper half of the diagram from S^{**} to S^*

and the shift in demand in the lower half of the diagram from D^{**} to D^*. Market value per unit increases, housing rent per unit declines, and the quantity of units increases. In effect, the ability to impose a tax on commercial and industrial property is of benefit to both housing consumers and the owners of housing units.

An extensive literature, beginning with Oates (1969), has established that higher property tax rates, holding public expenditures constant, reduce housing values. Similarly, an increase in public expenditures (especially on schools), holding the tax rate constant, will increase the value of a house. The effect of property taxes on commercial and industrial property has been the subject of very empirical few studies. One study by Wheaton (1984) found that differences across local jurisdictions in property taxes paid per square foot had no effect on gross rents in office buildings in metropolitan Boston. This finding means that none of the burden of the tax was being shifted forward from real estate capital and land onto tenants. Another study of office buildings in downtown Chicago (McDonald 1993) found that 45% of the property tax was being shifted forward to tenants in the form of higher gross rents, and that 55% of the tax was being absorbed by the owners of the real estate. More empirical studies of the commercial and industrial sectors are needed.

This discussion of the property tax has been rather lengthy, but we can now return to the questions raised at the beginning of this section. Who pays the property tax? If we ignore the expenditure side, Mieszkowski (1972) suggested that, if the property tax is a uniform tax on all capital and land and if both are in fixed supply, then the owners of capital and land pay the tax. Clearly the real estate tax is not uniform. The model depicted in Figure 13.4 shows that an increase in the property tax on housing in one jurisdiction is paid by both owners and housing consumers. Similarly, a decrease in the tax rate in one jurisdiction is of benefit to both. If the national average property tax rate is taken as the starting point for these changes, then housing consumers pay a portion of the local property tax that is above the national average and reap a benefit if the local property tax is below the national average. The analysis of the property tax on commercial and industrial property reaches the same conclusions. If the expenditure side of the local public sector is added to the model, then it is possible that relatively high property taxes on housing are matched by better local public services. In this Tiebout-type case the higher property tax is just a payment for better public services. However, this argument cannot be made in the case of commercial and industrial property. A higher property tax on these types of property is truly a tax, and the model in Figure 13.4 applies.

What is the impact of the property tax on location patterns within an urban area? One can presume that both residents and capital are, in the long run, mobile within an urban area. It is perilous for a local jurisdiction to raise its property tax rate to a level appreciably above the average for the urban area. Highly elastic demand and supply curves in Figure 13.4 mean that an increase in the tax rate leads to large changes in the quantity of housing located in the local jurisdiction. Indeed, you can show with the model in Figure 13.4 that sufficiently large demand and supply elasticities will mean that an increase in the tax rate will cause the local jurisdiction to cease to exist. Local officials and local voters must be cognizant of the fact that a high property tax rate, that is not offset by a high level of local public goods, will alter location patterns within the urban area to their detriment. The study by Ladd (1975) showed that they *are* aware of this fact and try to behave accordingly.

F. Intergovernmental Grants

The other chief source of revenue for local governments is grants from higher levels of government. State governments provide funds primarily for education, but they also fund a variety of other activities such as community development and highways and other transportation facilities. The federal government provides funds primarily for housing, transportation, community development, job training, and education. The provision of federal funds for income redistribution – direct support of the poor and the elderly – is not considered here.

Some of these funds are awarded to local governments automatically through complex distribution formulae. Other programs require that the local government prepare an application that documents eligibility and need. The larger units of local government employ sizable staffs of people to keep track of the distribution formulae and prepare these applications. Larger local governments also employ lobbyists in the state capital and in Washington, DC, to try to influence the rules and regulations of the funding programs. Why do the state and federal governments provide funds to local governments? What are the economic arguments for this kind of federalism? The matter of income redistribution policy has already been discussed, so the question here pertains to resource allocation policies.

The largest intergovernmental grants are provided by states for elementary and secondary education, so let us begin there. Education is the responsibility of the state government, and it has delegated this responsibility to local school districts. Clearly not all local school districts have the same ability to provide an education for their children, but clearly the society is also committed to some degree of equality of educational opportunity. State school aid tries to make up for the differences of school districts in their tax bases (per pupil). It does not succeed. School districts within the same state can have enormous differences in spending per pupil because spending is still based to a considerable degree on the local tax base. The crafting of a school-aid formula that tends to equalize educational opportunity is a tricky business.

Grant formulae can be categorized in two ways: categorical or noncategorical grants, and lump-sum or matching grants. Categorical grants are for specific purposes, such as education, while noncategorical grants can be used for a variety of purposes. These grants can be awarded as a lump sum, or they may require that the local jurisdiction put up matching funds. In other words, they can be awarded on the basis of need or on the basis of local effort to raise revenue. Indeed, some grant programs use both criteria at the same time. For example, a state's school-aid formula can provide a certain amount of funds per pupil as a function of the tax base per pupil, where districts with lower tax bases per pupil receive more funds. This formula can also contain a part that rewards the local district for imposing a higher real estate tax rate as well. This is done because a lump-sum grant provides little incentive for the local school district to use its own resources, limited as they are. Indeed, a lump-sum grant may induce the school district to give all property owners a tax cut with no net increase in spending on schools. Empirical studies reviewed by Inman (1979) show that this is not what happens, but the studies also show that a matching provision tends to stimulate total spending on the service in question more than does a lump-sum grant. These propositions regarding lump-sum and matching grants can be demonstrated theoretically.

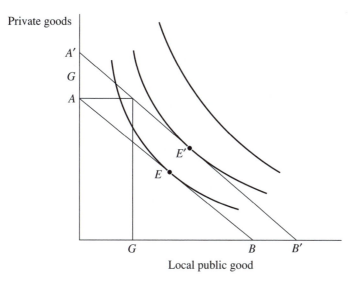

Figure 13.6   Effects of a lump-sum grant

To begin the theoretical demonstration, suppose that the preferences of the people in a local jurisdiction for the local public good and private goods can be depicted as the indifference curves in Figure 13.6. Given the income levels of the households in the jurisdiction, the community has a budget constraint of *AB*. With no intergovernmental grants, the local jurisdiction chooses a combination of private goods and the local public good designated by point *E*. Local taxes are imposed to raise the money for the local public good.

Now consider the effects of alternative intergovernmental grant programs. The simplest type of grant is the lump-sum grant. The local jurisdiction is simply given amount *G* shown in Figure 13.6. This grant can either be categorical or non-categorical. In other words, the rules may state that amount *G* must be spent on the local public good in question (categorical), or amount *G* can be spent on anything (noncategorical). Suppose first that the grant *G* is noncategorical. In this case the community's budget constraint shifts up to *A′B′*, and point *E′* is chosen. Note that the community, with the increase in income of *G*, has decided to increase its consumption of both the local public good and private goods. Some fraction of the grant amount *G* is spent on increasing the consumption of the local public good, and the remainder is used to cut local taxes. Indeed, the local jurisdiction could have decided to use all of the grant for tax cuts, or it could have decided to *increase* spending on the local public good by the entire amount of the grant and give no tax cut. We would expect that the actual outcome would fall between these two extremes.

Now suppose that the lump-sum grant is categorical. The rules state that the grant money received must be spent on the local public good in question, and records must be kept to document this use. However, the federal or state government cannot require that the local jurisdiction must *increase* its spending on the local public good in question by the amount of the grant. The only effective requirement is that at least amount *G* must be

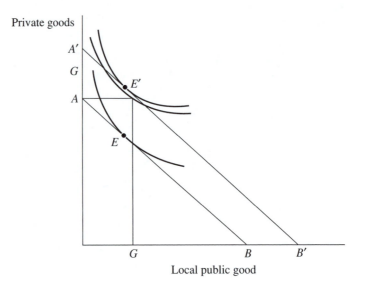

Figure 13.7   Effects of a categorical grant

spent on the local public good. In Figure 13.6 the local jurisdiction would have spent that much on the local public good even in the absence of the grant program. Therefore, the categorical lump-sum grant has the same effect as the noncategorical lump-sum grant.

The only case in which the effects of the two types of lump-sum grants differ occurs when the local jurisdiction, left completely to its own devices, would have spent less than amount *G* on the local public good *with the grant program in place*. Now the categorical grant rules force the local jurisdiction to increase this spending up to *G*. This case is shown in Figure 13.7, where the local jurisdiction starts with a low level of spending on the local public good (less than amount *G*), and prefers to take the entire grant as a tax cut. The rules of the grant program prohibit this move, spending on the local public good increases to *G*, and the local jurisdiction reaches a lower level of utility than it reaches if the grant were noncategorical.

Public finance economists argue that, except for the case shown in Figure 13.7, a categorical or noncategorical lump-sum grant is economically identical to an increase in income for the members of the local jurisdiction. In Figure 13.6 the grant shifts the budget constraint up, but an identical upward shift can be induced by an increase in the income of the households in the local jurisdiction. If this hypothesis is correct, then the grant money would be spent just as if it were an increase in disposable income for the households. However, several studies show that an increase in household income of $1 will increase spending on local public goods by $0.05 to $0.10, but a $1 increase in lump-sum grants will increase local public goods spending by $0.25 to $0.50. This result is known as the "flypaper effect" because grant money tends to stick where it hits – in the public sector. Somehow the households in the local jurisdiction do not view lump-sum grants as equivalent to ordinary income. What is going on here?

One possibility is that the studies are flawed. For example, the analysis in Figure 13.7 shows that a categorical lump-sum grant will increase spending on the local public good, but a general increase in income will not. Some lump-sum categorical grants may be provided for things that the local jurisdiction simply will not purchase with its own money. In the absence of the grant program, local demand is zero. This sort of argument may explain some of the flypaper effect, but there are several studies that seem to be without methodological flaws.

Suppose that the flypaper effect is real. What can explain it? The leading argument is that the nature of the political process leads to incorrect perceptions by local voters. There is reason to believe that local public officials are interested in having a larger budget. Local officials like to give tax cuts too, but they have some tendency to prefer to keep a good part of a lump-sum grant in the public sector. If local officials can control the public agenda, then decisions on taxes can be kept separate from decisions on the use of grant moneys. The basic idea is that local officials have some monopoly power that stems from a lack of complete information on the part of the local voters.

Next we turn to grants that require matching funds from the local jurisdiction. Most categorical grants require matching funds from the local jurisdiction. Many state and federal categorical grant programs specify a local matching rate m, which specifies the amount of money the local jurisdiction must spend for every dollar received from the grant program. For example, if $m = 1$, then the local jurisdiction must put up $1 for every dollar received. The local jurisdiction pays one-half of the cost of the local public good. In general, the share of the cost of the local public good paid by the local jurisdiction is $m/(1 + m)$. From the point of view of the local jurisdiction, the price of an additional dollar spent on the local public good is $m/(1 + m)$. If $m = 0.5$, then the local jurisdiction sees that an increase in spending on the local public good of $1 costs only $0.33 because the grant program matches every local dollar with two dollars.

The matching grant program can be depicted graphically. In Figure 13.8 the grant program provides a one-for-one match of local funds, so the price of the local public good facing the local jurisdiction has been reduced from $1 to $0.50. The community's budget constraint has shifted from AB to AB', and the local jurisdiction chooses point E'.

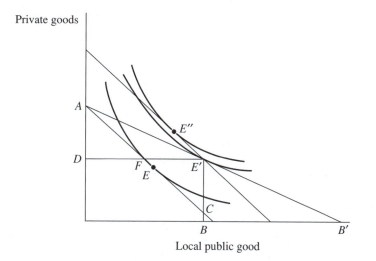

Figure 13.8   Effects of a matching grant

In the diagram the matching grant program has caused increases in consumption of both the local public good and private goods. However, because the consumption of private goods has increased, the case depicted in Figure 13.8 includes a local tax cut in response to the matching grant program. Even a matching grant cannot force the local jurisdiction to spend the entire grant on an increase in the local public good.

However, it is easy to show that the matching grant increases spending on the local public good more than does an equivalent lump-sum grant. The dollar amount of the matching grant is distance CE'. (How do we know this? Distance DE' is the total amount spent on the local public good. Amount DF is paid by the local jurisdiction, and the grant is the (equal) amount FE'. We know that $FE' = CE'$ because the original budget line AB makes a 45 degree angle with the axes.) Suppose that a lump-sum grant equal to amount CE' had been given instead. This grant enables the local jurisdiction to reach point E' if it so chooses. But remember that a lump-sum grant does not change the "price" at which the local public good can be purchased. The slope of the community's budget constraint with the lump-sum grant is -1, and the budget constraint passes through point E'. This means that the local jurisdiction can actually reach a higher indifference curve by choosing point E'' rather than point E'. Point E'' means less spending on the local public good with the equivalent lump-sum grant, compared to point E' with the matching grant. The lump-sum grant has a positive *income effect* on the local public good, but the matching grant has both an income effect and a *substitution effect* because the "price" of the local public good has been reduced by the rules of the program. Those of you who have had a course in microeconomic theory at the intermediate level will recall that the substitution effect always acts to increase consumption of the good that experiences the decline in relative price.

What types of grant programs are used by states to fund local public schools? The first grant programs were lump-sum categorical grants of a certain uniform dollar amount per pupil. The idea was to ensure a minimum level of education across the state, so this kind of grant is called foundation aid. The effects of this kind of grant program are shown in Figures 13.6 and 13.7. Now most states use some version of a foundation aid grant formula that is based on the amount of taxable real state per pupil. A general formula for this kind of grant program is

$$G = B - r(V - V^*) \text{ for } V > V^*, \text{ and}$$
$$G = B \text{ for } V < V^*,$$

where G is the grant per pupil, B is the basic per-pupil grant, V is the property tax base per pupil in the school district, V^* is a threshold property tax base per pupil, and r is a rate set by law. In this program, if the tax base per pupil in the school district is less than or equal to V^*, the grant per pupil is B. If the tax base per pupil is greater than V^*, then the grant per pupil is reduced by $r(V - V^*)$. Note that this kind of grant program is still a lump-sum grant because the grant does not depend upon the tax rate that is imposed by the local jurisdiction. There is no matching provision in the formula. Wealthier school districts receive smaller per-pupil grants from the state, but there is no assurance that this kind of grant program will equalize spending per pupil.

Despite the careful crafting of state school-aid formulae, the wide disparities in school expenditures per pupil remain. Some argue that these disparities violate the provisions in state constitutions for equal protection under the law and that education is the responsibility of the state. Lawsuits have been filed in most states; some of those cases have been won, some have been lost, and some are still pending. The plaintiffs (those who brought the lawsuits) who challenged the system for funding public schools have won their most significant victory in California in 1974. In that case, *Serrano v. Priest*, the plaintiff claimed that unequal funding for schools based on the local property tax violated the equal-protection clause in the California Constitution. The courts agreed, and ordered that the state must devise a system that keeps spending per pupil equal across districts (or within $100 per pupil). The equalization of spending across districts in California required a dramatic increase in the amount of state spending on schools, a topic that is discussed below. Cases in other states have led to changes in the system, but they have not equalized spending per pupil. Equality of spending per pupil may be a desirable goal for society to pursue, but the US Constitution, state constitutions, and current laws do not require it. In fact, the US Supreme Court ruled, in the case of *San Antonio Independent School District v. Rodriguez*, that the equal-protection clause in the US Constitution does not apply to education because education is not mentioned in the Constitution. This means that plaintiffs cannot win suits based on unequal spending on education across states. Sizable differences in spending per pupil will continue to exist within the same urban area (except in California), and these differences will continue to have impacts on the location choices of households and on the market value of housing.

State and federal funding programs for other local public expenditures such as transportation, community development, and job training can be justified on the grounds that each of these has substantial spillover effects outside the local jurisdiction. Programs that have sizable spillover benefits will be underfunded by local jurisdictions, so higher levels of government should subsidize these programs to some degree to induce local governments to do more. As discussed in Chapter 14, most major urban transportation projects are funded jointly by local, state and federal revenues (matching grants), and are also usually subjected to reasonably comprehensive cost-benefit and environmental impact studies. Other programs, such as community development and job training, are not analyzed as rigorously.

G. The Special Case of California

California is the first state to equalize spending per pupil in its public school districts. What is the nature of the system of local public finance that made this happen? The recent book by Fischel (2001) provides a detailed discussion of the California case, and other "tax revolt" examples from around the US.

The 1974 court case *Serrano v. Priest* was noted in the previous section. This is the case that ordered California to devise a system of financing local public schools so as to equalize spending per pupil. In response the state of California established a limit on spending by local school districts. The state also limited the rate at which spending could be increased, but allowed the districts with low spending per pupil to increase spending at a more rapid rate than districts with high spending. Spending differences narrowed over time during the 1970s.

The full equalization of spending per pupil across school districts was accomplished in the wake of the taxpayer revolt in California. In 1978 the voters of California enacted Proposition 13, a law that imposes strict limits on local real estate taxes. The law rolled back existing property taxes by over 50%, placed a 2 percent limit on annual reassessments (except at time of sale), and required that any other tax increase must be approved by a two-thirds vote. Local governments as a whole are allowed a property tax of only 1 percent of market value. Note that the property tax bill can increase only very slowly if the property is not sold to another owner, but that the assessment will "catch up" to the appreciation in market value when ownership changes. This feature is known as the "welcome stranger" tax increase. Some local jurisdictions have passed other tax increases by the required 2/3 vote. These taxes include a uniform parcel tax and local sales taxes.

How did Proposition 13 affect school spending? After the passage of Proposition 13, the state made an offer that school districts could not refuse. The state said that, if the maximum permissible property tax is imposed (i.e., 1%), then the state would pay the difference between the local revenue and the maximum amount of spending per pupil permitted by the state. All of the school districts accepted the offer, and it meant that all districts moved up to the state limit on spending per pupil. The state is now in complete control of the public school spending in California.

The passage of Proposition 13 left local governments, including school districts, with only very limited ability to raise taxes to finance infrastructure projects. Infrastructure needs to accommodate population growth can require more funds than are available through local taxes and intergovernmental grants. School districts need to build schools, and municipalities need to build public roads, fire stations, police stations, parks, jails, sewer mains, etc. This problem was addressed in 1982 by the passage of the Mello–Roos Community Facility Act, which permits local governments to set up special community facility districts. These special districts can issue tax-exempt bonds that are supported by special taxes levied on *new* properties in the special district. The new facilities are needed to accommodate the growth of population, so only the new properties must pay to support the bonds. Many local municipalities, counties and school districts have used this method of financing public facilities. As one would expect, the special tax on new houses has a strongly negative effect on their market prices. One study by Do and Sirmans (1994) found that an annual Mello–Roos payment of $705 per year for 25 years reduced the value of a house by $13,500, compared to neighboring properties in the same jurisdiction that were not subject to this tax.

Proposition 13 and the *Serrano v. Priest* decision have had a major impact on the financing of local public goods and services. Table 13.3 has been prepared to highlight the change. This table compares the sources of general revenue for all local governments in the US and in California for 1966–7 and 1986–7. The earlier year is prior to passage of Proposition 13, and also prior to the *Serrano v. Priest* decision. The later year is eight years after the passage of Proposition 13. Table 13.3 shows that local governments in California in 1966–7 obtained revenues in a manner that is very similar to the average for local governments nationwide. Local sources accounted for about 65% of general revenue, and the property tax was over four-tenths of local revenue. The state's share of local revenues was about one-third.

Now look at the figures for 1986–7. As we saw in Section B above, local governments around the nation shifted away from the property tax towards other taxes and charges and

Table 13.3 Sources of general revenue by local governments: US and California

	1966–7		1986–7	
	All local govt.	*California local govt.*	*All local govt.*	*California local govt.*
Local sources	65.3%	65.1%	62.0%	52.8%
Property tax	43.2	45.1	28.3	19.4
Other taxes	6.7	5.8	10.1	9.1
Charges and misc.	15.4	14.3	23.6	24.3
Intergovernmental	34.7	34.9	38.0	47.2
State	31.7	32.9	33.3	43.9
Federal	3.0	2.0	4.7	3.3

Source: Census of Governments (1967, 1987)

miscellaneous local revenue sources. The share of revenue raised through the local property tax dropped from 43.2% in 1966–7 to 28.3% in 1986–7. But look at California! The share of local revenues obtained through the local property tax dropped from 45.1% to 19.4% over this same period. Local governments in California increased their reliance on other taxes and charges and miscellaneous revenue sources as well, but the share of revenue that came from the state jumped from 32.9% to 43.9%. Almost half of local revenues (47.2%) for California local governments in 1986–87 came from intergovernmental sources. This increase in intergovernmental funds can be attributed largely to the system for funding the California public schools that is described above.

H. Central City Fiscal Problems

In a narrow sense a city's fiscal "problem" is that expenditures exceed revenues by amount large enough to make people think that a city is not a good credit risk. City officials wake up one morning and discover that the lenders are no longer willing to bail them out with short-term loans to cover the deficit. What do they do then? They can declare bankruptcy and refuse to honor their debt obligations. This strategy is not a good idea because it is likely that the city's ability to borrow will be negatively affected for many years. The better idea is to put in place a plan that includes a package of expenditure reductions, tax increases and other "revenue enhancements," and restructuring of debt. The idea of restructuring debts is to lengthen the repayment period so that current payments are reduced.

New York City was pushed to the brink of bankruptcy in 1975. However, we now know that New York was a special case that is not indicative of problems faced by other central cities. New York was (and is) required by the State of New York to pay 23% of the expenditures on welfare and Medicaid for poor city residents. Most cities pay none of these expenditures. Also on the expenditure side, New York City offered an extensive set of city services (including its own complete university system with very low tuition) and had powerful public-employee unions that had succeeded in increasing wage rates in the public sector. On the revenue side, the city was by state law not permitted to increase its real estate tax. The city was progressively getting into trouble in the early 1970s by borrowing large sums of money to cover current expenses, a policy that technically was illegal. The city also had a substantial amount of unfunded pension liability from the retirement pensions that had been promised to public employees. The house of cards came tumbling down in the recession of 1975, a time when federal aid to the city was also being cut. The banks refused to lend any more money to New York City. To resolve the crisis the state and federal governments stepped in to guarantee New York's bonds, and the federal government granted loans to New York City in exchange for a program of austerity. In short, New York City was trying to do too much and was guilty of shaky fiscal practices.

Now let us turn to the tragic case of East St. Louis, Illinois. East St. Louis is the old central city on the Illinois side of the Mississippi River across from St. Louis, Missouri. It is a very small city (population 45,000 in 1990) that has a population that is largely black. It is surrounded by suburban municipalities, so it has no ability to annex territory. The city once had a sizable economic base that included a major stockyards and meat-packing industry. The old economic base is now completely gone. The downtown office buildings are across the river in St. Louis. In short, East St. Louis is a city consisting entirely of badly depressed inner-city areas. The tax base of East St. Louis is insufficient to pay for anything remotely like decent urban public services; schools, police and fire, public health, and so on. The city is in fact a ward of the state of Illinois. In effect, the state operates the government of the city. East St. Louis is the living, barely breathing worst-case scenario. In recent years the city was sued by a citizen who charged the police force with brutality. The citizen won the case and was awarded a substantial amount of money in damages, which the city was unable to pay. The citizen was given title to city hall by the court until such time as other financial arrangements could be made. Thankfully, East St. Louis is obviously another special case.

Do central cities in general have fiscal problems? Some researchers, such as Clark (1985), point out that in a narrow sense, they really do not. A central city government can live within its means by carefully balancing the various demands on the budget with its revenue sources. The city can also take steps to strengthen the local economy, as discussed later in Chapter 21, although the payoff to these activities will take years to materialize. It is evident that since the New York City fiscal crisis of 1975 (and other fiscal crises experienced by Cleveland and a few other cities at about the same time), central cities have learned how to avoid fiscal crises, narrowly defined.

Central cities are avoiding fiscal crises, but Ladd and Yinger (1989) argued that what they are not doing is providing a standard package of public services at a standard local tax rate. Ladd and Yinger constructed an index of fiscal health for central cities that is based upon the assumption that a city offers a standard array of public services with a tax package that amounts to a tax of 3% on local income. The cost of the standard array of public services was determined by local conditions. The index measures how far the city falls short of this fiscal package as a percentage of the implied budget. The index for 1988 was −83% for New York City, −38% in Los Angeles, −45% in Chicago, −35% in

Philadelphia, and −64% in Detroit. The central city must make up for this implied deficit by aid from the state (and to a far lesser extent, the federal government), higher taxes, and/or lower spending on services. The cities in fact do make up for this shortage of funds using some combination of these strategies. The Ladd–Yinger index provides an interesting measure of the stress that city officials are under. They are under heavy pressure to find more revenue from state and federal sources. They constantly hear complaints about local taxes and fees from their constituents, and they are also forever being told that the public services, especially the public schools, are inadequate.

What are the sources of fiscal stress that have been documented by Ladd and Yinger (1989)? By now you should be able to answer this question. Your answer will probably include the following:

1   loss of commercial and industrial tax base;
2   retention of low-income population with heavy demands for public services such as education, health care, and housing;
3   high crime rates, which require more police and criminal justice facilities;
4   aging infrastructure, which requires expensive maintenance and rehabilitation;
5   population loss, which means that fixed costs must be spread over a smaller population;
6   old buildings, which create more fire hazards and demolition expenses;
7   inability to annex territory.

By the way, the loss of middle-class taxpayers to the suburbs may not have a strong negative effect on the fiscal situation of the central city. Middle-class households pay taxes, but they also demand public services. Indeed, the rule of thumb is that middle-class households and the houses that they own cost more in public services than they pay in taxes, largely because they send children to school. The trick is to get middle-class households that do not place demands on the public school system to live in the city.

What are the policy alternatives to address the problem of fiscal stress on central cities? One alternative is to permit the central city to annex territory or somehow to have access to the tax base of the urban area. Norton (1979) showed that many central cities in the sunbelt, such as Houston, Nashville, Jacksonville, and Phoenix, have been able to annex large amounts of territory. For example, under Texas law, Houston has extraterritorial rights over areas within five miles of its city limits. In this area new municipalities cannot be created and existing municipalities cannot annex territory without the approval of Houston. Houston has taken advantage of this system to prevent the creation of separate suburban municipalities. In a few other cases, most notably in Minneapolis–St. Paul, the urban area has a metropolitan governmental structure that requires the sharing of some of the tax base. A third option is to have state governments provide more support for the central cities. But what if none of these options can be made to work? Political power in many urban areas has shifted to the suburbs away from the central city. Suburbanites often have little enthusiasm for being taxed to provide better services for the central city. There are many central cities that find themselves in this position, and it means that they must daily fight the budget battles. As we pointed out earlier, one typical outcome is that expenditures per pupil in the public schools are generally lower in the central city than in suburban areas (with the exception of some poor suburbs).

I. Summary

This chapter has covered a great deal of material on the local public sector. The major points that were made are as follows.

1   The chief function of local government is to allocate resources to local public goods and services. Income redistribution and economic stabilization and growth are secondary functions.
2   The most important local public service is elementary and secondary education, but local governments provide many other goods and services.
3   There are two economic/political models of how public resource allocation decisions are made at the local level. One is the Tiebout model, which emphasizes the role of household mobility in enabling local jurisdictions to be set up that provide local public goods to match the preferences of households who choose to live there. The other theory, the median voter model, is a theory of voting that is based on the presumption that a local jurisdiction will contain households with different views regarding resource allocation decisions. The Tiebout model is a useful tool for understanding how local jurisdictions function in the suburbs. The median voter model is the realistic approach for studying the large central city's government.
4   The property tax is the most important local tax. Variations in this tax rate (as a percentage of the market value of property) within an urban area can have sizable effects on location patterns. A local jurisdiction with a property tax rate that is close to the average for the urban area will not suffer adverse consequences. A substantial increase in the tax rate, relative to the average, can cause housing rents to rise, housing values to fall, and capital to migrate to other locations. Similarly, a cut in the property tax rate relative to the average can have the opposite effects. Property tax incentives are used widely to stimulate local economic development. A discussion of property tax incentives for local economic development is included in Chapter 21.
5   The other major source of revenue for local governments is intergovernmental transfers. The largest grant program is the support for local schools provided by the states. State school-aid formulae are designed to offset part of the disparities in the tax bases of school districts. Sizable disparities in expenditures per pupil still exist, except in California. California has implemented a program that equalizes spending per pupil across school districts. The program has resulted in a major increase in the funding of local schools by the state.
6   Many central cities are under fiscal stress because they have lost tax base, contain populations with heavy demands for public services, and are unable to tap into the suburban tax base. One typical outcome is that spending per pupil in the public schools tends to be lower in the central city than in the suburbs.

Exercises

1   A local jurisdiction is (ala Tiebout) populated with 125 households who have identical demands for a local public good G that can be expressed as

$G = 100 - 0.5p,$

where p is the price per unit of the public good. Each unit of the public good costs \$5,000, and each household pays pG in taxes.

(a) What is the price per unit of the public good?
(b) What is the optimal amount of the public good for this jurisdiction?
(c) How much will each household pay in taxes?

2 Return to problem #1 above, and assume that the jurisdiction now includes the same 125 households *and* 175 households with the demand for the public good

$G = 50 - 0.5p.$

Suppose that the decision regarding the amount of public good to be supplied is determined by the median voter model.

(a) How much of the public good will be supplied and at what price per unit?
(b) How much will each household pay in taxes?

3 Suppose that the demand for housing in an urban area can be expressed as

$R = 10,000 - Q,$

where R is annual rent and Q is quantity of housing units. The supply of housing is a function of the market value, V, of a unit, or

$V = 50,000 + 2.5Q.$

Assume that the real rate of discount is 6% and that the annual property tax is 2% of the value of a unit.

(a) What are the market equilibrium quantity, annual rent, and market value?
(b) Assume that the annual property tax is increased to 4% of market value. What happens to quantity, annual rent, and market value? How much of the increase in the tax is borne by the consumers of housing (tenants), and how much is borne by the owners of the housing?
(c) Perform the graphical analysis mentioned in the text in which the supply of housing is fixed and the households are perfectly mobile across urban areas. What is the effect of reducing the property tax rate? Show using your diagrams.

4 There are two types of matching grants. The one presented in the text is actually an "open-ended" grant because there is no limit to the amount of money that will be provided by the grant program, as long as the local government allocates the required matching funds. The other type of matching grant is called "closed-ended" because there is a limit to the amount of the grant. For example, suppose that the matching grant program has a matching rate of \$1 for \$1, but that the maximum amount of the grant is \$1 million.

(a) Along the lines of Figure 13.8, draw the budget constraint for the local community under this closed-ended grant program.

(b) Compare the effects of these two types of matching grants on the amount spent for the local public good. Assume that both programs have a matching rate of $1 to $1, but that the closed-ended grant program has a maximum grant of $1 million.

References

Bernhard, A. and B. Stott, 1977, "Milwaukee Revenue Cost Analysis," *Urban Land*, vol. 36, no. 11, pp. 16–18.

Clark, Terry, 1985, "Fiscal Strain: How Different Are Snow Belt and Sun Belt Cities?" in P. Peterson (ed.), *The New Urban Reality*. Washington, DC: The Brookings Institution.

Enelow, James and M. Hinich, 1984, *The Spatial Theory of Voting*. New York: Cambridge University Press.

Fischel, William, 2001, *The Homevoter Hypothesis*. Cambridge: Harvard University Press.

Hamilton, Bruce, 1975, "Zoning and Property Taxation in a System of Local Governments," *Urban Studies*, vol. 12, pp. 205–11.

Inman, Robert, 1978, "Testing Political Economy's 'As If' Proposition: Is the Median Voter Really Decisive?" *Public Choice*, vol. 33, pp. 45–65.

Inman, Robert, 1979, "Fiscal Performance of Local Governments: An Interpretive Review," in P. Mieszkowski and M. Straszheim (eds.), *Current Issues in Urban Economics*. Baltimore: Johns Hopkins University Press.

Ladd, Helen, 1975, "Local Education Expenditures, Fiscal Capacity, and the Composition of the Property Tax Base," *National Tax Journal*, vol. 28, pp. 145–58.

Ladd, Helen and J. Yinger, 1989, *American's Ailing Cities: Fiscal Health and the Design of Urban Policy*. Baltimore: Johns Hopkins University Press.

Luce, Thomas and A. Summers, 1987, *Local Fiscal Issues in the Philadelphia Metropolitan Area*. Philadelphia: University of Pennsylvania Press.

McDonald, John, 1993, "Incidence of the Property Tax on Commercial Real Estate: The Case of Downtown Chicago," *National Tax Journal*, vol. 46, pp. 109–20.

McDonald, John, C. Orlebeke, A. Sen, and W. Wiewel, 1991, "Real Estate Development and Property Taxes in DuPage County," Center for Urban Economic Development, University of Illinois at Chicago.

Mieszkowski, Peter, 1972, "The Property Tax: An Excise Tax or a Profits Tax?" *Journal of Public Economics*, vol. 1, pp. 73–92.

Musgrave, Richard, 1959, *The Theory of Public Finance*. New York: McGraw-Hill.

Norton, R. D., 1979, *City Life-Cycles and American Urban Policy*. New York: Academic Press.

Oates, Wallace, 1969, "The Effects of Property Taxes and Local Public Spending on Property Values: An Empirical Study of Tax Capitalization and the Tiebout Hypothesis," *Journal of Political Economy*, vol. 77, pp. 957–70.

Samuelson, Paul, 1954, "The Pure Theory of Public Expenditures," *Review of Economics and Statistics*, vol. 36, pp. 387–9.

Samuelson, Paul, 1955, "Diagrammatic Exposition of the Pure Theory of Public Expenditures," *Review of Economics and Statistics*, vol. 37, pp. 350–6.

Tiebout, Charles, 1956, "A Pure Theory of Local Expenditures," *Journal of Political Economy*, vol. 64, pp. 416–24.

Wheaton, William, 1984, "The Incidence of Inter-Jurisdictional Differences in Commercial Property Taxes," *National Tax Journal*, vol. 37, pp. 515–27.

Chapter 14

Urban Transportation

There is no such thing as a free road.
Jack Hartman, Executive Director, Illinois Tollway

A. Introduction

Transportation in an urban area is used to move both people and freight. Transportation is a service that is demanded by people because of a desire to pursue an activity at some other location. These activities include work, shopping, school, entertainment, and many more. Streets and highways, buses, rail rapid transit lines and other facilities exist to transport people to their desired destinations. Freight transportation moves goods and services and to a desired location. The movement of goods by rail or truck has been discussed in previous chapters, but other systems exist to transport natural gas, sewerage, electricity, telephone calls, water, and cable television signals. In other words, there are many demands for transportation and several transportation systems in an urban area. The focus of this chapter is largely on one type of trip – the trip to work by those employed outside the home. This choice is based on two reasons:

- the trip to work is most important trip the adult worker makes; and
- trips to work are concentrated during the morning and afternoon "rush" hours, thus straining the capacity of the transportation system.

Other types of trips are also made at rush hour (e.g., trips to school or for shopping and trips by trucks), and these are included in the discussion. However, the peaking of demand for transportation during the rush hours is driven primarily by the trips to and from work.

Much of the discussion in this chapter is devoted to the use of streets and roads by autos and trucks, rather than public transportation or freight rail transportation. This focus is based on the overwhelming numbers of Americans who use the private auto (or truck or van) for the trip to work. Not all metropolitan areas are alike, of course. Table 14.1

Table 14.1   Choice of mode for trips to work: 2000

| | Total workers (thousands) | Auto[a] | | Public transit[b] | Other[c] | Work at home |
		Alone	Car pool			
CMSA[d]						
New York	9,319	56.3%	9.4%	24.9%	6.5%	3.0%
Los Angeles	6,768	72.4	15.2	4.7	4.2	3.6
Chicago	4,218	70.5	11.0	11.5	4.1	2.9
Washington, Baltimore	3,839	70.4	12.8	9.4	3.9	3.5
San Francisco	3,432	68.1	12.9	9.5	5.4	4.1
Boston	2,899	73.9	8.8	9.0	5.1	3.2
Philadelphia	2,815	73.3	10.3	8.7	4.9	2.8
Dallas–Fort Worth	2,528	78.8	14.0	1.8	2.5	3.0
Detroit	2,482	84.2	9.3	1.8	2.5	2.3
Houston	2,082	77.0	14.2	3.3	2.9	2.5

[a] Auto, truck and van.
[b] Includes taxicabs.
[c] Other includes walking, motorcycle, bicycle, and any other.
[d] Consolidated metropolitan statistical area.
Source: US Bureau of the Census, Census of 2000

shows that only 56.3% of trips to work in 2000 in the New York Consolidated Metropolitan Statistical Area were by workers driving alone. New York's subway and commuter rail systems and buses (and taxis) provided transportation for 24.9% of the workers. The use of public transportation by commuters in New York is, by far, the largest in the nation. Table 14.1 shows the top ten urban areas in terms of employment, and the next-biggest users of public transportation are the commuters of the Chicago metropolitan area (with 11.5%). Public transportation also has a sizable presence in Washington/Baltimore, San Francisco, Boston, and Philadelphia, but very little in Los Angeles, Dallas–Fort Worth, Detroit, and Houston. A small subway system was recently constructed in Los Angeles, but the percentage of commuters who used public transportation did not change from 1990 to 2000. Detroit leads the pack with 84.2% of workers who drive alone, and with 93.5% who use private auto (including car poolers). Detroit also has is tied for having the smallest percentage of public transit riders, with a paltry 1.8%. More workers work at home (2.3%) in the Detroit metro area than use public transit. Table 14.1 shows that there is more car-pooling in Los Angeles, Dallas–Fort Worth, and Houston than in the other top ten urban areas. Can you think of any reasons for this outcome? One guess is that the absence of public transportation in Los Angeles, Dallas–Fort Worth and Houston force more people to use car pools. [Note how car pool is now a thing, an activity (car-pooling), a group of people (car poolers, or maybe poolsters), and a verb (to car pool).] A cursory glance at the numbers in Table 14.1 certainly suggests that, in some urban areas, car-pooling makes the biggest contribution to reducing traffic. In any case, Table 14.1 provides ample justification for concentrating on autos and streets and highways.

The predominance of the auto for trips to work (and for most other purposes as well) is an overwhelming fact, but commuters will also tell you that traffic is getting worse. The book by Downs (2004) entitled *Still Stuck in Traffic* explains why traffic seems to be getting worse. The growth rate of population in the US as a whole is not very great, but some urban areas such as Los Angeles, Phoenix, Atlanta, and others in the sunbelt have experienced big population increases. More population means more trips in the urban area. More importantly, employment, licensed drivers, and autos and trucks in use have all increased rapidly. In addition, those vehicles are driven more miles per year than before. These changes are coupled with a slow response in building new highways. Downs (2004, p. 51) notes that total highway mileage in the US has increased very little (2.4%) from 1980 to 1998, a time period when total miles driven by autos and trucks increased by 80%. However, the better measure of road mileage is total lane miles. Lane miles in urban areas on expressways and major arterials increased by 36.6% from 1982 to 2000. Urban roads are being built, especially in the new suburbs, but not at a rate that is fast enough to keep up with the drivers. Downs (2004, p. 51) reports that roadway congestion as measured by the Texas Transportation Institute increased by an average of 43% from 1982 to 2000 in the 75 major metropolitan areas studied.

Traffic congestion is pretty bad and getting worse, so what can be done about it? This is the big question that is addressed in this chapter. However, you need to learn more about urban transportation before you can attempt to answer the question.

B. Transportation and Urban Location Patterns

The discussions so far in this book clearly suggest that transportation is a major force that shapes an urban area. The original cities in the United States began as ports, and the spatial patterns within those early cities around the port were determined by the rudimentary transportation methods of the early nineteenth century. The water and rail transportation revolution of the first half of the nineteenth century made large cities possible, and early rail systems also permitted cities to spread their growing populations over a wider area. Improvements in urban rail systems continued, but the shift to the truck and the automobile beginning roughly in 1920 was the truly revolutionary development in urban transportation.

As Table 14.1 shows, the system for moving people around an urban area is based mainly on the use of streets and highways by private automobiles. That system is supplemented by public transportation in the form of buses and, in a few larger urban areas, rail transit. The construction of commuter and freight rail lines once shaped urban areas, but now the highway system shapes the urban area. However, urban areas have also been shaped by the change in the methods used to travel to destinations outside the urban area. The increased use of air transportation for both passengers and freight has made the airport a center of economic activity, and has required the development of ground transportation facilities to serve the airport. The growth of trucking for inter-urban freight has meant a decline in demand for rail transportation. The construction of the highway system freed light manufacturers from locations near rail lines, and permitted any location within reasonable proximity of a major highway to be a "point of export" for the urban area.

At the same time, it is not correct to regard urban highways and bus and transit systems as completely independent forces that act on an urban area. Transportation facilities are built in response to current or projected future demands. Sometimes transportation facilities have been built ahead of demand, but often the construction of facilities is responding to demand forces that already exist. The construction of the urban expressway systems in the 1950s and 1960s was responding to a strong demand. Many people wished to live in suburban housing, but the lack of high-speed urban highways was preventing the fulfillment of this demand. Once those urban highways were constructed, the development of the suburbs was rapid. The era of massive urban highway construction is over. Now the construction of more urban highways is based more closely on existing demand – and costs, as well. The construction of public transportation facilities is also based on existing demand and careful projections of future demand. So it is true that urban transportation facilities are important in shaping an urban area, and strongly influence land-use patterns and the total amount and spatial patterns of urban travel. But it is also true that changes in urban transportation facilities are partly determined by changes on the demand side. A broader perspective would recognize that urban transportation systems and urban land use and travel demands are interdependent and evolve together over time.

Another factor to consider in urban transportation is the independent influence of public policy that is formulated at the federal, state, and local levels. Large-scale highway or transit projects often become political issues in which many actors play a role. These actors may be motivated by a variety of goals, including political power. Some political actors are swayed by a particular group that has a special interest. At other times local transportation policy is strongly influenced by budget and policy decisions that have been made by Congress and the President with little regard for local conditions and problems. Urban transportation policy would appear to be fertile ground for study by the conservative economists of the Chicago School of Political Economy, the people who enjoy uncovering the real motivations for particularly inefficient or inequitable policy decisions. And some Marxists see urban transportation policy as an inevitable outcome of the dynamics of monopoly capitalism.

It was noted in the introduction to this chapter that both the demand and the supply of transportation in an urban area are extremely complicated. Transportation analysts have made progress by breaking the general problem into smaller pieces and formulating models specific to each of those pieces. Models of the demand side are considered first.

C. Demand for Transportation in Urban Areas

One approach to the demand for transportation in an urban area would be to try to explain the total amount of travel demanded in an urban area in a period of time, such as a typical weekday. The total amount of travel demanded would be measured as the total number of miles traveled during the day. The researcher might gather data on a sample of urban areas, and suppose that total travel demand is a function of total population, average household income, age composition of the population, number of people who work, and perhaps some other variables. For example, one might wish to include variables that describe the location patterns of the urban area and the nature of the transportation system that is available. As a matter of fact, no one has used this approach to study the total demand for urban transportation. As Small (1992) discussed, several researchers have used this kind of approach to study the demand for public transportation in urban areas. But this aggregative approach has otherwise not been considered fruitful for the study of travel demand. The reasons are not difficult to determine, and they include the following:

- It is not clear how to measure the "price" of travel in this context.
- From a transportation planning standpoint, it is more important to know the demand for travel during the times of day when demand reaches its peaks.
- Also from a transportation planning standpoint, one needs to know the locations of the peak demands.

The study of the demand for transportation is usually undertaken in an individual urban area. The urban area is broken down into a set of small geographic zones. It is assumed that the location patterns by geographic zone of houses, jobs and shopping opportunities, as well as other possible trip destinations, are fixed. Travel demand analysis is then broken down into four steps. The first step is to study the generation of trips by a geographic zone during a particular time of day (e.g., the morning rush hour). Each zone is both an origin for trips and a destination for trips. The end of the first phase of the analysis yields models that explain (or predict) the number of trips that originate in a zone and the number of trips that have a zone as destination. Table 14.2 shows an actual urban area (in this case, Chicago in 1956) that consists of seven geographic rings, each of which is both an origin and a destination of trips to work. The seven rings as origins are listed down the left-hand side of the table, and the rings as destinations are displayed across the top of the table. The average distance of each ring from the central business district is also shown. The models from phase one of a transportation study will indicate the number of trips with rings 0–1 to 7 as origin, and they will also predict how many trips will have each ring as a destination. The number of trips with ring 0–1 (the central business district) as origin during the morning rush hour is 139,000, and is shown in the column labeled total. The number of trips with ring 0–1 as destination is 593,000, and this figure is shown in the row labeled total.

Table 14.2 contains some interesting patterns. The largest destination for work trips was, of course, the central business district (with 593,000 work trips), but an even larger number of workers lived in and worked in the same ring – 670,000. This figure is found by adding up the numbers on the "main diagonal" of the trip matrix. These numbers show, for example, that 88,000 workers lived and worked in ring 2. Far more workers traveled inward to a ring closer to the CBD than traveled away from the CBD; 979,000 commuted inward and 385,000 commuted outward. Indeed, only 158,000 commuted outward more than one ring away from the residence ring. Table 14.2 depicts an urban area that is a reasonable approximation of the monocentric city discussed in Chapter 5. This was Chicago in 1956, and times have changed. Employment in the CBD remained roughly constant as total employment increased enormously in the succeeding decades. In 2000 15% of total employment in the metropolitan area was located in the CBD compared to 29% in 1956.

The second phase of a travel demand study is known as trip distribution analysis, and its purpose is to fill in the elements of Table 14.2 by modeling how the trips from each

Table 14.2 Origins and destinations of work trips in a reasonably monocentric urban area: Chicago in 1956 (thousands of trips)

	Workplace ring							
	0–1	*2*	*3*	*4*	*5*	*6*	*7*	*Total*
Residence ring								
0–1	80	22	16	13	6	2	0	139
2	97 (58)[a]	88	50	25	13	5	1	280
3	125 (81)[a]	69	117	62	29	9	3	414
4	166 (101)[a]	60	91	162	52	18	4	553
5	57 (38)[a]	19	28	47	91	27	14	283
6	43 (29)[a]	12	14	25	42	74	14	224
7	25 (19)[a]	4	5	9	16	23	58	141
Total	593 (326)[a]	274	322	344	250	157	94	2,034
Distance to CBD (average in miles)	1.4	3.5	5.5	8.5	12.5	16.0	24.0	

[a] Trips to CBD by mass transit. Some columns do not add because of rounding.
Sources: Chicago Area Transportation Study (1959) and Meyer et al. (1965)

origin are distributed to the various destinations. We know that there are 139,000 trips with ring 0–1 as origin, but how many of those trips are taken to each possible destination? The third step is to assign to a particular means of travel the trips that are taken from an origin zone to some destination zone. The means of travel are auto, bus, walking, etc. This phase is known as mode split analysis. Given that 166,000 trips are taken from ring 4 to destination ring 0–1, how many are taken by auto and how many by public transit? As shown in Table 14.2, we know that 101,000 of these trips were by rail or bus transit. In fact, 326,000 of the work trips to the CBD (out of 593,000) were by public transit. The fourth and final step in the analysis is to assign the trips to a specific route in the transportation network. This step is known as trip assignment. Given that so many trips are taken *by auto* from origin ring 4 to destination ring 0–1, which specific routes will be used, and how many trips will be taken on each of these routes? Finally, a more complex analysis would involve all four of these steps for each *type* of trip, e.g., trips to work, trips for shopping, and truck trips. There would therefore be a table such as Table 14.2 and a set of demand models for each type of trip. Furthermore, the analysis might focus separately on the various particular times of day, such as the morning rush hour. The models that transportation economists have developed for each phase of the analysis are discussed in turn. The section then concludes with a discussion of the concentration of demand in peak periods of the day.

Trip generation models

Given that there are so many housing units located in zone A, how many trips to work will be generated by zone A? The answer depends upon several factors. Given the nature of the housing stock, what sorts of people will live in zone A, and what are their propensities to work? How accessible is zone A to employment? A study of trip generation will examine these questions. One approach is to formulate a model of bid rent for housing for each of several demographic groups, and to assign them to housing and locations on the basis of their bids. Models of this type were discussed in Chapter 5. Also, how many trips will have zone A as destination? How many jobs are located in zone A? What sort of shopping opportunities is available in zone A, and how do they influence shopping trips? Data gathered on travel origins and destinations by type of trip, along with demographic and housing and commercial information on the zones, will permit the analyst to estimate models of trip generation along the lines suggested here. Transportation studies normally begin with a survey of travel behavior that can be used to estimate trip generation models. The Census of Population that is taken every ten years includes (for a sample of households) information on the journey to work by each household member who is employed. This source is now widely used by local transportation planning agencies for statistical studies of travel demand for the journey to work. A survey of studies by Pickrell (1989) shows that the amount of daily travel by a household is a function of household size, income, urban area size, and residential density. The studies show that higher residential density has a modest negative effect on travel demand per household and trips by auto except at the highest densities for central cities in the US.

Trip distribution models

Given that the column and row totals in Table 14.2 are understood, how are the trips from the rings distributed among the possible destinations? Furthermore, how can it be assured that the trips distributed to a particular destination add up to the total number of trips to that destination? The model that is used to perform this complicated task is called the doubly constrained gravity model. The idea of a gravity model is explained first, and then the nature of the double constraint is examined.

   The gravity model of spatial interaction says that the number of trips taken from origin i to destination j increases with the number of trips with origin at zone i and with the number of trips with zone j as destination. A greater number of trips originating in zone i will result in more trips being taken to zone j. A greater number of trips with zone j as destination will mean that this zone is more attractive as a destination, and will therefore attract more trips from zone i. Also, the number of trips from i to j will depend upon the cost of the trip, which is often measured as the distance from i to j. The simple "unconstrained" gravity model in mathematical form is

$$T_{ij} = O_i^\alpha D_j^\beta / (d_{ij})^\tau,$$

where T_{ij} is the number of trips taken from i to j, O_i is the number of trips with i as origin, D_j is the number of trips with j as destination, and d_{ij} is the distance (cost of travel) from

i to j. The model is analogous to Newton's law of gravitational force between two bodies – especially if the distance variable appears in the denominator with an exponent of 2. In logarithmic form the model is

$$\log T_{ij} = \alpha \log O_i + \beta \log D_j + \tau \log d_{ij}.$$

In addition to urban travel, gravity models of this type are used to model spatial interactions of various kinds, such as population migration, air passenger travel, international trade, and financial flows. This simple model will usually yield a high level of explanatory power in statistical terms.

The "unconstrained" gravity model in the previous paragraph provides no guarantee that the columns and rows in Table 14.2 will add up properly to the column and row totals. There are two types of constraints that must be satisfied simultaneously. First, the total number of trips with zone i as origin must be equal to the sum across destinations of the trips with zone i as origin. In other words, the numbers entered in the columns of Table 14.2 must add up to the column sums. Second, the total number of trips with zone j as destination must equal the sum across origins of trips with zone j as destination. The numbers entered in the rows of Table 14.2 must add to the row sums. Those who would forecast travel demand by origin and destination zone must make sure that their forecasts are consistent, and the doubly constrained gravity model provides that consistency. The doubly constrained gravity model is of the form

$$T_{ij} = ABO_i^{\alpha}D_j^{\beta}/d_{ij}^{\tau},$$

where A and B are balancing factors that ensure that the two constraints are satisfied. Computational procedures exist to find A and B, but these computations are not based on economic analysis and are too complex to be discussed here.

The gravity model is probably not part of the standard tool kit of economists in general, but it is an important method in urban and regional economics and in transportation planning. As Niedercorn and Bechdolt (1969) first demonstrated, the gravity model has a basis in conventional microeconomic theory. Consider the three variables in the model. First, the distance variable (d_{ij}) is a proxy for the cost of traveling from zone i to zone j, so this is just the price of the trip. Modern versions of the gravity model include careful measures of the price of the trip, which includes both money and time. Also, the more sophisticated models make the price of the trip a function of the amount of traffic that uses each particular route to capture the cost of traffic congestion. Second, the total number of trips with zone j as destination (D_j) is a measure of the "attractiveness" of that destination. Niedercorn and Bechdolt suggested that D_{ij} is a measure of the utility one derives from traveling to zone j. Finally, the total number of trips with zone i as origin (O_{ij}) measures the scale of the demand for T_{ij}. It plays a role that is similar to the total number of households in conventional market demand analysis.

There is one theoretical weakness in the gravity model interpreted as a microeconomic model of trip distribution. The only "price" term that appears in the gravity model is the price of travel from origin i to destination j. The price of traveling to any other destination is not included. You learned in basic microeconomic theory that the demand for a good is a function of its price, income, the nature of preferences, and *the prices of other goods*. The price of *every* other good is not relevant, but the prices of goods that are close substitutes and complements can be important influences on the demand for a particular good. Urban transportation researchers who use the gravity model have essentially ignored this problem, although some have formulated what they call an intervening opportunities model. Such a model modifies the demand for trips from i to j to account for opportunities that are encountered along the way from i to j. An item that ought to be on the future research agenda is an investigation of which *prices* of trips to *other* destinations are important enough to include in the model. One destination that immediately comes to mind in this context is the central business district.

Mode split analysis

Given that a certain number of trips are being taken from origin i to destination j, how are those trips divided among the modes of travel? One approach to this problem is to gather data on actual urban travel patterns as shown in Table 14.2, including the number of trips taken between each pair of origins and destinations by each mode of travel. One would then estimate a model of the proportion of trips made using each mode as a function of the features of each mode. For example, suppose that there are just two modes – private auto and bus. What proportion of trips is taken by private auto? One approach is to make this proportion a linear function of the difference in money costs and time costs between the private auto and the bus. The *differences* in costs are relevant because the choice under study is which mode to use, not whether to make the trip in the first place. In equation form,

$$P_{ija} = T_{ija}/T_{ij} = b_0 + b_1(t_a - t_b) + b_2(m_a - m_b),$$

where the notation is as follows:

P_{ija} = the proportion of trips from i to j on mode a (auto).
t_a and t_b = time costs of auto and bus, respectively, for trip from zone i to zone j.
m_a and m_b = money costs of auto and bus, respectively, for trip from zone i to zone j.

The signs of both b_1 and b_2 are negative because increases in time or money costs for a mode reduce the proportion of travelers who make that choice. The constant term in the equation, b_0, should be 0.50 because, if the two modes have equal time and money costs, the choice between them is arbitrary – like flipping a coin.

This linear model is easy to understand and to estimate, but it has one major difficulty. The dependent variable is a proportion that is, of course, a number that cannot be less than zero or greater than one. The linear model is not restricted to the zero-one interval, so it can produce forecasts that are negative numbers or numbers that are greater than one. The solution to this problem that has been adopted by transportation analysts is to specify a model of mode choice that is inherently restricted to the zero-one interval. The most popular version of such a model is called the logistic transformation, which is written

$$\ln[P_{ijk}/(1 - P_{ijk})] = \alpha_0 + \alpha_1(t_a - t_b) + \alpha_2(m_a - m_b).$$

The dependent variable is the natural logarithm of P_{ijk} divided by one minus P_{ijk}, and the model can be estimated as a linear function. How does this model restrict forecasts to the zero-one interval? To see this, first simplify the notation by writing

$$z = \alpha_0 + \alpha_1(t_a - t_b) + \alpha_2(m_a - m_b) \text{ and } P_{ijk} = P.$$

Now we have

$$\ln(P/1 - P) = z.$$

The next step is to convert to the exponential form, which is

$$P/1 - P = e^z,$$

where e is the base of the natural logarithms. This equation is solved for P as follows:

$$P = e^z(1 - P),$$
$$P + Pe^z = e^z, \text{ and}$$
$$P = e^z/(1 + e^z).$$

Clearly P can never be zero or less because e raised to any exponent z is a positive number. And P can never be one or more because e^z is divided by $1 + e^z$. The shape of the logistic function is shown in Figure 14.1. The proportion P approaches 1 as z goes to positive infinity, and P approaches zero as z goes to negative infinity. As shown in Figure 14.1, when $z = 0$, $P = 0.5$. To see this last result, set

$$P = 0.5 = e^z/(1 + e^z), \text{ so}$$
$$1 + e^z = 2e^z, \text{ and}$$
$$1 = e^z, \text{ so that}$$
$$z = 0.$$

The natural logarithm of e^z is z, and the natural log of 1 is zero.

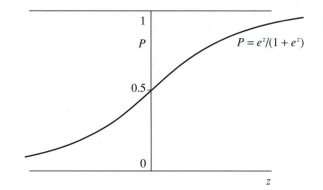

Figure 14.1   Logistic curve

Models of this type have been used extensively in transportation analysis, but actual applications of the model normally include more than just two independent variables. For example, empirical findings have demonstrated that it is important to divide the time cost into its walking, waiting, and actual travel time components. The proportion of people who choose the bus is strongly influenced by the amount of time spent walking to the bus stop, and by the amount of time spent waiting for the bus to arrive and waiting to transfer from one bus to another. The studies show clearly that urban commuters are willing to pay more if the bus can be made more convenient by cutting down on walking and waiting time.

Route choice analysis and the value of time

The final step in the analysis of urban travel demand is to model the choice of route, given that a particular mode has been chosen. (Do you know the way from i to j?) In the model of mode choice discussed above it was assumed implicitly that there was only one route for each mode. The measures of time and money cost are taken from that one route. This procedure is accurate also if alternative routes for the same mode have identical costs. This is often a reasonable assumption. However, there are situations in which the routes that might be chosen have quite different time and money costs. For example, in some places auto drivers have a choice of using a tollway or a free road. The tollway has a higher money cost and, because of the toll, will usually enable the traveler to save some time compared to the free road. In other instances bus riders may have a choice of an express bus with a higher fare that will drive on a limited-access highway versus the usual bus service on city streets with a lower fare. It is important for urban transportation policy to know how commuters make these choices.

Consider the choice of tollway versus free road. The same sort of logistic transformation model can be used in this situation, or

$$\ln(P_i/P_f) = \beta_0 + \beta_1(t_i - t_f) + \beta_2(m_i - m_f),$$

where P_i is the proportion taking the tollway and P_f is the proportion taking the free road. The signs of β_1 and β_2 are negative in this model as well because increases in the time or money cost of a route will reduce the proportion of people who choose it.

A model of route choice has the usual roles of explaining and forecasting the choice of route, but it also has another very important implication. Improvements in the transportation system are of benefit to people chiefly because of time saved. People are willing to pay money to save time in their urban travel, but how much are they willing to pay? If this willingness to pay were known, then benefits expressed in monetary terms can be compared to construction and land costs. The model for route choice does indeed provide an estimate of the money value of travel time saved. Consider variations in the time and money cost differences in the model that leave the proportion who choose the tollway *constant*. In equation form

$$\Delta\ln(P_i/P_f) = 0 = \beta_1\Delta(t_i - t_f) + \beta_2\Delta(m_i - m_f).$$

This equation says that the combinations of changes in time and money cost differences leave the commuters as a group indifferent to those combinations because the proportion who choose the tollway does not change. This equation can be rewritten as the value of a reduction in travel time, or

$$-\Delta(m_i - m_f)/\Delta(t_i - t_f) = \beta_1/\beta_2,$$

which is a number greater than zero. The ratio of coefficients β_1/β_2 equals the value of a reduction in travel time because it is negative one times the change in money cost that just compensates for a reduction in travel time. If $\Delta(t_i - t_f)$ is a negative number, then $\Delta(m_i - m_f)$ must be a positive number to keep constant the proportion who choose the tollway – hence the multiplication by −1.

Studies of mode choice also produce estimates of the value of travel time saved because mode choice studies also produce the coefficients on time and money cost differences. However, the studies of route choice provide a cleaner look at the value of time saved because mode choice can be influenced by the features of modes of travel that are not easy to measure and include in the model. The choice of private auto versus bus involves the fact that the bus can be crowded with other people who are noisy. On the other hand, the traveler does not have to drive the bus. The choice of route for the same mode is not complicated by such factors.

A very large number of studies have produced estimates of the value of travel time saved. A book by Bruzelius (1979) provides a survey of some of those studies. The value of travel time saved for the trip to work has been estimated to be 20% to 100% of the after-tax wage rate of the commuter. The average of these estimates is approximately 50% of the after-tax wage. However, the studies suggest that the value of commuting time saved does not rise proportionately with income. Also, there is evidence that commuters are willing to pay more to save time if their have longer commuting trips. In other words, the commuter who travels 45 minutes each way is willing to pay more to save 10 minutes than is the commuter who travels 30 minutes each way. This finding is consistent with the usual hypothesis in microeconomics of a declining marginal utility of a good, which is leisure time (or sleeping time) in this case. A longer commute means less time for leisure, and therefore a higher value for additional leisure.

Concentration of demand in peak periods

The discussion of urban travel demand concludes with a more detailed consideration of peak-load demand. As emphasized in section A, the demand for urban travel is greatest in the morning and afternoon rush hours because most work trips occur during these times. Trips to school also peak during these times, but other types of trips (such as shopping, delivery, and trucking for freight), do not have peak demand periods that are as pronounced. Traffic in urban areas on weekday mornings normally starts to build between 6 a.m. and 7 a.m. and peaks between 8 a.m. and 9 a.m. Traffic drops off sharply after that because few workers have a starting time later than 9 a.m. The afternoon peak period starts building between 3 p.m. and 4 p.m., reaches the peak around 5 p.m., and drops off sharply as commuters reach their homes.

It was also noted in the introduction to this chapter that in recent decades the total amount of travel, especially by auto, has grown much more rapidly than has the road and highway system. One implication of this growth in demand is that the "rush hour" has become longer. It is clear that some people choose to leave for work early, and in some cases employers have altered their schedules to permit employees to try to "beat the traffic." Hill et al. (1973) showed that urban areas in the US. with lower highway capacities compared to traffic volumes have longer rush hours. Also, there is evidence that improvements in the urban transportation system lead to a shortening of the rush hour. For example, Sherret (1975) showed that the opening of a mass transit line in the San Francisco diverted 8,750 auto trips to transit during the rush hour, but that additional auto trips were taken during the rush hour so that peak-period traffic levels declined very little. It is clear that a model of urban travel demand should include the fact that, for at least some people, the time of travel is flexible to some degree.

Two types of models have been developed to address the issue of flexible travel times. The older type of model is a set of conventional demand functions, with a demand function specified for each time period during the day. Suppose the task is to model the demand for travel between origin zone i and destination zone j. The model might break the day into six periods as follows:

- early portion of morning rush hour (6 a.m. to 7:30 a.m.);
- peak period of morning rush hour (7:30 a.m. to 9 a.m.);
- middle of day (9 a.m. to 3 p.m.);
- early portion of afternoon rush hour (3 p.m. to 4 p.m.);
- peak of afternoon rush hour (4 p.m. to 6:30 p.m.); and
- evening to early morning (6:30 p.m. to 6 a.m.).

Each period has its own demand function in which travel during that period is a function of the price during that period and the prices in the adjacent periods. In equation form

$$T_{ijk} = f(P_k, P_{k-1}, P_{k+1}),$$

where the subscript k refers to the time period in question, P refers to the price of travel (time and money combined), and subscripts $k - 1$ and $k + 1$ refer to the time periods before and after time period k. The adjacent time periods are viewed as substitutes for the time period in question, so reducing the price in either time period will reduce T_{ijk}. For example, an improvement in a highway will reduce travel times during the peak of the rush hour, increase traffic during the rush hour, and reduce traffic during the adjacent periods. More empirical research is needed to determine the magnitudes of these "cross-price" effects, i.e., the cross-elasticities of demand.

The second approach has been developed more recently, and it makes the time of departure for the trip a continuous variable. This type of model is discussed extensively in the urban transportation economics textbook by Small (1992). The model is based on the assumption that a cost is imposed on a person who arrives at a time other than the "desired" time. Work begins at 9 a.m. Early arrival means that there is some time spent at work that is neither as productive as regular working hours nor as pleasurable as leisure time at home. This cost of early arrival is a function of the amount of time spent in this state of limbo. The penalty for early arrival at work may not be very much, but the penalty for late arrival can be sizable. The worker can lose pay and, ultimately, be fired for lateness. The model assumes that this penalty for lateness is also a function of how late one arrives. In some cases it is reasonable to suppose that there is a lump-sum penalty for being late at all, and a further penalty that depends upon the degree of lateness. *Schedule delay* is the general term that is used to refer to amount of time by which these early and late arrivals do not correspond to the desired time.

Here is the problem confronted by the commuter in the schedule delay model. The commuter knows the function that describes the cost of being early and being late. The commuter also knows that the time spent to make the trip to work will be shorter if he avoids the peak of the rush hour. He can decide to go early, reduce travel time, and arrive early. Or he can decide to go late, reduce travel time, and arrive late. He makes the choice of departure time based on a balancing of these two costs – the time cost of travel versus the cost of schedule delay. It would seem that more people decide to arrive at work early than choose to arrive late, so consider the choice of departure time for the early bird. The top half of Figure 14.2 shows the cost of the commuting trip as a function of departure time. The cost is converted into money by using the value of travel time as discussed above. The function labeled trip cost rises as departure time gets later because of peak-period traffic. The other curve in the top half of Figure 14.2 is labeled schedule delay cost, and this cost declines as departure time is later because a later departure time means less time spent at the workplace prior to the actual beginning of the workday. Of course, if departure time gets too late, then the worker is late for work. This case is not depicted on Figure 14.2.

The lower half of Figure 14.2 depicts the marginal cost and the marginal benefit for the early bird of increasing departure time by one minute. The marginal cost (*MC*) is the increase in travel time cost if one departs one minute later, and marginal benefit (*MB*) is the reduction in schedule delay cost from delaying departure by one minute. The commuter determines departure time by equating marginal cost and marginal benefit. Departure time *H* is the point at which the marginal cost of delaying departure is just equal to the marginal benefit of delaying departure. Shifts in the marginal cost or marginal benefit function will change the departure time. For example, suppose that new devices are installed to coordinate the timing of the traffic lights. This improvement will increase driving speed and therefore reduce the travel time costs. As an exercise, use the model in Figure 14.2 to show how the commuter depicted will now depart later. (Hint: Be careful to show that the marginal cost of delaying departure *declines*.)

D. The Supply of Transportation in Urban Areas

Trips taken by persons, as opposed to freight, are partly supplied by the very person who demands the trip. You supply the time needed to get to the desired destination. Private firms supply the auto and the gasoline that you use, and the government supplies the streets and highways (and traffic lights). There is a school of thought based on a famous article by Becker (1965) that argues that many, if not all, consumer goods have this feature. All goods and services require some time for their use, so all consumption decisions are also decisions regarding the allocation of time. This line of thinking leads

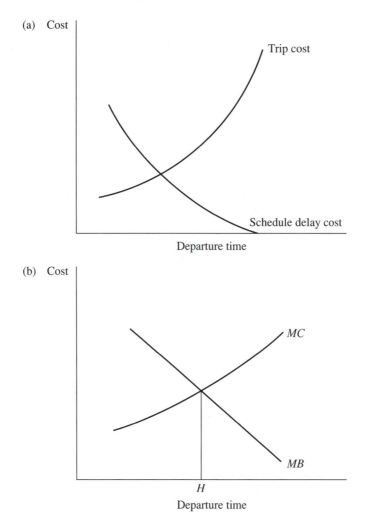

(a)   Cost

Trip cost

Schedule delay cost

Departure time

(b)   Cost

MC

MB

H

Departure time

Figure 14.2   Optimal departure time

to important insights into the demand for things such as dishwashers, frozen dinners, microwave ovens, and a host of other products that save time. In the case of urban transportation, the use of time by the traveler is central to the analysis. This discussion of supply begins with the short run, and then turns to the long run.

This section is devoted to the supply of travel by private vehicles on streets and highways. The following section examines public transportation.

Supply in the short run

As you know from basic microeconomics, the short run is the time period in which one of the basic inputs is fixed. In the case of auto and truck travel in urban areas, the fixed input is the capital stock supplied by the public sector – the streets and highways. The supply of travel in urban areas can be modeled using the production function that is a standard tool in economics. In order to characterize what happens on urban highways as a production function, it is necessary first to identify the output of the highway. Quantity of highway travel (Q) is measured by a physical distance (i.e., total miles traveled). On a given highway it is normal to record traffic volume V, traffic density D, and average speed S. Traffic volume is measured in vehicles per unit of time (i.e., vehicles per hour passing a particular point), while traffic density is the number of vehicles per unit of distance if a photograph were to be taken of the highway. For example, the photo shows that there were 50 cars per mile. Average speed is measured in units of distance per unit of time (e.g., miles per hour). In common usage V is normally referred to as flow. However, actually it is speed that measures the miles of travel produced per unit of time by an individual driver. This measure of output, miles per hour, is the same as any output measure in the sense that it is a quantity of output per unit of time. General Motors produced 4 million cars last year (4 million cars per year). You produced 35 miles of travel in an hour by driving at an average speed of 35 mph.

To establish the basic ideas, consider a road of fixed length and a time period of fixed duration. With no loss of generality choose the units of distance and time such that both are one (one mile and one hour). Assume that the highway is in a steady state over this unit of time, so that V, D and S are constant. It is helpful to imagine that the highway has only one lane and is a circle of one mile in circumference. Traffic density is the number of cars on the highway (i.e., the racetrack) at each point in time, so the total quantity of travel produced and consumed during one hour is

$$Q = DS = V.$$

Each car on the circular highway of unit length will pass a given point on the circle S times per hour; if $S = 35$ mph, then each car passes the "finish line" 35 times per hour. If there are 50 cars on the highway, then $35 \times 50 = 1{,}750$ cars pass the finish line each hour, and 1,750 miles are traveled per hour as well. The total quantity of travel Q is thus $DS = V$, which is the total number of vehicles which pass a given point on the circle each hour. This establishes the numerical identity between Q per unit of time and V. The assumption that the highway is a circle of unit length can be dropped. If a highway is in a steady state (with D, S, and V constant), then the $V = DS$ cars that pass a given point per hour are all different cars.

The key to converting this analysis into the conventional economics of production is to recognize that traffic density D is numerically equal to the time supplied by the driver and the vehicle, which is the variable input. Here it is assumed that the operating costs of the vehicle are a function of the amount of *time* the vehicle is in operation. The critical insight is that speed in the inverse of average variable cost *measured in units of time*. If speed is 35 mph, then the average variable cost measured in units of driver and vehicle time is 0.0286 hours per mile. Recall that the output of the highway is volume. Thus, average variable cost (AVC) in units of time is written

$$AVC = (1/S) = D/V.$$

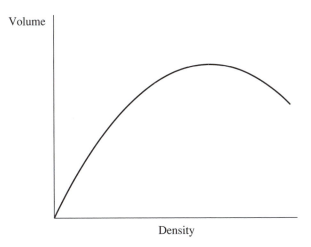

Figure 14.3   Fundamental diagram of traffic

Total variable costs (*VC*) in units of time are

$$VC = (AVC)V = D.$$

The total variable input measured in units of time is thus equal to traffic density. Go back to the example of the one-mile circular road with 50 cars each traveling at 35 mph. The variable cost of producing the 1,750 miles of travel in an hour is 50 hours of driver and vehicle time. This is the standard way to measure inputs – hours of labor and machine time. Variable cost can be converted to monetary units by using a value of driver time and the cost of operating a vehicle for an hour, but this conversion is not needed for the production function interpretation of the model. What is the shape of the short-run production function?

Highway engineers and other transportation researchers are familiar with the Fundamental Diagram of Traffic, which relates traffic volume and traffic density for a given highway facility. Figure 14.3 shows that the traffic volume increases with traffic density up to the capacity of the facility, and declines with further increases in density. The empirical relationship has been confirmed by numerous studies, one of which is discussed below. Given the definition of the variable input, the Fundamental Diagram of Traffic (Figure 14.3) can be interpreted as a short-run production function in which output is related to the variable input. As shown in Figure 14.4, the average and marginal production curves for the variable input can be derived from this short-run production function. The average product of the variable input (driver and vehicle time) is simply average speed: $S = V/D$. The marginal product of the variable input falls to zero at the density corresponding to the capacity of the highway, and is negative at higher densities.

The student of microeconomic theory learns this basic theory of production in the short run; as successive units of a variable input are added to a fixed input the marginal product of the variable input starts to decline at some point, and can possibly become negative if too much variable input is used. That student is also taught that no rational firm would

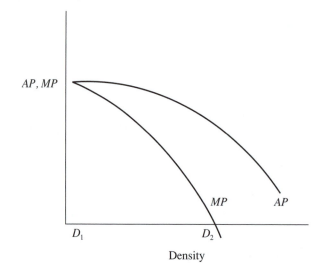

Figure 14.4   Average and marginal products of the variable input

hire units of the variable input with a negative marginal product. Those additional units of the variable input *reduce* total output. However, in the case of highway traffic, it is common to observe a highway operating in the region of negative marginal product. How is this possible? This situation arises because traffic flow is a classic example of a congestion externality in which there is no rational being present to prevent the addition of drivers and vehicles beyond the point at which marginal product is zero.

Traffic congestion is especially awful if the marginal product of the variable input is negative, but there is also the standard notion of traffic congestion. The normal idea of the traffic congestion externality corresponds to the portion of the short-run production function in which the average product of the variable input is declining and its marginal product is greater than zero. This portion of the short-run production function is shown in Figure 14.4 between traffic density levels D_1 and D_2. At low density levels (below D_1) the addition of more cars does not cause the average product (average speed) to fall, but beyond D_1 more cars on the highway will cause average speed to drop.

One study of traffic volume and density by Boardman and Lave estimated the short-run production function depicted in Figure 14.3 for a two-lane limited-access highway in the Washington, DC area on a day in 1968. Traffic volume is measured in vehicles in two lanes per hour, and density is vehicles per mile in the two lanes. The estimated function is

$$V = 2{,}882 + 21.73D - 0.052D^2,$$

and the three regression coefficients are all highly statistically significant. The point at which volume reached its maximum can be found by computing change in V with respect to D and setting the change equal to zero; i.e.,

$$\Delta V/\Delta D = 21.73 - 0.104D = 0.$$

The solution for D is 209, which means that traffic volume was at a maximum when traffic density was 104.5 vehicles per lane per mile. At $D = 209$, $V = 5,153$, or 2,576.5 vehicles per lane per hour. This empirical estimate of the maximum traffic volume per lane per hour is greater than the 2000 figure that is often used as a rule of thumb by traffic experts. Traffic density of 104.5 vehicles per mile means that each vehicle is allocated 50.5 feet of roadway. If the average car is 20 feet long, the cars are separated by about 1.5 car lengths (30 feet). Average speed can also be computed at the point of maximum traffic volume. Recall that $S = V/D$, so $S = 24.7$ mph. So there you have it. If traffic density on the expressway is so high that cars are separated by less then 30 feet, and if the average speed is less than 25 mph, then you are probably in the region of negative marginal product. You are now better informed. Does this information make you feel better when you are in a traffic jam? You are invited to take some perverse pleasure in announcing these facts to your companions in the auto.

Why does average speed fall as traffic density rises? Traffic engineers have complex mathematical theories of road traffic flow that explain this phenomenon. One of those theories is called the "follow the leader" model. In this model drivers react to events that happen in front of them so as to avoid accidents. For example, if a driver in fairly heavy traffic slows down slightly, the following driver will slow down by *slightly more* than the first. The third driver will slow down even more, and so on. Those of you who have driven on an expressway in a major urban area have probably experienced what is called a "rubber-necking" delay. Something worth observing, such as an accident on the other side of the highway, diverts the attention of drivers at some point. Drivers slow down slightly to look at the accident. Drivers in the chain of traffic overreact slightly to the driver in front, and at some point back in the chain of traffic, someone actually has to come to a complete stop. The impact of a rubber-necking delay on average speed is greater the higher is the density of traffic.

Another theory of road traffic flow is based on the safety rules that drivers are taught in driver's education. One is taught that the safe interval between cars on the expressway is larger at higher speeds. One fairly conservative rule of thumb is that the safe interval is one car length for each 10 mph. If people are following this rule, then an increase in traffic density will reduce the interval between cars and cause speed to drop. Normal drivers are not like racing drivers (we hope); they will not drive at the speed limit in "bumper-to-bumper" traffic conditions.

In standard microeconomic theory the short-run production function is converted into a set of short-run cost curves, and this conversion can be done for highway traffic volume as well. Recall that average variable cost, in terms of time, is the inverse of average speed, which in turn is the average product of the variable input. Therefore the average variable cost curve can be found as

$AVC = (1/S) = (1/\text{average product})$,

and this can be plotted as a function of output (traffic volume). This cost curve is shown in Figure 14.5. At low levels of traffic volume, average speed is constant (at the speed limit, presumably) and average cost is constant. As traffic volume rises, average speed falls and average cost rises. Marginal cost in the short run is defined as the change in total cost as output increases by one unit, or

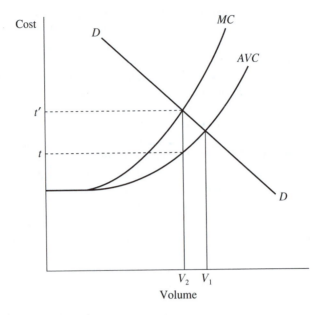

Figure 14.5   Cost and traffic volume

$MC = \Delta VC/\Delta V = \Delta(AVC \times V)/\Delta V.$

This marginal change consists of two parts, so that

$MC = (AVC)\Delta V/\Delta V + V(\Delta AVC/\Delta V) = AVC + V(\Delta AVC/\Delta V).$

This is a crucial result; it says that the marginal cost of output (traffic volume) is equal to average variable cost *plus* the change in average cost with respect to traffic volume times the traffic volume. Average variable cost rises as traffic volume rises, and this increase in cost (arising from the drop in speed) is multiplied by the total traffic volume. This term is the difference between *AVC* and *MC*, or

$MC - AVC = V(\Delta AVC/\Delta V).$

The marginal cost curve is also plotted on Figure 14.5.

Now consider the external cost involved in traffic congestion. An external cost involves a cost that is imposed directly on others by, in this case, an individual traveler. An increase in traffic volume has a cost equal to the marginal cost shown above, but the individual traveler does not pay all of that cost. In fact, the individual traveler makes the trip at average variable cost, i.e. at the inverse of average speed. That is the cost that the traveler sees, and is the price that the traveler uses to make the decision whether to travel on that highway at that time. The external cost is therefore the difference between marginal cost and average variable cost, or

External cost = $V(\Delta AVC/\Delta V).$

The external cost is the increase in cost imposed on each traveler ($\Delta AVC/\Delta V$) times the number of travelers (V).

Pricing in the short run

The demand for trips on the highway during the time period in question is also shown on Figure 14.5 as *DD*. Quantity demanded is expressed as a function of the cost of the trip that must be borne by the individual traveler, and that cost is expressed in units of time. Left to their own devices, travelers as a group will generate a traffic volume of V_1, where the demand curve intersects the average variable cost curve. At this point the marginal benefit of the trip, as measured by the height of the demand curve at V_1, is just equal to the cost borne by the last traveler, which is *AVC* at volume V_1.

You can see immediately that V_1 is an inefficient level of output because the *marginal cost* of the last unit of output exceeds its marginal benefit (*MB*). In fact, the marginal cost exceeds the marginal benefit by the size of the external cost, or

$$MC - MB = MC - AVC = V(\Delta AVC/\Delta V).$$

The efficient level of output in Figure 14.5 is V_2, where the marginal benefit of the output equals the marginal cost, which includes the externality. It is pretty obvious that the street and highway systems in urban areas are being used in this inefficient manner during the morning and afternoon rush hours. Is anything being done to cut back on traffic and use the system efficiently? The short answer is that virtually nothing is being done at this time. However, for many years urban economists have advocated the use of tolls to cut back on traffic congestion. A toll equal to the external cost *at efficient traffic volume* V_2 in Figure 14.5 would make the cost borne by the marginal traveler equal to true marginal cost of his trip. This toll is shown as amount *tt'*, which is expressed in units of time. An actual toll would be collected as money, so the units of time have to be converted to monetary units. Toll *tt'* is an efficient toll provided that the travelers who are induced not to use the highway at the time in question do *not* create more traffic congestion at some other location, and provided that the collection of the toll can be accomplished costlessly.

Consider first the actual collection of tolls. Conventional toll booths create traffic jams of their own, so this method cannot be used. However, methods do exist that can probably be made to work well on a large scale. One system is called automatic vehicle identification (AVI), in which each vehicle carries an electronic transponder. An electronic transponder is a device that automatically transmits an identifying signal when it receives a signal from a device buried in the highway. Wire loops are buried in the pavement, and the transponder is activated and sends out the signal when the car passes over the wire loop. The signal is sent to a central computer that computes the appropriate toll and prints up a bill to be sent out every month. The computer knows the traffic volume and density at the time the car's transponder sent out its signal, so the toll can be computed correctly. The system will work only if the drivers do not tamper with the transponder. Enforcement of the system can be done with the use of closed circuit television cameras. As Downs (2004) discusses, the effectiveness of both the electronic transponder system and the closed circuit TV cameras has been demonstrated in Hong

Kong. The imposition of congestion tolls without slowing the traffic is now technically feasible at some scale. Furthermore, it appears that the cost of the system itself is relatively modest compared to the gains in efficiency that are possible. Here is an example of the need for technology leading to its creation. In this case the need is for a method for low-cost monitoring of the use of a congestible public facility.

The more serious difficulty with the proposal for congestion tolls is the distinct possibility that not all (or most) of the urban street and highway system will be subjected to tolls. It may be relatively easy to impose a high-tech toll system on a few expressways, but expansion of the system to the bulk of the streets and secondary highways presents an enormous task that may prove to be too difficult and costly. At this point it is technically possible, through the use of global positioning systems (GPS) to monitor the position of every car, but the cost may be prohibitive. Second, there is a strong tradition of free access to local streets and highways. In fact, at the moment it is against the law to charge tolls on the interstate highway system. Some of the major urban expressways are part of the interstate highway system, so that law will have to be changed. More importantly, it is likely that the public will not stand for the imposition of tolls on local streets or secondary highways that provide immediate access to homes and businesses. What does all of this mean for congestion toll policy?

Suppose that only a portion of the urban highway network can be subjected to congestion tolls because of technical complexity and/or the tradition of free access to roads. Congestion toll policy must now be made under the constraint that some of the highway system cannot have a toll imposed. Does this constraint on policy mean that there are no gains to be made from a congestion pricing scheme? The answer to this question is "no," but the optimal congestion pricing scheme can be very different compared to the case in which tolls can be imposed on the entire highway system. The basic result is that, if the drivers view the tollway and the free road as substitutes, traffic will be diverted to the free road. If this traffic diversion causes congestion on the free road, then the optimal toll on the tollway is lower than the simple textbook toll shown in Figure 14.5. Indeed, in some cases the optimal toll on the tollway is far lower than the toll shown in Figure 14.5.

The problem is depicted in Figure 14.6, which displays the demand and short-run cost functions for two highways. These two highways are considered to be substitutes by the rush-hour commuters. In the initial situation there is no toll on either highway, and initial traffic volumes are V_t and V_f. Both highways are being used inefficiently because the marginal cost of the last unit of traffic volume exceeds its marginal benefit as measured by the height of the demand curve at that volume. The efficient traffic volumes are V_t^* and V_f^*, respectively, because these are the volumes at which marginal benefit equals marginal cost. Now suppose that a toll can be imposed on the tollway, but that the free road cannot have a toll. The imposition of the toll reduces volume on the tollway by two mechanisms. Some of those who no longer choose to travel on the tollway at this time do not travel at all or shift their trips to times during which the highways are not congested. This is the desired result. But the increase in the price of trips on the tollway also shifts outward the demand for trips on the free road. Traffic volume on the free road increases, which is a movement *away* from the efficient volume on this route and not the desired result. If *no* former tollway users switch to the free road (i.e., the two roads are not substitutes), then the toll can be set at the level that will cause volume on the tollway to be V_t^*. However, those travelers who *do* switch to the free road are causing additional

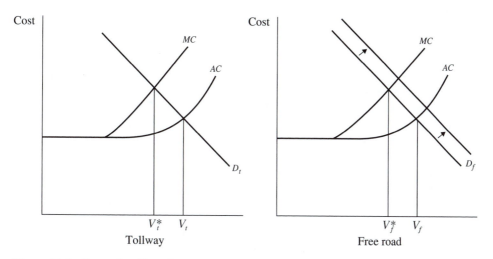

Cost   Cost

Figure 14.6 Cost and traffic volume: two routes

traffic congestion in the process, and this added congestion must be taken into account in setting the toll. The optimum toll is now less than the toll that pushes traffic volume on the tollway back to V_t^*.

How important is this problem of traffic diversion to substitute routes? First, it is known that some commuters will shift routes rather quickly. Commuters can be counted on to respond to incentives. There are no empirical studies of the exact situation depicted in Figure 14.6, but McDonald (1995) provided some fairly realistic numerical examples. One example sets up two routes with identical cost functions. The routes are assumed to be perfect substitutes. If optimum tolls can be imposed on both routes, that toll would be 23.4 cents per mile per vehicle. This is a fairly typical estimate of the optimum congestion toll on urban highways; if the commuter travels 10 miles each way for 240 days per year, the annual toll would be $1,123.20. However, if a toll can be imposed on only one route, the computations show that the optimum level for this toll is only 6.2 cents per mile. The inability to cover half the system with tolls makes a very large difference in the size of the congestion toll that should be imposed.

There is a growing interest around the world in implementing congestion tolls in some form. Congestion pricing methods can be categorized as:

1 city-center congestion pricing;
2 toll rings;
3 single facility congestion pricing; and
4 area-wide congestion pricing.

City-center congestion pricing has pioneered in Singapore in 1975, and their system for 23 years used a paper windshield sticker that permits a vehicle to enter the city center. An electronic "smart card" system was introduced in 1998. A fee for entering the restricted zone applies from 7:30 a.m. to 6:30 p.m., and the highest fee is charged for entry between 8 a.m. and 9 a.m. The amount of traffic entering the restricted zone dropped by 44% after the scheme was put into operation in 1975. However, traffic congestion was created just outside the zone.

The biggest news in recent years is the imposition in 2003 of city center congestion pricing in London. Those who wish to drive in Central London between the hours of 7 a.m. and 6:30 p.m. must pay a fee of £5. A driver who has paid the fee can enter and leave the zone as many times as desired on a given day. Vehicles are monitored by 230 cameras, and violators are fined £80 (£40 if payment is prompt). Residents of the zone receive a 90% discount. Taxis, motorcycles, and buses are exempt from the fee. The congestion fee has reduced the level of traffic in Central London by 15% to 20%, and cars are able to move about 38% faster than before (from 8 to 11 miles per hour). One can consult the Transport for London web site for the details of the system.

Toll ring systems exist in three cities in Norway (Bergen, Oslo, and Trondheim). These tolls are used primarily to raise revenue to pay for transportation facilities and do not vary by time day. Economists in Norway are studying alternative road pricing schemes.

It is fair to say that congestion tolls are not about to be imposed in the United States. However, the US Federal Highway Administration funded a small number of demonstration projects to test the viability of congestion tolls in carefully controlled circumstances. In one of those projects a tollway was inserted between the opposing sets of lanes of State Route 91, a freeway in southern California. State Route 91 originally had four lanes in each direction, and was heavily congested. The two lanes inserted in each direction and opened in 1995 were built by a private firm and financed by $134 million in bonds. The State of California subsequently purchased the lanes from the private firm and took over operating them. The toll varies by time of day and is assessed via a transponder mounted on the dashboard of the vehicle. While the new lanes have proven to be popular with commuters during rush hour, this is a perfect example of the problem discussed above in which the tollway and free road are substitutes. Also, since 1996 a high-occupancy lane on an expressway in San Diego has been available for use by low occupancy vehicles (that is, one person) if a permit is purchased. This fee is, in effect, a peak-period toll because ther is little or no incentive to buy a permit if one's use of the expressway does not occur in the peak periods. Public acceptance of both California projects has been good, probably because paying the toll can be seen as paying for access to additional road capacity. Proposals for other peak-period tolls on other individual facilities have been defeated by public opposition (in Seattle and San Francisco, for example).

Systems for area-wide congestion pricing have been under intensive study in the Netherlands and in London, but not implemented. Instead the decision in London was to impose the central city congestion toll. Various forms of area-wide pricing are also being studied in Osaka, Japan. The article by McDonald (2004) provides more information on road pricing and is an introduction to the more technical articles on traffic congestion and road pricing in that issue of *Review of Network Economics*.

In the absence of congestion tolls, are there any other policy measures that can be used to reduce the inefficiency of traffic congestion in the short run; i.e., without making major changes in the spatial patterns of households and firms in the urban area? One suggestion is to use gasoline taxes because such a tax targets road use pretty well. However, the problem of traffic congestion is one of road use at particular times and in particular places. A gasoline tax is a pretty blunt instrument that will tax the guy who works the night shift just as much as it taxes the rush-hour commuter. It would also tax non-work trips that already tend to avoid the rush hours to some extent. Most importantly, the gasoline tax would not encourage people to shift their trips to times of day when congestion is less. Many advocates of a higher gas tax believe that we should cut back on our use of petroleum in general because we rely to a considerable degree on oil imports. Their arguments are about the balance-of-payments problem and national security, and cannot be evaluated here.

Another suggestion is to impose taxes on parking in the central business district. The tax would be highest on those who arrive during the morning rush hour. The tax could thus be targeted to at least some of the people who are causing the traffic congestion problem, and it would encourage them to shift to public transit or car pools. The CBD parking tax has two relatively serious disadvantages, however. First of all, it misses the travelers who contribute to traffic congestion but do not have the CBD as their destination. In the dispersed urban area of today, that is a lot of people. Second, the parking tax does not tax the commuter according to the number of miles he drives on the congested highway. Everyone who shows up at the parking garage between 7:30 a.m. and 9:30 a.m. and leaves between 3:30 p.m. and 6 p.m. would pay the same tax. Despite these objections, the CBD parking tax has some potential to have an impact on the traffic congestion problem.

Yet another suggestion is to draw people out of their cars by subsidizing public transit. A related suggestion is to subsidize companies to set up car pools. The idea is to reduce the cost of alternative methods of getting to work. Public transportation is discussed below, but for now it is important to realize that public transit fares are already heavily subsidized by federal, state, and local governments. Transit agencies generally do not cover their all of their variable costs out of the fare box, and fixed (capital) costs are covered by general tax revenues. It is not clear how much further the general public is willing to subsidize public transportation. Programs to create car pools (or van pools) have met with some success. A study by Cervero (1989) shows that car poolers tend to be workers with lower level jobs who have longer commutes and quite regular work schedules. Workers who have more irregular schedules and travel patterns are not good candidates for car-pooling. One aspect of the federal Intermodal Surface Transportation Efficiency Act (ISTEA) of 1991 is to attempt to get large employers to increase the proportion of their workers who use car pools. However, the experiments along these lines have so far met with limited success. So, when all has been said and done, it is fair to say that commuters have little choice except to grimace and bear it and listen to the car radio.

Supply in the long run

In the long run the capital input embodied in the streets and highways is variable. The fact that the era of highway building of the 1950s and 1960s has reshaped urban areas has already been discussed. At this point the prospects for additions to the highway systems of most urban areas are few, but not zero. The emphasis in this chapter clearly is on the problem of traffic congestion and making more efficient use of our existing urban highway systems. This is a proper emphasis at this time, but there are still some possibilities for improvements in urban highways that can be of considerable benefit to the public.

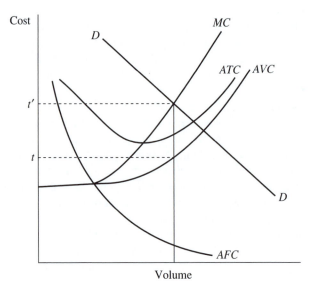

Figure 14.7   Cost and traffic volume

The analysis of highway improvements makes use of all of the concepts discussed so far in this chapter – models of demand, the value of reductions in travel time, production and cost functions under conditions of congestion, and pricing analysis.

Let us begin with a problem that is easy to study in theoretical terms. Suppose we have a highway with the same short-run cost curves as in Figure 14.5, marginal cost and average variable cost. To this set of cost curves we shall add the average *fixed* cost curve and the average *total* cost curve. Using a value of time, all costs are now stated in money terms rather than in terms of commuters' time. This complete set of short-run cost curves is shown in Figure 14.7. The new idea is the average fixed cost, but this is just the fixed cost divided by the volume of traffic. The fixed cost is the cost of the land and capital embodied in the highway for the time period that is being depicted – for example, one hour. What is the cost per hour of the land and capital embodied in the highway? Suppose the highway cost $100 million and the rate of interest is 6%. This means that the annual cost of the land and capital is $6 million. There are 8,760 hours in a year, so the cost of land and capital for one hour in this example is $685. Here we have ignored the cost of maintenance to keep the highway functioning. The fixed cost per hour should also include the annual maintenance cost divided by 8,760. Also, if the highway depreciates over time, then the hourly cost of capital should include a small amount to cover the eventual replacement of the facility. All of these ideas are built into the average fixed cost curve on Figure 14.7. The average total cost is simply the sum of average fixed cost and average variable cost.

Now consider the efficient congestion toll that should be imposed in Figure 14.7. Given demand curve *DD*, that toll is amount *tt'* as before. An interesting comparison to make is between the congestion toll and average fixed cost. As depicted in Figure 14.7, the congestion toll *tt'* exceeds the average fixed cost because the toll is larger than the vertical difference between average total cost and average variable cost. In other words,

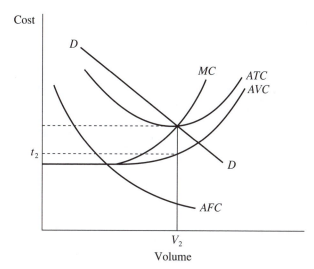

Figure 14.8   Congestion toll equals average fixed cost

the toll revenue collected over the time period exceeds the cost of the land and capital embodied in the highway. What is the significance of this outcome?

Suppose for the moment that demand curve DD is the demand curve for *every* time period during the year. Obviously this is a silly assumption because it ignores the fact that demand peaks during the rush hour, but play along for now. Given this assumption, toll revenues in excess of fixed costs are being collected in every time period. This would appear to be a signal that the highway should be expanded. An expansion of the highway is shown in Figure 14.8. This expansion is carefully designed so that the congestion toll revenue that is collected in each time period is just equal to the fixed cost. This means that the price that each commuter pays (average variable cost plus toll) is exactly equal to the average total cost of each trip. In Figure 14.8 all of this happens at traffic volume V_2, where the congestion toll of t_2 just equals the average fixed cost. Note that the expanded highway has been designed so that traffic volume V_2 coincides with the *minimum* average total cost that is possible for that facility. We see that efficient use of this particular highway (i.e., price equals marginal cost) involves setting a congestion toll equal to average fixed cost.

Figure 14.8 depicts a nice result for efficiency in the short run, but suppose further that the facility that was built is also the highway that provides for the minimum average cost in the *long run* at traffic volume V_2. In other words, suppose that the long-run average cost curve passes through the minimum point of the short-run average total cost curve. This can happen only if the long-run average cost curve is tangent to the short-run average total cost curve at volume V_2 and is therefore a horizontal line. Figure 14.9 depicts the situation. (Consider the alternative. If long-run average cost is not a horizontal line, then it exceeds short-run average total cost in some range. This is a contradiction. Long-run average cost is, by definition, the minimum average cost for each level of output.)

A horizontal long-run average cost curve means that the production of trips is subject to *constant long-run marginal cost*. Figure 14.9 therefore depicts a situation in which the

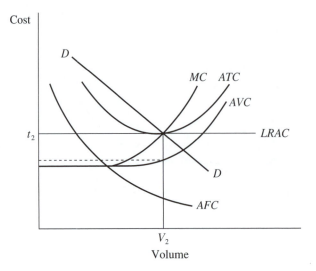

Figure 14.9   Optimum congestion toll in the long run

price paid by commuters is equal to long-run marginal cost as well as short-run marginal cost. The long-run marginal cost of a trip equals its marginal benefit, which is the usual condition for the optimal allocation of resources. Now we have another really nice result. If the production of trips is subject to constant marginal and average cost in the long run, then the efficient highway facility in the long run will be the one where the collection of congestion tolls just equals the cost of the land and capital embodied in the highway. The commuters just pay for their highway through the congestion toll! Is that not nice of them? As is discussed below, the real world is far more complex than the world depicted in Figure 14.9, but the general idea that proper congestion tolls could pay for the highways is intriguing.

Now let us turn to a more realistic view of highway construction projects. An important category of highway improvements is the addition of a link in the highway system. This kind of project is usually very expensive because it involves the acquisition of land and the construction of bridges and underpasses. Under what conditions do the benefits of such a project exceed the costs? Furthermore, how large should the project be? Consider Figure 14.10, which depicts the short-run and long-run cost curves for a particular highway facility. The short-run cost curves are now stated in money terms, but they are the same in essence as those depicted in Figure 14.5. The long-run average cost curve includes the costs that are variable in the short run *and* the capital costs of the highway scaled down to the time period under analysis. The time period under consideration in Figure 14.10 is *one hour* during the peak demand period of a typical weekday. Therefore, the capital cost of the highway is the cost of that highway for one hour out of its total lifetime.

In Figure 14.10, and in the real world, investment in a highway is lumpy. A limited number of investment options exists. It does not make sense to build a limited-access highway with only one lane in each direction, so that option is not depicted. Figure 14.10 depicts three options; a highway with two, three, or four lanes in each direction. Each of

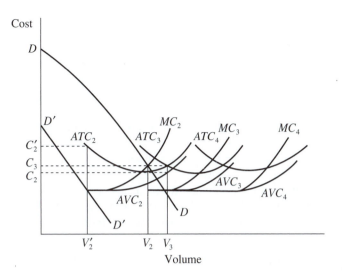

Figure 14.10   Cost and traffic volume: two lanes, three lanes, and four lanes

these three options has a set of short-run cost curves that includes the short-run average total cost curve. This average total cost includes the fixed cost of land and highway capital, but the average fixed cost curves have been omitted to reduce the clutter on the diagram. Average variable cost and marginal cost are the same concepts as in Figure 14.7. The long-run average cost curve consists of portions of the three short-run average total costs curves as shown. It is further assumed that the minimum points on each short-run average total cost curve occur at the same level of cost.

Now consider the investment decision. Demand curve DD shows the marginal benefits of traffic volume, and the problem is to decide whether to build a highway link and, if the decision is to build, how many lanes to construct. Let us first suppose the ideal world in which congestion tolls can be imposed on all relevant portions of the system. If the two-lane tollway were to be constructed, efficient traffic volume for this facility would be V_2, and the average total cost would be C_2. Should a facility of at least this size be con-structed? Clearly the answer is "yes" because the total benefit of the output is the area under the demand curve up to volume V_2 and the total cost is the area equal to V_2 times C_2. There is another category of benefits that may exist as well. It is possible that the construction of the project will cause a reduction in traffic congestion on other parts of the street and highway system. Any reduction in variable costs experienced by com-muters who still use those other parts of the system will count as benefits of the project in question.

Compare the result with demand curve DD in Figure 14.10 to the case if the demand curve instead is $D'D'$. In this case traffic volume V_2' is generated at an average cost of C_2'. Suppose that, because traffic volume V_2' is rather low, the benefits to commuters who continue to use the other parts of the system are negligible. The total cost of these trips (V_2') exceeds the total benefits because the area under the demand curve up to V_2' is less than the total cost (C_2' times V_2'). No highway link should be built in this case.

Return to demand curve DD. The next question is whether the project should be three lanes instead of two. The question is now whether the *additional* benefits of the third lane exceed the additional costs. If the project has three lanes, then traffic volume V_3 is generated at average total cost of C_3. Traffic volume increases from V_2 to V_3. In this particular case no congestion toll is needed because, at volume V_3, no traffic congestion exists. The additional benefits created by the third lane consist of the area under the demand curve between V_2 and V_3, and any added benefits to commuters who continue to use other routes. However, the total cost of producing traffic volume V_3 is now V_3 times C_3. Average total cost of trips has increased from C_2 to C_3 because the three-lane facility will be rather underutilized with demand curve DD. The addition to total cost is the increase in average total cost (C_3 minus C_2) times traffic volume V_3. The benefit of the additional traffic volume is the area under the demand curve from V_2 to V_3. The diagram has been drawn so that the *addition* to total costs exceeds the addition to benefits, and the third lane should be rejected. In this particular case the slight over-utilization of the two-lane highway is better than the underutilization of the three-lane highway. Note, however, that if the option to build the two-lane highway did not exist, the total benefits of building the three-lane highway (area under the demand curve up to V_3) exceed total costs (C_3 times V_3) and the three-lane project would be accepted. Still, the better choice is the two-lane highway.

The cost–benefit of the expansion of the highway from two to three lanes is usually done in another manner. The benefit side includes the value of the additional trips as above, but benefits also include the reduction in the cost of the trips taken by the original V_2 travelers. This benefit amounts to V_2 times the drop in the price paid by these drivers ($MC_2 - MC_3$ at volume V_2). Any benefits arising from reductions in traffic congestion on other routes would be added in as well. These benefits are then compared to the capital cost of the third lane scaled to the appropriate time period *plus* the loss of congestion toll revenue. The original V_2 drivers gain the toll revenue as part of the reduction in the price that they pay, and the public sector loses the toll revenue. The results of this computation are, of course, identical to the previous computation.

The analysis can be done over assuming that a congestion toll cannot be imposed. As in Figure 14.5, equilibrium traffic volume is set where the demand curve intersects the average variable cost curve. The computations of total benefits and costs then proceed as before. In this case the traffic volume with the two-lane project is somewhat greater and average total costs are a bit higher. The total benefits of the two-lane project still exceed total costs. As an exercise, show these points on Figure 14.10. Traffic volume with the three-lane project does not change because no toll was imposed under a tollway regime. Therefore, the addition of the third lane adds less to equilibrium traffic volume than it would under a tollway regime. It is still true that the benefits of the added trips are less than the addition to cost, so the third lane is rejected. You complete the exercise by demonstrating this conclusion on Figure 14.10.

One final problem needs to be addressed. How do we proceed to perform the cost–benefit study in the presence of peak and off-peak demands? Return to Figure 14.10 and suppose that demand curve DD represents peak demand and that $D'D'$ is off-peak demand. It was shown that the benefits of the two-lane highway link exceed costs during the peak periods, but that costs of this project exceed benefits during the off-peak times. Suppose that there are six hours of peak demand and 18 hours of off-peak demand during each day. The solution to the problem is simply to compute the sum of the 24 net benefit (i.e. benefit minus cost) figures. The positive net benefits with demand curve DD count 6 times, and the negative net benefits with demand curve $D'D'$ count 18 times. Given the situation depicted in Figure 14.10, the positive net benefits during the rush hours actually do exceed the negative net benefits generated at other times of day. However, it is quite possible that the evaluation of a project such as that depicted in Figure 14.10 could go the other way.

Two further points should be emphasized. The first point is that no congestion toll should be imposed in the off-peak periods because no congestion is generated at these times. It was previously emphasized that congestion tolls should vary with traffic conditions, and Figure 14.10 provides a simple example of this rule. Secondly, we should ask whether the congestion tolls collected during the peak periods are sufficient to pay for the land and capital embodied in the two-lane highway. In this case clearly those tolls do not cover the fixed costs. The congestion tolls roughly cover the fixed costs incurred during the peak demand periods, but the absence of congestion tolls in the off-peak periods means that toll revenue will fall short of total fixed costs.

E. Mass Transportation

Mass transportation is supplied using two basic technologies – internal combustion vehicles that operate on the streets and highways (i.e., buses), and electric vehicles that operate on fixed rail lines (e.g., commuter trains and subways). Both types of systems operate under conditions of economies of scale. However, because of those economies of scale, it is necessary to consider the costs of assembling the passengers at the points where they can be picked up and the costs of distributing the passengers to their final destinations after they leave the vehicles. The trip on mass transit is broken down into three parts, which are:

- the collection phase;
- the line-haul trip; and
- the distribution phase.

This basic framework is used to discuss each of the two mass transportation technologies.

Average costs of a complete trip on rail rapid transit were studied in detail by Meyer, Kain and Wohl (1965) in their important book *The Urban Transportation Problem*. The title of the book refers to the fact that the real problem faced by urban transportation planners stems from the decentralization of urban areas. In essence, the problem is transporting workers to jobs to dispersed locations in the suburbs. Further, the problem is particularly acute for black and Hispanic workers who live in the central city, and do not have the opportunity to reside in the suburbs. The problem is called "reverse commuting." After all those years this book is still important and quite relevant, even if the empirical evidence in the book is dated. But just why is reverse commuting such a problem?

Rail rapid transit systems are very good for moving large numbers of commuters to work in the CBD. Most of the urban areas listed in Table 14.1 that are the biggest users of rail rapid transit are ones with large numbers of jobs in a fairly small CBD – New York, Chicago, Philadelphia, and Boston. These cities were developed to a significant extent with rail rapid transit systems already in place. There are very large economies of scale in the line-haul portion of the trip, and the CBD is the destination for a very large number of commuters. Rail rapid transit is even more efficient if the residential areas that are served have high population densities, and in New York, Chicago, Philadelphia and Boston. A city with high population density can support several rail rapid transit lines, so the distance that the commuter must travel to get to the transit station is relatively short. The costs of the collection phase of the trip are low. And, because of the high employment density in the CBD, the costs of the distribution phase are also low.

Meyer et al. (1965) estimated that an hourly passenger volume of 20,000 on a line was needed to take reasonably full advantage of the economies of scale in line haul on rail rapid transit. At the time they wrote their book only five cities had hourly passenger volumes at this level or greater; they were New York, Chicago, Philadelphia, Boston, and Washington, DC. The first four already had extensive rail rapid transit systems and downtown subways at the time. An extensive subway system has since been built in Washington, DC, and this system is discussed below.

Meyer et al. (1965) also studied the costs of bus systems. The usual city bus system has buses that run on the major streets and pick and discharge passengers about every two blocks. Meyer et al. pointed out that this sort of system is inefficient for transporting workers to the CBD because the line-haul phase of the trip is slow. Instead, they suggested a system that they called bus rapid transit, or integrated bus service. The idea of bus rapid transit is to follow a route around a residential area until the bus is full of CBD workers, and then to proceed directly downtown by the quickest route possible (e.g., on the expressway). They showed that a fleet of buses can provide service that is much less costly than rail rapid transit. The bus can follow a flexible route to pick up passengers, so the costs in the collection phase are cut substantially compared to the rail system. Economies of scale arise because, if there are more passengers in an area to pick up, a single bus has to make very fewer stops to have a full load. Waiting time is reduced by running buses more frequently. Meyer et al. (1965) also studied the possibility of having "feeder" buses pick up passengers who are delivered to the rail rapid transit stations. They estimated that this sort of system works about as well as bus rapid transit, especially in residential areas with high population densities. The idea of bus rapid transit proved to be persuasive, and most urban transit systems provide some service of this type.

The data from Meyer et al. (1965) cited above suggested that Washington, DC might have been a good candidate for a rail rapid transit system because potential passenger volume might have been in excess of 20,000 per hour. The current Washington, DC, Metro system was completed in 1981 with a set of six major lines that run to the suburbs. As Mills and Hamilton (1994) pointed out, average ridership was 145,000 each way on the system, or an average of 24,167 per line. If the rush hour is approximately 2.5 hours in length, this works out to 9,667 riders per hour – far below the target of 20,000 per hour. Mills and Hamilton (1994, p. 304) computed the capital and operating cost of the system as of 1981, and found that capital costs were about $13.30 per round trip and operating costs were $2.60 per round trip. They further estimate that the time costs for the commuter were about $2.50 per round trip, so the average total cost per round trip in 1981 was $18.40. If we add $13.60 and $2.60, we see that, for the system to break even, the fare needed to be about $8.00 *each way*. Actual fares were, of course, much less. A bus rapid transit system could have provided much cheaper service. Indeed, Mills and Hamilton (1994) argue that a "system" based on commuting by private auto is probably cheaper. The Washington, DC, Metro ranks pretty high in the annals of transportation policy mistakes. It is fair to say that some goal other than economic efficiency was being pursued. What do you think it was?

Other studies of the heavy rail systems that have been built in recent decades show similar results. Furthermore, a study by Pickrell (1989) concluded that the analytical reports used to justify construction of these systems systematically exaggerated benefits and under-estimated costs. For example, the Miami system began service in 1986 and consists of two lines and 21 miles of track. Pickrell (1989) found that the original studies predicted a cost per rider of $1.73 (1987 dollars), and an actual cost per rider of $16.77. The primary cause of this gross error is the forecast of ridership; the forecast of weekday boardings was 240,000, but actual boardings were only 35,400. A recent book by Altshuler and Luberoff (2003) examines the history of "mega-projects" in urban areas and finds that political coalitions matter, and that the merits of the project often are of secondary importance. The politics and economics of a case study of a transit project in downtown Chicago are discussed below.

Thus far the discussion of mass transportation has concentrated on systems for moving commuters to the jobs in the CBD. There is good reason for this focus. As Meyer et al. (1965) and others since have shown, the private auto is almost always the cheapest method for getting people to and from work for locations outside the CBD. The full costs include time, vehicle operation, roadway, parking, and pollution. There are some exceptions to this finding. For example, the rail rapid transit system provides service to O'Hare Airport in Chicago, a major destination for workers that is outside the CBD. This rapid transit line mainly exists to deliver workers to the CBD, but the trains must return to O'Hare anyway. A good use of those returning trains is to carry the workers to the O'Hare employment center. In a few other instances a bus system might be a viable option for work trips to a major employment subcenter. Otherwise, the dispersed nature of residential locations and job locations makes the cost of a bus system high relative to private auto. Van-pooling was mentioned above, and this is also a viable option to the private auto for large employers. The key to making van-pooling competitive with the private auto is to have a full van of commuters who live in close proximity, who work for the same employer, and who have the same schedule. The results are a short collection phase and a very short distribution phase. But van pooling is not exactly mass transportation. There might be a valid argument for public subsidization of van-pooling because of it tends to reduce traffic congestion.

F. Politics and Transportation Projects: A Case Study

At the beginning of this chapter it was mentioned that proposed transportation projects can become hot political issues in an urban area. At any given time in most large urban areas there is a proposed transportation project that is the subject of political debate and controversy. What is it in your urban area? This last section takes a brief look at a proposed transportation project in Chicago that was the subject of debate for several years.

The proposed project is a light-rail transit system for downtown Chicago. Most observers agree that the movement of people within the downtown area of Chicago, and other large urban areas too, has become an increasingly important problem. Chicago's downtown area is large – about five miles long from north to south and 1.5 miles wide from east to west. Total employment in this area is approximately 600,000, and about 850,000 people enter the area on a typical weekday. There are about 1 million trips taken within the area per weekday. Some major businesses have resorted to private shuttle buses to transport their workers from commuter rail stations because of the shortage of mass transit and the difficulty the public transit buses have in moving through traffic.

Clearly there is a need for a transportation system that connects commuter stations, parking facilities, and transit stations and bus lines with offices, shopping areas, cultural centers, hotels, and convention facilities. What is more, there is a need to connect offices with shopping areas, office areas with other office areas, hotels with cultural centers and convention facilities, and all of the other possible combinations. Indeed, one of the major reasons for the economic vitality of a place such as downtown Chicago is the relative ease with which face-to-face contacts can be made. The downtown area has been spreading out over time, so the demand for a downtown transportation system has increased. Chicago's original downtown was confined roughly to the famous Chicago "Loop," which is an elevated mass transit line around the central square mile.

A light-rail transit system for downtown Chicago was first proposed in the 1980s by a local community group, and this proposal has been studied in detail by the City of Chicago. The US Department of Transportation has extensive requirements for the studies of proposed projects that involve the use of federal funds. Those requirements include a systematic examination of all reasonable alternatives. Those alternatives are briefly described as follows.

Null alternative

The null alternative is required by the US Department of Transportation's evaluation procedures, and serves as a baseline against which other policy options are compared. The basic idea is to estimate what will happen if nothing new is done. The null alternative included the existing public bus lines that serve the downtown area.

Transportation systems management alternative

This alternative involves some sizable operational and physical improvements in the bus system service. New bus stations would be added, new vehicles would be acquired, and better communications system would be added, and some routes would be changed. Several steps would be taken to improve the management of traffic in the downtown area. The cost of this alternative was estimated at around $100 million.

Bus-build alternative

The objective of the bus-build alternative was to create a bus system that is nearly separate from general traffic by means of both at-grade and below-grade bus facilities. The studies indicate that this option provides very limited benefits at substantial cost, and therefore received no further consideration.

Light-rail transit alternative

This alternative involves a new type of transit system that makes use of railway tracks embedded in the streets. The vehicles are powered by electricity, and are high-tech versions of the old trolley cars. The studies identify four corridors of high demand in the downtown area, so the plan includes four light-rail transit lines. The cost of the complete light-rail system is around $600 million.

Grade-separated alternative

This approach involves making use of existing railroad rights-of-way that exist below street level and constructing new elevated transit facilities. A grade-separated system could be implemented by extending rapid transit and commuter rail lines and/or by creating a new mode called automated guideway technology. Preliminary studies showed that this alternative is neither physically nor economically feasible.

The choices boil down to three; do nothing, improve the downtown bus system for a cost of $100 million, or build a light-rail system at a cost of $600 million. It turned out that the Mayor of Chicago and many other local officials and downtown businesses are attracted to the light-rail transit project. They like the idea of nifty and attractive high-tech trolley cars moving people around downtown in an efficient manner. Light-rail transit is a popular idea; transportation experts seem to be subject to fads (as are we all). Light-rail systems had been built recently in several cities such as San Diego, Pittsburgh, Buffalo, Sacramento, San Jose and Portland, Oregon, so Chicago perhaps was seeking to jump on this particular bandwagon.

Light-rail transit is a popular idea, but it has what Gómez-Ibáñez (1985) calls the "dark side" to light rail. Light rail has sizable capital costs compared to the bus system that can serve as a substitute. In the case of the San Diego light-rail system, he found that the cost per rider of light-rail transit was about 2.7 times the cost of the bus system that it replaced. Pickrell (1989) found a similar result for the light-rail systems in Buffalo, Pittsburgh, Portland, and Sacramento. Note that the light-rail system for downtown Chicago costs about six times as much as the improved bus system (the transportation systems management alternative). But what are the benefits of these two alternatives?

Detailed studies have been conducted of the amount of time that travelers would save under the light-rail and bus project alternatives. Passengers on the light-rail transit system will travel at 3 miles per hour faster than they do on the current bus system. The study showed that the average trip inside downtown is 1.5 miles (3 miles per day). If the original average speed is 8 mph and improves to 11 mph, then the typical person will reduce time spent traveling 3 miles from 22.5 minutes to 16.4 minutes – a saving of 6 minutes (0.1 hours) per day. Estimated ridership on the light-rail system is 50,000 per day (round trip), so the total amount of time saved per day is 5,000 hours. The total amount of time saved per year would then be 1.25 million hours (5,000 times 250 days). Recall that the value of time saved is about 50% of the after-tax wage rate. The average worker in downtown Chicago earned about $26,000 per year at the time of the study (or about $10 per hour after taxes), so the value of time saved was about $5 per hour. The value of the time saved per year was therefore about $6.25 million. This annual benefit is 1.04% of the cost of the project of $600 million. That is, of course, a very poor rate of return.

The improved bus system (transportation systems management alternative) costs only $100 million, but it is estimated to save only about 40% of the time that is saved by the light-rail system. The value of the time saved is therefore about $2.5 million per year, for a rate of return of 2.5%. In short, neither project appears to be a good investment.

In spite of the pessimistic cost–benefit analysis, plans for the light-rail transit system moved forward. The City of Chicago set up a special office to finalize plans and implement the project. The plan for financing the project was to split the cost equally between the local, state and federal governments. With the support of many downtown interests, the local government set up a special real estate taxing district in the downtown area to cover its one-third share. Some grumbling could be heard among downtown property owners when this action was taken in 1991, but only weak organized opposition to the project materialized at the local level. The Republican state legislature and governor of Illinois generally supported the project, in part because they opposed other projects that were favored by Chicago's Democratic mayor. For example, Republicans in state government opposed the mayor's plans to expand O'Hare Airport, and instead wished to build another airport in the suburbs. Under these circumstances, the political trade-off was to give the mayor the project that is of lesser importance.

What was the final disposition of the proposed light-rail transit system for downtown Chicago? The plans were complete, and both the local and federal governments were ready to start paying for its construction. However, the State of Illinois was forced to pull the plug on the project because of its fiscal problems. The state has growing expenses for medical care for the poor (Medicaid), education and criminal justice, and the political decision was made not to increase state taxes. One implication of this political situation is that many discretionary expenditure items were postponed, perhaps never to be undertaken at all. In the case of the light-rail transit project, it would appear that the proper decision has been made for the "wrong" reasons. As of this writing in 2004, the project is still dead.

G. Summary

The chapter began by posing the "big question" of whether anything can be done about the time-consuming and wasteful traffic congestion that is getting worse. You can now see that there are many little things that can be done. The battle must be fought on many fronts.

Consider first the demand side. There are several methods that can be used to encourage drivers to shift to time periods with less traffic congestion. Congestion tolls are the high-tech remedy that may never be implemented in a major fashion in the United States. Nevertheless, there may be specific places where a congestion toll can have the desired effect without creating too many traffic spillovers onto other routes. For example, congestion tolls on bridges seem to be workable. At a more practical level, CBD parking taxes, incentives for car-pooling, and providing incentives to employers to stagger work hours all seem to be workable. Higher taxes on gasoline (or autos themselves) are alternatives that are less attractive because they do not target the problem very well. Indeed, Downs (2004) argues that a higher tax on gasoline would cause drivers to switch to more fuel-efficient cars rather than to cut down on driving in the rush hour.

Even in an era of budgetary stringency, some improvements can be made on the supply side. There are bottlenecks out there that need to be widened. More advanced traffic control technology can be installed on major streets and minor highways. In the Chicago area a program known as "operation green light" has made life a bit easier. This project involved judicious widening of major streets and timing of the stoplights.

Another tactic is to provide drivers with better information about their route choices. Drivers need to know if there are accidents or other causes of traffic tie-ups, and they need to know *immediately*. Traffic information services exist in the major urban areas, but these services can be improved. A related policy is to make sure that accidents and other impediments are removed *very* promptly. Helicopters might be used. An expansion of accident-prevention programs is also worth thinking about.

All of the partial remedies listed so far take our location patterns and mode choices as given. Clearly these remedies will help, but the continued growth of population, employment and vehicles will soon overcome the improvements these remedies have brought. Are there more fundamental changes in the nature of urban areas in the United States that can have a big impact on traffic congestion? Downs (2004) considers a variety of policies to increase population density, increase the concentration of jobs, and reduce the imbalances that exist between residential and employment locations. All of these suggestions will involve a substantial amount of planning that is not likely to be very popular with Americans. Growth management policies may be feasible in some urban areas. Portland, Oregon, for example, has managed growth extensively – for an American urban area. But, as Garreau (1991) would surely point out, if you impose too many regulations, Americans are likely to create another edge city that the regulations cannot yet reach. A dilemma is defined as a situation requiring a choice between equally undesirable alternatives. Are the choices highly intrusive growth management or increasingly bad traffic congestion? If they are, then we truly face a dilemma. At this point we seem to be choosing traffic congestion – perhaps mainly by default. Or, as Mr. Hartman put it, "There is no such thing as a free road."

Exercises

1 Suppose a gravity model of trip distribution has been estimated as

$$T_{ij} = O_i^{0.5} D_j^{0.2}/(d_{ij})^2.$$

(a) What is T_{ij} if $O_i = 100$, $D_j = 200$, and $d_{ij} = 5$ miles? What if the distance is 10 miles instead of five miles?

(b) What happens to T_{ij} if both O_i and D_j double in size?

2 A model of mode split (with two modes) has been estimated as

$$\ln(P_{ija}/1 - P_{ija}) = -8(t_a - t_b) - 2(m_a - m_b),$$

where mode a is auto and mode b is public transit, t (travel time) is measured in minutes, and m (money cost) is measured in cents.

(a) At what values of $t^a - t^b$ and $m^a - m^b$ is the probability of using the auto equal to 0.5?

(b) Draw the graph of P_{ija} as a function of $z = -8(t_a - t_b) - 2(m_a - m_b)$.

(c) What is the value of reductions in commuting time implied by the estimated mode split function? What unit of measurement did you use to express the value of time?

3 You are supposed to be at your desk ready for work at 9:00 a.m. You cannot be late or you will be fired, but it is fine if you arrive early. You figure that each minute you spend at work before 9 a.m. costs you 3 cents. You also know that there is a function that describes the amount of time it will take you to get to work that is

Commute time = 15 minutes + 0.1(departure time minus 8 a.m.)
+ 0.02(departure time minus 8 a.m.)^2

Departure time minus 8 a.m. is measured in minutes. Your value of reductions in commuting time is 5 cents per minute.

(a) What is your optimal departure time?

(b) How much time do you spend commuting?

(c) When do you arrive at work?

(d) What happens if you decide that time spent at work before 9 a.m. costs you 4 cents per minute instead of 3 cents?

4 Consider a circular road with one lane that is two miles in length. There are 80 cars on this "track" travelling 50 miles per hour – speed (S) is 50.

(a) What is the traffic density (D)?

(b) What is traffic volume (V)?

(c) What units of measurement did you use?

5 Consider an urban highway that is subject to traffic congestion. The average cost of travel per mile on that highway is (in cents)

$$AC = 10 + 4V,$$

where V is traffic volume per hour, measured in 100s of vehicles per hour. For example, if $V = 500$ cars per hour, $AC = 30$ cents per mile. Assume that the demand for traffic volume per hour (during rush hour) is

$$V = 46 - P,$$

where P is the "price" paid by the driver.

(a)   Assume that no congestion toll is imposed. Compute V and P.
(b)   Assume that it is possible to impose the efficient congestion toll. Find the toll, and the efficient levels of V, P and AC.

6   The function that relates the inverse of speed $(1/S)$ to traffic volume on a highway is

$$1/S = (1/60) + 0.0005V,$$

where the inverse of speed is measured in hours per mile. What would this equation be if expressed in minutes per mile? The demand for traffic volume on this road is

$$V = 6{,}880 - 80(\text{travel time per mile}).$$

Travel time per mile is measured in minutes.

(a)   Find the equilibrium traffic volume in the absence of any congestion toll.
(b)   Find the marginal cost function for traffic volume, where cost is expressed as travel time per mile in minutes.
(c)   Find the optimal level of traffic volume.
(d)   Find the optimal congestion toll, expressed in *minutes*. (Imagine that the congestion toll consists of sitting in the "penalty box" for this period of time. The toll can also be assessed in money terms, of course.)

References

Altshuler, Alan and David Luberoff, 2003, *Mega-Projects: The Changing Politics of Urban Public Investment*. Washington, DC: The Brookings Institution.

Becker, Gary, 1965, "A Theory of the Allocation of Time," *Economic Journal*, vol. 75, pp. 493–517.

Boardman, Anthony and L. Lave, 1977, "Highway Congestion and Congestion Tolls," *Journal of Urban Economics*, vol. 4, pp. 340–59.

Bruzelius, Nils, 1979, *The Value of Time*. London: Croom Helm.

Cervero, Robert, 1989, *America's Suburban Centers*. Boston: Allen & Unwin.

Chicago Area Transportation Study, 1959, *Chicago Area Transportation Study: Final Report*. Chicago: CATS.

Downs, Anthony, 2004, *Still Stuck in Traffic: Coping with Peak-Hour Traffic Congestion*. Washington, DC: The Brookings Institution.

Garreau, Joel, 1991, *Edge City: Life on the New Frontier*. New York: Doubleday.

Gómez-Ibáñez, José, 1985, "A Dark Side to Light Rail," *Journal of the American Institute of Planners*, vol. 51, pp. 337–51.

Hill, Donald, L. Tittemore and D. Gendell, 1973, "Analysis of Urban Area Travel by Time of Day," *Highway Research Record*, vol. 472, pp. 108–19.

McDonald, John, 1995, "Urban Highway Congestion: An Analysis of Second-Best Tolls," *Transportation*, vol. 22, pp. 1–17.

McDonald, John, 2004, "Road Pricing in Practice and Theory," *Review of Network Economics*, vol. 3, pp. 347–55.

Meyer, John, J. Kain and M. Wohl, 1965, *The Urban Transportation Problem*. Cambridge, MA: Harvard University Press.

Mills, Edwin and B. Hamilton, 1994, *Urban Economics*, 5th edn. New York: Harper Collins.

Niedercorn, J. and B. Bechdolt, 1969, "An Economic Derivation of the 'Gravity Law' of Spatial Interaction," *Journal of Regional Science*, vol. 9, pp. 273–82.

Pickrell, Don, 1989, "Urban Rail Transit Projects: Forecast versus Actual Ridership and Costs," Cambridge, MA: Transport Systems Center, US Dept. of Transportation.

Sherret, Alistair, 1975, "Immediate Travel Impacts of Transbay BART," Report no. TM 15-3-75, Peat, Marwick, Mitchell & Co., for US Dept. of Transportation.

Small, Kenneth, 1992, *Urban Transportation Economics*. Chur, Switzerland: Harwood Academic Publishers.

Part V

Urban Social Problems

Chapter 15

An Overview of
Urban Social Problems

A. Introduction

This chapter is an introduction to urban social problems from the perspective of urban economics. In Chapter 1 we observed that many students take a course in urban economics because they are interested in and concerned about the economic and social problems that exist in urban areas. With the exception of Chapter 9, the first three parts of the book are largely devoted to economic models that help us understand urban economies. Chapter 9 concentrates on urban housing problems and policies, and this part of the book extends the discussion of urban problems to poverty, crime, education, and other topics of concern.

We also noted in Chapter 1 that many economists think that urban economics was founded as a separate field in the early 1960s. This was also the time in which the social and economic problems of the large cities were being recognized and documented more than ever before. The influential "Chicago School" of urban sociology had been founded in the 1920s, but the resurgence of interest in urban problems clearly began in the 1960s. One important contribution was *Dark Ghetto* by the social psychologist Kenneth B. Clark. This book was published in 1965, and it documented the economic, social, and psychological decay in the African American areas of the major cities. Some of Clark's chapter titles and subtitles give you an idea of his viewpoint:

- The cry of the ghetto
- Economic and social decay
- The dynamics of under-employment
- The Negro matriarchy and the distorted masculine image
- Emotional illness
- Homicide and suicide
- Drug addiction
- Ghetto schools: Separate and unequal
- Educational atrophy: The self-fulfilling prophecy.

Clark published his book just before the first major urban riot of the 1960s, the Watts Riot in Los Angeles in 1965. The older author of this book attended Professor Clark's class at the Harvard Summer School on the day the Watts Riot broke out, August 11, 1965. Professor Clark greeted the news with mixed emotions. Obviously, riots are not good. But he also felt that the rioting was partly an expression of desperation that could not be ignored.

An act of alleged police brutality sparked the Watts Riot. The violence was on a massive scale. In the rioting, which lasted five days, 34 people were killed, at least 1,000 were wounded, and about $200 million in property damage occurred. Much of the property damage was aimed at white-owned stores in the Watts area. It was estimated that 35,000 African Americans took part in the rioting, and 16,000 police and National Guardsmen were needed to quell it. The Watts Riot of 1965 foreshadowed the widespread urban rioting that took place in the latter years of the 1960s. The Summers of 1966 and 1967 saw many urban riots, including major riots in Detroit, Newark, New York, Cleveland, Washington, DC, and Chicago.

President Johnson appointed the National Advisory Commission on Civil Disorders on July 28, 1967 – five days after the Detroit Riot broke out. Johnson charged this commission with the task of determining the specific causes of the riots, studying the their deeper causes, and recommending policy. The commission's report (published in early 1968), known for its chairman as the Kerner Commission Report, concluded that the fundamental causes of urban violence were the racism that was deeply embedded in American society and the frustration that racism produces among African Americans. The Kerner Commission Report provided detailed evidence on overt discrimination, poverty, high unemployment, poor schools, poor health care, housing inadequacies, and police bias and brutality. The Report proposed large federal initiatives in housing, education, and employment – and called for a national system of income supplementation.

The Rev. Martin Luther King, Jr. said the the Kerner Commission Report was "a physician's warning of approaching death, with a prescription for life." Later that spring Dr. King was murdered, and his death sparked another round of massive urban rioting. Rioting was especially destructive on the west side of Chicago, where King had spent much of 1966 in an effort to highlight urban problems. In some ways the west side of Chicago is still trying to recover from the riot of 1968.

While many of the Kerner Commission's recommendations were not pursued, the riots of the 1960s and the reports that documented urban conditions clearly had an impact on the young field of urban economics. The chapters in this section of the book, as well as the Chapter 9 on housing policy and Chapter 21 on economic development policies for urban areas, are reflections of this influence.

At the outset it is important to realize that many social and urban problems are related. It is apparent that poverty, poor housing and homelessness, lack of education, and crime are correlated – not perfectly correlated, but correlated. These social problems have some of the same underlying causes. It is also true that a shift in the level of one problem can influence the others. For example, an increase in the poverty level from some outside cause can cause housing, education, crime to be worse as well. Then worsening conditions in housing, education, and crime can lead to further increases in poverty, and so on, ad infinitum. This idea is called the "vicious cycle." One problem getting worse makes another problem get worse, which in turn makes the first problem worse, and so on. Since the 1960s many observers of urban problems have emphasized the vicious cycle of poverty and other social conditions.

However, if urban problems are subject to the vicious cycle, they may also be subject to the "virtuous cycle" in which an improvement in one malady leads to improvements in other problems, which generates further improvements, and so on. In fact we shall argue that such a virtuous cycle has been at work in urban areas in the US since the early 1990s. This chapter documents the general improvement in social problems that has occurred in urban areas.

The notions of the vicious and virtuous cycles originate with the Swedish economist Gunnar Myrdal. He and a team of scholars applied these ideas to the problem of race in America in his monumental study *An American Dilemma*. He was commissioned in 1938 by the Carnegie Corporation to conduct a comprehensive study of the black population of the US as a social phenomenon. The study was undertaken from 1939 to 1942, and the 1,483-page *An American Dilemma* was published in 1944. Myrdal hypothesized that white prejudice and discrimination, and enforced segregation in the South, had been responsible in significant degree for holding down the standard of living, health, education, and other characteristics of the black population. In turn, he hypothesized that the low social and economic condition of the black population was an important cause of white prejudice and discrimination. If these hypotheses are correct, Myrdal (1996, p. 76) argued:

> If, for example, we assume that for some reason white prejudice could be decreased and discrimination mitigated, this is likely to cause a rise in black standards, which may decrease white prejudice still a little more, which would again allow black standards to rise, and so on through mutual interaction.

In spite of the deplorable condition of the black population in 1940 that he and his research team documented at great length, especially in the southern states, Myrdal believed that America was poised to begin an era in which the black population would experience great progress. He believed that the issue was one of fundamental morality, and that the "American Creed" of the essential dignity of individuals, the fundamental equality of all persons, and inalienable rights would move the nation in the right direction. Although he later acknowledged the lack of specific evidence in favor of this belief in the imminence of great change for the black Americans, in his preface in 1964 to the twentieth anniversary edition of *An American Dilemma* (1996, p. xxiii) he could not resist saying

> A student who has often been wrong in his forecasts will be excused for pointing to a case when he was right.

While Dr. Myrdal saw in 1964 that the Civil Rights Movement of the 1950s and 1960s was bringing great progress for black Americans, he also recognized that serious social and urban problems had not been addressed. Professor Clark had been one of the reseachers who provided material for *An American Dilemma* in the early 1940s, so his friend Dr. Myrdal wrote the foreward for *Dark Ghetto* in an effort to call attention to this important book.

As we noted above, by the 1960s attention had shifted to the social and economic problems of black Americans in major cities. It turned out that conditions in inner cities got much worse before they began to get better. This chapter includes a brief history of major urban problems since the 1960s.

B. Health

We turn first to one of the most important social indicators, health. Health, health care, and the financing of health care are and will continue to be near the top of the domestic policy agenda. Courses in health economics examine these matters in detail. The purpose here is simply to document dramatic improvements in the health of Americans, which is a critical piece of background information for the discussion of other social and urban problems.

Average life expectancy at birth has increased for all Americans. The largest gain has been made by black males, whose life expectancy increased from a pretty shockingly low 60 years in 1970 to 68.2 years in 2000. This group increased its expected life span by 3.7 years from 1990 to 2000 alone. Rates for black females also improved, from a life expectancy of 68.3 years in 1970 to 74.9 years in 2000. During this time, white males and females gained 6.8 years and 4.4 years, reaching life expectancies of 74.8 years and 80.0 years in 2000. Death rates have dropped as well. Actual death rates per 100,000 persons have declined (except for white females), but age-adjusted death rates, which control for the overall aging of the population, are lower by large numbers. The age-adjusted death rate for white males declined by 32.5% and for black males by 26.7% from 1970 to 2000.

The causes of the increase in life expectancy and the decline in the death rate are closely related to reductions in certain risk factors. The death rate from heart disease, still the largest cause of death, declined from 493 per 100,000 population in 1970 to 258 in 2000. This is a remarkable decline of 47.7%. The death rate from cerebro-vascular diseases dropped from 148 to 60 per 100,000 over these same thirty years, a decline of 59.8%. Evidently people are taking to heart the advice of their doctors regarding the prevention of heart and cerebro-vascular diseases. Unhappily, the death rate from cancer was unchanged: 199 per 100,000 in 1970 and 200 in 2000. However, the ongoing efforts to reduce smoking among Americans may mean that a decline in the cancer rate is on the horizon. The death rate from accidents dropped by almost half, from 62 to 34. And, remarkably, the age-adjusted death rate from AIDS went from 10.2 per 100,000 in 1990 to 16.3 in 1995, and then dropped by two-thirds to 5.4 in 1999.

Another critical health matter is the birth rate for teenagers. The birth rate for black young women aged 15–17 has declined from 113 per 100,000 in 1990 to 50 in 2000. This drop of 55.7% is a very good sign for the future because giving birth at this age interferes with the completion of high school. The birth rate for black young women aged 18–19 declined from 153 to 121 over this decade. The birth rates for white teenagers declined as well; from 30 to 24 for those aged 15–17 and from 78 to 73 for the 18–19 age group.

C. Poverty

Poverty and its concentration in urban areas are discussed in depth in the next chapter. This introductory section notes some basic trends in household incomes and poverty in the latter decades of the twentieth century.

The years of prosperity following World War II yielded substantial economic benefits to most Americans, but by the early 1960s it became clear that some people were being left behind. Poverty became a specific focus for federal policy at that time. A system for measuring the extent of poverty was initiated in 1963 by the federal government and back-dated to 1959. In 1959 22.4% of the population of the US was in poverty by this official standard. President Johnson declared a "War on Poverty" in 1964. The economic boom of the 1960s, coupled with numerous anti-poverty initiatives (the largest was Medicare, which provides support for health care among the elderly), produced a dramatic decline in the poverty rate up through 1973. The poverty rate of 11.1% in 1973 is still the lowest on record.

Since 1973 the poverty rate has roughly followed the business cycle. Slow economic growth in the 1970s, and the deep recession of the early 1980s, meant that the poverty rate drifted upward to 15.2% in 1983. Prosperity of the Reagan years in the 1980s is associated with a steady decline in poverty to 12.8% in 1989, but the recession of the early 1990s produced an increase in poverty that reached 15.1% in 1993. The economic boom period of 1993 to 2000 brought the rate of poverty down to 11.3% in 2000, but in the early years of the twenty-first century came overall job losses and an increase in poverty to 12.5% in 2003.

It is important to disaggregate the poverty figures because poverty varies appreciably by ethnic group and location. Table 15.1 shows some basic facts. The poverty rate for white Americans has remained relatively low at roughly 10% since 1970. Poverty among black Americans was above 30% until the 1990s (reaching 33.4% in 1992), but declined by one-third to 22.5% in 2000. The poverty rate for Hispanics increased from 22.8% in 1970 to 28.1% in 1990 (and 30.7% in 1994), but fell to 21.5% in 2000 – the lowest rate on record for this group. Table 15.1 also shows that the poverty rate in central cities was 14.2% in 1970 and a discouraging 19.0% in 1990. Poverty in central cities declined to 16.3% in 2000. The 1990s were years of economic progress for the poor of America's two largest minority groups and for the poor located in central cities.

Table 15.1   % poor in the US

	Total	Central City	White	Black	Hispanic
1970	12.6	14.2	9.9	33.5	22.8
1980	12.0	17.2	10.2	32.5	25.7
1990	13.5	19.0	10.7	31.9	28.1
2000	11.3	16.3	9.5	22.5	21.5

Source: US Bureau of the Census

Table 15.2   Household income in the US

Household income	Median ($ 2002)	% of households		
		Under 15,000	*15,000–25,000*	*Over 75,000*
White				
1980	38,621	17.3%	14.5%	15.0%
1990	41,668	15.4	13.5	20.5
2000	45,860	13.8	12.2	26.9
2002	45,086	14.5	12.8	26.6
Black				
1980	22,250	36.5	18.7	5.3
1990	24,917	34.6	15.5	8.5
2000	30,980	25.2	16.1	13.7
2002	29,177	27.4	16.4	12.9
Hispanic				
1980	28,218	24.7	17.2	7.1
1990	29,792	25.1	16.8	9.9
2000	34,636	18.2	17.8	14.8
2002	33,103	19.1	19.1	14.7

Source: Statistical Abstract of the US (2003)

Economic progress in the 1990s can also be documented with data on household incomes shown in Table 15.2. Buoyed by increased female labor force participation and earnings, household incomes have risen impressively since 1980. Moreover, the gains have been recorded across the income distribution – particularly at the lower end.

From 1980 to 2000 the median income of white households increased by 19% and the percentage of households with real incomes less than $25,000 fell from 32% to 26%. The improvements were far more pronounced for black households. Median income increased by 39%, and the percentage of households below $25,000 dropped from 55% to 41%. Meanwhile, black households with income exceeding $75,000 increased from 5.3% to 13.7%. During this period, Hispanic households experienced a gain in median income of 23%, and the proportion below $25,000 declined from 42% to 36%. The percentage with incomes above $75,000 more than doubled to 14.7%. Incomes did regress between 2000 and 2002, but this probably simply reflects the recession.

Many critics of the American economy rightly point out that inequality in the distribution of income has grown. But we would argue that absolute levels of income matter more than relative levels. Here the signs are positive. As Tables 15.1 and 15.2 show, the percentages of household with low and moderate incomes decreased significantly up to 2000. Further progress must depend upon the future resilience and growth of the American economy.

In addition to the overall level of poverty, urban scholars have called attention to the concentration of poverty in the inner cities of major metropolitan areas. As we pointed out, Clark (1965) was one of the first to document the deleterious effects of concentrated poverty. Wilson (1987, 1996) measured the extent to which poverty is concentrated in the inner city and conducted extensive research on these effects. Jargowsky (1997) conducted a comprehensive study of all metropolitan areas in the US for 1970, 1980, and 1990 and found that poverty in urban areas had become substantially more concentrated over those 20 years. Somewhat surprisingly, however, the trend towards increasing poverty concentration reversed in the 1990s. Recent studies by Jargowsky (2003) and McDonald (2004) document a dramatic reduction in the extent to which urban poverty is concentrated.

A related concern is that African Americans who remain in those high-poverty areas in the inner cities have experienced a decline in physical access to employment. This idea is known as the spatial "mismatch" hypothesis – where the mismatch refers to the residential location patterns of African Americans compared to the spatial patterns of employment (and employment growth) in large urban areas. Segregation in housing is alleged to have limited job opportunities for some African Americans.

D. Crime in Urban Areas

According to the FBI, crime in the US tripled between 1960 and 1980, the year in which crime hit its peak. Crime researchers think that the increase is somewhat exaggerated because the systems for reporting crime to the FBI have improved over the years, but no one thinks that crime did not increase dramatically in the 1960s and 1970s. Murders are almost always reported. The murder rate in 1960 was 5.0 per 100,000 population and barely changed to 5.1 in 1965. The murder rate per 100,000 people then began a steady increase to 7.8 in 1970, 9.6 in 1975, and 10.2 in 1980 – doubling in 15 years. The FBI crime index includes murder, rape, aggravated assault, robbery, auto theft, larceny-theft, and burglary. The total crime index for all of these crimes was 5,950 per 100,0000 people in 1980. In other words, on average one in 17 Americans was a victim of crime in 1980. Larceny-theft, the least "serious" of crimes in the FBI index, constitute 53% of all of these crimes. Nevertheless, there is no other way to say it, crime at this level is shocking. One in 9,800 Americans was murdered in 1980.

Since 1980 crime in America has declined substantially. The decline in crime has been especially pronounced in the 1990s. The murder rate in 1990 was 9.4 per 100,000, fell to 8.2 in 1995, and then dropped back to 1960s levels to 5.5 in 2000. The total crime index for 2000 was 4,124, which is a drop of 30% from 1980. Larceny-theft was 60.0% of total crime in 2000. The decline of crime in America is certainly an encouraging development, but the problem of crime has not been "solved." In 2000, on average, one in 24 Americans was a victim of crime.

Chapter 17 explores the causes of the increase and subsequent decrease in crime. The increase in crime is partly attributed to demographic changes; i.e., an increase in the proportion of the population who are young men. They are the most crime-prone people. But demography cannot account for the burst in crime in the 1960s and 1970s. Other factors implicated are the decline of two-parent families, segregation of African Americans in central cities (Kenneth Clark's *Dark Ghetto* effect), and an increase in what criminologists call violent predators. Violent predators are often involved in the illegal drug trade and commit large numbers of violent crimes. Can anything be done to reduce crime? Apparently the answer is "yes."

The decline in crime has been studied intensively, and some answers have emerged. Factors behind the decline in crime include demography (decline in the proportion of young men), increase in gun law enforcement, better policing strategies, the end of the crack cocaine epidemic, and better economic opportunity in the 1990s. Also, America has put many more people in jail. The number of people in prison increased by 73% in the 1990s, and reached 0.7% of the total population of the nation. Putting violent predators in state prison is one way to prevent them from committing crime. One study attributes 25% of the decline in crime to the increase in the prison population. But is this the kind of society we want? Crime in America remains a huge problem and a critical issue with many dimensions.

E. Education

Evidently Americans are "hooked on" education. The economic benefits to education are substantial, and the educational attainment of the population has increased substantially. In 1970, only 55% of white adults (age 25 and over) had completed high school. Thirty years later this figure was 85%. Among African American adults only 31% had earned the high school diploma in 1970, and this figure had jumped to 79%. The Hispanic population lagged in this category. Still, high-school completion rates did rise from 32% to 57% over this same period.

The numbers for higher education are also encouraging. In 1960 only 7.7% of adult Americans had graduated from college. By 2000, graduates exceeded 25%. The ethnic breakdown confirms that African Americans are narrowing the gap. The proportion of black adults with college degrees almost quadrupled since the last 1970s, rising from 4.4% to 16.5%. Latinos remained behind in this metric: some 10.6% had graduated from college in 2000 compared to 4.5% in 1970. But it is important to remember that many Latinos are immigrants, and that many are not fluent in English.

All of this is pretty good news. What is not good news is the fact that many students in the public school systems in large central cities do not perform well. And these are the school systems that enroll large numbers of minority children. America is struggling with the problem of how to increase the achievement of students in these school systems. Detailed consideration of this issue is beyond the scope of this book, but we would offer two observations. First, because education is so necessary to economic success in the modern economy, the society is demanding more of its schools than ever before. Secondly, there are many examples of very effective public schools all around us. Parents recognize these schools and, as we noted in the chapter (8) on housing markets, housing prices reflect access to good school systems. It seems to us that the goals of improving schools and providing better educational opportunity can be pursued with some success.

F. Summary

The next three chapters provide more detailed discussions of poverty, crime, and education. We recognize that students who enroll in urban economics classes often are motivated by the social and urban problems that they see around them. We encourage this concern, and we hope that this book is providing the concepts and factual background to help you make contributions to our society. The positive trends in social and urban problems that began in the 1990s need to be understood and made to continue. Myrdal's "virtuous cycle" seems to be working, but we do not know if its continuation is assured.

References

Clark, Kenneth B., 1965, *Dark Ghetto*. New York: Harper & Row.

Jargowsky, Paul, 1997, *Poverty and Place: Ghettos, Barrios, and the American City*, New York: Oxford University Press.

Jargowksy, Paul, 2003, "Stunning Progress, Hidden Problems: The Dramatic Decline of Concentrated Poverty in the 1990s," Living Cities Census Series Report. Washington, DC: The Brookings Institution.

McDonald, John, 2004, "The Deconcentration of Poverty in Chicago: 1990–2000. *Urban Studies*, vol. 41, pp. 2119–137.

Myrdal, Gunnar, 1996, *An American Dilemma*. New Brunswick, NJ: Transaction Publishers; 1st edn. 1944; New York: Harper & Row.

National Advisory Commission on Civil Disorders, 1968, *Report of the National Advisory Commission on Civil Disorders*. Washington, DC: Government Printing Office.

Wilson, W. J., 1980, *The Declining Significance of Race: Blacks and Changing American Institutions*. Chicago: University of Chicago Press.

Wilson, W. J., 1987, *The Truly Disadvantaged: The Inner City, the Underclass, and Public Policy*. Chicago: University of Chicago Press.

Wilson, W. J., 1996, *When Work Disappears: The New World of the Urban Poor*. New York: Knopf.

Chapter 16

Urban Poverty and
Its Spatial Concentration

A. Introduction

Poverty in the United States was not a major issue for public policy until the 1930s. It was not a major issue in the 1920s, when at least 50% of Americans could have been classified as poor. Prior to the 1930s relief for the poor was left to private charities and, to a lesser degree, local and state governments. The coming of the Great Depression in 1929 and the election of Franklin Roosevelt as President in 1932 changed all that. An examination of the Great Depression is beyond the scope of this book, but a few numbers will give you an idea of the motivating forces behind what Roosevelt called the "New Deal." From 1929 to 1933 the GNP dropped 31% in real terms, investment dropped to an amount that was less than capital depreciation, employment fell by almost 20%, and the unemployment rate shot up from 5% to 25%. The Great Depression shaped the attitudes and opinions of most of those who lived through it.

The people of the United States turned to the federal government to solve economic and social crises of the 1930s. The federal government took on many new responsibilities that carry on to this day. As you probably know, the English economist John Maynard Keynes provided the economic theory behind the idea that the national government must assume some responsibility for the overall performance of the economy. However, most of Roosevelt's New Dealers were pragmatic people who did not care about economic theory. They were trying to respond to immediate problems. Here is only a partial listing of the programs that were created in the 1930s:

- Federal Emergency Relief Agency provided emergency money for state and local relief agencies.
- Works Progress Administration (WPA) and Civilian Conservation Corps (CCC) employed millions of people on public works projects.
- Agricultural Adjustment Act (AAA) provides programs to support farmers and prices for farm products.
- Tennessee Valley Authority (TVA) and other programs provided electricity to the rural population.

- Social Security System provides pensions for retired or disabled people.
- Fair Labor Standards Act instituted a minimum wage.
- National Labor Relations Act (NLRA) gave workers the right to organize labor unions and to bargain collectively with employers.
- Aid to Families with Dependent Children (AFDC) was the nation's basic welfare program.
- Federal Housing Administration (FHA) helps people with average incomes become homeowners (as discussed in Chapter 9).

These and many other programs were established in the 1930s, and this partial listing makes it clear that the New Deal was addressed to the entire nation. A majority of the population was in poverty, and most people were at risk of losing their jobs, farms, or homes.

The nation did not really recover from the Great Depression until World War II called for the federal government to spend amounts of money that were unprecedented. The economy of 1939 and 1940 was operating at a level of GNP that was far below its capacity. In 1944 all governments (federal, state and local) spent an amount equal to 52% of the GNP, but the total amount of private spending in 1944 was roughly equal to the private spending in 1939!

World War II left the US economy in a dominant position in the world and the period of the late 1940s to the late 1960s was a period of growth and prosperity for the nation. However, by the late 1950s it became evident that growth and prosperity were not reaching down to a substantial minority of the population. The nature and extent of poverty had changed from the 1930s, so poverty became a different kind of problem for public concern and for public policy. For the first time we began to define the problem of poverty, to measure the extent of poverty (and its changes over time), and to design policies that focus specifically on the minority of the population that is in poverty.

This chapter concentrates on the measurement of poverty, causes of poverty, and the policies that have been used since the 1960s to alleviate poverty.

B. Definitions of Poverty

The first task was to define poverty. There is no ideal definition of poverty, but its definitions are of two basic types. One type of definition attempts to set an absolute standard for poverty that is based on an assessment of the minimum amount of income needed to sustain a healthy and minimally comfortable life. This approach might involve figuring out for households of various sizes a minimal budget for food, housing, health care, etc. The other approach is to define a poverty standard that is relative to the average standard of living in the nation. We might decide, for example, that poverty is defined as a household income level of less than 40% of the average for households of a given size. The idea is that people feel deprivation in relative terms – based on what they see around them. In addition, the definition of poverty probably should be based on a time period that is longer than one year. Many people in their early twenties (e.g., college students) who live in their own separate households have incomes that are low only temporarily. Other people have incomes that fluctuate from year to year, and they plan their lives and consumption expenditures accordingly. The problem of how to define poverty can never be resolved in a manner that satisfies everyone, but some sort of official definition is probably needed.

One or more official definitions of poverty are needed because we need to measure the extent of poverty and to assess the effectiveness of programs intended to alleviate poverty. Economists in the federal government set about establishing an official poverty standard, and they decided to use an absolute (rather than a relative) criterion. Their method is fairly simple. The US Department of Agriculture computes the minimum annual cost of a nutritious diet for low-income households, and then this number is multiplied by three because poor households spend about one-third of their incomes on food. Note that the official poverty line is defined as *annual money income*. The definition ignores assets and non-cash sources such as food stamps, housing assistance, publicly funded medical care, and non-cash gifts. The poverty line varies by size of household, and is updated annually to account for changes in food prices and for general inflation.

The poverty line for 2003 was set as a function of household size as follows:

One person	$9,244
Two persons	11,814
Three persons	14,441
Four persons	18,504
Five persons	21,885
Six persons	24,738
Seven persons	28,124
Eight persons	31,222

In addition, the poverty line is set at a slightly lower level for the elderly. Why is this done? Our conjecture is that the elderly need to eat less than others to maintain a healthy diet. What do you think about these poverty standards? Do they appear to be reasonable given what you know about the cost of living? Is an income of $18,504 a sensible standard for a family of four with two adults and two children? By the way, as of 2003, the minimum wage in the US was $5.15 per hour. One full-time, year-round job at this wage generated an income of $10,300. To put it another way, a single wage earner needed to make $9.25 per hour (40 hours per week for 50 weeks) to enable a family of four to reach the poverty line. Remember that these figures pertain to 2003, so you need to adjust them for inflation.

C. The Basic Facts of Poverty in the US

The official poverty line was established by the federal government in the early 1960s, and the first year for which an official poverty rate was computed is 1959. The history of poverty in the US from 1959 to 2003 based on the federal standard is shown in Table 16.1. This table reproduces most of a table in a government report, and it contains a lot of numbers. You have encountered many tables with economic data in this book, and by now you should have enhanced your skill at interpreting data presented in tabular form. Take a few minutes to look at this table, and then formulate some important facts

Table 16.1 Poverty in the US: 1959–2003

Year	All persons: number % (millions)		All persons in families: number % (millions)		Persons in female headed families: number % (millions)		Unrelated individuals: number % (millions)	
2003	35.8	12.5%	25.7	10.8%	11.7	28.0%	9.7	20.4%
2002	34.6	12.1	24.5	10.4	11.7	28.8	9.6	19.9
2001	32.9	11.7	23.2	9.9	11.2	28.6	9.2	19.9
2000	31.6	11.3	22.3	9.6	10.9	28.5	8.7	19.0
1999	32.8	10.3	23.8	10.3	11.8	30.5	8.4	19.1
1998	34.5	12.7	25.4	11.2	12.9	33.1	8.5	19.9
1997	35.6	13.3	26.2	11.6	13.5	35.1	8.7	20.8
1996	36.5	13.7	27.4	12.2	13.8	35.8	8.5	20.8
1995	36.4	13.8	27.5	12.3	14.2	36.5	8.2	20.9
1994	38.1	14.5	29.0	13.1	14.4	38.6	8.3	21.5
1993	39.3	15.1	29.9	13.6	14.6	38.7	8.4	22.1
1992	38.0	14.8	29.0	13.3	14.2	39.0	8.1	21.9
1991	35.7	14.2	27.1	12.8	13.8	39.7	7.8	21.1
1990	33.6	13.5	25.2	12.0	12.6	37.2	7.4	20.7
1989	31.5	12.8	24.1	11.5	11.7	35.9	6.8	19.2
1988	31.7	13.0	24.0	11.6	12.0	37.2	7.1	20.6
1987	32.2	13.4	24.7	12.0	12.1	38.1	6.9	20.8
1986	32.4	13.6	24.8	12.0	11.9	38.3	6.8	21.6
1985	33.1	14.0	25.7	12.6	11.6	37.6	6.7	21.5
1984	33.7	14.4	26.5	13.1	11.8	38.4	6.6	21.8
1983	35.3	15.2	27.9	13.9	12.1	40.2	6.7	23.1
1982	34.4	15.0	27.3	13.6	11.7	40.6	6.5	23.1
1981	31.8	14.0	24.8	12.5	11.1	38.7	6.5	23.4
1980	29.3	13.0	22.6	11.5	10.1	36.7	6.2	22.9
1979	26.1	11.7	20.0	10.2	9.4	34.9	5.7	21.9
1978	24.5	11.4	19.1	10.0	9.3	35.6	5.4	22.1
1977	24.7	11.6	19.5	10.2	9.2	36.2	5.2	22.6
1976	25.0	11.8	19.6	10.3	9.0	37.3	5.3	24.9
1975	25.9	12.3	20.8	10.9	8.8	37.5	5.1	25.1
1974	23.4	11.2	18.8	9.9	8.5	36.5	4.6	24.1
1973	23.0	11.1	18.3	9.7	8.2	37.5	4.7	25.6
1972	24.5	11.9	19.6	10.3	8.1	38.2	4.9	29.0
1971	25.6	12.5	20.4	10.8	7.8	38.7	5.2	31.6
1970	25.4	12.6	20.3	10.9	7.5	38.1	5.1	32.9
1969	24.1	12.1	19.2	10.4	6.9	38.2	5.0	34.0
1968	25.4	12.8	20.7	11.3	7.0	38.7	4.7	34.0
1967	27.8	14.2	22.8	12.5	6.9	38.8	5.0	38.1
1966	28.5	14.7	23.8	13.1	6.9	39.8	4.7	38.3
1965	33.2	17.3	28.4	15.8	7.5	46.0	4.8	39.8
1964	36.1	19.0	30.9	17.4	7.3	44.4	5.1	42.7
1963	36.4	19.5	31.5	17.9	7.6	47.7	4.9	44.2
1962	38.6	21.0	33.6	19.4	7.8	50.3	5.0	45.4
1961	39.9	21.9	34.5	20.3	7.3	48.1	5.1	45.9
1960	39.9	22.2	34.9	20.7	7.2	48.9	4.9	45.2
1959	39.5	22.4	34.6	20.8	7.0	49.4	4.9	46.1

Source: US Bureau of the Census (2003)

that it contains. This sort of exercise illustrates one of the critical skills an economist must develop – the ability to pull information from data. You will (we hope) recall from Chapter 1 that this is the second step in the creation of knowledge in a applied field such as urban economics. The data never speak for themselves. (The word data is plural; the singular is datum.) We must speak for the data.

Now let us give you our summary of important facts in Table 16.1.

- The poverty rate in 1959 was 22.4% of the population, and the poverty rate among people who lived in female-headed households and among unrelated individuals was much higher (almost 50%). While this fact is not shown, it is obvious that the poverty rate among people who lived in male-headed households was much lower than the average.
- The poverty rate in 2003 of 12.5% is lower than the poverty rate in 1959, but note that the total number of people in poverty was only slightly lower in 2003 (39 million versus 36 million).
- A closer look at the data over time reveals that the poverty rate declined sharply in the decade of the 1960s to 12.1% in 1969. Indeed, the sharp drop in the poverty rate began in 1961–62. The poverty rate remained in the rather narrow 11% to 12.6% range from 1969 to 1979, and then it increased in the early 1980s to 15.2% in 1983. This increase in the poverty rate was almost certainly caused by the deep recession of that period. The poverty rate drifted down after 1983 to 12.8% in 1989, but afterwards it increased steadily to the 15.1% of 1993. After 1993 it declined, reaching a low point of 11.3% in 2000, and then increased to 12.5% in 2003. Note that the all-time low for the poverty rate was 11.1% in 1973. What reasons would you hypothesize to explain these facts?
- The poverty rate among persons in female-headed families declined from 50.3% in 1962 to 38.2% in 1969, and this percentage was been stuck in the mid and high 30s until 1998. Recent years have seen a sizable decrease in this poverty rate – from 38.6% in 1994 to less than 30% since 2000. These data almost succeed in speaking for themselves, but we could add that people in female-headed families are at very high risk of being in poverty. The 7.0 million persons in poverty in female-headed families constituted 17.8% of the population in poverty in 1959, but that percentage increased dramatically, reaching 37% in the early 1990s. The total number of people in poverty was about the same in 1959 and 1993, but the number in poverty in female-headed families had more than doubled to 14.6 million.
- The poverty rate among unrelated individuals declined steadily from 1959 46.1% in 1959 to 21.9 in 1979. Many of the unrelated individuals are elderly, and the growth in Social Security benefits that began in the 1960s certainly helped this group. The nation has had far more success at reducing the poverty rate among unrelated individuals than among persons who live in female-headed families. However, the poverty rate among unrelated individuals has remained in the fairly narrow range of 19.0% to 23.4% since 1979. The low point of 19.0% was reached in 2000, but since then the rate has drifted upwards.

Table 16.1 provides a look at poverty over time, and it does highlight the poverty rates of people in female-headed families and unrelated individuals. However, there are many more ways to "cut" the data by population group. Table 16.2 has been prepared so we can

Table 16.2   Poverty rates for persons and families: 2003

	Number in poverty (millions)	Poverty rate (%)
Persons		
Total	35.8	12.5
White	25.0	10.6
Not of Hispanic origin	15.9	8.2
Black	8.8	24.4
Asian	1.4	11.8
Hispanic origin[a]	9.1	22.5
Persons by age		
Under 18 years	12.9	17.6
18–64	19.4	10.8
65 years and over	3.6	10.2
Persons by place of residence		
Inside metropolitan areas	28.4	12.1
Inside central cities	14.6	17.5
Outside central cities	13.8	9.1
Outside metropolitan areas	7.5	14.2
Northeast	6.1	11.3
Midwest	6.9	10.7
South	14.5	14.1
West	8.3	12.6
Families by type		
Married couple	3.1	5.4
Female householder, no husband present	3.9	28.0
Male householder, no wife present	0.6	13.5

[a] Persons of Hispanic origin may be of any race.
Source: US Bureau of the Census (2003)

look at several different groups of people for just one year – 2003. Tables 16.1 and 16.2 thus represent the two traditional methods that economist use to present and study data. The two methods are called the time-series approach and the cross-section approach. What does the cross-section approach shown in Table 16.2 tell us?

Once again, take a few minutes to form your own opinion of what important facts are contained in Table 16.2.

Are you finished? Here is our list.

- The poverty rate of white people is relatively low at 8.2%. The poverty rates for black people and people of Hispanic origin are both over 20%.
- The next group of figures shows the poverty rate by age group, and the group with the highest rate of poverty (at 17.6%) is *children* (people under age 18). The sensational way of saying it is that more than one out of six children in the United States of America lived in poverty in 2003. Surely there are serious consequences for our society in the long run because so many of our children live in poverty at any given time. At 10.2%, the poverty rate for the elderly is actually below the overall average.

- The next two sets of figures show that the poverty rate is higher in central cities than in suburbs or outside metropolitan areas, and that poverty is more prevalent in the South than in the other regions of the nation. A more detailed examination of poverty in urban areas is provided below.
- The final sets of data refer to families rather than to individual persons. In 2003, 10.0% of families were in poverty. As you would expect, the poverty rate was much higher among female-headed families than among married couples. The poverty rate was 28.0% for all female-headed families in 2003.

Table 16.2 includes the fact that the poverty rate is higher in central cities than in suburbs or non-metropolitan areas. It is also true that poverty in central cities tends to be concentrated in certain areas within central cities, and that this tendency towards the concentration of poverty has been increasing in some urban areas. Some recent studies define an "extreme poverty census tract" as one in which at least 40% of the population is in poverty. Several studies have shown that the number of extreme poverty tracts in central cities increased dramatically in the 1970s and the 1980s, as did the concentration of poverty in those tracts. Jargowsky (1997) found that 1.89 million poor people lived in these extreme poverty tracts in 1970 (12.4% of all people in poverty), and that this figure had increased to 3.75 million in 1990 (17.9% of all people in poverty).

These trends were particularly evident for the black population. Jargowsky (1997) estimated that the proportion of poor blacks who live in extreme poverty tracts increased from 26.1% to 33.5% over the 1970–90 period. This concentration of black poverty was particularly strong in certain cities such as Detroit, Milwaukee, Cleveland, Pittsburgh, and Buffalo. But cities on the East Coast (especially New York, Philadelphia, and Newark) actually saw reductions in the number of black extreme poverty tracts and the concentration of poverty in those tracts.

More recent studies by Jargowsky (2003) and McDonald (2004) show that the increasing concentration of poverty of the 1970s and 1980s reversed dramatically in the 1990s. Jargowsky (2003) found that the number high-poverty census tracts declined by 26.5% over the decade, and that the total population residing in high-poverty tracts dropped by 23.5%. McDonald (2004) conducted a study of the 77 traditional community areas in Chicago, and found that the number of high-poverty community areas increased from 1 in 1970 to 9 in 1980 and 11 in 1990. The reversal of trend in the 1990s resulted in only 6 community areas classified as high-poverty areas in 2000. McDonald (2004) found that the decline in the poverty rate among families in poverty areas was strongly associated with an increase in employment for females. The combination of employment opportunity and the changes in the public welfare system in the 1990s resulted in an increase in employment among females. The change in the welfare system in 1996 is discussed below.

D. Effects of Taxes and Transfers on the Poverty Rate

As we have seen, the official definition of poverty is based on before-tax money income from all sources except capital gains. This definition omits the effects of taxes and the value of noncash transfers (e.g., food stamps, public housing, Medicare, and Medicaid).

Table 16.3   The effects of taxes and transfers on poverty: 2002

	Persons in poverty (millions)	Poverty rate (%)
Definition 1	34.6	12.1
Definition 2 Def. 1 less government cash transfers	57.2	20.0

Definition 3
    Def. 2 plus capital gains, employee health benefits,
        and EITC and minus income and payroll taxes
	54.4	19.1

Definition 4 Def. 3 plus nonmeans-tested government cash transfers	34.0	11.9
Definition 5 Def. 4 plus value of medicare and school lunches	33.1	11.6
Definition 6 Def. 5 plus means-tested government cash transfers	31.1	10.9

Definition 7
    Def. 6 plus value of Medicaid and other means-tested
        government noncash transfers
	26.8	9.4

Number removed from poverty by		
Nonmeans-tested cash transfers (primarily Social Security)	20.4 million	
Capital gains and health insurance benefits	2.2	
Earned income tax credit	4.0	
Federal and state income taxes and payroll tax	−3.4	

Means-tested transfers
    (cash and noncash – welfare,
    Medicaid, food stamps, etc.)
	7.2	

Source: US Bureau of the Census (2003)

The US Bureau of the Census annually conducts a careful study of the effects of various taxes and transfer programs on the poverty rate. Some of their illuminating results are shown in Table 16.3. The bottom line on these results is that the poverty rate for 2002 is reduced by around 20% (from 12.1% to 9.4%) after capital gains, taxes, and transfers (cash and noncash) are included.

The official poverty rate is listed at the top of Table 16.3, and then several adjustments to this rate are made in succession. The first adjustment (definition 2) is to subtract out *all* government cash transfer payments, and to recompute the poverty rate based on the money income that remains. Government cash transfer programs include:

- Social Security payments (and US Railroad Retirement);
- unemployment compensation;

- education grants (Pell grants);
- Temporary Assistance for Needy Families (TANF);
- Supplemental Security Income (SSI); and
- veteran's benefits.

Social Security is, of course, the pensions paid to the elderly and to the disabled under the Social Security System. Unemployment compensation is the joint federal/state program that pays temporary benefits to workers who have been laid off. TANF is the main welfare program that primarily pays benefits to female-headed families with dependent children. This program replaced Aid to Families with Dependent Children (AFDC) in 1996. AFDC provided benefits for an unlimited time period, but TANF is limited to a lifetime total of 60 months. SSI is a transfer program that is run by the Social Security System for the elderly who are poor and do not qualify for regular Social Security benefits. Education grants and veteran's benefits are received by the relevant special groups.

Table 16.3 shows that, if all of these government transfer programs are subtracted, the poverty rate would be 20.0%. The number of people in poverty jumps from 34.6 million to 57.2 million. This figure of 20.0% is based simply on a subtraction of government transfers from the money incomes of households. No account is taken of the possibility that households would respond to the loss of government transfer payments by acting to increase other forms of money income – by working more, for example. Nevertheless, this first result in Table 16.3 gives us a pretty good idea of the extent to which all government transfer programs reduce poverty.

The next line on Table 16.3 is an intermediate step that shows the net effect of five items; income from capital gains, employee health insurance supplements (treated as part of total employee compensation), the earned income tax credit (EITC), federal and state income taxes, and the payroll (Social Security) tax. The only item in this list that needs comment in the earned income tax credit.

The current federal income tax includes a tax credit to workers who make low wages. A tax credit reduces one's tax liability and, in the case of the EITC, can result in the receipt of money from the federal government if one has a low income tax liability. The tax credit for the worker who has no children is very low, but the worker with one child can earn a sizable tax credit. Here is how the EITC works (as of 2001). If the worker had one child, the EITC increased by $340 per $1,000 of earnings up to a maximum tax credit of $2,428 at earnings of $7,100. The tax credit remained at $2,428 for earnings between $7,100 and $13,100, and then declined by $160 per $1,000 of earnings to zero at earnings of $28,250. A person with taxable income of $7,100 owed $1,061 in federal income taxes in 2001, so the tax credit of $2,428 meant that such a person actually received a check from the Internal Revenue Service for $1,367. The specific dollar figures are updated annually. The EITC effectively removed workers with earnings lesss than about $16,000 from the federal income tax roles, and actually provided a small *negative* tax to most of them. However, note that the EITC is indeed a tax credit for *earnings*. People who have no earnings do not benefit from the program, so EITC is not a welfare (or income maintenance) program.

As Table 16.3 shows, the net effect on the poverty rate of the five adjustments in definition 3 is very small. The inclusion of capital gains income, employee health insurance benefits, and the EITC moves some people above the poverty line. However, the federal and state income taxes and the payroll (Social Security) tax puts people below the poverty line, so the net effect is to reduce the number of people in poverty by 0.85 million.

The next step (definition 4) adds back in the government cash transfers that are *not* means tested. Means tested is the term used to describe transfer programs in which eligibility and benefits are based on the income (or wealth) of the potential recipient. The government cash transfer programs that are not means tested are Social Security payments (and Railroad Retirement), unemployment compensation, and most veteran's benefits and education grants. By far the largest program in this category is Social Security, and eligibility for this program is based on working on jobs that were covered by the program. Inclusion of these income sources brings the poverty rate down from 19.1% to 11.6%. In short, the Social Security System is the nation's largest anti-poverty program. Most of its payments are made to the elderly, but the program also covers people with disabilities.

The next line in Table 16.3 (definition 5) adds in the value of Medicare, the federal health care program for the elderly. This addition reduces the poverty rate to 11.6%. The value of Medicare included is not the cash amount paid by the government for health care for the elderly, but is, rather, an estimate of the value of Medicare benefits to the individuals in the program. The idea is to figure out how much income would have been spent on medical care in the absence of the program. This is called the "fungible value" of the benefits, and is assumed to be zero if the household has an income that is less than an estimated amount Y_b needed for basic food and housing needs. If household income exceeds Y_b, then the value of Medicare is assumed to equal the difference between actual income and Y_b (up to the actual Medicare benefit). The same method is used below to evaluate Medicaid benefits, the health care program for the poor.

The next step (definition 6) is very important. It shows the reduction in the poverty rate that results from the inclusion of *means-tested* government cash and noncash transfer programs; i.e. the public welfare programs. These programs include Temporary Assistance for Needy Families (TANF), Supplemental Security Income (SSI), public relief programs operated by the states, Medicaid, food stamps, and housing assistance. The largest of these programs is Medicaid. The means-tested programs reduce the poverty rate from 11.6% to 9.4%, and raise 6.3 million people above the poverty line.

This final line in Table 16.3 perhaps is the best available measure of the poverty rate because it includes the effects of the income and payroll taxes, and adds in the noncash government transfer programs as well. Recall that the official poverty rate in 1993 was 12.1%, but this adjusted figure is 9.4%.

E. Causes of Poverty

Table 16.1 shows that poverty rates have changed over time, and Table 16.2 shows that the poverty rate varies enormously by population group. Hypotheses about the causes of poverty must address both sets of facts.

Changes in the poverty rate over time are caused largely by three factors:

- macroeconomic conditions,
- demographic/social changes (e.g., increase in the proportion of households headed by females), and
- changes in public policy.

A substantial amount of research has shown that the poverty rate is sensitive to macro-economic conditions. For example, Blank and Blinder (1986) found that an increase in the unemployment rate for males of one percent increased the poverty rate by 0.7%. For an economist the first order of business in fighting poverty is keeping the unemployment rate low. The rate of growth of the American economy slowed down in the early 1970s. Wages of many workers, especially those without higher education, stagnated or even declined in real terms. The increase in the inequality of income tends to increase the poverty rate. As noted above, the rapid economic growth of the 1990s contributed to the decline in poverty. Macroeconomic policy is beyond the scope of this book, but the discussion of economic development policy for urban areas in Chapter 21 is relevant to fighting poverty.

Changes in the poverty rate are partly driven by social and demographic changes. We have seen that people who live in households headed by females are at very high risk of being in poverty. Thus, an increase in the relative size of this group will increase the overall poverty rate. Here the evidence is overwhelming. The population of the US increased by 35.5% from 1965 to 1993, but the number of people living in households headed by females increased by 131.3%. In 1993 14.6% of the population was living in households headed by females, and that proportion had increased from 8.6% in 1965. It is evident that far fewer women than men are able to earn enough money to escape poverty, so this trend towards more households headed by women makes it difficult to reduce the poverty rate. The status of women in the labor market is a subject that deserves a lengthy discussion, but that discussion is beyond the scope of this book. The topic of women in the labor market is normally included in courses in labor economics.

A purely demographic factor that tends to increase the overall rate of poverty is the recent rapid growth of the Hispanic population. As we have seen, people of Hispanic origin have a risk of being in poverty that is much higher than average. The proportion of the population that is of Hispanic origin increased from 6.56% in 1980 to 13.3% in 2000. Unless people of Hispanic origin are able to reduce their risk of being in poverty, the continued growth of this group will put upward pressure on the overall poverty rate. The poverty rate for the Hispanic population was 25.7% in 1980, 28.1% in 1990, and 21.5% in 2000, so this group did reduce its risk of being in poverty substantially in the 1990s.

The last factor to consider is changes in public policy. We saw that the poverty rate dropped sharply in the 1960s. That drop can be explained partly by the reduction in the unemployment rate that took place at that time. However, there was a large expansion of the income support system in the US at that time as well. Moffitt (1992) has provided a careful recounting of the history of means-tested transfer programs, and some of the most significant findings are as follows:

- The AFDC caseload increased from 3.0 million recipients in 1960 to 8.5 million recipients in 1970 and 11.3 million recipients in 1975. Eligibility criteria were reduced, and welfare rights organizations made the effort to inform potential recipients of their rights under the law.
- The number of recipients of food stamps increased from 0.4 million in 1965 to 4.3 million in 1970 and 17.1 million in 1975. The program was transformed from a minor program for the use of agricultural surpluses into a major means-tested transfer program.

- The Medicaid program was created in 1965, and the number of recipients was 15.5 million in 1970 and 22 million in 1975.

The number of recipients in all three of these major means-tested programs leveled off after 1975. It is clear that this major commitment on the part of government, largely the federal government, to income support for the poor resulted in a reduction in the poverty rate. Also, the Medicare program was created in 1965 to provide health benefits for the elderly population. At the same time the Social Security System started in increase benefits at a rate that exceeded the rate of inflation. These policy changes greatly reduced the poverty rate for the elderly.

Moffitt (1992) also shows that, from 1975 to 1990, the real value of the total of AFDC, food stamps, Medicaid, and housing assistance declined. The decline in the real value of AFDC benefits per recipient household actually began in 1970, and by 1985 the real decline in the average AFDC benefit was about 30%. The cause of this decline is the simple fact that states failed to increase benefit levels along with inflation. The consequence of this failure of benefits to grow with inflation is that the welfare package (AFDC, food stamps, Medicaid and housing assistance) is, over time, less capable of moving the household above the poverty level. The response of welfare recipients to this state of affairs is discussed below.

Now let us turn to the cross-section variations in the rate of poverty. Why does poverty vary so dramatically across population groups in the US? All of the determinants of the incomes of individuals and households matter. Any reasonably complete list of these factors will include:

- education level;
- job training;
- work experience;
- age and age discrimination;
- natural ability and intelligence;
- motivation;
- union membership;
- racial discrimination in the labor market;
- sex discrimination in the labor market;
- occupational segregation in the labor market;
- family background factors;
- geographic mobility (or immobility);
- racial segregation in housing, leading to spatial limitations on job opportunities.

The importance of education and training is emphasized in Chapter 17, and some of the other factors in this list will be discussed in this and the next section of the chapter. The net effect of all of these factors is a distribution of income that leads to the differences in the poverty statistics shown in Table 16.2. As you know, members of the black and Hispanic minority groups and women suffer from relatively high rates of poverty.

The poverty rate in 2003 was 12.5% of the population. The overall rate of poverty is a major national problem, but perhaps the most distressing aspect of the current poverty problem is the concentration of poverty in certain areas of major central cities in the form of what has been called the "urban underclass."

F. The End of Welfare as We Know It

No discussion of poverty and policies to alleviate poverty is complete without an examination of the major change in welfare policy that took place in 1996. Pavetti (2001) provides a fine history of welfare policy. The basic welfare program in the US, Aid to Families with Dependent Children (AFDC), was enacted during the depression of the 1930s. This program provided basic income support for female-headed families in poverty (and in some states also provided benefits for male-headed families). AFDC provided benefits to eligible families with no time limit, and was supposed to impose an implicit tax of 100% on earnings. The number of AFDC recipients grew slowly in the first thirty years of the program, reaching 4 million in 1966. The number of recipients grew rapidly over the next few years, and hit a plateau of 11 million in 1971. The number of AFDC recipients remained constant until the recession of the early 1990s, and reached a peak of 14 million in 1994. The number of recipients declined by 14% to 12 million in 1996 with the economic boom of the 1990s. Benefit levels were set by states, and varied from a maximum monthly benefit in 1996 of $120 in Mississippi to $703 in New York (and $712 in Hawaii and $923 in Alaska). The median for the maximum monthly benefit was $415 in 1996.

In 1996 the US Congress decided to change welfare as we know it. The Personal Responsibility and Work Opportunity Reconciliation Act (PRWORA) of 1996 was passed and signed into law by President Clinton just prior to the election of 1996. People who had been receiving AFDC had to apply to the state's Temporary Assistance for Needy Families (TANF) program. To be eligible for TANF, families must comply with work mandates and other requirements, and those that qualify for assistance are subject to time limits on the number of months they can receive assistance. Most states impose a time limit of 60 months, and recipients must be employed or engaged in job search. Failure to comply with work mandates will mean a gradual loss of TANF benefits for the entire family. This is in sharp contrast to AFDC. TANF recipiets continue to be eligible for other forms of assistance such as food stamps, public housing, and Medicaid, and strengthened the requirement that fathers provide child support. As Pavetti (2001) documents, the number of recipients dropped from 12 million on AFDC in 1996 to 5.8 million recipients in 2000, a decline of 52%. See Blank (2002) for a comprehensive evaluation of welfare reform.

TANF was created to achieve four important goals:

- provide assistance to needy families;
- end the dependence of needy families by promoting job preparation, work, and marriage;
- reduce out-of-wedlock births; and
- encourage the formation and maintenance of two-parent families.

The results of shifting from AFDC to TANF have been under intensive study, and Pavetti (2001) summarizes the findings as follows:

- Most parents (50% to 75%) who left the welfare roles obtained employment shortly thereafter, and as many as 87% have been employed at some time. However, earnings of welfare leavers in most cases are not sufficient to raise the family above the poverty line.

- Little is known about how welfare leavers who do not obtain employment make ends meet.
- The new system has increased child support payments from absent fathers, and these payments have reduced child poverty by two percentage points. For those families who receive it, child support is a substantial portion (26%) of income.
- Participation in the food stamp and Medicaid programs has declined, perhaps because of the overall climate that discourages families from applying for assistance.
- Some observers predicted severe hardship from the end of AFDC, and there is some evidence of severe and persistent economic hardship. Pavetti's (2001) review of studies finds that 9% to 27% of welfare leavers reported having difficulty providing enough food for their families.

One thing is certain. Studies of the largest change in social policy in our times will continue.

F. The Urban Underclass

The urban underclass consists of the groups of people who believe that they have little or no hope of joining the mainstream of American life in which people work for a living and look forward to their futures. The urban underclass displays behavioral symptoms that include:

- high unemployment;
- poverty;
- crime;
- illegitimacy;
- dependence on welfare;
- drug addiction and alcoholism;
- family instability;
- female-headed families;
- teen-age pregnancy;
- dropping out of school and poor education;
- low aspirations and low self-esteem;
- poor health; and
- early death.

Many people suffer from one or more of these problems at some times in their lives, but for the underclass these behaviors are the way of life. Richard Herrnstein and Charles Murray, in their controversial book *The Bell Curve* (1994), add that many of the people in the underclass also have low IQs (intelligence quotients) as measured by standard tests. There is no general agreement about how to define and measure the underclass in precise terms. But however the underclass is defined, a disproportionate number of the urban underclass is black. The existence, and apparent growth of, the urban underclass since the 1970s is a tragedy of immeasurable magnitude that confounds everyone.

Many social scientists have tried to understand the forces that perpetuate and increase the urban underclass. The leading scholar of underclass life is the sociologist William Julius Wilson. Wilson published two books that have had a major impact on thought about race and class. In the first book, *The Declining Significance of Race* (1978), Wilson argued that a growing number of blacks is being incorporated into the mainstream of modern middle-class American life, but that many are being left behind. The biggest social problem in America is no longer race, but class – especially the urban underclass. The emergence of the black middle class in large numbers is the reason that Wilson thinks that race, by itself, is of declining significance.

In the second book Wilson elaborated his thoughts on the urban underclass. That book is entitled *The Truly Disadvantaged: The Inner City, the Underclass, and Public Policy* (1987). Wilson documented the sharp increases in some of the symptoms of underclass behavior that have occurred since the 1960s. In 1960, 33% of black children were not living with two parents, and by 1988 that figure had increased to 61%. The number of black children born to an unwed mother increased from 23% to 61% over this same period. [However, Jencks (1992) pointed out that the main reason for this increase is the reduction in births by married women.] As we have seen, because families headed by women have a high risk of being in poverty, so black children have a high risk of being in poverty as well. In 1960, 51% of black women in the 15–44 age group were married, and that fraction had dropped to 29% by 1988.

Wilson argued that economic and social factors in the inner city can account for at least some of the growth in underclass behavior. He pointed out that poverty and unemployment have become more concentrated in certain areas of the inner city because those who are able to move out of such areas do so. The older black neighborhoods have lost their middle-class residents, so the remaining residents have lost contact with people who personify middle-class values. And the loss of decent jobs, primarily in manufacturing, from inner-city areas has reduced the employment prospects for black men. Wilson introduced what he called the male marriageable pool index, which is the number of employed men per 100 women in a particular age group. That index stood at 68 for black men aged 20–44 in the North in 1960, and it dropped to 56 by 1980 (Wilson 1987, p. 97). In contrast, the index for white men in the same age group in the North was 89 in 1960 and 86 in 1980.

Hammer (1992) has tested Wilson's hypotheses in a more rigorous statistical framework. Hammer posited the following model of labor force and family-related behavior:

- Reductions in blue-collar job opportunities reduce the labor-force participation of males.
- Reductions in male labor force participation reduce both the number of females who marry and the number of children who are born. The number of families headed by women increases.

Hammer tested these hypotheses using data on changes in the variables from 1970 to 1980 for 76 large urban areas. The model was estimated separately for blacks and whites in the 16–34 age group. He found that, as hypothesized, the decline in blue-collar employment for blacks was strongly related to the drop in black male labor force participation. The decline in the share of black women who were married with spouse present was strongly related to drop in male labor-force participation. The change in the fertility of black women was positively related to the change in the proportion of women who were married as expected, but the drop in male labor-force participation actually increased fertility (as was not expected). Hammer's explanation for this last result is that fertility may decline in urban areas where blacks had greater success in moving to middle-class status; i.e., where male labor force-participation increased. The results for whites came out generally as expected, but the magnitudes of the effects are considerably smaller for whites compared to blacks.

Hammer used his empirical results to trace through the effects of a loss of 1,000 blue-collar jobs for both blacks and whites. The loss of 1,000 blue collar jobs by blacks led to a decline in the labor force participation of black men of 253, while the same loss of blue collar jobs by whites reduced male labor force participation by 114. The number of black females with husbands present dropped by 104 (compared to 78 for whites). Whites responded to these changes by having 119 fewer children, but black children increased by 137. These changes resulted in 84 more female-headed families for blacks versus only 13 for whites. Based on Hammer's analysis, the loss of blue-collar jobs in urban areas appears to have had powerful effects on the black family and, in contrast to expectation, actually increased black fertility relative to what otherwise would have happened.

The linkages between the economy and underclass problems seem to be clear enough, but most researchers in the field think that the economic problems are insufficient to explain the massive changes that have taken place in society. Some blame the growth of the urban underclass on the welfare system but, as Ellwood (1988) and Moffitt (1992) pointed out, welfare programs became less generous during the 1970s as the underclass problems continued to grow at the same time. There is much that we do not know about the causes behind the underclass phenomenon, and economists (and others) must be modest in their claims of having the explanation at hand. Nevertheless, it is clear that the changes in the urban economy are implicated.

G. Life on Welfare

What sort of life do members of the urban underclass lead? This question cannot be answered because the underclass does not make itself available for detailed study. However, thanks to an ingenious study by Kathryn Edin that is reported in Jencks (1992), we have a pretty good idea about how welfare mothers lived in the 1980s. Edin interviewed a non-random sample of 50 welfare mothers in Cook County, Illinois during 1988–90 to find out how they get by on their meager welfare checks. The sample is not random because she had to interview people who would trust her. The sample was determined by the contacts of acquaintances.

The 50 welfare mothers had an average of 2.1 children and received a welfare check that was an average of $324 per month. They also received food stamps worth $200. Twenty-eight of the women resided in unsubsidized housing, and paid an average of $364 per month in rent and utilities. The remaining 22 who lived in subsidized housing paid only $123 per month in rent and utilities. The average food expenditure was $250 per month, so the food stamp allotment was not enough. Other expenses included clothing, laundry, cleaning supplies, school supplies, transportation, furniture, and so on. Average expenses for all of these other categories averaged $351 per month. Welfare mothers who did not live in subsidized housing had expenses of $940 per month, and those who lived in subsidized housing reported expenditures of $840 per month – compared to an average welfare check and food stamp allotment of $524.

From where does the rest of the money come? Almost half (43%) of the additional $316 or $416 in cash came from resident boyfriends, absent fathers, relatives, or friends. An equal amount (44%) came from money earned by the women themselves. Seven women had salaried jobs under another social security number, and 22 others had part-time jobs that were off the books (bartending, babysitting, catering). Five women sold drugs, and five worked occasionally as prostitutes. Of the five who sold drugs, one sold crack cocaine and was murdered shortly after the interview. The remaining 13% of the "supplemental" income came from various sources, including student loans. Not one of the 50 women lived just on the welfare check, food stamps, and subsidized housing. And only four reported any of the additional income to the welfare authorities. It is illegal not to report the additional income, but welfare authorities do not go looking for violations.

The only way a welfare mother can even come close to surviving without extra income is to live in subsidized housing. The option that is much preferred is the subsidized housing under the Section 8 program (as discussed in Chapter 9). These apartments are owned by private individuals or organizations, and are scattered throughout the city and inner suburbs. However, very few units of this type are available and there is a long waiting list. The other option is public housing in Chicago, which is horrible and dangerous. The waiting list is fairly short for public housing, but the welfare mothers in Edin's sample evidently will do almost anything to avoid having to live in public housing. And the welfare officials tacitly permit them to acquire the income necessary to stay out of public housing.

The choices that faced the welfare recipient can be depicted in a standard diagram that shows the labor–leisure trade-off. Figure 16.1 measures leisure time on the horizontal axis and income on the vertical axis. The total time budget for a person is assumed to be 480 hours per month (30 × 16). Consider the average welfare recipient from Edin's data who lives in unsubsidized housing. The family receives $524 in AFDC and Food Stamp benefits each month, and this amount is shown on the diagram. The total money income of the family is $940 per month, and about half of the additional amount (or $208) is received from others – boyfriends, other family members, etc. The rules of the AFDC program require that these funds be reported to the administrators of the program, and the AFDC benefit is supposed to be reduced by that amount. The welfare recipients in Edin's study do not report this income, so the family now has an income of $732 per month, as shown on Figure 16.1. Next, the welfare recipient considers working to earn additional money. The rules of the AFDC program regarding the taxation of earnings (the benefit reduction rate) for the first year on AFDC are rather complex but, after one full year on AFDC, benefits are supposed to be reduced by the amount of the earnings. In other words, the benefit reduction rate is 100%! No wonder the women in Edin's study failed to report their earnings.

Figure 16.1 depicts the various cases. If all of the rules of AFDC are followed, the AFDC family has an income of $524 per month regardless of the amount of time the woman works. The budget constraint is a horizontal line at an income of $524. If the unearned

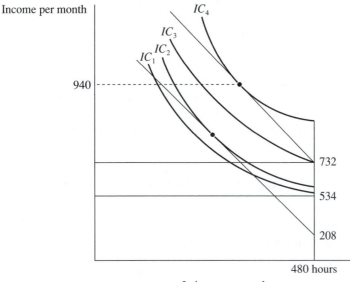

Figure 16.1   Welfare participation and work

income received from other people is not reported to the authorities but earnings are reported, then the AFDC family has an income of $732 regardless of the amount of time spent working. Now consider the option of working.

If the woman chooses not to receive AFDC and Food Stamps, then assume unearned income is $208 from other people. Suppose that the woman's wage rate is $5.00 per hour. The budget constraint starts with $208 and 480 hours of leisure. Income can be increased by $5.00 for each hour of leisure given up, so Figure 16.1 shows that the slope of the budget constraint is −5. If the woman chooses to be on AFDC and Food Stamps and to abide by all of the rules of the program, then monthly income will be $524. The woman who chooses *not* to be on AFDC and Food Stamps can reach this level of income by working 63 hours per month (or about 16 hours per week). Which option is preferable? The answer depends upon the woman's preferences, which are drawn to make the option of *not* participating in AFDC and Food Stamps the preferred choice.

Figure 16.1 depicts some better options. First, consider the option of participating in AFDC and Food Stamps and *not* reporting the unearned income received from others. Now the family has $732 per month. Including the $208 of unearned income received from others, the woman would have to work 105 hours per month (or about 26 hours per week) to have an income of this amount. Figure 16.1 is drawn so that participating in AFDC and Food Stamps, and not following all of the rules, is preferable to working and not receiving AFDC and Food Stamps. This choice is made presuming that it is extremely unlikely for the woman to be penalized for not following the rules of the AFDC program. Finally, consider the best option of all. Suppose that the woman receives AFDC and Food Stamps and fails to report *any* other forms of income, including her own earnings. As Edin's study indicated, this is done by working under another Social

Security number or working in the underground economy (where the few records that are kept are not available to the AFDC officials). The woman who makes this choice begins with a total of $732 in unearned income, and then decides how much time to work at a wage of $5.00 per hour. Edin's study showed that these families had an average income of $940 per month, so the woman earned $208. This level of earnings requires about 42 hours of work per month (about 10.5 hours per week). Figure 16.1 shows that this combination of $940 of income and 42 hours of work maximizes utility, given the constraint under which the woman must operate and given that the woman really does not face a penalty for failing to follow the rules of the AFDC program.

H. The Spatial Mismatch Hypothesis

The Urban Transportation Problem (1965), the book by Meyer et al., stated that the really serious urban transportation problem is the fact that the residents of the inner city do not have easy access to the jobs in the suburbs. The late John Kain (1968) elaborated this point in a classic article. Kain's hypothesis really has three parts:

- Housing segregation affects the distribution of black employment.
- Housing segregation reduces job opportunities for blacks.
- The process of suburbanization makes the problem worse.

Kain's (1968) statistical tests confirmed the first point; the residential location does affect the spatial distribution of employment. Blacks are viewed as being constrained in their choices of residential location by a segregated housing market, and this constraint is bound to have an influence on their job choices. This may or may not be particularly injurious to economic opportunity. What if urban blacks are constrained to live in areas in the city where there are many jobs? This was pretty much true in the 1950s, the time when the data used by Kain were collected. The social problem arises from Kain's other two hypotheses, but his empirical evidence in 1968 on these points was not completely convincing. However, it has now been established pretty definitively that all three of Kain's hypotheses are correct for teenagers. The evidence is not very convincing for adult male workers. It is worthwhile to review briefly the research that has been done on these important issues.

Kain (1968) tested his first hypothesis above by examining the racial composition of workers in a small zone (in Chicago or Detroit) as a linear function of the distance of that zone from the black housing area and the racial composition of the *residents* of that zone. The statistical significance of the distance variable (with a negative sign) confirms what can be called the direct effect of housing segregation on employment. Given that blacks have restricted residential location choices, the costs associated with distance will create the negative effect. The statistical significance of the racial composition of the residents of the zone (with a positive sign) is evidence that employers tend to hire workers who reflect the racial composition of the neighborhood in which the firm is located. This effect can be called the indirect effect of housing segregation on employment because it says that the movement of jobs from black to white residential areas will reduce black job opportunities apart from the effect of distance. The movement of jobs to distant, white suburbs is therefore doubly harmful to black job opportunities. Kain's (1968) empirical evidence indicated that both effects might be important.

Kain's study initiated a great deal of research, which has centered basically in two areas. First, several labor economists have argued that, while residential segregation restricts the opportunity to hold some jobs, the consequences for employment are relatively insignificant when compared to other factors that influence job opportunities for blacks such as the relative lack of education and training and racial discrimination. Second, it has been argued, most notably by Offner and Saks (1971), that the indirect effect of residential segregation on black job opportunities may be either positive or negative. It may be the case that residential integration will reduce disproportionately the jobs available to blacks because of the propensity of employers to hire workers who reflect the racial makeup of the surrounding residential area.

The labor market studies that are critical of Kain used different research strategies, but they all began with the observation that the demand for labor was stronger in central cities than in suburban areas. (This is no longer true in many urban areas.) Blacks were confined to residential locations that happened to be accessible to jobs. Noll (1970, p. 501) examined the spatial distribution of jobs in major urban areas in the 1960s and concluded that "jobs, particularly for the less skilled, are easier to find in the central city." Furthermore, studies by Lewis (1969) and Fremon (1970) demonstrated that the population in urban areas generally decentralized more rapidly than did total employment during the 1953–67 period. We now know that the reverse was true in the 1970s and 1980s; jobs "moved" to the suburbs more rapidly than did the people in these more recent periods. Friedlander (1972, p. 194) summed up the evidence at the time by noting that,

> The employment problems of city residents may be more affected by suburbanites commuting to the city for employment than by movement of jobs to the suburbs.

However, the real problem that was faced by minority residents of the central city may have been that employment opportunities in blue-collar and semiskilled and low-skilled jobs were moving to the suburbs so rapidly that a surplus of labor in these categories developed in the central city. This is the skills mismatch hypothesis. Several studies demonstrated that there had indeed been substantial shifts in the occupational mix of jobs in central cities. The most comprehensive study was done by Wilson (1979). Using the 1% public use samples from the 1960 and 1970 censuses for the 25 most populous states, he showed that there had been absolute declines in the craftsman, operative, and laborer categories in central cities over the period, while professional, sales, clerical, and service employment increased in central cities. Wilson did not determine whether these changes implied an increasing mismatch of skills between central city labor demand and supply, but it seems reasonably clear that the mismatch increased.

Partly because the direct test of the mismatch hypothesis requires a great deal of information about the supply of and demand for skills, a number of labor economists and other researchers have examined wage rates, earnings data, and unemployment rates for central city and suburban workers. However, as Wilson (1979) pointed out, evidence based on wage rates and other labor market data must be evaluated with care. There are four groups of black workers to be examined: those who live and work in the central city, those who live and work in the suburbs, those who live in the central city and work in the suburbs, and those who live in the suburbs and work in the central city. The best comparison to test Kain's hypothesis is, holding other factors constant, to examine the wages of workers who live and work in the suburbs with those who live and work in the central city. Workers who commute from the central city to the suburbs, for example, may only take jobs which pay more than the worker's expected wage because of the higher commuting costs involved. In other words, the data on wages earned by commuters from city to suburbs may contain a severe selection bias in the positive direction. Wilson (1979) made the appropriate comparisons and found that in both 1959 and 1969 the wages of blacks who lived and worked in the suburbs were not higher than the wages of blacks who lived and worked in the central city, holding constant schooling, experience, and industry. However, a more recent study by Price and Mills (1985) used data from the 1978 Current Population Survey and found that both black and white men who lived in the central city earned 6% to 8% less than their suburban counterparts, holding constant the effects of a large number of personal characteristics, industry, and amenities. Black workers who lived in the city earned 13% less than comparable white men who lived in the city, and black suburban residents earned 16% less than their white suburban counterparts. However, a study by McMillen (1993) found no evidence of the effect of the spatial mismatch on the earnings of black male workers in the Detroit urban area in 1980 because he found that blacks who worked in the central city had higher earnings there than if they had worked in the suburbs. Likewise, blacks who worked in the suburbs had higher earnings there than if they had worked in the central city.

Leonard (1987) conducted a study of black male employment in Chicago and Los Angeles using establishment data for 1974 and 1980 available from the Office of Federal Contract Compliance. The Chicago sample consists of 1,191 establishments that were observed in both years at their same locations. Regression analyses showed that the proportion of blue-collar employees in an establishment who were black males was strongly negatively related to the distance of the establishment from the border of the black residential area. Furthermore, this negative gradient in Chicago actually was steeper in 1980 than in 1974. No allowance was made for the movement of the border of the black residential area from 1974 to 1980, so the effect of the distance variable was actually underestimated. Furthermore, no attempt as made to consider the effects of establishments that decentralized over this period. It is telling that employment of black males in blue-collar jobs remained constant in the 547 suburban establishments in the sample of 1,191 given that total blue-collar employment in these establishments increased by 2.3% over the period. One might have expected that black workers would have been able to increase their ability of compete for suburban blue-collar jobs.

Ellwood (1986) completed an important study of the employment of male teenagers in metropolitan Chicago in 1970. This study is discussed in some detail because it has received a good deal of publicity. The study was designed to address two related issues; the effect of proximity to jobs on labor market outcomes, and whether the proximity effect can explain some of the differential in employment opportunities between black and white youth. Teenagers were chosen for the study because of concern for this group and because it is reasonable to assume that their residential locations are exogenous to the employment outcome. Many teenagers (even those not in school) live with their parents or guardians. However, Ellwood (1986) made no effort to determine whether the teenagers in his data lived at home. Two empirical research strategies were followed. The first used Census Tract data for 1970 and examined the employment rate for out-of-school male youths aged 16 to 21 living in the tract as a function of job accessibility, education, and demographic variables. The second approach used the special 1970 Census Employment Survey (CES) of low-income areas in Chicago.

The results using the Census Tract data indicate that employment rates were lower in tracts with more poor families, blacks, Spanish-speaking people, and children in single-parent families. Teenage employment for those not in school was greater if more teenagers were in school. The variable to measure job accessibility is the ratio of jobs (blue collar and service) located in the community to workers who live in the community. The variable is a measure of local demand relative to supply, and its regression coefficient is positive and statistically significant. But, as Ellwood (1986) pointed out, the magnitude of the coefficient is very small. The coefficient says that, if a neighborhood were changed from one with two workers per job to one with two jobs per worker, the employment rate of male teenagers would increase by less than one percentage point. This finding is consistent with the idea that locational factors are of minor importance compared to racial discrimination, education, and training.

The Census Employment Survey of 1970 was conducted on the west and south sides of Chicago. Blacks and whites in low-income areas were surveyed, and the survey was designed to gather information on the labor market. As Ellwood (1986) pointed out, this survey provides a natural experiment because access to employment was much higher on the west side than on the south side of Chicago. Ellwood (1986) simply calculated mean values for young black men (age 16–21) who resided in these two areas. The sample sizes are only about 100 for each area. The labor market outcomes for out-of-school young black men in the two areas are very similar. The employment (unemployment) rates were 51% (38%) for the south side and 54% (35%) on the west side. The outcomes for high school dropouts were very similar in the two areas. However, Ellwood (1986) did not point out that there might have been some differences in labor market outcomes for those young men who had graduated from high school. The employment (unemployment) rate for this group was 71% (19%) on the south side and 80% (10%) on the west side. The small sample sizes mean that these differences are not statistically significant, but the figures suggest that high school graduates did better on the west side than on the south side and that dropouts did poorly in both locations.

Ellwood (1986) was also able to use the CES data for the west side to compare labor market outcomes for black and white males who resided in the area. This tabulation reveals that the employment rate (unemployment rate) was 79% (11%) for whites and 54% (35%) for blacks who were not in school and in the 16–21 age group. Furthermore, the percentage of whites who had graduated from high school was 29% compared to 34% for blacks. Again it appears to be race, and not place.

Another approach to labor market studies was followed by Mooney (1969) and Masters (1974, 1975). Using a cross-section of urban areas, these studies related a measure of economic well-being of blacks to the degree of residential segregation and other variables. These studies failed to find an important relationship between these two variables. However, Kain (1974) has criticized both of these studies on the grounds that the measures of segregation used do not adequately measure the access of blacks to jobs. A related study by Moffitt (1977) examined changes in city/suburban relative wages for a cross-section of urban areas for 1960–70. The study found that wage rates in the central cities actually increased slightly relative to suburban wages during the period because of the extensive movement of the white population to the suburbs. Central city residents would thus appear to have had somewhat better wage opportunities in 1970 than in 1960.

The empirical evidence from the labor market appeared to be inconclusive until a series of studies on urban teenagers was conducted by Keith Ihlanfeldt and David Sjoquist. Ihlanfeldt (1992) has reviewed the literature and presented the Ihlanfeldt–Sjoquist findings. His review of the literature reveals that the studies that rejected Kain's hypotheses used flawed methods of some sort. For example, the Ellwood (1986) study is criticized on four grounds:

- The measures of access to employment may have been measured with error.
- It may not be true that the residential locations of the teenagers in Ellwood's study are exogenous. If residential location and work location are determined together, then the effect of residential location will appear to be zero.
- The comparison of white and black youths from the CES did not adequately control for other factors.
- The comparison of black youths who lived on the west and south sides may be flawed because it is not clear that residence on the west side provided better access to jobs that could be held by black youth.

In contrast, the research by Ihlanfeldt and Sjoquist (1990 and 1991) shows that poor access to employment is a significant factor in the low employment rates of black youth in a large number of urban areas. The measure of access to jobs that was used is the average travel time of low-wage workers who lived in the same residential zone as the youth in question. Only youths who still lived at home with a parent or guardian were included in the studies. The results for Philadelphia are that an increase in travel time of one standard deviation reduced the probability that a black youth had a job in 1980 by 4.0% to 6.3%. The effect of this same change on white youth was −3.8% to −5.1%. The difference in access to jobs between whites and blacks accounted for 33% to 50% of the difference in employment rates between the two groups. The studies by Ihlanfeldt and Sjoquist are superior to previous studies because they used a better measure of access to jobs, because they included only youths who live at home, and because their use of data on individuals permitted them to include a large number of control variables for individual and family characteristics. The results reported by Ihlanfeldt (1992) show that black female teenagers and Hispanic youths of both sexes faced the roughly the same problem with access to jobs as black males. At this point the work of Ihlanfeldt and Sjoquist is the definitive research on the narrow issue of access to jobs and chances for employment among black and Hispanic teenagers who still lived at home. The question for all black and Hispanic workers remains open. Is it race, or is it place for other groups of black and Hispanic workers?

Jencks (1992) argues rather persuasively that, for adult males, it is race and not place. Most teenagers are qualified only for jobs with low wages. It makes sense that they are not willing to search far and wide and to make lengthy commutes to jobs that pay very little. Other groups, such as women with children and adult men with little education, are probably in the same boat. The argument is not convincing for adult men with at least a high school diploma. These men conceivably can qualify for reasonably good jobs, including suburban jobs in manufacturing, construction, transportation and wholesale trade, and so on. As Jencks (1992, p. 123) puts it, "Distance is a problem only when employers let it become one." Distance is not a barrier for white men with at least a high school education. Firms in the central business district have no difficulty recruiting men who live in the suburbs. And people who work in the suburbs rarely live close to work. A good job pays enough to permit the worker to purchase a car; commuting is our way of life. Employers do not advertise their blue-collar jobs in places that are known to blacks in the inner city because they do not wish to hire these workers.

Jencks (1992) also provides a refreshing perspective on the problems that teenagers face in the labor market. He points out that variations in the employment rate of black and other teenagers can be explained by aggregate changes in demand and supply. For example, the boom in the Massachusetts economy in the 1980s reduced the unemployment rate of blacks to 5.6%, and Freeman (1991) found that tight labor markets substantially reduce unemployment among black teenagers. Macroeconomic evidence also shows that a high level of aggregate demand and a low unemployment rate benefit minority and teenage workers. The problem is that we may be reluctant to crank up aggregate demand enough to bring the unemployment rate down to levels such as 3.5% or 4% because we fear accelerating inflation. However, it is also true that the demand for unskilled labor has weakened as the supply of such labor has increased. This is the problem that labor economists used to call structural unemployment. The "structure" of demand for labor has changed; i.e., employers now demand more verbal, mathematical and analytical skills than before. At the same time the suppliers of labor have been slow to adjust. In some areas the supply of unskilled labor has been expanded by the immigration of Hispanic workers and other groups. The entry of the baby boom generation and many women into the labor force also tended to increase the supply of workers at all levels, especially at the unskilled and semi-skilled levels. In the 1980s there was something of a shortage of college-educated workers (at least in some fields), and an oversupply of workers with lesser skills. At this point in time the society is trying to grapple with the problem of how to upgrade the skills of our fellow Americans so that they can better match the demand for labor. Businesses, schools, colleges, and government in general are all engaged in a wide variety of serious efforts to understand and deal with this problem.

In his final publication Kain (2004) reviewed the history of research on spatial mismatch and pointed out that serious restrictions on residential choice have other, more serious consequences that may include higher housing prices or poor neighborhood quality, lack of opportunity for home ownership, and lack of educational opportunity. Indeed, Kain's last research project was the impact of residential segregation on educational opportunity. This topic in discussed in the next chapter.

Since the 1960s a debate has been going on about how to address the spatial mismatch problems discussed in this section. The policy debate also has some relevance to the problems of urban crime and underclass behavior as well. The debate has been framed as "ghetto development" versus "ghetto dispersal." We find the use of the word "ghetto" somewhat distasteful, but the idea is that policies might focus on building up the economy of the inner city as compared to policies designed to move low-income and minority households to locations where economic opportunities are better. Another shorthand phrase is bringing jobs to people or moving people to jobs. There is no reason why a comprehensive strategy cannot try to do both, but it may be useful to begin with a broader perspective.

Chapter 21 is a lengthy discussion of economic development strategy and policy for an urban area. An economic development strategy can be framed to provide greater or lesser benefits for the low-income residents of the inner city, but as Bartik's (1991) empirical results indicate, an effective strategy for economic development of any sort will generate enhanced economic opportunities for the residents of the urban area. It should be clear that the first thing to do is to put in place an economic development strategy that is designed to put some emphasis on low-income households. Economic growth at a sufficient rate in an urban area will translate into growth in the central city as well. Many people criticize what they derisively call "trickle down economics," but economic growth cannot be bad, and in a growing local economy it is easier to create opportunities for lower-income people. Let us work to expand the pie, and let us also try to make sure that some of the increase goes to the poor. With that said, what about "ghetto development" versus "ghetto dispersal?"

If politics is the art of the possible, then so is urban economic development. Is it possible to generate economic growth and development in the inner city outside of the downtown area? Perhaps it is, but the efforts to do so in urban areas that have experienced little growth overall have not been very successful. Inner city development efforts surely work better when the urban area is experiencing robust growth. That was the message from a study of enterprise zones in Cook County, Illinois. The one group of industries that was attracted to the inner city was wholesale trade and transportation, an industry group that was experiencing appreciable growth in the urban area as a whole. If the economic development strategy includes targeting of industries for special programs, then a program of inner city development should then target those industries that are experiencing substantial growth and that also would consider such a location. In particular, attempts to induce manufacturing to locate in the inner city of an urban area that is growing slowly are wasted efforts. It probably is true that, even when the urban area is growing, some special inducements will be needed to attract firms to the inner city. In would seem that some modest inducements are in order to bring about the result. Economic growth in the inner city might mean better job prospects for teenagers and women, at least. An improvement in job prospects for women might have a direct impact on the poverty rate, as McDonald (2004) found for the high-poverty areas in Chicago.

The conclusion is that some selective efforts to generate economic development in the inner city seem to make sense, but these policies are likely to work only after policies to promote the growth of the urban area as a whole have been put in place. In addition, the problem of structural unemployment of minority workers and others with low levels of education and training need to be addressed with labor market policies that will enhance educational and training opportunities. A full discussion of these matters is beyond the scope of this book, but the inherent difficulties must not be understated. Heckman (1994) points out that, between 1979 and 1989, the earnings of male high school dropouts per week decreased by 13%, high school graduates earned 4% less, and college graduates increased their weekly earnings by 11%. Heckman (1994) estimated the amount of investment in human capital that would restore the earnings of the high school dropouts and graduates to their 1979 levels. If the rate of return to investment in human capital is 10%, which is a decent rate of return to any investment, then each high school dropout would require an investment of $25,000 (in 1989 dollars) and each high school graduate would require $10,000 in human capital investment. The grand total for all males in these two categories is $426 billion (in 1989 dollars). Needless to say, high school dropouts do not have $25,000 to spend (and earnings to forego) to make the needed investment. They will need assistance from the public sector to obtain the education and training just to restore their earnings to 1979 levels, but the government is not contemplating a program of anything like the magnitude that Heckman suggests.

But what about "ghetto dispersal?" It turns out that there is solid evidence of the benefits of a limited program of "ghetto dispersal." The best studies of the strategy of "ghetto dispersal" have been done on an unusual program in Chicago (Rosenbaum 1993). In 1976 the Supreme Court of the United States ruled that, because the Chicago Housing Authority (the public housing agency in Chicago) had employed racially discriminatory policies in selecting locations for and administration of public housing, it must offer a program of rent certificates that permits the residents of public housing to move out to other locations. This program has succeeded in helping black people move to middle-class white suburbs; since 1976 some 4,000 families have participated in the program, and over half have moved to white suburbs. The evaluation studies compare those who moved to the suburbs to those who moved to another location in the city. This technique is a reasonable method for controlling for the level of motivation of the family. The adults in the study are women, and the ones who moved to the suburbs had a higher employment rate than did those who moved to a city location. Among those who claimed that they had never been employed before, 46% of suburban movers got jobs compared to 30% of city movers. (Note that moving out of public housing increased employment for both groups.) More importantly, the children in the families that moved to the suburbs did extremely well. These children were more likely to be in the college track in high school, to attend college, or to be employed full time if not in college. Those who were employed were far more likely to have decent earnings and job benefits (such as health insurance). After a period of adjustment to the higher standards that are imposed in suburban schools, the black students did much better in suburban schools than did their counterparts in city schools. The families that moved to middle-class suburbs, where the streets are pretty safe, jobs are plentiful, and schools have fairly high standards, learned how to take advantage of this better environment. In short, Rosenbaum and his associates have shown us that there is reason for hope.

The research that is available gives us a pretty clear message. The urban area with serious problems in its inner city should formulate and pursue a strategy of economic growth and development that includes some emphasis on attracting business to the inner city. At the same time, policies that move inner city residents to the suburbs provide positive results and should also be followed.

I. Homelessness

In Chapter 9 it was pointed out that the most serious problem facing low-income households in the housing market is the cost of housing, compared to (reported) income. The discussion above of the urban underclass included an examination of how 50 welfare mothers manage to provide for their families. The problem of housing loomed large in that discussion. Welfare mothers in Cook County, Illinois who did not live in subsidized housing paid an average of $364 per month in rent and utilities (electricity and natural gas for heat), an amount that was roughly equal to their welfare checks. Their solution to the problem of a severe shortage of money was to get income from a variety of other sources that were not reported to the welfare authorities (or to other government agencies, most likely).

The related problem of homelessness has been very much on the policy agenda in recent years. Several different attempts have been made to count the number of homeless people. The number will depend, of course, upon the definition of homelessness that is used. The official definition of homelessness that was written into the McKinney Homeless Assistance Act of 1987 defines the homeless as:

- individuals who lack a fixed, regular and adequate nighttime residence (e.g., those who use a tent, a highway underpass, a car, a sleeping bag on the street); and
- those whose nighttime residence is a temporary shelter or other institution that provides temporary housing; or
- a place not intended for human sleeping accommodations (e.g., a hallway in a public building).

This definition includes people who are living temporarily in welfare hotels or in shelters for battered women as well as those who are in homeless shelters. A narrow definition would include only those who sleep in homeless shelters and exclude the others who are in other forms of temporary accommodations. On the other hand, what about people who are doubling up in housing units or others who live in very crowded conditions? The number of people in these two categories also indicates a serious problem of access to housing that is affordable.

Many attempts have been made to estimate the number of homeless people, a group of people who are difficult to count because often they do not wish to be counted. The 1990 Census placed the number of homeless on the streets or in shelters at approximately 250,000 for the nation (as of March 1990). However, given that the homeless population changes constantly, a far larger number of people experiences a spell of homelessness during a year. The US Department of Housing and Urban Development (1984) used four independent methods to estimate the number of homeless, and came up with a range of 250,000 to 350,000 as of 1984. HUD also produced estimates of the homeless population for 60 cities in 1984. These estimates vary from 535.1 per 100,000 population in the city of San Francisco down to 6.8 per 100,000 in Fall River, Massachusetts. The top ten cities for homeless rates among the cities in the 1984 HUD study were as follows:

City	Homeless per 100,000
San Francisco	535.1
Los Angeles	412.0
Miami	348.8
New York	346.2
Chicago	323.9
Worcester, MA	259.9
Fort Wayne, IN	208.1
Las Vegas	205.0
Houston	200.7
Seattle	187.2

Note that the three largest cities in the nation (New York, Los Angeles and Chicago) were in the top five. These and other large cities have sizable absolute numbers of homeless people; for example, a rate of 412 per 100,000 in Los Angeles (population 3.5 million) translates into 14,400 homeless people on any given night. The McKinney Act of 1987 was passed to address the immediate problems of this sizable group of people by providing funds for homeless shelters, some funds for the rehabilitation of single-room occupancy dwellings, and some funds for community efforts to assist the homeless. However, many advocates for the homeless argue that the McKinney Act was a good start, but that more is needed.

If the number of homeless people is about 250,000, who are they? The HUD studies did not provide data on the characteristics of the homeless, but a fairly comprehensive national study by Burt and Cohen (1989) did. Their estimates of the homeless population are:

Sex/family status	Proportion
Single male adults	0.68
Single female adults	0.09
Male adults in families	0.01
Female adults in families	0.07
Children	0.15
Race	
Black	0.41
White	0.46
Hispanic	0.10
Other	0.03
Medical/criminal history	
Ever in mental hospital	0.19
Chemical dependency	0.33
Ever in prison	0.24

Note that most of the homeless in their study were adult males, but that 15% of the homeless were children. Homeless people suffer from high rates of mental illness and/or chemical dependency (e.g. addiction to alcohol), and they are disproportionately black. Presumably all the homeless are eligible for food stamps, but only 12% of the homeless adults in the Burt–Cohen study received them. Only 3% of homeless adults received welfare benefits (at that time Aid to Families with Dependent Children). The homeless in their study had very little cash income; the (reported) median for single adults was $64 per month and $300 for homeless families.

Now that you have a picture of the plight of the homeless, let us turn back to economic analysis to gain some insight into the causes of homelessness. It is obvious that many of the homeless have severe personal problems that take the homelessness issue beyond economics, but it turns out that economic factors can explain a good deal of the variations in homelessness. Nearly all homeless people all share one characteristic; at the time they are homeless they lack sufficient income to afford housing. More people will become homeless if the incomes of the poor decline and/or if the cost of housing rises.

It is helpful to use a model of the rental housing market that is similar to the one that was introduced in Chapter 8 (and similar to the models presented by O'Flaherty, 1996). Figure 16.2 shows a market for low-quality rental housing with a vacancy rate. The

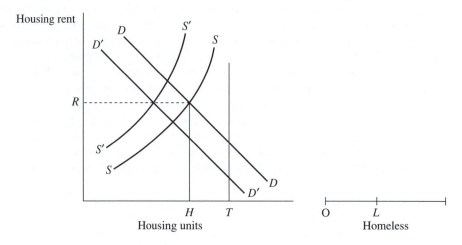

Figure 16.2   Market for housing and homelessness

demand for such housing is curve *DD*, and the supply in the short run is *SS* (with a total stock of units *T*). Housing rent is set at *R*, the number of units occupied is *H*, and the number of vacant units is *T − H*. It is assumed that, with rent at *R*, there are *L* households that are homeless – as shown on the right-hand diagram. The total number of low-income households is *H + L*. We have the seemingly anomalous situation of homeless people and vacant housing units at the same time.

Now let us consider alternative changes in the model that all tend to increase the number of homeless households.

- Suppose that the cost of providing housing rises because of increases in utility rates or other costs. The short-run supply curve shifts up to *S′S′*, housing rent rises, the number of occupied units drops, and the number of homeless households increases.
- Alternatively, suppose that the incomes of poor households decline, and this translates into a drop in the effective demand for housing units of low quality to *D′D′*. The housing rent will fall, but so will the number of occupied units. Homelessness increases.
- A third case is relevant in many older cities. Suppose that the housing for low-income households is old and depreciating. Units are removed from the stock when they become no longer fit for habitation, so both the total number of units (*T*) declines and the short-run supply curve (*SS*) shifts to the left. Housing rents rise and homelessness increases. Housing units can also be removed by redevelopment but, according to the filtering model, the construction of new units (in excess of the growth of the number of households) should free up other units for use by lower-income households.
- An even more sophisticated argument has been made by Apgar (1990). He argued that households in the lower-middle class are having greater difficulty becoming home-owners. Their incomes are not rising very much, if at all, and the cost of housing is rising. These trends mean that new houses are not being built and that households are failing to vacate rental housing. The filtering mechanism is not working. Low-income households are therefore caught in the squeeze caused by the high demand for rental units.

Some of the implications of this model were tested by Honig and Filer (1993) using the data on cities collected by HUD (1984). These data are based on informed opinions of the amount of homelessness in a metropolitan area. As noted above, the rate of homelessness varied very widely across cities, so Honig and Filer looked for economic variables that can explain that variation. They found that the rate of homelessness was positively related to the housing rent for low-quality housing units and negatively related to the vacancy rate for units of that type. As you might have expected, they found that recent employment growth had a strong negative effect on homelessness. Economic growth helps again! Also, they found that homelessness was lower if AFDC payments per recipient were greater. Homelessness may not be entirely an economic problem, but economic variables clearly influenced the rate of homelessness in the expected ways. Another empirical study by Quigley, Raphael, and Smolensky (2001) used all of the available data sets on homelessness, and found that the incidence of homelessness consistently is lower if the vacancy rate is greater, if rent is lower, and if incomes are higher. It appears that, based on the results obtained by Honig and Filer (1993) and Quigley et al. (2001), homelessness can be treated to a considerable degree as if it were just an economic problem. Indeed, the four most powerful variables in their analyses were the vacancy rate, housing rent level (for low-quality units), income, and employment growth. What can be done to reduce homelessness? Mansur et al. (2002) use a simulation model of urban housing markets to explore this question, and conclude that extending rent subsidies to all eligible households can reduce homelessness in the major urban areas in California by 25% to 33%.

G. Summary

This chapter has provided a brief tour through a most pressing economic and social problem in urban areas – poverty and some of its causes and effects. There are many other urban problems that could be discussed, such as youth gangs, drugs, guns, low school achievement, pollution, welfare policy, and so on. The choices of poverty and the underclass, housing–jobs mismatch, and homelessness were selected because of their close connection to the type of economic analysis developed in this book. Crime and education are discussed in the next two chapters.

References

Apgar, William Jr., 1990, "The Nation's Housing: A Review of Past Trends and Future Prospects for Housing in America," in D. DiPasquale and L. Keyes (eds.), *Building Foundations: Housing and Federal Policy*. Philadelphia: University of Pennsylvania Press.

Bartik, Timothy, 1991, *Who Benefits from State and Local Economic Development Policies?* Kalamazoo, MI: W. E. Upjohn Institute.

Blank, Rebecca, 2002, "Evaluating Welfare Reform in the United States," *Journal of Economic Literature*, vol. 40, pp. 1105–66.

Blank, Rebecca and A. Blinder, 1986, "Macroeconomics, Income Distribution, and Poverty," in S. Danziger and D. Weinberg (eds.), *Fighting Poverty: What Works and What Doesn't*. Cambridge, MA: Harvard University Press.

Burt, Martha and Barbara Cohen, 1989, *American Homeless: Numbers, Characteristics, and the Programs That Serve Them*. Washington, DC: Urban Institute Press.

Ellwood, David, 1986, "The Spatial Mismatch Hypothesis: Are There Teenage Jobs Missing in the Ghetto?, in R. Freeman and H. Holzer (eds.), *The Black Youth Employment Crisis*. Chicago: University of Chicago Press.

Ellwood, David, 1988, *Poor Support*. New York: Basic Books.

Freeman, Richard, 1991, "Employment and Earnings of Disadvantaged Young Men in a Labor Shortage Economy," in C. Jencks and P. Peterson (eds.), *The Urban Underclass*. Washington, DC: The Brookings Institution.

Fremon, Charlotte, 1970, *The Occupational Patterns of Urban Employment Change*. Washington, DC: Urban Institute Press.

Friedlander, Stanley, 1972, *Unemployment in the Urban Core*. New York: Praeger.

Hammer, Thomas, 1992, "Economic Determinants of Underclass Behavior," in E. Mills and J. McDonald (eds.), *Sources of Metropolitan Growth*. New Brunswick, NJ: Rutgers University Press.

Heckman, James, 1994, "Is Job Training Oversold?" *The Public Interest*, no. 115, pp. 91–115.

Herrnstein, Richard and C. Murray, 1994, *The Bell Curve: Intelligence and Class Structure in American Life*. New York: Free Press.

Honig, Marjorie and R. Filer, 1993, "Causes of Intercity Variations in Homelessness," *American Economic Review*, vol. 83, pp. 248–55.

Ihlanfeldt, Keith and D. Sjoquist, 1990, "Job Accessibility and Racial Differences in Youth Employment Rates," *American Economic Review*, vol. 80, pp. 267–76.

Ihlanfeldt, Keith and D. Sjoquist, 1991, "The Effect of Job Access on Black and White Youth Employment," *Urban Studies*, vol. 28, pp. 255–65.

Ihlanfeldt, Keith, 1992, *Job Accessibility and the Employment and School Enrollment of Teenagers*. Kalamazoo, MI: W. E. Upjohn Institute.

Jargowsky, Paul, 1997, *Poverty and Place*. New York: Russell Sage Foundation.

Jargowsky, Paul, 2003, *Stunning Progress, Hidden Problems: The Dramatic Decline of Concentrated Poverty in the 1990s*. Washington, DC: The Brookings Institution.

Jencks, Christopher, 1992, *Rethinking Social Policy: Race, Poverty, and the Underclass*. Cambridge, MA: Harvard University Press.

Kain, John, 1968, "Housing Segregation, Negro Employment, and Metropolitan Decentralization," *Quarterly Journal of Economics*, vol. 82, pp. 175–97.

Kain, John, 1974, "Housing Segregation, Black Employment, and Metropolitan Decentralization: A Retrospective View," in G. von Furstenberg (ed.), *Patterns of Racial Discrimination*. Lexington, MA: D. C. Heath.

Kain, John, 2004, "A Pioneer's Perspective on the Spatial Mismatch Literature," *Urban Studies*, vol. 41, pp. 1–32.

Leonard, Jonathon, 1987, "The Interaction of Residential Segregation and Employment Discrimination," *Journal of Urban Economics*, vol. 21, pp. 323–46.

Lewis, W., 1969, *Urban Growth and Suburbanization of Employment*. Washington, DC: The Brookings Institution.

Mansur, E., J. Quigley, S. Raphael, and E. Smolensky, 2002, "Examining Policies to Reduce Homelessness Using a General Equilibrium Model of the Housing Market," *Journal of Urban Economics*, vol. 52, pp. 316–40.

Masters, Stanley, 1974, "A Note on John Kain's Housing Segregation, Negro Employment, and Metropolitan Decentralization," *Quarterly Journal of Economics*, vol. 88, pp. 505–19.

Masters, Stanley, 1975, *Black–White Income Differentials: Empirical Studies and Policy Implications*. New York: Academic Press.

McDonald, John, 2004, "The Deconcentration of Poverty in Chicago: 1990–2000," *Urban Studies*, vol. 41, pp. 2119–137.

McMillen, Daniel, 1993, "Can Blacks Earn More in the Suburbs? Racial Differences in Intra-metropolitan Earnings Variation," *Journal of Urban Economics*, vol. 33, pp. 135–50.

Meyer, John, J. Kain and M. Wohl, 1965, *The Urban Transportation Problem*. Cambridge, MA: Harvard University Press.

Moffitt, Robert, 1977, "Metropolitan Decentralization and City–Suburb Wage Differentials," *International Regional Science Review*, vol. 2, 103–11.

Moffitt, Robert, 1992, "Incentive Effects of the US Welfare System: A Review," *Journal of Economic Literature*, vol. 30, pp. 1–61.

Mooney, Joseph, 1969, "Housing Segregation, Negro Employment, and Metropolitan Decentralization: An Alternative Perspective," *Quarterly Journal of Economics*, vol. 83, pp. 299–311.

Noll, Roger, 1970, "Metropolitan Employment and Population Distribution and the Conditions of the Urban Poor," in J. Crecine (ed.), *Financing the Metropolis*. Beverly Hills, CA: Sage Publications.

Offner, Paul and D. Saks, 1971, "A Note on John Kain's Housing Segregation, Negro Employment, and Metropolitan Decentralization," *Quarterly Journal of Economics*, vol. 85, pp. 147–60.

O'Flaherty, Brendan, 1996, *Making Room: The Economics of Homelessness*. Cambridge, MA: Harvard University Press.

Pavetti, Ladonna, 2001, "Welfare Policy in Transition: Redefining the Social Contract for Poor Citizen Families with Children and for Immigrants," in S. Danziger and R. Haveman (eds.), *Understanding Poverty*. New York: Russell Sage Foundation, pp. 229–77.

Price, Richard and E. Mills, 1985, "Race and Residence in Earnings Determination," *Journal of Urban Economics*, vol. 17, pp. 1–18.

Quigely, J., S. Raphael, and E. Smolensky, 2001, "Homeless in America, Homeless in California," *Review of Economics and Statistics*, vol. 83, pp. 37–51.

Rosenbaum, James, 1993, "Closing the Gap: Does Residential Integration Improve the Employment and Education of Low-Income Blacks?" in L. Joseph (ed.), *Affordable Housing and Public Policy*. Champaign, IL: University of Illinois Press.

US Bureau of the Census, 2003, Current Population Reports, Series P60–188, "Income, Poverty and the Value of Noncash Benefits: 2002," US Government Printing Office, Washington, DC.

US Department of Housing and Urban Development, 1984, *A Report to the Secretary on the Homeless and Emergency Shelters*. Washington, DC: Office of Policy Development and Research, HUD.

Wilson, Franklin, 1979, *Residential Consumption, Economic Opportunity, and Race*. New York: Academic Press.

Wilson, William, 1978, *The Declining Significance of Race*. Chicago: University of Chicago Press.

Wilson, William, 1987, *The Truly Disadvantaged: The Inner City, the Underclass, and Public Policy*. Chicago: University of Chicago Press.

Chapter 17

Crime in Urban Areas

A. Introduction

Compared to other economically advanced countries such as England, Japan, and Germany, crime in the United States is at shocking levels. The Federal Bureau of Investigation keeps track of serious crimes with victims that are reported to the local authorities in seven categories: murder, rape, aggravated assault, robbery, auto theft, larceny-theft, and burglary. Between 1960 and 1980 the reported amount of crime in the US in these seven categories per capita *tripled* from 1,867 crimes to 5,950 crimes per year per 100,000 population. Most crime researchers think that this increase is exaggerated because, in earlier years, some police departments did not have adequate systems for recording crimes and reporting them to the FBI. Nevertheless, no one thinks that crime did not increase sharply between 1960 and 1980. Crime per capita has declined dramatically since 1980 – especially since 1990, but crime is still a very serious problem in urban areas.

B. Facts About Crime in the US

A more detailed picture of crime in the US since 1960 is shown in Table 17.1. The murder rate doubled from 1960 to 1980 from 5.0 to 10.2 per 100,000, and the murder rates in 1990 was 9.4 per 100,000, but then dropped to 5.5 per 100,000 in 2000. The crime rate for rape increased by more than four times from 1960 to 1980, although this increase probably reflects an increase in the reporting of rapes as well as a real increase in crime. However the crime rate for rape dropped from 257 to 145 per 1,000,000 from 1990 to 2000. The robbery rate also increased by more than four times, and the rate of aggravated assaults increased by more than five times between 1960 and 1980 and continued to rise in the 1980s, but also dropped in the 1990s. The rate of burglary more than tripled from 1960 to 1980, and since then it has declined by over 50%. Larceny-theft tripled from 1960 to 1980, remained fairly constant up to 1995, and then declined along

Table 17.1   Crime in the United States: 1960–2000 (crimes per 100,000 population)

	Murder	Rape	Robbery	Assault	Burglary	Larceny-theft	Auto-theft
1960	5.0	9.5	59.9	85.1	502.1	1,024	181.7
1965	5.1	12.0	71.2	109.8	653.2	1,314	254.6
1970	7.8	18.5	171.4	163.0	1,071.2	2,079	453.7
1975	9.6	26.3	220.8	231.1	1,532.1	2,805	473.7
1980	10.2	36.8	251.1	298.5	1,684.1	3,167	502.2
1985	7.9	37.1	208.5	302.9	1,287.3	2,901	462.0
1990	9.4	41.2	257.0	424.1	1,235.9	3,195	657.8
1995	8.2	37.1	220.9	418.3	987.0	3,043	560.3
2000	5.5	32.0	144.9	323.6	728.4	2,475	414.2

Source: US Department of Justice, Federal Bureau of Investigation, *Crime in the United States* (various issues), Washington, DC: US Government Printing Office

with other crime rates. Auto theft almost tripled from 1960 to 1980, took a brief decline in the mid-1980s, then increased up to 1995, and declined.

Homicide is, of course, the most serious crime of all, and the crime with the best data because nearly all homicides are reported. The homicide rate increased from a low point in 1960 of 5 per 100,000 to 10.2 per 100,000 in 1980. Since then the homicide rate has dropped to 5.5 per 100,000 – nearly to its 1960 level. Some basic facts about murder are worth recounting. All of the following facts pertain to murders in 1993. First of all, murders are committed with firearms. In 1993, 69.6% of all murders – 16,200 murders – were committed with the use of a gun. Knives were used in 12.7%, blunt instruments in 4.4%, and personal physical force (e.g., hands, feet, pushing the victim) in 5.0%. Other means (including unknown means) accounted for 8.3% of all murders. For example, poison was used in 9 murders (0.04%). The means of choice for suicide victims is also usually a firearm, by the way. In our opinion this huge number of murders committed with firearms is a national scandal that we strangely seem unable to address.

The victims of murder are predominantly male (77%) and black (51%). About 49% of all murder victims are males between the ages of 15 and 34; and 34% of all murder victims are black males between the ages of 15 and 34. The single demographic group with the highest murder rate is black males aged 20 to 24; their murder rate is 206 per 100,000, which is 22 times the overall average rate of 9.4 per 100,000. Murderers are also predominantly male and black. Of the offenders in 1993 for whom the sex is known, 91% are male. Only 1,742 murders were known to have been committed by a female in that year. Among the offenders for whom sex and age are known, 62% are males between the ages of 15 and 29. Blacks make up 56% of murderers for whom the race is known, and black males between the ages of 15 and 29 are 41% of all murderers for whom sex, age, and race are known.

Even though crime has declined in recent years, it is fair to say that many of the residents of large urban areas in the United States still live in fear of crime. It is also true that the news media, especially local television stations, play up crime stories and probably make people more afraid than they otherwise would be. However, it may be that the effect of the news media can be overstated. A major topic of conversation among people who live in urban areas is the crime that they have experienced or seen themselves. As a piece of advice from these authors, college students who live on their own in dormitories or student apartments should not assume that they are immune to crime. You should at least be taking the normal precautions of keeping doors and cars locked, not leaving things within easy reach of thieves, and being aware of your surroundings. You have almost certainly been told these things since you were a small child, but they bear repeating. Our society has changed. Professor McDonald grew up in the 1950s in an urban area of about 80,000 people, and crime was never a concern. As far as we can remember, we did not lock our door.

Crime rates are higher in major central cities compared to other places, especially the suburbs of those same central cities. There is no other way to say it; some of the comparisons are shocking. In Atlanta the murder rate in the central city of 50.4 per 100,000 population in 1993 was 7.4 times the murder rate in the suburbs. The disparities between the central city and the suburbs of Atlanta are not as great for some of the other crimes; they are as follows:

Rape	3.9 times larger in central city
Robbery	7.2
Aggravated assault	10.1
Burglary	2.6
Larceny-theft	2.0
Auto theft	3.3

Note that the disparities are smaller in the non-violent property crimes of burglary, larceny and auto theft. This is a general pattern that exists in most other urban areas as well.

C. Causes of the Increase in Crime

Criminologists have investigated the factors behind the jump in crime rates between 1960 and 1980. One big factor is the baby boom. The bulk of crimes is committed by young men, so the high birth rates of the late 1940s and 1950s meant a large increase in the number of crime-prone individuals in the 1960s and early 1970s. However, demographic changes cannot account for the entire increase in crime during this period. By one estimate (Chaiken and Chaiken 1983), only 46% of the increase in the volume of arrests could be attributed to growth in the total population and changes in its age composition. However, empirical models that make use only of demographic data have been very successful in forecasting (if not explaining) crime rates.

One example of a crime forecasting model was estimated by Fox (1978). He was able to forecast various components of the FBI crime index very accurately using a model that contains only three variables;

- % of the population that is nonwhite and aged 14–17;
- % of the population that is nonwhite and aged 18–21; and
- the consumer price index.

Fox's model presents a rather stark depiction of the role of young black males in the perpetration of crimes – at least the ones that are reported to the FBI. The good news in the short run is that the drop in the birth rate (from a peak of 3.8 children per woman in the late 1950s to a low of 1.8 children per woman in 1976) means that crime rates should tend to be lower into the 1990s.

If purely demographic changes can account for only a fraction of the increase in the crime rate that took place during the 1960s and 1970s, what other factors were involved? This is the issue upon which criminologists have focused their attention, and they have some pretty reasonable answers. Young men are most prone to commit crimes between the time they reach puberty and the time they assume adult roles and responsibilities. This period of time has been growing longer because the age of the onset of puberty has been falling and, because of the increase in schooling needed to function in the modern economy, the age of the assumption of adult responsibilities has been rising. However, this factor does not appear to explain the sudden increase in crime during the 1960s and 1970s. Another factor that surely is involved is the decline in proportion of children in two-parent families. This decline in the role of fathers translates into a decline in the control that families have over teenage males. The timing of the sharp increase in the number of one-parent families in the 1960s and 1970s corresponds to the increase in the crime rate. The increase in the degree to which poor blacks are segregated in central cities is implicated as well. The role of the breakdown of social control in urban underclass communities is reasonably clear. Urban street gangs of mainly black and Hispanic young men dominate some neighborhoods and perpetrate a great deal of crime.

The factors behind the increase in crime discussed so far are demographic and socio-logical in nature, so they fail to pinpoint the direct causes of crime. The fact is that most young men in crime-prone groups do not commit serious crimes, and it is grossly unfair to label an individual on the basis of membership in a demographic group. We know that crimes are committed by a small minority of the population, and that a large number of violent crimes are committed by a small fraction of those who commit crimes. This group has been called violent predators by Chaiken and Chaiken (1983). They commit a very large number of robberies and assaults. Violent predators are different from other offenders. They began committing crimes at a young age, and were likely to have committed both property crimes and crimes of violence frequently before they were age 18. They tend to be more socially unstable than other offenders; few are married and they have trouble holding jobs. But perhaps their most important characteristic is their drug use. In the 1960s and 1970s use of heroin common among violent predators, and many of them combined heroin use with use of amphetamines, barbiturates, or alcohol. Violent predators also are often involved in drug dealing. In the 1980s and 1990s the use of cocaine became the largest drug problem. Offenders commit property crimes to pay for drugs, but it is also known that drug use can lead to the commission of violent crimes. In short, it appears that the increase in the number of violent predators, many of whom are multiple drug users, can account for the sudden and disproportionate increase in crime in the 1960s and 1970s *and* for the failure of crime rates to decline substantially in the 1980s.

Is it possible to identify violent predators? Chaiken and Chaiken (1983) found that it is very difficult to identify them from their official records. Records of juvenile offenders are, by design or by accident, often not very informative. And, because we need to identify violent predators at an early age, they usually do not have very extensive adult criminal records. The prospects for identifying and directing actions at the violent predators are not very good. It is true that violent predators cannot commit crimes when they are in jail, but the jailing of many more juvenile offenders may increase the criminality of those who are not violent predators.

D. Economics and Crime

What does economics have to say about crime? The above list of serious crimes includes four – robbery, auto theft, larceny, and burglary – that are economic crimes. Indeed, these four crimes make up 92% of all serious crimes. Most criminals, even the violent predators, are in the business of committing crimes for monetary gain. It is useful to think of criminals who commit crimes for economic reasons to be governed by economic incentives; the criminal commits a crime if his evaluation of the potential gain exceeds his evaluation of the loss that he may incur. By the way, the use of the male gender in the previous sentence is realistic; most crimes (not just murders) are committed by males. The gain to the criminal is the value of the loot that is acquired, of course. The loss to the criminal is the jail sentence and possible fine that will be imposed if he is caught and convicted of breaking the law. The possible loss really consists of two parts – the probability that the criminal will be caught and have a penalty imposed, and the size of that penalty. Numerous studies by economists have shown that criminals respond to both of these components, and some studies (e.g., Witte 1980) showed that increasing the probability of punishment (rather than increasing the size of the punishment) has the larger effect on the crime rate. This last finding means that the difficult and expensive work of apprehending and convicting criminals has a larger effect than does an increase in prison sentences. However, both of these policies are costly because prisons are expensive to build and to run.

The probability that an offender will actually suffer punishment depends upon the probability of arrest, the probability of conviction given that he is arrested, and the probability of punishment given that he is convicted. The probability of arrest for a *single* non-violent offense is known to be quite low, although offenders who commit many crimes eventually will be caught. According to the Federal Bureau of Investigation, the fractions of crimes cleared by arrests in 1993 (%) are as follows:

Murder	66
Rape	53
Aggravated assault	56
Robbery	24
Burglary	13
Larceny-theft	20
Auto theft	14

These figures pertain to offenses that have been "cleared" by the police by the arrest of an offender. The arrest of a single offender may "clear" several crimes that are on the books because the offender can be identified as the perpetrator of all of those crimes. Suppose that the probability of arrest for a single burglary is 0.05, but the offender committed five burglaries. The probability that he is *not* caught is $0.95 \times 0.95 \times 0.95 \times 0.95 \times 0.95$ = 0.77, so the probability that he is caught is $1 - 0.77 = 0.23$. A burglar who commits 20 burglaries has a $1 - 0.36 = 0.64$ probability of being caught, for example.

Forst (1983) conducted a detailed study of the dispositions of arrests for felonies. He found that, of 100 felonies, 35 were sent to the juvenile justice system. Of the remaining 65, 40 were accepted for prosecution. The 25 who were not prosecuted either were innocent or were guilty but could not be prosecuted for lack of evidence. Of the 40 who were prosecuted, 32 were convicted and 20 of these served time in jail. Therefore, Forst's (1983) estimate is that, if you are arrested for a felony and are considered to be an adult by the criminal justice system, you have a 0.49 probability of being convicted and a 0.31 probability of serving time in jail. Punishment in the US is neither swift nor sure.

Potential victims of economic crime can also be thought of as responding to economic incentives. People protect their homes with better locks, security alarm systems, and other devices. They also buy guns. To protect their cars they buy alarms and a well-known device that attaches to the steering wheel. People protect themselves when they are away from home largely by reducing their exposure to dangerous situations. These are rational responses to crime. It is also clear that crime has an effect on real estate markets, especially the residential market. Thaler (1978) found that crime rates have a negative effect on residential property values, and Mills (1992) found that crime in the central city increased the rate at which people moved to the suburbs.

The question of economic efficiency and crime was raised by Becker (1968) in a classic article. Becker's point is that, as long as crime has a marginal benefit for criminals that declines with the amount of crime committed, it is not worthwhile to prevent all crime through expenditures on police, courts, and prisons. If the crime rate is driven down to very low levels, there still are criminals out there who find that the benefits of crime exceed the cost to them. The cost of preventing crime at the margin is, at some point, greater than the cost of the crime to the victim. Figure 17.1 shows this last point graphically. The marginal cost of crime prevention is a declining function of the crime rate; the greater the number of crimes the lower is the cost of reducing the crime rate. This marginal cost of crime prevention is so labeled on Figure 17.1. The marginal cost of crime to the victim is assumed to be a constant amount in the figure, and the optimum amount of crime is crime rate CR_0. Note that the optimum crime rate rises if the marginal cost to the victim falls or if the marginal cost of prevention rises.

The analysis in Figure 17.1 presents the basic idea of an optimum crime rate, but it fails to depict the interaction between criminals and potential victims. Balkin and McDonald (1981) have devised a model of street crime that captures the idea of criminal–victim interaction. Street crime is crime that takes place outside the home (or workplace) and involves a direct confrontation of criminal and victim. Street crime can include murder and rape, but most often it is robbery or assault. Balkin and McDonald suppose that street crime is important enough to make ordinary citizens alter their behavior. They assume that people have two types of activities; one type of activity exposes them to street crime, and the other type of activity does not. The amount of time that one is exposed to street crime might be the amount of time spent outside after dark plus the amount of time that is spent during the daytime in areas where street crime can occur. It is assumed that the demand per day for activities that expose one to street crime is

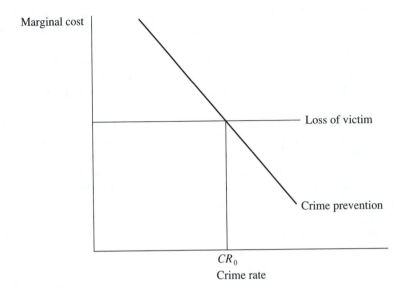

Figure 17.1   Optimum crime rate

inversely related to the risk of being a victim. Here the correct measure of risk; i.e., the "price" of this activity, is the probability of becoming a victim of street crime *per unit of time exposed* to crime. The demand for the activity that exposes potential victims to street crime is depicted in Figure 17.2 as curve *DD*.

Now consider the perpetrators of street crime. They spend part of their time outside looking for potential victims. We shall take the probability of apprehension and conviction and the prison sentence as given for the moment. If there are very few potential victims who expose themselves to street crime, then it will take a long time for a street criminal to find a victim. The criminal will have a low probability of finding a victim in a given amount of search time. On the other hand, if there are many potential victims out there, then the criminals will be able to find more victims per unit of time spent searching. It is hypothesized that there is a function that relates the amount of time street criminals are out there searching for victims and committing crimes to the rate at which victims can be found per hour spent. This is, in effect, the "wage rate" for the criminals. Suppose that this supply curve of criminal effort shows that the crime "wage rate" and the supply of time to criminal activities are positively related.

It was suggested that the probability of finding a victim is positively related to the amount of time that potential victims spent exposed to street crime. Therefore, the horizontal axis of Figure 17.2 is labeled "exposure time of potential victims" *and* "probability of finding a victim per unit of search time for criminals." An amount of exposure time by potential victims translates directly into a success rate for criminals. These two variables are measured in different units, but those two different units of measurement can both be displayed on the horizontal axis. Now consider the vertical axis of Figure 17.2, which is labeled "probability of victimization per unit of exposure time." This probability of victimization is determined directly by the amount of time that criminals devote to searching for victims and committing crimes. Both of these variables can be displayed on the

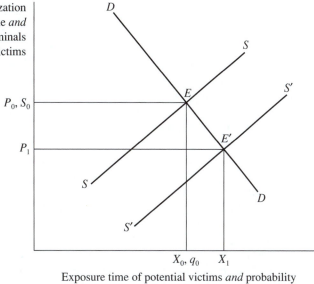

Figure 17.2   Market for street crime

vertical axis. Once again, the two variables are measured in different units, but a given amount of time supplied by criminals for criminal activity translates into a victimization rate. The two axes can therefore carry labels that correspond to the variables in the function that depicts the supply of criminal effort – the probability of finding a victim and the amount of time devoted to searching for victims and committing crimes. The supply of criminal effort is shown in Figure 17.2 as curve SS.

The equilibrium in this market for street crime is where the two functions intersect at point E. At this point the behavior of potential victims is consistent with the behavior of criminals. The equilibrium amount of time exposed to crime is X_0 and the probability of victimization per unit of time exposed to crime is p_0. Note that the actual crime rate for the time period (e.g., one day) in question is p_0 times X_0. Criminals spend amount of time S_0 in criminal activity, and they have a "success rate" of q_0 per unit of time spent "working" as street criminals.

Crime-control policies can enter the model by altering criminal behavior. Suppose that more police officers are put on the streets so that the probability of apprehension and conviction rises. This change means that, at any level of success rate for criminals (on the horizontal axis in Figure 17.2), the supply of time to criminal activities will fall. This drop in the supply of criminal "labor" is shown as curve $S'S'$. The decline in the amount of time devoted to criminal activity results in a new equilibrium point at E'; the citizens have increased the amount of time they are exposed to crime because the probability of victimization per unit of exposure time has dropped. However, the actual crime rate can rise of fall. Recall that the actual crime rate (per day) was p_0 times X_0. Now the actual crime rate is p_1 times X_1, which can be greater than, equal to, or less than the old crime rate.

What does this last result mean? It says that making an area safer (in terms of the probability of victimization per unit of time exposed to crime) may bring a lot of people out and exposed to crime so that the actual number of crimes rises. The story is analogous to the case of air travel. In the early days of air travel the accident rate per passenger mile was high, and few people chose to fly. Air travel was made much safer, a lot more people decided to fly, and more people (let us suppose) were involved in accidents. There are certain very dangerous places in urban areas where few crimes take place because hardly anyone is foolish enough to go there. This model has important implications for the allocation of crime prevention resources. If the objective is to reduce crime, then the crime prevention resources should be allocated to the places where with the highest actual crime rates. On the other hand, this policy would tend to ignore places that have relatively low crime but are extremely dangerous. In such places the residents are trapped inside their homes by the real fear of crime. A policy of allocating police resources to these areas will make the residents better off by permitting them to take back their streets, but there may or may not be actual reductions in crime.

This section has presented a brief introduction to the economic analysis of urban crime. Crime is perhaps the most pressing of urban problems, and it should be clear that economic analysis can make a contribution to the understanding of the motivations of criminals and potential victims. Economic analysis also provides some guidance for policy in that the economic motivations of criminals must not be ignored. The research shows clearly that criminals respond to punishment that is swifter and surer. However, it is far less clear that criminals can be induced away from a life of crime by positive economic incentives.

A good deal of research has examined the possible link between unemployment and crime. Freeman (1983) reviewed the studies up to the early 1980s and found that there is a relationship between higher unemployment and/or lower labor force participation and increases in crime. However, the link between the labor market and crime is far from sufficient to explain the rise in crime that took place during the 1960s and 1970s or the variations in crime rates from place to place. There are many reasons for us to pursue a policy of low unemployment rates and to provide improved economic opportunities for potential criminals (and everyone else) in general. One outcome of such a policy may be to reduce crime somewhat, but it is also clear that crime is a more complex social issue about which economists probably have little to say at this time. For example, a social experiment called the Supported Work Experiment (Manpower Demonstration Research Corporation 1981) provided ex-offenders with subsidized employment and social service support. This effort had no significant effect on subsequent crime (recidivism) or on the ability of the participant to get a job in the long run, compared to a control group. The reasons for this failure surely involve a complicated set of economic, social and psychological factors. At this time we do not know how to prevent the creation of violent predators.

E. Causes of the Decline in Crime

The decline in crime in the 1990s is a very hopeful sign. Some changes in crime rates in particular cities are quite remarkable. The total number of murders in New York City fell by 74%, from 2,245 in 1990 to 594 in 2003. Homicides in Los Angeles dropped by 54%

from 1992 to 2002. A critical need is an understanding of the causes of the decline in crime so that the trend can continue.

As the collection of studies in Blumstein and Wallman (2000) indicates, many factors contributed to the drop in crime, including:

- demography (decline in the proportion of the male population aged 18–24);
- increase in gun law enforcement (denying access to guns by convicted felons and minors) and decline in gun use that occurred after passage of the Brady bill in 1993;
- increase in incarceration;
- steady decline in adult violence (perhaps a result of the decline in the marriage rate);
- policing strategies;
- end of the crack cocaine epidemic, in part due to the extreme violence associated with the crack business; and
- economic opportunity.

All of these play some role in the reduction in crime. For example, the study by Spelman (2000) attributed 25% of the decline in crime to the increase in incarceration.

The increase in incarceration has received a great deal of attention, mostly negative. Here are a few facts. The number of inmates in federal and state prisons increased from 715,649 in 1990 to 1,305,253 in 2000 (91% in state prisons). The number of inmates in local jails increased from 405,320 in 1990 to 631,240 in 2000. Overall the number of people incarcerated increased by 72.8% over the decade. We had 1.9 million people in jail in 2000, which is about 0.7% of the total population.

The causes of the decline in crime are being debated actively. One prominent participant in that debate is economist Steven Levitt, who summarized his views in an article (2004). In his view the evidence shows that the following factors played little or no role in the decline in crime in the 1990s:

- the strong economy of the 1990s;
- the aging of the baby boomers;
- better policing strategies;
- gun control laws;
- laws allowing the public to carry concealed weapons; and
- increase in capital punishment.

Rather, Levitt (2004) contends that the chief causes of the decline in crime are:

- the increase in the number of police (police officers per capita increased 14% in the 1990s);
- the increase in the prison population (as noted above);
- the decline in the crack epidemic; and
- the legalization of abortion in the 1973 *Roe v. Wade* decision.

This last point has stimulated debate, but Levitt's evidence is that crime began its sizable decline eighteen years after abortions were made legal by the US Supreme Court. Furthermore, crime had already begun to decline in those five states that had legalized abortion before the Supreme Court issued its decision for the entire nation. Levitt (2004) cites a study by Dagg (1991) showing that children who were born because their mothers were denied an abortion were more likely to commit crimes. Levitt's summary of the factors (%) contributing to the decline in crime is:

1	Increase in prison population	35.8
2	Legalized abortion	30.0
3	Increase in police per capita	16.4
4	Reduction in crack	9.0
5	Other causes	8.8

Clearly the recent decline in the economy (in the early 2000s), coupled with an increase in the young adult male population, means that forces are at work that will tend to make the crime rate rise again. However, we now know about other factors that can be used to offset the tendency for crime to rise. One of those factors is incarceration, but some question whether increasing the prison population is worth the benefits in crime reduction. This choice represents a major dilemma of our time.

F. Summary

This chapter has documented the huge increase in crime that took place in the US from the 1960s to the 1990s, and it has also shown the dramatic decline in crime that began in the early 1990s. Explanations for these trends were discussed. Economic analysis clearly makes an important contribution to the study of crime – especially the economic crimes of robbery, burglary, larceny, and auto theft. However, explanations for violent crime seem to go beyond conventional economic analysis. The perpetrators of much of the violent crime are often associated with illegal drug dealing and use. Putting violent criminals in jail does reduce crime because it gets them off the street before more crimes are committed. Recent research suggests that the prevention of crime also depends upon having more police officers who contribute to the fight against crack cocaine. However, Levitt (2004) thinks that much of the decline in crime since the early 1990s can be attributed to the revulsion of society to the crack epidemic and to the legalization of abortion.

Exercise

1   Check the FBI web site for "Crime in the United States," and find out the crime rate for an urban area of your choice.

References

Balkin, Steven and J. McDonald, 1981, "The Market for Street Crime: An Economic Analysis of Victim–Offender Interaction," *Journal of Urban Economics*, vol. 10, pp. 390–405.
Becker, Gary, 1968, "Crime and Punishment: An Economic Approach," *Journal of Political Economy*, vol. 76, pp. 169–217.

Blumstein, Alfred and Joel Wallman, 2000, *The Crime Drop in America*. New York: Cambridge University Press.

Chaiken, Jan and Marcia Chaiken, 1983, "Crime Rates and the Active Criminal," in J. Wilson (ed.), *Crime and Public Policy*. San Francisco: ICS Press.

Dagg, P. K., 1991, "The Psychological Sequelae of Therapeutic Abortion: Denied and Completed," *American Journal of Psychiatry*, vol. 148, pp. 578–85.

Forst, Brian, 1983, "Prosecution and Sentencing," in J. Wilson (ed.), *Crime and Public Policy*. San Francisco: ICS Press.

Freeman, Richard, 1983, "Crime and Unemployment," in J. Wilson (ed.), *Crime and Public Policy*, San Francisco: ICS Press.

Levitt, Steven, 2004, "Understanding Why Crime Fell in the 1990s: Four Factors that Explain the Decline and Six That Do Not," *Journal of Economic Perspectives*, vol. 18, pp. 163–90.

Manpower Demonstration Research Corporation, 1981, *Final Report of the National Supported Work Demonstration*. New York: MDRC.

Mills, E., 1992, "The Measurements and Determinants of Urbanization," *Journal of Urban Economics*, vol. 32, pp. 377–87.

Spelman, William, 2000, "The Limited Importance of Prison Expansion," in A. Blumstein and J. Wallman (eds.), *The Crime Drop in America*. New York: Cambridge University Press.

Thaler, Richard, 1978, "A Note on the Value of Crime Control: Evidence from the Property Market," *Journal of Urban Economics*, vol. 5, pp. 137–45.

Witte, Ann, 1980, "Estimating the Economic of Crime with Individual Data," *Quarterly Journal of Economics*, vol. 94, pp. 57–84.

Chapter 18

Education, Labor Markets, and Migration

A. Introduction: Human Capital

The improvements in our overall standard of living depend in part upon investments that we have made in ourselves. Back in 1961 T. W. Schultz (1961) argued that those investments take several forms;

- formal education at the elementary, secondary, and higher levels;
- on-the-job training;
- adult education (both formal and informal);
- health services; and
- migration in response to economic opportunity.

Each of these activities contains a sizable element of giving up something in the current time period in order to enhance the potential for future earnings. The investment element of education and training is pretty obvious, but health services and migration may not seem to be human capital investments. Health services can be broadly conceived as expenditures that improve the life expectancy, strength and vigor of people. A great deal of health expenditures are made during a person's last few months of life, but other health programs and medical procedures prevent disease or permit younger people to live more productive lives. Migration can also be viewed as a form of investment inasmuch as the migrant bears the cost of moving to a new location in exchange for benefits that usually take the form of higher earnings. This section is a brief review of the theory of investment in human capital.

An investment consists of costs paid in the present in return for expected future benefits. Human capital investments involve costs that fall into three general categories:

- direct expenses (tuition, moving expenses for migration, etc.);
- foregone earnings during the investment period; and
- psychic costs (the challenge of learning, the loss of old attachments in migration).

The costs vary from person to person and by type of human capital investment. These variations are discussed below. The benefits of human capital investments are of two types:

- increased earnings; and
- psychic benefits.

The psychic benefits of human capital investment can arise from a more pleasant job (e.g., no heavy lifting), from feeling better through better health, and from education that permits one to enjoy more that life has to offer. All of these cost and benefit factors can make the human capital investment decision complicated in practice, but the outline of the basic theory is very simple.

Suppose that all of the costs and benefits of human capital investment somehow can be measured in terms of money. The decision is whether to make a proposed investment in human capital. If no investment is made, the individual continues to live life as is and receives a stream of benefits $b_0, b_1, \ldots, b_n$, where 0 is the current period and $1, \ldots, n$ are future periods. If the investment in human capital is made, the individual must pay a cost in the current period of C_0. The payment of this cost reduces benefits received in the current period to $B_0 = b_0 - C_0$. The investment results in a new stream of benefits beginning with B_1 and extending to B_n. Investment is made if the discounted present value of the new benefit stream exceeds that of the old benefit stream. In equation form, the investment is made if

$$B_0 + B_1/(1 + r) + \ldots + B_n/(1 + r)^n > b_0 + b_1/(1 + r) + \ldots + b_n/(1 + r)^n.$$

The discount rate is r, and it is a subjective rate which the individual applies to future benefits. Subtraction of terms for the same time period yields the investment criterion

$$(B_1 - b_1)/(1 + r) + \ldots + (B_n - b_n)/(1 + r)^n > C_0.$$

This inequality says that the investment is made if the present value of the increases in benefits (e.g., increases in earnings) exceeds the cost. Note that the model implicitly has the person making the decision every year. In year 0 the person decides to go to college. In year 1 the person decides whether to continue to attend college, and so one.

This basic model of human capital investment has some important implications. People who are "impatient" have high discount rates, and are therefore less apt to make an investment. Holding other factors constant, younger people are more likely to invest in human capital because they have longer lives to reap the benefits of the investment. Investment will increase if the costs of making the investment decline. Lastly, more investment will be made if the benefits increase. We shall consider each implication in turn.

Who has high discount rates and who has low discount rates? An answer to this question may require psychological explanations, but it is known that people do differ in the degree to which they are oriented towards the future. It may stem from the nature of the parenting one receives. One of the virtues of the middle class is its willingness to postpone gratification, and this is something that must be taught to children. Children do not automatically perceive the benefits of doing well in school. Decisions made by teenagers can close off options for the future, and a very important part of being a parent is to make children aware of the implications of their decisions. A related point is life expectancy. Younger people are more likely to make investments in human capital, but only if they have long life expectancies. One observation is that widespread school attendance at the elementary and secondary levels did not occur until life expectancies for the average person had improved in the latter half of the nineteenth century. In the current era consider the life expectancy of a male minority teenager who is a member of the urban underclass. His chances of surviving beyond the age of 30 are lower than for other groups, and his decisions probably reflect this realization.

The propensity to invest in human capital is inversely related to the cost of the investment. Cost can be influenced by many factors. Monetary costs obviously can be influenced by scholarships, health insurance payments (in the case of investment in health services), and other subsidies. But foregone earnings and psychic costs should not be ignored. For example, limitations on child labor reduce the foregone earnings of attending school. The availability of illegal activities (e.g., drug dealing) increases foregone earnings for those so inclined. More stringent law enforcement and higher penalties for breaking the law reduce foregone earnings for those who would pursue illegal activity. Psychic costs of education and job training can be reduced by making education and training institutions more friendly and in tune with the wishes of the students. Psychic costs can be reduced by giving all students high grades as well. Psychic costs of migration are reduced if you already know people in the place to which you migrate.

Benefits have their monetary and psychic sides as well. Some people go to college just to enhance their earning power, but that reason does not explain fully why some people choose to major in history, English and other fields (economics?) in the liberal arts that do not necessarily offer sizable monetary gain. For some people being an educated person is, to some degree, a reward in itself. Indeed, this is the "product" that liberal arts colleges are selling. If you want a real chance to make big money after graduating from a liberal arts college, you probably must go on to get an MBA degree, go to law school or medical school, get a Ph.D. in computer science, etc.

As you can see, the basic model of human capital investment is a very flexible analytical framework that can be applied to a wide variety of situations. There is one big potential pitfall with a model that is so flexible. We run the risk of making our "explanations" of behavior tautological. A tautology is the needless repetition of an idea in different words. Consider the following conversation.

Person A says, "It's too bad that Sam decided not to go to college. He is so smart, but he just doesn't care about the future."

Person B says, "I learned in my economics class that Sam doesn't care about the future because he has a high discount rate."

Person B has offered only a restatement of the idea expressed by person A, not an explanation of Sam's behavior. Person B has offered no hypothesis that can be tested and found to be *wrong*. A third person joins the conversation.

Person C says, "People who are left-handed are killed in accidents more often than right-handed people, and so they also tend to have lower life expectancies. Sam is left-handed, so that is why he decided not to go to college." Person C's hypothesis cannot be tested with just one observation (Sam), of course, but the idea can be tested (and possibly found to be wrong) using data on a large number of people. Holding other factors constant, are left-handers less likely to attend college?

The next sections use the human capital framework to discuss investment in education and training and in inter-urban migration.

B. Education and Training

Studies of national economic growth discussed in Chapter 19 indicate that about 13% of economic growth in recent years can be attributed to improvements in the level of education and training of the workforce. Denison (1985) estimated that 20% of the growth in output per worker over the period of 1929 to 1982 was associated with the increase in the general education level of workers. Education contributes to economic growth, but do investments in education offer high returns to individuals and to an entire urban area?

Labor economists and others have studied the monetary returns of education to individuals extensively since the early 1960s. The standard method in these studies is to find the discount rate at which the present value of the stream of monetary benefits is just equal to the monetary cost and foregone earnings, or find r^* such that

$$(B_1 - b_1)/(1 + r^*) + \ldots + (B_n - b_n)/(1 + r^*)^n = C_0.$$

Becker's (1975, p. 155) classic study of human capital includes a rate of return to a four-year college education for white males in 1939 that was estimated to have been about 14.5%. This figure is a rate of return in real terms (corrected for inflation). Becker's estimate for the 1949 cohort is 13%, which reflects the fact that federal income taxes had increased and, hence, the after-tax returns had dropped. White men of that era who invested in college earned high rates of return. The return for college dropouts was estimated to have been 9.5% for white males in 1939 and 8% in 1949. In other words, the men who attended college but did not graduate earned a return on their costs that was, on average, 9.5% (8%). These are still substantial real rates of return. Becker also estimated rates of return for nonwhite men for both the South and the North for 1939; the rate of return in the South was 12.3%, while the return in the North was 8.3%.

Another standard method for looking at the monetary returns to education is to plot the age–earnings profiles for people at various levels of education. Table 18.1 shows the age–earnings profiles for men who worked full time during 1999. Five different education levels are shown – from those with fewer than 12 years to those with an advanced degree. Two patterns are immediately obvious from this figure: men of a given age with greater education levels earn more, and earnings rise with age to a peak that occurs when the man is in his late forties or fifties. The table also reveals that the biggest jumps in earnings for men occur between "some college" and the bachelor's degree (four years). For example, men at age 35–44 earned $40,855 with some college and $56,923 with the bachelor's degree. Men in this age group with an advanced degree earned $69,764. As a point of comparison, high school graduates earned $34,002. Men in this same age group who did not graduate from high school earned $25,345. It is not for nothing that they say, "Stay in school."

Table 18.1   Earnings for males by age and education: 1999 (worked full-time)

	Age				
	21–24	*25–34*	*35–44*	*45–54*	*55–64*
Education					
Less than 12	17,170	21,470	25,345	26,687	27,980
High school grad.	21,078	28,262	34,002	36,634	36,519
Some college	22,088	32,063	40,855	42,852	43,036
Bachelor degree	30,358	41,854	56,923	57,663	59,420
Advanced degree	30,618	50,888	69,764	71,239	70,990

Source: US Bureau of the Census

Table 18.1 disguises that fact that earnings vary a great deal by race and ethnic group. For example average full-time earnings for men in the 25–34 age group in 1992 were:

	Whites	*Blacks*	*Hispanics*
Less than 9 years	$15,433	–	$14,992
High school dropout	19,918	$14,524	16,350
High school graduate	25,143	19,306	22,009
Some college	28,773	23,986	25,869
Associate degree	29,725	28,209	28,077
Bachelor's degree	38,558	27,922	30,945
Master's degree	46,348	–	–
Professional degree	54,950	–	–

(More recent data at this level of detail are not available.)

Note that the sample size for blacks and Hispanics with advanced degrees is too small to provide reliable estimates. The earnings of black men lag behind those of whites by a substantial amount with the exception of one category of education: blacks with the associate degree earn 95% of the amount earned by whites. The black man with the associate degree earned almost twice as much as a high school dropout. The earnings of Hispanic men lagged behind the earnings of whites at each level of education, but the discrepancies are smaller than between blacks and whites. Hispanics also show a high payoff to the associate degree. The associate degree that is offered by junior and community colleges can qualify one for many jobs that require fairly advanced technical training. Junior colleges are crucial institutions that enable workers to upgrade their skills to match the changing demands in the modern economy. However, it is somewhat puzzling that the associate degree does not offer such a high payoff for white men.

Age–earnings profiles for women who worked full-time in 1999 are shown in Table 18.2. The profiles for women at each education level are much flatter than those for men. For example, the woman high school graduate of age 25–34 earned $21,083, and the peak earnings for high school graduates was only $24,429 for the group at age 45–54. Also, the payoff to each additional amount of education is generally lower for women than for men. Full-time earnings for women vary by racial and ethnic group as well, but these variations are smaller than those for men. Full-time average earnings for women in the 25–34 age group in 1992 were:

Table 18.2   Earnings for females by age and education: 1999 (worked full-time)

	Age				
	21–24	*25–34*	*35–44*	*45–54*	*55–64*
Education					
Less than 12	14,211	16,068	16,956	17,671	18,500
High school grad.	17,054	21,083	23,064	24,429	23,977
Some college	19,104	25,292	29,133	30,534	29,926
Bachelor degree	25,981	32,860	40,072	39,939	39,175
Advanced degree	25,988	38,530	46,884	48,652	48,395

Source: US Bureau of the Census

	Whites	*Blacks*	*Hispanics*
Less than 9 years	$13,285	–	–
High school dropout	14,987	$14,265	–
High school graduate	19,272	17,491	$18,638
Some college	21,907	19,442	20,700
Associate degree	24,324	21,050	–
Bachelor's degree	29,063	27,121	28,949
Master's degree	35,067	–	–
Professional degree	45,810	–	–

Note that the average full-time earnings for Hispanic women are almost equal to the earnings of white women, and that the earnings of black women average 86.5% to 95.2% of the earnings of white women. Also, for all three groups, the bachelor's degree adds about $10,000 in comparison to the earnings of high school graduates.

The data examined so far show that there are strong economic incentives to pursue more education, but do these incentives vary over time? In fact, there have been substantial variations over time in the payoff to education. A full exploration of this point would take the discussion into the realm of labor economics rather than urban economics, but a few numbers can illustrate the idea. Some readers may recall that, during the 1970s, the payoff to education had dropped compared to previous time periods, and there was talk of the "overeducated" American. You will be happy to know that the return to higher education came back with a vengeance in the 1980s and early 1990s. One useful comparison is ratio of the full-time earnings of holders of bachelor's degrees to the earnings of high school graduates. These figures for males and females in the 25–34 age group (taken from various issues of the *Current Population Reports*) are as follows:

Ratio of bachelor's degree to high school graduate earnings

	Males	*Females*
1970	1.38	1.42
1975	1.16	1.29
1980	1.19	1.29
1985	1.27	1.35
1990	1.48	1.59
1999	1.48	1.56

The dip to the payoff to the college degree is clearly evident, but the recovery of the 1980s made the payoff to the degree even higher in 1990 than it was in 1970. It is no secret that the decades of the 1980s and 1990s were good decades for many college-educated workers.

Another technique that is used to study the relationships between earnings, schooling, age and experience, race, and other factors is to estimate a multiple regression model with earnings of individual workers as the dependent variable. Labor economists have been busy estimating earnings functions since the 1960s, and they now use a standard functional form. A study of the earnings of male adults in 1978 by Henderson (1982) can serve to illustrate the method and present a fairly typical set of results. The basic hypotheses are that earnings depend upon education and work experience. Work experience is valuable because the worker acquires training that is specific to the job or profession while he or she is on the job. Some firms offer formal programs of on-the-job training, while others provide for training that takes place in more informal settings. It is also true that a worker becomes more productive by doing the job and figuring out how to be more productive in the process. One of Becker's (1975) seminal contributions to the theory of human capital is to make the distinction between general training and specific training. General training is training that increases a worker's productivity in many firms, while specific training increases one's productivity more in one firm than in the others. General training is associated with formal education; educational institutions are useful for imparting knowledge that is of a general nature – knowledge that can be used in many settings. Some firms offer general training as well, but they prefer not to provide workers with training that will enhance their earning power in general. Instead, firms prefer to offer specific training to workers so that those workers become more productive only if they stay with the firm that provided the training.

Let us now see how these ideas have been applied in the study by Henderson (1982). It is possible to measure the worker's amount of formal education (i.e., general training), but it is extremely difficult to measure the amount of specific training that has been acquired on the job. Empirical studies of earnings usually use total work experience as a reasonable substitute for the worker's amount of on-the-job training. However, many studies of earnings do not have a measure of actual years of (relevant) work experience. Often they know only the age of the worker and the years of formal education. This is the case in Henderson's (1982) study of adult men, and he followed the conventional procedure in such a case. He assumed that the amount of work experience of adult men is equal to the man's age minus his years of formal education minus six. In other words, he assumed that the worker entered school at age six, went to school for the number of years indicated, and then worked without interruption since he left school. These assumptions are reasonable for most adult men. However, we know that some men (especially blacks and Hispanics) suffer from extended periods of unemployment or periods in which they are not in the labor force. Henderson's (1982) study, as well as many others, ignores the possibility that minority workers at a particular age and education level may have less work experience than white workers. There is one more complication. The age–earnings profiles shown in Table 13.1 show that earnings for adult men peak at an age of 45 to 55. It is apparent that age/experience does not continue to enhance earnings over one's entire working life; the effect is not linear.

With all of this as preface, what did Henderson (1982) find? The dependent variable in the analysis was the natural logarithm of earnings after taxes in 1977 for males who were fully employed at the time of the survey (March, 1978). His regression model included many control variables for some personal characteristics, occupation and the nature of the urban area in which the worker lived, and he found that

$$\ln(\text{earnings}) = 7.879 + 0.047 \text{ (Education)}$$
$$+ 0.032 \text{ (Age-Ed-6)} - 0.00058 \text{ (Age-Ed-6)}^2$$
$$-0.116 \text{ (Black)} + \text{other effects,}$$

where Age-Ed-6 is the measure of work experience. The equation says that the payoff to one more year of education was an increase in earnings of 4.7%, and that black workers earned 11.6% less than comparable whites. The payoff to experience declined in percentage terms as the worker gained more experience. The marginal effect of experience so measured at various amounts of experience is $\delta \ln E / \delta$ (Age-Ed-6) = 0.032 − 0.00116 (Age-Ed-6), or:

Age-education-6	Effect on earnings of one more year
0	3.2%
2	3.0
5	2.6
10	2.0
20	0.9
27.6	0.0

The last few paragraphs and Tables 18.1 and 18.2 contain a great deal of data on earnings and education levels, but one must take care in drawing implications from these data. The data only show the average earnings of people at various education levels. The data do *not* tell us that the average person at a particular education level can earn a certain greater amount if he or she acquired the additional education. First of all, many people with lower levels of education are not capable of pursuing higher levels of education. Furthermore, some did not pursue more education because they knew that, for them, the payoff was not sufficient to justify the cost. The other way to make the point is that part of the payoff to more education is a payoff to a person's basic intellectual ability. How much of the payoff of a college degree can be attributed strictly to the degree, and how much stems from the fact that college graduates have higher native ability and motivation than many other people? Labor economists and other researchers have wrestled with this question from the very beginning of the human capital "revolution," but they have not come up with a decisive answer. Surely the answer depends upon the field of endeavor. In some fields one can be self-taught. Remember that Abraham Lincoln taught the law to himself. Other fields require years of formal instruction. We prefer to have a doctor who has actually attended medical school. In recent years several fields that people learned on their own or through experience have become curricula in institutions of higher education. Charlie Chaplin did not attend film school. Walter Cronkite did not major in TV and radio.

Despite this caveat, it is illuminating to take a brief look at the educational attainment figures for adults in the United States. Table 18.3 displays data on educational attainment for adults aged 25 and over for 2002 by age and race. In that year 15.9% of adults did not have a high school diploma, 32.1% had the high school diploma (and no additional

Table 18.3 Educational attainment by age and race: 2002 (%)

	Less than high school	High school	Some college	Assoc. degree	BA/BS	Advanced degree
All	15.9	32.1	17.0	8.3	17.7	9.0
Age						
25–34	13.1	28.4	19.1	8.7	23.2	7.4
35–44	11.6	32.3	17.5	10.0	19.6	8.9
45–54	10.9	31.4	18.0	9.7	18.4	11.6
55–64	16.4	34.0	16.3	7.1	14.9	11.2
65–74	26.5	36.2	13.8	4.8	11.5	7.1
Race						
White	15.2	32.3	16.9	7.4	18.3	10.2
Black	21.3	33.9	19.8	8.0	11.8	5.2
Hispanic	43.0	27.9	12.7	5.3	8.1	3.0

Hispanic people can be of any race.
Source: US Bureau of the Census

formal education), and 26.7% had a college degree (9.0% with advanced degrees). Educational attainment varies somewhat by age group. As you probably would have guessed, more older adults who are still of working age (age 55–64) had not graduated from high school and fewer in this group had graduated from college. However, the variations in educational attainment across the younger groups (25–34, 35–44, and 45–54) were not very large. For example, 30.6% of the youngest group (age 25–34) had graduated from college compared to 28.5% for the 35–44 age group and 30.0% for the 45–54 age group. College graduates among the oldest group (55–64) number 26.1%.

The variations in educational attainment by race are far more telling. Table 18.3 shows that in 2002 15.2% of white adults had not graduated from high school, but the figures for black and Hispanic adults are 21.3% and 43.0%, respectively. Among whites 26.2% had graduated from college, but only 17.0% of black and 11.1% of Hispanic adults had graduated. Educational attainment for the two main minority groups in the United States has room for improvement.

One of the most perplexing problems is the tendency of students to drop out of high school. Some data on dropouts are shown in Table 18.4. This table shows dropout percentages by age group and race. A dropout is a person who is not enrolled in regular school and who has not completed 12 years of education or received a general equivalency degree (GED). The proportions of young people who dropped out of high school clearly have declined since 1970, but the figures show that a sizable problem still exists. Concentrate on the groups that are aged 18 to 21. The dropout percentage in 2000 was 12.6% for whites and 16.0% for blacks, but the Hispanic dropout figure was 30.0%. These figures do not tell us what policies should be adopted, but they do say something about the dimension of the problem.

What does the evidence concerning the monetary returns to education mean for an urban economy? Clearly it means that an urban area with a more highly educated labor

Table 18.4 High school dropouts: % of population group

	1970	1980	1990	2000
Total dropouts				
Age 18–21	16.4	15.8	13.4	12.9
Age 22–24	18.7	15.2	13.8	11.8
White				
Age 18–21	14.3	14.7	13.1	12.6
Age 22–24	16.3	14.0	14.0	11.7
Black				
Age 18–21	30.5	23.0	16.0	16.0
Age 22–24	37.8	24.0	13.5	14.3
Hispanic				
Age 18–21	n.a.	40.3	32.9	30.0
Age 22–24	n.a.	40.6	42.8	35.5

Source: Statistical Abstract of the United States (2003)

force will have higher output and income levels. And it means that improvements in education will lead to output and income growth. The evidence also presents an urban area with a challenge and a dilemma. We know that a sizable fraction of students in many of the public school systems in the large central cities are failing to graduate from high school. Many of those high school dropouts are black and Hispanic. We have seen that the minority high school graduate earns substantially more than the high school dropout, especially among males, but how much will it cost to increase the graduation rate? We have also seen that there are very large returns to the associate degree among black and Hispanic men. If the goal is to increase aggregate income in the minority population, the more efficient choice might be to concentrate on getting high school graduates through junior college rather than focusing on reducing the high school dropout rate. Alternatively, the more equitable choice is to concentrate on increasing the high school graduation rate because dropouts have the lowest income levels. If resources for education programs were unlimited, we could pursue all good programs at once. A more realistic view is that difficult choices must be made. One of the roles of the economist is to point out the nature of these choices so that the discussion over policy can be clearer.

C. Concerns about American Education

In recent years serious concerns have been raised about the quality of education in America in general. Stories abound of the large numbers of high school graduates who do not know when the Civil War took place. It is claimed that one-third of adults are functionally illiterate. In 1983, the National Commission on Excellence in Education published *A Nation at Risk*, a report that depicted American education in stark terms.

Criticisms abound of American education at virtually every level – from pre-school programs to graduate schools. (Some place the blame for failures of American businesses on MBA programs, for example.) What on earth is an urban area supposed to do? One place where many people would start is the elementary and secondary schools in the inner city that are producing people who are clearly poorly educated. We can let the MBAs and the firms that hire them fend for themselves, but the level of educational attainment of many black and Hispanic students in inner cities truly represents a huge problem for society. The implications for earnings of failing to graduate from high school have been spelled out in this chapter. Do we know what to do to improve public education in the inner cities?

One strategy that evidently does not work is to exhort everyone to "stay in school." If you enter high school reading at the fourth grade level, it is probably pointless for you to remain in a conventional high school program. You may scrape through ninth grade, but things will only get worse. Most likely it is true that people who drop out of high school when they reach their sixteenth birthday were in the process of dropping out for a considerable period of time. So why do many students reach high school unable to cope with a normal (or even watered down) high school program? We have a pretty good idea. It begins with parents who cannot or will not support children in their attempts to learn. Parents who are overwhelmed by their own economic and social problems have little energy left over to provide the necessary environment and encouragement. For example, the mobility of low-income households is notoriously high in some inner cities. Many children are forced to change schools frequently; a student turnover rate in inner city schools of 40% per year is fairly common. The next step is to place such children together in a school that is not particularly well funded. Finally, locate that school in a neighborhood where there are very few positive role models of people who have attained some measure of success through schooling. That ought to do it. We know pretty well what to do – change all of the factors that have just been mentioned. How can this be accomplished? It turns out that we know what to do, at least on a limited scale. A series of studies by Rosenbaum (1993) and his associates has shown that taking minority children and their welfare mothers out of public housing in Chicago and placing them in subsidized housing in white suburbs actually has significantly improved the educational attainment of the children, compared to others who remained in the city schools. This project was discussed in more detail in Chapter 16. Racial and economic integration seem to work. A comprehensive strategy for improving the human capital of an urban area includes school integration. What *else* can we do, you might ask?

An essay by Murnane and Levy (1992) provides a summary of what is known, and then they advocate a policy of systemic school reform that is backed up with support from the federal government. For Murnane and Levy, reform of our system of schooling involves:

- creating standards for student performance in crucial subjects such as math and reading, and creating valid methods for assessing progress in meeting those standards;
- creating incentives for students (especially high school students) to work harder in school and take more demanding subjects;
- forging better connections between school and work;

- creating better teachers by drawing in more of the better college graduates and giving them better training; and
- reforming the system for financing of the public schools by reducing the reliance on the local property tax. (As discussed in Chapter 13, the state of California now has a system that essentially equalizes spending per pupil across school districts.)

The federal government can support these reforms by supporting high-quality schooling for disadvantaged children, helping to recruit and train talented teachers, and assisting with the development of educational standards and assessment techniques.

Murnane and Levy (1992) and Ladd (2002) see an important role for parental choice in school reform as well, but they are quite skeptical of proposals for school vouchers. The matter of school vouchers to support students to attend any school of their (or their parents') choice was introduced in Chapter 13. Murnane and Levy (1992) and Ladd (2002) answered those who advocate such a broad voucher program. They argued that permitting parental choice within the public school system would improve accountability and might improve student achievement as well. However, they think that vouchers that can be used at any school (including private schools) would likely increase the inequalities that already exist in the education system. Schools will naturally wish to take good students and avoid the ones who are problems. They acknowledged that private schools in general do produce achievement results that are a bit better than results in public schools. Neal (2002) provided a survey of the evidence on this point. But they worried that schools that are in a market-like system will send the message that the parents wish to hear – that their student is doing well (even in he or she is not). They are far from convinced that schools that make their living by attracting students and their vouchers will actually produce better achievement results. They also pointed out that any voucher system must be structured so that disadvantaged or disabled students cannot be left out and so that fraud is controlled. For example, certain disadvantaged students might be given vouchers that are worth a good deal more to the school than the vouchers presented by other students. Their view is that there is a very small constituency for such a voucher system, but they could be wrong on this score.

Ladd (2002) reviewed the empirical evidence on the effects of voucher programs on educational outcomes. The main publicly funded voucher programs are in Milwaukee, Cleveland, and Florida, and some small, private programs exist around the US. In her view the available evidence, including the evidence on large programs in Chile and New Zealand, indicates that voucher programs do not produce large gains in student achievement, and may have detrimental impacts on some disadvantaged students. According to Ladd's survey of the studies, the program in Milwaukee, which served no more that 1,350 students out of 90,000 in the school system, seems to have produced small gains in math, but not in reading. The Florida system grades schools (A through F), and students in those schools that receive the lowest grade two times in four years are eligible for vouchers to attend private schools. The data show that those schools threatened with the voucher program (i.e., received on F grade) improved achievement relative to comparable schools. Ladd's (2002) interpretation of this outcome is that the state's grading system, with its increased scrutiny and assistance for low-performing schools, is the likely cause of the improved performance – not the existence of the voucher program.

D. Economics of Migration

Americans are a mobile group of people. Greenwood (1981) showed that every year about 3.5% of the population moved between states, an additional 3.0% or so moved across county boundaries within the same state, and about 12% moved within the same county. In other words, about 18% of the population moved in any given year. The most mobile group is young adults – about 9% of those aged 20–24 moved between states in any year. Migration has been studied from many perspectives; our focus is on labor migration as a source of economic growth and development of urban areas.

The first thing that you need to understand about migration is the distinction between gross and net migration. The change in the population of an urban area can be written as

change in population = births − deaths + in-migration − out-migration.

Births minus deaths is called the natural increase in the population, while in-migration minus out-migration is net migration. Gross migration refers both to the amount of in-migration and the amount of out-migration. Normally these gross migration flows are large compared to the amount of net migration. The natural rate of population growth varies from place to place, but migration flows are the main source of rapid population growth for an urban area. An urban area such as Los Angeles that experienced very rapid population growth had very large amounts of in-migration, sizable amounts of out-migration, and natural population growth as well. An urban area with little population growth, on the other hand, has negative net migration that roughly offsets the natural increase in the population. Negative net migration can involve large or small gross migration flows so long as the out-migration exceeds the in-migration.

The next thing to understand about migration is that the in-migrants are probably different from out-migrants in some way. People who move to the Chicago urban area include young college graduates who come to work in the financial or business service sector and young adults from Puerto Rico and Mexico who seek better economic opportunity. People who move away include retirees, factory workers who have lost their jobs, and students who are going away to college. In recent decades those who moved away have exceeded those who moved in. A good exercise would be to look up the data on migration for the urban area in which you live. The data from the 2000 Census is a good place to start.

The decision to migrate can be formulated in the human capital investment framework. The classic paper on this topic is by Sjaastad (1962); the migrant incurs money (including foregone earnings) and psychic costs in order to gain a stream of monetary rewards and/or non-monetary gains in the new location. The relevant benefits and costs are different for different types of migrants. The migrants who are moving primarily for labor market reasons should follow the basic monetary human capital model; moving is prompted by gains in earnings and reduced by higher costs of moving. The cost of moving is, for one thing, associated with distance, so migration is more likely to be for shorter distances. The benefits and costs of moving are influenced by the familiarity that the migrant has with the destination. For this reason, migrants often move to places where they have relatives or acquaintances. In addition, younger workers have more to gain from moving, and people who have a greater orientation towards the future (i.e., people with more education) are more likely to move. Numerous studies, many of which were reviewed by Greenwood (1981), have tested these and other hypotheses. Greenwood's (1981) study combined gross migration flows with economic growth in urban areas, so it will be discussed in detail below.

Before we turn to Greenwood's (1981) model, there is a third thing that you need to understand about migration – or rather, about studies of migration. There are two schools of thought about migration within the United States, or within any advanced national economy in which the population may move about freely. One school of thought is based on the idea that urban labor markets are generally in equilibrium most of the time. People are always migrating for a wide variety of reasons, and the net advantages to migration that open up tend to be closed fairly quickly by shifts in the flows of migrants. This model was discussed in the appendix to Chapter 8. Equilibrium wage rates for identical workers can vary substantially from place to place because of amenities and disamenities that people value. People who work in large urban areas are paid more because they face higher housing prices and longer commuting times, for example. People who work in places with nice weather get paid less than people who work in Minneapolis. Indeed, there is a substantial body of research on the quality of life in urban areas that is based on the assumption that variations in wage rates (and housing rents, as well) capture the values of amenities as they exist in various urban areas. For example, Blomquist, Berger, and Hoehn (1988) found that wages varied from urban area to urban area in statistically significant fashion with variations in human capital, occupation, industry, race, a few other factors, *and*:

- precipitation (negative effect);
- heating degree days (negative effect);
- cooling degree days (negative effect);
- windspeed (positive effect);
- violent crime in the urban area (positive effect);
- teacher/pupil ratio (negative effect);
- air pollution (negative effect);
- landfill waste in county (positive effect); and
- superfund hazardous waste sites in county (positive effect).

Note that the results generally are in accordance with intuition in that amenities (disamenities) were associated with lower (higher) wages. The exceptions are precipitation, heating degree days, and air pollution; more rain, colder weather, and more pollution were linked to lower wages. If labor markets and "markets" for amenities are in equilibrium across urban areas, then migration patterns will not be related to differences in wage rates.

The other school of thought in migration studies presumes that disequilibrium prevails most of the time, and that differences in wage rates and unemployment rates can therefore be used to predict migration patterns. All of the early research on migration was based on the presumption of disequilibrium; research that made use of a model of equilibrium began in the 1970s. Evans (1990) has reviewed the various studies and the logic that stands behind them, and concluded that the persistence of net migration in clear patterns is inconsistent with the presumption of equilibrium. Evans (1990) also concluded that urban area wage differentials, especially for occupations of lower skill, are too large to be consistent with equilibrium. Therefore, for purposes of this section it shall be presumed that there is disequilibrium in labor markets sufficient to cause migrants to respond to wages and/or other simple measures of opportunity in the labor market.

The basic model that Greenwood (1981) used originated with Muth (1971) in a paper entitled, "Migration: Chicken or Egg?" Migration should be in the direction of those urban areas with the most employment growth. But the migrants will create demand for goods and services produced locally and cause employment to rise. Muth (1971) argued that migration and employment growth are mutually dependent; employment growth causes migration *and* migration causes employment growth. His study of net migration to urban areas in the 1950s suggested that 60% to 70% of additional jobs in an urban area were taken by in-migrants, and that each net in-migrant generated one additional job (which had a 60% to 70% chance of being taken by another migrant). Muth's estimate that of 60% to 70% of new jobs were taken by in-migrants is in rough agreement with Bartik's (1991) estimate of 77%.

Greenwood (1981) built on the models of Borts and Stein (1964) (described in the appendix to Chapter 19) and Muth (1971), and developed a more comprehensive model of gross migration of the labor force, employment growth, and unemployment for urban areas. Table 18.5 shows a simplified version of Greenwood's model for urban areas for 1960 to 1970. The top half of Table 18.5 shows the results for four migration equations; the migration measures cover the five-year period from 1965 to 1970, and are:

- rate of gross out-migration to other urban areas;
- rate of gross out-migration to non-urban areas;
- rate of gross in-migration from other urban areas; and
- rate of gross in-migration from non-urban areas.

Note first that each rate of gross migration was positively related to its opposite variable; e.g., the rate of out-migration to other urban areas was positively related to the rate of in-migration from other urban areas. Most studies of gross migration have found that these opposite migration flows are positively related.

Beyond this relationship between opposing gross flows, gross migration for the most part responded to economic variables as expected. Income growth had a positive effect on out-migration to other urban areas (as was not expected), a negative effect on out-migration to non-urban areas, and positive effects on both in-migration flows. Employment growth had one negative effect on out-migration and one positive effect on in-migration. The per capita income level in 1960 had a positive effect on both out-migration to other urban areas and in-migration from non-urban areas. The level of unemployment in 1960 had negative effects on out-migration to other urban areas and on both measures of in-migration. The size of the labor force in 1960 (a measure of the size of the urban area) had a positive effect on out-migration to non-urban areas. Finally, both education and age were negatively related to both measures in out-migration. The asterisks in Table 18.5 indicate that the sign of the effect was opposite to that expected. The good news is that all of the statistically significant coefficients in the equations for in-migration have the expected sign, and the equation for out-migration to non-urban areas has only one "incorrect"

Table 18.5 Greenwood's model of migration and urban growth: 1960–1970

	Dependent variables: rates of			
	Out-migration to urban areas	Out-migration to non-urban areas	In-migration from urban areas	In-migration from non-urban areas
Out-migration to urban areas			+	
Out-migration to non-urban areas				+
In-migration from urban areas	+			
In-migration from non-urban areas		+		
Income growth	+*	−	+	+
Employment growth	−			+
Unemployment change	−*	+	−	−
Income, 1960	+*			+
Unemployment, 1960	−*		−	−
Labor force, 1960		+		−
Education, 1960	−*	−*		
Age, 1960	−	−		

	Growth rates of			
	Manufacturing employment	Government employment	Other employment	Unemployment
Out-migration	−	−	−	−
In-migration	+	+	+	
Natural population growth	+	+	+	+
Unemployment in 1960				−
Manufacturing emp. in 1960	−			
Government emp. in 1960		−		
Other employment in 1960			−	

Plus signs and minus signs refer to the sign of a stastically significant coefficient in the Greenwood (1981) study.
* Sign not as expected. Regression models include control variables for region.
Source: Greenwood (1981, p. 173)

sign. However, the equation for out-migration to other urban areas has five out of eight "incorrect" signs. Clearly the in-migrants to urban areas were responding to economic opportunities as represented by income and employment growth, declining unemployment rates, and low unemployment rates. The model of out-migration to non-urban areas also says that people responded to economic factors in the urban area of origin. However, the model of out-migration to other urban areas is not satisfactory.

The bottom half of Table 18.5 summarizes the Greenwood (1981) model for the employment growth rates of three broad industry categories (manufacturing, government employment, and all other employment) and for changes in the rate of unemployment. The models are quite simple and easy to interpret. The employment growth rate in each industry category was negatively related to out-migration, positively related to in-migration and natural population growth (births minus deaths), and negatively related to the initial employment level in the industry category. All of these results are as expected, including the results relating to the initial level of employment. The results for the change in the unemployment rate also make sense. Out-migration reduced the increase in unemployment, natural population increases increased the rise in unemployment, and the level of the unemployment rate in 1960 held back increases in unemployment.

All in all, the Greenwood (1981) study of gross migration of the labor force and employment growth in urban areas tells us that migrants, especially in-migrants, responded to measures of economic opportunity and also generated employment growth. The ability to attract the labor force is a prime mover in the growth of employment on a broad front, and the labor force can be attracted by conventional economic incentives such as income growth, employment growth, reductions in the unemployment rate, high income levels, and low unemployment levels. These findings are important as we consider the question of an overall economic growth strategy for an urban area in Chapter 21.

E. Summary

This chapter has documented the economic returns to formal education in the US. The return to higher education increased in the 1980s and 1990s. In spite of this increase in return, the percentage of adults who have graduated from college does not vary a great deal when one compares young adults (age 25–34) with older adults (age 35–44 and 45–54). However, the proportion of black and Hispanic youths who have dropped out of high school declined substantially from 1980 to 2000. The response of Americans to the incentive to attain higher levels of formal education is in evidence, but may not be as strong as one might have expected or hoped. We must remember that the data on education and earnings show average returns for those who completed the education level indicated. The data do not indicate the return that can be attained by someone who is the "marginal" investor in education. The raw data do not control for natural ability and motivation. Indeed, there is a school of thought that says that educational attainment is an indicator of some forms of natural ability and motivation. Employers therefore use educational attainment as a "screening" device to identify people with these basic traits. There is some truth to this argument, but how much is not clear.

This chapter has also examined inter-urban migration. Persistent migration patterns suggest that migration is not sufficiently prompt to wipe out wage (and unemployment rate) differentials across urban areas and regions.

Exercises

1   Suppose that there is a training program that will increase a trainee's earnings by $1,000 per year before taxes and by $750 after taxes. The actual cost of the program is $5,000 per trainee, and the trainee must forgo two months of earnings equal to $2,000 per month before taxes ($1,500 after taxes). Assume that the increase in earnings created by the training program lasts forever and that the trainee has a time horizon that is infinite.

(a) Assume that the trainee does not pay tuition because the training is a public program. What is the (private) rate of return to the trainee? What is the rate of return of the program for society? (Hint: The rate of return for society takes into account all of the costs and benefits of the program. Earnings are counted before taxes.)

(b) Suppose now that the trainee must pay $5,000 in tuition and that her discount rate is 6%. Assuming purely monetary motivation, will the person enroll in the training program?

2 Following the data depicted in Table 18.1, suppose that the average male high school graduate earns about $4,000 per year more (after taxes) from age 21 to 24 than does the man who did not earn the high school diploma. He then earns $9,000 (after taxes) per year more from age 25 to retirement (approximately an infinite time horizon). Assume to graduate from high school the person must forgo earnings of $15,000 per year for two years (everyone attends for two years, up to age 16). High school charges no tuition to the student but costs the taxpayers $7,000 per year per student. Assume a discount rate of 5%.

(a) Is earning a high school diploma a good investment for the individual? What are the present value of benefits and costs, dating your calculations at the beginning of the third year of high school?

(b) Is having the person complete high school a good investment for society?

References

Bartik, Timothy, 1991, *Who Benefits from State and Local Economic Development Policies?* Kalamazoo, MI: W. E. Upjohn Institute.

Becker, Gary, 1975, *Human Capital*, 2nd edn. New York: National Bureau of Economic Research and Columbia University Press.

Blomquist, Glenn, M. Berger, and J. Hoehn, 1988, "New Estimates of Quality of Life in Urban Areas," *American Economic Review*, vol. 78, pp. 89–107.

Borts, George and J. Stein, 1964, *Economic Growth in a Free Market*. New York: Columbia University Press.

Denison, Edward, 1985, *Trends in American Economic Growth*. Washington, DC: The Brookings Institution.

Evans, Alan, 1990, "The Assumption of Equilibrium in the Analysis of Migration and Interregional Differences: A Review of Some Recent Research," *Journal of Regional Science*, vol. 30, pp. 515–31.

Greenwood, Michael, 1981, *Migration and Economic Growth in the United States*. New York: Academic Press.

Henderson, J. Vernon, 1982, "Evaluating Consumer Amenities and Interregional Welfare Differences," *Journal of Urban Economics*, vol. 11, pp. 32–59.

Ladd, Helen, 2002, "School Vouchers: A Critical View," *Journal of Economic Perspectives*, vol. 16, pp. 3–24.

Murnane, Richard and F. Levy, 1992, "Education and Training," in H. Aaron and C. Schultze (eds.), *Setting Domestic Priorities*. Washington, DC: The Brookings Institution.

Muth, Richard, 1971, "Migration: Chicken or Egg?" *Southern Economic Journal*, vol. 37, pp. 295–306.

National Commission on Excellence in Education, 1983, *A Nation At Risk*. Washington, DC: US Dept. of Education.

Neal, Derek, 2002, "How Could Vouchers Change the Market for Education?" *Journal of Economic Perspectives*, vol. 16, pp. 25–44.

Rosenbaum, James, 1993, "Closing the Gap: Does Residential Integration Improve the Employment and Education of Low-Income Blacks?" in L. Joseph (ed.), *Affordable Housing and Public Policy*. Champaign, IL: University of Illinois Press.

Schultz, Theodore, 1961, "Investment in Human Capital," *American Economic Review*, vol. 51, pp. 1–17.

Sjaastad, Larry, 1962, "The Costs and Returns of Human Migration," *Journal of Political Economy*, vol. 70, no. 5, part 2, pp. 80–93.

Part VI

Urban Growth

Chapter 19

Models of Metropolitan Economic Growth

A. Introduction

Economic growth is a topic that is central to the entire discipline of economics. Adam Smith thought about it deeply in the book that many will argue founded economics in 1776, *An Inquiry into the Nature and Causes of the Wealth of Nations*. In the first years of the nineteenth century Parson Malthus worried what would happen when the growth of population outstripped the growth of food and other necessities of life. Modern thinking about economic growth at the national level started just after World War II when the field of economic development was founded. This field in economics concentrates on the problems of economic growth in less-developed countries such as India, China, and Mexico. More recently, urban planners and public officials in the US have decided to use the term economic development to refer to the study of the problems of growth of state and local economies in the US. You should be aware that different people will use the term "economic development" in these two senses. An economist (with gray hair) will probably be referring to places like India, while a younger person with a background in state and local policy studies will probably mean places like Cleveland.

The hope that less-developed countries might be placed on a growth path that would increase significantly their standards of living stimulated economic theorists in the 1950s to devise models that can explain national economic growth. The most famous contributor to the theory of economic growth is Robert Solow, who received the Nobel Prize in 1987 for his analysis of economic growth. It is fair to say that nearly all of the subsequent research on economic growth either augments Solow's model or is an attempt to criticize and replace Solow's basic framework. Solow used a fundamental idea from microeconomics – the production function, a function that relates inputs to potential outputs at the level of the firm (or industry). But Solow was frying bigger fish; he asserted that there exists a production function for an entire national economy that relates real gross domestic product (GDP) to capital and labor inputs and an autonomous growth factor that might be called "technological change." This production function can be written

$Y = AF(K,L)$.

Here Y is real GDP for a year, K is an index of the capital input, L is the labor input, A is the autonomous growth factor, and F denotes a function of K and L. The appendix to this book includes an introductory discussion of functions of this type, and you should review the material in this appendix as needed as you read this chapter.

At this point you should recall that GDP is *value added* by the primary inputs capital and labor. One way to measure GDP is to measure "final" output – consumption, investment, government purchases of goods and services, and net exports. The other way to measure GDP is to compute the value added by firms at each step of the production process. Auto companies purchase steel from steel companies, glass from glass manufacturers, mufflers from muffler firms, and so on – and then add value to these intermediate inputs by assembling them into automobiles. The auto companies hire labor and use their own plants and equipment to add the value.

What did Solow say about this basic production function? He stated that the growth in GDP stems from the growth in the capital input, the growth of the labor input, and the growth of the autonomous factor. In other words, growth in GDP has two basic causes – growth in the basic inputs and growth in output relative to the growth in the basic inputs. He also pointed out that growth in GDP per worker is generated by growth in capital per worker in the economy and by growth in the autonomous factor. Since Solow wrote in 1950s much of the debate has centered on just what is included in the autonomous factor, which is a pure public good. This question is discussed at length in this and the next three chapters in the context of urban areas.

Public officials, urban and regional planners, economists, and the public in general are concerned about the rate of economic growth in their state and local economies. State and local governments have been trying to increase the rate of economic growth through a wide variety of policies. Does your local government have an office of economic development or some similar department? What are your local officials doing to stimulate the local economy? Chances are they are doing something. Despite the widespread use of economic growth policies at the state and local level, research on the determinants of state and local economic growth has lagged far behind policy formulation and implementation. State and local officials are using policies that have unknown effects. For example, some 37 states have an enterprise zone program, a program that designates certain areas for some state and local tax breaks and subsidies. What are the effects of these enterprise zone programs in various types of locations? At this point we simply are not sure. The purpose of this section of this book is to help you to understand the various models of economic growth that can be used to examine an urban area, to learn what is known empirically about the determinants of local economic growth, and to gain a perspective on local "economic development" policy. We shall begin with what was once a popular model for the local economy, economic base analysis, and then turn to models of the Solow type. The next sections of the chapter add more local economic growth models to the mix.

B. Economic Base Analysis

The first economic model that was used to study the local economy was invented in the late 1930s, and is called economic base analysis. Given when it was invented, it is not surprising that economic base analysis is similar to Keynesian multiplier models. This would be a good time to review the basics of the Keynesian multiplier. We suppose that there is a national economy (with no government, for simplicity) that is suffering from unemployment. The GDP of the nation is written using the final output approach as

$$Y = C + I,$$

where C is consumption spending and I is investment spending. This really just an accounting identity that says all final output is either consumption or investment. The GDP of the nation is also the income earned by the primary inputs, capital and labor. Consequently, there is the behavioral relationship for consumption spending, written as a linear function

$$C = a + bY.$$

Here the propensity of consume is b, the fraction of additional income that is spent on consumption. The consumption function implies that there is also a function for saving – or non-consumption. By another accounting identity, $C + S = Y$, where S is saving. This identity and the consumption function imply that

$$S = Y - C, \text{ or that}$$
$$S = (1 - b)Y - a.$$

The propensity to save is $1 - b$, or one minus the proportion of additional income that is spent on consumption.

A critical insight supplied by Keynes is that income that is not spent on consumption is spent on investment goods. The critical purpose of the financial sector is to channel savings by households to those firms and households who make investments. Investment spending is regarded in the simple multiplier model as being exogenous – determined outside the model. Because $I = S$,

$$I = (1 - b)Y - a, \text{ or}$$
$$Y = (a + I)/(1 - b).$$

An increase in I of \$1 will increase Y by $1/(1 - b)$; this is the Keynesian multiplier. It says that an increase in investment spending will increase Y by the inverse of the propensity to save, which is $1 - b$. If the propensity of consume is 3/4, the propensity to save is 1/4, and the multiplier is 4.

Before we go on to the economic base model, note that this simple Keynesian model has no foreign trade sector. Also, note that the exogenous category of spending is investment. You should also recall from your study of macroeconomics that the multiplier works to increase real output (GDP) only when the economy is operating as less than full employment. If the economy is at full employment, an increase in investment spending cannot increase GDP in real terms.

The economic base model for urban areas focuses attention on trade with the rest of the economy. One good way to focus on exports and imports is to add them to the basic Keynesian model. For this purpose, assume that exports are exogenous (as investment is exogenous), and that imports are a function of income (as consumption is a function of income). The import function can specified as

$$M = c + dY,$$

where d is the propensity to spend an increase in income on imports. We now have two "leakages" of spending in the local economy, saving and imports. In this model gross "urban" product is

$$Y = C + I + X - M,$$

where X is exports. Assume that the spending on imports is for consumption activity. Consequently, total output of the local economy includes exports, but we must net out imports from C, consumption spending. As defined here, C includes some imports.

Instead of $S = I$ as in the simpler model without trade, the relevant condition is that $S + M = I + X$, or that "leakages" equal exogenous spending. In this model imports do not have to equal exports. Why not? Because, if you decide to import more than you export, you pay by having less savings at a given level of investment.

Substitution of the behavioral equations for C and M into the above income equation produces:

$$Y = (a + bY) - (c + dY) + I + X, \text{ or}$$
$$Y = (a - c + I + X)/(1 - b + d).$$

In this case an exogenous increase in investment or exports of \$1 increases local income by $1/(1 - b + d)$. This is the multiplier for a model with trade. For example, if $b = 0.75$ (as before), but $d = 0.25$, then the multiplier is 2. Recall that the multiplier was 4 when there were no imports ($d = 0$).

Now suppose we add a government to the model. We will suppose that the government spends amount G in the local economy and collects taxes according to a proportional income tax at rate t, or that taxes collected from the local economy are

$$T = tY.$$

Consumption spending is now regarded as a function of disposable income, which equals income minus taxes, i.e. $(1 - t)Y$. The consumption function is now

$$C = a + b(1 - t)Y,$$

and the saving function of income after taxes is

$$S = (1 - t)Y - C = -a + (1 - b)(1 - t)Y.$$

All government spending in the local economy shall be assumed to be exogenous and for the services of local labor.

With government in the model the definition of total local expenditure and income is

$$Y = C + I + G + X - M.$$

Given that $Y = C + S + T$, this equation can be manipulated to yield

$$S + T + M = I + G + X,$$

or that the total "leakages" of saving, taxes, and imports equal the total of exogenous spending.

Substitution for S, T and M in the above equation produces

$$(1 - b)(1 - t)Y - a + tY + c + dY = I + G + X, \text{ or}$$
$$Y = (a - c + I + G + X)/(1 - b + bt + d).$$

Now the local multiplier is $1/(1 - b + bt + d)$; an increase in spending for investment, government, or exports will increase local income by this amount. If $b = 0.75$ and $d = 0.25$ as before, and $t = 0.3$ (30% tax rate), then the local multiplier is 1.38. In other words, an increase in exports of \$1 will increase local income by \$1.38. A local multiplier inherently is not very large because the "leakages," including saving, imports, and taxes, are sizable fractions of additional income in a local economy.

Now let us turn to the economic base model. The local economy is partitioned into two parts, the sector that produces goods and services for export outside the urban area and the sector that produces for local use. This partition of the local economy can be based on income or employment – employment is probably the more popular choice because of better data availability. The fundamental equation for total employment T is

$$T = B + L,$$

where B is basic (export) employment and L is employment for the production of locally consumed goods and services. As in the Keynesian model, employment in the export sector is exogenous. A behavioral relationship is specified as

$$L = a + bT;$$

employment in the local sector is a function of total employment just as consumption is a function of income. The propensity to employ additional workers in the local sector for each additional worker is b. Substitution for L in the total employment equation yields the basic result that

$$T = (a + B)/(1 - b).$$

This equation implies that an increase in basic (export) employment of 1 will increase total local employment by $1/(1 - b)$. This is the local multiplier.

In some cases it is assumed that $a = 0$, so that

$$L = bT.$$

In other words,

$$b = L/T \text{ and}$$
$$1 - b = 1 - (L/T) = (T - L)/T = B/T.$$

In short, the local multiplier is just T/B, the ratio of total to basic (export) employment. This method for estimating the local multiplier simply requires an estimate of basic (export) employment. Total employment for a local economy is provided by standard government data sources.

This last simple economic base model is indeed very simple – too simple. Using the Keynesian multiplier model, we found that multipliers for a local economy are likely to be pretty low because of savings, imports and taxes. Suppose we take the previous multiplier of 1.38. The economic base model produces a multiplier of $T/B = 1.38$, or if $B = 0.8T$. Basic (export) employment must be 72% of total employment! Clearly something is wrong here. Employment in local economies is not 72% for export and 28% for local use or anything even close to those proportions. The problem stems from the assumption that $a = 0$ in the equation $L = a + bT$. If $a = 0$, the average and marginal propensities to employ workers in the local sector are equal. If a is greater than zero, the average propensity is greater than the marginal propensity. We want the marginal propensity for purposes of estimating the multiplier; but there is no justification for assuming that the marginal and average propensities are equal.

Let us take one final look at the algebra of the model. We know that the local multiplier is $1/(1 - b)$ and that $L = a + bT$. The crucial quantity is b, which equals

$$b = (L - a)/T = (L/T) - (a/T).$$

Substitution into the multiplier equation yields

$$1/(1 - b) = 1/[1 - (L/T) + (a/T)].$$

We know that $1 - (L/T) = B/T$, so

$$1/(1 - b) = 1/[(B/T) + (a/T)]$$
$$= T/(B + a).$$

As before, if $a = 0$, then the multiplier is T/B. But if a is greater than zero, the multiplier is smaller than T/B. The greater is a, the smaller is the local (marginal) multiplier. The economic base model has been used widely, but we do not recommend use of the simple economic base model with a local multiplier of T/B.

There are two further problems with this sort of model as a model of the economic growth of an urban area. First, as indicated above, Keynesian multiplier models (and economic base models) presume that there is unemployment. Total output is surely constrained by the supply of inputs, but this kind of model has nothing to say about the supply side. Even more importantly, the model emphasizes exports (and other exogenous spending) as the engine of growth. That is fine as far as it goes, but it does not go very far. Why does an urban area have a demand for its exports? What causes that demand to increase or decrease? The model is silent on these vital questions. The other models of urban economic growth provide some answers. In truth, the economic base model is an adaptation of the Keynesian multiplier model, which was expressly intended as a tool for short-run analysis. Economic growth is ultimately a long-run business. These are harsh criticisms, but we do not mean to suggest that we should ignore that fact that exports and imports are very important aspects of an urban economy. An alternative model with exports and imports is proposed in section F below.

C. Neoclassical Growth Theory

Solow's model of economic growth is called neoclassical because it is based on a production function for the economy in which it is possible to substitute capital for labor continuously, holding output constant. This idea of continuous substitution between inputs in production, holding output constant (and between consumer goods along an indifference curve), was devised in what is known as the neoclassical period of economics – about from 1870 to 1914. Suppose we begin with a particular neoclassical production function, the familiar Cobb–Douglas function, which is written

$$Y = AK^{\alpha}L^{1-\alpha}.$$

From the appendix to the book you know that, because the exponents sum to one, the production function has constant returns to scale. To see this again, multiply both inputs by 2. The implications are as follows:

$$A(2K)^{\alpha}(2L)^{1-\alpha} = A2^{\alpha+1-\alpha}K^{\alpha}L^{1-\alpha} = 2Y.$$

Doubling both inputs doubles output. Another important property is output per worker (average product), which is also called productivity, or

$$Y/L = A(K/L)^{\alpha}.$$

Output per worker is a function of the autonomous growth factor and capital per worker. The growth in productivity thus depends upon the growth in the autonomous growth factor and in capital per worker.

The basic equation for growth can be easily derived from the general form of the aggregate production function. If

$$Y = AF(K,L),$$

then, from the mathematics covered in the appendix to this book, the change in output can be written

$$\Delta Y = \Delta AF(K,L) + MP_K\Delta K + MP_L\Delta L.$$

Here MP_K and MP_L are the marginal products of capital and labor. This equation can be converted to percentage change form by dividing by Y, or

$$\Delta Y/Y = \Delta A/A + MP_K(K/Y)(\Delta K/K) + MP_L(L/Y)(\Delta L/L).$$

Since MP_K is just $\Delta Y/\Delta K$, $MP_K(K/Y)$ is the elasticity of output with respect to the capital input, which is $(\Delta Y/Y)/(\Delta K/K)$. Similarly, MP_L is $\Delta Y/\Delta L$, and $MP_L(L/Y)$ is the elasticity of output with respect to the labor input. The basic growth equation can be written

$$\Delta Y/Y = \Delta A/A + E_K(\Delta K/K) + E_L(\Delta L/L),$$

with E_K and E_L denoting the elasticities of output with respect to capital and labor. This equation says that the growth rate of GDP equals the growth rate of the autonomous growth factor, plus the growth rates of the two basic inputs weighted by the proper elasticities of output.

If we use the Cobb–Douglas production function, the elasticity of output with respect to capital is α, (the exponent of capital in the Cobb–Douglas function), and the elasticity of output with respect to labor is $1 - \alpha$ (the exponent of labor). To see this, consider the change in output with respect to a change in K using the power-function rule, or

$$\Delta Y / \Delta K = \alpha A K^{\alpha-1} L^{1-\alpha} = \alpha A (L/K)^{1-\alpha}.$$

The marginal product of K is determined by the ratio of labor to capital (L/K). Multiplication by K/Y will convert the equation to elasticity form;

$$E_K = (\Delta Y / \Delta K)(K/Y) = \alpha A K^{\alpha} L^{1-\alpha} / Y = \alpha.$$

The proof for the labor input follows the same method. Finally, suppose that each input is paid its marginal product, as would be the case with perfectly competitive markets for the two inputs. Denote the payment to each unit of capital as r, and denote the wage paid to labor as w. These assumptions mean that

$$\alpha = rK/Y \text{ and}$$
$$1 - \alpha = wL/Y.$$

The elasticities of output are the shares of total output paid to each of the inputs. With constant returns to scale these elasticities just sum to 1, and the total output is exhausted by the payments to the two inputs.

Now you understand the basic mechanics of neoclassical growth theory. Before we turn to its use in the explanation of growth in urban areas, you need to understand how the model has been used to examine growth at the national level. Use of the model at the national level did not proceed smoothly, and a heated controversy ensued.

D. Explanations of US Economic Growth

It is helpful first to examine some empirical estimates of the sources of economic growth at the national level. Substantial progress has been made in quantifying the sources of national growth, so those who seek to understand economic growth at the urban or regional level must have an understanding of this work.

One of the articles for which Robert Solow received the Nobel prize is a study of the sources of US economic growth from 1909 to 1949 (Solow, 1957). In that study 87.5% of the increase in gross output per man hour was attributed to technical change in the broadest sense (the autonomous growth factor), and the remaining 12.5% was attributed to increased use of capital. Solow used the phrase "technical change" to refer to the autonomous growth factor. Solow's 1957 paper is justifiably famous, but it had at least one unintended consequence. Taken by itself, Solow's paper leaves the false impression that economists have no coherent explanation for economic growth. Indeed, one still hears the basic result of this paper cited in conversation and in popular literature today. Solow's study lead Edward F. Denison to produce his first study (1962) of the sources of economic growth in which technical change is still regarded as the main source of growth.

In contrast to these studies, Dale Jorgenson and Zvi Griliches (1967), in a controversial paper, claimed that they measured the quantities of output and inputs with greater accuracy and found that disembodied (or residual) technical change contributed very little to growth. Their chief innovation was to devise methods for measuring the changes in the *quality* of the capital and labor inputs. This study set off a heated exchange between Denison and Jorgenson and Griliches that was published in the *Survey of Current Business* in 1969 and 1972. Denison's comments on the original Jorgenson-Griliches paper induced some revisions in the estimation methods; the revised estimates for 1950–62 published by Jorgenson and Griliches (1972) are as follows:

Sources of US economic growth 1950–1962

Capital	1.71% per annum
capital stock	1.30
quality change	0.30
utilization	0.11
Labor	0.71%
labor stock	0.37
quality change	0.44
utilization	−0.10
Autonomous growth factor	1.03%
Growth of gross private domestic product	3.47%

In these estimates technical change (autonomous growth factor) accounts for 30% of the growth in gross private domestic product and 33% of the growth in real output per worker. The growth in the measured capital stock accounts for a somewhat larger proportion of total growth over this period. And the changes in capital and labor quality (as measured by the change in the distributions of capital and labor toward more highly priced input forms) are significant contributors to growth.

Denison has continued to study the sources of US economic growth, and his latest estimates (1985) for the 1929–82 period are:

Sources of growth of potential national income 1929–1982

Labor	34%
Education per worker	13%
Capital	17%
Advances in knowledge	26%
Improvements in resource allocation	8%
Economies of scale	8%
Other factors	−6%
Total	100%

The proportion of growth attributed to advances in knowledge is 26%, which agrees fairly well with the earlier Jorgenson–Griliches estimates, but Denison attributes a smaller fraction of growth to capital than do Jorgenson and Griliches.

A major study by Jorgenson et al. (1987) is the best empirical study of the sources of national growth over the period of 1948 to 1979 both from the theoretical and empirical standpoints. Their perspective on economic growth emphasizes the contribution of the mobilization of resources within individual industries using a neoclassical framework. The explanatory force of this perspective is powerful at the sector level. For 46 of the 51 industrial sectors included in their study, the contributions of intermediate, capital, and labor inputs were the predominant source of the growth of output. Technical change (the autonomous growth factor) accounts for the major portion of growth in output in only five industries.

For the nation as a whole, Jorgenson et al. (1987) found that capital (both quantity and quality increases) accounted for 45.6% of the 3.42% annual average growth in aggregate output from 1948 to 1979. Labor (both quantity and quality) accounted for 30.7% of growth, and the autonomous growth factor explained 23.7% of total growth. Improvements in the quality of capital were associated with only about one-fourth of the growth that can be attributed to capital, but the growth in the quality of labor accounted for almost 50% of the growth attributed to the labor input. In short, the sheer quantity of capital is very important to growth, and improvements in the quality of labor and technical change (the autonomous growth factor) make big contributions as well.

One message to urban economics is clear from this brief examination of empirical studies of economic growth. Understanding economic growth is a complicated matter. No study as comprehensive as the Jorgenson et al. (1987) has been done at the urban or regional level. Indeed, given the data requirements, there is little prospect that such a study can be done for urban areas anytime soon. Another message from these studies is pretty clear. Economic growth policy at the national level can focus first on investment in capital goods, although policy might also focus on labor quality and technical change.

Despite the sophisticated work of Jorgenson, Gollop, and Fraumeni, there is still much that we do not understand about economic growth. For Americans the unsolved mystery is the slowdown in productivity growth that has occurred since 1973. As defined above, productivity is real GDP divided by the total amount of labor employed in its production. According to various issues of the *Economic Report of the President*, from 1948 to 1973 productivity in the US economy grew by an average of 2.5% per year, but from 1973 to 1991 the average growth rate for productivity was only 0.7% per year. This sharp drop in productivity growth has been translated into stagnant household incomes and wages. The median household income in real terms increased by 2.7% per year from 1948 to 1973, but from 1973 to 1989 (the peak year) the annual average increase was only 0.5%. This stagnation of household income took place during a period when the percentage of the population over the age of 16 who were employed increased from 58% to 63%. During this same period, 1973 to 1989, the average hourly earnings in the private sector declined in 1982 dollars from $8.55 to $7.64, an average annual decline of 0.7%. (However, there is evidence that fringe benefits grew by more than enough to make up for this decline in hourly pay. Total hourly compensation grew from $10.45 to $11.89 over this period, an average annual increase of 0.8%, a figure that is line with the productivity growth rate.)

Why did the productivity growth rate drop? There are many causes, and there is no consensus of opinion. One expert in empirical macroeconomics, Robert Gordon (1993, pp. 363–72), shows that slower growth in capital explains only a small part of the slowdown in productivity growth. Many economists cite a decline in the average quality of workers because of the increase in the labor force participation of teenagers and women since 1973. Others claim that the nation has failed to invest enough in public capital, the infrastructure. Still others point out that we are running out of raw materials; it costs more to recover the same amount of oil, natural gas, and other natural resources. The impacts of increases in governmental rules and regulations, particularly environmental and safety rules, are blamed by some. These impacts seem to be concentrated in particular industries, such as electric power generation. All of these arguments have merit, but at this point we do not know enough to determine how much of the decline in productivity growth can be attributed to each one. Paul Krugman, a prominent member of the younger generation of economists, puts it (perhaps a bit too pessimistically) as follows (1990, p. 15):

> So we really don't know why productivity growth ground to a near-halt. That makes it hard to answer the other question: What can we do to speed it up?

The good news is that US economic growth has been quite brisk since Krugman (1990) wrote this statement.

The rapid growth in GDP during the 1993–2001 period of 3.55% is attributed to the wide-scale adoption of computer technology, the internet, electronic commerce, and so on. William Nordhaus (2002) concluded that there was definitely an increase in labor productivity growth beginning in 1995. He estimated the acceleration of the growth rate of labor productivity at 1.1% to 1.6% per year for 1995–2000 compared to 1977–95. The growth rate of labor productivity during 1995–2000 was 2.87%, and this growth can be attributed to a "pure" productivity effect (controlling for the changing composition of output). Productivity growth was especially rapid in the "new economy," defined as the nonelectrical machinery, electrical machinery, telephone and telegraph, and software industries. Production of computers and semiconductors, two components of electrical machinery, were responsible for roughly 25% of the growth in labor productivity. However, sectors that are not part of the "new economy" also contributed to the rebound in productivity growth by adopting new technologies.

E. Neoclassical Models of Metropolitan Growth

The basic neoclassical model has been used to study economic growth at the metropolitan level. This section outlines the methods for such a study, and reviews some of the empirical findings. Growth models for urban areas concentrate attention on the growth rates of capital and labor, which depend critically on migration from or to other parts of the nation. While somewhat dated, a good example of a basic, straightforward model was developed by Ghali, Akiyama, and Fujiwara (1978). They applied the model of the states of the US, but the same principles can be used.

Consider again a one-sector model in which the relationship between aggregate output and inputs for an urban area is expressed as a Cobb–Douglas production function

$$Y_{it} = Ae^{rt}K_{it}^{\alpha}L_{it}^{1-\alpha},$$

where the subscript i refers to the urban area and t refers to year t. Recall that α and $1 - \alpha$ are the elasticities of output with respect to K and L. The term e refers to the base of the natural logarithms, and the parameter r is the rate of technical change. Parameter r is a decimal, such as 0.04, which means 4% per year. Ghali et al. (1978) assumed that output elasticities and the rate of technical change are the same in all urban areas, but this assumption might not be tenable in some applications of the model. However, the model allows for differences across urban areas in the marginal products of capital and labor because, as was shown above in section C, marginal products are determined by the capital–labor ratio in the urban area.

If factor markets are competitive, the wage (w) will equal the value of the marginal product of labor, and the rental rate of capital (r) will equal the marginal product of capital in equilibrium. Thus

$$w_{it} = P_t(\Delta Y/\Delta L)_{it}, \text{ and}$$
$$r_{it} = P_t(\Delta Y/\Delta K)_{it},$$

where P_t is the price of output, which is assumed to be the same in all urban areas. It is clear that the capital–labor ratio determines interurban factor price differentials. The factor prices above and the ratio of capital to labor will change over time if the rates of growth of the two inputs differ.

It is conventional to assume that capital and labor move from urban area to urban area in response to factor price differentials. Thus the rate of growth of labor in an urban area is the natural increase in the labor force plus a component that is a function of the difference between the wage in the urban area in question and average for all other urban areas. Similarly, the rate of growth of capital in an urban area is the "natural" increase in capital derived from saving and investment within the urban area plus interurban capital movement that is a function of the difference between the rental price of capital in that urban area and the average rental price for all other urban areas. It is also conventional to assume that labor and capital do not respond instantly to such price differentials. A "partial adjustment" mechanism is assumed; labor and capital respond to price differentials, but not enough so that the price differential is eliminated in one year.

The movement of labor and capital in response to factor price differentials should, in the long run, eliminate those factor price differentials. Urban areas (or states or regions) with high ratios of labor to capital presumably have low wages and high rental prices of capital. Labor migrates away from and capital migrates to such areas. Similarly, urban areas with high ratios of capital to labor have low rental prices of capital and high wages. If capital responds more rapidly than labor to factor price differentials, then the lower wage regions will grow more rapidly than higher wage regions. In the end wages in all urban areas (or states or regions) converge to the national average – except for wage differences related to amenities associated with living in particular places. For example, places with good weather will have lower measured wages as compensation. The hypothesis of the convergence of wages (and per capita income) across regions of the US has been the subject of a great deal of research. For the most part, researchers have observed a long-run convergence of per capita incomes across regions, but there are enough exceptions to this result to suggest that more complicated forces are at work. Borts and Stein, in an influential book that was published in 1964, found that there have been time periods when growth was higher in states with high wages. Also, there have been times when both wages and the rental price of capital were relatively high in the same state. Borts and Stein (1964) set out to devise a neoclassical growth model for states that can explain this more complicated set of empirical findings. Their model is discussed below.

The model proposed by Ghali et al. (1978) admits one other determinant of factor movements. Specifically, they suggest that growth differentials may carry information on the probability of gaining employment at the prevailing wage and on other factors that might influence the migration of labor and capital. The implications of the possibility that growth in output can encourage further growth in inputs will be explored below. Input growth equations can be written

$$L_{it}^* = \beta_0 + \beta_1(w_i/w)_{t-1} + \beta_2(g_i)_{t-1}, \text{ and}$$
$$K_{it}^* = \beta_3 + \beta_4(r_i/r)_{t-1} + \beta_6(g_i)_{t-1},$$

where L^* and K^* are the growth rates of L and K, w and r and the national average wage rate and rental rate on capital, and $(g_i)_{t-1}$ is the growth rate differential for urban area i relative to the national average growth rate (expressed as a percentage of the national growth rate). In equation form

$$(g_i)_{t-1} = [(Y_i^* - Y^*)/Y^*]_{t-1},$$

where Y_i^* and Y^* are the growth rates for urban area i and the national average.

The study by Ghali et al. (1978) estimated the model for 1958–63 using the states of the US as observations, and they also estimated the basic growth accounting equation

$$Y_{it}^* = r + \alpha K_{it}^* + (1 - \alpha)L_{it}^*.$$

The growth rate Y_{it}^* is the estimated rate of growth of gross state product, and the rate of growth of capital was approximated as the rate of growth of nonwage income. The equations estimated by multiple regression analysis are:

$$Y_i^* = 0.013 + 0.457K_i^* + 0.769L_i^*, \qquad R^2 = 0.486$$
$$L_i^* = 0.017 + 0.031(w_i/w)_{t-1} + 0.020(g_i)_{t-1} \quad R^2 = 0.620$$
$$K_i^* = 0.050 + 0.024(r_i/r)_{t-1} + 0.009(g_i)_{t-1} \quad R^2 = 0.583.$$

All estimated coefficients are statistically significant at conventional levels. The term R^2 refers to the percentage of the variance of the dependent variable accounted for by the independent variables included in the regression analysis. Note that the equation for the growth of output suggests increasing returns to scale (0.457 + 0.769 = 1.226). However, the figure 1.226 is not statistically significantly different from 1.0. This model is dynamic; the rates of growth of inputs influence the rate of growth of output in the state during the same time period. This rate of growth of output affects the rate of growth of inputs in the following period, leading to further changes in the rate of growth of output.

Simulation experiments were carried out with the above model. These experiments indicate that interstate disparities in the *level* of output per worker are quite persistent over time (out 15 years), but the wide disparities in the rates of growth of output and output per worker narrow quite rapidly. The neoclassical model estimated by Ghali et al. (1978) thus generates long run convergence of *growth rates*, but if the levels of output per worker are compared, little convergence will be found as long as the initial levels of output per worker differ.

Research by John Crihfield and Martin Panggabean (1993) has used a model very similar to that of Ghali et al. (1978) to study growth and per capita income convergence in metropolitan areas. They also seek to test for the effects of investment in public infrastructure at the metropolitan level. Their model is estimated for 288 metropolitan areas in the US for the period 1963–1977. They specify a production function for a metropolitan area at time t as the Cobb–Douglas function

$$Y_t = A_t K_t^{\alpha} H_t^{\beta} L_t^{1-\alpha-\beta},$$

where K includes public sector capital as well as private sector capital, and H is human capital. The growth rate of the autonomous growth factor, A, is assumed to exogenous to an urban area, but the growth rates of labor and private capital are functions of several variables. Output is measured as the total personal income for the metropolitan area, K is measured as the share of local income invested in private and public sector capital, and H is approximated by the percentage of residents over age 25 with at least 12 years of schooling. The production function is converted to a growth equation for per capita income. Their empirical results for the parameters in the production function are that $\alpha = 0.113$, $\beta = 0.204$, and $1 - \alpha - \beta = 0.683$. Crihfield and Panggabean acknowledge that the estimate of α, which is also supposed to be capital's share in total income, is low compared to studies at the national level. The share of capital is actually about 0.25. This inaccuracy may be the result of an imperfect measure of capital. Otherwise, the results appear to be quite reasonable. Note particularly that the measure of the quality of the labor input is a significant factor. Crihfield and Panggabean also found that metropolitan areas with higher per capita incomes in 1960 had lower growth rates. This result supports the hypothesis that per capita incomes of metropolitan areas are converging over time, in line with the neoclassical model.

Other research uses the neoclassical framework to examine employment growth (instead of output growth) at the metropolitan level. These studies will be discussed in Chapter 20.

F. Neoclassical Export Base Models of Urban Growth

This section will examine a two-sector neoclassical model of urban growth in which one sector produces a product for export and the other sector produces a good only for local consumption. This model shall be called a "neoclassical export base model." This type of model is more complex than the one-sector models discussed above, but the greater complexity also yields a richer set of possible outcomes that can be explained by the model. A mathematical version of this model is presented in the appendix to this chapter for more advanced students.

Borts and Stein (1964) developed the model presented in this section. They turned to a more complex neoclassical model because the one-sector model was unable to account for some empirical findings for states of the US. There have been periods in which high-wage states grew more rapidly than low-wage states. At times regions may have returns to labor and capital that are both above the national average and other regions where both returns are below the national average. And the former regions may grow more rapidly than the latter. It is clear that, even though it is many years old, the book by Borts and Stein (1964) is one of the best works on regional growth. It may also be true that it is not well understood. For example, Clark, Gertler et al. (1986, p. 41) stated that,

> Any reading of Borts and Stein (1964) would show that their own neoclassical production function models lacked much empirical validity.

They note that (1986, p. 258),

> Taking changes over three intervals (1919–29, 1929–48) and (1948–53), Borts and Stein (1964) measured the growth of capital, expecting it to grow fastest in low-wage states. In fact, this occurred only in one period (1929–48), casting some doubt on this aspect of the simple model they had chosen to test.

Richardson (1973, p. 221) argued that,

> However, it must be recognized that some of these findings, particularly that both capital and wages increased more rapidly in high wage areas in the first and third periods, are compatible with views of the regional growth process that are not extensions of but are quite contradictory to the neoclassical approach.

In fact, Borts and Stein (1964) took the findings referred to in these quotations as the starting point for their more sophisticated investigation. Borts and Stein (1964, p. 20) state,

> We have found that neoclassical price theory, suitably developed, provides the explanation of interstate differences in growth rates.

Instead it seems that the critics of neoclassical theory are prepared to discard it because its simplest version failed to explain some important facts about state growth rates.

The model developed by Borts and Stein is a conventional two-sector model of growth for an individual state. If the economy of the state is disaggregated to two sectors, then the growth rate in the real wage does not depend solely upon the growth in the auto-nomous growth factor and the capital–labor ratio (as in the one sector model). An increase in the ratio of capital to labor in a state may not lead to a rise in the ratio of capital to labor in each of the two sectors; a reallocation of output may occur in favor of the commodity produced by the relatively capital-intensive sector. This reallocation of output releases a relatively large amount of labor from the labor-intensive sector. This labor is employed in the capital-intensive sector, but these workers who shift sectors now require a greater amount of capital per worker than before. For the wage to rise capital accumulation must raise the ratio of capital to labor in both output sectors. This requires that capital accumulation be accompanied by an increase in the relative price of output in the sector that is relatively labor intensive. If, during capital accumulation, the relative output prices remain unchanged, the factor proportions do not change in both sectors. All that happens is a reallocation of output in favor of the sector that is relatively capital intensive and the wage does not increase. The empirical evidence presented by Borts and Stein confirmed their view of the growth process. Reallocation in favor of the labor-intensive services sector occurred in the group of states that underwent the greatest growth of capital relative to labor (during the 1929–53 period). This reallocation produced the observed increase in the marginal product of labor (i.e., wage rate) in those states.

The neoclassical economic base model as developed by Borts and Stein assumes that all markets within the urban area are perfectly competitive, capital is perfectly mobile and hence can be imported at the going price, and the growth rate of labor in the urban area is a given. This last assumption means that labor does *not* respond to wage rate differentials across urban areas – an assumption that empirical evidence has shown is not tenable. An exogenous growth in labor will cause the urban area to grow in the Borts–Stein model. Some of the critical results of the model pertain to the impacts of a change in the *price* of the export product. An increase in this price represents an increase in the demand for exports. A fundamental result of the model is that an increase in the price of exports will increase the wage rate. The wage increases because the increase in the price of the export product leads to importation of capital at its going (national) price. If the price of the exported output rises, but the price of capital does not increase, then the wage rate in the export sector must increase. This increase in the wage is transmitted to the local sector.

G. A Synthesis of Mainstream Economics: Preliminary Version

The Keynesian model in section B and the two-sector neoclassical models in sections E and F are two types of mainstream economic models. The Keynesian model generates growth through increases on the demand side, while the neoclassical model relies on growth of supply – labor in particular. It is useful to depict both models on a diagram for a local labor market.

Consider Figure 19.1, which shows the local market for labor. There is only one kind of labor in the market, and therefore everyone makes the same wage rate. The Keynesian model, in labor market terms, presumes that curve AA is the supply curve of labor. The supply is perfectly elastic at the current wage rate (at least in the relevant range of supplies). The demand for labor is curve BB. A given level of aggregate demand $(C + I + G + X - M)$ requires amount of labor L_0 at the current wage. The supplies of labor and all other inputs are perfectly elastic in the relevant range, so that employment in

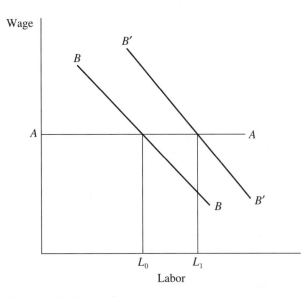

Figure 19.1   The labor market in an urban area

the local economy can grow only if demand increases. An increase in aggregate demand which increases the demand for labor to $B'B'$ will increase employment to L_1.

The two-sector neoclassical growth model has a perfectly elastic *demand* for labor because more exports can be sold at the prevailing price, capital can be freely imported at the prevailing price, and the local industries produce under constant returns to scale. The wage equals the value of the marginal product of labor in the export industry. The value of the marginal product is the price of output times the marginal product of labor. The price of output is taken as a constant, and the marginal product of labor can always be adjusted and kept constant by importing the appropriate amount of capital. Therefore, in Figure 19.2 the horizontal line AA is the demand for labor in the local economy. The supply of labor from the current residents is curve BB, so equilibrium employment is L_0. With a perfectly elastic demand for labor (and other inputs), growth occurs when the supply of labor increases. If the labor supply increases to curve $B'B'$, by natural population growth or by net in-migration, then employment increases to L_1.

Few economists are prepared to believe that either labor supply curves or demand curves are perfectly elastic at the level of an entire metropolitan area. There may be limitations on the ability of an urban area to sell its export good at a constant price. In nothing else, an expansion of exports will require that the good be transported greater distances and incur greater transportation costs. The price received by exporters will have to be reduced to offset the increase in transportation costs as more distant markets are penetrated. Likewise, even Keynes believed in the perfectly elastic supply of labor only under conditions of high unemployment.

A synthesis of the two mainstream economic models is shown in Figure 19.3. The demand for labor is labeled DD, the supply of labor is SS, the current wage is W_0 and the employment level is L_0. Employment growth can be generated by either an increase in demand (to $D'D'$), or an increase in supply (to $S'S'$). An increase in the demand for

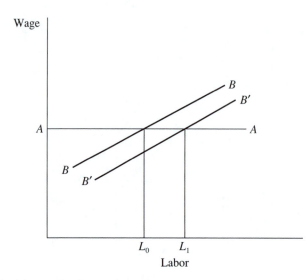

Figure 19.2   The labor market in an urban area

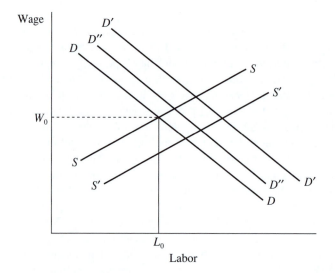

Figure 19.3   The labor market in an urban area

exports will generate an increase in demand for labor directly and indirectly through the local multiplier effect. Note that an increase in demand causes both employment and the wage to increase; part of the potential employment increase is choked off by a wage increase.

An increase in labor supply increases employment and decreases the wage. The decrease in the wage depends upon the elasticity of demand for labor, of course. If Borts and Stein (1964) are correct in asserting that the demand for labor in a local economy is highly elastic, then employment will increase and the wage will not decline very much.

Assuming that the increase in employment increases aggregate demand in the local economy, there will be an increase in the demand for local good (and imports, as well). This further increase in the demand for labor to produce local goods is shown as $D''D''$ in Figure 19.3. These increases in employment can then stimulate further increases in labor supply through migration, and the process can start again.

An early study by Muth (1971) found that an increase in migration to an urban area (in the 1950s) caused a direct increase in employment in that urban area equal to the increase in migration, and that the direct increase in employment induced migration of about 2/3 of that employment increase. In equation form;

$$\Delta E = \alpha M, \text{ and}$$
$$M = \beta(\Delta E) + \Theta,$$

where ΔE is the change in employment, M is migration, and α, β and Θ are coefficients. Muth's (1971) estimates are that $\alpha = 1$ and $\beta = 0.67$. The two equations can be solved for δE, or

$$\Delta E = \alpha\Theta/(1 - \alpha\beta) = \Theta/(1 - 0.67) = 3\Theta.$$

This result means that an increase in migration of 1 (brought about by increasing Θ by 1) will lead directly and indirectly to an increase in employment of 3. The indirect effect includes further in-migration that is induced by the increases in employment. Note that, for Muth's (1971) model to be stable, it must be true that $\alpha\beta$ is less than 1.0.

The simple synthesis of mainstream economic models is called "preliminary" because the impacts of changes in the autonomous growth factor have been ignored. The details of the autonomous growth factor are considered in Chapter 20, and then another synthesis of models is offered.

H. Input–Output Analysis

So far this chapter has introduced the export base and the basic one-sector and two-sector neoclassical models of urban economic growth. These models come straight from the Keynesian and neoclassical models of mainstream economics, and it is probably true that most researchers of urban economic growth are not happy with these tools. The search is on for models that will explain more of the variety and the detail of urban growth and decline. The purpose of the remainder of this chapter is to provide an account of the leading models that either supplement, or are intended to replace, the models that have been discussed thus far.

The first model included here is an expanded version of the Keynesian multiplier model discussed at the beginning of the chapter. The input–output model was invented by Wassily Leontief of Harvard in the 1930s, and he received the Nobel prize for his stunning accomplishment. The model is called input–output because it explicitly includes all of the intermediate goods and services that are used in the production of final goods and services. Recall that the Keynesian model and the neoclassical growth model are both

Table 19.1   Transactions table for a local economy

Inputs supplied by	Output sold to			Final demand		Gross output
	Manuf.	*Serv.*	*Trade*	*Households*	*Exports*	
Manufactures	6	4	10	0	20	40
Services	5	8	2	25	10	50
Trade	0	0	0	30	0	30
Local labor, capital, land	14	33	8	0	0	55
Imports	15	5	10	0	–	30
Total inputs	40	50	30	55	30	

models of *value added* only. Leontief rightly believes that much of the detail – and reality – of the economy is omitted by the concentration on value added. Leontief took a direct approach to the problem, and in so doing, invented a brilliant scheme for keeping track of an economy. Input–output analysis is a valuable accounting system, but can also be used to make projections and examine impacts of policy in the short run. As with the Keynesian multiplier models, the value of input–output models is not primarily as a method for analyzing long-run growth. Nevertheless, it is included because it clarifies one's thinking about any economy, including an urban economy.

The basic data for the input–output model is a transactions table, a simplified example of which is shown in Table 19.1. This table of transactions has been drawn up to resemble an urban economy, so the model presented here is intended to be at least somewhat realistic. Notice first that the local economy consists of four sectors; manufacturing, services, trade, and households. Across the top of the table the columns carry the labels of the sectors to which output is *sold*. Output is sold to the four local sectors, and there are exports to buyers outside the urban area. Down the left-hand side of the table are listed the sectors that supply *inputs* to the production activity that is carried on in the urban area. The manufacturing, service, and trade sectors are listed here as suppliers of intermediate inputs. The other inputs used in local production include the services of local labor, capital and land. These inputs create the *value added* by the local economy. To simplify the model we shall assume that local labor, capital and land are all owned by local households. This means that the income earned by these basic factors of production will accrue entirely to the local economy. The last input used in local production is imports from outside the urban area. Imports are shown as the fifth line in Table 19.1.

Let us pause for a moment to consider each of the three basic production sectors of this economy. Manufacturers produce a wide variety of goods; a good deal of local manufacturing output is exported, and some is also purchased by local manufacturing, service and trade firms. Some manufacturers produce parts and equipment used by other local businesses, but in this model it is assumed that manufacturers do not sell directly to households. Instead, manufactured products are sold to households by firms in the trade sector. Indeed, this is all the local trade sector does in this model – sell to local households. The service sector in an urban area is a very large and diverse collection of activities, including health care (14% of the economy!), business services (accountants, lawyers, computer firms, financial services, etc.), and other sorts of personal services. Services are purchased by local businesses and households, and some services are also exported. For example, financial services supplied by firms in an urban area can be performed for clients who live elsewhere, and some medical services can be provided for patients who come to the urban area for that purpose.

Local residents supply the labor, capital and land used by the three production sectors. The production of services is assumed to require a great deal of labor, and some land and capital as well. Manufacturing uses labor and factories, which require capital and land. The trade sector purchases goods from local suppliers and from firms outside the urban area, and requires a relatively small amount of local labor, capital and land compared to the total sales volume. Goods and services that are imported are presumed to be imported by firms, and households then purchase some of those imports from local service and trade firms. The other imports are used as intermediate inputs into local production.

Now return to Table 19.1. The numbers in each column represent the dollar amounts of the *inputs* used in the sector shown at the top of the column. In particular, manufacturing in the urban area used $6 worth of manufactured goods (made locally); $5 in local services; $14 in local labor, capital and land; and $15 worth of imports. The total value of the inputs in the local manufacturing sector is therefore $40. Note that manufacturing is assumed to use a good deal of imported products – parts, equipment, etc. Similarly, the local service sector bought $4 from local manufacturer, $8 from the local service sector itself, $33 from local households (labor, capital and land), and $5 in imports. What was purchased by the local trade sector?

Consider the column labeled households. This column does not represent "inputs" into a production process, but rather it lists final consumption activity. Households bought nothing from local manufacturers (as mentioned above), and purchased $25 in services and spent $30 with the local trade sector. In this model there is no saving; households spend all of their incomes. The model could be expanded to include saving and investment. Next, the column for exports shows the amounts sold to customers outside the urban area by the manufacturing and services sectors. The final column is called gross output. Gross output is the dollar value of *total sales* for a sector. For example, the local manufacturing sector had sales of $40. This is *not* value added (which was $14), but the value of *sales*. This entry of $40 is the sum of the figures in the first row, the row that shows the sales by local manufacturers to the various sectors. The $40 is also equal to the total value of the inputs purchased by the local manufacturing sector. Total purchases of inputs equal total sales because profits are included in the payments to local households. Note that the local service sector had a grand total of $50 in sales, distributed across the sectors as shown in the second row of the table. The local trade sector had $30 in sales, all of which were to local households.

The last column also lists a "gross output" figure for households. This figure of $55 is really the total income earned by households in the urban area from the sale of the services of labor, capital and land. Total income is also equal to total value added in the local economy, hence the local gross domestic product was $55. Finally, total exports were $30, which equals the total imports shown in the fifth row. The fourth and fifth columns together constitute the final demands for goods and services. The accounts balance. Table 19.1 shows why input–output analysis is highly useful as an accounting system.

Table 19.2   Input coefficients for a local economy

	Manuf.	*Serv.*	*Trade*	*Households*
Manufactures	0.150	0.080	0.333	0.000
Services	0.125	0.160	0.067	0.455
Trade	0.000	0.000	0.000	0.545
Value added	0.350	0.660	0.267	0.000
Imports	0.375	0.100	0.333	0.000

The accounts shown in Table 19.1 can be converted into a model of the local economy. The first step is to compute the input coefficients for each sector. An input coefficient is the proportion of the total value of inputs spent on one particular input. For example, the local manufacturing sector purchased $6 from the local manufacturing sector out of a total of $40. The input coefficient is thus $6/40 = 0.15$. The remaining input coefficients for manufacturing are 0.125 for services, 0.35 for local value added (labor, capital, and land), and 0.375 for imports. These proportions add up to 1.0, and together they are the "recipe" for the goods manufactured locally. At this point is necessary to make some behavioral assumptions. It shall be assumed that the prices of all goods and services in this economy are constant. It is further assumed that the goods and services in the economy are produced under constant returns to scale, and that input proportions do not change as the scale of production is changed. Therefore, if we wish to increase local manufacturing output by $1, we will need $0.15 in manufactured goods, $0.125 in services, $0.35 is value added, and $0.375 in imported goods and services. The increase in output of $1 is the same thing as an increase in one unit of output because the price of output is constant. The input coefficients have been computed for each sector, and are shown in Table 19.2.

The input coefficients shown in Table 19.2 can be used to set up a system of equations to represent the local economy. We shall use the following notation:

M = gross output in manufacturing,
S = gross output in services,
T = gross output in trade,
Y = total income (value added) in the local economy,
X_m = exports of manufactured goods, and
X_s = exports of services.

Now pay close attention. Reading across Table 19.2, we know that the gross output in manufacturing is 0.15 of the gross output in manufacturing, plus 0.08 of the gross output of services, plus 0.333 of the gross output in the trade sector, plus exports of manufactured goods. In equation form

$$M = 0.150M + 0.080S + 0.333T + X_m,$$
$$S = 0.125M + 0.160S + 0.067T + 0.455Y + X_s,$$
$$T = 0.545Y, \text{ and}$$
$$Y = 0.350M + 0.660S + 0.267T.$$

The usual assumption is to take exports as exogenous variables, so this system of four equations can be solved for the four unknowns (M, S, T and Y) in terms of the two export variables.

Finding the solution even to this simple system of four equations in not easy, so the usual technique is to convert the model to matrix form and use a computer to find the solution. Real input–output models can contain hundreds of sectors, so use of the computer to solve them is mandatory. The system of equations can be solved by successive substitution to eliminate variables (otherwise known as brute force), and the solutions are:

$$M = 1.613X_m + 0.772X_s,$$
$$S = 3.236X_s + 1.141X_m,$$
$$Y = 2.413X_s + 1.542X_m, \text{ and}$$
$$T = 0.545Y.$$

These solutions provide various multipliers associated with an increase in exports. An increase in manufacturing exports of \$1 will increase gross manufacturing output by \$1.61, gross output in services by \$1.14, local income (value added) by \$1.54, and gross sales in trade by \$0.84. The multipliers associated with service exports are; 0.77 on manufacturing output, 3.24 on output of services themselves, 2.41 on income, and 1.32 on gross sales in trade. In this model exports of services have the larger effect on local income because there is more "local content" in services; value added is 66% of service gross output, but only 35% of gross output in manufacturing, and the two income multipliers are 2.41 and 1.54. Recall that total income is 55 and total exports are 30, so the ratio of income to exports is 1.83. This figure is just the weighted average of the two export multipliers, where the service sector export multiplier of 2.41 gets half the weight of the manufacturing export multiplier of 1.54. (Manufacturing exports are 20 and service exports are 10.)

Input–output analysis as a model of the economy in the short run has provided some useful results. It has shown that different types of exports have different multiplier effects on the local economy. It also shows the full increases in output in all of the sectors of the local economy that are needed to respond to increased exports. The solutions to the model above tell us, that to expand manufacturing exports by \$1, the local economy needs to produce \$1.61 worth of manufactures and \$0.77 in services. An added dollar of service exports requires \$3.24 in services and \$1.14 in manufactured goods. Coupled with information on potential supplies in various sectors, the input–output model can thus be used to determine whether the local economy has the capacity to handle the requirements of a large increase in exports.

The model can also be used to estimate changes in imports used in each sector. From Table 20.2, the equation for imports is

$$I = 0.375M + 0.100S + 0.333T.$$

Hence, knowledge of the changes in M, S and T produces a projection of the change in imports. The total change in imports should equal the change in exports, of course. As an exercise, you can confirm that a \$1 increase in manufactured exports generates a \$1 increase in total imports.

Input–output models have become a popular analytical tool for local economic development officials. Several types of studies are conducted with the help of such a model. For one thing, the table of input coefficients can tell local officials whether the local economy supplies a lot or a little of the intermediate inputs needed by the export industries. If local suppliers appear to be weak, the next step is to find out why and consider whether the intermediate suppliers can be strengthened. On the other hand, if the suppliers of intermediate inputs are abundant, perhaps more of the export product can be attracted to the local economy. One can imagine the advertisements in industry trade journals that say, "We have the suppliers that you need right here in Ourtown." Another, less obvious, use of the model is to examine the impacts on the local economy of a change in technology – changes in the input coefficients. We run the model with a given set of export demands and the old input coefficients, and then we rerun the model with the same export demands and a new set of input coefficients. What happens? Is local income increased? What are the changes in output requirements?

As one might suppose, the usual use of the model is to make projections that show the impact of a particular exogenous change in final demands. For example, the Chicago input–output model recently has been used to estimate the effects of a proposed theme park and legal gambling casino to be located near downtown. So many tourists are expected to visit these attractions each year, and to spend money at hotels, restaurants, museums, etc. What will be the increases in output and employment in the various sectors of the Chicago economy? The input–output model provides a set of answers that is internally consistent. All of the rows and columns add up properly; no fudging is required to make all of the changes in all of the sectors balance. Indeed, the model does all of this automatically. Clearly Leontief deserved his Nobel Prize.

The input–output model is a useful and popular tool, but there are some limitations that one must bear in mind. The biggest problem with the framework is the requirement for data. The transactions table needs data on transactions. For each sector we need to know how much of the intermediate inputs were purchased locally versus imported. The task of collection of original survey data is costly, so model builders turn to cheaper alternatives. One approach is to use data that exist (only for manufacturing) at the US Bureau of the Census on the identities of suppliers and customers for a sample of establishments from around the nation. The sample of establishments includes enough observations from major metropolitan areas to permit the estimation of input coefficients. Another approach is to adapt the national input–output table for the local economy. It is assumed that the local sector has the same input requirements as does the industry at the national level. These input requirements are divided between local suppliers and imports based on the relative size of the relevant local sectors. For example, if a local industry needs computer chips for its product but there no local producers, we can conclude that the computer chips are imported. These alternatives to original survey research usually work fairly well in the sense that the input–output model that is generated is capable of replicating past data on the local economy with reasonable accuracy.

A more serious problem with input–output models for a local economy is the stability of the input coefficients. The input coefficients must, of necessity, be derived from data on the past record of the local economy. However, input coefficients can change suddenly when a local sector decides to import an intermediate input rather than to purchase it locally (or purchase it locally rather than import it, for that matter). Input coefficients are rather stable over time in the national input–output model, but the national model does not have to include trade among urban areas and regions. This problem may be particularly acute in an industry that is undergoing rapid technical change or growth, and such an industry may just be the kind of industry with which the local analyst in concerned. Input coefficients can be unstable because of price changes as well. The basic input–output model explicitly assumes that all prices are constant, but a change in relative input prices should lead to some substitution effects. Input–output models are not designed to handle this kind of problem easily, although changes in the input coefficients can be made. Changes in input coefficients must also be made when there is technical change. These problems mean that the model needs to be updated periodically.

Recall that the input–output model is also based on the assumption of constant returns to scale for the local industries. The projections of the model are inaccurate if there are increasing (or decreasing) returns to scale. A related point is that the model is also inaccurate if agglomeration economies exist of the types discussed in Chapter 3. Localization economies essentially are economies of scale for the industry, and urbanization economies are economies that stem from the size of the local economy as a whole. Input-output models do not account for these phenomena.

Finally, as we have emphasized, input–output analysis is a short-run tool. It is useful for making projections and performing impact analyses that are of short duration. It is not really a tool for the analysis of long-run growth because the model really has no supply side. The model presumes that the needed supplies of labor, capital, land, and inter-mediate products will be forthcoming when there is an exogenous increase in final demand. It may be perfectly reasonable to assume all of this in the short run, but the long run is a different story, as the neoclassical growth model tells us.

I. Economic History and Urban Growth and Development

Now we turn from the world of formal models to the more informal and eclectic field of economic history. Economic history is an important tool for understanding urban economies. The best modern economic historians combine analyses of the institutions and historical context of the urban area and its region, economic analysis, and political economy to provide a convincing narrative of what happened and why. This explanation may also have considerable relevance for current economic development policy. Two excellent examples of economic history as applied to an American city or region are discussed in this section. William Cronon's *Nature's Metropolis* is the story of Chicago and the Midwest in the nineteenth century, and *Old South, New South* by Gavin Wright tells the story of the transformation of the southern economy since the 1930s. Wright's book does not deal specifically with urban areas in the South, but the connections between the region and its urban areas are pretty obvious. Both of these books are outstanding works of scholarship and written for a pretty wide general audience, so we strongly recommend that you read them. If you are assigned to do a book report or book review in one of your courses, these would make good choices.

William Cronon's book (1991) is a chronicle of the intimate connections between the growth and development of Chicago and the rest of the Midwest. The book contains rich descriptions of the lumber industry of the Midwest, the development of the grain trade and futures markets, the meat packing industry, the coming of the railroad, and much more. As such, it provides the historical background needed to understand the evolution of Chicago's economic functions in the larger economy. This brief discussion cannot do this great book justice – only basic themes and a few examples can be covered here.

Chicago essentially did not exist before the State of Illinois announced in 1833 that it was going to build a canal that would connect the Chicago River to the Illinois River about twenty miles to the Southwest. Why was this important? First, it represented the most convenient connection between the waterway systems of the Great Lakes and the Mississippi River. The Chicago River is a very short river that flowed into Lake Michigan, and the Illinois River is a long, wide and fairly deep river that flows southwest to the Mississippi. Second, the Erie Canal had opened in 1825. This man-made waterway permitted freight to move from New York City to the Great Lakes system and, hence to Chicago. The connection at Chicago would permit freight to move between New York and the great Midwestern hinterland, which was largely vacant in 1833. The announcement of the construction of the Illinois and Michigan Canal created a boom in land values in the muddy place called Chicago the likes of which has not been seen since. Chicago suddenly had become the chief transshipment point for much of the continent. Because of the economic turbulence of the late 1830s and early 1840s, the canal itself was not completed until 1848. The State of Illinois in fact defaulted on its original canal bonds. Nevertheless, the city of Chicago had been created.

Chicago got its start shipping agricultural products that could be transported from the nearby farms even without the canal in place. But the place really took off when the canal opened in 1848 and when the construction of the railway network centered on Chicago was begun at roughly the same time. Agricultural products could be shipped in from a wider hinterland, and various products needed by farmers could be supplied from Chicago. One of those products required by the farmers of the Midwest was lumber. The original lumber industry of the Midwest harvested wood in northern Wisconsin and Michigan, shipped the rough lumber to Chicago by water, produced the more finished lumber in Chicago, and then shipped the lumber to its final users by rail and water. The owners of the lumber firms often hired their lumberjacks and other workers for the season in Chicago. Lumber was cut down in the winter so it could slide on snow to nearby rivers. In the spring the logs moved down river to the sawmills, and then the ships transported the sawn lumber to Chicago. Chicago was the Mecca for the lumber firms because its market for lumber was so large that the lumber buyer in Chicago could purchase an entire shipload of lumber for cash right at the dock on the Chicago River. The buyer then moved the lumber a short distance up the Chicago River to the lumber district, where the lumber wholesalers maintained their inventories. The lumber district was served both by rail and water transportation. So this is another example of how Chicago was "nature's metropolis," a metropolis created by the natural resources of the great midwestern region.

Another instructive story that was already mentioned in Chapter 5 is the saga of cattle, hogs and meatpacking. The business of packing meat began in Chicago in its earliest years, but the business really boomed during the Civil War. In 1865 the various stockyards and meat packers in Chicago decided to create the Union Stockyards, stockyards large enough to serve the entire industry. Prior to 1865 the stockyards and meat packing plants were scattered throughout the city. One might add that cattle and hogs (alive or dead) do not make very good neighbors. This facility was located at the southwestern edge of the city, where good access to both rail and transportation was provided. The meat packing plants soon followed to this location. Then, in the early 1870s, the hunters cleared most of the western plains of the bison. This hunting, which was unrivaled in its savagery, permitted the cattle ranchers to take over large expanses of territory from Texas to Montana. The construction of railroads connected these far-flung places to the market for livestock in Chicago. We are all familiar with the fabled cattle drives from Texas to places in Kansas like Abilene and Dodge City. Perhaps we tend to forget that from there the cattle were transported to Chicago by rail, or they were fattened up on corn on farms in Iowa or Illinois (and then shipped to Chicago). Here we have it again. An entire complex of industries was created in Chicago by the natural resources of the Midwest.

One final example tells the other side of the story. Chicago, with its excellent transportation connections to a wide area, was a natural site for manufacturers and wholesalers who catered to the farmers and the residents of the smaller towns. All of this was not lost on Cyrus McCormick, who invented the mechanical reaper in the 1830s and opened a factory in Chicago in the 1840s. Another entrepreneur of great renown was one Montgomery Ward, who figured out that a mail-order business could eliminate the middle man and make money. His business was greatly enhanced by the introduction of rural free delivery by the US Post Office. A couple of guys named Sears and Roebuck soon followed.

Cronon's book (1991) demonstrates that Chicago was, to some degree, a special case of a special place. However, perhaps the more important point is that his methods of historical and economic scholarship can be applied to many other urban areas around the nation (and world, for that matter). Indeed, Cronon stopped his story in 1893. Chicago's story in the twentieth century is awaiting another Cronon.

Now let us move forward in time and look to the South. The South is the region of the nation that has attracted the greatest attention of the economic historians. The reason is obvious; as a region the economy of the South was, until quite recently, very different from the rest of the nation. It is to the South that we must look for the best regional economic history. And the best of the best is the book by Gavin Wright (1986) entitled *Old South, New South*.

The relevant part of Wright's analysis is his account of how and why the South was transformed from an economic backwater in 1930 to an integral part of the economy of the nation in 1980. Wright's analysis is that the economy of the South in 1930 was based on a low-wage labor market and an associated cultural isolation. Political power was used to maintain an economy based on low-wage labor. The abolition of slavery had not eliminated the historical legacy of separateness, which continued until modern times. However, because the South lost the Civil War and could not set up its own national government, during the twentieth century it increasingly came under the political jurisdiction of the larger nation. It was subject to the laws and policies of the New Deal of the 1930s, as well as the market forces and technologies of the nation. In Wright's view, the critical economic event was the imposition of national wage and labor standards beginning in the 1930s. These actions eventually eliminated the stake that southern property owners had in keeping a separate labor market. Decisions were made to invite in flows of capital and labor, and the distinct "southern economy" has largely disappeared.

Once change was underway, several factors as summarized by Wright (1986, pp. 239–40) contributed to southern economic development:

1   Market incentives brought capital and skilled and educated labor to the South, particularly to its urban areas.
2   Federal spending (defense spending in particular) that the South once shunned was now sought.
3   Favorable climate and other amenities worked in the South's favor (especially after the invention of air conditioning).
4   The South invented state and local economic development policies such as industrial revenue bonds, long-term tax exemptions, active local economic development corporations, etc.
5   The South had a relatively clean slate in terms of absence of labor unions, entrenched bureaucracies, restrictive legislation – a good "business climate."
6   Lastly, a shift was made from relatively high to relatively low taxes on business.

Does Wright the economic historian provide a formula for policy for other places at other times? Perhaps some of these elements are relevant, but we must remember the context in which these policies were adopted and generated successful outcomes.

Another facet of the work of economic historians is the explanation of economic growth in part using the notion of strategic industries. A strategic industry is one whose growth induces growth of a complex of industries, and thus creates a substantially new economy. Growth is thought of as being induced by backward linkages to suppliers and forward linkages to customers. These industries generate rapid changes in technology in complex combinations and sequences. The standard example from economic history is the English cotton textile industry of the late eighteenth century, as described in rich detail by Landes (1969). Other examples abound in the literature; railroads and machine tools in the US in the nineteenth century and chemicals in nineteenth-century Germany are good examples. Examples in urban areas in the US include autos in Detroit, steel in Pittsburgh, financial services in New York, microelectronics in Silicon Valley in northern California, and risk management financial services in Chicago.

The issues regarding strategic industries for those concerned with the growth of particular urban areas are:

•   Can strategic industries be identified?
•   Are there any local policies that can foster the growth of strategic industries?

It would seem that both of these questions can be answered in the affirmative, at least at a broad level. Economic analysis of an urban economy should be able to identify the key export sectors and to determine if any of these sectors also induces growth in other sectors through market or technological linkages. And once these sectors are identified, it should be possible to determine if there are any public policies that inhibit growth or if such sectors have special needs for public services, infrastructure, particular labor skills, and other important inputs. At the very least, it should be possible to devise public policies that do not stand in the way of progress. For example, Ferguson and Ladd (1988) have argued that this was the essential contribution of state policy to the "Massachusetts miracle" of the 1980s. However, it is fair to say that not much research has been done that validates the cost-effectiveness for urban areas or states of targeting programs to strategic industries. Also, there is little evidence that local governments are really very capable of identifying an emerging strategic industry. It may be easy to identify an industry that *once was* a strategic industry. The problem is to identify industries with appreciable potential for further growth, and then to foster that growth. There really is little evidence at this time to suggest that local governments can successfully pursue such a course. Indeed, the *national* debate over industrial policy seems to have subsided with the general conclusion that the public sector is probably not very effective at targeting industries as strategic industries.

This guarded conclusion regarding local public policy does not, however, suggest that researchers should abandon work that uncovers the historic roots of a local economy. Also, methods for improving the studies that are done of the local economy should be pursued. Some of these methods are discussed below.

J. The Product Cycle and Urban Growth

Another important perspective on urban and regional growth has been derived from the field of economic history. Currently it is known as the product cycle model, or the long wave model, or the product–profit cycle. Its adherents include scholars such as Norton and Rees (1979), Markusen (1985), and Booth (1986). Norton and Rees (1979) provided an early description of the regional shift in manufacturing in the US during 1966–77. Booth (1986) has provided a succinct statement of the model, so this section follows his presentation.

Historical studies have established the existence of industrial lifecycles. New industries experience a period of rapid growth after an initial phase of incubation, and, as a consequence of competition from still new industries, eventually face a retardation of growth or absolute decline. The existence of industrial lifecycles may be related to the Schumpeter's (1942) concept of competition involving a constant struggle in the market place between entrepreneurs to gain a monopoly position in a new commodity, a new technology, a new source of supply, or a new type of organization. Any competitive edge gained in this struggle is ultimately eliminated by competition from still new innovations in the market. The private enterprise economy thus involves a constantly changing mix of products, technologies, sources of supply, and forms of business organization. New industries periodically emerge to replace older industries as growth leaders in the economy. For a while these industries may be the strategic industries that were discussed above. The early stages of the industrial lifecycle exhibit rapid technical change requiring flexible, labor-intensive production processes. The later stages involve a stabilizing of technology, saturation of product markets, and increasing concern with cutting unit production costs through the attainment of scale economies.

There may be a connection between industrial lifecycles and urban growth and decline. The growth of an urban area or a region is stimulated by the presence of industries in the rapid growth phase of their lifecycles, and retarded by the presence of industries in the slow growth or decline phase. Indeed, firms that are intent on cutting production costs may relocate from large urban areas with high costs of labor and real estate. An urban area with an appropriate mix of growing and stable industries will not experience a period of decline in its growth rate, but the scholars mentioned above believe that urban areas with ageing industries suffer through relatively lengthy periods of time without developing substantial amounts of economic activity in new, growth industries. If this is true, there must be barriers to the formation of new industries in urban areas with a mature industrial base.

Generally it is true that new industries are formed by new businesses. Only rarely do existing large firms in already established industries become the driving force for the creation of entirely new industries. Consequently, Booth (1986) states that the central issue is whether there are impediments to new business formation in older urban areas with mature industries. One factor is that firms in mature industries focus on management rather than entrepreneurship because their central problem is achieving scale economies and cutting costs. Such firms train managers, not entrepreneurs who would be capable of starting new firms in the area. Such firms provide (seemingly) secure, well-paying jobs for capable people, so the push to become an entrepreneur may be absent. Also, the presence of large mature firms in a urban area could place a limit on the availability of venture capital for new businesses. Mature enterprises provide stable and secure returns on investment compared to start-up companies.

However, once employment opportunities begin to decline in mature industries in an urban area, then the prospects for the formation of new businesses begin to change. Managerial opportunities in mature firms begin to disappear, and those with business skills who do not migrate to other regions will start to turn to the formation of new businesses. Also, capital and labor will be attracted to new firms as opportunities in the mature sectors decline. But the adherents to the product-cycle model suggest that the fundamental problem is that a lengthy period is often required before new businesses that manage to survive grow to the point where they become major employers. In the meantime, an older urban area with mature industries in a state of decline will experience slow economic growth and social problems associated with inadequate employment opportunities. Eventually, new industries will emerge and the growth rate will recover, but the time lapse between the growth phase of one wave and another could be lengthy. An auxiliary part of the story is that large, mature firms do not engage in the development of new products and technologies at the rate required to keep the urban area growing evenly. Booth (1986) hypothesizes that the bureaucratic form of management in large firms is partly designed to inhibit product and process innovation because there is a strong desire to control the activities of the employees. Whether this is true, empirical evidence summarized by Scherer (1980) suggests that very large corporations are only infrequently the source of major new innovations. While there are exceptions, large firms have not felt a strong pressure to innovate until their traditional business activity is seriously threatened, and the time lapse between feeling this pressure and developing major new sources of economic activity will be lengthy.

The product-cycle story is certainly plausible, and daily reports in the newspapers seem to validate the idea that large firms have difficulty being truly innovative. However, there are problems with the model at this point:

- The empirical evidence in support of the model is weak and subject to alternative interpretation.
- The model provides very limited policy prescriptions for lagging urban areas (besides the suggestion to "wait").

The empirical evidence in support of the model begins with the observations that much of the growth in newer science-based industries has been in southern and western urban areas, and that the New England area seemed to have entered a new long wave in the late 1970s and 1980s. However, these developments might also be explained by the presence of specific human and non-human capital, factor costs, threshold effects, and federal government procurement policies. In our opinion, more sharply focused empirical tests are needed.

Markusen (1985) has modified the product cycle model to consider profits (and well and output and employment) and oligopoly as key elements in the historical development of an industry. Markusen's version of the model is called the profit-cycle model. The profit-cycle model has five characteristic stages;

- *zero profit*, corresponding to the initial birth and design stage of the industry;
- *super profit*, corresponding to the era of excess profit from an innovative edge;
- *normal profit*, corresponding to the stage of open entry and movement toward market saturation;
- *normal plus or normal minus profit*, corresponding to the post-saturation stage in which the industry becomes an oligopoly or excessively competitive; and
- *negative profit*, corresponding to the obsolescence stage.

The industry is spatially concentrated in the first two stages, and begins to disperse in the third stage. The presence of oligopoly will retard dispersal in the fourth stage, and may accelerate dispersal and disinvestment in the fifth stage.

Markusen (1985) conducted 18 case studies of US industries over the period 1947 to 1977 to test the profit-cycle model. These case studies are of six producer goods industries, six consumer goods industries, and six resource-based industries. Markusen claims that the case studies lend strong support to the model. In the producer goods industries, the rapidly innovating industries of computers and semiconductors displayed increasing employment shares in the top states, while the more mature industries (two textile industries, steel and aluminum) dispersed continuously. Oligopoly played a role in the steel and aluminum industries – production remained more spatially concentrated than would have been the case under competitive conditions.

The consumer goods sectors examined are pharmaceuticals, women's clothing (suits and dresses), auto assembly and parts, brewing, and shoes. All of these sectors show the expected geographical agglomeration and dispersion tendencies. In two mature sectors (apparel and shoes), oligopoly never appeared (according to Markusen) and dispersal occurred soon after innovation subsided. Oligopolies, and organized labor in autos, in the other sectors slowed dispersal. Because their location patterns are more constrained by resource supplies, the resource-oriented sectors display a more varied pattern with respect to the profit-cycle model, as one might expect.

The profit-cycle model is a useful method for organizing information about industries, and it can be quite useful to know the stage of the cycle for a particular industry at a particular time. However, there are two fundamental difficulties with the profit-cycle model. First of all, it is not really a theory. It is a tautological method for organizing information about industries. New industries are born somewhere, and then disperse once the basic innovations have been made. They either become oligopolies or they do not. Eventually products developed by someone else displace some (or all) of the demand for the original products. All of this is true essentially by definition. The model seems to make only one testable hypothesis that can be refuted; oligopoly slows down the dispersal of the industry in stage 3. Otherwise, the model cannot really be subjected to empirical testing that can lead to its rejection. Secondly, the profit-cycle model has no policy implications at the urban or regional level. Evidently the important thing for an urban area is to be the site of major product innovation, but the model is silent on how products are born. Others are silent on this point as well, but the profit-cycle model has no alternative policy handle.

K. What *Is* Correlated with Metropolitan Growth?

As this chapter demonstrates, economists are adept at devising theories about growth. But as a more practical matter, what is known empirically about metropolitan growth? A recent study by Glaeser and Shapiro (2003) answers this question. Theirs is a study population growth of the largest 275 metropolitan areas in the US for 1980 to 1990 and 1990 to 2000. They found that the average population growth for metropolitan areas was 10.5% in the 1980s and somewhat faster growth of 11.8% in the 1990s. Growth rates varied widely – from −16.0% to 65.7% in the 1980s, and −7.5% to 58.9% in the 1990s. There is a great deal of variation to "explain," but the basic patterns are actually quite clear. Metropolitan areas in the West and the South regions of the nation grew more rapidly than did metropolitan areas in the Northeast and Midwest regions. Holding constant the effect of location within one of these regions, metropolitan areas in which manufacturing initially was a greater share of total employment grew less rapidly. Also, larger metropolitan areas actually grew slightly more rapidly than did smaller metropolitan areas, but metropolitan areas with greater population density grew less rapidly. Perhaps the most interesting findings in the Glaeser–Shapiro study pertain to the education or income levels of the population. Metropolitan growth in the 1990s is positively correlated with the percentage of adults (age 25 and over) with a high school diploma, and with the percentage who have college degrees (or higher). Another way of making the point is that growth is positively associated with per capita income and negatively related to the poverty rate of the population in the metropolitan area. In short, growth is positively related to the level of human capital embodied in the local population. Furthermore, this result is stronger in the decade of the 1990s than it was in the 1980s.

L. Summary

This chapter has introduced three basic models of economic growth that can be applied to urban areas. The first is a simple Keynesian multiplier model with exports and imports, which is also called the economic base model. This model is really a model of short-run impacts of changes in exports (and other changes), and it is not really a model of long-run growth. However, its emphasis on exports and imports is on target. Other more complex models presented in this book also emphasize exports and imports.

The second model discussed in this chapter is the one-sector neoclassical growth model, as developed by Robert Solow. This model ignores exports and imports; instead it concentrates on the growth of inputs and technical change. This model has been applied extensively to the analysis of economic growth at the national level. However, a complete explanation for the national slowdown in the growth of labor productivity from 1973 to 1991 remains elusive. The one-sector model has also been applied to the economic growth of states and urban areas. However, those applications have not yielded results that are fully satisfactory.

The failure of the one-sector neoclassical growth model to explain some important empirical findings for states led Borts and Stein (1964) to develop a two-sector neo-classical growth model. In this model the local economy produces a good for export and another good only for local consumption. The export good faces a perfectly elastic demand curve, and capital can be imported freely at the national price. Under these circumstances the growth of the local economy is determined by the growth rate of the labor force and by technical change. An increase in the demand for exports means that the price of exports rises. An increase in the price of the export good will increase the wage in the local economy.

The Keynesian and two-sector neoclassical growth models can be combined into a more general mainstream economic model that acknowledges the importance of both the demand and supply sides. An even more general synthesis of models will be discussed at the end of Chapter 20.

In addition, this chapter has surveyed several other approaches to urban economic growth. The mechanics of input–output analysis have been presented to clarify our thinking about the structure of a local economy, and to emphasize the intermediate inputs as well as value added. The eclectic works of urban and regional economic history have been discussed briefly to point out the importance of historical factors in the development of an area. Urban areas in the South had very different histories compared to urban areas in the Northeast or Midwest. This distinction used to matter a great deal. Does it still matter for purposes of understanding the local economy? One should not rule out the importance of history. The potential importance of the product cycle for urban areas was explored as well. As an empirical matter, metropolitan population growth in the 1990s is positively associated with location in the South and West, smaller amounts of manu-facturing employment, lower population density, and the human capital embodied in the local population.

Up until now we have not taken a systematic look at the autonomous growth factor, what Solow called technological change. This is the task of the next chapter.

Appendix to Chapter 19: The Borts–Stein Model of State Economic Growth

It is useful to present more formally the Borts–Stein model of state economic growth because it can be adapted to contemporary urban areas. The keys to the model are the equations for the growth of wage payments and payments to capital. These equations can be used to study, for example, the effects of a change in export prices, which leads to a movement of capital between states. It is assumed that the economy of the state produces two goods; X, a capital-intensive export good, and Y, a labor-intensive domestic good (consumed within the state). Capital K and labor L are freely mobile between the two industries. The economy consumes three goods; X, Y, and M an imported good that is not produced in the state. C_x denotes domestic consumption of X. The relevant prices are P_x, P_y, P_m, W (wage), P_k (purchase price of a unit of capital), and r (rate of return for capital). It is assumed that the labor force is growing at a fixed percentage rate L^*. The * will denote the rate of growth for the variable in question. The price of X is fixed in the national market, as are the import prices of M and K and the rate of return of capital. The wage rate and the price of Y are determined inside the model.

The production functions for X and Y are assumed to be Cobb–Douglas with constant returns to scale. Export production is assumed to be capital intensive relative to domestic goods production. The two production functions can be written

$$X = AK_x^{\alpha}L_x^{1-\alpha}, \text{ and}$$
$$Y = BK_y^{\beta}L_y^{1-\beta}.$$

The assumption about capital intensity in the two industries means that α is greater than β. The wages in these two sectors equal their respective values of the marginal products of labor, or

$$W_x = P_x[(1 - \alpha)A(K/L)_x^{\alpha}] \text{ and}$$
$$W_y = P_y[(1 - \beta)B(K/L)_y^{\beta}].$$

Wages in the two sectors are equal, or $W_x = W_y = W$.

Full employment of capital and labor in the state means that

$$L_x + L_y = L \text{ and}$$
$$K_x + K_y = K.$$

The return on capital in both sectors must equal the borrowing rate set in the national market, or

$$rP_K = P_x \text{ (marginal product of } K \text{ in } X) \text{ and}$$
$$rP_K = P_y \text{ (marginal product of } K \text{ in } Y).$$

The total product of a state equals the value of the final goods and services produced;

$$Z = XP_x + YP_y.$$

The expenditure of the total product is divided between savings and the consumption of the three types of goods in given proportions. Assuming no income payments to foreign owners of capital,

$$Z = S + C_x + MP_m + YP_y,$$

$$C_x P_x = cZ,$$
$$YP_y = eZ, \text{ and}$$
$$S = sZ,$$

where S is saving. The other terms have already been defined. Note that $MP_m = (1 - c - e - s)Z$. The growth rate of labor is assumed to be exogenous, or

$$(\delta L/\delta t)/L = L^*,$$

where t is time. The growth rate of capital is defined as the ratio of investment to the capital stock, or

$$(\delta K/\delta t)/K = K^* = I/K,$$

where I is net investment. The proportion of the labor force employed in the export sector is defined as.
Total income Z is the sum of the wage bill WL and the payments to capital $rP_k K$, or

$$Z = WL + rP_k K, \text{ where}$$
$$WL = W(L_x + L_y) \text{ and}$$
$$rP_k K = rP_k(K_x + K_y).$$

Borts and Stein showed that, in the absence of technical change and exogenous disturbances such as a change in the price of exports, the state's economy will grow in a balanced fashion determined by the rate of growth of labor, L^*. In this case $L^* = K^* = I^* = S^* = Z^*$. To see this result recall that the price of exports (P_x) is fixed, as are the prices of capital and imports. The state can freely import capital to match the growth in its labor force. The state will expand its export production along a perfectly elastic demand curve. Because of this, the wage rate will remain constant because it will be determined by the wage in the export sector. The additional workers in the export sector will call forth production of the domestic good Y, and factor prices are constant in this industry as well. Output proportions remain constant as the state's economy grows. The growth in the labor force thus calls for an equal growth rate for capital (and investment and saving) and total output. In short, in this economy with capital freely imported at a constant price and with perfectly elastic export demand, the growth rate is set by the growth rate of the other input, labor.

The critical results pertain to the impacts of a change in the price of the export product, P_x. An increase in P_x represents an increase in the demand for exports, so this is where the idea of the "neoclassical export base model" originates. The fundamental result of the model is that

$$W^* = P_x^*/(1 - \alpha).$$

This equation says that the growth rate of the wage rate equals the growth rate of the price of the export product divided by $1 - \alpha$, which is the share of income going to labor in the export sector.

To see this result, we need to solve the model for the equation that relates W^* to P_x^*. Return to the production function for X and solve for the marginal product of K_x, or

$$\delta X/\delta K_x = \alpha A K_x^{\alpha-1} L_x^{1-\alpha} = \alpha X/K_x.$$

Now set the value of the marginal product of capital equal to its price as in

$$P_x(\alpha X/K_x) = rP_k,$$

and solve for K_x, so that

$$K_x = \alpha X(P_x/rP_k).$$

The demand for capital is thus a function of the quantity of output, the price of output, and the price of capital. Similarly, find the marginal product of labor in X, set the value of the marginal product of labor equal to the wage, and solve for L_x as follows:

$$\delta X/\delta L_x = (1 - \alpha)AK_x^{\alpha}L_x^{-\alpha} = (1 - \alpha)X/L_x;$$
$$P_x[(1 - \alpha)X/L_x)] = W; \text{ and}$$
$$L_x = (1 - \alpha)X(P_x/W).$$

The demand for labor is thus a function of the output level, the price of output, and the wage rate.
    Now substitute these equations for K_x and L_x into the production function, or

$$X = A[\alpha X(P_x/rP_k)]^{\alpha}[(1 - \alpha)X(P_x/W)]^{1-\alpha}.$$

Note that X on the right-hand side of the equation has exponents α and $1 - \alpha$, so X appears on both sides of the equation and cancels out. We wish to solve the equation for W. After some manipulation, we have

$$W^{1-\alpha} = A\alpha^{\alpha} (1 - \alpha)^{1-\alpha}P_x(rP_k)^{-\alpha}.$$

Let E stand for the collection of constant terms;

$$E = A\alpha^{\alpha}(1 - \alpha)^{1-\alpha}.$$

Therefore the final equation for W is

$$W = [EP_x(rP_k)^{-\alpha}]^{1/1-\alpha}.$$

This equation can be solved for P_x, and the result is that

$$P_x = (1/E)(rP_k)^{\alpha}W^{1-\alpha}.$$

This equation says that the supply price (i.e., marginal cost) of the good is a Cobb–Douglas function of the input prices. In short, a Cobb–Douglas production function generates a Cobb–Douglas function for supply price. However, we must remember that, in the Borts-Stein model, P_x is an exogenous variable that helps to determine W (and not the other way around).
    The computation of the derivative of W with respect to P_x is a bit messy, but straightforward using the chain rule. Define the terms inside the brackets as J, so $W = J^{1/1-\alpha}$. Therefore

$$dW/dP_x = (dW/dJ)(dJ/dP_x).$$
$$dW/dP_x = (1/1 - \alpha)J^{\alpha/1-\alpha}J/P_x = (1/1 - \alpha)W/P_x.$$

Conversion to elasticity form gives us the percentage change in the wage resulting for a one percent change in P_x, or

$$(dW/dP_x)(P_x/W) = 1/1 - \alpha.$$

This is the result we sought. It says that a one-percent increase in the price of the export good will increase the wage rate by the inverse of the share of labor. If the share of labor is 0.75, then the increase in the wage rate will be 1.33%. Assuming that the labor market in the urban area is perfectly competitive, this increase in the wage rate will be transmitted to workers in the domestic good industry as well.

Exercises

1   You are the economist for the Department of Economic Development of Ruston, Pennsylvania. You know that employment in export industries is 25,000 and that total employment in the urban area is 60,000. You receive word that Volkswagen has decided to locate a plant in your community and that they plan to hire 3,000 workers.

(a)   Can you use the information in the question to predict the effect of the increase in export employment on total employment in the urban area? How would you go about generating such a forecast?
(b)   Make a careful listing of the assumptions that you made in making your forecast so that you can make clear the potential weaknesses in that forecast.

2   You have estimated a Keynesian model for Ruston as follows:

$$C = 100 + 0.9(1 - t)Y$$
$$T = tY = 0.3Y$$
$$M = 0.23(1 - t)Y$$
$$I = 150$$
$$G = 200$$
$$X = 300$$

Remember that import (M) are part of total consumption spending C and that disposable income is $Y - tY$, where t is the tax rate.

(a)   Compute equilibrium income (Y) and taxes (T), imports (M), consumption C, and saving.
(b)   What is the multiplier for Ruston?
(c)   What happens to Y, T, M, and C if exports increase by 100?
(d)   Return to the original value for exports. What happens if the propensity to consume out of disposable income falls from 0.9 to 0.8?

3   Suppose that the growth rate of gross urban product for an urban area is

$$y = 0.25(k) + 0.75(l) + t$$
$$k = (s/v) + j$$
$$l = n + m$$

where y is the growth rate of GUP, k the growth rate of capital, l the growth rate of labor, t the rate of technical change, s the saving rate, v the capital/output ratio, j the rate of in-migration of capital, n the natural rate of growth of labor in the urban area, and m the rate of in-migration of labor.

(a)   Assume that $s = 0.1$, $v = 4$, $j = 0.05$, $n = 0.02$, $m = 0.03$, and $t = 0.03$. Calculate y.

(b)   Calculate the percentage growth in y that can be attributed to
    1.   Labor force growth
        a.   Natural growth
        b.   Migration
    2.   Capital growth
        a.   Natural growth through local saving
        b.   Migration of capital
    3.   Technical change.

4   Suppose that the aggregate production function for the urban area is

$$Y = Ae^{rt}L^{\alpha}K^{\beta},$$

where Y is output, r the rate of technical change, t is time, L the labor input, K the capital input, and α and β are the elasticities of output with respect to labor and capital. Assume that $r = 0.02$, $\alpha = 0.75$, and $\beta = 0.25$.

(a)   Prove that α and β are the elasticities of output with respect to labor and capital.

(b)   Derive the basic growth equation in Section C for this model.

(c)   What is the rate of growth of this economy if labor grows at 1% per year and capital grows at 2% per year? What is the rate of growth of the wage rate under these conditions (assuming that labor is paid its marginal product)?

5   Consider Muth's famous "chicken or egg" model of urban growth. It is written that

$$\delta E = \alpha M$$
$$M = \beta(\delta E) + \theta$$

where E is employment in the urban area, δE is the change in employment, M is migration into the urban area, and θ is an exogenous amount of in-migration.

(a)   Why might migration increase when the change in employment (δE) increases?

(b)   Suppose that $\alpha = 0.5$ and $\beta = 0.4$. What is the change in employment (δE) when θ changes by 1?

(c)   For the model to be "stable," it must be true that $\alpha\beta$ is less than 1.0. Why? What is meant by stability here?

6   Assume the following input–output table for a local economy:

	Purchasing industry		Final demand	Gross output
	A	B		
Producing A	10	50	40	100
Industry B	30	10	30	70
Value added	60	10		
Total inputs	100	70	70	170

Assume that value added is entirely attributable to local labor and capital inputs.

(a) What are the direct input (technical) coefficients?
(b) What is gross output, and how are the figures obtained?
(c) Write the model in equation form as shown in Section H
(d) Assume that final demand is now $A = 50$ and $B = 30$. Recalculate the entire table. What is the multiplier implied by these results?
(e) You will note that final demand does not include separate entries for exports outside the urban area. Does this urban area export anything? How do you know?

7 Return to the local economy depicted in Table 19.1. Suppose that exports double (manufactures increase to 40 and services increase to 20).

(a) Recalculate the entire table.
(b) Does the size of the local economy double?

8 Find out if there are any books on the economic history of the urban area of your choice. Most of the older, large urban areas have rather extensive bibliographies. Select one of these books. Does the author of this book use a conceptual framework that resembles one of those covered in this chapter? If so, what is it? Is some other conceptual framework used? Is so, what is it? If there is no conceptual framework used, which one would you suggest? Why?

References

Borts, George and Jerome Stein, 1964, *Economic Growth in a Free Market*. New York: Columbia University Press.

Booth, Douglas, 1986, "Long Waves and Uneven Regional Growth," *Southern Economic Journal*, vol. 53, pp. 495–518.

Clark, Gordon, M. Gertler, and J. Whiteman, 1986, *Regional Dynamics*. Boston: Allen & Unwin.

Crihfield, John and M. Panggabean, 1993, "Growth Convergence in US Cities," *Journal of Regional Science*, vol. 38, pp. 138–65.

Cronon, William, 1991, *Nature's Metropolis*. New York: Norton.

Dension, Edward, 1962, *The Sources of Economic Growth in the United States*. Washington, DC: Committee for Economic Development.

Dension, Edward, 1985, *Trends in American Economic Growth*. Washington, DC: The Brookings Institution.

Ferguson, Ronald and H. Ladd, 1988, "Massachusetts," in R. Fosler (ed.), *The New Economic Role of the States*. New York: Oxford University Press.

Ghali, Mohab, M. Akiyama and J. Fujiwara, 1978, "Factor Mobility and Regional Growth," *Review of Economics and Statistics*, vol. 60, pp. 78–84.

Glaeser, Edward and J. Shapiro, 2003, "Urban Growth in the 1990s: Is City Living Back?" *Journal of Regional Science*, vol. 43, pp. 139–65.

Gordon, Robert, 1993, *Macroeconomics*, 6th edn. New York: Harper Collins College Publishers.

Jorgenson, Dale and Zvi Griliches, 1967, "The Explanation of Productivity Change," *Review of Economic Studies*, vol. 34, pp. 249–83.

Jorgenson, Dale and Zvi Griliches, 1972, "Issues in Growth Accounting: A Reply to Edward F. Dension," *Survey of Current Business*, vol. 52, pp. 65–94.

Jorgenson, Dale, F. Gollop and B. Fraumeni, 1987, *Productivity and US Economic Growth*. Cambridge, MA: Harvard University Press.

Krugman, Paul, 1991, *The Age of Diminished Expectations*. Cambridge, MA: MIT Press.

Landes, David, 1969, *The Unbound Prometheus: Technological Change and Industrial Development in Western Europe from 1750 to the Present*. Cambridge: Cambridge University Press.

Leontief, Wassily, 1951, *The Structure of the American Economy 1919–1939*, 2nd edn. Fair Lawn, NJ: Oxford University Press.

Markusen, Ann, 1985, *Profit Cycles, Oligopoly and Regional Development*. Cambridge: Cambridge University Press.

Muth, Richard, 1971, "Migration: Chicken or Egg?" *Southern Economic Journal*, vol. 37, pp. 295–306.

Nordhaus, William, 2002, "Productivity Growth and the New Economy," *Brookings Papers on Economic Activity*, no. 2, pp. 211–44.

Norton, Robert and J. Rees, 1979, "The Product Cycle and the Spatial Deconcentration of American Manufacturing," *Regional Studies*, vol. 13, pp. 141–51.

Richardson, Harry, 1973, *Regional Growth Theory*. New York: Wiley.

Scherer, Frederick, 1980, *Industrial Market Structure and Economic Performance*. Chicago: Rand McNally.

Schumpeter, Joseph, 1942, *Capitalism, Socialism and Democracy*. New York: Harper and Row.

Solow, Robert, 1957, "Technical Change and the Aggregate Production Function," *Review of Economics and Statistics*, vol. 39, pp. 312–20.

Wright, Gavin, 1986, *Old South, New South*. New York: Basic Books.

Chapter 20

Agglomeration Economies, Technical Change, and Urban Growth

A. Introduction

The basic neoclassical growth model was discussed in Chapter 19, and the survey of the variety of approaches to the study of economic growth in that chapter has made us sensitive to complicating factors such as input–output relationships and product cycles. The discussion of the neoclassical models in Chapter 19 introduced the "autonomous growth factor," but included no detailed discussion of this factor for urban areas. The time has come to correct this deficiency. Agglomeration economies were discussed in Chapter 3 as creating cost advantages for firms in an industry that are concentrated in a particular urban area (localization economies), or that are located in larger urban areas (urbanization economies). And the role of technical change was emphasized in Chapter 19 as a factor of considerable importance in determining the national growth rate. What are the contributions of these kinds of factors to urban growth? Just how do these factors work in an urban area to generate growth? In recent years these are questions that have engaged some of the very best researchers.

These questions have also engaged some of the best researchers in earlier years. Benjamin Chinitz, one of the researchers in the New York Metropolitan Area Study of the 1950s, went on to study Pittsburgh in the early 1960s. The contrast between these two urban areas led Chinitz (1961), in a classic paper, to ask, "How does the growth of one industry in an area affect the area's suitability as a location for other industries?" How might industrial diversity foster growth? Chinitz supplied hypotheses that remain fresh today. He suggested that competitive industries, as opposed to oligopolistic industries, have more entrepreneurs – people who are willing and able to take the risk of starting a new business. An urban area full of competitive industries is likely to create new businesses and more growth. A similar point was made about the supply of capital. The presence of competitive industries means that financial institutions that supply loans to businesses must be prepared to deal with smaller borrowers and, therefore, be more receptive to the entrepreneur. A more diversified local economy will have a more diversified demand for labor, and will therefore call forth a greater supply of labor, especially among women.

All of these factors suggest that an urban economy with competitive and diversified industry will grow more rapidly than one with oligopolistic and undiversified industry. These ideas, and others, have been tested empirically and largely confirmed in recent research. That research is reviewed in this chapter. The chapter concludes with two industry case studies of agglomeration economies – the automobile industry in Detroit and the semiconductor industry in the San Francisco metropolitan area (Silicon Valley).

B. The Neoclassical Production Function Revisited

Let us return to the basic concept of the production function, but following the two-sector neoclassical model in Chapter 19, we shall assume that a particular production function pertains to an *industry* in an urban area. We shall not assume that a single production function can be used for an entire urban area. For example, suppose that a production function can be specified for the manufacturing sector of an urban area as follows:

$$Q = A(z,t)F(K,L).$$

Here z is a collection of factors that create agglomeration economies, t is the level of technology, and $F(K,L)$ is the function of capital and labor, as usual. However, it shall now be assumed that $F(K,L)$ can exhibit economies of scale for the local industry. In fact, most of the empirical studies of manufacturing industries in urban areas indicate that economies of scale exist at the industry level for some industries. The studies by Henderson (1986, 2003) were discussed in Chapter 3. Such economies of scale are external to the individual firm in the urban area, but are internal to the industry. This is precisely what is meant by localization economies, so localization economies are not being included in the collection of factors called z.

There is a critical distinction between agglomeration economies and technical progress. Technical progress means that a *firm* that adopts the new technology can produce more output with the same amounts of capital and labor inputs. Technical progress, when implemented, is internal to the individual firm. Agglomeration economies are, by definition, external to the individual firm in an urban area. However, it may be that some agglomeration economies act by *increasing* the rate of technical change for firms in a particular urban area. There may be agglomeration economies in the invention and development of new technologies, and there may be agglomeration economies in the adoption of new technologies. Other agglomeration economies, such as economies of scale in transportation facilities, create lower costs that are passed along to individual firms.

Now is a good time to review the theory of agglomeration economies that was presented in Chapter 3. Figure 20.1 reproduces Figure 3.7 for an industry in an urban area. The average and marginal cost curves for the industry have negative slopes because of localization economies, i.e., economies of scale at the industry level in the urban area. The demand curve DD intersects the average cost curve AC at output level Q, the equilibrium level of output. Ignore cost curves AC' and MC' for now. Because of localization economies, the local industry is larger than it would be if the industry operates with constant average costs.

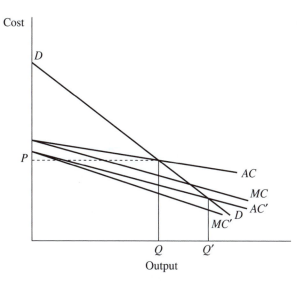

Figure 20.1   Cost and output for an urban industry

With Figure 20.1 in mind, it is possible to classify the different types of agglomeration economies. One distinction is between agglomeration economies that are *static* and those that are *dynamic*. Static agglomeration economies mean that the *level* of some agglomerative factor is associated with some *level* of industry output. In the production function for the local industry,

$$Q = A(z,t)F(K,L),$$

the level of z creates a level for $A(z,t)$ and, thus, for output. For example, a larger urban area has better and cheaper air transportation (the z factor). This creates a one-time increase in $A(z,t)$ and a one-time shift downward in the industry's cost curves in Figure 20.1. In contrast, a dynamic agglomeration economy means that the *level* of the agglomerative factor is associated with an *increase* in industry output that *continues* through time. For example, a larger urban area has more inventive inventors, who in turn create a continuous stream of technical change that is larger than in smaller urban areas. The size of the urban area (the z factor) causes technology (the t factor) to increase continuously.

The other essential distinction is, of course, between localization and urbanization economies. Both types can be static or dynamic. We now see that Figure 20.1 is depicting a static localization economy. For example, economies of scale in the production of some intermediate input mean that the size of the local industry in question is associated with a one-time reduction in average cost. Figure 20.1 also depicts a static urbanization economy because the positions of the average and marginal cost curves for the industry are based on an assumption about the size of the urban area. With static urbanization economies, an increase in the size of the urban area will shift the average and marginal cost curves down to AC' and MC'. The industry experiences a one-time increase in output to Q'.

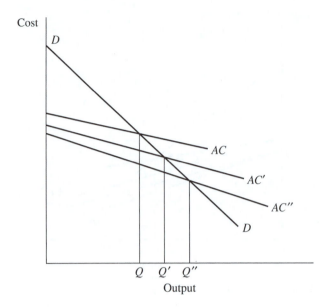

Figure 20.2   Dynamic agglomeration economies

What about dynamic agglomeration economies? Dynamic agglomeration economies mean that the level of the agglomerative factor creates continuous reductions in costs for the industry. The effect of a dynamic urbanization economy is depicted in Figure 20.2. The size of the urban area is given, but the dynamic urbanization economy shifts the average and marginal cost curves down again and again. The output of the industry grows from Q to Q' in the first year, for Q' to Q'' in the second year, and so on. Figure 20.2 can also be used to depict a dynamic localization economy. It this case the *size* of the industry itself causes the average and marginal cost curves to shift down again and again. What is more, the resulting growth of the industry means that the size of the industry is larger in the next time period, which will influence the size of the next shift downward in the cost curves. For example, a larger local industry may generate a more rapid rate of technical change (changes in *t*). This idea of dynamic localization economies is closely related to the notion of cumulative causation – an effect that feeds back on itself positively.

One final distinction needs to be made concerning dynamic agglomeration economies. Figure 20.2 shows that they lead to continuous increases in the output of the industry, but it does not indicate whether a higher level of an agglomeration factor is associated with increases in output that are larger in absolute or percentage terms. Turn to Figure 20.3, which depicts the same industry in two different urban areas. In the upper half of the diagram, the industry is relatively small. The dynamic localization economy leads to small absolute increases in the output of the industry, but these increases are large in percentage terms. In the lower half of the diagram, the industry is relatively large. The dynamic localization economy produces fairly large increases in the level of output, but those increases are small in percentage terms. Thus, this particular dynamic localization economy produces a larger absolute continuous increase in output, but not an increase in

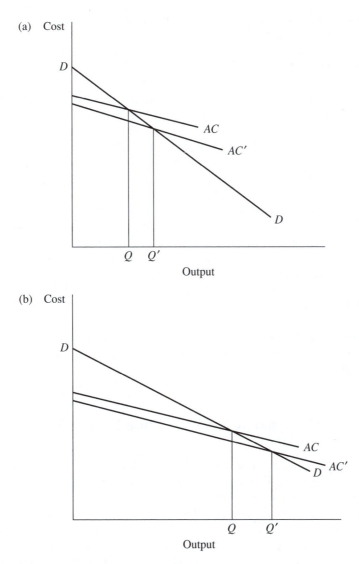

Figure 20.3   Dynamic agglomeration economies

the rate of growth of output. Figure 20.3 has been drawn to show this case because the empirical results discussed below are consistent with this story. However, another diagram could have been drawn showing a dynamic localization economy which results in a higher rate of growth of output – the larger the local industry, the larger is the rate of growth.

The expanded neoclassical production can be used to obtain a growth equation that is similar to the growth equation in Chapter 19, or

$$\Delta Q/Q = \Delta A/A + E_K(\Delta K/K) + E_L(\Delta L/L),$$

where E_K and E_L are the elasticities of output with respect to capital and labor. It is now assumed that these two elasticities may add up to a number that is greater than 1.0 (increasing returns to scale for the industry, i.e., static localization economies). The crucial term in the equation is $\Delta A/A$. How are the other types of agglomeration economies specified?

The answer can be found by writing down an equation for the total change in A (ΔA_T) alone. For simplicity assume for the moment that there is only one z factor, so

$$\Delta A_T = (\Delta A/\Delta z)\Delta z + \Delta A(z,Q) + (\Delta A/\Delta t)\Delta t(z,Q,\Delta z,\Delta Q).$$

This equation includes the following:

- $(\Delta A/\Delta z)\Delta z$ is a static urbanization economy.
- $\Delta A(z,Q)$ represent dynamic urbanization and localization economics because ΔA is written as a function of the *levels* of z and Q (industry output).
- $(\Delta A/\Delta t)\Delta t(z,Q,\Delta z,\Delta Q)$ represents the effects of both static and dynamic urbanization and localization economies on the level of technology because Δt is made a function of both the levels and changes in z and Q. These three terms will be mentioned in the succeeding discussion.

Now we understand the mechanics of a growth equation that includes agglomeration economies and technical change. What we need now is insight into the actual market and non-market processes that might be at work.

C. Dynamic Agglomeration Economies

What can create dynamic agglomeration economies in urban areas? Most of the leading scholars of this topic seem to agree at least on one thing. At the heart of dynamic agglomeration economies is the production and use of knowledge. Krugman (1991) is an exception to this statement; he thinks that knowledge is an important part of the story, but that dynamic agglomeration economies can be associated with labor market and intermediate input markets effects as well. This section reviews the arguments that are made in favor of putting knowledge at the center of the story, and the following section examines the empirical studies that have been done to test hypotheses.

Something of a revolution has been going on in economic growth theory since the 1990s. External economies arising from knowledge spillovers are thought to be critical to the productivity level or the rate of economic growth of a nation. This point of view has been stated by several leading scholars, including Romer (1986), Lucas (1988), and Porter (1990). If knowledge spillovers are important, then it is logical to think that the spillovers are more important in urban areas, where people and firms are in close proximity. This point of view harks back to an earlier book by Jane Jacobs, *The Economy of Cities*, that was published in 1969. Her book is insightful and easy to read, and you should add it to your reading list. (We have thoughtfully compiled your reading list in the preface to this book.)

The general idea of knowledge spillovers is too vague to generate hypotheses that can be tested. More details about how knowledge spillovers work are needed, and it turns out that there are three somewhat different theories that all fall into the category of knowledge spillovers. These three theories are set out nicely in an article by Glaeser et al. (1992). This article appeared in the *Journal of Political Economy*, a leading journal that usually publishes very technical articles. However, this article is quite readable by someone who is majoring in economics and who has familiarity with multiple regression analysis. Glaeser et al. (1992) point out that the theories of dynamic agglomeration economies based on knowledge spillovers differ along two dimensions. First, do knowledge spillovers come primarily from firms within one's own industry or from firms in other industries? Second, what is the impact of market structure (competition versus oligopoly) on knowledge spillovers? We shall consider these two questions in turn.

The first theory argues that the knowledge spillovers occur largely within a local industry. This is one form of localization economies. In Chapter 3 you learned that static localization economies can stem from economies of scale and specialization among the suppliers of intermediate inputs and services, and from specialization and better training of workers. You also learned that firms can learn about the most efficient production process from other firms in an urban area. However, these ideas were presented as static, not dynamic, cost advantages. As discussed above, a dynamic theory must posit a mechanism for *continued* reductions in costs for firms in an urban area. The knowledge spillover idea is that a greater concentration of firms in a particular industry in an urban area will cause there to be a greater rate of new product development, improvements in existing products, and improvements in the methods for producing those products. The rate of innovation will be more rapid because there are more highly trained people around who are thinking about how to improve the industry. An idea created by one person will stimulate another, and another, and so on. Ten isolated innovators are less productive than ten innovators located in the same urban area. There will also be a rapid transmission of all of this new knowledge to firms if they are located in close proximity. The information is transmitted in several ways; through highly trained workers who move from firm to firm, through business meetings and conferences, through industrial spying, through copying of a competitor's product, and through more formal education and training programs that exist in the urban area to serve the industry. In short, dynamic localization economies act to increase the rate of technical change, so Q (the output level in the urban area) appears in the technical change term $(\Delta A/\Delta t)\Delta t(z,Q,\Delta z,\Delta Q)$.

At this point you may ask about the modern technologies for the transmission of information. Is it not true that information can be transmitted easily around the nation (indeed, the world) on the internet? Do innovators and imitators have to be located in the same urban area? In some cases, clearly they do not. But there are other cases, perhaps the most important cases, where proximity is needed. Edwin Mills (1992) has called this situation the one of transmitting "ambiguous information." Mills (1992, p. 11) offers the definition that

> Ambiguous information is information that requires an interactive and convergent set of exchanges before the final exchange can be consummated.

Consider a few examples. An industrial buyer and a seller of a specialized piece of electronic equipment will need to hold a series of meetings between specialists in design, production, marketing and other departments before the contract is signed. A second example occurs within one firm. The development of a new product requires that a great deal of information be exchanged between the R&D people, production people, marketing specialists, legal experts, and others. A third example is the research seminar. Such seminars occur in universities, but they also are held by one firm for its own employees or by an industry, professional or trade association for a wider audience. The seminar speaker presents some new ideas to fellow specialists, but often the most valuable part of the seminar is the discussion that ensues. Thoughts can be offered, and new ideas are sometimes generated. This kind of exchange of ambiguous information, with its frequent generation of new ideas, can take place in any field of endeavor that relies on ideas.

Does the idea of the exchange of ambiguous information apply to localization economies? Clearly it does. An industry that is undergoing change is an industry that is generating new ideas. Those ten innovators who live in close proximity are more productive than if they are isolated precisely because they communicate in the interactive way that Mills describes. However, the concept of the exchange of ambiguous information can also apply to a sector of the economy that is broader than an industry. Indeed, the first example offered by Mills (1992, p. 11) is that of a customer and a supplier, not of firms in the same narrow industry. This argument means that the urbanization factor z appears in the terms $\Delta A(z,Q)$ and $(\Delta A/\Delta t)\Delta t(z,Q,\Delta z,\Delta Q)$.

Jane Jacobs (1969) stressed that knowledge spillovers take place across different industries and lines of work. She argued that diversity of industry in an urban area is more stimulating for the production of new ideas than is the greater size of an individual industry. In fact, some industries are born because the firms in one particular industry perceive the need for new products or services, and act to develop them. For example, in the nineteenth-century grain and cotton merchants saw the need for better systems for making financial transactions. The financial services industry was born, including the futures and options industry. The futures and options industry is concentrated in Chicago, and the exchanges compete over the development of new products for the management of risk (a localization economy). For Jacobs, it is diversity, rather than uniformity, that produces the new products and the new technologies. For her the essential function of urban areas is the creation of "new work." The knowledge spillover is wider than an individual industry, but not as wide as the entire urban economy.

Now let us turn to the second dimension along which these theories differ. The effect of market structure on technical change has been debated in the literature of industrial organization economics for many years. Does monopoly (or oligopoly) foster technical change because only they can afford the costs of R&D? Or do competitive industries generate technical change because the competitors are always seeking to gain a competitive edge? Some of the most influential books on economics in modern times have grappled with this issue, and it is worthwhile to do a brief tour of this literature.

Joseph Schumpeter's 1942 book *Capitalism, Socialism and Democracy* has been a big seller, and a staple of college reading lists, since the 1940s. Schumpeter has been justifiably renowned for what he called the process of creative destruction inherent in the capitalist economy. Schumpeter's (1942, p. 32) summary of this process states that

Possibilities of gains to be reaped by producing new things or by producing old things more cheaply are constantly materializing and calling for new investments. These new products and new methods compete with the old products and old methods not on equal terms but at a decisive advantage that may mean death to the latter. This is how 'progress' comes about in a capitalist society.

These concepts are taught in today's schools of business administration (along with the related product cycle framework). But, with good reason, those schools rarely teach the second half of Schumpeter's story – that capitalism was being killed by its own success. We shall tell the whole story here because you should know it, and because it may have been the case that Schumpeter made his arguments to fit his end result. Economists no longer take the second part of Schumpeter's story seriously.

Schumpeter recognized that modern capitalism in his day produced industrial enterprises that operate at a very large scale and have some monopoly power, but that this monopoly power is not of great concern because of the "perennial gale of creative destruction." Indeed, those large firms are the ones with the wherewithal to turn the process of creating new products and new processes into a routine function. In short, Schumpeter believed that the existence of large firms would increase the rate of product and process innovation. He did not stop there, but went on to state that the people who made the innovations would be employees of large firms. In this process the class of entrepreneurs and small business owners are largely wiped out. As firms become larger and larger, ownership is divorced from control. The owners of these firms lose their entrepreneurial function, and the firms are operated by professional managers. In addition, the success of the large firms will drive many smaller firms out of business. Few people are vitally concerned with the sanctity of private property and freedom of private contracting. With fewer people left to defend the institution of private property, its opponents win the day. The opponents include intellectuals, who will persuade the mass of workers through the written and spoken word that socialism will improve the conditions of the working class, and that the grossly unequal income distribution produced by capitalism is not needed to ensure economic progress. Capitalism thus destroys its own institutional framework, and sets the stage for the socialistic takeover of those large firms.

What a prophesy! Schumpeter thought that the balance of forces he described would lead to the advent of socialism in the US in about fifty years from the time he wrote his book (in 1947). Clearly his prophesy was wrong! By the way, Schumpeter died in 1950, shortly after he reiterated his prophesy at the American Economic Association meetings.

John Kenneth Galbraith, the most popular interpreter of the US economy of the 1950s, also wrote that oligopoly would foster technical change. *American Capitalism*, which was published in 1956, was his first best-seller and is a major work of political economy written with Galbraithian flair. His point of departure was to note the oligopolistic nature of many modern industries, especially in manufacturing. He argued that oligopoly is the natural outcome in industries in which firms have sizable economies of scale. Entry into such industries is easy only when they are new; as the industries mature the surviving firms gather both economies of scale and experience. Latecomers face barriers to entry that are all but insurmountable. Galbraith saw that firms in oligopolistic industries usually do not engage in price competition, but instead compete using advertising, product differentiation (if feasible), and technical change. He contended that these firms charge excessive prices and engage in wasteful advertising and product differentiation, but that they also produce socially beneficial technical progress. In this regard Galbraith's model is similar to Schumpeter's framework. Large firms in oligopolized industries can afford the expense of technical change and have the market power to reap its benefits. As Galbraith (1956, p. 88) put it,

> The net of all this is that there must be some element of monopoly in an industry if it is to be progressive.

He concluded that we must learn to live with oligopoly, warts and all. He saw no connection between oligopoly and socialism.

Modern economists who study technical change argue that Schumpeter and Galbraith may have a point because, compared to a firm in a competitive industry, a large firm in an oligopolized industry is able to reap more of the immediate benefits of technical change, and therefore has a greater incentive to invest in R&D. The lack of property rights may slow down the pace of innovation. Oligopolies may be good for growth because they are more able to "internalize the externality" of a new discovery. On the other hand, it may also be true that the ability to appropriate the benefits of a new discovery is determined by many other factors as well. In contrast to Schumpeter and Galbraith, Jacobs (1969) and Porter (1990) believe that competition will foster innovation. Jacobs argues that monopolies limit alternative methods and products, and Porter believes that stiff competition leads to the creation and adoption of innovations.

Industrial organization economists study the economics of technical change without giving much consideration to the spatial dimension. It is generally agreed that both the development and the adoption of new technology depends upon:

- appropriability (ability to capture the benefits);
- market structure; and
- technological opportunity.

In fact, modern economists generally agree that R&D spending depends primarily upon appropriability and technological opportunity, and not on market concentration. The adoption of new technologies, however, is probably stimulated by competitive markets. Note that appropriability is a matter that can be considered to be separate from market structure, an idea that eluded Schumpeter and Galbraith. These conclusions are based on studies of specific industries at the national level, and have not really been seen as applicable to matters of urban growth.

A geographer, Edward Malecki, has done several studies of specific industries in urban areas. His survey article (1983) indicates that the adoption of new technologies tends to be associated with larger firms, lower-cost innovations, more flexible management, and more complete information. There is no apparent association with the size of the urban area. In addition, there is evidence both supportive of and contrary to the notion that large firms adopt innovations earliest. In short, what is known about technological change from the industrial organization literature is generally too specific to an industry to provide general implications for urban growth theory and policy.

The bottom line on the market structure argument is that the nature of the market structure for the industry in an urban area may be a separate dynamic localization economy. The equation for ΔA_T should therefore be revised to read

$$\Delta A_T = (\Delta A/\Delta z)\Delta z + \Delta A(z,Q) + (\Delta A/\Delta t)\Delta t(z,Q,m,\Delta z,\Delta Q),$$

where m stands for market structure.

D. Empirical Studies of Agglomeration Economies

There are two types of empirical studies that seek to test for the presence of agglomeration economies in urban areas. Studies of the first type estimate a version of the growth equation for output

$$\Delta Q/Q = \Delta A/A + E_K(\Delta K/K) + E_L(\Delta L/L).$$

These studies are confined to the aggregate manufacturing sector in urban areas because only the industries in this sector have the required data for output (value added). These studies also require data on growth in capital and labor. In particular, the researcher must construct estimates of the urban area's capital stock in manufacturing for each year of the study. Mullen and Williams (1987) and Fogarty and Garofalo (1988) have been the pioneers in this laborious task, and the interested reader can consult their articles for the details. The labor input used in the studies is simply man-hours of work. No attempt is made to adjust the measure of the labor input for changes in the educational level of the workers. The second type of study is of specific industries in urban areas. Most studies are based on industry-level data, but recent studies increasingly make use of data on individual establishments. Employment growth is easily observed; it is reported annually by county for very detailed industry categories. Consequently, employment data can be used to study urban industry growth in narrowly defined industries. Other studies have examined the births of establishments, wages, or rents paid. One study by Henderson (2003) discussed below used output data at the establishment level.

First we turn to the studies that use the production function equation to test hypotheses regarding agglomeration economies at the metropolitan level. The first study is by Fogarty and Garofalo (1988), and it examined manufacturing output (value added) in 13 urban areas over the period of 1957 to 1977. Their study is based on the production function

$$Q = A(z,t)F(K,L),$$

and they permit increasing returns to scale with respect to the capital and labor inputs. They hypothesize that the z variables, the factors that create agglomeration economies, include:

- population of the urban area;
- age of the urban area (1977 minus the year the central reached population of 50,000);

- the central density of manufacturing employment in 1963; and
- the gradient of manufacturing employment density in 1963.

Note that they are testing for *static* urbanization economies and localization economies for the manufacturing sector as a whole, and that they are not testing a market-structure hypothesis. In addition to testing for a standard static urbanization effect (the size of the urban area), they are testing whether the age of the urban area and the spatial pattern of manufacturing have impacts on productivity. These are static urbanization and localization economies, respectively.

The equation estimated is

$$\ln Q = a_0 + a_1 t + b_0 \ln K + b_1 \ln L \ln K + b_2 \ln L + c_1 z_1 + \ldots + c_n z_n,$$

where t is time (1957 = 0), and $z_1, \ldots, z_n$ are the factors that create agglomeration economies. They also tested variables that indicate the time periods 1965–72 and 1973–7. All of the variables enter the estimated equation with statistically significant coefficients, and the results are as follows:

- Urban area population is positively related to output up to a population level of 2.9 million, but has a negative effect thereafter.
- Age of the urban area has a strong negative effect on productivity.
- Central density of manufacturing employment in 1963 has a positive effect on productivity.
- The steeper manufacturing employment density gradient has a positive effect on productivity up to a gradient of 50% per mile, but has a negative effect at steeper gradient levels.

The results also indicate that the manufacturing sector in an urban area is subject to increasing returns to scale; at the mean values of K and L, the sum of their output elasticities is 1.19. Finally, as other productivity studies find, there is evidence of a slowdown in productivity growth after 1973.

Together these results provide intriguing confirmation of several ideas about static agglomeration economies. The result for economies of scale indicates the presence of economies external to the firm but internal to the manufacturing sector as a whole. However, given that the manufacturing sector is such a broad definition of an industry, it is questionable whether the Fogarty–Garofalo findings should really be called evidence of static localization economies. Rather, the result suggests something that falls between static localization economies and static urbanization economies. The findings pertaining to the size of the urban area indicate the presence of urbanization economies up to a point (2.9 million), but that further growth in the population of the urban area detracts from productivity in manufacturing. Finally, the findings regarding the spatial structure of the manufacturing sector are quite interesting. The results say that a greater spatial concentration (higher central density, and steeper density gradient – up to a point) contributes to productivity. Are static localization economies stronger when the industry is spatially concentrated in the urban area? The results are pointing in that direction.

Fogarty and Garofalo (1988) used their estimated equation to provide an explanation for the changes in productivity in the 13 urban areas over the 1957–77 period. The observed average growth rate for the 13 urban areas over the period was 3.35% per year. Excluding the increasing returns to scale, growth of capital and labor provided accounted for 1.17% of that growth. Productivity growth accounted for the remaining growth. Increasing returns to scale added 0.44% to the growth rate, and population growth added a very small 0.13% to growth. However, on average the decentralization of the urban areas (lower central density and flatter density gradient) *reduced* productivity growth by an estimated 1.22%. The remaining 2.83% is growth not related to the static agglomeration economies included in the analysis. In summary, the Fogarty–Garofalo study does not test for any dynamic agglomeration economies, but finds strong evidence of static localization economies. The particularly interesting finding is that the spatial pattern of local manufacturing is a static localization economy.

A second study of this type is by Mullen and Williams (1990), and examined productivity growth in the entire manufacturing sector in 24 urban areas over the period of 1958 to 1977. They estimated productivity growth as

$$\Delta Q/Q - \alpha(\Delta K/K) - \beta(\Delta L/L),$$

where α and β are the factor shares. They then used their estimate of productivity growth as the dependent variable. They found that productivity *growth* was positively influenced by faster growth in manufacturing output and by urbanization economies (population level in the urban area). These findings are very important. The finding that productivity growth is related to output *growth* is a finding of a *static* localization economy. Return to Figure 20.1. An increase in demand (outward shift in the demand curve) will increase both output and productivity along the given average cost curve (*AC*). On the other hand, the finding that the level of population positively influenced the rate of output growth is evidence of a *dynamic* urbanization economy.

In the Mullen–Williams (1990) results, productivity growth was negatively related to the population growth rate and the rate of growth of the manufacturing capital stock in the most recent period (1974–8). They think that the positive effect of the output growth rate on productivity growth is caused by use of more modern capital, which embodies later technology. We learned in Chapter 19 that Jorgenson and Griliches and others argue that new technology often comes embodied in new capital of higher quality. Mullen and Williams (1990) have found some indirect confirmation of this idea for urban areas. However, the negative effect of capital growth in the last four years of the study period may be caused by the energy crisis of that period or by the increase in environmental regulations that were instituted at that time. Also, rapid population *growth* seems to cause diseconomies, perhaps because of congestion and other effects (which may be only temporary).

Next we come to the studies of specific industries in urban areas. Rosenthal and Strange (2003) surveyed this rich and growing literature. As we noted in Chapter 3, they suggest that the dimensions of agglomeration economies consist of four types:

- *industry effects* (localization economies, urbanization economies, and every possibility in between);
- *geographic effects*, in which distance attenuates the agglomeration effect;

- *temporal* (i.e., dynamic agglomeration economies); and
- *organizational*; the degree of competitiveness of the local industry/economy.

As we shall see, there is evidence for the existence of agglomeration economies along each of these dimensions. Rosenthal and Strange (2003) list the possible microeconomic sources of agglomeration economies as:

- *labor market pooling effects*;
- *input sharing* (economies of scale in input production);
- *knowledge spillovers*;
- *natural advantages* (natural resources, and so on);
- *home-market effects* (local demand stimulates the industry);
- *consumption opportunities* (primarily for productive and highly paid workers); and
- *rent seeking*, which means that firms are attracted to cities where the politically powerful reside.

Rosenthal and Strange (2003) found at least one study that provides evidence for each of these sources of agglomeration economies. In the remainder of this section we shall discuss a few examples of the best studies that they identified.

Two influential studies were published in 1992; one by Glaeser, Kallal, Scheinkman and Shleifer, and the other by O'hUallachain and Satterthwaite. These two studies seemingly reach sharply different conclusions regarding the presence of dynamic localization economies, so they must be examined in detail in order to determine the sources of the different results. It turns out that the two studies have reasonably consistent results concerning localization economies. They find that localization economies are rarely strong enough to increase the *growth rate* of employment in a local industry, but that some larger absolute increases in employment are often generated. Recall Figure 21.3 and the discussion surrounding it.

It must be remembered that studying employment growth is not the same thing as studying output growth. Employment data are available for all industries in an urban area, but output data available only for manufacturing, Glaeser et al. (1992) and O'hUallachain and Satterthwaite (1992) did not wish to restrict their studies to manufacturing. It is helpful first to consider the neoclassical model for *employment* demand in an industry in an urban area. That model says that employment demand depends upon the wage rate, the rental price of capital, demand for output, the level of technology, and agglomeration economies. Holding the other factors constant, an increase in the wage rate reduces employment because of both the substitution effect (towards the capital input) and the output effect (resulting from a higher marginal cost and price of output). An increase in the price of capital may increase or decrease employment because the substitution effect operates to increase employment, but the output effect works to reduce employment. An increase in demand increases output and employment, of course. Finally, technical change and agglomeration economies can increase or decrease employment. An improvement in technology or an increase in an agglomeration economy (e.g., an increase in the size of the urban area) will mean that the same output can be produced with fewer labor (and capital) inputs. If output remains constant, employment falls. However, output will not remain constant because of the reduction in cost and output price brought about by the increase in productivity. If demand is responsive to the reduction in price, output may increase enough to generate more employment. In short, it is possible that employment can either rise or fall as output rises.

A study by McDonald (1992) examined employment growth in entire manufacturing sector in 263 urban areas for the period 1983–6. This study found that changes in the local wage rate and in local demand are important factors in manufacturing employment change. The model that was estimated followed closely the theoretical discussion in the previous paragraph, and the following elasticities of employment change were found.

Variable	Effect of 1% increase on % employment change
Wage rate in urban area	−0.71
Population of urban area	0.84
Real income per capita in urban area	0.81
Share of employment in declining industries	−0.18
Federal procurement	0.04

All of these variables attained high levels of statistical significance. The elasticity of demand for labor in manufacturing is estimated to be −0.71. Employment is responsive to increases in local demand – population and real income per capita have elasticities of slightly over 0.8. Employment growth is lower the greater is the share of local employment in the declining parts of the manufacturing sector at the national level. The declining industries are food products, tobacco, textile mills, apparel, chemicals, petroleum and coal products, leather products, and primary metals. Federal procurement has a positive effect on employment, as expected. This study also tested for the presence of dynamic localization economies for employment in the manufacturing sector as a whole, with the result that the employment level in the base year had no effect on employment growth in the subsequent three-year period.

Now we are ready to examine the study by Glaeser et al. (1992). They examined employment growth from 1956 to 1987 in the six largest industries at the two-digit SIC code level in the 170 largest urban areas. The SIC code system is described in Chapter 4 above. The six largest industries were selected because they wanted to focus on industries that represent specialties for the urban area, and because they wished to avoid small industries that may have volatile growth records. They assume that there are national markets for labor and capital, so they assume that the changes in the wage rate and the rental rate of capital were the same for all of the industries and urban areas. This assumption concerning the wage rate clearly is incorrect, and may have had a serious effect on the empirical results. They also assume that technical change in an industry consists of a national rate of change and local dynamic agglomeration economies. Assuming that changes in input prices can be ignored and that there is technical change that occurs at the national rate for the industry, the growth in employment depends upon demand growth and dynamic agglomeration economies. Their measures of dynamic agglomeration economies are:

- employment in the industry in the urban area in 1956;
- average size of establishments in the local industry relative to the nation;

- urban area's other top five industries' share of total employment in the urban area; and
- the location quotient for the industry in the urban area.

The first variable tests for dynamic localization economies as a function of the size of the local industry, and the second is aimed at the market-structure hypothesis. The third variable tests for Jacobs' idea that diversity in the local economy enhances growth – a form of dynamic urbanization economy. Finally, the location quotient (share of industry in local economy divided by the industry's share in the national economy) tests whether a high degree of specialization in the industry fosters growth. This seems to be a combination of a dynamic localization effect and a dynamic urbanization effect. The study includes a variable for demand growth–employment growth in the industry at the national level (excluding the urban area in question). They also included variables for the wage level in the industry in 1956 and for location of the urban area in the South.

The findings of the study are as follows:

Variable	Sign of effect on employment growth
Employment growth in industry in US	+
Wage level in 1956	not significant
Employment in industry in urban area in 1956	−
Location in South	+
Location quotient	−
Average size of establishment (relative to nation)	−
Employment share of other top five industries	−

Note that the employment level in the industry in 1956, the initial year, had a negative effect on the employment growth rate. The estimated coefficient is highly statistically significant, but not very large in its effect. The estimated coefficient says that, if the initial employment level in the local industry was 10,000 larger, the growth from 1956 to 1987 was 4% less than it otherwise would have been. The effect is only −0.13% per year. This result no doubt reflects the fact that many of the older urban areas of the Northeast lost a sizable amount of employment in their largest industries during the 1970s and 1980s. Pittsburgh lost most of its steel industry because of competition from foreigners and domestic mini-mills. Chicago suffered a sharp drop in meatpacking (food products). Employment in the apparel manufacturing business dropped in New York. The empirical result certainly suggests that the reasons for the concentration of those basic industries in a few urban areas seem to have evaporated. However, there is one problem with this statistical finding. Employment growth would be negatively related to the employment level if the wage rate tended to increase more in these large local industries. In fact, Glaeser et al. (1992, p. 1147) include evidence that this is precisely what happened. Wage increases were positively related to the urban area's employment level in the industry in 1956. This is not a new story; there is evidence to suggest that wages in some of the basic industries in northern urban areas were pushed up in the 1950s and 1960s, and that the loss of jobs can be attributed partly to this factor. As discussed above, McDonald (1992) tested and confirmed the importance of changes in local wages. Recall also that greater localization economies do not necessarily lead to an increase in employment. The positive effect on output must be large enough to cause employment to expand. Finally, recall from Figure 20.3 that greater localization economies may not be associated with a larger percentage increase in the industry, but only a larger absolute increase in the industry.

The other findings of Glaeser et al. (1992) provide confirmation that both diversity and competition in local industry foster growth. Employment growth was greater the less specialized was the local economy in the industry in question and in the other top six industries. And employment growth was greater the smaller were the establishments in the industry, compared to average establishment size for the industry in the nation. These are *dynamic* agglomeration economies as defined above in section B. The hypotheses of Benjamin Chinitz (1961) and Jane Jacobs (1969) come out looking good. As discussed above, the finding regarding the presence of localization "diseconomies" can be questioned.

Another influential study of urban employment growth was completed by Breandan O'hUallachain and Mark Satterthwaite (1992). They also examined individual industries, but their selection criterion was different from that used by Glaeser et al. (1992). They selected 37 industries that grew rapidly during the period of their study, 1977–84. Nine of the industries are in manufacturing, and the rest are wholesale trade, six industries in transportation and communications, four industries in FIRE (finance, insurance and real estate), and 17 services. Data were collected from the urban areas in which the industry existed in 1977 and in which growth occurred. A regression model was estimated for each of the 37 industries.

For each industry they postulated the model

$$E_1 - E_0 = aE_0^\alpha L^\beta \exp(bX + cZ + \varepsilon).$$

The notation is as follows:

- E_1, E_0 are employment in the industry in 1977 and 1984.
- L is the size of the labor force in the urban area.
- X is a group of variables that describe economic development incentive programs in the urban area.
- Z is a group of variables that describe the urban area.
- ε is a random error term.
- exp stands for e, the base of the natural logarithms. Here e is raised to the power $bX + cZ + \varepsilon$.

Taking the natural log of both sides of the equation produces the equation that was estimated;

$$\ln(E_1 - E_0) = \ln a + \alpha \ln E_0 + \beta \ln L + bX + cZ + \varepsilon.$$

This equation requires that $E_1 - E_0$ be positive, of course, because the logarithm of a negative number or zero does not exist. This dependent variable, the log of the absolute change in employment, was chosen rather than the percentage change in employment because some urban areas with very small initial levels of employment for an industry can experience huge percentage increases that are really indicative of nothing in particular.

The O'hUallachain–Satterthwaite model has an interesting implication concerning dynamic localization economies. As in Glaeser et al. (1992), base year employment in the industry is included in the model to test for localization economies. The model can be written in percentage growth terms as

$$(E_1 - E_0)/E_0 = aE_0^{\alpha-1}L^\beta \exp(bX + cZ + \varepsilon),$$

which means that the employment growth rate is higher the greater is E_0 if α is greater than 1.0. If α is less than 1.0 and greater than zero, then the employment growth rate is lower when E_0 is greater. If α is positive, an increase in E_0 means that the absolute growth $(E_1 - E_0)$ is larger. But $\alpha = 1$ is the dividing line between a localization economy that increases the growth rate of employment in the industry and a weaker localization economy that increases employment, but not its growth rate. Once again, refer to Figure 20.3. If α exceeds 1, employment in a growing industry becomes concentrated in the urban areas with the largest initial levels of employment. If α is less than 1, employment growth in the industry will be more dispersed across urban areas.

The results obtained by O'hUallachain and Satterthwaite include the following findings. First, the initial employment level had a statistically significant and positive effect in 33 out of the 37 industries. No other variable even comes close to this overwhelming result. A more detailed discussion of this finding is provided below. The size of the labor force in the urban area produced the expected result in 17 industries, which is strong confirmation of dynamic urbanization economies for a variety of industries. The average size of the firms in the local industry had a negative effect in 17 industries, a result that is in full agreement with the Glaeser et al. (1992) findings. A more competitive market structure seems to foster growth in a variety of industries. High wages and unions deterred employment growth in some industries (14 and 9, respectively), while labor quality (college graduates) stimulated some growth in 9 industries. The last variable to show any consistent result was a measure of market strength, total income in the urban area divided by employment in the industry in the base year (1977). This variable had the expected positive effect in seven industries. A large collection of other variables that was included had no consistent effects. These variables include various local amenity and policy variables. Notable is the absence of effects for public policy; taxes, education, industrial revenue bonds, and enterprise zones. University R&D parks did have the expected positive effect in six industries. It would seem that, at least with some of these policy variables, the policy has been instituted in response to unfavorable changes in the local economy. It such is the case, then it will be difficult to identify a positive effect of policy.

Let us now return to the findings regarding dynamic localization economies. Recall from the previous discussion that a coefficient of 1.0 for base year employment is the dividing line between a strong dynamic localization economy that increases the local employment growth *rate* in the industry and a weaker localization economy that lowers this employment growth rate but increases the employment level. Of the 33 statistically significant and positive effects, the average is 0.75 and only five exceed 1.0. Of these five, only three are statistically significantly greater than 1.0. These are:

Industry	Localization effect
Wholesale trade	1.19
Legal services	1.14
Accounting services	1.18

In these industries a higher base year employment level is associated with a higher employment growth rate. These three industries centralized as they grew. The other industries did not. In short, O'hUallachain and Satterthwaite (1992) found very few instances in which the effect of the localization economy is so strong that it increases the growth rate of employment. Their finding is thus almost completely consistent with the findings of Glaeser et al. (1992), who found that base year employment had a slight negative effect on the employment growth rate.

We have taken a good deal of time and energy to review some important recent studies of dynamic agglomeration economies. Empirical findings can always be subjected to further study, but some fairly clear results already have emerged. Dynamic localization economies exist in growing industries, but not in a form that is strong enough to cause the rate of employment growth in a local industry to increase. Dynamic urbanization economies also exist in some industries. Fogarty and Garofalo (1988) found a small static urbanization effect in total manufacturing up to a population level of 2.9 million. Mullen and Williams (1990) found evidence of dynamic urbanization economies in the manufacturing sector, and O'hUallachain and Satterthwaite (1992) found the presence of dynamic urbanization economies in 14 out of 37 growth industries. Curiously, Glaeser et al. (1992) did not test for urbanization economies by using a simple measure of the size of the urban area. Both Glaeser et al. (1992) and O'hUallachain and Satterthwaite (1992) confirmed the hypothesis that a more competitive local industry (in terms of smaller firms) generates more employment growth, and Glaeser et al. (1992) found that diversity in the local economy also contributes to employment growth in an industry. Fogarty and Garofalo (1988) found that the spatial pattern of the manufacturing sector can influence its growth – a very neat connection between the two basic topics (urban location patterns and urban growth) in this book.

The study by Henderson (2003) made use of what Rosenthal and Strange (2003) regard as the best data base to date. This study uses plant level data from 1972 to 1992 for 742 counties in 317 metropolitan areas on five machinery industries and four high-tech industries. The machinery industries are:

- construction equipment;
- metal working;
- special industrial;
- general industrial; and
- refrigeration machinery and equipment.

The high-tech industries are:

- computers;
- electronic components;
- aircraft; and
- medical instruments.

These are all major industries in the US.

Henderson (2003) estimated an equation for *output* at the *plant* level as a function of plant inputs of capital, labor, and materials, and other variables to capture agglomeration economies. Although he acknowledges that it is not the best choice, book value of initial capital stock was used. The basic result for high-tech plants is as follows:

$$\ln(\text{output}) = 0.50 \ln(\text{hours worked}) + 0.39 \ln(\text{materials}) + 0.06 \ln(\text{capital})$$
$$+ 0.08 \ln(\text{number of plants in same industry in county}).$$

The estimated equation controls for time and for location effects. All four variables are highly statistically significant. The equation says that a doubling of the number of plants in the same industry in the county increased output by 8%. A very similar result was obtained when the sample was restricted to single-plant high-tech firms. However, there is no evidence of this static localization economy in the machinery industries. Further analysis of the high-tech industries showed that the number of plants in the industry in the county five or ten years ago had a positive effect on output. This result confirms the existence of a form of dynamic localization economies that pertains to single-plant firms – those plants that do not have other plants in the firm with which to interact. Once again, this effect was not found for the machinery industries. Tests for urbanization economies showed no significant effects for the high-tech industries. The diversity of the local economy did not matter, nor did the overall size of the local economy. On the other hand, both the diversity and the size of the local economy did have a positive effect on the machinery industries, but only for the plants that are part of a multi-plant firm. Henderson (2003) is somewhat puzzled by this last result, and suspects that it may reflect unmeasured business service inputs provided by the firm to its plants.

E. Identification of Industries with Dynamic Agglomeration Economies

Is it possible to identify the industries that are experiencing dynamic agglomeration economies? This kind of information has high value for many people in a local economy. Those who hope to work in or those who supply inputs for such an industry have an obvious interest in this knowledge. Officials who plan public infrastructure programs or education and job training programs need this information. Public officials who are trying to promote the growth of the local economy are also keenly interested in knowing about these areas of strength. Unfortunately, there is no fool-proof method for identifying industries that will continue to grow as a result of dynamic agglomeration economies.

The research reported in the previous section does provide some suggestions that one might follow. Recent employment growth is a good clue, but the industry should also already be large enough to generate its own dynamic localization economies. Smaller firms also lead to more rapid growth. A more diverse local economy may also help (Henderson, 2003, to the contrary), but this factor does not help one pick the industries with dynamic agglomeration economies within a given local economy.

How much recent growth is indicative of dynamic agglomeration economies? The more the better, one might suppose. However, there is one immediate problem. Some urban areas, such as Los Angeles (see Chapter 1) have been growing rapidly in nearly all categories, while many other urban areas are not growing very rapidly as a whole. An urban area that is growing rapidly overall may indeed have dynamic agglomeration economies operating in a large number of sectors, but it is unlikely that all those sectors are growing more rapidly than "average" in some sense. An economy that is growing rapidly as a whole will pull along industries that are not dynamic generators of growth, and it is reasonable to suppose that such industries perform no better than the average for the local economy. What is more, an urban area that is not growing rapidly as a whole (e.g., New York and Chicago) may contain dynamic industries. How can such industries be identified in that sort of environment?

A technique exists that puts these thoughts into numerical terms. The method is known as shift–share analysis, and it is a method for dividing the growth of an industry in an urban area into components that are helpful in identifying dynamic agglomeration economies. In the conventional form of shift–share analysis, the percentage change in employment in a particular industry i in a local economy can be written down as

$$\Delta e_i / e_i = \Delta US/US + [(\Delta US_i/US_i) - (\Delta US/US)] + [(\Delta e_i/e_i) - (\Delta US_i/US_i)],$$

where the notation is as follows.

US is total employment in the United States.
US_i is employment in the US in industry i.
e_i is employment in the local economy in industry i.

As always, ΔUS means "change in" employment in the US. Employment growth in the local industry has been divided into three parts; the part attributable to total employment growth in the nation, the part attributable to the fact that national employment growth in the particular industry was more rapid (or slower) than the nation as a whole, and the third term that compares the employment growth in the local industry to that industry's national growth rate. This last term is normally called the competitive position of the local industry because it is a direct comparison of the industry's growth locally and nationally. The method is called shift–share analysis because the first term in the equation can be called the (national) share term, and the sum of the two other terms represents a shift relative to the overall national growth rate.

The critical term for purposes of identifying local industries with dynamic agglomeration economies is the third term – the competitive position. If an industry is growing more rapidly in the local economy than in the national economy, then perhaps it is exhibiting dynamic agglomeration economies. The word "perhaps" is used because this is a very weak criterion. In fact, nearly all industries in the Los Angeles urban area grew more rapidly than their national counterparts during the 1980s. Does this mean that nearly all industries in Los Angeles had dynamic agglomeration economies? Clearly one cannot reach that conclusion. Conventional shift–share analysis does not appear to provide a very discriminating criterion.

Let us not give up on the idea of shift–share analysis just yet. One problem with the conventional form of shift–share analysis is that the growth rate of the local economy as a whole does not appear in the formula. Many industries in Los Angeles grew rapidly simply because they were located in Los Angeles and the rising tide lifted all of the boats. Our version of shift–share analysis is

$$\Delta e_i/e_i = \Delta E/E + (\Delta US/US - \Delta E/E) + [(\Delta US_i/US_i) - (\Delta US/US)] + [(\Delta e_i/e_i) - (\Delta US_i/US_i)].$$

The new notation is E, which denotes total employment in the local economy. Our share term is $\Delta E/E$, the percentage change in total employment in the local economy. The rest of the formula represents the shift relative to $\Delta E/E$. The competitive position is now defined to be

$$(\Delta e_i/e_i) - (\Delta US_i/US_i) + (\Delta US/US - \Delta E/E).$$

The competitive position in conventional shift–share analysis has now been adjusted by the difference between the national and local growth rates in total employment. For example, suppose that an industry in Los Angeles grew by 15% and that its national counterpart grew by 8%. However, suppose that total employment in the US grew by 5% compared to 10% in Los Angeles. The conventional shift–share method would say that the local industry has a competitive position of +7%. On the other hand, the M&M shift–share method says that the competitive position is +2%, because 5% of that growth was more rapid general growth in the local economy. One can say that the local industry grew by 2% more than might have been expected, given the identity of the industry and the fact that it is located in Los Angeles.

To repeat, there is no foolproof method for identifying industries in the local economy that may be exhibiting dynamic agglomeration economies. The M&M competitive position is a tool that may prove to be useful. It will be used in the next chapter in the discussion of local economic development policy.

F. A Synthesis of Mainstream Economics: Later Version

Recall that Chapter 19 includes a preliminary synthesis of Keynesian and neoclassical models of urban growth. This section updates that synthesis to take into account what has been learned about agglomeration economies. This synthesis is called a "later version" because no version of a model is the final version. Actually, Figures 20.1, 20.2, and 20.3 present the synthesis of mainstream economics as it pertains to the level and growth of *output* of an industry in an urban area. This section will examine employment and employment growth in a particular industry in an urban area. Recall that the model depicted in Figure 19.3 is the market for labor for an entire urban area.

Figure 20.4 depicts the initial demand curve for labor by the industry as DD, and the supply curve is SS. The labor supply curve is drawn with a positive slope, indicating that the industry can recruit more workers only by increasing the wage rate a bit. The industry is only a part of a larger labor market in the urban area, so it faces a fairly elastic labor supply curve.

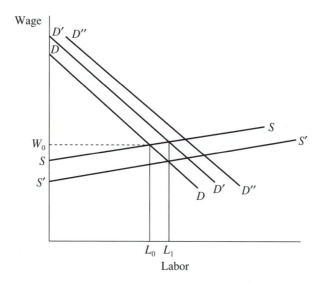

Figure 20.4 Dynamic localization economies

The market demand for labor by the industry is a bit complicated because of the static localization economy. Individual firms in the local industry operate under constant returns to scale, but the local industry operates under increasing returns to scale. The market demand for labor in the long run is the value of the marginal product of labor *as seen by the firms*, which is less than the value of the marginal product of labor for the industry as a whole. The individual firm presumes that, given the price of capital services and the wage rate, it can expand at constant marginal cost, i.e. at a constant marginal product of labor. Therefore, the firms in the industry think that the marginal product of labor is a constant MP^*. The value of the marginal product is the price of output times MP^*, but the price of output for the industry is given by the demand curve for output. The price of output falls as the industry output and employment expand, and this declining output price is incorporated into demand curve DD.

The initial wage rate and employment level are W_0 and L_0. The empirical results found in the studies by Glaeser et al. (1992), O'hUallachain and Satterthwaite (1992), and Henderson (2003) indicate the presence of dynamic localization economies, at least in some sectors such as high-tech. The dynamic localization economies increase the productivity of the inputs, leading to reductions in cost and market price and an increase in output. The empirical evidence indicates that the output effect outweighs the productivity effect for a local industry, so the labor demand increases rather than decreases. The demand for labor shifts to $D'D'$. This means that, at employment level L_0, reductions in costs are generated by the industry which cause output and employment to rise in the next time period. The increase in the size of the industry (to employment level L_1 and its corresponding output level) generates a further increase in productivity that reduces costs and market price again. This further shift in the demand curve for labor (to $D''D''$) results in an employment increase to L_2. In Figure 20.4 this series of increases in employment is declining in percentage terms, but increasing in absolute terms.

As increase in the supply of labor, shown as a shift from SS to $S'S'$, will increase employment and reduce wages as usual. However, the presence of dynamic localization economies means that the employment and output increases will lead to even larger improvements in productivity than otherwise would occur at that time. The demand curve for labor is constantly shifting outward, but an increase in labor supply will cause a one-time jump in labor demand that may have further dynamic effects.

G. Two Case Studies

The models and econometric results reviewed in this chapter may appear to be lifeless to some readers, so it is useful to examine some case studies that highlight some static and dynamic agglomeration economies. Two cases have been chosen because of their importance for both the US economy and their home urban areas. The first case is the automobile industry and Detroit, and the second is the semiconductor industry and metropolitan San Francisco. The first case is the story of events that took place a hundred years ago, while the second case is from the recent past. It is clear that both of these cases are quite exceptional. They represent extreme examples of the exploitation of agglomeration economies. But extreme examples have their uses in that they demonstrate the existence of particular phenomena, including in these cases the phenomenon of dynamic localization economies.

Detroit and the automobile industry

The first American automobile producer was not located in Detroit. The Duryea Company of Springfield, Massachusetts was the first to begin production of a gasoline powered car in the US in 1896. Olds, the first Detroit producer, began in 1899, but by 1904, 42% of American autos were being produced in the Detroit area. And by 1914 Detroit was making 78% of a vastly expanded auto industry output. What accounts for this concentration of the industry in one urban area?

Jackson (1988) argues that Detroit possessed concentrations of crucial industries, skilled workers, available local venture capital, and entrepreneurs. He argues that this combination of factors, combined with strong consumer demand, created the critical mass that resulted in continued innovation that other urban areas simply could not match. In short, Jackson thinks that a dynamic localization economy was at work that operated through the rate of technical change. But what are the details of this argument?

The critical antecedent industry was the shipbuilding industry. It was here that the internal combustion gasoline engine was developed into a practical engine for powering boats. This kind of engine, rather than the steam engines that were used for ocean vessels, was designed to be used on the rivers and lakes in and around the Michigan area. And the gasoline engine, rather than steam or electric engines, turned out to be the best engine for the auto. Several early Detroit automobile men had backgrounds in the boat engine business. Olds produced them, Leland made parts for them, and Dodge and Ford repaired them. Other industries that were present in Michigan supported the auto industry

– examples include the carriage industry, steel, wheelwrights, and the machine-tool industry. The firms and workers in these industries had the skills to produce the components needed for the auto. Another important factor was the availability of financing for the fledgling auto companies. Considerable fortunes had been made in lumber, mining, food processing, and other industries. What is more, the investors in Detroit were willing to learn about the potential of the auto industry. All of this created what Jackson (1988, p. 95) calls "an innovative contagion, in which the development of ideas, products, and markets acquires its own momentum and energy, continuing until the industry matures."

A good deal of the story of the early Detroit auto industry can be told through the life of one man – Henry Ford. Ford's story is included in a massive history of the auto industry by David Halberstam titled *The Reckoning* (1986). Halberstam's book is fascinating and I recommend that you read it – after the school term is over and when you have plenty of spare time. Henry Ford was born on a farm in Michigan in 1863. As a boy he grew to hate farming and to love tinkering with machines. In 1879, at the age of sixteen, he walked to Detroit to look for some interesting work. At the time Detroit was full of small foundries, machine shops, boat builders, and carriage makers. He worked in a machine shop for a while, and later worked repairing boat engines for a company called Detroit Dry Docks. He returned to the farm in 1886 in response to an offer from his father, but by 1891 he was back in Detroit. His reading of technical magazines had convinced him that important new inventions were imminent.

He told his wife that he intended to invent the horseless carriage, but before he could do that he needed to learn more about electricity. He took a job with Detroit Edison (the local electric power company) as an engineer to support his family and his tinkering and inventing activities. He had his first experimental car on the street by 1896. The vehicle was really a four-wheel bicycle with an engine. He followed up with a better car, and in 1899 he started his first car company. At this time dozens of engineers and inventors were starting car companies in Detroit. Ford's company folded within eighteen months, but he continued to improve his experimental models. With Henry Ford at the wheel, one of his improved models won an important auto race in 1901 in nearby Grosse Pointe. This bit of notoriety moved him ahead of many of his competitors.

Ford was ready to start another auto company in 1903. At this point he was forty years old, and he knew just about everything there was to know about the car business at that time. Furthermore, he had the vision that the future of the business was to build a car that was cheap enough to be marketed on a massive scale to the farmers and artisans of the day. In 1903 cars were expensive, and only well-to-do people bought them. There were only about 800 cars in Detroit at the time, and many of Ford's financial backers were quite dubious about his plan. Nevertheless, Ford's new company was successful from the beginning. The company made money, and some of the money was ploughed back into additional design work.

The year 1908 stands as a landmark year in industrial and urban economic history. In that year Henry Ford introduced the Model T Ford. The Model T was reliable, durable and compact. It benefited from recent improvements in steel technology that permitted steel parts to be both lighter and stronger. Ford realized immediately the implications of improvements in steel for the auto industry. Ford's Model T was very successful from the beginning. In 1908 Ford had a 9.4% share of the American market. But now the nature of the story changes. Up until 1908 Ford had been only a part of the Detroit auto industry and its dynamic localization economies.

When the Model T was introduced in 1908, Ford began the process of creating economies of scale for his company. He did this by inventing the assembly line. At first assembly lines were developed for various parts of the Model T – motors, transmissions, etc. Then, in 1914, the first moving assembly line was introduced. The chassis of the Model T was pulled along by a conveyer belt that was fashioned after the system used by Chicago meat packers to "disassemble" cattle into cuts of beef. These improvements in production methods permitted Ford to cut the price of the Model T from $780 in 1910 to $360 in 1914. Halberstam (1986, p. 81) informs us that, in 1914, Ford produced 268,000 cars with 13,000 employees while the other 299 US auto makers produced 287,000 cars with 66,000 employees. Ford's share of the market (in terms of cars produced) had increased from 9.4% in 1908 to 48% in 1914. The chief source of this tremendous growth in the Ford Motor Company was economies of scale that were *internal to the firm*. As Mr. Ford once put it, "I invented the modern age."

Ford did not stop with the Model T assembly line. Beginning in 1918 he created his River Rouge complex, which eventually became a fully integrated manufacturing facility that took iron ore in at one end and shipped cars out the other end. "The Rouge" began as a boat factory in 1918, added a pig-iron plant in 1920, branched out to tractors, auto engines and a steel plant in 1925, and then became the plant for the Model A Ford that was introduced in 1928. The Rouge employed 75,000 workers, was 1.5 miles long by 0.75 miles wide, and had 23 major buildings and 93 miles of railroad track. The glass for the Model A was even made there. At the Rouge it took four days to produce a complete car from raw materials. Halberstam (1986) thinks that Henry Ford invented "just-in-time" inventory and production methods.

So there we have it. The early years of the auto industry in Detroit were characterized by dynamic localization economies as dozens of little firms and their inventor-owners created several products and an industry. They were assisted also by static localization economies in the labor market, capital market, and the markets for intermediate inputs. However, after 1908 the story changes as Ford made his drive for mass production through the development and use of huge economies of scale at the firm level. As you know, huge economies of scale create cities too. But Ford's internalization of scale economies means that they are not externalities. It was noted above that, in 1914, Detroit had a 78% share of American auto production. Ford had 62% of Detroit's share. The tremendous growth of the Detroit auto industry was therefore a combination of static and dynamic localization economies *and* the exploitation of theretofore unimagined economies of scale by Ford Motor Company.

Silicon Valley and the semiconductor industry

The transistor was invented on December 23, 1947 at the Bell Laboratories in Murray Hill, New Jersey. Many people have come to regard the transistor as the major invention of the twentieth century. Its three inventors, John Bardeen, Walter Brattain, and William Shockley, in 1956 received the Nobel Prize in physics for this major scientific and technological breakthrough, but just what is the transistor and why is it so important?

You need to understand just a little bit of the science and technology to understand the origins of the Silicon Valley industry agglomeration. My source for the information is the book by Braun and Macdonald (1982), which is a nice nontechnical history of the semiconductor industry up to the beginning of the 1980s.

The transistor is a device that uses semiconductor material to amplify or switch an electrical signal. The *New York Times* of July 1, 1948 described it as follows:

> The working parts of the device consist solely of two fine wires that run down to a pinhead of solid semi-conductive material soldered to a metal base. The substance on the metal base amplifies the current carried to it by one wire and the other wire carries away the amplified current.

Scientists at Bell Labs, MIT, Purdue, and other centers of scientific research had been experimenting with semiconductor materials since the 1930s for a variety of purposes. The article in the *New York Times* reported on the demonstration at Bell Labs of a transistor radio – a radio that contained none of the standard vacuum tubes, but instead used solid-state amplifiers. But what is a semiconductor?

A semiconductor is a substance that conducts electricity poorly at low (room) temperatures, but will conduct electricity if minute quantities of certain substances (called impurities) are added, or if heat, light, or voltage is applied. In other words, a semiconductor is an insulator of electric current in its normal state, but it can become a conductor of electricity that can be *modulated*, or controlled, by one of these alterations in its state. For example, the addition of the proper impurity alters the configuration of the electrons in the semiconductor so that electricity is conducted. The elements germanium and silicon were two of the semiconductor materials that were under basic scientific study before and during World War II. Both are strong and hard substance that seemed to have promising semiconductor properties.

The first transistor that was invented at Bell Labs in 1947 was in fact a germanium crystal with two wires attached. Bardeen and Brattain discovered that the application of a small positive electric charge greatly increased the capacity of germanium to carry current. This meant that an amplifier could be achieved by the close spacing of two conducting wires on a germanium crystal. By the way, the term transistor is a combination of the two words transfer and resistor to indicate that current is transferred across a resistor. The Bardeen–Brattain transistor is called a point contact transistor. A much more practical transistor, called the junction transistor, was invented by William Shockley and was first constructed in 1951 – also at Bell Labs. Shockley's idea is to make a sandwich of two types of semiconductors to create the needed reconfiguration of electrons. Limited application of both types of transistors began in the early 1950s, but the reliability of the early devices was not very good. Bell decided to publish the findings from the lab, hold symposiums, and license the technologies widely in the hope that other firms would help to improve the devices. The benefits of a practical transistor for the telephone business were obvious, but Bell also hoped to enhance its reputation and avoid charges that it was a monopoly. Indeed, the first practical application of the junction transistor was made in hearing aids by another company – Raytheon. But the early and mid-1950s was a time far removed from today's world with its powerful computers, communication satellites, electronic calculators, and other miniature electronic devices of almost every conceivable sort.

Several companies, such as Raytheon, RCA, General Electric, Philco, and Texas Instruments, began working on the transistor right after a Bell symposium in 1952. In 1954 Texas Instruments announced that it had succeeded in making a silicon junction transistor. Silicon had the ability to work at much higher temperatures than germanium, so this transistor was of great interest to the military. By 1957 there were 26 firms that were making some 600 different types of transistors commercially. It turned out that relatively small groups of physicists who were trained in solid-state physics could develop new transistors for various purposes. These people soon learned that the knowledge gained by working for one company could be quite valuable for another company. Frequent movement of semiconductor experts from one company to another became routine. For California's Silicon Valley the most important move of this kind was the decision by William Shockley in 1954 to leave Bell Labs and start his own company in Palo Alto, Shockley's home town. Shockley Semiconductor Laboratory was established in 1955, and because of his great reputation, Shockley was able to lure some of the best young semiconductor experts away from older firms in the East.

Shockley's company was only moderately successful, but in 1957 eight of his men decided to leave and create their own company, Fairchild Semiconductor. The influence of Fairchild has been felt throughout the entire semiconductor industry, and its impact in Silicon Valley is incomparable. Braun and Macdonald (1982, p. 126) noted that by the early 1970s some 41 companies had been founded by former Fairchild employees. Most of these companies are (or were) in Silicon Valley. These companies include industry giants such as Intel and National Semiconductor. But before we get ahead of ourselves with the story of Silicon Valley, we need a little more technical information.

The next great breakthrough was the invention of the integrated circuit in 1959 at Texas Instruments in Dallas. An integrated circuit is a device in which the functions of a number of components are performed inside a single chip of semiconductor material. The first simple integrated circuit was invented at Texas Instruments, but the device was first put into production at Fairchild Semiconductor in 1960. In the early 1960s the entire output of integrated circuits was purchased by the federal government, but numerous private commercial uses for such devices were introduced within a few years.

The experience of Fairchild and other firms with integrated circuit technologies led to the major breakthrough that has created the world as we now know it. In 1968 three men, Robert Noyce, Gordon Moore, and Andrew Grove, left Fairchild to start a new firm – a little outfit called Intel (also located in Silicon Valley, of course). Does your personal computer have an "Intel inside?" Chances are pretty high that it does. Intel's work on an electronic calculator for a Japanese firm led in 1969 to the invention of the microprocessor, or the silicon chip that is programmable. The world's first microprocessor was announced on November 15, 1971. At the time it was called a "micro-programmable computer on a chip." This chip could be combined with more ordinary chips and input–output devices to create a complete microprocessor. Between 1972 and 1982 the 120 chipmaking companies grew to over 3,000 firms that offer an enormous variety of high-technology products and services for the private market.

Now we can address the question of why Silicon Valley became the center of the semiconductor industry and its explosive growth. It would seem that there might have been other candidates. What about Dallas, with Texas Instruments? How about New Jersey (near Bell Labs) or Boston or somewhere else? Sure, Shockley started his own company in Silicon Valley, and his company spawned Fairchild Semiconductor, but what else was involved? We will probably never know with certainty, but several factors have been suggested by various experts.

One fairly conventional account of these factors has been provided by Henton and Waldhorn (1988). The role of the federal government was supportive by providing the market for integrated circuits in the 1960s and by supplying funds for solid-state physics research and graduate students at various universities. They give a great deal of credit to the growth of the commercial market beginning in the late 1960s, and the availability of venture capital was critical in the creation of new firms. Venture capitalists must have intimate knowledge of the industry because they play an important organizing and planning role in the early years of a company. However, these factors do not tell us why Silicon Valley was uniquely successful. Henton and Waldhorn (1988) also mention the role of Stanford University and electrical engineering professors Fred Terman and John Linvill. They recruited the brightest graduate students and trained them to work in the semiconductor industry, and in 1951 Terman was instrumental in establishing the first university-based research and industrial park at Stanford. These factors tell us something about how Silicon Valley grew through export demand and the exploitation of agglomeration economies. It is clear that venture capital and the training of solid-state physicists and electrical engineers at Stanford are, at least, static localization economies. They may even lead to dynamic localization economies, but this point is not clear.

Braun and Macdonald (1982) provide a more detailed account of how growth took place in Silicon Valley. To Henton and Waldhorn's list of factors they add suppliers of intermediate inputs and good weather, but their main argument concerns the benefits one firm gains from proximity to the others. Information about the latest technological and commercial developments is vital. The latest information is extremely valuable, but its value lasts only for a short time. Under these conditions it behooves one to be located as close to sources of information as possible. Information is not shared on a formal basis, but is transmitted through informal contacts. A certain establishment called the Waggonwheel Bar, which is located only a block from Intel, Raytheon, and Fairchild, was known as the fountainhead of the industry because this was where the semiconductor men socialized, exchanged information, and hired employees. As mentioned above, often the hiring involved "stealing" key people from other firms. The inducements usually included both high salaries and stock options because the success of a firm in the semiconductor industry usually depends upon the expertise of a few key people. The industry is one with an extremely rapid rate of technical change, and it is clear that the density of firms and the highly competitive environment in Silicon Valley enhanced that rate of technical progress. A reasonable hypothesis is one of dynamic localization economies operating through the rate of technical change that were related to the size of the local industry and its competitive market structure. It is pretty clear that, early in the 1960s, these dynamic localization economies began to function in Silicon Valley.

G. Metropolitan Growth and Urban Spatial Patterns

The basic economic functions of urban areas were discussed in Section I of the book, and urban location patterns were studied in Section II. This chapter and the previous chapter constitute a detailed look at metropolitan growth. Recall that, in Chapter 1, we hypothesized that urban growth and changes in location patterns are related. We illustrated this connection with data from New York, Los Angeles, and Chicago. Now it is time to take a look at the research that has put these two topics together in systematic fashion. In our view this is a fruitful area for further research.

The first study of the topic is the book by Norton (1979). He began with the observation that older central cities lost population in the 1950–75 period but that younger central cities gained population during this period. Some old central cities, such as St. Louis, Pittsburgh, Detroit, Buffalo, and Cleveland, experienced huge population losses, while San Diego, Phoenix, and Houston showed large gains in population. At the time many argued that the old, industrial cities were obsolete and that large areas within their boundaries had essentially been abandoned by all except the poor. At the same time economic growth in general had shifted from the Northeast to the sunbelt.

Norton (1979) conducted his study by assembling data on the 30 largest urban areas as of 1970 and then ranking them according to their population levels in 1910. The top 12 are, with the exception of San Francisco, all in the Northeast and include New York, Chicago, Philadelphia, Detroit, St. Louis, and so on. These are the old, industrial urban areas. The bottom 12 urban areas are called young urban areas because they had not grown to prominence as of 1910. Ten of the 12 are in the sunbelt; the other two are Indianapolis and Columbus. The six urban areas in the middle are a mixed group, including Los Angeles, Washington, DC, Milwaukee, Kansas City, New Orleans, and Seattle. Employment in the 12 old, industrial urban areas was dominated by manufacturing; their average percentage of employment in manufacturing in 1950 was 34.6%. In contrast, the average for employment in manufacturing for 1950 for the 12 young urban areas was 18.9%.

Norton's old, industrial urban areas and young urban areas differed sharply in metropolitan population growth, central city population growth, and annexation by the central city. Average population growth for the old, industrial urban areas was 32% from 1950 to 1975, while the young urban areas grew by 111% over this period. The central cities of the old, industrial urban areas declined in population by 21% during this period, while the central cities in the young urban areas increased by 124%. Part of this huge difference can be attributed to the fact that the young central cities were able to annex territory and old, industrial cities were not. The percentage increase in land area for the old, industrial central cities was 2% while the young central cities expanded their land areas by 704%! It should be noted that much of this annexation was "preemptive" in the sense that the city annexed territory in advance of population growth.

Norton (1979) summarized the information on population growth in a particularly clever way. He used the population growth data for 1950–70 for the 30 urban areas to estimate a linear equation that relates population growth in the central city to population growth in the urban area and the increase in land area of the central city over the period. The estimated equation is

$$CPOPGRO = -61.9 + 1.1 \ UPOPGRO + 0.06L,$$

where CPOPGRO is the percentage growth in the population of the central city from 1950 to 1970, UPOPGRO is the corresponding growth figure for the urban area (including the central city), and L is the percentage increase in the land area of the central city. The R^2

for the estimated equation is 0.88; the equation "explains" 88% of the variation in central city population growth for the 30 urban areas. All three coefficients (including the constant term of −61.9) are highly statistically significant. Look carefully at this equation and see what it says. First, it says that an increase in the growth of the population of the urban area of 1% actually increased the population growth of the central city by 1.1% (although 1.1 is not significantly different from 1.0). However, the equation also says that, if the urban area did not grow at all and if the central city annexed no territory, the population of the central city would have decreased by 61.9% over 20 years! No urban area had zero population growth during this period, so this did not happen. (Here is a small project. Look up the data on the Detroit urban area for 1970–2000. The population of the city of Detroit has dropped by over 50% from its peak.) Another way to interpret the equation is to find the increase in the population of the urban area that results in no change in the population of the central city. Assuming that annexation is zero, this growth for the urban area is 57%. Finally, the coefficient of the annexation variable says that an increase in the land area of the central city of 1% increased its population growth by 0.06%. A doubling of the land area would have increased central city growth by 6%.

Norton gave his empirical result an interpretation that is related to the population density function from Chapter 6. He argued that during the 1950–70 period there was a strong tendency for population to move to the suburbs in all urban areas because of declining commuting costs and rising real incomes. This means that the population density function was getting flatter and the peak population density was falling, as was shown in Chapter 6 for the case of Chicago. On the other hand, population growth will shift the population density function up – density will tend to increase at all locations. The change in the population of the central city is the net outcome of these two forces: suburbanization and growth of the urban area. Recall that this was the basic idea behind the discussion of population change in New York, Los Angeles, and Chicago in Chapter 1 as well.

Norton (1979) succeeded in showing the powerful connections between growth in the urban area and the fortunes of the central city. Growth that was sufficiently robust (along with the ability to annex territory) was able to offset the forces of suburbanization, but the urban areas that date from the industrial age did not have that kind of growth (or the ability to annex territory). Norton attributed this slow growth of the old, industrial urban areas to the decentralization of the economic growth incubator function away from the old, industrial Northeast to the sunbelt. Norton's analysis leaves us with no policy "handles" to change the situation. There was something inevitable about the decline of the old, industrial urban areas. Economic growth policies for urban areas are discussed in the next chapter.

A more recent study of urban areas was conducted by Stanback (2002). This study was discussed in Chapter 4 for its method of classifying urban areas by economic function. Stanback's proposition – his compilation of important facts – is that the national economy has undergone a dramatic change that involves a large shift in the composition of employment away from industries that produce goods to those that produce services. Furthermore, the goods-producing industries increasingly have needed producer services such as transportation, and communications, wholesaling, finance, advertising, and the professional services of accountants, lawyers, and management consultants. A great deal of this transformation is associated with the use of computer technology in all phases of production of goods and services. The shift of the economy toward the production of services has taken place in urban areas that are experiencing decline in the industrial sector of the central city and development of suburbs with more diverse industrial and office employment bases. The economies of the suburbs have become much broader and the relationship between the central city and the suburban has changed significantly. Stanback notes three important changes in urban areas that have taken place since the 1970s:

1   The downtown areas of major cities have been transformed and rebuilt by the growth of the service sector – finance, insurance, real estate, professional services, and so on. Downtown employers still rely on commuters from the suburbs, although an increasing number of downtown workers have decided to live in certain areas of the central city.
2   As we saw in Chapter 7, the new suburbanization has created large centers of employment and agglomeration economies that place the suburbs in direct competition with downtown and other older employment areas. Suburban employment centers have become the centers of economic growth in urban areas. Suburban employment growth has been robust on a broad front and manufacturing employment in the suburbs has generally been stable.
3   The demand for workers has shifted sharply in favor of workers with higher levels of education and training.

Except for the last of these three points, all of this has been discussed extensively in Chapter 7. These changes in the economy of urban areas have created even greater challenges for the central city outside the downtown area because employers find that such locations (e.g., old industrial areas) are not suitable for service-sector activity.

The success of suburban developments since the 1970s has raised the question of whether the suburbs really "need" the central city any longer. Are the economies of the suburbs and the central city sufficiently independent that the suburbs would be capable of the same growth even if the central city were to disappear? Stated in this way the question sounds absurd. Nevertheless, just what do the suburbs gain by their association with the central city? Ihlanfeldt (1995) did a careful review of the evidence on this question and found that there are several connections that are potentially important. He placed these connections into four general categories:

1   The conditions of the central city influence the perceptions that outsiders have of the urban area. These perceptions can influence their willingness to make investments in the urban area as a whole.
2   Central cities provide amenities of various kinds that are valuable for all residents of the urban area. These amenities include cultural, recreational, and educational facilities.
3   The central city may provide a "sense of place" or a sense of community pride for all who live in the urban area. This point is difficult to study empirically, but that does not mean that community pride is not important.
4   Central cities still offer certain types of agglomeration economies that are not available in the suburbs.

The bulk of the existing evidence pertains to agglomeration economies in the central business districts of major central cities. The basic idea is that face-to-face contacts are still important for a variety of activities in the business and public sectors and that location in the central business district offers a lower coset for making those contacts. What are the services provided in the central business district for firms located in the suburbs? A study by Schwartz (1992) examined the purchase of five business services by firms in the New York, Los Angeles, and Chicago urban areas. Those five services are actuarial consulting, auditing, banking, investment banking, and legal services. He found that firms located in the suburbs relied primarily on central city firms for these services, and very few companies in the central city relied on suburban providers of these services. Suburban firms in the Chicago area relied on the central city more than did their counterparts in New York or Los Angeles, and reliance on the central city by suburban firms was generally greatest for legal services. Ihlanfeldt (1995) suspected that this reliance on the central city for such services may be eroding over time, and more research will be needed to investigate this possibility. Nevertheless, the reliance of the suburbs on the central city in the three largest urban areas for accounting, banking, and legal services is impressive. These services are included in the category of urbanization economies that was introduced in Chapter 3.

H. Summary

As the survey by Rosenthal and Strange (2003) shows, the empirical study of static and dynamic agglomeration economies has become quite popular among researchers. As recounted in section E, some findings are emerging that confirm the existence of agglomeration economies that have enhanced growth in urban areas. The size of the local industry (localization economies) seems to matter, but dynamic localization economies may not be as strong as some have thought, except in some fairly unusual cases such as the early auto industry in Detroit, the semiconductor industry in Silicon Valley, and other high-tech industries. Urbanization economies have an influence in some industries, but urbanization economies also may not be as pervasive as some have suggested. A more competitive urban industry, as measured by smaller size of the firms, grows more rapidly. This is a very important recent finding that adds greatly to our knowledge. Also, some evidence points toward diversity in the local economy as a contributor to the growth of an industry. In brief, what we think we know at the moment is that an industry in an urban area will grow more rapidly if it produces a product that is in demand, is competitive, is already of some size in the urban area (and was of some size in the past), is located in a larger urban area (but not too large), and is surrounded by a diverse collection of industries (maybe). All of this is not complete conjecture, but the result of solid, time-consuming empirical research. Hard work – there is no substitute for it.

Finally, we considered briefly the research on the relationship between urban growth and development and changing spatial patterns in urban areas. The shift to the "service economy" has major implications for urban areas. Research on the topic shows that the suburbs are growing on a broad front and downtowns in major urban areas are doing reasonably well. However, central city neighborhoods outside the downtown area struggle unless they are located in an urban area that is growing rapidly or somehow become part of the downtown growth (e.g., condos for those downtown lawyers). The connections between urban growth and development and urban location patterns are good topics for further research. The business of local economic development policy is considered in the next chapter.

Exercises

1   Suppose that the growth rate of an industry in an urban area has been found to be a function of:

- the growth rate of labor, with a coefficient of 0.75;
- the growth rate of capital, with a coefficient of 0.4;
- the employment level in the industry;
- the rate of growth of employment in the urban area;
- the number of flights departing daily from the local airport.

Is growth in this local industry subject to:

- Static localization economies?
- Dynamic localization economies?
- Static urbanization economies?
- Dynamic urbanization economies?

2   You conduct a study of a growth industry in a large number of urban areas and find that

$$\ln(E_1 - E_0) = 0.44 + 0.62 \ln E_0 + 0.48\text{Pop} + \ldots$$

Where E_0 is employment in the industry in the base year, E_1 is employment in a subsequent year, Pop is population of the urban area, and ... stands for other variables that have been included in the study.

(a)   Is this industry subject to dynamic localization economies? Why? What is the magnitude of the effect, if any?
(b)   Do these results tell us whether the industry is subject to static localization economies? Why or why not?
(c)   Is this industry subject to dynamic urbanization economies? How do you know?

3   Assume that the nation and an urban area have the following employment figures in the base year.

	Industry A	Industry B	Industry C
US	1,000	2,000	500
Urban area	100	100	100

Assume national growth rates of A (10%), B (5%), and C (30%), and assume local growth rates of A (5%), B (10%), and C (25%).

(a)   Use conventional shift–share analysis to compute, for each industry, the three components of growth; the part attributable to total employment growth in the nation, the part attributable to national growth in the industry as faster (or slower) than total national growth, and the competitive position of the local industry.

(b) Use the M&M version of shift–share analysis to compute the four components of growth for each industry as shown in the text. Does the nature of the results change compared to conventional shift–share analysis?

References

Beeson, Patricia, 1990, "Sources of the Decline in Manufacturing in Large Metropolitan Areas," *Journal of Urban Economics*, vol. 28, pp. 71–86.

Braun, Ernest and S. Macdonald, 1982, *Revolution in Miniature: The History and Impact of Semi-conductor Electronics*, 2nd edn. Cambridge: Cambridge University Press.

Chinitz, Benjamin, 1961, "Contrasts in Agglomeration: New York and Pittsburgh," *American Economic Review, Papers and Proceedings*, vol. 51, pp. 279–89.

Fogarty, Michael and G. Garofalo, 1988, "Urban Spatial Structure and Productivity Growth in the Manufacturing Sector of Cities," *Journal of Urban Economics*, vol. 23, pp. 60–70.

Galbraith, John K., 1956, *American Capitalism*. Boston: Houghton Mifflin Co.

Glaeser, Edward, H. Kallal, J. Scheinkman, and A. Shleifer, 1992, "Growth in Cities," *Journal of Political Economy*, vol. 100, pp. 1126–54.

Halberstam, David, 1986, *The Reckoning*. New York: William Morrow and Co.

Henderson, J. Vernon, 1986, "Efficiency of Resource Usage and City Size," *Journal of Urban Economics*, vol. 19, pp. 47–70.

Henderson. J. Vernon, 2003, "Marshall's Scale Economies," *Journal of Urban Economics*, vol. 53, pp. 1–28.

Henton, Douglas and S. Waldhorn, 1988, "The Megastate Economy," in S. Fosler (ed.), The New *Economic Role of American States*. New York: Oxford University Press.

Ihlanfeldt, Keith, 1995, "The Importance of the Central City to the Regional and National Economy: A Review of the Arguments and Empirical Evidence," *Cityscape*, vol. 1, pp. 125–50.

Jackson, John, 1988, "Michigan," in S. Fosler (ed.), *The New Economic Role of American States*, New York: Oxford University Press.

Jacobs, Jane, 1969, *The Economy of Cities*. New York: Vintage.

Krugman, Paul, 1991, *Geography and Trade*. Cambridge: MIT Press.

Lucas, Robert, 1988, "On the Mechanics of Economic Development," *Journal of Monetary Economics*, vol. 22, pp. 3–42.

Malecki, Edward, 1983, "Technology and Regional Development: A Survey," *International Regional Science Review*, vol. 8, pp. 89–125.

McDonald, John, 1992, "Assessing the Development Status of Metropolitan Areas," in E. Mills and J. McDonald (eds.), *Sources of Metropolitan Growth*, New Brunswick, NJ: Rutgers University Press.

Mills, Edwin, 1992, "Sectoral Clustering and Metropolitan Development," in E. Mills and J. McDonald (eds.), *Sources of Metropolitan Growth*, New Brunswick, NJ: Rutgers University.

Mullen, John and M. Williams, 1990, "Explaining Total Factor Productivity Differentials in Urban Manufacturing," *Journal of Urban Economics*, vol. 28, pp. 103–23.

Norton, R. D., 1979, *City Life-Cycles and American Urban Policy*. New York: Academic Press.

O'hUallachain, Breandan and M. Satterthwaite, 1992, "Sectoral Growth Patterns at the Metropolitan Level: An Evaluation of Economic Development Incentives," *Journal of Urban Economics*, vol. 31, pp. 25–58.

Porter, Michael, 1990, *The Competitive Advantage of Nations*. New York: Free Press.

Romer, Paul, 1986, "Increasing Returns and Long-Run Growth," *Journal of Political Economy*, vol. 94, pp. 1002–37.

Rosenthal, Stuart, and William Strange, 2003, "Evidence on the Nature and Sources of Agglomeration Economies," in J. Henderson and J. Thisse (eds.), *Handbook of Regional and Urban Economics*, vol. 4. Amsterdam: North Holland.

Schumpeter, Joseph, 1942, *Capitalism, Socialism and Democracy*, 2nd edn. 1947. New York: Harper & Brothers.

Schwartz, Alex, 1992, "Corporate Service Linkages in Large Metropolitan Areas: A Study of New York, Los Angeles, and Chicago," *Urban Affairs Quarterly*, vol. 28, pp. 276–96.

Stanback, Thomas, 2002, *The Transforming Metropolitan Economy*, New Brunswick, NJ: Center for Urban Policy Research, Rutgers University.

Chapter 21

Economic Development Policies for Urban Areas

A. Introduction

It is quite likely that some of you, the readers of this book, one day will be engaged in the formulation, implementation and evaluation of economic development policy at the state and local level. In order to perform this role well, you will need to think about and formulate basic goals, set measurable goals that are consistent with these basic objectives, devise overall economic development strategies and supporting policies, and conduct evaluations of the results. This chapter takes you through this policy process for local economic development in a systematic fashion, and concludes with a discussion of local economic development policy in practice.

B. The Goals of Economic Development Policy

The first task in formulating a policy for economic development is to think well about the goals that the community wishes to pursue. In this section we pause to think about basic goals. The usual statements that are made by state and local public officials boil the goals down to two things – jobs and tax base. There may be nothing wrong with jobs and tax base as goals, but what is the logic that supports them? What about consumption and leisure time as goals? For whom are these jobs being created? What about efficient use of resources, equitable distribution of income, and personal freedom? The discipline of economics provides a coherent framework that can be used to formulate the goals for an economic system.

Throughout the book the goal of policy has been the one derived from the mainstream economist's notion of Pareto optimality. A Pareto-optimal (i.e., efficient) allocation of resources is one in which it is not possible to increase the welfare of one person unless the welfare of another person is reduced. The goal of policy is to move towards a Pareto-optimal allocation of resources by identifying policies that increase the welfare of someone without reducing the welfare of anyone else. In the language of cost–benefit analysis, the value of benefits exceeds the value of the costs, and those upon whom costs are imposed receive compensation or side payments so as to restore them to their original levels of utility. However, in practice often it is not possible to compensate fully those upon whom costs are imposed. If the value of benefits exceed costs, but compensation is not paid to keep everyone at or above their initial levels of utility, then the policy or project in question is said to offer a *potential* Pareto improvement in the allocation of resources. Clearly the use of the potential Pareto improvement criterion by itself can be dangerous; for example, it would signal approval of a project that taxes the poor to provide some large benefit for the rich.

It was pointed out in Chapter 2 that mainstream economists also acknowledge that even an efficient economy can produce a distribution of income that is highly unequal. Society may wish to alter that distribution through a variety of policy measures. Equity in the distribution of the fruits of the economy is a goal that is separate from the goal of Pareto optimality. These are the goals of the mainstream economist – efficient use of resources in the sense of Pareto, and an equitable distribution of income in accordance with the society's notion of equity.

Can these goals be used to formulate policies for economic growth and development? The essence of a policy to promote economic growth and development is that the society must give up something now in order to gain a return later. A condition for Pareto optimality exists in this problem of *intertemporal* (now versus later) choice. To focus merely on Pareto optimality, suppose that the economy consists of just one farmer. (An economy with only one person has no income distribution problems, of course.)

The lonely farmer can allocate his time to working in his field, or he can devote his time to clearing more ground for cultivation. If he clears one acre for cultivation, he can grow more food and fiber next year and in all the succeeding years. It is assumed that each succeeding acre of newly cleared land adds less to output because the farmer has only a limited amount of time to work in any given year; investment is assumed to have a declining marginal product. The time devoted to clearing land subtracts from this year's food and fiber production. The farmer can grow more food and fiber this year by working harder in his field. In this model land is, in effect, unlimited. The farmer's time is the scarce resource that must be allocated between producing for now and investing for the future.

Let us suppose that the farmer can clear an additional unit of land in one week. The farmer gives up ΔQ units of output for use this year, and gains Δq units of output in all future years. Once cleared, the land produces a stream of output forever, so the rate of return in terms of output is $\Delta q / \Delta Q$. This trade-off between current and future output is shown as line qQ in Figure 21.1.

How does the farmer evaluate this trade-off in terms of his own utility? We must assume that the farmer's utility depends upon the quantity of output produced and consumed in the current year and in the future, or

$$U = U(Q,q),$$

where Q is the current output and q is future output. It is assumed that the farmer has indifference curves for current and future output of the usual sort, with a declining marginal rate of substitution of one output for the other, as discussed in the appendix to the book. The decision to spend one more week clearing land means that the farmer must

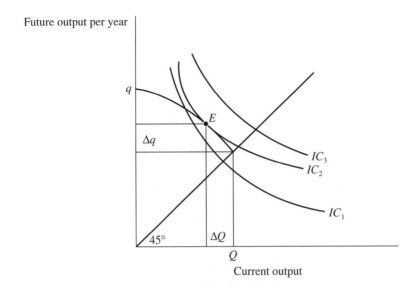

Figure 21.1 Choice of current versus future output

give up utility in the current period. The gain in utility terms is the subsequent increase in utility in future periods. This willingness to give up current output for future output is shown by a set of indifference curves in Figure 21.1. These indifference curves are labeled IC_1, IC_2, and so on.

The farmer chooses point E on his highest possible indifference curve, as shown in Figure 22.1. The condition for efficient use of the farmer's time says that the rate of return to investment ($\Delta q/\Delta Q$) equals the marginal rate of substitution of output in future years to output in the current year.

Suppose that the farmer's utility function is the same in each year, and that all of his remaining years count equally in his mind. In the absence of investment in the clearing of land, his output, consumption, and marginal utility would be the same every year. He would therefore go ahead and clear the next unit of land as long as

$$\Delta q/\Delta Q > 1/n.$$

If the farmer is 30 years old, and his life expectancy is 70 years, then he clears the next unit of land if $\Delta q/\Delta Q$ is greater than or equal to 0.025; i.e., the rate of return to investment is 2.5%. Note that the required rate of return is higher the shorter is the farmer's life expectancy. If he expects to live only one more year, then the condition for investment is $\Delta q/\Delta Q > 1$.

How does this condition for efficient investment translate to a market economy with many people? Now the farmer is not self-sufficient. A crop is produced and sold in the market, and consumer goods are purchased with the income earned. The farmer's utility is a function of income, but the optimality condition is still the same;

$$\Delta y/\Delta Y = \text{MRS of future for current income},$$

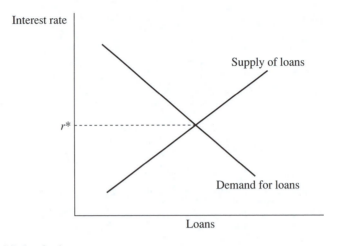

Figure 21.2   Market for loans

where *y* is the permanent gain in income earned by giving up *Y* income in the current year. What makes this model different is that the economy consists of many producers who are facing the same decision. They have the choice of allocating their time to investment or to current production for sale, but they also have the option of producing for sale and lending part of the income to someone else who wishes to make an investment but not suffer the a drop in consumption in the current year. Such a person is willing to pay interest on the loan because the loan enables him or her to consume more in the future and consume no less in the present year. The borrower may be a person with such excellent investment opportunities that attempting to invest in all of them would quickly use up all of current income. Suppose that the loan is one year in duration, but the borrower has the ability to borrow again next year. A market for these loans is formed; borrowers demand loans and lenders supply loans. Figure 21.2 shows the competitive market for loans. The demand for loans is a declining function of the interest rate that must be paid, and the supply of loans is an increasing function of the interest rate that is received. An interest rate on one-year loans is set at r^*.

Now return to the farmer's original problem. The farmer can invest and earn a return of $\Delta y / \Delta Y$, or he can lend money and earn a return of r^*. The optimality condition for the individual farmer is now

$$\Delta y / \Delta Y = r^* = \text{MRS of future for current income.}$$

The return on investment in clearing land (or whatever the real investments are) must be equal to the interest rate that can be earned on loans. If this equality does not hold, then the farmer can reallocate his current income and earn a higher return. The same thing holds for the borrower. This person borrows money as long as the return on the real investment exceeds the interest rate that must be paid on the loan. Under these conditions, all members of the economy equate their marginal rates of substitution to the same r^*. Everyone has the same marginal rate of substitution of current for future utility. The economy is adding to capital, so both capital per person and output per person are also growing.

In this market economy everyone begins with some endowment of resources that can be used to produce income for current consumption or invest in improving those resources for future use. In the end everyone has the same rate of return to investment and the same marginal rate of substitution of current for future utility. It is therefore not possible to make someone better off unless someone else is made worse off. For example, suppose that we ordered person A to invest one unit less and person B to invest one unit more. Remember that we assume that the marginal product of investment declines, so this means that person A must give up more income than person B gains. Person A gives up a return of r^* or more, and person B gains a return of r^* or less. We do not wish to make person A unhappy, so we order person B to compensate A for the loss. But this makes B worse off because the additional return earned on the investment is not enough to compensate A. Our competitive market economy is at a Pareto optimal allocation of resources. An optimal amount of resources available in the current year is being used to invest in the expansion of resources and output in the future. In this economy, there is no need for government to alter that allocation of resources.

What can go wrong with the market allocation? The market outcome can be inefficient for all the usual reasons:

- monopoly and oligopoly;
- public goods;
- externalities (e.g., agglomeration economies); and
- failure of actors to have perfect information about current and future tastes, technologies and prices.

This last item points to an important feature of investment; its returns usually are risky. Risk-averse investors require a higher expected rate of return on risky investment than on investments with certain outcomes. However, what is very risky for the individual investor may not be very risky at all for society. Suppose a new product is developed, and a large number of firms consider entering the market. For the individual firm the prospects may be very risky because some firms may lose out in the competition. However, for the society, the total investment made in the entire industry produces a return with little risk. The individual firm cannot diversify its investment into all of the other firms that are entering the industry. Individual risk-averse firms will require a rate of return that is too high from the point of view of society, so there is justification for subsidizing investment in this case.

Setting Pareto optimality as a goal has yielded an extensive list of reasons to formulate an economic growth and development policy. These reasons include the following:

1 Investment in industries that are monopolized should be increased.
2 Some public goods involve investment, not simply current expenditures for currently consumed goods and services. The public capital stock includes everything from airports to zoos.
3 The presence of externalities creates the usual problems. A good example is the presence of localization economies, where the firms in the urban area do not invest the efficient amount on their own. Another critical example is expenditures on research and development. The patent and copyright systems provide incentives for inventors

and innovators in many areas, but the creation of basic knowledge (for example) usually cannot be patented or copyrighted.

4   The distinction between social risk and the risk faced by an individual firm can mean that investment in something such as a new product should be subsidized.

Next consider the goal of equity. Establishing equity as a goal means that we must decide on a way to add together the utility levels of the members of the society. We need to know whether the society is better off if we reduce person A's utility as we increase person B's utility, so we must assume that these changes can be measured and compared. A general form of a *social welfare function* is

$$W = W(U_1, U_2, \ldots, U_m),$$

where there are m people in the society. This social welfare function will tell us how much, for example, U_1 can be reduced as U_2 is increased in order to leave social welfare constant. One form of the social welfare function is the classical utilitarian or Benthamite welfare function, written as the sum

$$W = U_1 + U_2 + \ldots + U_m.$$

A slightly more general form would attach different weights to the utilities of different people, or

$$W = a_1 U_1 + a_2 U_2 + \ldots + a_m U_m,$$

where the weights $a_1, \ldots, a_m$ are positive numbers. For example, McDonald (1987) proposed that criminals have lower weights and victims of crime have higher weights.

The field of pure economic theory includes an extensive literature on optimal economic growth that has been summarized by Solow (1970). In this literature the goal of the economy is to maximize the stream of consumption per capita over time. This is a pure case of the classical social welfare function in which all members of society count equally. A reallocation of consumption that leaves the per capita amount constant has no impact on social welfare under this assumption. What this social welfare function is really doing is separating efficiency matters from distributional matters. The idea is that we will figure out how to maximize our consumption possibilities, and then later we can worry about the distribution of the goods. Others argue that it is not really possible to in practice to separate efficiency and distribution, so some kind of equity goal must be built in from the beginning. Reasonable people are in disagreement over this issue. A social welfare function that attempts to address this issue was proposed by the moral philosopher John Rawls (1971); what is now known as the Rawlsian social welfare function is

$$W(U_1, U_2, \ldots, U_m) = \min\{U_1, U_2, \ldots, U_m\}.$$

This function says that social welfare is not improved unless the utility of the person with the lowest level of utility is increased. How does Rawls justify this proposed social welfare function? He thinks that this is the social welfare function that the members of society would agree upon in what he calls the "original position." The original position refers to the hypothetical time when people come together to make up the rules for a society without specific knowledge of their positions within that society. They do not know whether they will be rich or poor, intelligent or dull. Rawls thinks that a rational person would not agree "in advance" to a classical social welfare function that would permit society to reduce his or her welfare to enhance the welfare of someone else. Instead, the rational person adopts what is called the "maximin" rule that ranks alternatives by their worst outcomes. This is a rule for pessimists – those who presume that the worst is likely to happen. Few mainstream economists advocate the use of the Rawlsian social welfare function with the maximin rule. In addition, the rational person in Rawls' initial position would set up a society with liberty and equal rights for all and equal opportunities for all to attain positions and offices. Note that, for Rawls, the social contract does not require equal *outcomes*, but rather equal rights, liberties, and opportunities coupled with the maximin rule.

You might be wondering why a chapter on local economic development policy has ventured into moral philosophy. It so happens that one of the most thoughtful practitioners of local economic development, the late Robert Mier, wrote a book entitled *Social Justice and Local Development Policy* (1993) in which a Rawlsian view is adopted. As Commissioner of Economic Development for the City of Chicago in the 1980s, Mier tried to be consistent in favoring policies and processes for policy formulation that tended to increase the welfare of those with the least. As you can imagine, it was not easy to stick to this principle. His book recounts his experiences as a public official in the administration of Mayor Harold Washington of Chicago.

Mainstream economics offers two goals: Pareto optimality (efficiency) in resource allocation, and equity. In contrast, conservative economists such as Milton Friedman offer the goals of freedom and liberty, but Friedman also advocates a policy of income redistribution for the reasons discussed in Chapter 2. His proposal for a policy of income redistribution, the negative income tax, is consistent with freedom and liberty for those who receive the transfer payments and those who pay for them. Conservatives naturally take a dim view of policies that interfere with the operation of the market, but they do acknowledge the need for public investments in urban infrastructure and other public goods. Marxists must surely approach local economic development policy with mixed emotions. They wish to see the urban proletariat get organized and eventually overthrow the capitalist class and establish a socialist state. However, when the proletariat gets organized, it may succeed in winning some real concessions from its capitalist masters that, in effect, prevents the revolution from happening. This process is what is known as being "co-opted." Real Marxists worry a great deal about co-optation, but non-Marxist urban community organizers worry about winning real concessions.

C. The Goals of Local Economic Development

The theoretical literature in economics on optimal growth pertains almost exclusively to the national economy. The location of people and economic activity is ignored. Yet it must be stated frankly at the outset that much of local economic development policy is designed to alter the location of certain kinds of economic activity. An urban area can build a nice, modern airport that provides economies of scale and makes a lot of people more efficient, but the people of that urban area are also aiming to attract economic activity that otherwise would be located elsewhere. Local economic development policy inherently has an impact both on efficiency and distribution. What is more, we can expect that policy makers at the local level are really only concerned with the welfare of their constituents, the residents of their area.

A consideration of local economic development policy is also complicated by the fact that there are many actors in the drama, but that probably there is no one in authority who is responsible for designing policies for the urban area as a whole. Large central cities have their economic development officials and programs, and most counties and larger suburban municipalities have economic development programs. States are engaged in economic development programs in a big way as well. With a small number of notable exceptions (e.g. Minneapolis–St. Paul), real metropolitan government does not exist in the United States. Urban areas are economic units, but they do not have a government that just encompasses that unit. In this situation perhaps we look to the states as the makers of economic development policy that can come closest to matching the interests of a large urban area. The state level for making policy also has the advantage that the interests of all people who live in the state are (we hope) being taken into account. State officials would likely think twice about a policy that simply shifts economic activity from one part of the state to another. In any case, the structure of government in the United States is a serious complication that influences local economic development policy. Now let us get down to business. What do state and local officials want from economic development policy, and why do they want it? How do those goals stack up against the general goals of efficiency and equity?

The goal of expanding the tax base has already been discussed extensively in Chapter 13. Local public officials are interested in attracting commercial and industrial property so long as the benefits of the expansion of the tax base are greater than any diminution of the quality of the local environment. The added tax base permits the local government to provide better public services for the residents and/or impose lower taxes or charges or other user fees on local residents. The expansion of the tax base may create benefits for all local residents, rich and poor alike. If the effort to expand the tax base is successful, local officials and legislators (as agents for the local residents) must decide how those benefits shall be used – tax cuts, increased spending on public schools, more police protection, etc. Pursuit of the goal of expanded tax base can largely be considered an effort to redistribute benefits from other communities to one's own. Whether the efficiency of the economy is improved in the process is incidental, and depends upon the specific means that are used to attract the tax base. Specific policies are discussed in the next section. Now consider the goal of expanding employment in the local economy. The pursuit of this goal by an entire urban area can possibly lead to a shift in the demand for labor in the local economy that is large enough to increase wage rates for everyone who works there. However, a general increase in wage rates usually is not the motivating idea. Rather, local officials wish to expand employment opportunities because sizable numbers of local residents are unemployed, underemployed, or not seeking work because they are discouraged about their chances. Unemployment means that the worker is actively seeking work, but is unable to find work at the current wage rate. Unemployment is a serious problem in most large central cities, but underemployment may be an even greater problem. A person who is underemployed is employed, but is working at less than his or her capacity. Some part-time workers wish to work on a full-time basis. Many others work in jobs that do not make full use of their skills and abilities, and get paid less than they might be able to earn if better jobs were available. Lastly, discouraged workers are workers who would be drawn into the labor market if they thought that jobs were available to them. Official data are collected on unemployment and part-time workers, but we do not really know how many people fall into the underemployed and discouraged worker categories. However, it is reasonable to presume that a substantial number of people who earn very low wages are underemployed. These are people who work and cannot lift themselves out of poverty but, if given the chance, are capable of holding better jobs with higher pay.

Local economic development officials must be careful to distinguish short-run economic fluctuations and long-run economic growth and development. The local rates of unemployment and underemployment may be high temporarily because the national economy is in recession. The local economy must rely upon recovery of the national economy to bring local employment up to the level that is consistent with what is regarded as full employment at the national level. At this time macroeconomic policy makers at the Federal Reserve regard national full employment to be an unemployment rate in the range of 5% to 5.5%. A lower level of unemployment is believed to cause an *accelerating* rate of inflation. However, a national unemployment rate of 5% to 5.5% can still mean that some local economies, especially central cities, have serious economic problems and high levels of poverty.

The goal of enhancing employment opportunities for unemployed, underemployed and discouraged workers has merit both on efficiency and equity grounds. Unemployed and underemployed resources are wasted resources. Putting an unemployed or discouraged worker to work adds to society's available output at an opportunity cost that is the value of the worker's "leisure time." An apparent benefit is the reduction in unemployment compensation or welfare payments that were being paid to the unemployed person, but we shall see precisely how to figure the benefits. Suppose that a job is found for the unemployed worker at a wage rate of $6.00 per hour, and that the worker values his or her own leisure time at $2.50 per hour. Assume that the unemployed worker had been receiving $350.00 per month in welfare payments. The worker now earns an income of $960.00 per month (i.e., four weeks). Previously monthly income had been $350.00, and the leisure time that is given up to work was worth $400.00 per month. The worker is now better off by $210.00 per month, and the rest of society is better off by $350.00 per month from the reduction in welfare benefits. The benefits therefore total $560.00 per month. Another way to think of it is that, while unemployed, the worker was producing leisure time that was worth $400.00 per month. Employment at a wage of $6.00 per hour produces output worth $960.00 per month, for a net gain of $560.00. In this case, society chooses to distribute this net gain by reducing the welfare payment to zero. This distributional scheme results in a gain of $210.00 for the worker and $350.00 for the rest of society.

The case of the underemployed worker is essentially the same. Society gives up the value of whatever the underemployed worker had been producing, but gains the value of his or her new output. The new output is assumed to be more valuable than the old output. Assuming the worker is paid the value of the marginal product, the net gain to society accrues entirely to the individual worker.

In addition to the direct employment effect, the increase in employment, output and income may have a multiplier effect on the local economy that will result in putting more unemployed, underemployed or discouraged workers to work. The computation of multiplier benefits is the same as for the direct employment benefits above.

The policies that put unemployed, underemployed, or discouraged workers to work (either directly or through the multiplier effect) also have distributional consequences that most people favor. At least some of the benefits accrue to the worker who is the target of the policy, and it is probable that this person has a low income. The exception would be proposals to make welfare recipients work at wages that are so low that they really experience no gain. This analysis suggests that one criterion for judging proposals to change the welfare system is whether both the welfare recipients and the rest of society benefit from the changes.

The previous section introduced two very different social welfare functions that society might wish to use to evaluate distributional changes. The weighted classical social welfare function adds together the (weighted) utility levels of all members of the society, while the Rawlsian social welfare function evaluates a change on the basis of whether it benefits the person with the lowest level of utility. These two different ways of specifying the goal can lead to very different policies. Even if the weighted classical social welfare function that is used puts heavy weights on the utility levels of those people with low incomes, it is possible that a policy would be chosen that primarily increases the utility levels of higher-income people. This outcome would not be selected with the Rawlsian social welfare function.

Consider a concrete example that is not unlike the choices that economic development officials sometimes must make. Suppose that the city has an amount of money available to subsidize the redevelopment of one of two sites. In this example possible multiplier effects are ignored. One site will be used by the developer of an office building, which will be used by lawyers, accountants, and management consultants. Because of localization economies, the incomes of these professionals will be enhanced somewhat. The office building will also provide some jobs for local unemployed or underemployed janitors, low-level clerks, and some other lower-income people. The other site will be used by a manufacturer in food processing. The manufacturer hires semi-skilled workers who are roughly at the level as the janitor or low-level clerk. An evaluation of these alternatives based on the Rawlsian social welfare function would examine only the benefits experienced by the lower-income workers. Who hires the larger number of lower-income workers – the manufacturer or the firms that occupy the office building? How much are these workers paid? Use of the weighted classical social welfare function would include the benefits to other workers, and to the owners of the firms and real estate properties involved.

D. Local Economic Development: Strategies and Policies

A strategy is a plan for reaching a goal, and policies are the individual actions or elements that support the strategy. Local economic development policy makers have invented alternative methods for defining strategy, and these will be discussed first. We will then turn to an examination of policies.

Strategies for local economic development

Strategies are discussed in various ways, but local economic development officials will most often classify strategies as business attraction, business retention, or local business growth. This can be a useful way to organize one's thoughts; there is a distinct set of activities that is used to support each of these strategies. These three strategies also reflect an evolution in the thinking of many local economic development officials. Serious efforts at local economic development probably began in the 1940s and 1950s with the efforts of southern states and localities to attract manufacturing plants from the older manufacturing areas of the Northeast. Those efforts that were based on publicizing low wages, lack of unions, low taxes, supporting infrastructure, southern hospitality and warm weather, met with considerable success in some places. The idea of business attraction caught on, and many states and local governments copied the southern strategy. However, many of the state and local governments that followed this strategy found little success, or found that businesses were demanding large subsidies. The strategy of business attraction has been given the mildly derogatory term "smokestack chasing" because of these problems.

Beginning in the 1950s and 1960s states and local governments in the industrial Northeast realized that they were losing businesses to the suburbs and to the sunbelt. Large companies were closing their old plants in the older central cities and opening new plants in other locations. Smaller companies that were growing were running out of space and moving out. As Hoover and Vernon (1959) discussed, the New York Metropolitan Region Study of the late 1950s devoted a good deal of attention to this phenomenon. The strategy of business retention was devised to prevent these plant closings if possible. The idea is to discover and address the problems that the company is having with its current site. Is more land needed? Is there a problem with crime and security? Are real estate taxes a problem? The city can help the company find more land, improve police services, and grant a real estate tax break for plant expansion. Perhaps most importantly, the city can show that it cares about the business and wants to keep the lines of communication open. Business retention efforts have met with some success, but often state and local officials found that there was really nothing that they could do to prevent an old plant from closing. Besides, they found that they were responding to emergency situations involving the impending closing of a plant rather than formulating a coherent strategy for the local economy.

After experience with business attraction and retention efforts, state and local officials realized that their most productive strategy might well be to concentrate on the businesses that are actually located in their communities and are not planning to move away. The strategy of local business growth has evolved into a comprehensive economic growth and development strategy that includes assistance for new enterprises, and the policies that are used to support this strategy are discussed below. It is fair to say that states and localities still devote some efforts to business attraction, and that business retention still receives high priority, but the modern program for local economic development is a comprehensive economic growth and development strategy.

There is a second method for classifying economic development strategies that makes the distinction between a sectoral strategy and an area strategy. The idea of a sectoral strategy is to identify the industries, or groups of industries, that can be promoted in order to achieve the goals that have been articulated. For example, employment gains are possible in industries that are subject to localization economies. Also, additional investment is called for in industries that are subject to monopolization or represent low social risk compared to individual risk. Then policies are designed to support the growth of the "target" industries. An area strategy targets a particular geographic area because the residents of that area are in particular need. Then the idea is to design policies that will improve the economic prospects for these residents. The enterprise zone program that exists in most states is a package of policies aimed at particular small areas that are in economic distress. In 1994 the federal government started a program called "Empowerment Zones" to provide federal tax incentives and other benefits for businesses and workers located in six particular areas. Sectoral and area strategies may or may not be complementary. An industry with a high potential for growth may have no interest in locating in an impoverished neighborhood and hiring low-income residents. An area strategy may imply policies aimed at a simple redistribution of existing economic activity, such as commercial and retail development. Firms attracted to such developments will tend to hire some local residents, and will at least enhance the shopping in the area.

Policies for local economic development

We already know from Chapters 19 and 20 that the sources of urban economic growth fall into the following general categories:

- export demand;
- import replacement;
- private capital;
- public capital (infrastructure);
- labor quality;
- technical change;
- entrepreneurship;
- agglomeration economies (static and dynamic); and
- amenities.

Now is a good time to review briefly what we know about each of these sources of growth.

Export demand and import replacement

The models presented in Chapter 19 emphasized export demand as a source of urban growth. The Keynesian models are driven by the quantity of exports, while the two-sector neoclassical models are driven by the price of exports. Either way, exports are important. Furthermore, the economic functions of an urban economy in the larger economy were discussed in Chapter 4. The task of local economic development policy is to identify export sectors that have potential for further growth. This analytical task is discussed below.

The Keynesian models in Chapter 19 also included imports into the urban area. In those models there is a propensity to import that helps to determine both the level of local income and the size of the local income multiplier. In particular, recall that the local income multiplier from Chapter 19 is

$$1/(1 - b + bt + d - dt),$$

where b is the propensity to consume, t the tax rate, and d the propensity to import. Clearly a reduction in the propensity to import will increase the multiplier. The importation of goods and services also plays an important role in the input–output model of a local economy (Chapter 19). In that model the local economy imports inputs into local production processes. Close examination of the input–output model showed that the local multiplier is greater for the sector with the greater "local content" in its output.

The task for local economic development policy then is to identify points where greater use of local inputs is possible. Clearly, this task requires a great deal of data on the use of local and imported inputs by various industries. One reasonably simple method for approaching this task is to concentrate on the local labor content of goods and services. Data on total sales and payments of wages and salaries are generally available by industry for local economies (e.g., in *County Business Patterns*), so this approach is feasible. However, concentration on labor content omits other local inputs (capital, land, intermediate inputs). A complete input–output model is needed to consider all of the possibilities for import substitution for inputs.

Capital

The empirical evidence reviewed in Chapter 19 showed that the growth of capital is instrumental in the growth of both national and local economies. We also know that capital investment fluctuates widely, and sometimes investment has not been allocated to its best use. For example, there was serious over-investment in commercial real estate in the late 1980s and early 1990s and in telecommunications and other high-tech gear in the late 1990s. In addition, both the level and best allocation of public-sector investments are continuing sources of controversy.

The federal government takes the lead in formulating policies designed to increase the overall level of private investment, and federal policies also influence greatly the allocation of private investment to alternative uses (such as commercial real estate versus capital equipment). Decisions about federal tax policy regarding depreciation allowances, capital gains, small-business loan programs, and investment tax credits can have important consequences for local economies. At the same time, the growth of the local economy can depend upon local programs that pertain to private capital. The local real estate tax is an obvious policy handle. Most states and major municipalities also have business loan programs that provide some financing, for example, to newer and smaller businesses. It appears that local economic development officials need to have a more comprehensive view of private capital and its potential to further local economic growth. Decisions regarding investment in public capital are made by all three levels of government: federal, state, and local. A good deal of investment in public capital in urban areas is funded by the federal government. Examples include public transit, airports, highways, sewer lines, and many other important items. At this point sizable investments are needed to maintain the existing capital stock. A review of the issues by the Congressional Budget Office (1998) concluded that the most productive investments are to be found in maintenance of existing facilities, selected highway projects, and airports.

Labor

The growth of the labor force is a primary determinant of the growth of an economy. The primary source of labor force growth for an urban area is in-migration of population, and studies of migration show that a greater in-migration increases the demand for labor and stimulates more in-migration. One can conclude that a local economy with unemployed, underemployed, and discouraged workers should not fear the in-migration of population. Studies by Bartik (1991, 1994) reveal that households at the lower end of the income distribution are the primary beneficiaries of employment growth. These studies are discussed in detail below.

Education and training

The importance of education and training has emerged consistently in studies of the sources of economic growth. Indeed, the recent data show that the returns to higher education have increased in the United States because the real earnings of workers with a high school education or less declined in the 1980s and early 1990s and real earnings of those with college experience have increased sharply. The fraction of the labor force that has graduated from college is increasing, but society still faces the huge task of providing better education and training for the other 70% of the work force that does not graduate from college. It is fair to say that improvements are needed at every level from preschool to junior college and adult job training programs – but especially in the large public school systems in the central cities. The critical importance for cities of education embodied in creative and talented people has been emphasized recently by Richard Florida (2005).

Local governments are the primary providers of education from preschool to junior college, and they are also responsible for providing job training programs that are funded by the federal government. The policy issues in the field of education and training are many and varied and cannot be covered fully in a book on urban economics. Should more education be provided by the private sector through voucher programs? How can high schools, junior colleges, and adult job training programs be connected to employers more effectively? How can elementary and secondary education be improved so that disadvantaged and minority groups in the society are better prepared for the job market? These are issues that will not go away soon, and they are the basic stuff of local economic development policy.

Technical change

Technical change can take the form of new, improved products, better production processes, and diffusion of new technologies to a larger number of producers. Historically, the formulation of policies to enhance technical change has been within the purview of the federal government. The federal government supports a great deal of basic and applied research, is sometimes the main customer for new high-tech products, and provides assistance to small businesses to help with the adoption of new technologies. However, dissatisfaction with the rate of technical change in the 1970s prompted many state and local governments to introduce their own policies designed to improve the rate of technical change. For example, many state and local governments operate technology assistance centers for business. Some states, including Michigan with the auto industry, support research efforts that are connected to one of the state's industries. Recall that the study by O'hUallachain and Satterthwaite (1992) tested for the effects of university R&D parks on local industry growth and found that this variable did contribute to growth in 6 of 37 industries. At this point we have no studies of the cost-effectiveness of these kinds of state and local efforts. (Agricultural states have, of course, for many years funded agricultural research through their state universities.)

Entrepreneurship

The creation of new business ventures requires entrepreneurship, the undertaking of risky business activities. Entrepreneurship calls for the ability to assess market opportunities, and to organize an enterprise that is capable of seizing those opportunities. Entrepreneurship has recently become a part of the curriculum of schools of business administration as well as a field of academic research. Some of the skills needed to assess opportunities and organize a business can be taught, and students now have the opportunity to major (or minor) in the field of entrepreneurship in some MBA programs (and in a few undergraduate programs, too). Entrepreneurs are part of what Florida (2005) calls the creative class.

Many state and local governments have sought to encourage entrepreneurs by providing what are called business incubators. A business incubator is a facility that provides some institutional support for the fledgling business, such as a cheap office or lab space, secretarial assistance, and telecommunications equipment. As the name indicates, the idea is that the business will thrive in the incubator and eventually move out and be on its own. Sometimes business incubators are supported through a university, and the hope is that professors and other researchers associated with the university will transform their scientific and technological discoveries into marketable products. Some business incubators have been quite successful, while others have languished. A great deal of anecdotal information exists, but at this time, there is no comprehensive study that demonstrates the factors involved in creating a successful business incubator.

Amenities

Most local economic development specialists believe that local environment, cultural, public goods, and social amenities are important to the success of a local economy. Amenities are becoming increasingly important because, so the argument goes, many industries have become less tied down by the traditional locations factors of access to raw materials, intermediate inputs, and markets. A high level of "quality of life" in an urban area permits its firms to recruit critical personnel more easily. Recall that this is thought to have been a factor in the success of Silicon Valley. However, we have no solid estimates of the effects of various amenities on local growth. The study of growth in 37 industries by O'hUallachain and Satterthwaite (1992) found that two measures of local amenities, good climate and recreation facilities, had essentially no effect. Would it be worthwhile for an urban area to create a first-rate symphony orchestra? The answer is (in our view) undoubtedly in the affirmative, the growth rate of the local economy might increase.

Table 21.1   Sources of economic growth and examples of growth policies

Sources of growth	Policies
1 Export demand	Export promotion offices, ads, etc.
	Assistance for businesses to enter export markets
	Convention and tourism bureau
	Create new products (see technical change below)
2 Import replacement	General campaign to buy local goods
	Public purchasing to local firms
	Identify imports and target industries
3 Capital (private)	Direct loans (revolving loan funds)
	Industrial revenue bonds
	Venture capital funds
	Loans from public pension funds
	Real estate tax incentives
	Assistance with real estate planning
	Land assembly and sale at low price
4 Capital (public)	Infrastructure replacement, maintenance and development
5 Labor quality	Basic education
	Higher education
	Vocational education
	Job training programs (Job Training Partnership Act)
6 Technical change	
A New products	Support basic R&D
	Public/private industrial research centers
	University research
B New production	Support applied R&D processes
	Public/private industrial labs
C Diffusion of new technology	Business technology assistance centers
7 Entrepreneurship	Entrepreneurship education programs in colleges, etc.
	Small business assistance centers
	Business incubator facilities
8 Amenities	Promotion of local cultural, educational, recreational facilities
	Provision of high-quality basic public services with low taxes
9 Agglomeration economies	
A Urbanization economies	Infrastructure – transportation, etc.
	All of above to promote growth of the urban economy in general
B Localization economies	All of above targeted at particular industries

Agglomeration economies

Chapter 20 is a reasonably comprehensive review of what is known about urban agglomeration economies. In that chapter it was concluded that:

1   Static localization economies (i.e., scale economies for individual industries in an urban area) exist in several industries, but more testing is needed in non-manufacturing sectors.
2   Dynamic localization economies clearly have been quite strong in a few cases, such as in Silicon Valley, and evidence exists of a weaker form of dynamic localization economies in a large number of high-tech and other growth industries.
3   Both static and dynamic urbanization economies have been found to exist in some studies, but the results are not as conclusive as with localization economies.
4   A more competitive local industry tends to grow more rapidly, other things equal.
5   Diversity in the local economy contributes to the growth of particular industries.

A comprehensive strategy for state or local economic development recognizes all of these sources of growth and selects individual policies that clearly have the potential to make a contribution to the basic goals as expressed through an economic development strategy. Numerous policies exist to enhance each of these sources of growth, and several examples for each source of growth are listed in Table 21.1.

The choice of the package of policies depends, of course, on the statement of goals and selection of the economic development strategy. For example, suppose that the basic goal is simply to increase the per capita income of the residents of an urban area, and suppose that the chosen strategy is to support growth without attempting to select target industries or areas. Given this goal and this strategy, the local officials might select these policies:

Growth policies without distributional goals or industry targeting

Export demand	General national/international ad campaign
	Tourism bureau
Import replacement	General ad campaign to buy locally
Capital (private)	Loan programs to which any business may apply
	Real estate tax incentives for new business property
	Land assembly assistance
Capital (public)	Infrastructure replacement, maintenance, and development
Labor quality	Improve basic education
Technical change	Research grant program to which any business or
	university researcher can apply
Entrepreneurship	Entrepreneurship education programs
	Small business assistance centers
	Business incubators
Amenities	Provide good public services with low tax rates
	Promote local culture, education, recreation
Agglomeration economies	Concentrate on urbanization economies

This policy package makes no particular attempt to worry about the distribution of income, and it avoids the selection of target industries. Because it avoids the selection of target industries, there are many policy options listed in Table 21.1 that cannot be included. Only so much can be done to promote exports or replace imports without targeting specific export industries or imports and thereby targeting the export promotion or import substitution campaign. Some types of programs to support the growth of private capital require that particular industries be identified. Loan programs work better if the lending officers can specialize in particular industries, for example. The enhancement of labor quality beyond basic education requires that some choices be made concerning the type of education or training programs to be offered. Programs to increase technical change must normally have an industry or group of industries in mind. Industrial research centers and business technology assistance centers must focus on particular research topics and types of assistance. Entrepreneurship programs can be of a general nature up to a point, but learning how to be an entrepreneur in a sophisticated line of business requires teachers with specialized knowledge. Finally, we have learned that localization economies exist in many lines of business. Programs to exploit possible localization economies require first that the industries be identified. Many local economic development officials think that some industry targeting is necessary in order to make effective use of their limited resources.

An example of a different economic development program is outlined by Mier (1993). Mier was the top economic development official for the City of Chicago during the period of 1983 to 1989. It has already been noted that he advocated a Rawlsian social welfare function for the evaluation of economic development strategies and policies. He opposed programs unless he could see that benefits would accrue to the lower-income and minority residents of Chicago. He also believed strongly that a coherent policy required the identification of target industries, and that policies for those target industries should always emphasize jobs for the needy. He fought against economic development strategies that emphasized downtown office growth in the financial and services sectors on the grounds that suburbanites held most of the jobs and few benefits "trickled down" to the needy. He saw one role of the city's department of economic development as supporting grassroots community organizations across the city that would then exercise some influence over policy decisions. Together with other city officials, he drew up a strategic plan known as "Chicago Works Together." The basic strategy was to promote "balanced growth" (i.e., not just downtown growth) and neighborhood development, to create job opportunities for lower-income Chicagoans, and to provide for greater public participation in the formulation of specific policies. Mier envisioned both sectoral and area development strategies. The policies that were used to pursue this agenda included:

1 local preference in public sector hiring and buying;
2 selection of target industries for support with loan programs, technical assistance centers, export promotion and other programs;
3 neighborhood planning;
4 skilled labor force development related to target industries;
5 job retention efforts, especially in manufacturing;
6 infrastructure investment related to job development;
7 linked development; and
8 planned manufacturing districts.

These last two require some explanation. Under Mier's leadership, the City of Chicago attempted to extract from developers and firms in highly successful areas such as downtown and the O'Hare Airport area promises to create links to the lower-income areas of Chicago in exchange for the city's support. For example, if a developer needs a zoning change and some infrastructure improvements for a downtown site, the city bargains for goals in hiring city residents or requires that the developer also develop another site in one of the target neighborhoods. Planned manufacturing districts are designed to slow down the conversion of land zoned for industry to commercial or residential use. Under ordinary circumstances the owner of property zoned for industry can apply for a change in zoning on the basis of a plan for redevelopment to another use, and that application normally will be approved by the zoning board. Mier believed that this process caused what he called industrial displacement, which resulted in a loss of manufacturing jobs in the city. The worst-case scenario is one in which a factory that employs city residents at good pay is displaced by condominiums and shopping areas for high-income people who work downtown. Under the planned manufacturing district ordinance industrial properties in such a designated district can be converted to other uses only if they are first marketed for manufacturing use in good faith and if the new uses do not affect industry negatively.

Under Mier's guidance, target industries were selected based on their historic locations in Chicago's industrial areas outside of downtown and on the fact that they hire semi-skilled workers at reasonably good pay. Task forces were set up to study the prospects for job growth in the steel and apparel industries. Once it had been possible for a semi-skilled worker to find a job easily in these and other manufacturing industries in Chicago. Indeed, such job prospects were a big reason for the massive migration of black workers from the South in the 1940s, 1950s, and 1960s. Industrial employment had been a way out of poverty for many, but that avenue had largely been closed by the massive loss of manufacturing jobs in the city. Manufacturing employment in the city of Chicago had dropped almost continuously from 668,000 in 1947 to 277,000 in 1982. Mier's task forces were set up to find out what could be done in the steel and apparel industries, two large industries that had been especially hard hit by employment declines. The task forces concluded that there are some smaller sub-sectors in both industries that represent opportunities for employment growth.

This section has outlined two very different economic development strategies. One attempts to promote economic growth in general and avoids the targeting of industries. The other promotes economic growth that can have obvious tangible benefits for lower-income households in a large central city, and attempts to target both industries and areas accordingly. How effective are these (and other) strategies? The matter of evaluation of both strategy and individual policies is taken up later in this chapter.

E. The Selection of Target Industries

Many, if not most, states and large municipalities with economic development programs have attempted to focus their efforts through the selection of target industries. It is difficult to resist the temptation to select target industries because, once selected, those industries give guidance to decisions about policy – from selection of trade journals for ad campaigns to worker training programs to the focus of business assistance centers. But what is the theory behind the selection of target industries? After all, some have questioned the usefulness of target industries because forecasts for individual industries for an urban area are subject to large errors. Furthermore, focusing attention on a short list of industries may cause policy makers to neglect the more basic conditions for general economic growth and development. Policy makers must be sensitive to these problems. With these points made, it still may be that the industries that represent the economic future of the urban area can be identified and targeted. This section looks at the question of industry targeting for two urban areas, Philadelphia and Des Moines.

This chapter and previous discussions in this book have supplied the theoretical argument for target industries. Target industries are industries for which the level of investment supplied by the private market falls short of the efficient level. As we have seen, the private market fails to be efficient in the presence of monopoly, public goods, externalities, and information gaps. We have seen that localization economies are an important category of externalities in the context of local economic development. Also, while this topic is in need of research, a difference between individual risk and social risk can exist for some types of investments. Individual firms may be applying a discount rate to the future returns of some investments that is too high from society's point of view.

Philadelphia

One well-known study of target industries for the Philadelphia urban area by Stull and Madden (1990) suggests that the objective of economic development policies should be to eliminate impediments to and promote the growth of the industries that are well suited to the Philadelphia environment. This statement of objectives is somewhat vague because it mentions two types of target industries: (1) industries that are growing slowly because of some local constraints and falling short of their potential, and (2) industries that are growing rapidly that might be induced to grow even more rapidly. In the end Stull and Madden (1990) opt for the latter group of industries because it is difficult to identify industries that are growing slowly simply because of some local impediment (as opposed to slow growth for fundamental reasons). Their method then is to identify industries or sectors that have shown rapid growth in recent years and have additional potential for growth. They are sensitive to the "product cycle" model, which implies that an industry with rapid growth in the past may pass into a phase of slow growth. Such industries should be avoided as targets because probably they will not respond to policy initiatives. A more detailed examination of the Stull–Madden (1990) study is useful.

The book begins with an examination of manufacturing in the Philadelphia urban area by Richard Bernstein (1990). An industry is defined by the three-digit SIC codes. The list of potential target industries is created using a single criterion; employment in the industry grew from 1978 to 1986. Out of 136 manufacturing industries, 31 qualified on this criterion. Twelve of the industries were eliminated because they are in printing and publishing or construction materials, two sectors that produced almost entirely for the local market. Three more can be eliminated because they employed fewer than 1,000 workers in 1986. Eight industries are members of the high-technology group, and include:

- pharmaceuticals;
- ordnance;
- computers;
- communications equipment;
- electronic components;
- aircraft and parts;
- optical instruments; and
- medical instruments.

Some of these industries may be good candidates for being target industries, although Stull and Madden (1990) think that the growth of all except pharmaceuticals and medical instruments was tied to federal defense spending. They rightly conclude that reliance on federal defense spending can no longer serve as a basis for local economic growth.

The remaining eight industries include five in metal products and machinery; hand tools, structural metal products, refrigeration machinery, miscellaneous non-electrical machinery, and railroad equipment. The other three are miscellaneous food products, miscellaneous textile products, and miscellaneous plastic products. These eight, plus pharmaceuticals and medical instruments, represent a list of potential target manufacturing industries. The ten industries employed 55,400 workers in the Philadelphia urban area in 1986, so this group of industries clearly is large enough to matter a great deal to the Philadelphia economy. Stull and Madden (1990) conclude that attention should focus on the industries in this group that are characterized by small establishments and customized products or rapid changes in technology. They do not say it, but these criteria may also be reasonable proxies for localization economies. However, it is fair to say that Stull and Madden (1990) think that manufacturing generally represents very limited opportunities for future growth in Philadelphia. They look elsewhere for sources of substantial growth.

The large producer services sector appears to be a good place to look for target industries. Stull and Madden (1990) include finance, insurance and real estate (FIRE), business services, legal services and other professional services, and administrative and auxiliary establishments in this sector. They argue that these industries may represent good opportunities because their services sometimes are exported outside the urban area, the jobs usually offer good pay, and a solid producer services sector can attract firms in other industries. Their analytical procedure is to compare the industries in the producer services sector in Philadelphia with their counterparts in the other 19 largest urban areas in the US. Using location quotient analysis, they find that Philadelphia is somewhat less concentrated in this sector than are the other urban areas, but that insurance and legal services are clearly sources of strength and growth. They also find that Philadelphia appears to be importing an unusually large amount of its computer programming and data processing services, so a program of import replacement might be pursued in this industry. Otherwise, they conclude the producer services in the Philadelphia urban area are sufficiently strong and comprehensive to represent attractions for firms that require these services.

Another critical service sector is health care. Erwin Blackstone and Kathleen Carr-Possai (1990) examined this sector in Philadelphia and found it to be a strong export sector. Leading medical schools and teaching hospitals make Philadelphia one of the nation's leading centers of medical education, research, and training. Philadelphia ranks second among the 20 largest urban areas in the fraction of total employment engaged in health care. Blackstone and Carr-Possai point out that some hospitals will close or be consolidated as the provision of health services shifts to other entities, and Philadelphia's concentration in hospitals makes it especially vulnerable to this change in the organization of medical practice. Nevertheless, they argue that a good economic development strategy would include the continued strengthening of Philadelphia's health education sector.

The final sector that was examined in the Stull–Madden volume (1990) is research and development. Stull and Madden wish to call attention to the idea that Philadelphia's opportunities for growth may be in activities that are in the early stages of the product cycle. A special survey was conducted that revealed that Philadelphia has concentration of R&D activity in the medical/biology field, aerospace, chemicals, and electronics/computers. The R&D in the medical/biology field is particularly extensive and includes activity in pharmaceuticals, biology/biotechnology, medical research, and medicine. This R&D activity fits in both with the pharmaceutical and medical instruments industries and the medical education and training sector. Stull and Madden (1990) conclude that the best target sector for Philadelphia is its vast and diverse health care complex, which includes related manufacturing, R&D and education and training providers. Given that the demand for more and better health care shows no signs of slowing down, why not?

Des Moines

The economy of Des Moines was studied in some detail in Chapter 4 using the idea of industry clusters. In that examination it was found that manufacturing employment in Des Moines had declined over the 1980–7 period by 13.1%, compared to a national decline of 10.2%. This kind of lackluster performance suggested that manufacturing does not represent a very good opportunity for growth in the Des Moines economy. That judgment is too hasty because there may be individual manufacturing industries, or clusters of industries, in Des Moines that benefit for localization economies. We have already seen in Chapter 20 that some individual manufacturing industries do indeed display localization economies. The question is whether such industries can be identified in Des Moines. The method of shift–share analysis was proposed in Chapter 20 as a device that might be useful for the identification of industries that may possess localization economies. That method is used here to examine the manufacturing sector in Des Moines.

The study of manufacturing in Des Moines is shown in Table 21.2. The table includes industries that had at least 500 employees in either 1980 or 1987. The employment level for each industry in Des Moines in 1987 is shown, along with the percentage changes in employment and pay per employee in the industry for both Des Moines and the US as a whole. For example, employment in the food products industry in Des Moines in 1987 was 3,580. Employment in the industry in Des Moines had grown by 21.1% from 1980 to 1987 compared to a decline of 6.1% in the nation. Pay per employee in nominal terms (not corrected for inflation) increased by 25.8% in Des Moines and 37.8% in the nation over this same period. Table 21.2 shows that Des Moines has two other large manufacturing industries – printing and publishing and non-electrical machinery. Four of the nine industries in Des Moines lost more than 30% of their employment over the 1980–7 period, but three others show substantial employment gains. The manufacturing sector in

Table 21.2   Shift–share analysis of manufacturing employment in Des Moines: 1980–1987

Industry	Employment in 1987 in DM	Employment change (%) 1980–7		Wage change (%) 1980–7		Competitive position	
		DM	US	DM	US	Basic	adj.
Food products	3,580	21.1	−6.1	25.8	37.8	29.9	21.4
Paper products	987	3.4	−4.4	71.3	53.0	10.5	23.3
Printing & publish.	6,661	3.8	19.1	48.7	50.0	−12.6	−13.5
Chemicals	477	−30.4	−12.0	45.5	53.3	−15.7	−21.2
Stone, clay, & glass	371	−55.0	−14.1	61.7	48.5	−38.2	−29.0
Fabricated metals	872	−52.9	−13.7	63.1	48.8	−36.5	−26.5
Machinery, nonelec.	3,595	−32.9	−23.4	49.5	50.0	−6.8	−7.1
Transp. equip.	948	47.2	−1.7	65.9	54.3	51.6	59.7
Misc. manuf.	785	38.9	−11.4	29.6	51.6	53.0	37.6

Source: County Business Patterns 1982 and 1989

Des Moines represents what might be called a "mixed bag," so it is worthwhile to proceed with some further analysis.

The first technique is to compute the competitive position as defined in Chapter 20, or

$$CP = (\delta e_i/e_i) - (\delta US_i/US_i) + (\delta US/US - \delta E/E),$$

where e_i is employment in industry i in the local economy, US_i is employment in the same industry in the US, and US and E are total employment in the US and the local economy. This equation says that the competitive position for an industry is the difference between the growth rate of the industry in the local economy and in the reference economy (the nation) *plus* the adjustment for the extent to which the reference economy as a whole grew faster than the local economy. In this case employment in the nation grew by 14.2% from 1980 to 1987 and employment in Des Moines grew by 11.5%, so the adjustment is +2.7%. The competitive positions so defined are shown in Table 21.2 under the heading "Competitive position – basic." Three manufacturing industries in Des Moines had strongly positive competitive positions; these were food products, transportation equipment, and miscellaneous manufacturing. The food products industry has a sizable presence in Des Moines, and is discussed further below. The other two industries each had fewer than 1,000 employees in 1987, so the large percentage increases in employment from 1980 to 1987 were not very large in absolute terms. Industries that are so small do not make good target industries, but they should be watched to see if the growth continues.

Two other industries in Des Moines, paper products and printing and publishing, experienced modest employment growth during the 1980–7 period. Paper products are a small industry in Des Moines, but it shows a positive competitive position and deserves to be watched for further developments. Printing and publishing is the largest manufacturing industry in Des Moines, but its modest employment growth of 3.8% over the period compares unfavorably with the national growth of 19.1%. The competitive position in printing and publishing is −12.6% over these seven years. The other three industries listed in Table 21.2 have a small presence in Des Moines and strongly negative competitive positions.

This brief look at manufacturing in Des Moines has identified one possible target industry – food products. You may recall from Chapter 3 that food products are one of the industries that exhibited static localization economies in the Henderson (1986) study. In other words, there are economies of scale at the industry level in an urban area. It is not known whether there are dynamic agglomeration economies associated with this industry. More insight can be gained from a closer look at the industry in Des Moines. The total manufacturing employment in Des Moines in 1987 of 3,580 consisted of 1,150 workers in meat products, 571 in dairy products (down from 701 in 1980), and the rest scattered across the remaining categories of food products. Furthermore, County Business Patterns shows that Des Moines has one major meatpacking plant that experienced a substantial increase in employment from 1980 to 1987. We do not know exactly how large was the employment increase in this plant, but we do know that it went from size class of 250–499 workers to 500–999 over the seven years. The employment increase in food products in Des Moines was 624 over this period, so it is quite possible that much of the increase in the industry took place in this one plant. No doubt a knowledgeable resident of Des Moines can tell us the identity of this plant. Further investigation is needed to determine whether the growth in employment in meatpacking was the result of localization economies or simply scale economies at the plant level. If it was the latter, then there is no particular justification for making the industry the target of public economic development efforts.

Table 21.2 contains one final column that makes use of the data on pay per employee that is provided in County Business Patterns. Recall from Chapter 20 that employment growth in an industry can be influenced by the growth of the wage rate. The study by McDonald (1992), for example, found that the elasticity of demand for labor in manufacturing with respect to the wage rate was −0.7. We would expect that employment growth in an industry would be lower the greater is the increase in the wage rate, but the shift–share computations introduced so far fail to take this factor into account. Shift-share analysis measures the performance of an industry in the local economy compared to the nation, so a correction is needed for the change in the local wage rate compared to the national average wage rate in the industry. The comparative wage change figures are shown in Table 21.2. For example, the wage in food products in Des Moines increased by 25.8% over the 1980–7 period, and the national average wage change in the industry was 37.8%. These are nominal wage changes (not corrected for inflation). The consumer price index increased by 37.9% over this period, so the real wage did not change at the national level and dropped by 12.1% in Des Moines. We therefore expect that employment would have increased more in Des Moines simply because of the drop in the wage rate relative to the national wage. If we apply an elasticity of demand for labor of −0.7, then employment in the industry in Des Moines should have increased by 8.5% more than if its wage had not dropped relative to the national wage. We therefore adjust the Des Moines competitive position *down* by 8.5% to reflect the employment growth that occurred because of the local wage change relative to the nation. The final column in Table 21.2 shows these adjusted competitive positions for the manufacturing industries in Des Moines.

These adjustments for the wage effect do not change dramatically how we evaluate these industries, but note the paper products industry. In this industry the wage rate increased by 71.3% in Des Moines compared to a 53% increase in the nation. This 18.3% increase in the wage relative to the nation means that this industry had more strength in Des Moines that we previously had thought. An adjustment of +12.8 (18.3 × 0.7) is made to the competitive position.

This section has examined the problem of the selection of target industries through the use of Philadelphia and Des Moines as examples. Target industry selection is obviously a risky business, but careful study of the recent trends in the local economy should cut down on the risk.

F. Evaluation of Economic Development Strategies and Policies

Now we come to the most difficult part of the topic of local economic development – evaluation. As economists we seek to discover the results produced by economic development strategies and policies that would not have occurred otherwise. It is fair to say that experimentation with policies has outstripped efforts at evaluation. It is also true that state and local officials often have shown a disinterest in evaluation research. Indeed, some officials who are responsible for operating particular programs are interested largely in self-serving evaluation efforts. More competent and unbiased evaluation efforts are needed. The improvement of evaluation efforts is an important issue that the readers of this book will face in their careers. This section is a basic introduction to evaluation research in the context of local economic development policy.

Evaluation of strategy and policies must begin with the goals that are being pursued. A misunderstanding about goals leads to evaluation that is not on target. For example, many critics of local economic development policies point out that the result is to shift the location of some economic activity. This result may have been the goal of policy, so the critics are complaining about the goal rather than the policies themselves. This chapter began with a lengthy discussion of the basic goals of economic policy – to improve efficiency and to create a more equitable distribution of income. These goals are adopted here as the standards against which to judge local economic development efforts. All strategies and their attendant policies will affect both efficiency and equity, so evaluation work should try to measure both. This chapter also discussed the more immediate goals of increasing the local tax base and the local employment level. At the very least, evaluation research should be directed at the measurement of these variables.

The evaluation researcher can contemplate making an evaluation of the overall economic development strategy and/or the individual policies that make up the implementation of that strategy. As a practical matter it is usually, but not always, easier to evaluate the impacts of a particular policy rather than to determine the total effects of an overall strategy. Indeed, one approach to the evaluation of an overall strategy is to perform an evaluation of each policy and sum the effects. This approach has the advantage that it will tell us (we hope) which policy elements of the strategy had the largest effects on the desired outcomes. This information can then be used to allocate more effectively the resources available for economic development. Let us turn to the evaluation of individual economic development policies.

Economists use two basic methods for policy evaluation: they estimate economic models using non-experimental data, and they use experimental (or "quasi-experimental") data. Both of these methods were introduced in the discussion of housing policy. The estimation of an economic model using non-experimental data means that the data that are used have been generated by the normal operation of the economy. For example, data gathered by the Federal Housing Administration were used to estimate the price and income elasticities of demand for housing. These estimated elasticities can then be used to perform an economic evaluation of housing policies. Alternatively, the US Department of Housing and Urban Development ran two experiments in which low-income households were given housing allowances, and other households were members of the "control" group. Data were gathered during the experiments to determine the effects of the policy.

Both techniques can be used to evaluate local economic development policies, but the experimental method is used only rarely. The use of non-experimental data has already been illustrated in the study by O'hUallachain and Satterthwaite (1992) that was discussed in Chapter 20. They tested for the effects of policies such as enterprise zones, research parks, and industrial revenue bond programs on employment growth in growth industries. They found that both enterprise zone programs and research parks had positive effects on employment growth in manufacturing as a whole. The research strategy is to gather data on a large number of local economies, and to measure and test for the statistical significance of the many factors that may contribute to growth in employment and tax base. In the experimental method individual firms or workers are selected for participation in a program or to be members of the control group, and data on both groups are collected for several years of participation in the program.

A survey of evaluation research on local economic development policies up through 1990 has been provided by Timothy Bartik in his 1991 book *Who Benefits from State and Local Economic Development Policies?* This book is an excellent source of information on this topic, and it would make a good required text for a course on economic development policy. Tax incentives are the local policies that have been studied most extensively. Newman and Sullivan (1988) have also done a survey of research on this topic. The surveys of research on tax effects find that local taxes have strong effects within an urban area, but that the effects are much weaker across urban areas. Bartik (1991, p. 40) found that 7 out of 10 studies of intra-urban growth found statistically significant local tax effects. The average size of the local tax effect is an elasticity of -1.92; i.e., if a small suburban jurisdiction reduces its local real estate tax on business by 10%, in the long run business activity will increase by an average of 19%. Bartik's (1991) survey of inter-area studies shows that 24 out of 30 found a statistically significant tax effect, controlling for the amount of public services. The average size of these effects is an elasticity of -0.33, so a state or urban area that cuts its taxes on business by 10% (holding public services constant) can expect an increase of about 3% in business activity. Capital and labor resources are highly mobile within an urban area but much less mobile across states or urban areas, so these empirical findings make sense.

Bartik (1991) also surveyed research on a variety of other economic development programs. Six of the studies surveyed were of state enterprise zones, a program that is of recent vintage. The first proposal for enterprise zones was made in 1978 by Sir Geoffrey

Howe, a Conservative member of the British House of Commons who later served as a minister in the government of Prime Minister Margaret Thatcher. Stuart Butler, a researcher with the Heritage Foundation, introduced the idea in the US in 1979. Jack Kemp, the former conservative Republican congressman and former Secretary of Housing and Urban Development, immediately became a strong advocate for enterprise zone programs. The basic idea of an enterprise zone program is to provide incentives in the form of tax breaks and regulatory relief to businesses located in depressed parts of urban areas. Kemp and his congressional colleagues did not succeed in creating a federal program in the 1980s, although a federal program called "Empowerment Zones" was created in 1994. However, the enterprise zone idea was received enthusiastically by many state and local public officials, and an enterprise zone program in some form was begun in 37 states in the 1980s.

The enterprise zone programs in the states differ widely. Some states have a small number of zones, and others have many zones. As Erickson (1992) discusses, the criteria for the designation of enterprise zones can be generous or stringent, and are usually based on unemployment and/or poverty. Economic development incentives in enterprise zone programs fall into three general categories; investment incentives (e.g., tax rate reductions or tax credits), labor incentives (e.g., tax credits for jobs created, job training tax credits, incentives for hiring zone residents), and financing programs (e.g., investment fund linked to zone location). Indeed, some state enterprise zone programs approximate a comprehensive economic development strategy for a small, depressed area within a larger urban area.

Bartik (1991) and James (1991) conducted careful surveys of the evaluation research on state enterprise zone programs. They found that the evaluations have not been convincing one way or another because the programs were not designed from the beginning for effective evaluation and because little high-quality research has been done. A few studies have used the "before and after" method, and others have used surveys of zone businesses. Bartik (1991) and James (1991) concluded that the best feasible evaluation method would make use of "comparison areas" to determine the impacts of an enterprise zone program. The "before and after" method, which looks for discontinuities in economic trends, may attribute an effect to the enterprise zone program when in fact some other broader economic force is at work. Surveys of zone businesses, which are usually conducted after a program has been in operation, fail to gather information from businesses that failed or moved away in the interim. Also, these surveys usually do not include businesses that are *not* located in enterprise zones.

The first study of a state enterprise zone program that compared enterprise zones with comparable areas that did not participate in the program was conducted for the Illinois program by McDonald (1993). The use of regression analysis controlled for other factors that influence economic growth in both types of areas. The Illinois enterprise zone program includes a sales tax exemption on building supplies, a state income tax credit for investment in machinery, equipment or buildings, and a local property tax abatement. The program also includes a tax credit for each job created in a zone if certified dislocated or disadvantaged workers are hired to fill them, and a loan program was set up for zone businesses. Clearly the program promotes investment in buildings. As one local enterprise zone administrator put it, "The enterprise zone program is mainly a bricks and mortar program."

What were the goals of the Illinois enterprise zone program? The Illinois law that created the program states that the goal is to stimulate business growth and retention in depressed areas of the state. The original statement of the program's goals and regulations from the state agency responsible for implementing the program included the goal of causing some investment to be made in enterprise zones rather than elsewhere in the state. Thus, the program had, as one of its original objectives, the stimulation of economic activity in depressed areas of Illinois even if that would have meant a reduction in economic growth in other areas of the state. Enterprise zones were designated in all of the largest urban areas in the state, including 12 enterprise zones in Cook County (the central county in the Chicago urban area).

The research performed by McDonald (1993) showed that the enterprise zone program had no statistically significant effect on total employment in the zones, but that the program stimulated growth in the distribution sector (wholesale trade and transportation) over the period from 1983 to 1987 by about 25% beyond what it would have been. The evidence strongly suggests that the enterprise zones attracted economic activity in this sector that they would not otherwise have attracted in the absence of the program. Two other findings are worth noting. First, the enterprise zone program tended to be targeted at depressed areas. Therefore, a failure to control for past employment growth performance (including decline) may lead to the incorrect impression that the enterprise zone program had a negative impact on employment growth. This is a case of a "treatment" being given to a non-random group of subjects. One must take special care in evaluating programs with this characteristic. Second, the distribution sector was characterized by fairly rapid growth during the period under study and by sizable demands for investment in real estate capital. The enterprise zone incentives appear to be targeted at industries with these characteristics. The program really does nothing for an industry that is experiencing declining demand for its products. It is possible that different types of industries respond to different kinds of incentives.

Studies of enterprise zone programs in other states have been conducted. O'Keefe (2004) provides a survey of recent studies and a careful examination of the California program. Her survey of studies shows mixed results; some studies show positive effects on employment in the zone and some show no effect. O'Keefe's study of California in the 1990s shows that employment growth in the enterprise zones was about 3% greater per year compared to similar areas that were not part of the program. This larger employment growth continued for the first six years of the program, but it did not persist in later years.

The results of the McDonald (1993) study of the Illinois enterprise zone program suggested some more general implications for policy. First of all, the focus of the enterprise zone program on depressed areas of the state has been lost because there are now 88 designated zones in the state. The program will be less successful at stimulating investment and employment growth in depressed areas if other areas of the state also contain enterprise zones. Secondly, the emphasis on subsidizing capital investment should be reconsidered. The results of the study suggest that the subsidies in the program are successful at stimulating growth in enterprise zones in a growth sector that is capital intensive – the distribution sector. Other types of incentives are needed to attract other sectors to enterprise zones. For example, larger wage subsidies and job training programs might be needed if the objective of the program is to stimulate more employment in enterprise zones. Finally, the State of Illinois did not keep records concerning the cost of the enterprise zone program. It was not possible to retrieve data on the sales tax exemptions and the state income tax deductions and credits earned by the participating firms. The lack of this information means that the benefits of the program could not be compared to the costs. It also means that the responses of the firms could not be estimated as a function of the magnitudes of the incentives in the program.

The studies surveyed by Bartik (1991) also include two studies of incentive to attract foreign investment and one study of export promotion programs. Both policies were found to be effective. The study by Coughlin and Cartwright (1987) of state manufacturing exports found that $1 of added state spending on export promotion increased exports by $432! Bartik (1991) examined the studies of public services and public infrastructure, and found that education expenditures and infrastructure had positive effects more often than other forms of public spending. More research on these and other local economic development policies is needed, and it is likely that this area of research will be an active one for some years to come. One clear need is for greater use of the experimental method in the evaluation of economic development policies.

Bartik's (1991) examination of the research on local economic development policies convinced him that those policies probably do have positive effects on employment. The next question he asked was how that employment growth was of benefit to local residents. Bartik's book contains extensive empirical research on the various impacts of employment growth in urban areas over the 1979–86 period. An increase in employment in an urban area will reduce unemployment and increase labor force participation of the current residents, but most of the new jobs will be taken by migrants to the urban area. Bartik's summary (1991, p. 95) is that, in the long run, 6% to 7% of new jobs will be filled by unemployed residents, 16% will go to residents who enter the labor force, and migrants will take 77% to 78% of the new jobs. These results are very important because they say that a one-time increase in employment will reduce unemployment and increase labor force participation permanently. Furthermore, a 1% permanent increase in employment increases average earnings by 0.4%, but real wages per hour for a given occupation do not increase. The one-time increase in employment also permits some residents to move to better-paying occupations. This effect is strongest for black, less-educated and younger workers. What is more, Bartik's evidence is that the effects of an employment increase are highly progressive; the lowest-income people have the highest percentage gains in earnings. The long-run earnings gains from a 1% increase in employment by quintile found by Bartik (1991, p. 173) are:

Quintile	% gain in earnings
1	4.64
2	0.66
3	0.42
4	0.32
5	0.21
Average	0.41

Clearly Bartik's findings come close to saying that about the best thing that can be done for poor people is to increase overall employment in the urban area. He makes no distinction between the different sources of employment growth; he has estimated the effects of the actual employment growth in the urban areas included in the study over the period of 1979 to 1986. Most of that actual employment growth was, of course, in the service sector. Bartik (1991) takes the view that the competition among localities in economic development policies is not necessarily wasted effort. If localities with the economies that are the most depressed are also the most active in economic development policy, then economic activity will tend to shift towards those areas. This result is both efficient and equitable because underemployed people are being put to work, and the poorest workers reap the largest benefits.

Bartik (1994) has completed another study that demonstrates the same idea. In this study job growth from 1979 to 1988 in an urban area increased income for the poorest 20% of the households by more than the average household. A 1% increase in employment over this decade increased labor income for the lowest 20% of households by 2.6%, while the gains for other quintiles were (in order, from low to high) 1.4%, 1.2%, 0.6%, and 0.5%. Bartik (1994) concluded that policies to stimulate job growth in an urban area are progressive as long as the public cost per job created is not too high and provided that those costs are financed by taxes (e.g., income or sales tax) rather than by cuts in welfare spending.

We reach the end of this section with the finding that local economic development policy can be both efficient and equitable, provided that those policies result in employment gains in the more economically depressed areas. This is an important finding, and it is why this book has devoted so much material to the topic of urban economic growth and development. However, at this time we do not know much about the cost side of these policies in relation to benefits.

G. Local Economic Development Policy in Practice

Most of this chapter has been written as if it is possible to have a coherent economic development strategy for an entire urban area. In section C it was noted briefly that for the most part, economic development policy is carried out by local governments and by state governments. In this section we take a look at policy at both levels, starting with local government.

Local governments and economic development

In most major urban areas in the United States there is no local government that encompasses all, or even most, of the urban area. There are a few exceptions, such as Indianapolis, Minneapolis–St. Paul, and Houston, but these are indeed exceptions. The other basic fact is that local governments still depend heavily on the local real estate tax (and on local sales tax revenue and local charges and fees). The result is that local governments within an urban area have an incentive to compete against one another for commercial and industrial development rather than to engage in policies to increase growth of the entire urban area.

Table 21.3   Local economic development game

	Edge County		
	Do nothing	*Draw firms from central*	*Create new jobs*
Central County			
Do nothing	200[a]	300	250
	500	400	500
Draw firms from edge	100	200	150
	600	500	600
Create new jobs	200	300	250
	550	450	550

[a] The top number is jobs in Edge County; the bottom number is jobs in Central County.

Consider a numerical example in a form similar to the "prisoner's dilemma" game. Suppose that an urban area has two counties, Central and Edge, and each county can pursue three kinds of economic development strategies: (1) do nothing, (2) try to draw firms away from the other county (using tax breaks, etc.), and (3) engage in efforts to assist existing firms in the county to grow and to attract new businesses. Table 21.3 shows the outcomes in terms of the number of jobs in each county for the nine possible combinations of strategies. If both counties do nothing, Central has 500 jobs and Edge has 200 jobs. If the counties only try to draw firms away from each other, their efforts cancel out (and are wasted). If only one county tries to draw firms away from the other, 100 jobs will move. If only one county, instead, engages in efforts to assist existing firms to grow and to attract new businesses, 50 new jobs will be created. It is more difficult to have success with these creative efforts than it is simply to draw firms away from the adjacent county. The rest of Table 21.3 is filled in using these assumptions.

Now we are ready to play the game of local economic development. For example, if Edge engages in efforts to attract business from Central while Central works to create new jobs, the net result is 300 jobs (200 + 100) in Edge and 450 jobs (500 − 100 + 50) in Central. The message from this example is simple; the urban area has more total jobs (250 + 550) if both counties work to create new jobs. But each county has a stronger incentive to go after the jobs in its sister county because that strategy leads to more jobs in that county regardless of what strategy is followed by the other county. This is the dilemma of the game of local economic development. What can be done about this inherent problem? Leaders are needed who can see the possibilities for the urban area as a whole, and incentives are needed for local policies to be cooperative rather than competitive.

The problem described above is particularly acute when the suburban jurisdictions are playing the game to attract jobs away from the central city. Central cities are the home of most of society's social and economic problems: poverty, crime, fiscal difficulties, and many others. These problems are discussed at length in Part IV of the book, but for now it is worth noting that efforts of the suburbs to attract jobs from the central city will tend to make those problems worse. As it is, suburbs have an incentive to do things that may tend to make central city problems worse.

What do central cities do in response to the decline in their job base? New York City is a good example of a central city that is an active player of the game. According to the *New York Times* (July 5, 1995), during the period January 1994 to July 1995 the city approved 11 deals that gave $348 million in sales tax breaks to various companies. New York City has also expanded its programs for low-interest financing, energy subsidies, property tax breaks, and other benefits. The city began its aggressive program in the early 1980s in response to the exodus of firms to New Jersey and Connecticut. Some major firms, including CBS, Morgan Stanley, First Boston, the New York Mercantile Exchange, and the New York Times, have received large benefits not to leave the city. The use of property tax breaks is especially popular because they are easy to administer and require no direct expenditure of city funds. The term tax expenditures is used to describe tax breaks for firms. A program known as the Industrial and Commercial Incentive Program was created in 1981 and provides property tax breaks to companies that build, move to, or expand in any of the four boroughs other than Manhattan. (The area of Manhattan above 96th Street is also eligible for the program.) Also, a program exists to provide property tax breaks under special circumstances for firms in central and lower Manhattan. Those special circumstances include the building of "smart" buildings that are highly efficient in their use of energy.

Most of the larger municipalities (central city or suburb) have an economic development strategy, and the policies that are used most frequently include tax abatement, tax-increment financing districts, loan subsidies, and direct loans to businesses. Tax-increment financing (TIF) districts are small districts within a municipality in which increases in property tax revenues are devoted to infrastructure and other improvements within the district. The use of TIF districts has grown rapidly, and there is now some good empirical research on their effects. The best study was done by Weber et al. (2002). This study shows that industrial parcels in mixed-use TIF districts (those that contain commercial and/or residential properties along with industrial properties) have values that are about double the value of parcels not located in TIF districts. However, parcels located in TIF districts that are exclusively industrial do not have higher values than industrial parcels located elsewhere. These results suggest that, for TIF districts to be successful economic engines, flexibility in their use of land should be provided.

Economic development incentives have become part of the game of local politics. The executives of major recipients of local tax breaks and other assistance are sometimes major contributors to the campaigns of local candidates. This fact draws attention to some obvious problems. The potential exists for firms to buy influence and, ultimately, tax breaks in the guise of "economic development" policy. On the other side of the coin, public officials have learned that firms do not necessarily keep the promises they make to retain and/or create jobs when they accept assistance. Newer versions of economic development programs include requirements that firms make commitments about jobs and that benefits will be lost if those commitments are not met. The local government must also monitor the performance of those firms to ensure compliance. The city of New York has run into problems with the performance of some of the firms that have received tax breaks and other benefits, and the city has imposed stronger performance requirements and instituted closer monitoring of performance. But do not lose sight of the fact that all of New York City's efforts are designed to prevent further movement of firms to New Jersey and Connecticut! By the way, the state of New Jersey apparently has no intention of standing by and doing nothing while New York expands its economic development efforts. Read the *New York Times* for further movements in the game.

As major central cities such as New York City work to keep jobs that are already there, many local governments in the suburbs and in the sunbelt are working to attract new firms. Many of those efforts meet with little success, but some localities have a great deal of success – and success can create its own problems.

Consider the case of Rio Rancho, New Mexico. Rio Rancho is a suburb of Albuquerque that is a big player in the economic development game. In the early 1980s they attracted a large Intel plant that makes semiconductor chips. Note that the Silicon Valley firm, Intel, sought a cheaper site away from the San Francisco area for its manufacturing operations. The deal that attracted the plant includes the provision that Intel does not have to pay any real estate taxes for 30 years. Then, in 1993, Rio Rancho landed the huge Intel plant that makes the Pentium chip, the main component of some of the best personal computers. The deal to land the Pentium plant includes:

1 exemption from real estate taxes for 30 years;
2 lower state corporate income tax rate;
3 exemption from the gross receipts tax on equipment purchases;
4 recruitment and training of workers;
5 deep discounts on moving and storage fees and utility deposits for Intel employees who moved in;
6 guaranteed fast action on such things as building permits.

Rio Rancho is also very effective in recruiting smaller firms. They have a recruiting team of experts who will go anywhere to cut a deal. Their team includes a city planner, a banker, and a builder, so Rio Rancho can promise that a firm can plan, gain approval, and build its facility in four months.

Rio Rancho is wildly successful in the economic development game, its municipal services have not kept up with its job growth. As of 1995 the town had no high school, and its middle school had an enrollment that was double the planned capacity of the building. The high school students were bused to an overcrowded school in Albuquerque. The failure to build schools stems from the fact that the school district relies on real estate taxes, but Intel and other firms are exempt from the tax. The real estate tax in Rio Rancho on residential property was at the limit permitted by state law, but the tax collections fell far short of their needs. Intel points out that their employees earn high incomes and pay income and sales taxes to the state, so the problem is with the system of financing schools and is not caused by Intel or the other firms. In any event, success can have its pitfalls.

State governments and economic development

Since the 1970s most state governments have become very active in the economic development game. The first states to play the game were the southern states that worked to attract industry from the North starting in the 1950s, but by the 1970s nearly all states realized that they had to be in the game. Some states have actually designed very creative economic development strategies that are adapted to their particular circumstances. A book edited by Fosler (1988) titled *The New Economic Role of American States* contains several useful case studies that describe how states responded in the 1970s and 80s to the need for economic development. A few examples from Fosler (1988) will give you a flavor of what has been going on.

In response to the decline in the domestic auto industry, in the 1980s the state of Michigan designed a comprehensive strategy to update its industrial base by promoting research and development, product development, and venture capital, and by helping workers retrain for the new industrial jobs. The focus was on creating new products and new businesses, not on attracting firms from elsewhere. In the 1990s (after the recession of 1990–1) Michigan did very well in participating in the growth of manufacturing in the Midwest.

Tennessee followed a strategy of attracting firms to the state. Tennessee has inherent advantages that derive from its location near the center of the nation and from its low wages and level of unionization. The Tennessee government has been helpful to businesses that are in need of a location for a new plant, and its low-key approach has been quite attractive to Japanese auto firms. Tennessee has attracted several Japanese auto plants as well as the General Motors Saturn plant by using relatively modest financial incentives coupled with an atmosphere of patience and trust. Tennessee has been successful in attracting branch plants of major manufacturing firms, but this success has left the state with a relative lack of business services. A large and diverse business services sector helps a local economy create new firms, so Tennessee may wish to employ a more diversified strategy.

As a final example of a state's strategy, the state of Minnesota has long followed a policy of developing its own human resources through high-quality education at all levels. Economic pressures on some of its older industries, such as agriculture and mining, have led the state into some more conventional economic development programs and "smokestack chasing." Some observers of the Minnesota scene were very skeptical of these targeted incentive efforts and argued for a return to the older strategy of keeping the public sector focused on the quality of basic public services. In any event, Minnesota succeeded in attracting the Mall of America, the nation's largest shopping mall. It is brilliantly located close to the state's major airport in the suburbs of Minneapolis, so shoppers can fly in from anywhere in the Midwest for a day (or more) of shopping. The Mall of America is more than just a shopping mall: it has hotels, live entertainment, and an indoor amusement park. Is this mall the wave of the future, or will shopping over the internet make such real estate obsolete?

The message of Fosler's (1988) book is that states are, and probably will continue to be, the most creative players in the local economic development field. You may find that state government will be an exciting place to work in the future. If you do go to work in state government in the field of economic development, try to remember who you know about urban economies and their problems. Be sensitive to equity considerations as you pursue economic growth for your state.

H. Summary

This chapter is a broad survey of local economic development policy. It began with a discussion of the basic goals of any economic policy – efficient use of resources and equity in the distribution of income. A more efficient use of resources occurs when there is a gain in the welfare of some individual with no reduction in the welfare of someone else. It was pointed out that perfectly competitive markets can produce an efficient intertemporal allocation of resources, i.e., an efficient amount of investment in future productive capacity. However, all of the reasons for the failure of markets to be efficient in a static economy also operate over time. The standard problems of monopoly, public goods, externalities, and lack of information still apply. Furthermore, there is the added problem of social risk versus individual risk. Investments in future productive capacity can be highly risky for an individual firm, but the risk for society is less because that social risk is spread out over many firms. This observation suggests that some investments, such as investments in new technologies, should be subsidized because individual firms are applying discount rates to future returns that include a risk premium that is too high from society's point of view. In short, strong arguments can be made on efficiency grounds for economic growth policy.

The goal of equity in the distribution of income requires that the society agree upon the nature of that goal. Reasonable people can have widely differing views about this goal, and often a difference in policy recommendations stems from different views about the goal of equity. For example, some would place very heavy weight on increasing the incomes of the poorest members of the society, while others would distribute the weights more evenly. Given these overall goals of economic policy, the specific goals of local job growth and an increased tax base were examined. The view is offered that job growth that employs unemployed or underemployed workers offers benefits on both efficiency and equity grounds.

The choice of goals leads to the selection of an overall economic development strategy and the policies to be pursued in support of that strategy. A strategy to increase growth with no special reference to the poorest members of the urban area leads to one set of policies, while a strategy to emphasize economic opportunity for the disadvantaged can lead to another package of policies. A policy can be categorized according to the underlying factor in economic growth that it enhances. From your study of Chapters 19–20, you know that these underlying economic growth factors are;

- export demand;
- import substitution;
- capital (private and public);
- labor force quality;
- technical change:
    - new products,
    - new production processes, and
    - diffusion of new technology;
- entrepreneurship;
- amenities;
- agglomeration economies;
    - urbanization economies, and
    - localization economies.

One topic that is debated by experts in local economic development is whether the local programs should select "target" industries as the focus of much of the strategy and policy.

A target industry is one that will respond well to policy initiatives because of the existence market failure of some sort: e.g., localization economies or individual risk that is high compared to social risk. At this point it is not clear that local officials are very adept at selecting good targets, but it is also true that the use of scarce resources for economic development programs may require that some choices be made. Some economic development policies can be of a general nature: e.g., improvements in basic education, general training in entrepreneurship, support for cultural, social and recreational amenities, provision of good public services at low tax rates, and so on. Indeed, it is quite possible that general policies of these kinds represent the best use of scarce public and philanthropic resources. However, many local economic development officials cannot resist the urge to select target industries. Some analytical methods are offered to assist in this selection.

The final topic in the chapter is the evaluation of economic development strategies and policies. A good deal of research has concentrated on the effects of local taxes on economic activity, and the recent studies generally have found that variations in local taxes for small jurisdictions within an urban area can have sizable impacts on business location. The figure obtained by Bartik (1991) in his survey of the research is that a 1% decrease in local taxes, compared to the rest of the urban area, can result in about a 1.9% increase in economic activity. This finding is consistent with the discussion of the local public sector in Chapter 13. State and local taxes are less powerful influences on the location of economic activity across states and urban areas.

The only other local program that has been studied very much is the state enterprise program. As of 1991, 37 states had enterprise zone programs, but very few of those programs had been subjected to an evaluation of decent quality. The study of the Illinois enterprise zone program by McDonald (1993) found that the program did stimulate employment in the distribution sector (wholesale trade and transportation) in the enterprise zones. However, total employment did not increase in the zones compared to other areas. However, O'Keefe (2004) found that the enterprise zone program in California did increase total employment growth in the zones. Bartik's (1991) survey of other evaluation research found that other policies, such as export assistance and programs to attract foreign investment, had positive effects.

Clearly more research on the effects of economic development policies is needed. Assuming that effective policies do exist, Bartik's (1991) examination of the impacts of employment increases on the local labor market produced striking results. Job growth does most of the right things. A one-time increase in employment reduces the unemployment rate, increases the rate of labor force participation, increases earnings, and produces the greatest benefits for the poor. In short, labor resources are used more efficiently and the distribution of income becomes more equitable. The favorable effects of local economic growth in general, and employment growth in particular, are sufficient justification for devoting three chapters of this book to these topics.

The real world of economic development policy at the local level often consists of competition between jurisdictions within the same urban area. This competition can be harmful because it comes at the cost of a lost opportunity – the opportunity to devise strategies that will enhance the growth of the entire urban area. This problem of policy coordination and cooperation has not been solved in most of America's major urban areas, but some state governments have developed creative economic development strategies that are more in keeping with the message of this chapter.

This is the concluding chapter of the book, and we hope that we have ended on a hopeful note. Chapters 19 and 20 have demonstrated that we do have some understanding of how to increase the growth rate of an urban economy. This chapter has outlined alternative goals and strategies and policies that can be used to pursue those goals. Local economic development officials can serve their constituencies well by thinking carefully about goals, strategies, policies, and program evaluation.

Exercises

1   Suppose that you are the economic development czar of your urban area. You have decided to pursue the goal of increasing the per capita income of residents of the urban area (without regard to income distribution), and your strategy is to support growth by selecting target industries.

  (a)   Select a package of specific policies from Table 21.1 that is consistent with this strategy.
  (b)   Conduct an analysis of that local economy along the lines shown in Table 21.2 to identify possible candidates for target industries. Use County Business Patterns for 1998 and 2002 from their web site.

2   Contact a public economic development agency that operates within an urban area of your choice. This agency might be a department of the central city government, for example. What are the primary goals and strategies of this agency, as nearly as you can determine? Are they smokestack chasers? Do they concentrate on industry retention? Do they have a more comprehensive economic development strategy? Was it difficult to find out about basic goals and strategies? What are the policies used to support that strategy? Are policies being pursued that seem to be in pursuit of no coherent strategy? What goals would you pursue?

References

Baily, Martin, G. Burtless, and R. Litan, 1993, *Growth with Equity*. Washington, DC: The Brookings Institution.

Bartik, Timothy, 1991, *Who Benefits from State and Local Economic Development Policies?* Kalamazoo, MI: W. E. Upjohn Institute.

Bartik, Timothy, 1994, "The Effects of Metropolitan Job Growth on the Size Distribution of Family Income," *Journal of Regional Science*, vol. 34, pp. 483–501.

Bernstein, Richard, 1990, "The Restructuring of Manufacturing within the Philadelphia Region," in W. Stull and J. Madden (eds.), *Post-Industrial Philadelphia*, Philadelphia: University of Pennsylvania Press.

Blackstone, Erwin and K. Carr-Possai, 1990, "Growth and Change in Health Care Employment within the Metropolitan Area," in W. Stull and J. Madden (eds.), *Post-Industrial Philadelphia*, Philadelphia: University of Pennsylvania Press.

Congressional Budget Office, 1988, *New Directions for the Nation's Public Works*. Washington, DC: CBO.

Coughlin, Cletus and P. Cartwright, 1987, "An Examination of State Foreign Export Promotion and Manufacturing Exports," *Journal of Regional Science*, vol. 27, pp. 439–49.

Erickson, Rodney, 1992, "Enterprise Zones: Lessons from the State Government Experience," in E. Mills and J. McDonald (eds.), *Sources of Metropolitan Growth*, New Brunswick, NJ: Rutgers University Press.

Florida, Richard, 2005, *Cities and the Creative Class*, New York: Routledge.

Fosler, R. Scott (ed.), 1988, *The New Economic Role of the States*. New York: Oxford University Press.

Hoover, Edgar and R. Vernon, 1959, *Anatomy of a Metropolis*, Cambridge: Harvard University Press.

James, Franklin, 1991, "The Evaluation of Enterprise Zone Programs," in R. Green (ed.), *Enterprise Zones: New Directions in Economic Development*, Newbury Park, CA: Sage Publications.

McDonald, John, 1987, "Crime and Punishment: A Social Welfare Analysis," *Journal of Criminal Justice*, vol. pp. 245–54.

McDonald, John, 1992, "Assessing the Development Status of Metropolitan Areas," in E. Mills and J. McDonald (eds.), *Sources of Metropolitan Growth*. New Brunswick, NJ: Rutgers University Press.

McDonald, John, 1993, "Tax Expenditures for Local Economic Growth: An Econometric Evaluation of the Illinois Enterprise Zone Program," *Public Budgeting and Financial Management*, vol. 5, pp. 477–505.

Mier, Robert, 1993, *Social Justice and Local Development Policy*, Newbury Park, CA: Sage Publications.

Muth, Richard, 1971. "Migration: Chicken or Egg?" *Southern Economic Journal*, vol. 37, pp. 295–306.

Newman, Robert and D. Sullivan, 1988, "Econometric Analysis of Business Tax Impacts on Industrial Location: What Do We Know and How Do We Know It?" *Journal of Urban Economics*, vol. 23, pp. 215–34.

O'hUallachain, Breandon and M. Satterthwaite, 1992, "Sectoral Growth Patterns at the Metropolitan Level: An Evaluation of Economic Development Incentives," *Journal of Urban Economics*, vol. 31, pp. 25–58.

O'Keefe, Suzanne, 2004, "Job Creation in California's Enterprise Zones: A Comparison Using a Propensity Score Matching Model," *Journal of Urban Economics*, vol. 55, pp. 131–50.

Rawls, John, 1971, *A Theory of Justice*, Cambridge, MA: Harvard University Press.

Solow, Robert, 1970, *Growth Theory: An Exposition*, New York: Oxford University Press.

Stull, William and J. Madden, 1990, *Post-Industrial Philadelphia*, Philadelphia: University of Pennsylvania Press.

Weber, R., D. Bhatta, and D. Merriman, 2002, "Does Tax Increment Financing Raise Urban Industrial Property Values?" *Urban Studies*, vol. 40, pp. 2001–21.

Appendix: A Review of Some Mathematics and Microeconomic Theory

Some fundamental results in microeconomic theory and mathematics are used repeatedly in this book, so this appendix provides a discussion of all of the results that you will need to read the rest of the book. All of the concepts will be familiar to one who has studied intermediate microeconomics and one term of calculus. Some of the material will be new to those of you who have not taken these two courses – you will need to study this appendix carefully.

A. Some Basic Mathematics of Functions

Basic concepts in mathematics will be presented first. Economics always makes use of functions, an example of which is

$$Q = f(K,L).$$

This equation says that the quantity of output (Q) is a function (f) of the quantities of inputs capital (K) and labor (L). A function means that, for a given combination of K and L, there is only *one* value of Q. An example of a linear function is

$$Q = 5K + 7L.$$

If $K = 1$ and $L = 5$, $Q = 40$. An example of a quadratic function is

$$Q = K^2 + 5L.$$

Another example of a function is

$$Q = 4KL.$$

Often in economics one is interested in finding out how much the variable on the left-hand side of a function changes when a variable on the right-hand side of the function changes. From the linear function above that says $Q = 5K + 7L$, we know that Q changes by 5 when K changes by 1, or

$$\Delta Q/\Delta K = 5.$$

Here Δ (delta) denotes "change in." Similarly, if $Q = 4KL$, then the change in Q when K increases by 1 can be written

$$\Delta Q/\Delta K = 4L.$$

What about the change in Q as K increases in the function $Q = K^2 + 5L$? This question is a bit more complicated, but a simple rule can be found. A helpful way to write this equation is

$$Q = K(K) + 5L.$$

If K increases, both of the K's increase, which means that

$$\Delta Q = K(\Delta K) + (\Delta K)K, \text{ or}$$
$$\Delta Q = 2K(\Delta K), \text{ and}$$
$$\Delta Q/\Delta K = 2K.$$

Notice that K is multiplied by the exponent 2, and the exponent on K is now 1. This is an example of the exponent rule for finding derivatives in calculus. The more general rule is: If

$$Q = K^b, \text{ then}$$
$$\Delta Q/\Delta K = bK^{b-1}.$$

This result can be demonstrated if we write

$$Q = K \times K \times K \dots K \quad (b \text{ times}), \text{ so that}$$
$$\Delta Q = \Delta K(K^{b-1}) \times \Delta K(K^{b-1}) \dots \times \Delta K(K^{b-1}) \quad (b \text{ times}).$$

Therefore

$$\Delta Q/\Delta K = bK^{b-1}.$$

Often we wish to know how Q changes if both K and L change. The linear form $Q = 5K + 7L$ yields the simple result that

$$\Delta Q = 5\Delta Q + 7\Delta L.$$

The change in Q in the multiplicative form $Q = 4KL$ can be found by varying K and L separately and adding the two changes together, or

$$\Delta Q = 4L(\Delta K) + 4K(\Delta L).$$

One final mathematical concept is needed. This idea is known as the chain rule, and it applies when K on the right-hand side of a function for Q is itself a function of some other variable X; i.e.,

$$Q = f(K), \text{ and}$$
$$K = g(X),$$

where g indicates a different function with K as a function of X.

The basic result of the chain rule is that

$$\Delta Q/\Delta X = (\Delta Q/\Delta K)(\Delta K/\Delta X).$$

Suppose that $Q = 6 + 5K$ and $K = 2X$. We have

$\Delta Q/\Delta K = 5$,
$\Delta K/\Delta X = 2$, and
$\Delta Q/\Delta X = 10$

by the chain rule. This result can also be obtained by substituting for $2X$ for K in $Q = 6 + 5K$, which yields $Q = 6 + 10X$. Obviously $\Delta Q = 10\Delta X$.

B. Production Theory

These mathematical concepts can be used to demonstrate some of the basic results in microeconomic theory. Begin with the production function

$Q = f(K,L)$.

The change in output when one of the inputs is changed (holding the other constant) is called the marginal product (MP) of that input, which can be written

$MP_K = \Delta Q/\Delta K$, and
$MP_L = \Delta Q/\Delta L$.

Here it shall be assumed that the marginal product on an input declines as more of the input is used; this is the law of diminishing (marginal) returns. Figure A.1 shows a marginal product curve for

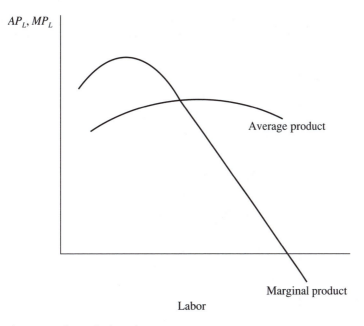

Figure A.1   Average and marginal product

labor. Note that the curve is drawn so that, at some point, the marginal product of the input falls to zero and then becomes negative. The idea is that, holding other inputs constant, adding more of the worker will eventually create a situation in which one more worker hampers the ability of the other workers to produce output.

Given the production function, we can also define the average product of an input, or

$AP_K = Q/K$, and
$AP_L = Q/L$.

An average product curve for labor is also shown in Figure A.1. The average product is rising if the marginal product exceeds the average product, and the average product is falling in the marginal product is less than the average product. If average product equals marginal product, then the average product is not changing. This is what we like to call the "old average – marginal relationship," a concept that you learned in the basic microeconomics course.

The change in output if both inputs change is

$\Delta Q = MP_K(\Delta K) + MP_L(\Delta L)$.

If K and L change so as to leave output the same,

$\Delta Q = 0 = MP_K(\Delta K) + MP_L(\Delta L)$.

This equation defines an isoquant, the curve that shows the various combinations of inputs that produce the same output level. Figure A.2 shows a set of isoquants. The *slope* of the isoquant can be found by solving the equation for the tradeoff between K and L, which is

$\Delta K/\Delta L = -MP_L/MP_K$.

This is the familiar result that the slope of the isoquant is the ratio marginal products times −1. See the isoquants in Figure A.2. The slope gives the trade-off between capital and labor that holds

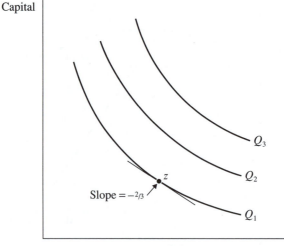

Figure A.2   Isoquant map

output constant. For example, suppose that $MP_K = 3$ and $MP_L = 2$ at point z in Figure A.2. If you increase the labor input by one unit, how much capital can you subtract and keep output constant? Increasing the labor input by one unit increases output by 2 units, so you can subtract 2/3 units of capital and hold output constant. The figure 2/3 is just

$MP_L/MP_K = 2/3$.

C. Theory of the Firm

Suppose that the firm with the production function wishes to maximize profits (π). The firm faces a demand curve and must pay for the two inputs. The quantity demanded (Q) is a function of the price that is charged, or

$Q = g(P)$.

For example, suppose that

$Q = 100 - 2P$.

This demand curve is shown in Figure A.3.

Profits equal total revenue minus total costs. Total revenue (TR) is the price of output times the quantity sold, and total costs (TC) are the sum of the expenditures on each input, or

$\pi = TR - TC = PQ - TC = PQ - rK - wL$,

where r and w are the prices that the firm must pay for the use of capital and labor. The firm must decide how much output to produce, so we wish to know how profits change as output is increased. The profit-maximizing level of output occurs where the additional profit generated by producing one more unit of output has dropped to zero. One result needed is that

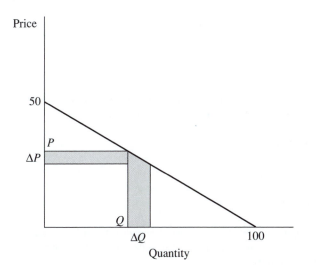

Figure A.3   Demand function

$$\Delta\pi = (\Delta TR/\Delta Q)\Delta Q - (\Delta TC/\Delta Q)\Delta Q = 0.$$

The change in total revenue when output changes is called marginal revenue (*MR*), and the change in total cost when output changes is called marginal cost (*MC*). Therefore,

$$\Delta\pi = 0 = MR\Delta Q - MC\Delta Q,$$

and the change in profits ($\Delta\pi/\Delta Q$) drops to zero where

$$MR = MC.$$

This is the familiar condition for maximizing profits that you learned in the basic microeconomics course. The result is normative; it says that in order to achieve the goal of maximizing profits, the firm *should* produce where marginal revenue equals marginal cost. In more general terms, the firm sets output where the marginal benefit of output (the marginal revenue) equals the marginal cost.

Take a closer look at marginal revenue. Recall that total revenue is *PQ*, which means that the change in total revenue consists of two parts, i.e.,

$$\Delta TR = Q\Delta P + P\Delta Q.$$

These two components are depicted in Figure A.3. As *Q* is increased we see that $P\Delta Q$ is a positive number and $Q\Delta P$ is a negative number (because *P* must be reduced so that more output can be sold). Marginal revenue is the net outcome of these two offsetting forces.

We also know that *Q* is a function of *P*, written $Q = g(P)$. However, we are contemplating changes in *Q*, not *P*. We need to invert the demand function and instead make *P* and function of *Q*. This can be done if *Q* always declines as *P* increases, because *P* then will always decline as *Q* increases. Write down the inverted function as

$$P = g^{-1}(Q).$$

For example, if $Q = 100 - 2P$, then

$$P = 50 - Q/2.$$

The change in *P* can be written simply as

$$\Delta P = (\Delta P/\Delta Q)\Delta Q.$$

The term $\Delta P/\Delta Q$ is just the slope of the demand curve, and it has a negative sign. Substitution of this expression for ΔP into the equation for ΔTR gives the result that

$$\Delta TR = Q(\Delta P/\Delta Q)\Delta Q + P\Delta Q.$$

Marginal revenue is given by

$$MR = \Delta TR/\Delta Q = Q(\Delta P/\Delta Q) + P.$$

This equation simply says that the marginal revenue is the price of output plus an adjustment for the fact that the price had to be reduced in order to sell more output. The reduction in price ($\Delta P/\Delta Q$) is multiplied by *Q*.

If the firm is in a perfectly competitive market for output, the price does not have to be reduced to sell more ($\Delta P/\Delta Q = 0$), and

$MR = P.$

A closer look at marginal cost is also useful. Recall that

$TC = rK + wL.$

There are two simple ways to increase output – use more capital or hire more labor. Suppose more labor is used, so

$\Delta TC = w(\Delta L/\Delta Q)\Delta Q.$

The expression $\Delta L/\Delta Q$ is the amount of labor that is needed to produce one more unit of output, which is just the inverse of the marginal product of labor ($\Delta Q/\Delta L$). Therefore

$MC = \Delta TC/\Delta Q = w/MP_L.$

Recall Figure A.1, which depicts MP_L. The declining MP_L as output rises translates into a *rising* marginal cost of output, as shown in Figure A.4.

A sensible firm will use the cheaper method for increasing output. Suppose that more capital is hired instead. The same logic produces the result that

$MC = \Delta TC/\Delta Q = r/MP_K.$

The firm's managers know that something is amiss if these two figures for marginal cost are different. If the marginal cost of increasing output by using more capital exceeds the marginal cost of increasing output by hiring more labor, then the firm should cut back on its use of capital and hire more labor. These changes can keep output at the same level and reduce total costs. Therefore, a firm that is maximizing profits must have

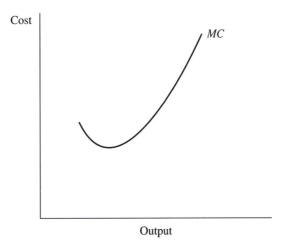

Figure A.4   Marginal cost

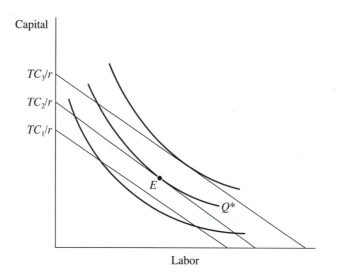

Figure A.5   Cost minimization in the long run

$r/MP_K = w/MP_L.$

This condition can be rewritten as

$MP_L/MP_K = w/r,$

which is the familiar condition that, for profit-maximization, the firm should have the ratio of input prices equal to the ratio of marginal products. This is another normative proposition. Recall that the ratio of marginal products is the slope of the isoquant times −1. Figure A.5 shows this condition graphically.

In Figure A.5 the firm has a target of producing an output level of Q^*. The parallel lines on the diagram are *isocost* (equal total cost) lines with slope $-w/r$. Each line is based on the equation

$TC = rK + wL$, so that
$K = (TC/r) - (w/r)L.$

Given a level of TC, the straight line of K as a function of L is defined. Varying TC produces the set of parallel lines shown in Figure A.5. The firm minimizes cost in the long run by selecting point E on the Q^* isoquant. Point E is defined by a tangency between the Q^* isoquant and an isocost line. The lowest possible total cost occurs at point E.

As a final exercise with the theory of the firm, return to the condition that $MR = MC$ for the maximization of profits, and substitute for MR and MC from the above results. The new statement is that

$MR = Q(\Delta P/\Delta Q) + P = r/MP_K = w/MP_L = MC.$

This group of equations can be manipulated to produce some interesting results, two of which are that

$MR(MP_K) = r$, and
$MR(MP_L) = w.$

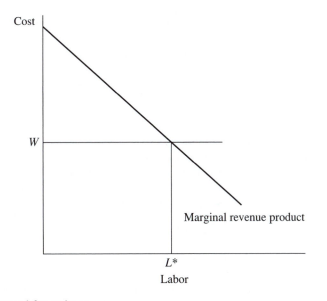

Figure A.6   Demand for an input

The left-hand sides of these equations are called the marginal revenue product of capital and labor, respectively. They tell us the amount of added revenue that is generated when the firm uses one more unit of capital or hires one more unit of labor. Figure A.6 shows the marginal revenue product for labor. Maximization of profits means that this added revenue is set equal to the price of the input. If the last unit of an input hired is generating more revenue than it costs, then the firm is not maximizing profits and more of the input should be hired. (Note the use of the word "should" again.) In Figure A.6 the price of a unit of labor is w, and profit-maximizing employment is L^*.

If the firm sells output in a perfectly competitive market, then $\Delta P/\Delta Q = 0$, and the conditions reduce to

$$P(MP_K) = r, \text{ and}$$
$$P(MP_L) = w.$$

The left hand sides of these equations are called the *value of the marginal product*, the added output produced by the marginal unit of the input times the price of the output.

D. Theory of the Consumer

The basic theory of the consumer is used to examine how households allocate their resources and respond to changes in their economic circumstances. The theory contains two separate elements; the preferences of the consumer for various economic goods, and the budget constraint that the consumer faces.

Consumer preferences are summarized in the utility function, the function which describes the consumer's level of well being as a function of the amounts of economic goods consumed. For example, the utility function for a particular consumer might be written

$$U = U(x_1, x_2, x_3, \ldots, x_n),$$

where x_1 through x_n are various economic goods such as housing, food, clothing, and leisure time. The utility function says that, for a given combination of the goods, the consumer achieves some unique level of utility.

Now suppose that the amount of one of the goods (x_1) changes. We can write

$$\Delta U = (\Delta U / \Delta x_1) \Delta x_1.$$

What do we know about the crucial quantity $(\Delta U / \Delta x_1)$? The usual assumption is that we know only that $(\Delta U / \Delta x_1)$ is greater than zero; we do not know by *how much* utility increases when x_1 increases. We do not presume that utility is measurable in the same sense that we presume that output in a production function is measurable. What we *do* assume is that the utility function can tell us how much of one good can be substituted for another good to keep utility *constant*.

Suppose that good x_1 is decreased and that good x_2 is increased so as to keep utility constant at some level. We can use the mathematics of functions to write

$$\Delta U = (\Delta U / \Delta x_1) \Delta x_1 + (\Delta U / \Delta x_2) \Delta x_2 = 0$$

because the net change in utility is zero. This is the basic equation for an indifference curve, the curve that shows the combinations of x_1 and x_2 (given certain amounts of the other goods x_3 to x_n) that yield the same level of utility. The equation can be solved to yield

$$-\Delta x_1 / \Delta x_2 = (\Delta U / \Delta x_2) / (\Delta U / \Delta x_1).$$

The negative sign on the left-hand side has to be there because we know that Δx_1 is a negative number, Δx_2 is a positive number, and the right-hand side of the equation is greater than zero.

The quantity $(\Delta U / \Delta x_1) / (\Delta U / \Delta x_2)$ is called the *marginal rate of substitution* of x_1 for x_2 because it tells us the amount of x_1 which can be given up when x_2 increases by one unit so as to keep utility constant. The marginal rate of substitution is -1 times the slope of the indifference curve shown in Figure A.7 because this figure has the quantity of x_1 on the vertical axis and the quantity of x_2 on

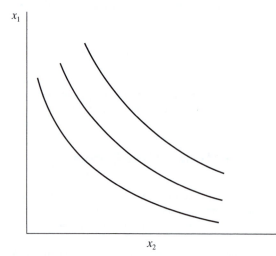

Figure A.7   Indifference curves

the horizontal axis. The standard assumption is that the indifference curve is bowed in toward the origin of the graph as shown. This shape implies that the amount of the good x_1 that is substituted for another unit of x_2, to keep utility constant, *declines* as the amount of x_2 increases and x_1 decreases. This is a sensible assumption because it means that, as the consumer has more of x_2 and less of x_1, he is less willing to trade away x_1 for more x_2 as utility is being held constant. The shorthand method for stating this assumption is to say that the marginal rate of substitution declines.

An indifference curve for goods x_1 and x_2 is assumed to exist for each level of utility, so a family of indifference curves can be drawn on the same diagram, as shown in Figure A.7. A higher level of utility corresponds to higher indifference curves, of course, because both of the goods are assumed to be *goods*.

Now we turn to the other half of the story – the budget constraint. We assume that the consumer has a given amount of resources to allocate to the goods in the utility function. The usual problem involves allocating a given amount of money income to the various consumer goods that can be purchased in the market. For simplicity suppose that there are only two such goods, x_1 and x_2, and that the consumer has an amount M to allocate to purchases of these two goods. In order to proceed we must know the prices of these two goods. Suppose that they are p_1 and p_2, respectively.

We now have all of the information needed to write down the budget constraint for this problem, and it is

$$M = p_1 x_1 + p_2 x_2.$$

Amount M is spent only on the two goods. The budget constraint can be placed on Figure A.8 by solving the budget constraint for x_1 in terms of x_2. This solution is

$$x_1 = (M/p_1) - (p_2/p_1)x_2.$$

As an exercise, confirm that this equation is correct. This new equation says two things very clearly. First, if the consumer buys no units of x_2, then the amount of x_1 that can be purchased is M/p_1. This makes perfect sense – the maximum amount of x_1 that the consumer can buy is M divided by the price of x_1. Second, the equation says that, if x_2 is increased by one unit, then x_1 must be reduced by p_2/p_1 units.

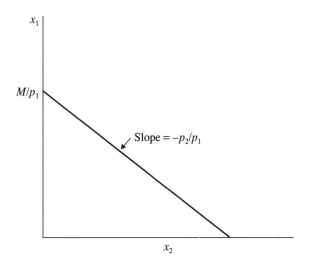

Figure A.8   Budget constraint

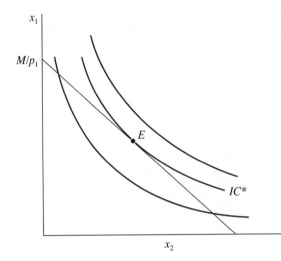

Figure A.9 Consumer equilibrium

Consider a numerical example to reinforce this second point. Suppose that the price of x_1 is \$2 per unit and that the price of x_2 is \$6 per unit. If the consumer decides to buy one more unit of x_2 he will spend \$6 more dollars on x_2. Where can he find \$6? He can find \$6 by reducing his purchases of x_1 by 3 units because each unit of x_1 has a price of \$2. Note that $p_2/p_1 = 6/2 = 3$.

We bring the indifference curves and the budget constraint together in Figure A.9 and present a graphical solution to the consumer's allocation problem. The objective of the consumer is to get the most utility possible from his purchases, so the idea is to get to the highest indifference curve that is possible given a budget of M. The highest feasible indifference curve is labelled IC^* in Figure A.9; it is the indifference curve that comes into contact with the budget constraint only at one point.

Note that indifference curves below IC^* come into contact with the budget constraint *twice*, and that indifference curves above IC^* do touch the budget constraint at all – they cannot be reached.

Indifference curve IC^* comes into contact with the budget constraint only once because the two curves are tangent – their slopes are equal at point E. Recall that the slope of an indifference curve is −1 times the marginal rate of substitution, and the slope of the budget constraint is − p_2/p_1. Therefore the mathematical expression for the maximization of the consumer's utility subject to the budget M is

$$\Delta x_1/\Delta x_2 = -p_2/p_1 = -MRS_{12},$$

where MRS_{12} is the marginal rate of substitution of x_1 for x_2.

One different application of this model of the consumer is used in the book. In this application x_1 is assumed to be money income (M) and x_2 is leisure time (L, measured in hours). People regard both of these as goods, so the indifference curves are of the usual sort. The only tricky part is the budget constraint. Here the constraint is the number hours the individual has to devote to leisure time and to activities that yield money income.

Suppose that the individual has total time T per week to devote to leisure (L) and work, and suppose that he can earn wage rate w at work. The equation for his budget can therefore be written as

$$M = w(T - L) = wT - wL.$$

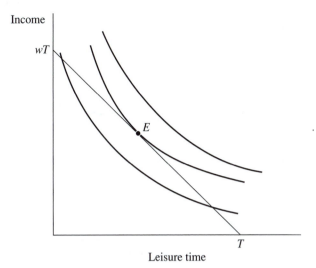

Figure A.10   Allocation of time to work and leisure

Here M is graphed on the vertical axis and L is shown on the horizontal axis of Figure A.10. The slope of the budget constraint is $-w$, which means that if the individual increases leisure time by one hour, $\$w$ of money income must be given up. This case is depicted in Figure A.10. The maximization of utility occurs at point E. In this case point E represents an allocation of time to its competing uses – work and leisure.

E. Efficiency and the Market Economy

So far only a single firm or household has been considered in this review of microeconomic concepts. Let us broaden the picture to consider the interests of an entire economy, focusing on the market for a single good. That good has a demand function

$$Q = (P)$$

and an inverse of the demand function

$$P = g^{-1}(Q).$$

The demand function tells the quantity demanded at each price, while the inverse demand function tells the price offered at each quantity. In other words, the inverse demand function indicates that someone out there in the market for the good is willing to pay a particular price for the next unit of the good. That willingness to pay is lower the greater is the quantity. The inverse demand function can therefore be interpreted as the marginal benefit curve for the good in question. The inverse demand curve has been depicted in Figure A.11 and labeled "marginal benefit." The

If the good is produced under conditions of perfect competition, the supply curve of the good is also the marginal cost curve for the industry. This is the fundamental result for supply that is taught in the principles of economics course. The marginal cost curve is also depicted in Figure A.11. The

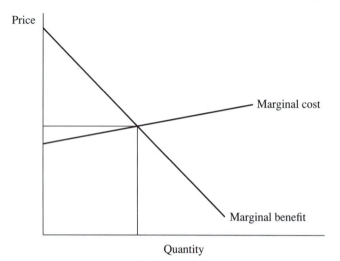

Figure A.11 Equilibrium in a competitive market

competitive market equilibrium price and quantity is also the point at which the marginal benefit of the good to its last purchaser is just equal to the marginal cost of the good. The perfectly competitive outcome is therefore an efficient outcome, in the economic sense that it is the level of output at which it is not possible to make someone better off unless someone else is made worse off. To see this point, suppose that suppliers are ordered by the Pope to increase the quantity supplied beyond the competitive equilibrium output shown in Figure A.11. There are benefits attached to this increased output, but the cost to the producers of producing the additional output exceeds that benefit. The Pope notices his mistake, and then orders the consumers of these additional units to pay the suppliers for their expenses. This transfer keeps the suppliers on the same level of well being, but the consumers are now worse off because they have had to transfer to suppliers an amount of money in excess of the value of the additional benefits of the good.

Alternatively, suppose that the output of the good has been restricted by a monopolist. A monopolist sets output where marginal cost equals marginal revenue, and then sets price from the demand curve so that

$$MC = MR < p.$$

Refer to Figure A.12. The monopolist faces demand curve DD, and has a marginal revenue function MR. She maximizes profits by equating MR and MC at output level Q^*, and sets the price P^* from the demand curve.

At the monopoly output the marginal cost is less than the marginal benefit of the good, represented by the price as read from the inverse demand function. This is clearly an inefficient allocation of resources because there is room for a consumer to bribe the monopolist to produce more of the good. A clever bribe can make both the consumer and the monopolist better off. For example, at output Q^*, a clever consumer could make a private deal to offer a price of $P^* - 1$ for the next unit of output. Suppose that the other consumers do not learn of this private deal. The consumer is better off because she gets to consume one more unit of the good at a price below her marginal benefit, and the monopolist is better off because the price paid exceeds the cost of producing that additional unit. Bribery can continue until the marginal benefit of the good is just equal to the marginal cost. At this point the consumer has no further room to make a bribe.

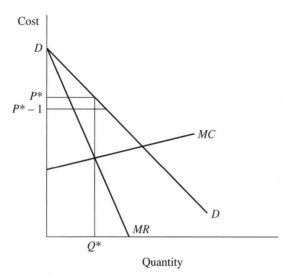

Figure A.12   Monopoly price and output

The monopoly example in the previous paragraph is closely related to the basic idea of cost–benefit analysis. In the cost–benefit analysis of a public good or service the idea is to produce more if the marginal benefits exceed marginal costs, of if

$MB/MC > 1$;

the marginal benefit–cost ratio exceeds one. If the benefits and/or costs of the public good extend beyond one year, then one must compare the present value of the stream of benefits to the present value of the stream of costs. The benefits and costs that occur in the future must be discounted by an interest rate that represents the willingness of society to trade the present for the future. For example, if society is willing to wait one year to receive benefits only if 5% interest is paid (in real terms), then benefits in amount MB that occur one year in the future have a present value of $MB/(1.05)$. A finding that MB/MC exceeds 1.0 means that enough benefits exist to pay all of the costs of the public good and have something left over. This means that the potential exists for the project in question to make someone better off while leaving no one else worse off. Projects that do not at least have this potential should be rejected.

F. Interest and Discounting

The concepts of compound interest and discounting are used frequently in urban economics and real estate, and in everyday life as well. As an educated person, you *must* understand these ideas. There is no alternative. The basic ideas are presented here, and they are used often in the body of the text. Some sophisticated compound interest and discounting concepts are developed in Chapter 8, the chapter on urban housing.

Suppose you know that your local bank is paying a 5% interest rate on one-year certificates of deposit. This means, of course, that if you deposit $100 today, you will receive $105 one year from today. The formula for this computation is

$$A_1 = A_0(1 + r),$$

where A_1 is the amount one year from today, A_0 is the initial deposit, and r is the interest rate expressed as a decimal (e.g., .05).

Now answer the following question. If you can answer this question, you understand the basic idea from which all of the rest of the ideas follow. Given that you, or anyone else, can earn 5% on bank deposits, what is the most you are willing to pay for a promise to pay you $100 one year from today? Are you willing to pay $100 now? Of course not, because you can put your $100 in the bank and have $105 one year from today. What about $99? If you put $99 in the bank today, you will have $103.95 one year later. So what is the answer? The answer is $95.24. If you were to put $95.24 in the bank at 5% interest, you would have $100 in one year. You can always earn interest on your money at the bank, so a promise to pay $100 one year from today is worth $95.24 today.

How did you (or I) get the answer of $95.24. This amount is, in fact, equal to 100/(1.05), or 100/(1 + r). This computation is just a manipulation of

$$A_1 = A_0(1 + r) \text{ to read}$$
$$A_0 = A_1/(1 + r).$$

If we know A_0, then we use the top formula to compute A_1. If we know A_1, then we use the bottom formula to compute A_0, the initial deposit needed to produce A_1.

Now suppose that you decide to roll over your certificate of deposit for a second year, and suppose that the interest remains at 5% for the second year. (The interest rate probably will have changed in a year, but ignore this complication.) In two years you will have an amount that is computed as

$$A_2 = A_1(1 + r) = A_0(1 + r)(1 + r) = A_0(1 + r)^2.$$

If the initial deposit is $100, then the amount in two years is $110.25. This is compound interest because you earned interest on your interest earnings. You earned $5 in interest in the first year, and you earned $.25 on that $5 in the second year in addition to the $5 in interest on your original deposit of $100.

Now answer the question, "How much is the promise to pay $100 in *two* years worth *today*?" Manipulation of the above formula produces the answer:

$$A_0 = A_2/(1 + r)^2 = 100/(1.05)^2 = 90.70.$$

This is the answer because, if you were to deposit $90.70 today at 5% interest, you would have $100 in two years. Use your pocket calculator to check this out.

The next step is to compute the current value of a promise to pay $100 one year from today *and* $100 two year from today. You already know the answer to this one. You add $95.24 and $90.70 to get $185.94. The more general formula for this computation is

$$A_0 = A_1/(1 + r) + A_2/(1 + r)^2,$$

where A_1 and A_2 are the amounts to be received at the end of one and two years. This is, in fact, a general formula for the computation of the *present value* of a series of payments.

Suppose the series of payments extends for 10 years. The present value of that series of payments is computed as

$$PV = A_1/(1 + r) + A_2/(1 + r)^2 + \ldots + A_{10}/(1 + r)^{10},$$

where the . . . stands for the third through the ninth terms.

What if the series of payments goes on forever? Does a series of payments ever go on forever? Sure. Land in an urban area never wears out. The payments of land rent for the privilege of using the land go on forever. The present value of an infinite series of payments is

$$PV = A_1/(1 + r) + A_2/(1 + r) + \ldots + A_{n-1}/(1 + r)^{n-1} + A_n/(1 + r)^n.$$

Note that the payment in time period "infinity" is A_n, and that this amount is divided by $(1 + r)^n$, which is a number that is infinitely large (because $1 + r$ is greater than 1). Therefore the present value of A_n is actually zero.

The formula for the present value of an infinite series of payments simplifies very neatly if the amount that is paid each year is a constant amount A. Now the formula is

$$PV = A/(1 + r) + A/(1 + r)^2 + \ldots + A/(1 + r)^{n-1} + A/(1 + r)^n.$$

Multiply both sides of this equation by $(1 + r)$ to obtain

$$(1 + r)PV = A + A/(1 + r) + \ldots + A/(1 + r)^{n-2} + A/(1 + r)^{n-1}.$$

Subtract the top equation from the bottom equation to obtain

$$(1 + r)PV - PV = A - A/(1 + r)^n = A.$$

Remember that the present value of amount A to be received an infinite number of years from now is zero. Therefore,

$$rPV = A, \text{ or}$$
$$PV = A/r.$$

The present value of an infinite series of payments equal to A is just A/r. For example, if $A = 100$ and $r = .05$, then $PV = 2000$. An investment of $2000 at 5% interest forever will produce an infinite series of payments of $100.

G. Mathematics of Exponential Functions

Exponential functions are used frequently in urban economics (and in economics in general) to create models of economic growth, urban population density, and many other economic phenomena.

We define e at the limit, as m approaches infinity, of

$$(1 + 1/m)^m.$$

It so happens that e equals about 2.718, and is known as the base of the natural logarithms. To convince yourself of this numerical result, use you pocket calculator to compute the above expression when $m = 5$, $m = 10$, $m = 15$, etc.

The natural logarithm of a (positive) number is the power to which e is raised to get the number, or

$$x = e^{\ln x}.$$

Here ln x means "natural logarithm," the logarithm with base e.

Consider a compound interest problem where amount A earns interest rate r per year, and interest is compounded m times per year. Then the value (V) of A after t years is

$$V = A(1 + r/m)^{mt}.$$

For example, if $m = 1$ (annual compounding), $V = A(1 + r)^t$. If $m = 2$ (semi-annual compounding), $V = A(1 + r/2)^{2t}$. With quarterly compounding, $V = A(1 + r/4)^{4t}$. And so forth. This formula can be written as

$$V = A((1 + 1/x)^x)^{rt},$$

where $x = m/r$. This result follows from the standard laws of exponents, and the proof is left as an exercise. This last formula means that

$$V = Ae^{rt}$$

as m approaches infinity (since x approaches infinity as m approaches infinity). This is the standard formula for exponential growth of amount A at interest rate r with continuous compounding. A graphical example is shown in Figure A.13.

For exponential decay, we can write

$$V = A(1 - r/m)^{mt} = A((1 + 1/x)^x)^{-rt},$$

where $x = -m/r$. This means that

$$V = Ae^{-rt}$$

as m approaches infinity. This is the standard formula for exponential decay at rate r with continuous compounding, and Figure A.13 shows an example. Note that the value of the function (V)

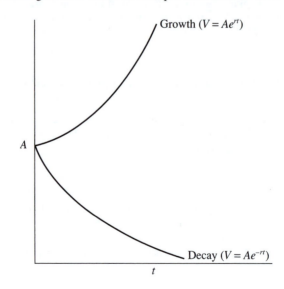

Figure A.13   Exponential growth and decay

declines by the same percentage in each time period, which means that the actual numerical value of the *decline* gets smaller and smaller as time passes.

These exponential functions have important properties that make them very convenient functions for empirical work. In particular, if $V = Ae^{rt}$, then (using the calculus symbol dx/dy as the symbol for the derivative of x with respect to y)

$$dV/dt = rAe^{rt}, \text{ or}$$
$$(dV/dt)/V = r.$$

Likewise, if $(dV/dt)/V = r$, then $V = Ke^{rt}$ (where K is some constant). In other words, if the percentage rate of change per time period is r, then V with continuous compounding at any time period is $V = Ae^{rt}$, where A is the initial value (at time zero).

The basic exponential growth and decay functions are very useful in urban economics. For example, population density in an urban area is usually described reasonably well by the exponential decay function written

$$D(x) = D_0 e^{-gx},$$

where $D(x)$ is population density at distance x from the central business district, D_0 is the hypothetical population density at distance zero, and g is called the density gradient. From the discussion of changes above we know that

$$(dD(x)/dx)/D(x) = -g,$$

or that the percentage decline in population density per unit distance is g. Also, the exponential decay function for population density can be written in logarithmic form as

$$\ln D(x) = \ln D_0 - gx.$$

The natural logarithm of population density is a linear function of distance to the central business district.

This change property of the exponential function can be proved quite easily. These proofs require familiarity with basic calculus, and can be skipped. Let us begin the proof by using the simplified function $V = e^t$. We define the natural logarithm as the power to which e is raised to obtain a specified (positive) number, or

$$\ln V = t,$$

where ln stands for natural logarithm. It is easy to show that $dt/dV = 1/V$. From the definition of a derivative,

$$dt/dV = \text{limit (as } V \text{ approaches } N\text{) of } (\ln V - \ln N)/(V - N)$$
$$= \text{limit } \ln(V/N)/(V - N).$$

This result follows because the logarithm of a quotient (such as V/N) is the same as the difference in logarithms. Here N is simply some specific value for V at which we have chosen to find the derivative. Next define $m = N/(V - N)$. Now we have

$$dt/dV = \text{limit}(m/N) \ln(1 + 1/m),$$

as result that follows because $1/m = (V - N)/N = V/N - 1$. Therefore,

$dt/dV = \text{limit}(1/N) \ln(1 + 1/m)^m$.

As V approaches N it so happens that $m = N/(V - N)$ approaches infinity, so

$dt/dV = (1/N) \ln e = 1/N$,

since the natural logarithm of e itself is 1. Remember that N is a value of V that V approaches in the definition of the derivative. This simple result can be inverted to yield

$dV/dt = N$,

which means that the derivative of $V = e^t$ is always itself!

Now if $V = Ae^{rt}$, then we can find dV/dt by using the chain rule for derivatives, which states that

$dV/dt = (dV/dz)(dz/dt)$,

where z is some intermediate function. In this case let $z = rt$, so $V = Ae^z$. This means that $dV/dz = Ae^z$ and $dz/dt = r$, so

$dV/dt = rAe^{rt}$

and

$(dV/dt)/V = r$.

Answers to Selected Exercises

Chapter 3

1 (a) Cost per ton is $175 if the trees are transported, compared to $160 if the firewood is transported. Thus, the trees should be cut into firewood at the forest. You actually only needed the transport cost data to determine the cost-minimizing location.

   (b) The price of firewood is $150, it is not profitable to produce, but at a price of $175 a profit can be made.

2 (a) With 23 customers, the median is customer #12 located 25 miles from Lubbock.

   (b) With 27 customers (10 in Amarillo), the median customer is #14 – still 25 miles from Lubbock.

   (c) Now with 27 customers (4 more in Lubbock), the median customer is in Lubbock.

3 (a) There are 11 customers. The profit-maximizing equilibrium locations are both at the median customer (#6). Any other location is not an equilibrium because one vendor has an incentive to move. Aggregate travel costs are

   $$(1/2)2(5 + 4 + 3 + 2 + 1) = 15 \text{ cents}$$

   (b) The socially optimal location pattern is to have the vendors locate at the one-quarter and three-quarter points along the beach. These points correspond to customers #3 and #9. Aggregate travel costs are

   $$(1/2)2(2 + 1) + (1/2)2(2 + 1) + (1/2)3 = 7.5 \text{ cents}$$

   However, this location pattern is unstable because either firm can increase sales by moving toward the center.

4 (a) $AC = 10 - 0.001Q$ (because $TC = q(ac)n$).
       $TC = n(10q - 0.001qQ)$. Since $Q = nq$,
       $TC = Q(10 - 0.001Q) = Q(AC)$.

   (b) $TC = 10Q - 0.001Q^2$, so
       $MC = 10 - 0.002Q$.

   (c) The industry produces where $AC = P$, so $Q = 1,000$, $AC = 9$, and $MC = 8$.

Chapter 5

1   Initial value $= R/r = 10,000/0.05 = \$200,000$. With the tax

$V = (r - tV)/r$, where t is the tax rate, and
$V = R/(r + t) = 10,000/0.08 = \$125,000$.

2   (a)   The bid-rent function with profits equal to zero is:

Profit $= 0 = pQ - TC = 1,000 - 100(0.25)x -$ other costs $-$ rent/acre,

where x is distance to the CBD.
Other costs are $5 per unit, or $5,000, so
Rent/acre $= R = 500 - 25x$.
(b) $R = 500 - 25x$, or $x = 16$ miles.

3   (a)   Marginal cost of distance is $(\$4/8)250 = \$125$ per mile per year.
(b)   Marginal benefit of moving one mile farther out is $3,000(\$.05) = \$150$ per mile per year. Thus MC of travel is less than the marginal benefits of travel.
(c)   Locational equilibrium requires that

$3,000(\Delta R/\Delta x) = 125$, so
$\Delta R/\Delta x = \$0.0417$ per mile.

Chapter 6

1   (a)   The second industry has "other costs" of $10 per unit, so:

Profit $= 0 = 1,500 - 75x - 750 - R$, or
$R = 750 - 75x$.

(b)   The two bid-rent functions cross at $x = 5$.

2   (a)   For the land rent function, let $x =$ distance to the CBD. The slope of the land rent function is $-2t$. The area of the city is PK, so the radius x^* of the city is found as

$PK = \pi(x^*)^2$, or $x^* = (PK/\pi)^{0.5}$.

The key to the problem is to realize that land rent at the CBD $(x = 0)$ equals travel cost at x^*, which is

$2tx^* = 2t(PK/\pi)^{0.5}$.

Thus the land rent function is

$R(x) = 2t(PK/\pi)^{0.5} - 2tx$.

(b)   Aggregate land rent is the volume of the land rent cone with base equal to the area of the city and height equal to land rent at the CBD, or

Agg $R = (1/3)PK[2\pi(PK/\pi)^{0.5}] = (2/3)t(PK)^{1.5}/\pi^{0.5}$.

Aggregate travel costs equal the volume of the cylinder of base PK and height of the land-rent function at the CBD minus the aggregate land rent, so aggregate travel costs are 2 times the aggregate land rent.

(c) A decline in marginal travel cost t reduces the land rent at the CBD and flattens the rent function because

$R(x) = 2t(PK/\pi)^{0.5} - 2tx$.

In other words, land rent falls everywhere in the city except at the edge, where it is still zero.

(d) The results in answer c happened because the population of the city is fixed, as is the land area of the city (fixed at PK). Land rent at the edge of the city is always zero, and the amount of the transportation cost avoided by living at any given location in the city has declined.

3 (a) Equation c says that the marginal cost of moving a marginal distance away (t) equals the marginal benefit of this move $[R'(x)l_D(x)]$, the savings in land rent.

(b) $l_D = B/R(x)$, so $R'(x)/R(x) = -t$.

The land rent gradient is a constant percentage change per unit of distance, and this percentage change is just equal to the marginal transportation cost.

(c) From equation (6), setting $L_D = L_S$,

$N(x)/L(x) = 1/l_D(x) = R(x)/B$.

Thus the population density gradient is $(1/B)$ times the land rent gradient.

(d) If t rises, the population density gradient gets steeper.

Chapter 7

1

Distance	Gross density
0	7,500
1	6,140
2	5,027
4	3,370
10	1,015
3.14	4,000
8	1,514

Chapter 8

1 (a) $V = (6,000 - 4,000)/0.05 = 40,000$.

(b) Market value is still $40,000. Compute present value of rents received at end of years 1, 2, and 3, and the house sold for $40,000 at the end of year 3.

(c) Selling price of $50,000 adds $8,636 to present value.

Chapter 9

1   Substitution of 0.4 for A and m_L in the final formula for t yields $t = 0.12$ (instead of 0.14).

2   (a)   If $Y = 15,000$ and $p = 100$, then $H = 500/10$ and $Hp = \$5,000$.
    (b)   If $Y = 20,000$, then $H = 666.7/10 = 66.67$ and $Hp = \$6,667$.
    (c)   If $p = 70$, then $H = 500/8.367 = 59.76$. $Hp = 70 \times 59.76 = \$4,183.20$. Total expenditures fall because demand is inelastic.

Chapter 10

2   (a)   Potential gross income equals \$2,250,000 per year, and effective gross income (with vacancy rate of 10%) is \$2,025,000.
    (b)   Net operating income (NOI) is EGI minus expenses of \$1,001,250, so NOI = \$1,023,750.
    (c)   The market value of the building is \$10,237,500, with a cap rate of 10%, or \$9,306,818 with a cap rate of 11%.

Chapter 11

1   (a)   In the short run, set

$$V + Q = 110 = 25 - R + 150 - 3R = 175 - 4R, \text{ so}$$
$$R = 16.25$$
$$\text{At } R = 16.25, V = 8.75 \text{ and } Q = 101.25, \text{ so } Q/K = 0.9205.$$

This is compared to $C/R = 12.5/16.15 = .769$, so there is an incentive to build more office space.

    (b)   In the long run we have the equilibrium condition $R = C(K/Q)$, so

$$R = (12.5)(175 - 4R)/(150 - 3R), \text{ which leads to}$$
$$150R - 3R^2 = 2,187.5 - 50\,R, \text{ giving the quadratic}$$
$$3R^2 - 200R + 2,187.5 = 0.$$

Application of the quadratic formula yields

$$R = 13.79.$$

At $R = 13.79$, $Q = 108.63$ and $V = 11.21$, so $K = 119.84$. The market supplies 9.84 msf more office space. We check our answer by noting that:

$$C/R = 12.5/13.79 = .9065 = Q/K = 108.63/119.84.$$

Chapter 12

1   Before-tax cash flow (BTCF) is \$10,000. Net selling price (NSP) is

\$100,000. After-tax cash flow (ATCF) is figured as follows:

ATCF = BTCF − tax
    Tax = 0.35(BTCF − interest − depreciation)
        = 0.35(10,000 − 3,000 − 2,051) = 1,732.
Thus, ATCF = 8,268.

After-tax return to equity = (8,268 − 3,000)/50,000 = 10.54%, which exceeds the cost of equity of 10%.

2 Front-door method with 50% loan. Equity and loan are both equal to $10,568,903. Required return to equity is $1,056,890 and debt service is $906,928. Thus, required NOI is $1,963,818, which exceeds the one-year profit estimate of $1,836,763.

Chapter 13

1 (a) The price for a household is 5,000/125 = 40.
    (b) $G = 100 − 0.5p = 80$ units.
    (c) Tax bill = 80 × 5,000/125 = $3,200.

2 (a) The median voter is a household with demand equal to $G = 50 − 0.5p$. The price for a household is 5,000/300 = 16.67, so $G = 41.67$ units.
    (b) The tax bill for each household is $pG = 694.6$.

3 (a) $V = R/(r + t)$, so the demand function translated into $V − Q$ space is $V = 125,000 − 12.5Q$. Setting supply equal to demand yields

$$50,000 + 2.5Q = 125,000 − 12.5Q, \text{ or}$$
$$Q = 5,000.$$
$$\text{At } Q = 5,000, V = 62,500 \text{ and } R = 5,000.$$

    (b) If t increases to 0.4, then $Q = 4,000$, $V = 60,000$, and $R = 6,000$. Under the old situation (with $t = 0.02$) the tax was $0.02 × 62,400 = 1,250$. The new tax is $0.04 × 60,000 = 2,400$. The tax increases by 1,150, of which 1,000 is paid by the tenants in the form of higher rent. The owner pays 150 of the increase in the tax, which makes sense because the present value of 150 per year is $150/0.06 = 2,500$, which is the decline in the value of the house.

Chapter 14

1 (a) $\ln T_{ij} = 0.5(\ln 100) + 0.2(\ln 200) − 2(\ln 5)$
        $= 2.30 + 1.06 − 3.22 = 0.14$, so
    $T_{ij} = 1.15$.

    If distance is 10, then $\ln T_{ij} = −2.25$ and $T_{ij} = 0.1$ (i.e., trips fall from 1 to 0).
    (b) If both O and D double in size, the $T = 1.88$; T does not double because the exponents of O and D add up to a number that is less than 1.

2 (a) Probability of using the auto of 0.5 means that

$$\ln(P/1 − P) = \ln(1) = 0 = −8(t_a − t_b) − 2(m_a − m_b).$$

   (b)   Thus any combination of $(m_a - m_b)/(t_a - t_b) = -4$ leads to $P = 0.5$.

   (c)   The value of reductions in commuting time is 4 cents per minute.

3 (a)   Define m as the departure time in minutes after 8 a.m. Commuting time is therefore

$$CT = 15 + 0.1m + 0.04m^2.$$

The value of commuting time is $5CT$. Time spent at work before 9 a.m. is $60 - m - CT$, and the cost of the time wasted is $3(60 - m - CT)$. The total cost of time is therefore $5CT + 3(60 - m - CT)$. Substitution for CT produces:

$$\text{Total cost} = 75 + 0.5m + 0.2m^2 + 180 - 3m - 45 - 0.3m - 0.06m^2$$
$$= 210 - 2.8m + 0.08m^2.$$

Minimization of total cost requires that $dTC/dm = -2.8 + 0.16m = 0$, or $m = 17.5$ (minutes past 8).

   (b)   Commuting time is computed from the CT function, and it equals 29 minutes.

   (c)   Arrival time is thus 8:46.5.

   (d)   If the cost of time spent at work increases to 3.1 cents per minute, departure time changes to 19.14 minutes past 8, commuting time increases to 31.6 minutes, and arrival time is now 8:50.74.

4 (a) $D = 80/2 = 40$ cars per mile.

   (b) $V = DS = 40$ cars per mile times 50 miles per hour $= 2,000$ cars per hour.

5 (a)   Supply is $AC = 10 + 4V$ and demand is $V = 46 - P$, so:

$$P = 46 - V \text{ and } AC = P, \text{ or}$$
$$10 + 4V = 46 - V, \text{ which yields } V = 7.2.$$

   (b)   Marginal cost is $10 + 8V$ and $V = 4$.

6 (a) $(1/S) = 1 + 0.03V$ in minutes per mile. Substitution into the demand function yields $V = 2,000$.

   (b)   If average travel time is $1 + 0.03V$, the total travel time is $V(1 + 0.03V)$ and marginal travel time is thus $1 + 0.06V$.

   (c)   Optimal traffic volume is found by substituting into the demand function, or $V = 1,172$.

   (d)   The optimal congestion toll is the difference between average and marginal cost at optimal V. This difference is $0.03V$, which is 35.16 minutes.

Chapter 18

1 (a)   Private return is computed from $3,000 = 750/r$, so $r = 25\%$. Social return is computed from $9,000 = 1,000/r$, so $r = 11.1\%$. Social costs include \$5,000 in program cost and \$4,000 in foregone earnings before taxes, and social benefits are the increase in before-tax earnings.

   (b)   Private cost is now \$8,000. Present value of private benefits equals

$$\$750/.06 = \$12,500,$$

so the individual does enroll in the program.

2   The idea is to compute the costs and benefits of the last two years of high school. The worker has a stream of benefits of $4,000 per year for four years (age 21 to 24), followed by an infinite stream of benefits of $9,000 per year beginning at age 25. These benefits are discounted back to age 17. Costs consist of $15,000 at age 17 and $15,000 at age 18. A real discount rate of 5% is used, so private costs equal $29,286. The benefits of completing high school easily exceed this amount.

Chapter 19

1   (a) $T/B = 2.4$, so the local multiplier is 2.4. An increase in basic employment of 3,000 would yield an increase in total employment of 7,200.
    (b)   This forecast assumes that $L = a + bT$ with $a = 0$, so the multiplier is B/T. The forecast also assumes that B and L workers are paid equally.

2   (a)   With this function for imports $[M = 0.23(1 - t)Y]$, then:

$$Y = C + I + G + (X - M)$$
$$Y = 100 + 0.9(0.7)Y + 650 - 0.161Y$$
$$0.531Y = 750$$
$$Y = 1,412.$$

The values of C, T, and M follow.
    (b)   The multiplier for Ruston is $1/(0.531) = 1.88$.

3   (a) $y = 0.25k + 0.75l + t$. Successive substitution for k, l, and t yields $y = 8.625\%$.
    (b)   The growth rate can be decomposed as follows:

Labor force	3.75%
Natural growth	1.50
Migration	2.25
Capital	1.875
Local saving	0.625
Migration	1.25
Technical change	3.00

4   (a) $\Delta Y = \alpha A e^{rt} L^{\alpha-1} K^{\beta} \Delta L$, so substitution into the definition of elasticity produces $(\Delta Y/\Delta L)(L/Y) = \alpha$. The same procedure works for K.

    (b) $\Delta Y/Y = \Delta A/A + E_K(\Delta K/K) + E_L(\Delta L/L)$
          $= r + \beta(\Delta K/K) + \alpha(\Delta L/L)$

because Ae^{rt} grows at rate r.
    (c)   The growth rate of Y is 3.25%.

5   (a)   Larger employment growth tells potential migrants that they have a better chance of finding a job when they arrive.
    (b) $\Delta E = \alpha\theta/(1 - \alpha\beta) = 0.625\theta$.
    (c)   Note that the denominator in the equation for ΔE is $(1 - \alpha\beta)$. If $\alpha\beta > 1$, then this denominator is negative, which yields a nonsense result that an increase in θ makes M increase without limit.

602 Answers to Selected Exercises

6 (a) The technical coefficients are:

	A	B
A	0.1	0.714
B	0.3	0.143

(b) Gross output is the total value of output of an industry, which also equals the total value of all of the inputs.

(c) $A = 0.14A + 0.714B + X_A$
$B = 0.3A + 0.143B + X_B$

(d) If final demand for A increases from 40 to 50, then:

	A	B	Final demand	Gross output
A	11.5	53.8	50	115.3
B	34.6	10.8	30	75.4
VA	69.2	10.8		
Total	115.3	75.4	80	190.7

Gross output of A increased by 15.3/10 = 1.53, and gross output of B increased by 5.4/10 = 0.54. Value added increased by 10/10 = 1, of course.

(e) There are no exports because there are no imports; all output is sold locally.

Chapter 20

1 Static localization economies exist because the industry has increasing returns to scale (0.75 + 0.4 = 1.15). Dynamic localization economies exist because industry growth is a function of the employment level. Static urbanization economies exist because industry growth is a function of employment growth in the urban area (holding other factors constant), and dynamic urbanization economies exist because industry growth depends on the level of air service.

2 (a) Because the coefficient of $\ln E_0$ is less than 1.0, the dynamic localization economy is of the weaker form; employment in the base year leads to greater employment growth in absolute (but not percentage) terms.

(b) The model includes no variable that captures a static localization economy effect.

(c) The Pop variable tells us that the industry is also subject to a dynamic urbanization economy.

Index